Johannes Kepler

and the New Astronomy

IOANNES KEPPLERVS. S. CÆS. MAIEST. ET ORDD. SVP. AVSTRIÆ MATHEMATICVS. &c.

Argentina

Owen Gingerich
General Editor

Johannes Kepler

and the New Astronomy

James R. Voelkel

Oxford University Press
New York • Oxford

for Katy

Oxford University Press

Oxford   New York
Athens   Auckland   Bangkok   Bogotá   Buenos Aires   Calcutta
Cape Town   Chennai   Dar es Salaam   Delhi   Florence   Hong Kong
Istanbul   Karachi   Kuala Lumpur   Madrid   Melbourne   Mexico City
Mumbai   Nairobi   Paris   São Paulo   Singapore   Taipei   Tokyo
Toronto   Warsaw

and associated companies in

Berlin   Ibadan

Design: Design Oasis
Layout: Leonard Levitsky
Picture research: Lisa Kirchner

Library of Congress Cataloging-in-Publication Data
Voelkel, James R. (James Robert)
Johannes Kepler and the New Astronomy / James R. Voelkel
p. cm. -- (Oxford portraits in science)
Includes bibliographical references and index.
Summary: A biography of the German astronomer who discovered three
laws of planetary motion.
ISBN 0-19-511680-1 (hardcover); 0-19-515021-X (paperback)
1. Kepler, Johannes, 1571-1630 Juvenile literature. [1. Kepler, Johannes,
1571-1630. 2. Astronomers.] I. Title. II. Series.
QB36.K4V64 1999
520'.92--dc21   99-23844
[B]   CIP

9 8 7 6 5 4 3 2

Printed in the United States of America
on acid-free paper

On the cover: Portrait of Kepler by Hans von Aachen (1612). Scholars are not entirely certain that this portrait depicts Kepler. Inset: Detail of the frontispiece of the Rudolfine Tables showing Kepler at work.
Frontispiece: Copperplate engraving of Kepler (1620) by Jacob von Heyden, after a portrait by an unknown artist.

Contents

OXFORD PORTRAITS IN SCIENCE

"It can be said that among the men whose genius enriched and deep-ened human knowledge by creative achievements in the area of exact science there is hardly one who enjoys the sympathy of as many as does Kepler, despite the facts that his principal field of activity is unfamiliar to most and that the result of his labors is difficult to understand and appreciate. It is the halo of his personality which draws many under his spell, the nobility of his character which makes friends for him, the vicissitudes of his life which arouse sympathy, and the secret of his union with nature that attracts all those who seek something in the universe beyond, and different from, that which rigorous science offers. In their hearts they all quietly bear veneration and love for this exceptional man. For no one who has once entered the magic sphere that surrounds him can ever escape from it."

—**Max Caspar**, *Kepler*

This contemporary woodcut depicts the Comet of 1577. The artist has included himself in the foreground, sketching the comet with the help of an assistant who holds a lantern.

CHAPTER

I

The Comet

The year 1577 was graced with one of the most spectacular comets in recorded history. With a resplendent head that outshone any star and a tail 50 times the breadth of the full moon, it wheeled majestically through the heavens, exciting attention and comment throughout Europe. Deep in southern Germany in the duchy of Württemberg, Katharina Kepler led her five-year-old son Johannes up the hill overlooking the village of Leonberg to view the spectacle. His weak vision made more bleary by the late hour, the comet did not make much of an impression on him. But he would always remember his mother's kind gesture from an otherwise harsh and difficult childhood. At the same moment, far to the north on his private island in the Danish Sound, a young nobleman took time out from the task of building the world's greatest astronomical observatory to make detailed nightly observations of the comet.

Comets appear without warning in the heavens, which are otherwise the most regular and enduring feature of our environment. As such, at the time comets were viewed as fateful omens, signs that a change was in store. If the magnificence of the sign were any indication of its significance, this change would be very, very big. Perhaps it foretold the death of the emperor or of the sultan of the Turks, or maybe even the second coming of Christ was at hand. As it turned out, the comet did foretell a change, for along with the thousands of people who flocked out at night to gawk fearfully at the specter, here and there a handful of astronomers took careful, precise measurements that would eventually lead to a revolution in thought. The Scientific Revolution was dawning. And the little boy who stood yawning on the hill would be one of its most important thinkers.

Johannes Kepler was born on December 27, 1571, at 2:30 P.M. in his grandfather Sebald's small but commodious house in the city of Weil der Stadt. He was his parents' first child, and his father Heinrich was still living with his parents. The Keplers were a once proud and noble family, now in decline. Generations before, in 1433, Kepler's great-great-great-great-grandfather had been knighted by Emperor Sigismund in recognition of his valiant military service. Since then, in gradual steps, the family had left imperial service, fallen out of the nobility, entered the craftsman class, and moved to the small, sleepy city of Weil der Stadt. But the Keplers still cherished their former glory. They still had their family coat of arms, and tales were told of the military honors won by Kepler's great-grandfather and grandfather under Emperor Charles V and his successors.

Although not as illustrious as they had once been, the Kepler family had a respectable place in the life of Weil der Stadt. Grandfather Sebald, with his red, fleshy face, distinguished-looking beard, and fine clothes, was an authoritative man who had been mayor for ten years when Kepler was born. His election as mayor was a reflection of his high standing in the community, especially since the Keplers were members of the minority Protestant community there. As a leader, Sebald was more dictator than negotiator, but his advice was sound and the community trusted him. Still, he struck young Johannes as irascible and stubborn.

Sebald was the patriarch of the family and the closest thing Johannes would have to a father figure. The Kepler family's long slide seems to have reached bottom with Johannes's father Heinrich, Sebald's fourth son. He was a brutal, uneducated man who was absent for much of Kepler's childhood. Kepler wrote of his father, "He destroyed everything. He was a wrongdoer, abrupt, and quarrelsome." The martial spirit by which generations of Keplers had distinguished themselves in service to the emperor seems to have overflowed in Heinrich. Oppressed by the tight quarters of his father's house, Heinrich left before his son was three years old to seek adventure as a mercenary soldier fighting in Holland. This would be a pattern throughout Johannes's childhood: his father would return for a time, but the lure of the battlefield would call him back. When he was home, he was a hard and bad-tempered man. Finally, in 1588, when Kepler was sixteen, his father left, never to be seen again. It was rumored that he fought as a naval captain for the Kingdom of Naples and perished in Augsburg on his way home, but no one ever knew for sure.

Kepler was raised mostly by his mother, Katharina, the daughter of Melchior Guldenmann, who was the innkeeper and mayor of the village of Eltingen. Kepler took after her in many ways. Like her, he was small, wiry, and dark. They both possessed restless, inquisitive minds. Kepler's mother did not have formal schooling, but she was interested in the healing power of herbs and homemade potions, a pastime that would have very unfortunate consequences when she was an old woman and was put on trial as a suspected witch. There is no doubt that Katharina Kepler was also a strange, unpleasant woman whom people did not like. She too easily turned her sharp wit to the attack. Kepler himself described her as "sharp-tongued, quarrelsome, and possessing a bad spirit." The relationship between Kepler's brutal father and shrewish mother was certainly explosive, and it must have created an unbearable atmosphere in the home when Heinrich was not off soldiering somewhere. Years later, when Kepler used astrological principles to calculate the time of his conception, he arrived at the answer 4:37 in the morning on May 17, 1571. Since he had been a small and sickly baby, he disregarded the fact that his parents had only been married on May 15 and concluded he had been born prematurely, a "seven-months baby." If we view his conclusion with skepticism, the image of a hasty marriage precipitated by an unplanned pregnancy completes the picture of his parents' unhappy relationship.

Kepler was the first of seven children borne by his mother. Of these, only four grew to adulthood, a level of infant mortality not uncommon in the sixteenth century. Two years later, another son, Heinrich, was born. Like his namesake, he became a restless and unlucky man, whose life became a series of misadventures in which he was continually the victim of life-threatening accidents, beatings, and robberies. Kepler's other siblings were far less adventurous and led quite ordinary lives. His sister Margarethe grew up and married a clergyman. The youngest child, Christoph, later entered the craftsman class, as his forebears had done, and became a respectable tinsmith.

Despite its small size of 200 or so citizens and their families, Weil der Stadt was an imperial free city. It was a free city in the sense that, although surrounded by the duchy of Württemberg, it was an independent unit in the patchwork of duchies, principalities, bishoprics, and cities that made up the Holy Roman Empire of the German Nation. The Holy Roman Empire stretched across all of Germany and Austria and included Bohemia in the east (the Czech Republic today) and parts of France and Holland in the west. It was ruled by the Holy Roman Emperor Rudolf II from his seat in distant Prague in Bohemia. As an imperial free city, Weil der Stadt owed its allegiance only to the emperor and sent its own representative to the Imperial Diet, the occasional mass assembly of all of the powers of the empire. Weil der Stadt's status and history also meant that the practice of both Catholicism and Protestantism was allowed there, even though surrounding Württemberg was an aggressively Protestant state. The practice of religion in Germany at that time was an intensely disputed subject and one that would be of the utmost importance in Kepler's material, intellectual, and spiritual life.

The confessional struggles that would mark and mar Kepler's life had a history that was just over 50 years long at the time of his birth. After Martin Luther had broken with the Catholic church in 1517, proclaiming that faith alone justified man before God and that every person should read the Scriptures for himself, chaos had reigned for some time. The need for a reform of the Christian church—which was at that time almost exclusively Catholic in Western Europe—was deeply felt in the hearts of many people, especially in northern Europe. But political considerations clouded the picture as well. The Catholic church was a rich and powerful institution with its center of power located across the Alps in Rome. The prospect of seizing local assets from the Catholic church and evading its political power by joining with the Protestants appealed to many dukes and princes.

On the other hand, many felt a sincere loyalty to the Catholic church, which had upheld Christianity for more than a thousand years. Since Germany was not a unified country but a political patchwork, widespread religious and political upheaval engulfed the region. Finally, in an effort to restore order, an agreement was reached in the Religious Peace of Augsburg (1555), according to which each local leader would determine whether Catholicism or Protestantism would be practiced in his domain. The exception was the imperial free cities, like Weil der Stadt, in which both religions could continue to be practiced if they had previously done so. The situation in Weil der Stadt was further complicated by the fact that its urban area was entirely

Martin Luther broke with the Catholic church in 1517. The resulting religious upheaval had a strong effect on Kepler throughout his life.

surrounded by the duchy of Württemberg, whose duke was an important and powerful promoter of Protestantism. Thus, the Keplers found themselves in the unusual position of being members of a Protestant minority in a free city within a Protestant duchy.

Issues of religion played a powerful role in Kepler's education. Alone among his siblings, he was destined for a university education. By the time he set the first foot on this path at the age of five in 1577, his parents had moved the family from Weil der Stadt to the nearby town of Leonberg. Unlike the free city, Leonberg was part of the duchy of Württemberg, and so Kepler had access to the fine educational system the dukes had established for their subjects. He began in the ordinary German school, but was quickly moved to the Latin school, which was part of a parallel school system leading to the university. Whereas students in the German school learned the German they would need for their everyday life, students in the Latin school were taught to read and write in Latin, the international language of learning. Indeed, they were even required to speak only Latin to one another. Throughout Europe, serious study in any discipline was conducted in Latin, both in books and at universities, where even lectures and debates were in Latin. One strange result of Kepler's education was that, although his style in Latin was quite elegant, he never learned to write as well in his native language. He wrote all of his serious books and letters—even those to other Germans—in Latin.

A smooth ascent through the educational system was by no means assured for Kepler. He lost some time when the family moved again to Ellmendingen. Worse still, between 1580 and 1582, when he was eight to ten years old, he was set to hard agricultural labor by his parents. A small, weak child, he was unsuited to work in the fields, and it may have been a relief to parents and child alike to reenroll him in school. He gained a more serious foothold in the educational system when he passed state examinations and was admitted to the lower seminary at Adelberg on October 16, 1584. Lower seminary was the first of two steps leading to admission to the university. He did well and, two years later, proceeded to the higher seminary at the former Cistercian monastery at Maulbronn.

Perhaps because he was a small and sickly child or to escape from the unpleasant atmosphere of his childhood, Kepler delighted in difficult mental exercises, and he thrived in school. He became interested in poetry and meter and took pleasure in composing poems in difficult classical styles. Jokes and puzzles delighted him, and many of his poems employed tricks like anagrams (in which the letters can be rearranged to spell another word or phrase) and acrostics (in which the first letter of each line read downward forms a new word or phrase). To train his memory, he selected the longest Psalms to memorize.

Like his mother, he had a restless and inquisitive mind. As a result, his compositions would be full of digressions, as he leapt from one uncompleted thought to another. This quickness of mind and tendency to jump from one thought to another stayed with him throughout his life. And like his father, he expressed a certain amount of quarrelsomeness and violence. He was fiercely competitive. He made a list of his "enemies" from school (significantly, he left no list of friends), many of whom competed with him for high rankings in the class lists. When the lists were posted, spirits sometimes ran so high that fist fights broke out. Most of the time, a reconciliation was reached only when Kepler's rivals stopped challenging his academic supremacy.

Despite his occasional high spirits, Kepler was a serious and pious student. Even as a boy, he approached his religious studies with the greatest earnestness. He was never content simply to accept what he had been taught but always had to work it out for himself. So if he heard a sermon denouncing one Christian sect or another, he always made sure to follow the argument, compare it to what was actually said in the Bible, and come to his own conclusion. There were many subtle points of dogma that were erected as walls to separate the "true believers" from heretics, those who would not accept the standard teachings of the church. The ramparts of these walls were manned by serious young preachers who in their lessons and sermons fiercely denounced others' beliefs. Contentious disagreements existed not only with the Catholics but even more so between the various Protestant sects, chiefly the Lutherans and Calvinists. Most often Kepler saw the truth to lie somewhere between the positions staked out by the various sects, and he acknowledged that there was an element of truth even in "heretical" opinions. His willingness to concede the positive points of conflicting theological interpretations revealed his sincere faith and his good-hearted nature. His teachers tolerated his investigation of unorthodox and suspect beliefs because of his earnestness, but in his life he would learn that no amount of good faith and reasoned argument was sufficient to forge understanding between the Christian sects. Indeed, his efforts would end up alienating him from his own precious Lutheran community.

The culmination of Kepler's efforts in school came when Kepler passed the baccalaureate examination at the University of Tübingen on September 25, 1588. Even though he was still at the higher seminary at Maulbronn, he had officially been registered as a student at Tübingen for almost a year. He thus completed his undergraduate studies at Maulbronn and passed by examination at Tübingen, earning a B.A. degree without yet having attended classes there. The way was now open to proceed to the university to pursue an M.A. degree, and then to study at the university's seminary, where he would get advanced training in theology. After all these years of education, he would be able to enter service in the church, which had long become his greatest aspiration.

In early September of the following year, Duke Ludwig named five scholarship students to the *Stift*, the Lutheran seminary, at the University of Tübingen. Kepler was among them. By accepting the scholarship, Kepler was committing himself to lifelong service to the duke of Württemberg. In exchange, everything would be provided for him. The *Stift* would house and look after him while he completed two years of studies leading to his master's degree, and then take over responsibility for his additional three years of theological studies. He packed some personal possessions and set out for Tübingen. Around September 17, 1589, he signed his name in the registration book at the *Stift*:

Johannes Kepler from Leonberg

Born December 27, 1571

He was 17 years old. Following the normal course of study, Kepler would study two more years in the arts faculty of the university before devoting himself purely to theology. The two areas of his studies that interested him above the others and that remained his primary concerns for the rest of his life were mathematics (which included astronomy) and theology. The two subjects were alike in a way: both transcended our earthly experience in their quest for eternal truths. For Kepler, geometrical proofs seemed the closest we can come to certain knowledge in our mortal existence. And in astronomy, he saw in the layout of the solar system the image of God.

Kepler's teacher in mathematics and astronomy was Michael Maestlin, a solid and gruff-looking man whom Kepler admired deeply. The mathematical sciences were a specialty of Lutheran universities in Germany, and Maestlin was well qualified to teach Kepler the latest in astronomical theory: the heliocentric system of Nicolaus Copernicus, a Polish astronomer who had died 50 years earlier. In the heliocentric system, which means literally "sun-centered,"

This engraving of Tübingen is by Matthäus Merian, who published a series of 16 books, the Topographia, that depicted many European towns and cities. Kepler attended the university in Tübingen.

the sun is at rest in the center of the solar system and the planets travel around it. Maestlin was quite unusual in actually believing this heliocentric system to be true. But he still taught the older geocentric (earth-centered) Ptolemaic astronomy to his beginning students.

Ptolemaic astronomy had been the dominant cosmological system, or view of the universe, for 1,500 years since its development by Claudius Ptolemy in the second century A.D. Ptolemy began with the knowledge—ancient even in his time—that the world is a sphere. In addition, he adopted the universal belief that it was at rest in the center of the universe, which was bounded on the outside by the sphere of stars. To this basic cosmological framework, Ptolemy added detailed mathematical theories for the motion of every planet. With some slight adjustments, these theories were sufficient to predict the planets' motions pretty well up until Kepler's time.

Ptolemy's cosmology was consistent with Aristotle's much older theory of the elements. Aristotle, the great and influential Greek philosopher of the fourth century B.C., had taught that the heavens are made up of a substance called

aether. Unlike the earthly elements, earth, air, fire, and water, whose natural motions were finite (toward and away from the center of the earth), the heavenly aether alone had a natural, unending circular motion.

In the 50 years since Copernicus published his heliocentric system in 1543, not many people seriously entertained the possibility that it might be true. It was too unbelievable that the earth should move without us sensing it. Just the earth's daily rotation would have to be a dizzying 900 miles per hour, not counting its annual motion around the sun. And yet objects fell straight down, not away from the direction of the earth's rotation, and birds and objects in the air did not fall behind as the earth rotated out from underneath them. The motion of the earth seemed physically impossible. Ptolemy's geocentric system, on the other hand, was perfectly consistent with Aristotle's physics.

In the second half of the sixteenth century, however, problems had arisen with the theory of the aether. According to Aristotle, aether was unchanging and immutable. But in 1572, a dazzling *nova,* or "new star," appeared. Careful observations showed that it was not below the moon in the earthly region but somewhere high in the aether. And then came the magnificent comet of 1577.

While Kepler was holding his mother's hand on the hill outside Leonberg, far to the north on the Island of Hven, the Danish nobleman Tycho Brahe (who, like Galileo and Michelangelo, is known by his first name) had made exhaustive, precise observations of the comet. They showed that it, too, was above the moon, not just below the moon in the realm of fire where comets had been thought to be. In addition, the comet was moving somewhere through regions thought to be full of aether spheres. In 1588, after 11 years of patient preparation, Tycho declared with meticulous justification that the aether spheres did not exist. It was not enough for him to become a Copernican—the physical absurdity of heliocentrism and the testimony of Holy Scripture stood in the way—but the Ptolemaic system was under threat.

For Kepler, studying under Maestlin in the early 1590s, the physical objections to a moving earth seemed a small thing. For him, the Copernican system had a wider, religious significance. The universe, as he saw it, was nothing less than the image of God, its Creator. The sun, the most resplendent body, was situated in the center, whence it distributed light, heat, and motion to the planets. It represented God the Father. Outermost in the system were the stars. They were located on a fixed sphere—the most perfect of geometrical bodies—centered on the sun that enclosed the universe and defined its space. It represented God the Son, Jesus Christ. A sphere is generated by an infinite number of

text continues on page 22

COPERNICUS'S MODEL OF RETROGRADE MOTION

Nicolaus Copernicus published his heliocentric system in 1543, the year of his death.

In Ptolemy's geocentric system, the earth was at rest in the center of the universe, and all the motions we see in the heavens were attributed to the stars and planets. In Copernicus's heliocentric system, many of the motions are attributed to the motion of the earth, our vantage point. It is just as if you are in a train at the station: when you look out the window at another train and it starts to move, it is not immediately clear whether it is your train or the other that is moving. For instance, according to Copernicus, the daily motion all celestial bodies share—rising in the east and setting in the west—is really caused by the eastward rotation of the earth on its axis. The heavens do not move over us; we move under them.

The situation with our view of another planet is more complicated, because both the earth and the planet have their own motion around the sun, and our perception of the planet's location depends on both where the earth is and where the planet is. Mars is a good example. Much of the time, we perceive Mars's motion as it moves slowly eastward with respect to background stars. But when the earth and Mars are on the same side of the sun, the earth passes Mars because the earth travels faster and its orbit is smaller. As the earth moves by, our motion makes Mars look like it is falling behind. And during that period of time, from the earth it looks like Mars stops moving and even moves backward for a time.

text continued from page 20

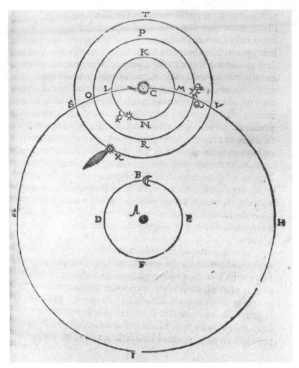

This is Tycho Brahe's diagram of the location of the Comet of 1577 from his book De mundi aetherei recentioribus phaenomenis (On the More Recent Phenomena of the Aetherial World) (1588). The comet is moving around the sun on the path marked XVTS near Venus, which moves on the path QPOR. Mercury is innermost, on path NMKL.

equal straight lines coming forth from its center, which fill out the space between the sphere and its center. This intervening space represented the Holy Spirit. As in the Trinitarian concept of God, in which Father, Son, and Holy Spirit unite in the one God, so in the sphere, no one of the elements—center, surface, or volume—can exist without the others. The periods of the planets and their distances also made sense in the Copernican arrangement: the closer they are to the sun, the source of all change and motion, the faster they move around. During his time at the University of Tübingen, Kepler defended the reality of the Copernican system in two separate formal academic debates, using just this type of argument. But he always considered astronomy and the Copernican system to be just a side interest to his religious studies.

In the meantime, Kepler's theological studies were proceeding according to schedule. On August 11, 1591, he completed his required two-year advanced study in the arts and received his master's degree. Two months later, the university senate wrote to the mayor and city council of Weil der Stadt requesting that his scholarship be renewed. "Young Kepler," they wrote, "has such an extraordinary and splendid intellect that something special can be expected from him."

In early 1594, however, came a devastating change of plans. Within months of completing an additional three years of theological studies, Kepler was forced to cut them off. The previous year, Georg Stadius, the mathematics teacher at a

Protestant seminary school in Graz, Styria (a district of Austria), had passed away. In November, the Styrian representatives appealed to the prominent Lutheran University of Tübingen to recommend a replacement, preferably one who also knew history and Greek. Kepler had distinguished himself in his enthusiastic study with Maestlin and had otherwise done well, so the theological faculty selected him.

It was a bitter personal struggle, as Kepler was torn between his calling and his duty. Previously, when his friends at the *Stift* had received far-flung postings, they had complained openly and attempted to avoid them. Seeing this, Kepler resolved that when the call came to him, he would accept it promptly and with dignity. Now his smugness came back to haunt him. It was not so much that Graz was far away in a foreign country that bothered him but rather that he was being taken away from the chance to be a pastor and serve the church. He did not want to be in the lowly position of a mathematics teacher. On top of that, he did not see that he had any particular aptitude in mathematics. On the other hand, he did not want to be selfish; one is not put in this world for himself alone. Finally, he proposed a compromise that left open the possibility that he could return to church service in the future.

The paperwork was quickly put in place. The head of the Tübingen *Stift*, and the inspectors of the Protestant school in Graz wrote to the duke of Württemberg requesting permission for Kepler to leave Württemberg and take up the job. The duke signed off on March 5. Kepler hurriedly tied up his affairs in Tübingen. On March 13, 1594, he left his beloved university for far-off Styria.

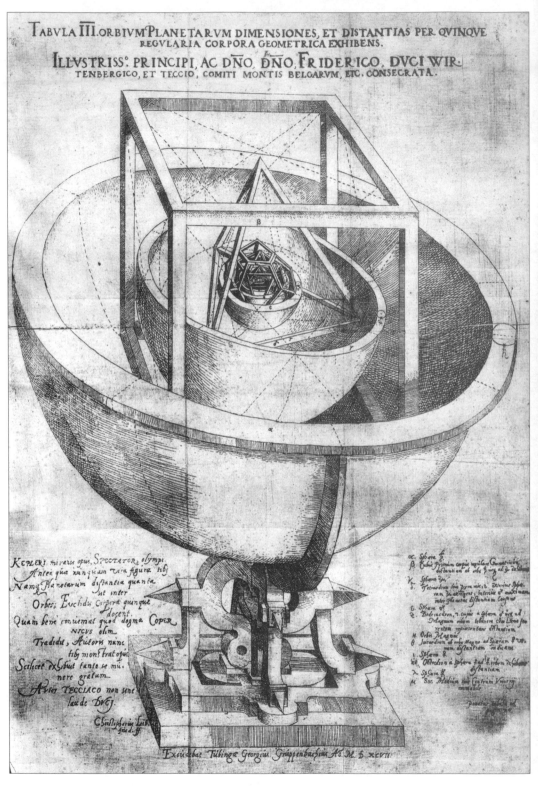

Kepler's cosmological hypothesis from the Mysterium cosmographicum (1596) provides a geometrical explanation of the distances between the planets in their orbits..

The Secret of the Universe

It took Kepler nearly a month to travel from Württemberg, through Bavaria, into Austria, and then across Austria toward its southern frontier. On April 11, 1594, he reached the hilltop fortress town of Graz, the capital of Styria, one of the districts of Inner Austria. He ascended the narrow streets and found the squat, square building housing the Protestant college, where he was shown into the colonnaded courtyard and taken to his new lodging.

The long journey underscored the remoteness of the place and the foreignness of his new situation. The most significant change was the charged religious climate in which he found himself. Unlike Württemberg, which was staunchly Lutheran, in Styria, Catholics and Protestants lived side by side in uneasy coexistence. Ideally, this situation should never have come to pass. Under the terms of the Religious Peace of Augsburg, Styria should have been Catholic like its Hapsburg rulers. Decreeing the practice of religion, however, required the power to enforce it, and almost all of the powerful land-owning nobility in Inner Austria had converted to Lutheranism. Twenty years before, Archduke Charles had granted the Protestant nobility the concession under the Pacification of Bruck (1578) that Protestant nobles in the countryside and Protestant citizens of cities like Graz could freely exercise their religion. Almost ever since, there had existed a religious stalemate.

Kepler's position in this conflict was not neutral. The Protestant seminary school had been set up in 1574 in deliberate opposition to the Catholic Jesuit college founded the previous year. It had developed into the principal seat of the Protestant party in Graz, and its staff were important representatives of the Protestant community.

Matthäus Merian created this view of Graz, the capital of Stryia, for the Topographia. In addition to his work as a school-teacher, Kepler was the district mathematician of Styria.

There were four preachers and about a dozen teachers at the all-male school, which comprised two levels, a boy's school and an upper school. Kepler taught in the philosophical division of the highest of the four classes in the upper school. Though he was called to teach advanced mathematics, which included astronomy, his classes were not well attended. His first year, he had only a few students, and the second, none at all. The school inspectors realized that it

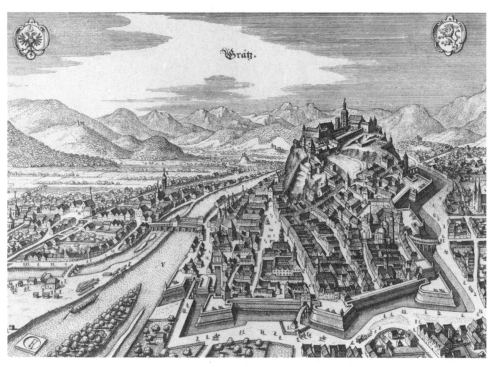

was the subject matter and not their new young professor that was at fault. Instead, Kepler was reassigned to teach other topics, and, during the following years, taught a variety of courses, including rhetoric, Virgil, basic arithmetic, history, and ethics.

In addition to his duties as a schoolteacher, Kepler carried the joint appointment of district mathematician. As such, it was his duty to compile an annual calendar and astrological prognostication, a prediction for the coming year. Throughout his life, Kepler had mixed feelings about astrology. On the one hand, as he wrote a few years later in his book *De fundamentis astrologiae certioribus* (On the More Certain Principles of Astrology) (1601), he disliked the idea of "nourishing the superstition of fatheads." On the other hand, he sincerely believed that alignments of the planets had subtle but important influences on man and nature. Kepler seems to have struck the right balance for his *Prognostication for 1595*. In his first prognostication, he predicted bitter cold, an attack by the Turks on Austria's southern flank, and a peasant uprising. That winter was so cold, it was said, that shepherds in the mountains broke off their noses when they blew them. Kepler's other unpleasant prophesies came true as well. He was an instant success.

Of course, Kepler had another motivation for composing pubic prognostications and for the private astrological consulting he did: it was a valuable source of income. As he wrote justifying his astrological activities to his disapproving former professor Michael Maestlin, "If God gave every animal tools for maintaining life, what harm is there if for the same purpose He joined astrology to astronomy?" For his prognostication for 1595, Kepler received a bonus of 20 florins, worth seven weeks of his 150 florin salary as a teacher. His subsequent annual prognostications were regularly rewarded in the same way.

Kepler had accepted the assignment to teach mathematics in Graz more or less unwillingly. He resolved, however, now

Michael Maestlin was Kepler's astronomy professor in Tübingen. Maestlin was very supportive of his student's work, and was instrumental in getting Kepler's first book published in Tübingen.

that he was a professional mathematician—or an astronomer, which was really the same thing then—to elevate his studies to a suitably philosophic level. He began by reconsidering Copernicus's heliocentric system of the world, and he noticed that there were some unexplained elements in it.

One of the most satisfying features of the heliocentric system had been that it fit the orbits of the planets together into a harmonious, commensurable system. That is to say, Copernicus's heliocentric system required that the planets be located in precise distances relative to the earth, so the distances of all of the planets from the sun were determined with respect to one another, or the system was "commensurable." In the old Ptolemaic cosmology, the relative distance of the planets had been determined simply by stacking up the systems of spheres belonging to the different planets one on top of another, like the layers of an onion. But in Copernicus's heliocentric system, the planets all had to be located at specific distances from the sun. Mercury's orbit had to be about one third the size of the earth's, Venus about two thirds, Mars about one and a half, Jupiter five times, and Saturn ten times.

As Kepler began looking more closely at the heliocentric system, he realized that Copernicus had offered no fundamental reason why the planets were located at these particular distances. Kepler began to wonder, why these particular distances? For that matter, why were there six and only six planets? Or, as Kepler considered the question, why did God choose to construct the solar system in this way and not another?

The basis for an answer to these questions came to him while he was in front of his class teaching on July 19, 1595, when he drew a diagram of an equilateral triangle inscribed within a circle, so that the vertices of the triangle just touched the surrounding circle. He noticed that if he inscribed another circle within the triangle, so that it just touched the midpoints of the sides of the surrounding triangle, the ratio of the size of the large circle to the small circle was about the same as the relative size of Saturn's orbit to Jupiter's orbit. If he then inscribed a square within the inner circle and incribed a smaller circle within it, its size relative to the other circles might be the same as Mars's orbit to Saturn's and Jupiter's orbit. He immediately began to suspect that the relative sizes of all of the planets' orbits had some such geometrical basis, that God had used geometry as an archetype while creating the universe.

text continues on page 31

I n Greek antiquity, it was already known that there are five and only five regular polyhedra, that is, three-dimensional geometrical figures with all identical equilateral faces, which are also called "Platonic" solids. A cube is the most common example of a regular solid. How can one tell that there are four and only four possible others?

Start by thinking about how one might construct a regular solid, starting with the sides around one point. There have to be at least three sides; otherwise, a three-dimensional body cannot be formed. Arrange three squares around a point, and then fold them up to form a three-sided figure, which is half a cube. An identical figure attached to the first will complete the cube with six sides. Equilateral triangles will fold up more tightly, leaving a space at the top the same size as the other sides. Attach one more side, and one has a tetrahedron with four faces. Pentagons will fold up like a shallow dish, but additional pentagons can be attached to the edges. If one adds more sides to these and then more sides to the next set of edges, a dodecahedron with twelve identical pentagonal faces eventually will be formed. Hexagonal faces will not work. Three hexagons meet in a flush plane, and they cannot be folded up to form the sides of a solid.

If we go back to triangles, we see that we could try four equilateral triangles around a point. Fold them up, and one has a pyramid shape. An identical pyramid joined to the top forms a regular octahedron with eight faces. Five equilateral triangles will also fit around a point. Fold them up, and the figure is very shallow, but if one keeps adding on sides, a regular twenty-sided icosahedron eventually will be formed. Six equilateral triangles will form a flush plane which cannot be folded into a three-dimensional figure. Four squares will also form a flush plane. Nor can any other combination of regular polygons be fit around a single point. Therefore, these are the only possible regular solids.

text continued from page 65

The use of plane geometry was unsatisfactory, and he quickly realized that he would have to use solid geometry. The universe is three dimensional, after all. With three dimensions, he would have to work with spheres instead of circles and regular solids instead of polygons. It had been known to mathematicians since antiquity that there are five and only five regular solids, the tetrahedron (four-sided), the cube (six-sided), the octahedron (eight-sided), the dodecahedron (twelve-sided), and the icosahedron (twenty-sided). As soon as Kepler remembered that, the answer became clear to him. Later, in the Preface to his book *Mysterium cosmographicum*, he quoted the proposition just as it had come to him at that moment:

> The earth's circle is the measure of all things. Circumscribe a dodecahedron around it. The circle surrounding it will be Mars. Circumscribe a tetrahedron around Mars. The circle surrounding it will be Jupiter. Circumscribe a cube around Jupiter. The surrounding circle will be Saturn. Now, inscribe an icosahedron inside the earth. The circle inscribed in it will be Venus. Inscribe an octahedron inside Venus. The circle inscribed in it will be Mercury.

This detail of a plate from Kepler's Harmonice mundi shows the construction of the Platonic solids: the tetrahedron (top left), the octahedron (Oo), icosahedron (Pp), cube (Qq), and dodecahedron (Rr).

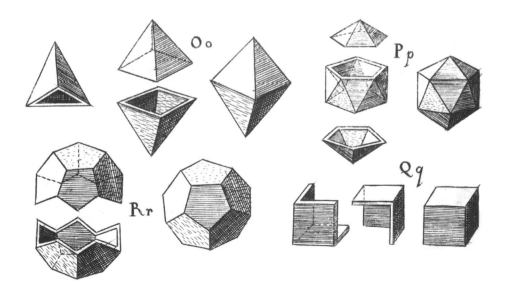

The spacing of the planets within the polyhedra seemed just about right. More importantly, Kepler knew immediately why there are six and only six planets. Since there were only five possible regular polyhedra, they could be inscribed between only six different spheres. The discovery he made on July 20, 1595, was so profound he wept tears of joy. As he wrote in a letter to Maestlin, he regarded his discoveries as "stupendous miracles of God."

By October 1595, Kepler had resolved to publish his findings in a book. It would be, as he saw it, a physical proof of the truth of Copernicus's heliocentric system and, at the same time, a testament to God's glory. In so making known God's plan of the world, Kepler found a way to make meaningful the assignment he had been given to become a mathematician. As he wrote in a letter to Maestlin at the beginning of October,

> I am in haste to publish, dearest teacher, but not for my benefit . . . I am devoting my effort so that these things can be published as quickly as possible for the glory of God, who wants to be recognized from the Book of Nature . . . Just as I pledged myself to God, so my intention remains. I wanted to be a theologian, and for a while I was anguished. But now, see how, God is also glorified in astronomy through my work.

There would be many details to be ironed out before he was ready. Among other things, there was another fundamental question about the Copernican system to address: why did the planets have their particular periods? Here, Kepler's thinking took a very important turn. Ever since he was a student, he had thought that the reason the nearer planets go around faster was their proximity to the sun, which is somehow the source of the force that makes them go around. Now, he tried to derive a mathematical formula based on his physical intuition that would relate the planets' periods to their distances. There were two effects to take into account. The first is just geometry: the further a planet is from the sun, the longer its orbit will be and the longer it will take to get around. But in addition, the further away it is, the weaker the planet-moving force will be. So he added these effects to come up with the formula: from one planet to another, the increase in the period will be twice the difference of their distances. He himself later realized the formula was incorrect, but remarkably it yielded planetary distances that were similar to those derived from the polyhedral hypothesis. Again, he wept tears of joy and excitedly wrote to Maestlin about his new hypothesis, "Behold how near the truth I have come!"

Kepler sent his first outline of the two main arguments he would include in his book to Maestlin in October 1595. Throughout that cold winter, he filled out that outline with a number of auxiliary arguments. Since the polyhedral hypothesis was founded on the idea that God had rationally structured the universe based on the five regular solids, Kepler turned his attention to seeing what meaning he could discern in the particular arrangement of the solids. In the process, he ended up having a lot more to say about the polyhedral hypothesis than the planet-moving force hypothesis, but he did come up with one additional argument based on the planet-moving force hypothesis that would be extremely influential in his later thinking about planetary theory.

Around March 1596, when he was putting the finishing touches on his manuscript, he noticed a very interesting application of the planet-moving force hypothesis. Previously, he had only seen the planet-moving force as a way to relate the periods and distances of different planets to one another. After some more thought, he realized that it could be applied to a single planet as it moved on its own orbit around the sun. As the planet approached nearer to the sun, the planet-moving force would be stronger and the planet would move more quickly. Later on in its orbit, as it receded from the sun, the force would be weaker and the planet would slow down. This general change of speed of a planet with its distance from the sun had been built into

Ptolemy's and Copernicus's mathematical models of the motion of the planets, but neither of them had interpreted this change in speed physically.

This idea was, in fact, the single element of the book that would worry Maestlin. He later admonished Kepler not to make too much of this planet-moving force hypothesis "lest it should lead to the ruin of astronomy." What troubled Maestlin was that Kepler seemed to be trampling on a delicate division line between two parts of astronomy. In the sixteenth century, astronomy was widely regarded to consist of a physical part, which dealt with the nature and structure of the universe, otherwise known as cosmology, and a mathematical part, devoted to producing accurate mathematical theories of the planets' motion. Everything else in Kepler's book seemed to fall into the physical part. But by saying that his planet-moving force could explain certain mathematical details of Ptolemy's and Copernicus's planetary theories, Kepler seemed to be importing physical reasoning into mathematical astronomy. As far as Maestlin was concerned, it seemed this would only mess up the theories of the planets.

In January 1596, Kepler received word from home that both his grandfathers were ailing, and at the end of the month, he left Graz to visit them. Sadly, old Sebald died during his visit home. While Kepler was in Württemberg, he took the opportunity to promote his new hypotheses. In February, he traveled up to the capital, Stuttgart, to try his luck at the ducal court.

The aristocracy were patrons of science and the arts generally, but Kepler had a curiosity to market: a model of his new system of nested polyhedra in silver. Or, if something really splashy was desired, Kepler outlined how the model could be realized in the form of a huge punch bowl. The spaces between the different planetary spheres could be filled with various beverages, and by means of hidden pipes and valves, the party guests could fill their glasses from seven taps spaced around the rim. The duke was skeptical at first, but after seeing a paper model Kepler had painstakingly constructed and consulting with his astronomical expert (Maestlin), he advanced Kepler some money to fabricate the more restrained silver model.

The next three months were a frustrating disaster. Kepler was stuck in Stuttgart pestering the goldsmith, and the project hardly got anywhere. In the end, he had to go back to Styria, leaving the project in the goldsmith's hands. Although the matter dragged out for a few years, the entertaining model of Kepler's polyhedra was never built. It would have been wondrous to see.

In the meantime, Kepler had the opportunity to travel to Tübingen, visit with Maestlin, and begin negotiations with a printer to publish his book. None of the printers back in Graz were competent to print a complex astronomical book, but Tübingen had a serious printer named Gruppenbach. Gruppenbach agreed to publish the book on condition that it be approved by the university senate. The senate asked Maestlin for his expert opinion of the astronomical content, and he responded enthusiastically. The only part that the theological faculty demanded to be removed was Kepler's chapter on how to reconcile heliocentrism with passages in the bible that seemed to support geocentrism, such as Psalm 104:5, which states that God "laid the foundations of the earth that it should not be removed for ever." The real meaning of Holy Scripture was not Kepler's business. As he was admonished in a letter from Matthias Hafenreffer, a professor of theology, Kepler was to restrict himself to "playing the part of the abstract mathematician." It was frustrating to Kepler, since he had conceived his work as a physical proof of the truth of heliocentrism. How was he to glorify God speaking only hypothetically? But he obediently went along with the Lutheran authorities.

When Kepler returned to Graz in August 1596, there was some damage to repair from his long absence. To begin with, he had received leave for two months, and he had

These miniature portraits of Johannes Kepler and his wife Barbara date from around the time of their wedding in 1597.

been absent for seven. But he carried a letter from the duke of Württemberg asking for Kepler's superiors' forgiveness since Kepler had been delayed in his service. This was excuse enough. Unfortunately, Kepler's neglect of his love life would not prove so easy to repair.

As early as the previous December, Kepler had made the acquaintance of a young woman with whom he quickly fell in love. Her name was Barbara Müller. Among other things, we know that she was pretty, plump, and extremely fond of cooked tortoise. She was the eldest daughter of a wealthy mill owner and entrepreneur, Jobst Müller, who resided on an estate about two hours south of Graz. Although she was only 23, Barbara had recently become a widow for the second time. Both of Barbara's previous husbands had been significantly older than she was—both were 40—which was not an uncommon state of affairs in days when family and community played so great a role in determining whom one was to marry. An older man would have shown his capacity to be a success and to provide for his family. By contrast, Kepler was scarcely 24 when he began to woo her. Although he had a university education, he was still only a schoolteacher with unknown prospects. It would not prove easy to convince Herr Müller that Kepler was a suitable match for her. Herr Müller was a businessman who kept his eye on the bottom line. Barbara had financial assets. Kepler was a penniless scholar.

Probably as early as January 1596, a delegation of respectable members of the Protestant community was assembled to present and recommend Kepler to Jobst Müller as a suitor for Barbara. Kepler left his matrimonial affairs in their hands when he left for his long trip to Württemberg. In June, during his stay there, he received word that they had been successful. He was advised to hurry home, but not before purchasing silk (or at least double taffeta) wedding clothes for himself and his fiancee on the way in Ulm.

As Kepler's failing attempt to construct the model of his celestial discovery dragged out through the summer, the arrangements for the wedding also fell through. In his absence, Herr Müller had become convinced that he could do better for his daughter. When Kepler returned in the fall, he learned that his longed-for union had been canceled. Fortunately, he received support from his school and church, which weighed in on his behalf. Before he had left for Württemberg, he had given Barbara his word. By the middle of January, Kepler appealed to the church: either it must get involved and convince Barbara's father, or Kepler needed to be released from his promise. In short order, the church had set things right again. A solemn promise of marriage was celebrated on February 9 and the wedding on April 27, 1597.

For a while at least, joy reigned supreme in the Kepler household. Kepler received a silver cup as a wedding gift from the school authorities, as well as a raise of 50 florins, to 200 florins a year, to accommodate his move out of the school grounds. Kepler loved his seven-year-old stepdaughter Regina. Barbara quickly became pregnant and bore him a son on February 2, 1598. He was christened Heinrich, Kepler's father's and brother's name. Kepler cast a horoscope for his firstborn son. He would be like his father, only better—charming, noble in character, nimble of body and mind, with mathematical and mechanical aptitude. It was a crushing blow when after only two months of life, his little son Heinrich became ill and passed away. "The passage of time does not lessen my wife's grief," Kepler wrote, quoting Ecclesiastes, "the passage strikes at my heart: 'O vanity of vanities, and all is vanity.'"

The first happy days of Kepler's marriage saw the arrival of the first copies of his book, whose complicated printing was not finished until March 1597. Although the volume was slim, its title was long. It read *Prodromus dissertationum cosmographicarum, continens mysterium cosmographicum, de admirabili proportione orbium coelestium, deque causis coelorum numeri, magnitudinis, motuumque periodicorum genuinis & proprijs, demonstratum per quinque regularia corpora geometrica*, or in English, The Forerunner of Cosmographical Essays, Containing the Cosmographical Secret: On the Marvelous Proportion of the Celestial Spheres, and on the True and Particular Causes of the Number, Size, and Periodic Motions of the Heavens, Demonstrated by Means of the Five Regular Geometric Bodies. It is known by the abbreviated Latin title, the *Mysterium cosmographicum*, which translates roughly as The Secret of the Universe. Kepler called it a "forerunner" because he foresaw writing a series of treatises on the Copernican system. This book contained his premier discovery, and so he wanted to get it out first and see how people responded to it.

He now began sending copies of the book to astronomers for their opinions. The two copies he dispatched blindly to Italy found their way into the hands of a then little-known mathematics professor at the University of Padua. The man confided to Kepler in a letter that he too had been a Copernican for many years and had been collecting physical proofs of the motion of the earth but had kept them to himself, "terrified as I am by the fortune of our teacher Copernicus himself, who although he earned

Prodròmus

DISSERTATIONVM COSMOGRA-
PHICARVM, CONTINENS MYSTE-
RIVM COSMOGRAPHI-
CVM,

DE ADMIRABILI
PROPORTIONE ORBIVM
COELESTIVM, DEQVE CAVSIS
cœlorum numeri, magnitudinis, motuumque periodicorum genuinis & pro-
prijs,

DEMONSTRATVM, PER QVINQVE
regularia corpora Geometrica,

A

M. IOANNE KEPLERO, VVIRTEM-
bergico, Illuftrium Styriæ prouincia-
lium Mathematico.

Quotidiè morior, fateorque: fed inter Olympi
Dum tenet affiduas me mea cura vias:
Non pedibus terram contingo: fed ante Tonantem
Nectare, diuina pafcor & ambrofiâ.

Addita eft erudita NARRATIO M. GEORGII IOACHIMI
RHETICI, de Libris Reuolutionum, atq̃, admirandis de numero, or-
dine, & diftantijs Sphararum Mundi hypothefibus, excellentiffimi Ma-
thematici, totiusq̃, Aftronomia Reftauratoris D. NICOLAI
COPERNICI.

TVBINGÆ.
Excudebat Georgius Gruppenbachius,
ANNO M. D. XCVI.

The title page of the first edition of the Mysterium cosmographicum carries the publication date 1596 (MDXCVI), although the printing was not finished until 1597.

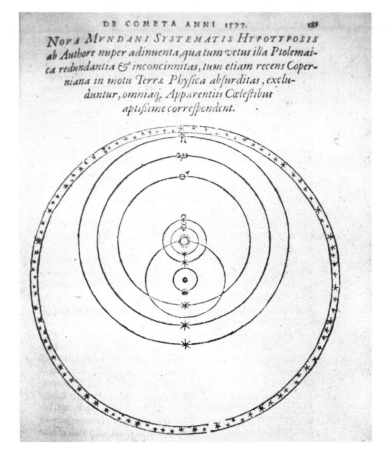

immortal fame among some, nevertheless among a vast number (for such is the number of fools) appeared fit to be ridiculed and hissed off the stage." Kepler was especially tickled by the unknown man's name. His first name was the same as his last, like an echo: Galileo Galilei. Kepler urged Galileo to come out publicly in support of Copernicus. "Have confidence, Galileo," he wrote, "and step forward. If I guess correctly, few of Europe's principal mathematicians will want to distance themselves from us; so great a force is truth." But for the time being, Galileo kept silent. Kepler would not hear from him again for many years.

Kepler next became involved in a scandal and a bitter dispute, which he would desperately regret but which did much to shape his future. One of the people who asked for a copy of the book was the emperor's mathematician, Nicholas Reimer, who used the Latin last name Ursus, meaning "bear." Kepler had written to Ursus a year and a half earlier relating his discovery, but he had never written back. Now, suddenly, Ursus was interested. What Kepler did not know was that Ursus was planning to use him as a pawn in his vicious intellectual dispute with the Danish nobleman Tycho Brahe, Europe's leading astronomer. Both men were claiming to have invented a new cosmological system. It was like Copernicus's system in that the planets went around the sun, but to keep the earth unmoved at the center, the sun moved around the earth with all of the planets in train. In his earlier letter, as a way of being nice and without really knowing what he was saying, Kepler had written "I love your hypotheses." Ursus planned to reprint Kepler's letter in his own book *On Astronomical Hypotheses* (1597) to make it look like Kepler was on his side.

Ursus was a coarse man, the son of illiterate pig herders, who had worked his way up from the filth to become mathematician to the emperor. He was not going to let Tycho Brahe, a privileged aristocrat, accuse him of stealing his idea. On the title page of *On Astronomical Hypotheses*, Ursus printed a motto, a pun on his name, which read "I shall meet them as a bear separated from her cubs." As the motto suggested, it was a wild attack. He crossed every line of civility, making lewd suggestions about Tycho's family and insinuating that Tycho had recently left Denmark because he had committed a horrible crime. In the end, Tycho managed to round up most of the copies and burn them. Only a handful of copies survived the flames.

In the meantime, Kepler was innocently trying to send a copy of his book to Tycho Brahe, whose opinion he was anxious to know. Tycho had moved to northern Germany and it took a long time for Kepler's letter to catch up to him. By a fateful coincidence, it finally arrived on the very same day as Ursus's horrible new book. Tycho was not normally an even-tempered man. For once, however, he reacted with moderation. He could not imagine, he wrote, that Kepler had known his letter would be used in Ursus's "defamatory and criminal publication." For his part, Tycho only wanted a statement of Kepler's opinion of Ursus's behavior, which he could use in his planned lawsuit against Ursus.

With regard to Kepler's book, Tycho mentioned that he had glanced at it and he thought Kepler's speculation was ingenious, but that Copernicus's values for the planetary distances were not accurate enough for his purpose. But he suggested Kepler might make good use of the collection of accurate observations he had amassed over his lifetime as an astronomer. It was a tantalizing possibility. From that moment on, Kepler knew that he would have to meet Tycho face-to-face. Following roundabout routes, their exchange of letters had taken over a year. If he was ever going to straighten out this disaster involving Ursus, he would have to see Tycho in person.

Even as it was becoming clear to Kepler that he needed to confer with Tycho Brahe regarding his research, other events were afoot in Styria that pushed him into Tycho's arms. Shortly after his marriage, Kepler had remarked to Maestlin that, because of his wife's extensive holdings and family connections, he was now effectively bound to Styria, unless "the land was no longer safe for a Lutheran." He had reason to have such concerns. A few months earlier, Archduke Ferdinand II had come of age and assumed rule over Inner Austria, the part of Austria which included Styria. Although his father Archduke Charles had tolerated the Protestants in his lands, Ferdinand's mother had been fervently Catholic and had tried to reverse his concessions. Ferdinand had been raised in Catholic Bavaria and educated at Ingolstadt under the direction of Jesuit advisors. It was feared that he would make good the threat to enforce his rights under the Peace of Augsburg and force all people in his lands to share his Catholic faith. The fear was not misplaced.

There was tension early in Kepler's time in Graz, but the new prince made no overt hostile move. Only after a meeting with Pope Clement VIII in Rome in the summer of 1598, during which, the story went, he vowed to return his lands to Catholicism, did he begin taking measures against the Protestants. The Protestants viewed his return from Italy with apprehension. It was rumored that he would return at the head of an army of Italian soldiers.

When Ferdinand returned, with tension high, there were incidents between the Catholics and Protestants. The balance of power had long been in the Protestant hands. They did not sense the shift underway and brashly taunted the Catholics. Kepler watched in despair as his people brought on their own ruin. Rude caricatures of the Pope were distributed. A Protestant preacher in the pulpit ridiculed the worship of Mary with an obscene gesture. Arrests were made. Poor Protestants in the hospital were refused care, and Protestants were overtaxed for burials.

Then came the beginning of the end. The Catholic archpriest, the highest-ranking priest in the city, forbade the practice of every Protestant sacrament, including communion and marriage. The Protestants appealed to the archduke, and it only made things worse. On September 13, 1598, he decreed that the Protestant college and all church and school ministries were to be dissolved within 14 days. Ten days later, the archbishop ordered all Protestant ministers and teachers to leave the city within a week, under penalty of death. Again, the Protestants protested; they summoned the assembly of the Estates of Styria, and the counselors anxiously begged the prince to repeal the decree. Instead, he issued a stunning new order. On September 28, 1598, he decreed that all the collegiate preachers, rectors, and school employees had to leave the city of Graz and its environs by nightfall, that they then had to clear out of Styria altogether within the previously given deadline of one week, and that any of them who showed themselves again faced "the loss of life and limb." Kepler and his colleagues were banished. They hastily gathered together some supplies, and leaving their wives behind, they dispersed out of the city into the countryside. They hoped for a future reprieve, but only Kepler was ever allowed to return.

At the end of October, Kepler's petition to be allowed to return was granted, and he came from wherever he had been sheltering back into the city. Because he held the dual job of mathematics teacher and district mathematician, he was allowed to return in the latter capacity, as his friends and supporters had pleaded. For the time being, Kepler was safe.

The screw continued to turn on the Protestants in Graz, as they were forbidden the practice of their religion. At first, they simply left the city to attend services at the country estates of noblemen whose Protestant clergy had not been expelled, but soon that was prohibited. Protestants were required to have their children baptized as Catholics and to marry in the Catholic ceremony. A grief-stricken Kepler confronted these oppressive measures after the death of his second child, a daughter named Susanna who was born in June 1599 but lived only 35 days. He refused a Catholic burial for her and was fined. He appealed, and the fine was halved, but he still had to pay before the dead infant could be buried. Luther's German translation of the Bible and all "heretical" books were banned. Searches were undertaken and guards were set at the gates to keep them out. In a spectacular display, 10,000 seized books were burned in a huge bonfire in Graz.

Relieved of his teaching duties, Kepler escaped from the tumult in the streets to his heavenly speculations, developing thoughts on the harmony of the heavens that he would only publish some twenty years later. But he kept his eyes open for an avenue of escape. He inquired about the possibility of an appointment at the University of Tübingen without success. He learned that Tycho had become the emperor's new mathematician, making a triumphant entrance into Prague while

Ursus fled the city. In December, Tycho reissued the invitation to Kepler to come join him for astronomical consultations. When the opportunity arose at the beginning of January 1600 to travel to Prague in the company of Baron Johann Friedrich Hoffmann free of charge, Kepler jumped at the chance. He was on his way before Tycho's second invitation even arrived.

This portrait depicts Tycho Brahe in 1586, at the age of 46. On the arch around him are the crests of important noble families to which he was related.

The New
Astronomy

On January 11, 1600, Kepler set off from Graz to meet
Tycho Brahe. After a journey of about ten days, the party
arrived in Prague, the seat of the Holy Roman Emperor.
High on the hill overlooking the city sat the Hradschin, the
emperor's sprawling compound incorporating castle, cathedral, palace, and imperial offices. Clustered around it, as
though drawn to the seat of power, were the palaces of aristocrats and ambassadors in the district called Hradcany. The
Lesser Town, home of courtiers and craftsmen, spilled down
the hillside to the Molda. Across the long stone bridge, the
city spread out into the patrician Old Town, and further
into New Town. Compared to Graz, it was a busy and
chaotic place, with numerous open markets among the city's
narrow, stinking streets. Prague was an important city in its
own right as capital of prosperous Bohemia. But the presence of the emperor had also attracted a diverse international community of ambassadors, aristocrats, power-seekers,
and hangers-on, as well as scholars, alchemists, artists, and
skilled craftsmen.

Tycho did not live in the city but in Benatky castle in
the countryside northeast of the city, which had been put at

his disposal by the emperor. Consequently, it took some time before Kepler could send out a note announcing his presence in Prague. The next day, Tycho sent his son, Tycho Jr., and a trusted associate, Franz Tengnagel, into town with instructions to bring Kepler back out with them in the carriage.

The meeting of Johannes Kepler and Tycho Brahe on February 4, 1600, is extraordinarily significant in the history of science. The two men could not have been more different. Tycho was a nobleman, self-assured, domineering, and combative. Kepler was a commoner, sincere, reflective, peace-loving, and unassuming. Yet they fit together like a lock and key. Tycho was the observer, with a lifetime's accomplishment behind him in the form of 20 volumes of astronomical observations stretching back more than 35 years. Kepler was the young theorist, with one slim, highly speculative volume to his credit. Both were brilliant, and each one's skills complemented the other's. But neither was there by choice. Tycho had abandoned his native Denmark after a haughty dispute with his patron the king, and now was an expatriate, if not an exile. Kepler had fled oppressive atmosphere of religious intolerance in Styria. The bringing together of these two men at this place and time would change astronomy.

Tycho Brahe was an unusual man, to say the least. The first thing that would have struck Kepler about him was that he had a prosthetic nose made of gold and silver blended to a flesh color, a souvenir of a duel dating back to Tycho's student days. He had close-cropped, receding reddish hair, with a trim beard overhung by a large handlebar mustache. His personality was regal and overbearing.

Tycho had been born into the highest level of Danish society, a small class of aristocratic families that owned and ran the country. With the lavish support of the Danish crown, he had established an unprecedented observatory, Uraniborg, and engaged scores of scholars and craftsmen to aid him in his investigations of the heavens. Tycho had spent most of the last twenty years holed up on his private island devoting his attention—and a great deal of the king of Denmark's gold—to a total reformation of astronomical theory founded on an unprecedentedly complete and accurate collection of observations of the planets. He had trained assistants, cultivated instrument makers, and sent agents to collect astronomical books and manuscripts. Then, just when his 20 years of astronomical activity seemed to be coming to fruition, his royal support had suddenly eroded and he had had to leave Denmark in search of a new patron. After a couple years of uncertainty, he had secured the support of a most important and devoted patron, the Holy Roman Emperor Rudolf II.

When Kepler arrived, Benatky castle was abuzz with activity. Tycho was never comfortable without his great astronomical instruments set up, and masons and carpenters were in the process of making modifications to the castle to accommodate them. Interconnected instrument bays were being erected along the bluff overlooking the river Iser and the flat plain to the south. Here, he would regather his forces and found a "New Uraniborg."

A large and varied staff was being assembled to assist Tycho in his efforts. In addition to Tycho Jr. and Franz Tengnagel, there was Christian Severin Longomontanus, a talented Danish astronomer who had spent his entire career working for Tycho. Johannes Müller, mathematician to the elector of Brandenburg, and his family arrived the following month, pushing Kepler further down in the hierarchy. With Tycho's common-law wife, Kirsten Jørgensdatter, their other children, various other assistants, and servants, the small castle was crowded.

Kepler was rather bewildered by the scene and felt lost amid Tycho's large household. Nor was their collaboration what he had hoped for. He came to use Tycho's superior observational data to test and develop his polyhedral cosmo-

text continues on page 49

In 1575, the king of Denmark granted Tycho Brahe the Island of Hven in the Øresund (the strait between present-day Denmark and Sweden) along with enough money to build and run an observatory. During the next twenty years, Tycho made Uraniborg, "the castle of Urania," into Europe's first scientific research institute. Starting in 1576, he had a Renaissance castle custom-built there to correspond to his needs. Its main feature was two second-story observing decks where instruments were permanently installed under removable conical roofs. There was also a library, where Tycho had a huge brass globe five feet in diameter, on which the positions of stars were patiently engraved when they were known with sufficient accuracy. In the basement, there were 16 furnaces of different kinds for alchemical experiments. Eight small rooms under the roof gables on the third floor housed assistants and students.

Tycho had instrument shops, where he was constantly producing more refined and accurate instruments, and a printing press, so he could publish his findings. In the watchtower of his castle wall, he even had a jail. Elsewhere on the island, he built his own paper mill and fishponds. Later on, Tycho decided that it would be better to have a separate observatory, where larger instruments could be installed down out of the wind. This subterranean observatory, called Stjerneborg, "the castle of the stars," housed Tycho's largest and most sophisticated instruments.

text continued from page 65

logical hypothesis from the *Mysterium cosmographicum*. But he found Tycho to be secretive with his data. For his part, Tycho was not about to give his data away, and he did not particularly trust Kepler, especially given his suspicious connection with Ursus.

Tycho was at the stage in his career when he needed to spend time analyzing his many years of observations to distill accurate planetary theories from the raw data. For this, he needed many assistants to do the calculations. Tycho assigned Kepler to work under Longomontanus's supervision on the theory of Mars. The situation was galling to Kepler. He found himself lost in the commotion at Benatky, picking up dribs and drabs of greatly-desired information as Tycho casually let fall a reference to the location of a planet's apogee (its furthest distance from the earth) or node (where its orbit intersected the sun's orbit) as he held court during dinner in the crowded second floor dining room.

Even though Kepler could not get on with the development of the polyhedral hypothesis, for which he needed data on all of the planets, there was still work he could do on his planet-moving force hypothesis, for which he could use just the Mars observations. And within a few months he had come up with some remarkable confirmation. If the planets were really moved by a force coming from the sun, then the geometry of the planets' theories should reflect that. First, he found that, no matter what he tried, Mars's orbit had to take into account the sun's actual position, which made sense if it was the source of motion. Second, and more importantly, by ingeniously manipulating the observations of Mars, Kepler was able to investigate the earth's orbit, and he found that the earth shared the physically non-uniform motion of the other planets; it too speeded up when it approached the sun and slowed down as it receded. Astronomers had never previously understood that the theory of the earth was so similar to the theories of other planets. In fact, in the *Mysterium cosmographicum*,

Kepler had had to acknowledge that the planet-moving force hypothesis did not work with the earth's orbit. Now, suddenly, the earth's motion confirmed the planet-moving force hypothesis. Though the result was immensely gratifying to Kepler, Tycho Brahe, like Maestlin, objected vehemently to his use of physical analysis in the derivation of planetary theory.

The first summer of Kepler's collaboration with Tycho Brahe was also marred by some friction between the two astronomers over Kepler's status and professional prospects. Facing the extreme uncertainty of how events would unfold in Styria, Kepler pressured Tycho for a formal position and contract. To Tycho, Kepler's demands were an affront. He had problems of his own collecting his salary from the emperor and pushing on with the renovation of Benatky. However, he was working behind the scenes to secure an imperial salary for Kepler, by having the emperor officially summon Kepler to assist Tycho Brahe for two years in his astronomical work. During this time, Kepler would continue to receive his 200 florin salary as district mathematician in Styria, and the emperor would supplement it with another 100 florins. Since the request to release Kepler for this assignment would come from the emperor, it was believed the representatives of the Estates of Styria would not be able to turn it down.

With his future prospects looking much better, Kepler prepared to return home in May. As a final gesture of goodwill, Tycho arranged for Kepler to travel with his third cousin, Frederick Rosenkrantz, as far as Vienna. They departed on June 1. Rosenkrantz would have had tales to tell as they traveled southeast through Bohemia into Austria. Like his cousin, Rosenkrantz was a Danish nobleman whose relations with his native land were strained. He had fled Denmark after getting a young lady-in-waiting pregnant, but had been captured and sentenced to the loss of two fingers and his nobility. But then, the sentence had been commuted to service in the Christian campaign against the

Islamic Turks, who had advanced through the Balkans and were threatening Austria's southern border. After stopping to visit his cousin at Benatky, he was traveling to Vienna to join the Austrian troops. Unbeknownst to him, Rosenkrantz was already being immortalized in a way. In 1592, when on a diplomatic mission to England with another cousin of Tycho's, Knud Gyldenstierne, he had made an impression on the young playwright William Shakespeare and had earned himself a bit part in *Hamlet*.

The hopeful joy that attended the preliminary results of

In this mural, printed in Tycho's Mechanica, Tycho points to the heavens. A cutaway image of Uraniborg shows the observing decks, the library with the great celestial globe, and the alchemical furnaces in the basement.

his research on Mars and the prospect of returning to Prague to continue his work with Tycho Brahe quickly dissipated upon Kepler's return to Graz. The Styrian councilors were not well disposed toward releasing Kepler to return to Prague. Kepler's astronomical speculations were out of place in the uneasy atmosphere that gripped Styria. It would be better, they concluded, if Kepler were to turn his attention to something useful, like going to Italy to study medicine and then returning to practice as a physician.

That summer, Kepler tried to interest Archduke Ferdinand to hire him as his personal mathematician, as his cousin the emperor had done with Tycho Brahe, but Ferdinand had other plans. On July 27, 1600, a notice appeared: an ecclesiastical commission was coming to Graz. At 6 A.M. on July 31, all citizens would present themselves for an examination of their faith. Anyone who was not Catholic or did not pledge to convert to Catholicism would be expelled from the country. Archduke Ferdinand himself accompanied the commissioners. They set up a large table in the middle of the church. During the course of three days, one by one, more than a thousand people approached the table and declared themselves. When Kepler's turn came, he declared himself a Lutheran and unwilling to convert. His name was inscribed on the list of banished men, 15th of 61. He was given six weeks and three days to be out of the country.

Kepler began to make preparations to leave. He only had to figure out where to go. The arrangement with Tycho Brahe was ruined, for it presupposed his receiving the greater part of his pay from Styria. Desperately, he wrote to Maestlin, again asking whether some "little professorship" might be found for him at Tübingen. Not hearing from Maestlin and having no other options, he would head back to Prague. He had been advised that Tycho would find a way to take care of him, and, indeed, Tycho responded to his distress by writing that the collapse of their arrangement did not matter; Kepler should not hesitate but should return with confidence.

On September 30, 1600, two weeks beyond the expulsion deadline, Kepler left Graz with his wife and daughter and two wagons containing all their possessions. His stay in Graz was over.

Kepler had grave misgivings about returning to Tycho's service. He was too proud and insecure to depend entirely on Tycho's mercy, but there was nowhere else to go. Underway, he was struck with a terrible fever. When he arrived in Prague on October 19, Baron Hoffmann took him in, a sick, exhausted, and depressed man. When Maestlin finally reported that there was no prospect of a job for him in Tübingen, Kepler was shattered. He replied with pathetic resignation, "I cannot describe what paroxysm of melancholy your letter caused me . . . For here in Prague I have found everything uncertain, even my life. The only certainty is staying here until I get well or die." A serious cough joined the fever, and Kepler feared he had tuberculosis. His wife became ill as well.

When he was finally well enough to go to work, he found Tycho's circumstances substantially changed as well. Tycho had abandoned his unfinished "New Uraniborg" at Benatky for cramped quarters in the city. When the plague that had gripped Prague the previous year had receded, Emperor Rudolf II and his court had returned, and the emperor desired the presence of his astrologer, Tycho Brahe. It was precisely the kind of work Tycho disliked—it was difficult to convince the emperor of the limit of astrological prognostications—but it was essential to satisfy his patron. He had packed up the instruments and was doing his best to accommodate them at his new home in the city. Kepler and his family were also squeezed in somewhere when they left Baron Hoffmann's. Tycho's personnel had also changed. Longomontanus had left him after many years of service and returned to Denmark to make a career for himself independent of Tycho. None of the various Germans Tycho had tried to attract, including Johannes Müller, had worked out either.

Kepler's fever raged on intermittently for months through the spring of 1601, and he was unable to work much on his Mars research. His fever subsided only that summer, during a visit back to Styria. Old Jobst Müller had died, and Kepler went back to look after his wife's inheritance, hoping to convert her assets into cash. His effort was fruitless, but after he returned from his four month visit around the end of August, he felt really well and rested. When he returned to Prague, Tycho had a scheme to secure for him a formal imperial appointment. The fact of the matter was, Kepler was about the only assistant Tycho had left. Longomontanus was gone. Tengnagel had married Tycho's daughter Elizabeth that summer and gone off to Deventer, Holland, taking another assistant, Johannes Erikson, with him.

Tycho worked as astrologer to Holy Roman Emperor Rudolf II (below) and proposed a great set of astronomical tables that were named the Rudolfine Tables *in his honor.*

Putting a great deal of faith in Kepler, Tycho took him to court and introduced him to the emperor, a strange, shy man with round childlike eyes set in a face anchored by a prominent chin, the characteristic feature of the Hapsburg family. Tycho presented a plan to compile a great set of astronomical tables and asked permission to name them *The Rudolfine Tables*, after the emperor. It was a grand gesture.

The great astronomical tables, like the *Alphonsine* (Ptolemaic) or the *Prutenic* (Copernican), had been named after their sponsors, ensuring them a kind of immortality. If Tycho's lived up to their promise, they would be a magnificent monument indeed. Rudolf liked the idea very much. The only thing Tycho would require would be a salary for his assistant, Johannes Kepler.

The paperwork for Kepler's salary does not seem even to have been put in motion when it became obsolete. Ever since moving into the city, Tycho's social circle had expanded, and without much observing being done at night, he got back into the noble pastime of attending parties where a great deal of hard drinking was done. On October 13, 1601, he attended a party at the house of Peter Vok Rozmberk. In order to avoid some breach of etiquette, Tycho remained seated at the table for far longer than his bladder allowed. It was a fatal miscalculation. By the time he got home, he could no longer urinate, and it quickly became clear that he was in serious trouble. It is impossible to know precisely what afflicted Tycho. Passing even a little urine was excruciatingly painful, and as the wastes built up in his body, he suffered from what Kepler called "intestinal fever," probably what we now call uremia. He passed sleepless nights in agony. Knowing that he would die, he spoke to Kepler, and begged him to present his research in the Tychonic system of the world rather than the Copernican. Then he became delirious, repeating over and over, "Let me not be seen to have lived in vain." Finally, as Kepler inscribed on the final page of Tycho's observation log,

> On October 24, 1601, when his delirium had subsided for a few hours, amid the prayers, tears, and efforts of his family to console him, his strength failed and he passed away very peacefully.
>
> At this time, then, his series of celestial observations was interrupted, and the observations of thirty-eight years came to an end.

On November 4, draped in black cloth and decorated in gold with the Brahe coat of arms, Tycho's casket was carried by twelve imperial officers, all of them noblemen, in a procession to the Protestant Tyne Cathedral. Accompanying it were black banners carrying lists of his titles and accomplishments in gold letters. His riderless horse and men carrying his arms and armor followed behind. Then followed a parade of people: noblemen, barons, ambassadors, his assistants, including Kepler, Tycho's family, and distinguished citizens. A solid wall of humanity lined the route as the procession snaked through the city. And in the church, there was scarcely any room to be found. Tycho was interred in the nave, his grave marked by a magnificent red marble frieze depicting him in full armor. He rests there still.

Kepler had scarcely any time to ponder his future. Within two days, he was informed the he would become the emperor's new mathematician, with responsibility to care for Tycho's instruments and to complete Tycho's unfinished publications, the most important of which would be the *Rudolfine Tables*. At the time of his appointment, Kepler was the obvious choice. There was no other qualified candidate around, and only weeks earlier Tycho had presented him as his primary collaborator in the *Rudolfine Tables*. Still, the emperor recognized that Tycho's instruments and observing logs rightly belonged to his heirs, so he simply bought them for the extraordinary sum of 20,000 florins—an amount sufficient to pay Kepler's previous salary in Styria for a century

Tycho's renowned instruments include the Great Equitorial Armillary (left) and the Trigonal Sextant (right). After Tycho's death, Emperor Rudolf II bought these instruments and made Kepler responsible for looking after them.

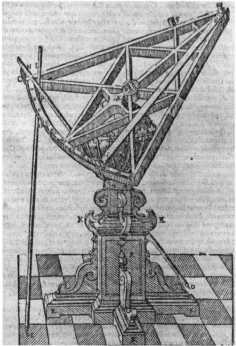

or to buy a half dozen country estates in Bohemia. However, money at the court of Rudolf II had an unearthly quality. The emperor promised whatever he wanted; collecting it from the imperial treasury was another matter. Kepler consistently had problems collecting even his 500 florin annual salary.

The terms of Kepler's succession to Tycho's position sowed the seeds for a conflict with Tycho Brahe's heirs that would exercise a significant influence on the form of Kepler's future scientific work. When Tengnagel returned from England the following summer, he discovered that the heirs had hardly received any money from the treasury. Tengnagel was a nobleman, and Tycho's son-in-law by virtue of his marriage to Elizabeth, so he represented the family's interests. First, he thought he could exert some pressure by suing to get the observing logs back until they were paid for. But then it occurred to him that there was money in the *Rudolfine Tables* project. In October 1602, he managed to get responsibility for the *Rudolfine Tables* transferred to himself, at double Kepler's salary. To add insult to injury, he accused Kepler of sloth and saw to it that someone was assigned to check up on what Kepler was doing.

At this point, the emperor had two mathematicians, and he may well have wondered what he was paying Kepler to do. Kepler was compelled to name the books he would compose to justify his continuing employment. It was a fateful moment, for in grasping among his half-finished projects Kepler named what would be two of the most significant books of seventeenth-century science. As he described the situation in a letter to a friend,

> . . . because I have had my diligence called into doubt, I have assumed the obligation for two works. The one to be ready for Easter 1603 will be Commentaries on the Theory of Mars (or whatever else the name might be), or The Key to a Universal Astronomy . . . The other, to be completed within 8 weeks, will be the Astronomiae pars optica [The Optical Part of Astronomy].

The *Astronomiae pars optica*, whose full title ended up being *Ad Vitellionem paralipomena, quibus astronomiae pars optica traditur* (Supplements to Witelo, in which the Astronomical Part of Astronomy is Treated), had its origin in an essay Kepler had composed in the summer of 1600 on the formation of pinhole images. Earlier that year, Tycho had told him about his observations of a partial solar eclipse, in which the moon passed in front of the sun without completely covering it. Tycho had observed the event without looking directly at the sun by allowing sunlight to fall through a pinhole onto a white screen, where it formed an image of the eclipsed sun. Using his measurements, Tycho concluded that total solar eclipses, in which the moon would completely cover the sun, were impossible. Kepler was skeptical regarding this claim, for there were ample accounts of total solar eclipses in the historic record. After observing a partial solar eclipse for himself from Graz on July 10, 1600, Kepler had carefully analyzed the formation of pinhole images and come to the correct conclusion that their accuracy depended on the size of the aperture. This finding explained Tycho's incorrect conclusion about the possibility of solar eclipses; his pinhole image of the sun was distorted by the size of the aperture and slightly too large, which had led Tycho to believe the moon could never totally cover it. Kepler's essay was a nice little supplement, as he put it, to Witelo's *Optics*, the standard 13th-century treatise on optical theory.

Kepler's essay had clear implications for astronomical observations, and two years later, he grasped for it as something that he could easily get ready for publication within a few weeks. But here, Kepler's legendary inability to focus on one problem at a time got the better of him. First, he wanted to add the other elements of optics that were relevant to astronomy, such as atmospheric refraction. And then he got the work tangled up with a comprehensive treatise on eclipses and the sizes and distances of the sun and moon that he had also been working on. Ultimately, he decided that he could not really write on astronomical observation without taking into account the function of the human eye.

He managed to disentangle the treatise on the sizes and distances of the sun and moon and put it aside, but the material on the function of the eye was a great success. In addition to pinhole images, he was able to publish the first correct account of vision and the eye. For centuries, how we see, a complicated question involving the nature of light, geometrical optics, and the anatomy of the eye, had been a topic of investigation by natural philosophers and optical theorists. By rigorously building on his other optical analyses, Kepler realized that, rather than rays of light being "captured" somehow in the fluid of the eyeball, the lens in the eye *projects* the image of the outside world onto the surface of the retina. Kepler's optical principles dictated that such an image is formed upside down and backwards on the retina; how that image is taken into the mind and rectified to be right side up and frontwards, he could not say. With the help of his new account of vision, he was able to add to this a precise description of the function of different eyeglasses in the correction of nearsightedness and farsightedness. Finally, in the introductory chapter on the nature of light, he was able to deduce the correct relationship for the intensity of light as a function of its distance from the source. Reasoning that light spreads out from a point in a sphere, he concluded that its intensity should be proportional to the area of that sphere, or the intensity should be inversely proportional to the square of the distance.

Some of the problems Kepler attacked did not yield, such as a precise account of the theory of refraction, the bending of light rays as they pass from one medium to another. Nevertheless, starting from an analysis of a limited problem in Witelo's *Optics*, he ended up with such a thorough reworking of optical theory that his *The Optical Part of Astronomy* became the foundation work of seventeenth-century optical theory. It was not a bad performance for some-

Kepler's theory of retinal vision as depicted in René Descartes's Dioptrique. The triangle (V) is projected onto the retina at R and the circle (Y) at T. Thus the image of the outside world is projected upside down and backwards onto the retina.

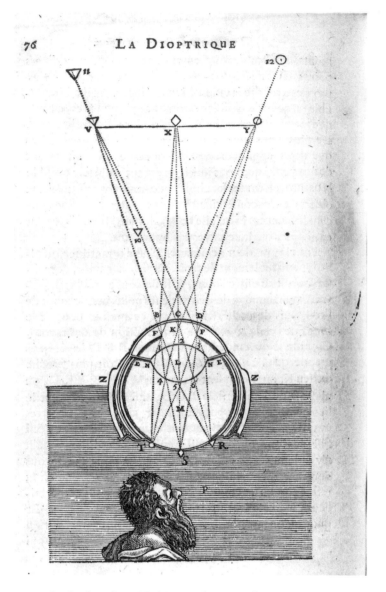

one who had to "justify his employment."

Kepler had originally promised the *Astronomiae pars optica* in time for Christmas 1602. As it swelled to become a tome of 450 pages, publication was delayed, and he did not finally present the finished manuscript to the emperor until January 1604. It was printed in Frankfurt, and appeared in time for the great Frankfurt book fair in the fall of 1604.

When the book was out of his hands, Kepler turned his attention to the other project he had promised the emperor, a work he referred to as *The Commentaries on Mars*, or *The Key to a Universal Astronomy*. It was an odd genre for an astronomical book; a single planet's motion had never before been the subject of a book-length treatment. This tight focus was in some sense contrived, because Tengnagel had snatched away responsibility for the larger project of coming up with tables for all of the planets. But Kepler realized that it would be a work of great significance, for it was by using observations of Mars that he had discovered that a major change was needed in the theory of the earth's orbit. He recognized the significance of this finding even before committing to the *Commentaries*, writing in a letter, "In short, I have beheld the sun in the theory of Mars as though in a mirror, in that I see how and to what extent it affects all planets. I take from Mars the example for treating the others. And thus I hope presently for all the best for every part of astronomy."

So far, Kepler's work on Mars had vindicated his novel, physical approach to deriving the orbits of the planets. He had had the hunch, based upon his notion of a planet-moving force coming forth from the sun, that the earth's orbit had to be like the other planets, so that it would move faster when it was closer to the sun and slower when it was further away. And he had been right. If he could demonstrate that his "celestial physics" was valid, he would be able to argue that only the Copernican system of the universe made physical sense and that it was true. Since, as he believed, the heliocentric system was a material symbol of God in His creation, establishing its truth continued to have an important religious dimension as well.

Since Tycho's death, Kepler's Mars research had taken a turn toward becoming ever more physical. He had started with the planet-moving force hypothesis put forward in the *Mysterium cosmographicum*, but he had realized that his formulation was flawed. He had then begun using the simple principle that a planet's speed around the sun was inversely proportional to its distance: the closer it is, the faster it goes around. But how could one describe the ensuing motion mathematically? It was a difficult question, because on an eccentric orbit the planet would be slightly changing its distance, and therefore its speed, all the way around. A modern mathematician would use calculus to calculate the effect, but it had not been invented yet.

Kepler first took a brute-force approach. He calculated the distance from the sun to Mars at each and every degree around an eccentric circular orbit and used the sum of those distances as a measure of the time it took to get from one place to another. It was a tedious and unsatisfactory experience, but as he was thinking about it, he remembered that Archimedes, the Greek mathematician who lived at the turn of the second century B.C., had used a similar trick with sums of distances to calculate the area of a circle. Surely, the area swept out by Mars as it went around its orbit would be a good measurement of the sum of the distances. In this way, Kepler came to the approximating principle that the area swept out by a planet as it goes around its orbit will be equal in equal time intervals. This later came to be known, through an historical accident, as Kepler's "second law" of planetary motion, even though he came upon it first.

He tried applying his new area law on a circular orbit that was slightly eccentric, so that the sun was located off center along an axis that passed through the center of the circle and defined Mars's closest and furthest positions from the sun. When he did so, he realized that, in his calculated position, Mars was spending too much time along the sides of its orbit away from the axis. It would have to be speeded up there, which meant that the orbit would have to be squeezed in a little along the sides to redistribute that area, or time, into other parts of the orbit. As he put it, it was as though you held a fat-bellied sausage and squeezed it in the

KEPLER'S FIRST TWO LAWS

Kepler's first two laws are:

1. The planets move in elliptical orbits, with the sun at one focus.

2. The line connecting the planet and the sun sweeps out equal areas in equal times.

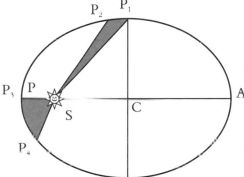

The two laws are illustrated in the figure above, which shows the elliptical orbit of a planet, with the sun at the focus marked S. The size of an ellipse is usually given in terms of the *semimajor axis*, which is half the long axis PA, or the distance PC. And the eccentricity is defined as the ratio of the distance of the sun from the center to the size of the semimajor axis, or $e = \frac{SC}{PC}$. The ellipse depicted above has an extraordinarily large eccentricity compared to the orbits of the planets, which would look like perfect circles if shown at this scale.

Kepler's second law states the area swept out by the planet as it moves along its orbit from position P_1 to P_2 (the shaded area P_1SP_2) must be the same as the area swept out in an equal time interval as it moves from P_3 to P_4 (area P_3SP_4). As is apparent in the diagram, this means that when a planet's distance to the sun is smaller, it must move correspondingly further around its orbit in the same time interval. Consequently, the planet moves most quickly around perihelion (P) and most slowly around aphelion (A), or as Kepler would have expressed it, it moves most quickly when it is near the source of the planet-moving force and most slowly when it is furthest away.

middle, forcing the meat out into the ends. Thus, by exercising his physical intuition, Kepler came to the conclusion that the orbit must be some kind of oval, rather than a perfect circle. The rest of his effort would be devoted to determining which oval, in conjunction with his area law, produced positions that agreed with Tycho's exquisitely accurate observations.

The task of determining exactly which oval was appropriate and how to generate it was a torturously complex process that took all of 1604. Kepler wrote to Longomontanus that he had tried it twenty different ways. Eventually, he resorted to using an ellipse as an approximation of a likely oval orbit. Ellipses are a subset of ovals that have mathematical properties that make them much easier to use, especially when calculating areas. With this approximating elliptical orbit and the area law, the error was almost precisely opposite what it had been with a circular orbit. The sausage had been squeezed too much. He then concluded that the correct orbit must lie somewhere in between.

This new in-between ellipse had the interesting feature that the sun precisely occupied one of its foci. Indeed, Kepler's interest in this new orbit had originally been spurred by considering exactly how far in from a circle Mars had come at the point one quarter of the way around its orbit. He knew that it should come in about half as far as his previous attempt, and then suddenly realized that, measured from the sun, there was a concise trigonometrical way to describe that distance, and it entailed an elliptical orbit. Moreover, he understood precisely how Mars's distance from the sun changed throughout its orbit, and this particular ellipse resolved a nagging problem about the accuracy of his area law approximation. This flood of considerations came to him at once. It was, he wrote, "as if I were roused from a dream and saw a new light." Thus, he came to his "first law" of planetary motion, that the orbits of the planets are ellipses with the sun at one focus.

The book was not supposed to be merely about a new theory for Mars. It was the debut of a whole new physical approach to astronomical theory, which happened to be based on Kepler's Mars research. Therefore he entitled it *Astronomia nova AITIOΛOGHTOΣ, seu physica coelestis, tradita commentariis de motibus stellae Martis*, that is, A New Astronomy Based upon Causes, or Celestial Physics, Treated by Means of Commentaries on the Motions of Mars. He knew it could not *prove* that his physical astronomy or the Copernican system was true. Mathematical astronomers would be all too willing to disregard what he thought would be the most compelling feature of the book, the physical basis of his new astronomical theories. His journey through astronomical theory carries the weight of his argument. "No other approach," he wrote, "would succeed than that founded upon the very physical causes of the motions." In the end, the argument is rhetorical: the fact that Kepler discovered the ellipse and the area law following certain hunches does not logically establish that his reasoning is correct.

Around Easter 1605, Kepler realized that Mars's orbit was an ellipse, but he still had much more to write. Before Kepler could publish he also had to settle with Tengnagel, who had the right to approve any of Kepler's work based on Tycho's observations. The prospect of having Tengnagel meddling in his work was almost more than Kepler could bear, especially since Tengnagel had essentially abandoned his work on the *Rudolfine Tables*. Kepler agreed to let Tengnagel write a preface to his book, in which Tengnagel admonished the reader "not to be swayed by anything of Kepler's, especially his liberty in disagreeing with Brahe in physical arguments."

Everything went slowly, and it was not until 1609 that the *Astronomia nova* finally appeared. The emperor had reserved the right to distribute every copy of his personal mathematician's work, but in the end Kepler had to turn the entire edition over to the printer to cover unpaid costs. It was not a very auspicious launching for what would turn out to be one of the most important astronomical works in history.

The *Astronomia nova* was a tall, handsome—if slightly austere—volume of some 340 pages. It is considered to be Kepler's masterpiece. It is a work of great mathematical genius and breathtaking inventiveness. His contentious point that knowledge of the planet's motions can only be determined by consideration of the physical cause of those motions eventually came to be recognized as true. It is interesting, however, that, though he showed that astronomy should be physical, his particular physics was ultimately discarded. In the generations after his death, it came to be recognized that there is no force coming from the sun that pushes the planets around. The celestial mechanics that Isaac Newton developed is entirely different. The planets' tendency is to continue moving in straight lines, and the gravitational attraction of the sun pulling them in constrains them to move around it. But even with this different physics, Kepler's first two laws necessarily follow: the orbits of the planets are elliptical with the sun at one focus and the area swept out by a planet is equal in equal times.

The great work of the *Astronomia nova* now completed, Kepler took a break from his studies, and his mind turned to Galileo. How would the Italian, who also sought physical proofs of Copernicus's system, react to Kepler's painstaking presentation of his physical astronomy? Little did he know that Galileo was not studying the *Astronomia nova* but making the astronomical discoveries that would make him the talk of Europe and secure his reputation for all time.

On March 15, 1610, the startling news came to Prague that Galileo had discovered four new planets. Kepler's friend the imperial councilor Johann Matthäus Wackher von Wackenfels was so excited by the report that he stopped his carriage at Kepler's house and called him down to the street to tell him. The two were so overcome that they could scarcely talk. They babbled and laughed in excitement at the news. Kepler was excited but ashamed and confused as well. What did the discovery mean for his polyhedral hypothesis? He had already determined the necessary number of planets, and there was room for no more.

Galileo's book had not even left the press when the news first flew to Prague. The first copy of his *Sidereus nuncius* (The Starry Messenger) (1610) to reach the city belonged to the curious emperor, who lent it to his mathematician for his opinion. Kepler was immediately relieved. The new planets were previously-unknown satellites of Jupiter, discovered by Galileo using the newly invented telescope. In addition to Jupiter's moons, Galileo demonstrated definitively that the surface of the moon was rough and earthlike. He also turned his telescope to the stars, revealing thousands that had previously remained unseen. The Milky Way he resolved into a myriad of stars whose faint light combined into the nebulous streak across the sky.

The advent of telescopic observation would open a new era for astronomy. In the meantime, Galileo's announce-

These images from Galileo's Sidereus nuncius depict the surface of the moon as viewed through the telescope. Galileo's observations showed that the moon was mountainous and earthlike.

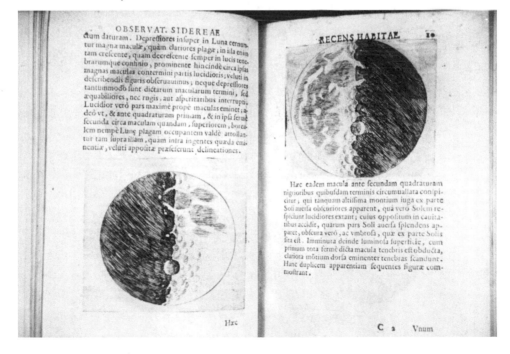

ment was so radical that many could scarcely believe it. Because Kepler was imperial mathematician, his opinion would carry some weight and lend Galileo important credibility. Galileo sent a copy of his book along with a letter asking for Kepler's judgment to the Tuscan ambassador in Prague, who had the book delivered to Kepler. On April 13, Kepler visited the ambassador's residence, where Galileo's request was read to him. An official courier was returning to Tuscany within a week, and Kepler promised his reply would be ready for the return trip. He finished his letter to Galileo on April 19.

So many other people were anxious to know what Kepler had said that he had the letter printed as a small 35-page book with the title *Dissertatio cum nunceo sidereo* (A Conversation with the Starry Messenger) (1610). It was an unusual work. Kepler did not have a telescope, so he could not confirm the observations. (Try as he might he could not get Galileo to send him one and eventually had to borrow one to see the new phenomena for himself.) In the meantime, the most Kepler could do to lend Galileo support was establish the plausibility of what Galileo had reported, beginning with the telescope itself. In some ways the principle of magnifying images using a combination of lenses had been alluded to in previous optical theory. But it was something Kepler had missed in his *Astronomia pars optica*. Five months later, he had cracked the problem and the next year Kepler published the first detailed optical theory of two lens systems in his *Dioptrice* (1611), including a superior telescope design using two convex lenses, now called the "astronomical" or "Keplerian" telescope.

Otherwise, Kepler could only respond enthusiastically to Galileo's discoveries and speculate about their meaning. With regard to Galileo's account of lunar geography, Kepler admitted that he was totally convinced by Galileo's observations and analysis of mountains and craters on the moon, and he speculated that the cratered appearance was due perhaps to the moon being light and porous (which according to Kepler's physical astronomy would explain its rapid revolution around the earth). Or perhaps the craters were great circular ramparts built by lunar inhabitants, in whose shade they could shelter during the inhospitable 14 days of continuous sunlight on the moon's surface.

Jupiter's moons were by far the most spectacular of Galileo's discoveries. For Kepler, they were significant because they had implications in favor of heliocentrism. First, the fact that Jupiter also had moons seemed to remove the objection that the earth could not travel around the sun without losing its moon. Also, the fact that the moons revolved in the plane of Jupiter's rotation implied that the moons were being swept around by a planet-moving force coming from Jupiter, just as Kepler had suggested in the *Astronomia nova* that the moon is moved by the earth's rotation. Finally, Jupiter's moons suggested to Kepler that Jupiter must be inhabited by intelligent beings. Why else would God have endowed Jupiter with this feature we cannot see?

With the publication of the *Dissertatio,* Kepler became the first astronomer to come out publicly in favor of Galileo and his discoveries. The support of the imperial mathematician helped to subdue the sniping Galileo faced from his critics. Yet, in return, Kepler received from Galileo scarcely a word of thanks and no acknowledgment of Kepler's more substantial achievements in astronomy. Though Kepler tried a few more times to engage the Italian in correspondence, apart from one inconsequential note some 17 years later, he never heard from Galileo again. Though two of the greatest astronomers in history lived at the same time, and even communicated, there was barely a connection between them. In his unassuming way, Kepler never complained of Galileo's offensive disregard. And Galileo apparently took little notice of Kepler's reform of astronomical theory.

It was now 1611; Kepler was 39 years old. In the 11 years since coming to Prague, Johannes Kepler had grown from an insecure refugee into a leading figure in the imperial capital's learned circles and a man of international scientific reputation. His status as scientific heir to Tycho Brahe and the flow of important works that issued from his pen lent him an air of astronomical omniscience that the English poet John Donne described in his satire *Ignatius his Conclave* (1611), where he wrote that "ever since Tycho Brahe's death [Kepler] hath received it into his care, that no new thing should be done in heaven without his knowledge."

The same period that saw Kepler's rise to fame saw the decline of his eccentric patron into madness. Observing the emperor's governance from afar before moving to Prague, Kepler had marveled at the emperor's "Archimedian manner," a kind of dynamic immobility, as he saw it, in which the emperor nonetheless managed to maintain a long, stalemated war against the Ottoman Turks and, at the same time, kept the empire's fractious states from disintegrating. But since Kepler's arrival in Prague in 1600, the emperor's pathological shyness and extreme stubbornness had given way to isolation, paralyzing indecision, and paranoia. Turning away from the world, he became a recluse, shut in among his precious collections in Hradschin, a virtual prisoner in his own castle. It was widely reported that his erratic mental state had deteriorated into insanity.

As Rudolf's intransigence and inactivity began to imperil the house of Hapsburg and the empire, a conspiracy was hatched against him. At a secret meeting of the Austrian Hapsburgs in Vienna in April 1606, the family agreed to recognize Rudolf's estranged, ambitious younger brother Matthias as head of the family. Two years later, Matthias moved against his brother under force of arms, leading an army of 20,000 men from Vienna, through Moravia, into Bohemia, and to within a day's march of Prague. Facing certain defeat, the emperor capitulated. He ceded Matthias the kingdom of Hungary and archduchies of Austria and Moravia effective immediately, retaining only Bohemia,

Silesia, and Lusatia to himself, though Rudolf had to ensure Matthias's succession as king of Bohemia after his death.

The weakened emperor now faced pressure from the powerful Protestant representatives of the Bohemian Estates, the representative assembly in Bohemia, who exacted from him a Letter of Majesty (1609) guaranteeing freedom of religion. Chaffing under the concessions they had extorted and descending into insanity, Rudolf made a desperate bid to regain control of his country and its capital. The following winter, Rudolf inexplicably invited his cousin, Archduke Leopold V, bishop of Passua, to invade Bohemia. Leopold's army pillaged its way through Bohemia to Prague, invading and looting the Hradcany and the Lesser Town.

A spirited defense by Protestant troops (who for their part also looted Catholic churches and monasteries in the Old Town) and a large bribe put an end to Leopold's attack, but Rudolf was finished. In the midst of the crisis, the Protestant representatives sided with Matthias. Rudolf was deposed, and on May 23, 1611, Matthias was crowned king of Bohemia. Deranged and powerless, the emperor lived out his days in the Hradschin, where he died within a year on January 20, 1612.

Kepler stayed loyal to his patron to the end. Though he was consulted for advice, he did his best to keep astrology out of the gullible emperor's troubled mind. And when the emperor's enemies approached Kepler, he spun the astrological analysis in the emperor's favor, predicting long life for him and trouble for Matthias. Still, Kepler could see that the situation was deteriorating. He took care to have backup plans ready and found a promising situation in the Upper Austrian capital of Linz. After the emperor's death, nothing held Kepler in Prague, and in the middle of April he left the city for Linz.

A portrait by Hans von Aachen, probably of Kepler, from around 1612.

The Harmony of the World

When Kepler arrived in Linz in May 1612, he was emotionally exhausted. The splendid intellectual society in the imperial capital in which he had been intensely creative and productive had submerged into civil war. The horrible events of the previous year had robbed him of the will to continue his astronomical studies.

The year 1611 had been devastating and sorrowful, not only for Prague but also for Kepler's family. As the year opened, his wife Barbara was sick with Hungarian fever and showed signs of a mental disorder. As she was recovering, all three children were struck with smallpox. Eight-year-old Susanna (his second daughter with that name) and three-year-old Ludwig survived, but Kepler's favorite, darling six-year-old Friedrich, died on February 19, and Barbara sank into a depression. Then, Archduke Leopold's troops invaded, and Kepler's neighborhood in Old Town was overrun by unruly Bohemian peasants loosely organized for the Protestant cause. At this point, Kepler redoubled his efforts to move his family away from Prague. But even as he was returning from a trip to Linz to make arrangements in June 1611, he found Barbara deathly ill from a contagious fever brought into Prague by Matthias's Austrian troops. She died on July 3, 1611.

Though he was glad to be away from the charged and uncertain atmosphere in Prague, his arrival in quiet Linz was accompanied by pangs of guilt. Three years before, he had begun planning the move to accommodate his wife, whose simple nature had never been at ease in the imperial capital. He had chosen the place because of its similarity to Barbara's native Graz. Linz was the provincial capital of Upper Austria, the duchy northeast of Styria. Like its neighbor before Archduke Ferdinand's confessional cleansing, Upper Austria was predominantly Protestant. Yet it was within the Hapsburgs' hereditary lands, so Kepler was able to arrange to continue his work there. Now, without his wife, the imperial mathematician felt out of place in a city that did not boast a university or printing press and whose Protestant school was inferior even to Graz's.

Finding a position for a man of Kepler's stature had been ticklish. At the invitation of some Upper Austrian lords, Kepler had tendered his services to the representatives of the Estates of Upper Austria after Rudolf's abdication. A contract was drawn up according to which Kepler would continue work on the *Rudolfine Tables*, compose a map of Upper Austria, and produce whatever mathematical, philosophical, or historical studies were "useful and suitable." In practice, he had the same job he had had in Graz: district mathematician and teacher in the district school. It was a rather ordinary position for the man he had become, but the authorities in Linz paid him his 400 florins regularly, which was far more than he could say for his exalted imperial appointment.

Kepler's high profile unfortunately exposed him to unwelcome scrutiny from his coreligionists in Linz. Immediately upon his arrival, Kepler sought communion from the chief pastor, Daniel Hitzler, himself an alumnus of the Tübingen theological seminary. Since his seminary days, Kepler's questioning of Lutheran dogma had grown into a refusal to sign the Formula of Concord, the Lutherans' strict charter of belief. The issue that particularly concerned him was the interpretation of the Eucharist, in which Kepler sided with the Lutherans' hated rivals, the Calvinists. Hitzler required Kepler to sign the Formula of Concord. Kepler declined to subscribe to the relevant clause regarding the interpretation of the Eucharist and Hitzler denied him communion, thereby excluding him from the congregation.

That his strongly held personal convictions should exclude him from the Protestant community was intensely painful to Kepler, especially since it was on a fine point of dogma only theologians could appreciate. In August, he appealed Hitzler's ruling to the church consistory in Stuttgart. His petition was swiftly rejected in a shaming letter that upheld Hitzler on all points and advised Kepler to refrain from "theological speculations" and concern himself with his mathematical studies. As a "lost little sheep" he should obediently follow the voice of the arch-shepherd. Although Kepler was incapable of being "sheepish" about matters of conscience, he promised to be quiet and make no trouble.

Nevertheless, he became the object of rampant gossip about his unorthodox views. Unlike those who sought to police belief and vilify their opponents, Kepler drew elements of religious truth from Lutheranism, Calvinism, and Catholicism. He was alternately accused of being fickle and wanting to found his own unique Keplerian creed. He responded bitterly, "It makes me heartsick that the three big factions have so miserably torn up the truth among themselves that I have to gather the little scraps together wherever I find them." Even as the German-speaking lands were inching inexorably toward a devastating religious war, he never ceased to try to act as a conciliator among the faiths. He was repaid with suspicion, backbiting, and threats. The final chapter of Kepler's exclusion from communion came in the wake of a painful and awkward visit to his old theology professor Matthias Hafenreffer in Tübingen in the fall of

1617. In the desperate hope of being readmitted to communion, he began a passionate and detailed correspondence with Hafenreffer about his refusal in conscience to sign the Formula of Concord. After an exchange of two letters, Hafenreffer laid their correspondence before the theological faculty and the consistory for a decision. The time for discussion was over. On July 31, 1619, he delivered their official verdict: "Either you will abandon your erroneous and wholly fallacious fantasies and embrace the divine truth with humble faith, or stay away from the fellowship of our church and of our creed." Kepler was effectively excommunicated from the Lutheran church.

After his arrival in Linz in 1612, the first project upon which Kepler embarked was finding a new wife to care for his children and run his new household. He undertook this search in deadly earnest but with his characteristic inability to keep any one thing on his mind. Kepler's tortured route toward finding a bride is preserved in a letter to an unnamed noble friend, in which the various candidates are referred to only by number, which gives the procedure a comical mathematical overtone. He had called his many years of trial and error in planetary theory his "warfare with Mars." He likewise waged a battle in his mind over which candidate to pick.

Number One was a widow he and his wife had known in Prague, whom his wife had seemed to recommend before her death. It seemed fitting that a mature man like Kepler, now past the passion of youth, should settle down with a woman experienced in running a household. But she had two marriageable daughters and her assets were controlled by a trustee whom she did not want to alienate. Besides, though she looked healthy enough, her breath stank, and when Kepler saw her again after six years, he did not find her attractive. To confuse matters, one of her daughters had become Number Two in the interim, an unseemly turn of affairs. The daughter was attractive and well educated, but used to luxury and immature for running a household. She would be more glittering than useful. At this point, bewildered by the choice and questioning whether it was a good idea to consider what his wife would have wanted, Kepler had left Prague.

Putting those prospects aside, there was Number Three, another widow from Bohemia who was attractive and good with the children. She was willing, but betrothed to another, who had in the meantime gotten a prostitute pregnant, so she felt released from that obligation. But it did not work out.

The series continued in Linz with Number Four. She was from an honorable family, attractive and athletic in stature, and the match might well have gone through, had Kepler not been distracted by Five. Compared with Four, Five's family was less respectable and she had less property and a smaller dowry, but she distinguished herself with her seriousness and independence, and above all with her love and Kepler's faith in her humility, frugality, diligence, and love of the stepchildren.

Kepler vacillated, waiting for advice on whether he should marry Three after all. When he abandoned that prospect, he started to favor Four, but in the meantime she had grown tired of waiting and become engaged to someone else. By this time, Five was losing her luster as well. Number Six had a certain nobility, but she was immature and possibly conceited. He felt awkward abandoning Five and went back to her. But then friends, concerned with her common origins, recommended Number Seven, a noblewoman. She was a good candidate, but he could not make up his mind, so she rejected him.

By now the imperial mathematician's inept wooing had become the talk of Linz, but the parade of candidates went on. Number Eight had religious scruples due to Kepler's exclusion from communion. Number Nine had lung disease, and Kepler foolishly tested her by telling her he was in love with someone else. Number Ten was ugly and so fat that Kepler was afraid people would laugh at the comical contrast to his thinness. Finally, Number Eleven was with-drawn after a long wait because she was too young.

Five had long been in his mind. He summoned up his courage, returned to her, offered her his hand, and she accepted. She was Susanna Reuttinger, the orphaned daugh-ter of a cabinetmaker, who had lived for many years as the ward of Baroness von Starhemberg, whose husband was one of Kepler's patrons in Linz. At 24 years old, she was much younger than Kepler's 41 years, which occasioned some twittering. Even Kepler's stepdaughter Regina wrote to say that Susanna was not old enough to act as stepmother to Kepler's children. But he loved and trusted her. They were married on October 30, 1613, and in time, she bore him seven more children, only one or two of whom survived to adulthood. We hear little more about her during his life, but in Kepler's life, no news is generally good news.

Though the document in which Kepler pours out to his noble friend the misadventure of selecting a new bride is pathetic, even comedic, Kepler found the process profound. He could do nothing more than question the role of divine providence in the series of events that tore him one way and then another before revealing his true love. Throughout, he had been diverted by considerations of his prospective bride's status, family encumbrances, wealth, and his standing in the community, but in the end he had chosen an honest com-mon woman. His actions caused him to question his own character, as he asked, "Can I find God, Who in the con-templation of the entire universe I can almost feel in my hands, also in myself?"

Kepler eased back into scholarly work. Still unable to immerse himself in the astronomical work that consumed him, he addressed his skills to an interesting mathematical problem having to do with wine barrels. In the summer of 1613, Kepler was summoned to Regensburg by Emperor Matthias, who had succeeded Rudolf upon his death and confirmed Kepler's appointment as imperial mathematician

STEREOMETRIA DO-

lit, ut æquentur capacitate, quia vix vnquam profunditates ventrium ad diametrum orbis lignei, attingunt proportionem sefquitertiam,

Hactenus de figura Dolij Auftriaci, fequitur,

De virga cubicá eiufq; certitudine.

THEOREMA XXVI.

In dolijs, quæ funt inter fe figuræ fimilis: proportio capacitatum eft tripla ad proportionem illarum longitudinum, quæ funt ab orificio fummo, ad imum calcem alterutrius Orbis lignei.

Sint dolia diverfæ magnitudinis, fpecie eadem SQKT, XGCZ, quorum orificia OA, diametri orbium ligneorum QK, ST & GC, XZ, eo-

Schema XXII.

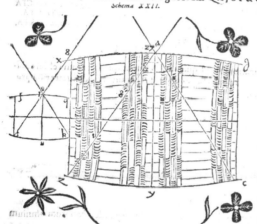

runq; ima T, K & Z. C. longitudines OK, OT æquales, fic & AC, AZ Diro, capacitates doliorú, effe in tripla proportione longitudinis OK, AC. Agantur enim per O, A, plana OV, AY, parallela orbibus ligneis, & fint duo trunci Conici, SV & VQ,

fic XY, & YG inter fe fimiles. Quæ igitur de proportione dimidiorum doliorum funt vera, illa etiam de duplicatis erunt vera. Sint igitur propofitæ figuræ OVKQ. AYCG, conici trunci, fintq; latera figurarum OQ, VK, & AG, YC. Diametri Bafium minorum QK, GC, diametri bafium maiorum OV, AY; & OQKV, AGCY fectiones quadrilateræ figurarum per fuos axes, fimiles inter fe, earumq; diagonij OK, AC.

Ergò cum figuræ fimiles, fint ad feinvicem in tripla proportione analogorum laterum, erit proportionis AG lateris ad OQ latus, aut GC diametri, ad QK diametrum tripla, proportio GY corporis ad QV corpus. At in figuris planis trilateris AGC & QK fimilibus, ut GC ad analogum QK, vel ut AG ad analogum OQ, fic etiam diagonios AC ad analogon diago.

In Nova stereometria doliorum vinariorum *(1615), Kepler discussed the problem of the measurement of the volume of wine barrels. Wine merchants calculated the volume of a barrel from a linear measure of the diagonal from the fill hole (a) to the side of the bottom (z). Kepler simplified the process of measurement by treating the cask as the sum of two truncated cones.*

shortly thereafter. On the way back down the Danube to Linz, Kepler noticed that the banks of the river were lined with wine casks of various shapes and sizes and he became interested in the problem of how to express their volumes mathematically.

Since their sides were not straight, he had to think of a way to approximate their volume as the sum of a large number of thin disks, each of which was slightly larger or smaller than the next. In a characteristically Keplerian manner, he soon realized that similar techniques could be used to calculate the volume of whole families of solid figures. In particular, he wanted to generalize the study to include shapes generated by conic sections (the family of curves including the circle, ellipse, and parabola) rotated around any line in their plane. Though some of his demonstrations may have lacked mathematical rigor, this work became an important part of the history of the development of the integral calculus in the 17th century, even though it had the apparently prosaic title *Nova Stereometria doliorum vinariorum* (A New Stereometry of Wine Casks).

The book was not a tremendous success. In fact, after failing to interest any publisher, Kepler took the initiative of having a printer, Johannes Plank, brought to Linz and in 1615 the *Nova Stereometria doliorum vinariorum* became the first book ever published in the city. Kepler's superiors, the representatives of the Estates, were unimpressed, and they advised their mathematician to concentrate on the matters specified in the contract: the *Rudolfine Tables* and the map. Kepler had found working on the map uninteresting and odious, not least because, as he wrote in a report on his work, his information-gathering trips had been marred by "scolding and threats from inexperienced, coarse, and suspicious peasants." Besides, he argued, the map distracted his attention from the *Rudolfine Tables*. The representatives took the hint and transferred responsibility for the map to their district engineer.

His experience with the *Nova Stereometria doliorum vinariorum* had the important consequence of forcing Kepler to become his own publisher. In the following years, he fed Plank a series of works he composed in Linz. A German edition was prompted in part by having Plank sitting idle and also by the opportunity it presented of widening the circle of presentation copies for which Kepler would receive the customary financial reward. Such honoraria were often more lucrative than the actual sale of the book. In the case of the German edition, Kepler already had the woodblocks for the illustrations, so he only had to pay for new typesetting and printing. Once he had distributed the presentation copies and tallied up the honoraria he received in return, he covered the production costs and raked in at least 40 florins pure profit before actually selling a single copy. In addition, he resumed publishing annual prognostications in 1616 after a hiatus of 11 years. He considered this "a little more honorable than begging," and he needed the money for his next big publishing venture, an astronomical textbook.

Even during the composition of the *Astronomia nova,* it had been clear to Kepler that his new astronomy would be incomprehensible to most readers. In addition to being philosophically alien, the ellipse and the area law made calculations much more complicated. As early as 1611, Kepler had begun planning a more textbook-like exposition that would reach students down to "the low schoolbenches," and yet also contain the theoretical basis of the *Rudolfine Tables.*

He named the book the *Epitome astronomiae Copernicanae* (The Epitome of Copernican Astronomy) in conscious imitation of his own teacher Maestlin's oft-reprinted textbook, the *Epitome astronomiae.* But whereas Maestlin had taught introductory astronomy from a geocentric standpoint, Kepler became the first person to present heliocentric astronomy in textbook form. Kepler gave Planck the manuscript of the first volume in 1616, which contained basic material on the nature and scope of astronomy, the shape of the earth, the celestial sphere, the earth's motion around the sun, and the sun's consequent risings and settings, up to some problems in spherical trigonometry.

Immediately after finishing this volume, Kepler gave Planck his *Ephemeris for 1618.* An ephemeris ("ephemerides" is the plural) contains tables that give the position of each of the planets for every day of the year. Since ephemerides were essential reference books for astrologers and navigators, they were a lucrative product for astronomers of Kepler's time. The *Rudolfine Tables* would give the theory and means for anyone to calculate ephemerides that were just as accurate as his own, so Kepler got a head start on cashing in on their commercial potential by starting to calculate his own ephemerides before giving others the means to do so.

He had had a good theory for Mars in the *Astronomia nova*. When his life began to settle down in Linz in 1614, he had worked on the other planets off and on, and by May 1616, he was far enough along to begin grinding out ephemerides. But then, there was the problem of printing. Ephemerides were mostly numbers and printers did not normally have enough. Kepler therefore decided to invest in his own set of numerical type. The tedious calculations took time too. Kepler had help from assistants now and then but had to do much of it himself.

With the help of Kepler's type, Planck's press kept cranking. A prognostication for 1618 finished off 1617, to be ready for the new year. Then, in 1618, followed an ephemeris for 1617, an ephemeris for 1619, and a prognostication for 1619.

Even as Planck was clearing the backlog of publications, mounting troubles in Kepler's personal life diverted him from the task of completing the *Rudolfine Tables*. To begin with, the problem of his exclusion from communion weighed heavily on his mind. He began also to get wind of family problems back home in Württemberg. At the end of December 1615, he had gotten word from his relatives that accusations of witchcraft had been leveled against his 68-year-old mother. Almost a year later, to keep her from making matters worse for herself, they had sent her to Linz to live with her son.

The storm in Kepler's personal life mounted in the fall

of 1617. First, his two-and-a-half-year-old daughter Margarethe Regina, the first of his children with Susanna, died on September 8, 1617, of cough, consumption, and epilepsy. Shortly thereafter, her namesake, his stepdaughter Regina, died on October 4, 1617. She had been seven years old when Kepler married her mother, Barbara, and he had loved her from the start. Through the subsequent years in Prague as he battled with the theory of Mars, he had watched as she grew into a young woman. In 1608, he had seen her married in a good match to Philip Ehem, a descendant of a prominent Augsburg family, then representative at the imperial court of Elector Frederick IV of the Palatinate. In the disorder of 1610 they had moved back to the Palatinate, though she still kept in touch with her father in letters. She and her husband had just moved to Walderbach, near Regensburg, when she died at the age of twenty-seven.

Philip Ehem was desperate for help with Kepler's three grandchildren and begged him to send his eldest daughter, 15-year-old Susanna, to help him temporarily. Kepler agreed, and accompanied her personally on the trip up the Danube to Regensburg. From there, he went on to Württemberg, where his mother had gone earlier in the month, to see what he could do to put an end to the nonsense about sorcery.

As diversion on his trip, he took with him Vincenzo Galilei's *Dialogo della musica antica e moderne* (Dialogue Concerning Ancient and Modern Music), in which the astronomer Galileo's father had defended the Pythagorean theory of harmony. Kepler had long been interested in theories of harmony because of their mathematical basis. Though he found the Italian a little rough going, it was similar enough to Latin, and he read through three-quarters of it with relish during the trip.

The trip to Württemberg ended up being fruitless, as proceedings against his mother were once again delayed. He did get a chance to visit Tübingen, where he discussed every aspect of his new tables with old Maestlin and met an impressive young man, Wilhelm Schickard, who was not only mathematically talented but also an expert in oriental languages, such as Hebrew and Arabic. But Kepler's attempt to reconcile himself with Hafenreffer and his faith was rebuffed. On the way back, he stopped to visit Susanna to see how she was settling in, and then returned to Linz.

He arrived in Linz on December 22, 1617, just at the beginning of the Christmas festivities. The final blow came when he found his six-month-old daughter Katharina, his second child with Susanna, deathly ill, and on February 9, 1618, she, too, died. Kepler had lost three children in less than six months.

His spirit was too weighed down to go back to his work on the *Rudolfine Tables*, which he had broken off in the fall. Instead, he sought solace from the terrible dissonances in his personal life in another study, writing to a friend "Since the *Tables* require peace, I have abandoned them and turned my mind to developing the *Harmony*."

Kepler had first conceived of a work devoted to certain kinds of mathematical regularities in the world—which he called "harmonies"—during the dark period in 1599, after the death of his first daughter named Susanna and during the time when the measures against the Protestants in Styria were becoming ever more oppressive. He had sketched out his thoughts on mathematical harmony at that time in considerable detail, even going so far as to describe the structure of the book he would one day write.

When he succeeded in getting a copy of Claudius Ptolemy's *Harmony*—first in a Latin translation and then in a manuscript in the original Greek—he had been stunned by the similarity. That two men separated by a millennium and a half in time should converge on the same findings showed Kepler that he had surpassed time and space in his contemplation of the divine. "That the very nature of things was revealing itself to men through interpreters separated by the distance of centuries was the finger of God," he wrote.

The inquiry to which Kepler was returning in 1618 was the one he had turned to when his career changed from the church to science: to proclaim the glory of God from the Book of Nature. As in the *Mysterium*, he sought by revealing the underlying mathematical regularities in nature to make manifest the wisdom of its Creator. The unfamiliarity of the study should not make us think that Kepler resorted to mysticism, the irrational spiritual union with God. On the contrary, Kepler's work was supremely rational. Though his logic was strained at times by the effort to find the rational explanation underlying every aspect of harmony, he relentlessly pursued the questions until he had reasonable answers.

Harmony was the earliest human experience of fundamental mathematical relationships in nature. Already, in the 6th century B.C. the Pythagoreans had recognized the role of number in harmony with a religious awe. The first phenomena were those found in music. A string plucked once, then held down midway and plucked again, sounds an octave. The ratio of the length of the strings is 1:2. There are a limited number of additional harmonious tones. A ratio of 2:3 sounds a fifth, 3:4 a fourth, 3:5 a major third, 5:8 a minor third, 4:5 a major sixth, and 5:6 a minor sixth. But why these lengths, and why are they harmonious?

Harmony was also considered to be the explanation for the spacing of the distances of planets from the earth; the planets would be arranged at certain distances that corresponded to harmonic intervals. These harmonious spacings gave rise to the notion that there was a "music of the spheres."

The Pythagoreans and Plato saw the numbers as being fundamental. But Kepler never saw numbers, or quantities, as primary. Thus, when he asked why there were six and only six planets in the *Mysterium cosmographicum*, he did not ruminate on the significance of the number six. Instead, he saw geometry as primary. "Before the origin of things," he wrote, "geometry was coeternal with the divine Mind."

The foundation of his work on harmony therefore began with two substantial parts on geometry. He defined different levels of "knowability" for figures that could be constructed with the classical Euclidean tools of ruler and compass, the equilateral triangle, square, pentagon, hexagon, octagon, and a few others. Since the seven-sided heptagon was not constructable in this way, he reckoned God Himself could not have used it in the construction of the world. He expressed his conclusion best in a letter to a friend, where he wrote that, in the area of mathematics, "these things alone we know properly, and, if it can be said piously, with the same kind of comprehension as God, at least as much as we comprehend anything in this mortal life."

Much of the first two parts of Kepler's book was original mathematics. For instance, his definition of "congruence" was the foundation of a field of mathematics still actively practiced today. Kepler's "congruence" was the property of plane polygons to tessellate, or to fill a plane regularly and completely. Squares, triangles, and hexagons are perfectly congruent and can thus be used to tile floors, hence the modern name for this area of mathematics is "tiling theory." Kepler also published his discovery of two new perfect solids, the so-called star solids, both having 60 sides. But since they are constructed on top of Platonic solids (for instance by attaching a tetrahedron to each face of an icosahedron), Kepler considered them secondary in importance to the fundamental five Platonic solids.

Kepler applied his mathematics to musical harmony by arguing that only knowable polygons that divide the circumference of a circle into integral sections that are themselves the number of sides of knowable polygons form consonant proportions. For instance, the octagon and the pentagon are both knowable figures, that is, they are constructable with

ruler and compass. An octagon divides a circle into 8 equal arcs. Since the pentagon is also a knowable polygon, it is allowed to combine five of those arcs and to compare their length to the circumference of the circle. In this case, the ratio of lengths will be 5:8, the same as the ratio of strings in a minor third. On the other hand, since a heptagon is not a knowable polygon, the arcs combined in the ratio 7:8 will be inharmonious. The reason for both types of harmony came ultimately from the relation between God and His creation. As people are made in the image of God, so they have in them the inherent appreciation of consonant ratios determined by the knowable polyhedra, even if they are ignorant of mathematics.

The crowning part of Kepler's book on harmony was the fifth part, in which he addressed himself to the spacing of the planets and its relation to musical harmony. He had already argued in the *Mysterium cosmographicum* that God had based the spacing of the planets on the five Platonic solids. He did not now abandon that idea but sought to find the causes of two more phenomena. One was the size of the planetary eccentricities, that is, how far the sun is from the center of each of the planets' orbits. The eccentricity determines how close a planet gets to the sun at its closest approach, called "perhelion," and how far away it gets at its furthest distance, called "aphelion." Consequently, as governed by Kepler's second law, the eccentricity determines how quickly a planet moves at perihelion and how slowly it moves at aphelion. The eccentricities of the planets are not the same. Mars has a comparatively large eccentricity, while Venus has scarcely any eccentricity at all. Much as he had done some 20 years earlier in the *Mysterium cosmographicum*, Kepler set himself the problem of explaining why the planets had the seemingly arbitrary eccentricities they had. The second new phenomenon whose cause he sought had occupied his thoughts for 25 years. He wanted to know the precise mathematical relationship between the planets' mean distances from the sun and their orbital periods (how long it took for them to return to the same place in their orbits).

Kepler thought that the answer to both of these questions would be related to harmony. But a straightforward comparison of the various planets' closest (perihelial), mean, and furthest (aphelial) distances did not reveal harmonious relationships. Kepler now began another search for harmonious relationships between the planets' angular speeds as viewed from the sun. These could be within one planet's orbit, between its slowest speed at aphelion and its fastest speed at perihelion. If such a harmonious relationship existed, it would explain why the planet had the eccentricity it did. Or the relationship could exist between two planets, say between the aphelial speed of one and the perihelial speed of the next. Such a relationship would bear on the spacing of the planets with respect to one another. It was a vexing problem, but Kepler eventually succeeded in finding an arrangement that embodied all musical harmonies and corresponded to the planets' observed distances and eccentricities.

Kepler composed the book in a frenzy of activity during which every thought he had ever had about harmony came back to him and was included somewhere. At the very end, on May 15, 1618, the final piece of the puzzle fell into place. For 25 years, he had been seeking the relationship between the periods of the planets and their distances from the sun. It was as simple as imaginable: the ratio of the period squared over the distance cubed was the same for all planets. This was "Kepler's third law of planetary motion."

The fact that this final mystery was revealed to Kepler just as he was finishing up a book that was the culmination of his life's work made him exultant:

> Now, eighteen months since the twilight, three months since sunrise, but just a few days since the dazzling sunlight of my most wonderful contemplation shone forth, nothing can restrain me. I want to give in to the sacred frenzy, I want to taunt mortal men with my candid confession: I have stolen the golden vessels of the Egyptians to construct a tabernacle for my God far from the boundaries of Egypt. If you forgive me, I will rejoice. If you are incensed, I will endure. I am throwing the dice and writing the book, whether for my contemporaries or for posterity, it does not matter. It can await its reader for a hundred years, if God Himself waited six thousand years for His contemplator.

On May 27, 1618, Kepler put down his pen. His masterpiece, *Harmonices mundi libri V* (Five Books on the Harmony of the World) was complete. It was dedicated to King James I of England, whom Kepler had selected because he hoped that James might act as a peacemaker between Europe's warring faiths. He offered it so that his examples of the brilliant harmony God had put in His creation might give James strength in his quest for harmony and peace among the churches and the states.

However unrealistic that hope might have been, it was too late: four days earlier neighboring Bohemia had erupted into revolution, igniting the Thirty Years War.

The planets' periods had been known rather accurately for centuries. The relative distances of the planets were harder to determine, but Tycho Brahe's accurate observations had also provided Kepler with good values for the distances during his work on the *Rudolfine Tables*. These are the data Kepler had:

	Mercury	Venus	Earth	Mars	Jupiter	Saturn
Period	88	225	365	687	4,333	10,759
Distance	388	724	1,000	1,524	5,200	9,510

The periods are given in days, and the distances in $\frac{1}{1000}$ ths of the earth's average distance from the sun. If we convert the periods into years and define the earth's average distance to be 1 Astronomical Unit (A.U.), we have:

	Mercury	Venus	Earth	Mars	Jupiter	Saturn
Period	0.24	0.616	1.00	1.88	11.87	29.477
Distance	0.388	0.724	1.00	1.524	5.20	9.51

Already, we can see the relationship Copernicus noted, the clear correlation between the planet's distances and their periods. But Kepler was seeking an exact relationship between period and distance that would be the same for all of the planets. Let us begin by calculating the ratio of the period to the distance.

	Mercury	Venus	Earth	Mars	Jupiter	Saturn
$\frac{\text{Period}}{\text{Distance}}$	0.62	0.851	1.00	1.23	2.28	3.10

The spread in the values between Mercury and Saturn indicates that the ratio is not constant for all planets. Dividing another factor of distance into the denominator should increase Mercury's value while decreasing Saturn's value.

	Mercury	Venus	Earth	Mars	Jupiter	Saturn
$\frac{\text{Period}}{\text{Distance}^2}$	1.6	1.18	1.00	0.809	0.439	0.326

But now, we have gone too far the other way; the ratio for Saturn is smaller than that for Mercury. We will have to multiply another factor of period into the numerator.

	Mercury	Venus	Earth	Mars	Jupiter	Saturn
$\frac{\text{Period}^2}{\text{Distance}^2}$	0.38	0.724	1.00	1.52	5.21	9.61

At first, it might seem like we are not getting anywhere. The spread in the val
ues is wider than when we started out. But the ratios look suspiciously similar
to the planets' distances. Dividing one more factor of the distance into the
denominator should even them out.

	Mercury	Venus	Earth	Mars	Jupiter	Saturn
$\dfrac{\text{Period}^2}{\text{Distance}^3}$	0.99	1.00	1.00	1.00	1.00	1.01

As though by magic, it works out that the period squared over the distance
cubed is very nearly the same for all of the planets. This was the relationship
linking the planets' individual periods and distances that Kepler had been seeking for 20 years.

Expressed in modern notation, Kepler's third law is that for all bodies orbiting
another body,

$$\frac{p^2}{a^3} = k$$

where p is the period, a is the mean distance, and k is a constant that depends
on the body being orbited and the units used. In the case above, for the solar
system, using years and Astronomical Units, it just turns out to be $1.00 \; {}^{\text{year}^2}\!/_{\text{A.U.}^3}$.
Other units will not yield such elegant constants. Nor is the constant the same
for other orbital systems.

In 1618, irate Protestant representatives threw two Catholic regents and their secretary out of the window of the Hradschin in Prague. This act was the beginning of the Thirty Years War.

Witch Trial

On May 23, 1618, a gang of dissatisfied Protestant representatives had stormed the council chamber in the Hradschin in Prague, where they grabbed two Catholic officials and, in a time-honored Bohemian expression of revolt, threw them out of the castle window. This "defenestration of Prague," as it is called, marked the beginning of the Thirty Years War, an insane and devastating conflict that would lay waste to Germany as pillaging armies of ever-increasing size swept across her. In the process, one third of the population would be killed, either directly or indirectly from disease and starvation, and Germany would be reduced to a mere shadow of her former glory. By the time the warring parties had finally exhausted themselves and brought an end to the conflict with the Peace of Westphalia (1648), Kepler would be long dead.

Although the tensions came to a head in 1618, they had been building for some time. The conflict between the Catholics and the Protestants had put the delicate patchwork of duchies and principalities that made up the Holy Roman Empire under increasing strain. Even within the Hapsburg emperor's own hereditary lands, such as Upper and Lower Austria, there was considerable potential for religious conflict, with the powerful landed Estates being primarily Protestant while their sovereigns were Catholic. Archduke Ferdinand II had begun the process of converting his share of the family lands back to Catholicism, but they represented a small fraction. Outside the Hapsburg lands, the independent states of the empire formed self-defense pacts based on their faith, the Protestant Union (1608) and the Catholic League (1609). These pacts looked to coreligionists in countries outside the empire for monetary and military support, creating faultlines that would ensure that war, when it began, would involve all of Europe's major powers.

The war began with an uprising in Bohemia. The predominately Protestant Bohemians had long jealously defended their freedom of religion. In 1617, when they named Archduke Ferdinand II "king designate" to succeed Matthias upon his death, it was with the expectation that he would honor the concessions ensuring religious rights they had forced from his predecessors, Rudolf and Matthias. They had reason to regard Ferdinand with suspicion, since many of the refugees of his religious persecution had settled in Bohemia. The Bohemians soon came to regret their choice of Ferdinand as "king designate." When Ferdinand went to negotiate his claim to become the next emperor at the imperial court in Vienna—where Matthias had returned it, ending Prague's golden age as the capital of the empire—he left Prague in the hands of ten regents, seven of whom were Catholic, with explicit instructions to curb Protestant power.

In the spring of 1618, the Protestants summoned a meeting of the Bohemian Estates to discuss the anti-Protestant policies. The order came down from the Hradschin, where the Catholic regents sat, for the delegates to disperse. Such a command was regarded as unconstitutional. The delegates of the Estates responded by marching on the Hradschin and throwing two of the regents and their secretary out of the window. The revolt had begun.

While the Estates organized a provisional government and started to raise an army, Ferdinand organized a counter-attack, but it took time. In the meantime, Lusatia, Silesia, and Upper Austria joined the revolt in the summer of 1618. By the following summer, Moravia and Lower Austria had joined as well. In a stunning move, the rebel army marched south into Lower Austria and laid siege to the imperial capital Vienna. By then, Ferdinand had raised an imperial army of 30,000 men with help from the Spanish Hapsburgs and the Pope. They invaded southern Bohemia, cutting off the rebel army at Vienna and lifting the siege.

Political events now took center stage. In July 1619, the Estates of the Bohemian Crown signed a treaty of alliance with the Estates of Upper and Lower Austria. In the meantime, Matthias, emperor and king of the Bohemians, had passed away. In August, the Bohemians nullified Ferdinand's election as "king designate," and offered the crown to Frederick V, the prominent Calvinist prince of the Protestant Palatinate. At just the same time, a meeting of the seven imperial electors in Frankfurt elected Ferdinand II holy Roman emperor on August 28, 1619. Thereafter, he immediately went south to Munich for negotiations with Maximilian of Bavaria, the powerful leader of the Catholic League.

It was agreed that Maximilian's Catholic League forces would drive east into Bohemia through Upper Austria. At the same time, imperial troops from Vienna would attack the Bohemian forces in Lower Austria, and troops from the Spanish Netherlands would invade the Palatinate,

Holy Roman Emperor Ferdinand II fought with Protestants from his time as Archduke of Styria through his reign as emperor, creating a great deal of political unrest.

protecting the Bavarians' rear flank. On July 17, 1620, 30,000 Catholic League troops invaded Upper Austria. Recapturing Linz was their first objective.

For the Estates of Upper Austria, joining the Bohemian rebellion had been a foolhardy move. Once Linz was occupied by Bavarian forces, a swift retribution could be expected. Kepler immediately began worrying about his future. He had already experienced Ferdinand's Counter-Reformation measures once. On the other hand, though his appointment had not yet been confirmed by Ferdinand, he had been imperial mathematician to the two previous emperors for 18 years. This history and his ongoing work on the *Rudolfine Tables* tied him to the house of Hapsburg. But would he be able to continue his astronomical work and remain a Protestant?

In the fall of 1620, after Bavarian forces had taken the city, Kepler had to leave Linz to return to Württemberg. The course of his mother's witch trial demanded his presence. Because of the increasing uncertainty in Linz, he decided it was prudent to remove his family from harm's way, so he packed them up and took them with him as far as Regensburg, where he found them a place to stay. It was too shameful to tell anyone why he was going, so the Keplers left town secretly. Kepler did not even tell his assistant Gringalletus where they were going. When it was discovered that they were all missing, the people of Linz naturally assumed that the imperial mathematician and his family had fled the town for good.

The series of events that had now reached a climax in his mother's witch trial had begun more than five years before. It was a petty and sordid tale, one that had more to do with personal grudges, gossip, and intrigues involving money than sorcery. Even so, the supernatural connotation does not mean that it was an uncommon event. Indeed, the frequency of witch trials reached a frenetic peak in southern Germany in the late 16th and early 17th centuries. At the

time when Kepler's mother's trouble began, no fewer than six women were sentenced to death in her town of Leonberg within a few months.

Frau Kepler's trouble was rooted in her unpleasant and meddling personality. Kepler himself conceded that she suffered from "trifling, nosiness, fury, and obstinate complaining," but he attributed such character flaws to the feeble-mindedness of a seventy-year-old. Her avid interest in folk medicine and herbal cures also made her an easy target for accusations of witchcraft.

Her particular adversary was an unstable woman named Ursula Reinbold, the glazier's wife, whom Kepler called "the crazy." Frau Reinbold had had some unsatisfactory business dealings with Kepler's brother Christoph, the tinsmith. After a heated exchange, Christoph denounced her, upbraiding her with her record of imprisonment for prostitution. When Frau Reinbold complained to her friend Frau

The Landhaus, or country house, in Linz. The Protestant school where Kepler was hired to teach is behind and to the right; its tower is visible above the Landhaus.

Kepler about what her son had said, she got no support. Frau Kepler sided with her son, echoing his denunciation of her bad reputation. Frau Reinbold thereafter nursed a grudge against both of them.

Frau Reinbold made a habit of taking potions to abort illicit pregnancies. When one of these made her very ill, she attributed her sickness not to the drug, nor the botched treatment she had received from her brother, the court barber-surgeon of the prince of Württemberg, but to a "witch's drink" Frau Kepler had given her three and a half years earlier. Her brother, while drinking with the bailiff of Leonberg, Lutherus Einhorn, drunkenly insulted and threatened Frau Kepler. He went so far as to hold the tip of his sword to her throat, and threatened to run her through if she did not produce a "witch's antidote" for his sister. It was an impossible situation, for complying would have meant admitting that she was a witch. Standing her ground, though trembling all over, Frau Kepler energetically responded: she had not made Frau Reinbold sick, she said, and she could not make her better. Finally, Einhorn sobered up enough to put an end to the ugly scene.

Frau Kepler could not let this disgraceful encounter go unpunished. Unchallenged, the rumors of witchcraft Ursula Reinbold was spreading would fester and become ever more dangerous. In August 1615, with the support of her son Christoph and her son-in-law Georg Binder, a village pastor, she brought a libel suit against Ursula Reinbold for accusing her of being a witch. In October, Margarethe Binder, Kepler's sister, wrote to him in Linz informing him of these developments.

His sister's letter did not arrive until December 29. Kepler responded swiftly and decisively, writing an indignant letter to the Leonberg town senate on January 2, 1616. Mustering all of his status as imperial mathematician he strenuously objected to his mother's treatment, to the bailiff's behavior, and to the outrageous rumors that he, too, was somehow involved in "forbidden arts." He demanded that written copies of all legal proceedings involving his mother be forwarded to him.

Kepler had bitter suspicions that he himself was the origin of his mother's problem. A few years earlier, he had rewritten a student essay on heavenly appearances as viewed from the moon in the form of a playful piece of fiction. He had to give the narrator a way to find out about the moon, so he used the unfortunate literary device of having the narrator informed by a daemon summoned by the narrator's mother, an old woman skilled in folk magic. The similarity to Kepler's own mother was perhaps somewhat intentional but not to the point of implying that she was a witch. Kepler supposed that a handwritten copy of this little essay had found its way to Tübingen in 1611, where he imagined it had been "chattered about in barbers' shops." The court barber-surgeon would then have had good reason to suspect the imperial mathematician's mother of being a witch. In fact, however heartfelt Kepler's guilt, the essay may well have had little to do with the dark events in Leonberg.

In Leonberg, Lutherus Einhorn was in an awkward position. As bailiff he was the representative of the law in the town. But he had been a participant in the actions that precipitated Frau Kepler's suit. In order to avoid having to be a witness or reveal his part in them, he stalled the case of *Kepler* v. *Reinbold* as long as possible, so no evidence was scheduled to be taken before October 21, 1616.

Then, six days before the proceeding was scheduled to begin, matters took a turn for the worse. When Frau Kepler was out walking one day, she came across a group of girls carrying bricks to the kiln. The path was narrow, and the girls stepped aside to give a wide berth to the rumored witch. There was some kind of altercation. Frau Kepler claimed merely to have brushed their clothing and given them a dirty look. One of the girls claimed she had been hit on the arm, and that, thereafter, the pain increased hour by hour until she could not feel or move her hand.

Over the next two days, a conspiracy was hatched. The girl's mother, Walburga Haller, the wife of a day laborer, was in debt to Ursula Reinbold, and she and her family joined the Reinbold side. The barber-surgeon appeared on horseback from Tübingen. Suddenly, three days after the incident, Frau Haller went after Frau Kepler with a knife, screaming at her to heal her daughter. The Reinbolds and the Hallers wanted to press charges against her, so Frau Kepler was taken before the bailiff and interrogated. Einhorn examined the bruises on the girl's arm. After a convenient consultation with his friend the barber-surgeon, he authoritatively concluded, "It is a witch's grip; it's even got the right impression."

Frau Kepler now did a very foolish thing. She approached the bailiff with the offer of a silver goblet if he would forget about the whole incident and get on with taking evidence in her lawsuit. It was just what the bailiff needed to avoid exposing his part in the earlier attack on Frau Kepler. He suspended her case, and forwarded the charges of "witch's drink," "witch's grip," and bribery to the High Council in Stuttgart. The councilors returned the order to arrest her on sight, interrogate her, and "examine her strenuously" with regard to the accusations against her and her theological beliefs. It was the preliminary stage of a witch trial.

By the time the arrest order came back from Stuttgart, Frau Kepler had been hustled off to safety, first to her daughter's house in Heumaden and from there to Linz, where she stayed with her son from the end of 1616 to September 1617. When he heard about the turn of affairs, Kepler took the case into his hands. He immediately hired lawyers for his mother in Leonberg and for himself in Tübingen and Stuttgart. And he wrote a letter to the duke of Württemberg's vice chancellor detailing the bailiff's bias and bad behavior in the case and denying the rumors that his mother had fled jurisdiction because of her bad conscience.

In the fall of 1617, Kepler accompanied his mother home and attempted to get her civil suit in motion, but to no avail. The proceeding was delayed by the Reinbolds' legal maneuvering, possibly assisted by the barber-surgeon's influence at the ducal court in Stuttgart. At least, the interest in arresting and interrogating Frau Kepler seemed to have passed. Kepler finally had to suspend his effort and returned to Linz in early 1618. Things were moving very slowly.

The following summer, Kepler received a letter from his old classmate Christoph Besold, now a member of the law faculty at Tübingen and probably his lawyer there. Besold mentioned a danger to watch out for: the Reinbolds and the bailiff might contrive things so that Frau Kepler's civil suit could be turned around and become a criminal charge of witchcraft against her. He turned out to be exactly right. In October 1619, the Reinbolds filed a counter civil suit against Frau Kepler, demanding 1,000 florins in damages for poisoning Frau Reinbold with the "witch's drink." In effect, they were defending themselves against the libel charge by demonstrating that she really *was* a witch.

Their 49-count indictment against her was made possible by the flood of gossip unleashed by rumors of Frau Kepler's witchcraft. Everyone, it seemed, remembered some eerie, unnatural encounter with Frau Kepler. Among other things, she was supposed to be responsible for the death of pets and livestock, to have ridden a calf to death, to have attempted to lure a young girl to witchcraft, to have caused mysterious pains without touching people, to have passed through locked doors, to have killed infants by saying a blessing over their cribs, and to have asked the gravedigger for her father's skull so she could have it set in silver to be a goblet for her son, the mathematician. The last of the charges had the distinction of at least being true. Her defense was that she had heard of the ancient custom of making cups from deceased relatives' skulls in a sermon.

The legal situation had become very dangerous. With the bailiff on their side, testimony in the case of *Reinbold* v. *Kepler* began almost immediately, in November 1619. Thirty or forty witnesses were called, and their testimony was taken down in thick volumes.

In July 1620, the Reinbolds succeeded in getting the duke to turn their complaint into a criminal case. The high council ordered that Katharina Kepler be arrested and interrogated, under torture if necessary. In order to avoid commotion, on August 7, 1620, she was roused from her sleep, bundled into a large chest, and carried out of Heumaden in the dead of night.

The sudden turn of events disheartened the Kepler camp. Christoph Kepler and Georg Binder, Margarethe's husband, were ready to abandon Frau Kepler to her fate. They had too much to lose. Christoph was a young man and could not endure the shame of the community. It was more than he could take to have the spectacle of his mother's witch trial under his nose in Leonberg. He succeeded in having the trial transferred to Güglingen. Georg Binder was a pastor and had his position in the church to think about.

Margarethe seems to have been the only one who still held out hope. She wrote at once to her brother Johannes, telling him that his mother needed his help. He, in turn, wrote from Linz to the duke of Württemberg, asking him to stay the trial until he could arrive. It was his "God-given and natural right," he wrote, to come to his mother's aid. The trial was delayed five to six weeks. On September 26, 1620, Kepler met with his mother in prison.

The poor, bewildered, now-74-year-old woman was kept in chains, watched over by two hired guards, whom she had to pay out of her own pocket. She likewise had to pay her upkeep during the delay of the trial. These expenses revealed the naked greed of the Reinbold camp. Part of the reason for their suit had always been the hope of cashing in on Frau Kepler's assets. They had petitioned early on to have her property inventoried. When it now turned out that the two lackeys being paid to watch her were wastefully using firewood, threatening with their expenses to consume all of her assets during the trial, Frau Reinbold petitioned "in the name of God's mercy" to protect the defendant's funds.

Kepler took charge of the defense. There is a funny note in the transcripts of the trial that attests to the force of his presence. "The prisoner," the scribe writes, "appears *unfortunately* with the support of her son Johannes Kepler, the mathematician." Kepler directed his mother's lawyer, Johannes Rueff, to do all of his arguments in written form. It was a slower and costlier way of proceeding, but he had been advised that it more often led to a positive outcome. It can hardly be believed, therefore, that he was criticized by his brother Christoph for the higher costs. Kepler and Rueff submitted their written defense on October 2. The bailiff of Güglingen, sensing that he was being outmaneuvered, brought in Hieronymous Gabelkofer, the prince's counsel, to prosecute for the state.

New witnesses were heard in January 1621. In May, the defense submitted further written arguments. At this point, Kepler went to the capital, Stuttgart, to work on the final summation with his lawyer. Their conclusion was a 126-page brief rebutting all of the charges. Although composed with legal assistance, elements of it are in Kepler's hand and much of it represents his own work. It was very much his presence and his effort writing in his mother's defense that began to turn the balance.

The concluding defense was submitted on August 22. As was usual, the trial proceedings were sent to the law faculty at the University of Tübingen for a decision. Luckily, Kepler's ally, Christoph Besold, would be able to exert some inside influence there. It is perhaps an indication of the difficulty of escaping charges of witchcraft that, even after Kepler's devoted efforts and with Besold on the inside, they were still not able to achieve an acquittal. The best the court could decide was that it was not certain. It ordered that Frau Kepler be examined again under the lightest form of torture, the "territio verbalis," verbal terrification.

On September 28, 1621, the verdict was carried out as ordered. Against her protestations, Frau Kepler was taken to the appointed place in the company of Bailiff Aulber, three representatives of the court, and a scribe and was presented to the torturer. He showed her his instruments and, under threat of great pain and suffering, strenuously commanded her to tell the truth. She denied any involvement with witch-craft. The report of the bailiff reads, "She announced one should do with her what one would. Should one pull one vein after another out of her body, she knew that she had nothing to say. With that, she fell on her knees, said the Lord's prayer, and declared that God should make a sign if she were a witch or a demon or ever had anything to do with sorcery. Should she be killed, God would see that the truth came to light and reveal after her death that injustice and vio-lence had been done to her, for she knew that He would not take His Holy Spirit from her but would stand by her."

In light of her testimony under threat of torture, the charges were dismissed. On October 3, 1621, the duke of Württemberg ordered that she should be set free. Of the outstanding costs of the trial, Jacob Reinbold was ordered to pay 10 florins for having initiated the proceedings and Christoph Kepler was to pay 30 florins for having incurred extraordinary expenses by having them transferred to Güglingen. Her spirit broken by the ordeal, Katharina Kepler died six months later, on April 13, 1622.

Immediately after his mother's interrogation, Kepler returned to Linz. The Linz Kepler returned to in November 1621 was far different from the one he had left. Shortly after his departure, Frederick V and the Bohemian

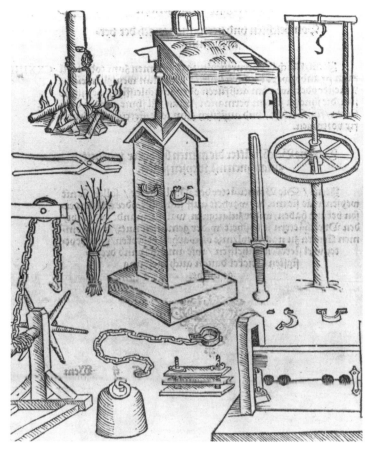

The standard tools of the torturer, as shown in this 16th-century woodcut, included the strappado (bottom left), thumbscrews (bottom center), the Catherine wheel (bottom right), and the stake (top left). Kepler's mother was shown the tools and instructed in their use during her final interrogation.

rebel army had been swiftly defeated at the Battle of White Mountain. The Protestant revolution in Bohemia and the Austrian territories along the Danube had been repressed.

The city was still under occupation by the Bavarian army, and Ferdinand II would make use of their presence to stage a replay of the Counter-Reformation moves he had made in Styria 20 years before. For the time being, it was the prominent Protestant leaders of the rebellion he was after. In June, 27 Protestant ringleaders had been executed in Prague. Kepler's old friend Jessenius had been among them; he had had his tongue cut out before being quartered. A dozen of their heads were put on pikes on the bridge tower, where they remained as mute warnings for ten years before they disintegrated and fell off. In Linz, the actions were less lethal. Among other people, Kepler's nemesis Daniel Hitzler was thrown in prison.

Kepler found himself in a strange position. It had been widely known that his brother Protestants in Linz had rejected him. Now, when they were being oppressed, he was being spared. Still, his open admiration of Frederick V's father-in-law, James I, in the dedication of the *Harmonice mundi* and his sudden flight the previous year had given rise to rumors that the emperor had put a price on his head. His equally sudden reappearance was a real surprise. It was surprising to Kepler that almost the first thing that happened upon his return was that Ferdinand II confirmed his appointment as imperial mathematician on December 30, 1621.

As imperial mathematician, Kepler was left unmolested even while measures were taken the next year against other Protestant teachers and preachers. And then, a few years later, when all the rest of the Protestants were required to convert or leave (as they had been many years before in Styria), not only was Kepler allowed to stay but his printer Planck as well and as many skilled assistants as Planck needed.

By 1622, Kepler's many years of work on the *Rudolfine Tables* were beginning to come to an end. To many astronomers, it was about time. To them, it seemed that work on books like the *Harmonice mundi* or the second edition of the *Mysterium cosmographicum* (1621) had been a distraction from Kepler's "important" work of composing new astronomical tables based on Tycho Brahe's observations. To them, Kepler replied, "Do not sentence me completely to the treadmill of mathematical calculations, and leave me time for philosophical speculations, which are my only delight." But by the end of 1623, Kepler felt as though he were going through labor pains, "The *Rudolfine Tables*, which I received from Tycho Brahe as the father, I have now carried and formed within me for 22 whole years, as little by little the foetus forms in the mother's body. Now the labor pains torment me."

Die ficht man die 12. Köpff auff den Prager Bruckenthurn auffgesteckt

The heads of the leaders of the Bohemian revolution were displayed on pikes on the bridge tower in Prague as a public warning.

Part of the torment was finding a suitable place to print them. To Ferdinand, it was an important sign of normalcy that the astronomical achievement that had been supported by the Hapsburg house for so long should be printed in Austria. He would not allow Kepler to have the book printed in Ulm, where it was peaceful and there were more experienced printers. Money was also a problem, which led Kepler on a ten-month wild-goose chase from the imperial treasury in Vienna to various cities that were supposed to turn imperial payments over to Kepler but would not. He finally returned to Linz in the fall of 1625 with little to show for his travels. He was left with no alternative but to try out Planck and see how he would handle the high-prestige job of printing the imperial *Rudolfine Tables*. But before they could even get started, Linz erupted in civil disorder.

On October 10, 1625, Ferdinand II's government decided to become serious about the measures they were taking against the Protestants. The familiar pattern of repression from Styria was repeated in Linz. The previous expulsion of teachers and preachers had had time to take effect. It was now renewed with the threat of capital punishment. It was time to force the people to convert, too. All avenues for Protestant practice were forbidden. The measures culminated in the order that all people convert to Catholicism or leave the land by Easter 1626. Because of his position, Kepler was exempted from all of these measures. His only annoyance was that the Catholic Reformation Commission sealed his personal library on the grounds that it might contain heretical books. Ironically, when Kepler's friend the Jesuit Paul Guldin wanted to borrow a book, he had to tell him he could not get into his own library.

In the spring of 1626, Upper Austria reached a breaking point. Five thousand Bavarian troops still occupied Linz as surety for the debt owed Maximilian by Ferdinand II for his part in repressing the Bohemian rebellion. In lieu of interest on the debt, the Bavarians taxed Upper Austria. For his part, Ferdinand was relying on their presence to keep a lid on the country while he carried out his plan for compulsory conversion to Catholicism. This put the Bavarian occupiers in a dangerously unstable position. On May 15, 1626, in retaliation for the harrassment of Italian priests who had been brought in to return the parishes of Upper Austria to Catholicism, the leader of the Bavarian authorities ordered the summary execution of 17 randomly selected men. A peasant uprising erupted, which all but succeeded in driving the Bavarians and Ferdinand's forces out of Upper Austria.

The peasants formed themselves into large troops and roamed Upper Austria, burning and looting. On June 24, 1626, they besieged the capital, Linz. "By the help of God and the protection of His angels, I survived the siege intact," Kepler wrote to a friend. But the two months spent behind city walls waiting for the arrival of imperial relief forces had been an ordeal. Kepler's house was part of the city wall, and it was constantly occupied by soldiers who disturbed him with their comings and goings at all times of the day and night.

Worse still, shortly after the beginning of the siege, on June 30, the peasants started a fire in the outskirts of the city. Luckily, as the fire spread, no harm came to the hand-written copy of the *Rudolfine Tables* on which Kepler had worked so long. But the fire did consume Planck's press. With the press gone, there was no longer any reason to remain in Linz. Linz had gone from the peaceful haven Kepler had come to 14 years before to a repressive and disturbed place. When the siege was lifted in August, he wrote to the emperor requesting permission to leave. By November 20, he and his family were on a boat traveling up the Danube, and Kepler was looking for another place to print the *Rudolfine Tables*.

The frontispiece from Kepler's Rudolfine Tables (1627) shows the contributions of various astronomers. In the center, Tycho Brahe (with arm raised) and Copernicus (seated) discuss the merits of the Tychonic system. Kepler is shown in the lower left panel.

The Dream

When the storm is raging and the shipwreck of the state is threatening, there is nothing nobler for us to do than let down our anchor of peaceful studies into the depths of eternity.

—from a letter to Jacob Bartsch, November 6, 1628

With the onset of winter, November was not a very advantageous month for moving, but Kepler was possessed by the desire to be away from the disorder in Linz and to get on with the publication of the *Rudolfine Tables*. The boat carrying the Kepler family got as far up the Danube as Regensburg, but beyond there the river was iced over. Regensburg had by now become a familiar refuge for them, so Kepler settled his family there, loaded his type onto a wagon, and set out alone for Ulm.

When he got there on December 10, 1626, Kepler moved in across the street from Jonas Saur's printing shop. Having constant access to the shop was a necessity. Kepler had completed the 538-page manuscript, but it was complicated enough—especially with the layout of the many tables—that the author himself was needed on hand at all times. All the materials were in readiness as well. During his fruitless travels the previous year trying to collect his back salary, Kepler had ordered four bales of paper from the cities of Memmingen and Kempten in the expectation that he could barter for them with written orders from the emperor for the cities to pay him. But as it turned out, he ended up paying for the paper out of his own pocket. Anticipating that he would be allowed to print the *Rudolfine Tables* in Ulm, he had had it delivered directly there. He himself had brought along his set of numerical type and the special astronomical-symbol type he had had custom-molded for the *Rudolfine Tables*.

Despite some friction over cost, the printing proceeded at a frantic pace. Kepler had set the goal of completing the printing in time for the fall 1627 book fair in Frankfurt. He supervised the layout of the tables and proofread the sheets as they came out of the press. There were to be no errors. He wanted the tables to be perfect, a fitting capstone of his collaboration with Tycho Brahe and of his career as an astronomer.

There were still some details to be worked out. The book would need a dedication to the emperor from Brahe's heirs, who still had not been paid in full for Tycho's observing logs and so still owned them. Kepler wrote informing them that the book was being printed. Tycho had begun the work and it was based on his lifetime of observations, so he would be listed on the title page as the primary author, where he was called "that Phoenix of astronomers." Even though it was Kepler who had written the entire book, he did not begrudge Tycho this honor in any way.

In addition, the *Rudolfine Tables* would be Kepler's first book with a frontispiece, a common feature of 16th- and 17th-century books. A frontispiece was a magnificent engraving that was packed with symbolism and meaning. Kepler had Schickard draw up a sketch of what he wanted and sent it to Tycho's heirs for approval.

The frontispiece as it finally appeared was a representation of a temple to Urania, the muse of astronomy. The development of astronomy is represented by the 12 columns supporting the roof. In the rear, where the columns are only rough-hewn logs, stands a Babylonian astronomer making an observation using only his fingers. He represents the ancient Babylonian observations to which astronomy traced its roots. Nearer the front, where Hipparchus and Ptolemy are seated, the columns are brick, representing the improvement in astronomy in ancient Greece. Copernicus has an Ionic column. And Tycho Brahe has a magnificent Corinthian column, on which his sophisticated instruments are hanging. In the center, Copernicus and Tycho discuss the merits of the heliocentric and Tychonic systems, with Tycho pointing toward the ceiling of the temple where his system is depicted and asking "Quid si sic?" or "What if it is like this?"

Standing around the roof of the temple are allegorical figures who assisted Kepler with his accomplishment. To the right are Magnetica with her compass needle and Stathmica with her balance and lever. They represent the celestial physics upon which Kepler's reform of astronomical theory was based. Then there are Kepler's mathematical helpers, Geometria and Logarithmica, who has the natural log of one half in her halo. On the left are the optical parts of astronomy, one of them holding the recently-invented telescope. Above them flies an eagle wearing the imperial crown dropping coins from its beak. It represents the three Hapsburg emperors who provided financial support for the project.

There was one aspect of the frontispiece that was not in the sketch shown to the heirs, with whom Kepler had always had difficulty. Below the figures in the base of the temple are panels depicting different scenes. In the center, for instance, is a map of Tycho's island Hven, where his observatory was located. And to the left is Kepler himself. He is looking out at the viewer, seated at a table under a banner listing his publications *Mysterium cosmographicum,*

Astronomiae pars optica, Commentarium Martis (that is, the *Astronomia nova*), and *Epitome astronomiae Copernicanae*. He is working by candlelight, having sketched some numbers on the tablecloth. On the table is his project: a model of the roof of the temple itself. Kepler has made a subtle but unmistakable statement about his role in this undertaking: though those on whom he based his work occupy places of honor on the stage above him, it is Kepler alone who is the architect of this achievement.

And it was a magnificent achievement. The tables them-

This detail of the frontispiece of the Rudolfine Tables shows Kepler as the architect of the achievement. He works by candlelight on a model of the temple above him. The banner lists his important publications. A few coins dropped by the Hapsburg eagle have reached his desk.

selves provided the means to calculate the position of any planet for any time thousands of years into the future or the past. It was only the third truly new set of planetary tables in European history. And whereas Copernicus's and Ptolemy's tables were more or less equally accurate, Kepler's were some 50 times more so. Within a few years, it was possible to pinpoint the time of a transit of Mercury across the face of the sun so that it was possible to observe it in transit for the first time in human history. It would be a spectacular demonstration of the accuracy of Kepler's tables. Of course, Kepler's theories were more difficult, especially since he had incorporated logarithms, which had only been invented a few years earlier. Much of the book, therefore, was made up of explanatory text that told the reader how to use the tables. There were also a geographical register of the longitudes and latitudes of the earth's major cities and Tycho Brahe's catalogue of the positions of 1,000 stars.

The printing of the *Rudolfine Tables* was finished on time in September 1627, and on September 15, Kepler set out with the copies for the Frankfurt fall book fair. He left the copies with the publisher Gottfried Tampach to sell on commission at an agreed-upon price, but he was not optimistic that sales would be brisk, noting, "There will be few purchasers, as is always the case with mathematical works, especially in the present chaos."

By the end of November, he was reunited with his family in Regensburg. Nearly a year had passed since he had left them to print the *Tables*. For many months, he had been thinking about what to do after the *Tables* were finished. During the summer, a series of imperial decrees had been issued, ordering the discharge of all non-Catholic officials in Upper Austria. Kepler had often escaped this sort of decree, but with the tables now finished, there was reason to think that the emperor might really fire him.

It was with some trepidation that Kepler went to the imperial court just after Christmas to present a copy of the

Duke Albrecht Wallenstein is received at the imperial court after defeating King Christian IV of Denmark. Wallenstein was immensely successful but a threat because of his power.

Rudolfine Tables to the emperor personally. He found the court in high spirits. By virtue of Ferdinand's ceaseless and creative diplomacy and major victories on the battlefield, the Protestant revolt had been completely put down. To seal their victory, Ferdinand had brought the court to Prague, where he was overseeing the installation of his son as king of Bohemia.

Much of the credit was due to the emperor's new favorite, General Albrecht Wallenstein. Born and educated as a Lutheran, Wallenstein set a course for success when he

converted to Catholicism in 1606, which enabled him subsequently to marry an elderly widow with vast land holdings in Moravia. Wallenstein used his new-found wealth to
good advantage, supporting Ferdinand II in putting down
the Bohemian rebellion in 1619–1621. His financial speculation in the aftermath of the rebellion gave him the money
to buy up 60 estates of banished or executed Protestant
noblemen. Soon, he owned almost all of the northwestern
quarter of Bohemia. His immense resources enabled him to
speculate financially in warfare. With Ferdinand's blessing,
he raised an imperial army of 24,000 men without charge
to the treasury; the army would pay for itself with booty
and tribute from conquered territories. Following the trend
of the Thirty Years' War, his army soon numbered more
than 100,000 men. Ferdinand, who was then no longer mil-
itarily dependent on Maximilian of Bavaria, gave Wallenstein the title of supreme commander of imperial troops
and shortly thereafter elevated him to be Duke of Friedland.

Wallenstein was immensely successful as a general. In
association with the commander of Catholic League forces,
Count von Tilly, Catholic forces were able to defeat various
Protestant threats through the mid- to late-1620s, most
importantly invasions from the north by the Protestant King
Christian IV of Denmark. In late 1627, when Kepler
arrived at the imperial court, they were just celebrating
Wallenstein's total victory over the Danish king. Christian
had not only been driven off German soil but entirely off
the Danish peninsula of Jutland. As his reward, Wallenstein
was immediately given the Silesian principality of Sagan and
was subsequently also made Duke of Mecklenburg.

Kepler's experience of the unhappy state of affairs in
Linz had deceived him about what to expect at the imperial
court. He was surprised to find that he had many admirers
and well-wishers at the court in Prague. Some of them, of
course, were old friends and acquaintances from his previous years there, although there was a sobering absence of

any Protestants. The court had been as decisively cleansed as the lands under Ferdinand's control.

The emperor received Kepler graciously, pronouncing himself well pleased with the tables. The notion that Kepler might already have lost his job in the wake of the previous summer's imperial decrees was laughed off. In fact, for his 25 years of effort on the *Rudolfine Tables*, Kepler was given a grant of 4,000 florins, worth ten years' salary. Of course, Kepler had learned that a grant from the emperor was an unreliable asset. As it was, it brought the amount of money the emperor owed him to nearly 12,000 florins. If he ever hoped to collect on that debt, how could he leave imperial service?

However, Ferdinand did make it clear that the condition of his future service in the Hapsburg's lands was firmly conditional on Kepler's conversion to Catholicism, and the Jesuit Paul Guldin was assigned the task of convincing Kepler to convert. Needless to say, Guldin was unsuccessful. But there was another possibility. Kepler could remain in imperial service in one of the lands now held by General Wallenstein. Wallenstein himself had declared that he believed in the peaceful coexistence of the different faiths, a point of view with which Kepler agreed heartily. And the open practice of Protestant religion was still allowed in Wallenstein's Silesian duchy of Sagan.

Kepler and Wallenstein had a relationship of sorts going back 20 years. In 1608, Kepler had cast a horoscope for an anonymous nobleman. On the basis of the birth information, he described the man as "alert, quick, industrious," uninterested in ordinary things, brutal, hard on his subjects, and so forth. But also, he wrote, "with him can also be seen great thirst for glory and striving for temporal honors and power, by which he would make many great, dangerous, public and concealed enemies for himself but also he would mostly overcome and conquer these." It was a good description of Wallenstein, who had secretly commissioned it. Sixteen years later, after the Thirty Years War had begun, and Wallenstein had begun to amass those "temporal honors and power," Kepler received his first horoscope back, with the request for certain elaborations. He updated the horoscope but stopped with the year 1634 due to some "horrible disorder" in that year. In an eerie coincidence, 1634 would turn out to be the year in which Wallenstein was murdered.

The advantage of having Kepler working for him was that the ambitious general would have state-of-the-art astrological advice. Kepler himself had long recognized the inherent danger in providing astrological advice to men of great military and political power and had strenuously resisted being put in that position, so he and Wallenstein probably worked out an arrangement in which Kepler would supply the planetary positions—for which he was now the undisputed master—and the interpretation would be done by somebody else, probably Wallenstein's personal astrologer

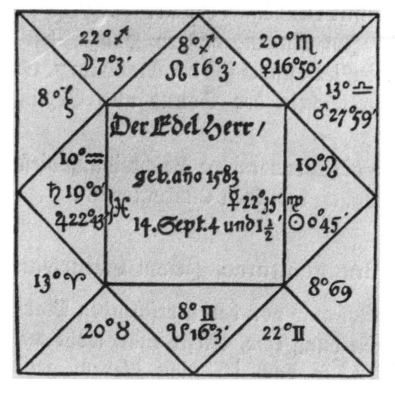

Kepler prepared this horoscope for Wallenstein in 1608. Surrounding the center box are 12 triangles representing the astrological houses. House I (left) is ascendant, the most important house, containing the stars about to rise at the time of birth. It contains Saturn and Jupiter, which would be considered the important planets governing Wallenstein's character.

Gianbattista Zeno.

Kepler would also be a status symbol for Wallenstein, whose growing collection of duchies were rewards for his military victories. Wallenstein's support of Kepler's studies would show that he was not only a military strongman but also a civilized patron of the arts and sciences. Indeed, Wallenstein later tried to move Kepler to his newly-acquired city of Rostock, so that Kepler's presence might raise the status of the university there.

The outlines of an agreement were struck in February 1628 but were not finalized until April. Kepler would receive a house in Sagan, a printing press, and a rich stipend of 1000 florins a year. His duties were not spelled out but were minimal. In addition, Ferdinand "requested" that Wallenstein take into his own hands the problem of collecting the 11,817 florins Kepler was owed by the imperial treasury. In the past, Kepler had been written drafts on imperial cities that the cities had not honored. They were little better than bounced checks. The warrior Wallenstein might have more success. With the job and Wallenstein's responsibility for the collection of Kepler's back pay, as of the summer of 1628, it was clear that Kepler's future lay in Wallenstein's hands.

In May, Kepler returned to his family in Regensburg. The following month, he sent them on to Prague with their possessions while he himself traveled for one last time to Linz. Again, he was well received. He was even paid 200 florins for his presentation copy of the *Rudolfine Tables*, a generous gesture Kepler had not expected from a country so stricken by the recent war. Kepler described what had happened since leaving the city, including his arrangements with Wallenstein, and requested to be released from his contract. His request was granted, and afterwards he traveled immediately north to Prague to meet his family. Together, they traveled north to Sagan, where they arrived on July 20.

Kepler never felt at home there. He could barely understand the dialect of the local people, and his own German was regarded as barbarous. Sagan also had no intellectual culture to speak of, so he was almost completely unknown and he felt like a fish out of water. The combined effect was to make him feel very lonely. Idleness added to his discontent when the promised printing press was so slow to appear that even a year after his arrival it had not been provided. In the meantime, he made arrangements to use a press in nearby Görlitz, but he had to set all the type himself by hand. Only around the beginning of 1630 was he able to put a typesetter and a printer to work at his own personal press.

In an almost unimaginably heart-wrenching turn of events, Kepler's arrival in Sagan coincided with the beginning of the Counter-Reformation there. Though Sagan was almost exclusively Protestant and Wallenstein personally believed in the coexistence of the faiths, the political reality of working for Ferdinand II demanded that he comply. Needless to say, forced conversions on this massive scale were accompanied by bitter resentment and suffering. To Kepler, the measures unfolded in a predictable sequence, as the Protestant school gave way to one founded by Jesuits specially brought in for the purpose, "heretical" books were seized, Protestants were forbidden the practice of their religion, and finally those who refused to convert were ordered to leave. Kepler was again exempted, but experiencing the calamity of the Counter-Reformation for a third time could not have been easy.

To ease his loneliness and isolation, Kepler relied on his correspondence, especially with his good friend Matthias Bernegger in Strasbourg and with Wilhelm Schickard in Tübingen. This link to the outside world became all the more important when Bernegger began to play an active role in the wedding plans of Kepler's daughter Susanna. The prospective bridegroom was a young scholar of mathematics and medicine named Jacob Bartsch, who had gained Kepler's respect by publishing an ephemeris based on the inquiries into the kind of life he had led, how much money he spent, etc. Much of the planning for the match went on in a three-way correspondence between Kepler, Bernegger, and Bartsch. Indeed, Bartsch was well on the way to getting engaged to Susanna before even meeting her. But Kepler did require that in addition to his blessing, Susanna would have to approve of the match.

When it came time to plan the wedding itself, Kepler decided that the best place to hold it would be in Strasbourg. It was too far for him to travel, so Bernegger stood in for him, acting as the father of the bride. Kepler could only read the glowing account of the festivities that Bernegger wrote to him. The wedding was celebrated on the afternoon of March 12, 1630, after Bartsch had received his medical degree that very morning. Kepler's brother Christoph, his sister Margarethe, and his son Ludwig had all been there. The astronomer's daughter in the midst of her bridesmaids "shone out like the moon among the smaller stars," Bernegger reported. Huge crowds lined the street and Strasbourg's elite made up the wedding procession. "It was meant," Bernegger had to remind him, "especially to honor you."

Jacob Bartsch married Kepler's daughter Susanna in 1630. Bartsch was the first person to publish ephemerides based on the Rudolfine Tables.

In addition to the distance and his age—he was then 59—one other thing had kept Kepler from the wedding festivities in Strasbourg: his wife Susanna was eight months pregnant. The following month on April 18, she gave birth to a baby girl, Anna Maria, her seventh child, counting the two who had died in infancy. She now had two grown stepchildren and five of her own.

At the beginning of April, Kepler had spent some weeks consulting with Wallenstein. Tending to his wife after she gave birth also took Kepler away from the print shop, and without his presence, the printing of his next batch of ephemerides could not proceed. Kepler therefore instructed them to get to work on his book about the moon, entitled *Somnium* (The Dream).

The *Somnium* was a project that Kepler had begun more than 25 years earlier, when he was a student at Tübingen. As we have seen, when he was a student, he was convinced that Copernicus's heliocentrism was true. But he ran into trouble convincing people of its truth because they could not imagine that the earth was moving without feeling it. In order to highlight the ambiguous experience of the observer, in 1593 he composed an essay on what the celestial appearances would look like for beings on the moon.

He had kept the essay, and some years later in Prague, he expanded it into a piece of fiction, full of double meanings and clever allusions that would delight his learned friends in the imperial court. This was the essay he thought was responsible in part for his mother's witch trial. Once she was freed, he decided that he would avenge the gossip about his story by publishing it openly with explanatory notes that would show everyone just how foolishly it had been taken out of context and inflated. These notes soon exceeded the story in length. A decade later, he had 50 pages of notes and diagrams for a 28-page short story.

The story of Kepler's *Dream* is set in a series of concentric frames. The outermost narrator is Kepler himself, who, after going out to watch the stars and the moon, falls into a deep sleep. He dreams he is reading a book, which begins "My name is Duracotus; my native land Iceland, which the ancients called Thule. My mother was Fiolxhilde . . ." (these lines alone have three footnotes covering a page and a half).

This second narrator's mother, Fiolxhilde, is a wise woman who gathers herbs, carries on mysterious rites, and sells magical wind charms to Icelandic sailors. After Duracotus ruins one of her charms by peeking inside, she sells

Kepler's last book, the
Somnium, *was a short
work of fiction. The printing of this book was not
completed until after
Kepler's death.*

JOANNIS KEPPLERI
Somnium, sivè Astronomia
Lunaris.

Um anno 1608. ferverent diſſidia inter
fratres Imp: Rudolphum et Matthiam Archiduⁱ
cem ; eorumque actiones vulgo ad exempla re-
ferrent, ex hiſtoria Bohemica petita ; ego publi-
ca vulgi curioſitate excitus, ad Bohemica legenda animum
appuli. Cumque incidiſſem in hiſtoriam Libuſſæ Viragi-
nis, arte Magica celebratiſſimæ: factum quadam nocte, vt
poſt contemplationem ſiderum et Lunæ, lecto compoſi-
tus, altius obdormiſcerem: atque mihi per ſomnum viſus
ſum librum ex Nundinis allatum perlegere, cuius hic erat
tenor:

Mihi¹ Duracoto nomen eſt, patria ² Islandia, quam veteres
Thulen dixère: ³ mater erat Fiolxhildis, quæ ⁴ nuper mortua, ſcri-
bendi mihi peperit licentiam, cujus rei cupiditate pridè arſi. ⁵ Dum
viveret, hoc diligenter egit, ne ſcriberem. Dicebat enim, multos
eſſe pernicioſos oſores artium, ⁶ qui quod præ hebetudine mentis non
capiunt, id calumnientur; ⁷ legeſ ſigant injurioſas humano gene-
ri; ⁸ quibus ſanè legibus non pauci damnati, ⁹ Heclæ voraginibus
fuerint abſorpti. ¹⁰ Quod nomen eſſet patri meo, ipſa nunquam di-
xit, ¹¹ piſcatorem fuiſſe, & centum quinquaginta annorum ſenem
A   deceſ-

him to a sea captain, who takes him to Tycho Brahe's island
Hven, where he learns astronomy. After five years, he finds
his way home. His remorseful mother is delighted by his
return and his new knowledge of astronomy. What he has
learned from books, she says, she was taught by a gentle and
innocuous daemon. She agrees to summon the daemon to
teach Duracotus about "Levania," as the moon is known by
its inhabitants. They foregather at a crossroads, Fiolxhilde
speaks some words, and after covering their heads with their
coats, they hear the raspy, indistinct voice of the daemon.

The daemon, now the third narrator, tells about how
the heavens appear viewed from the moon. The day-to-day

phenomena are quite different, as Kepler knew. On the earth, a day is 24 hours long, during which time the moon goes around the sky once, while it takes a month to return to where it was among the stars, going from new moon to full moon to new moon again as it does so. On the moon, because one side always faces toward the earth, the earth just hangs in one place on the sky, "as though," Kepler writes, "it were affixed to the heavens with a nail." It revolves in 24 hours as it hangs there, for which reason Kepler's lunar inhabitants call it "Volva." Their day corresponds to a cycle of lunar phases, so it lasts a whole month.

Of course, if one face of the moon always faces the earth, the other hemisphere always faces away. For this reason, the near side of the moon is called "Subvolva" (under Volva) and the far side is called "Privolva" (deprived of Volva). Lacking the moderating influence Volva has on the long, hot days and the long, cold nights, Privolva is a wilderness roamed by hoards of scavenging nomads, while in Subvolva civilization has taken root.

Unfortunately, Kepler did not say much more about the alien creatures who inhabit the moon. His emphasis throughout is on astronomy and on astronomical appearances as viewed from the moon, and he does not exploit his set-up for any broader literary purpose. Almost as soon as he begins to stray into fanciful descriptions of creatures, he wakes up with his head covered by his pillow, a joke referring back to the ritual of summoning the demon in the dream.

It is not the story line of the *Somnium* but the literary genre that is of interest. Some say that Kepler's use of scientific knowledge to create a detailed framework for a fictional account of another world makes the *Somnium* an important early work of science fiction. The notes—although they are inserted so thickly that they make it nearly impossible to concentrate on the story—are more interesting in themselves, for they reveal some of Kepler's speculative insights.

For example, he describes quite clearly the point between the earth and the moon where the gravitational attractions of each body exactly cancel.

The printing of the *Somnium* was suspended when Kepler was able to help again with the ephemerides. But it was resumed when it became necessary for him to go on a business trip in October. His finances were in trouble again. First, he had 3,500 florins invested in Upper Austria. After a year of getting the runaround, he had been promised the payment of his interest if he presented himself on November 11 in Linz. Second, Wallenstein had been deposed as supreme general of the imperial army in August. Emperor Ferdinand II never called a meeting of the Imperial Diet, but he did need the support of the seven powerful electoral states, those states of the empire that had a vote in the election of a new emperor. At the meeting of the imperial electors in Regensburg in the summer of 1630, Ferdinand came under pressure from the electors, who feared Wallenstein's great power. They demanded Wallenstein's resignation, and Ferdinand complied. Since Kepler had become so dependent on Wallenstein, his patron's fall from grace was serious business, especially in the matter of the nearly 12,000 florins he was owed by the emperor. It would be strategic to visit the meeting of the electors in Regensburg and see for himself how things stood.

Kepler set off on October 8, 1630. In order to be ready for any eventuality, he took with him nearly every scrap of documentation concerning his wealth. In addition, he shipped a huge stock of books ahead to Leipzig, including 57 copies of the ephemerides for the years 1621–1636, which they had been printing furiously in order to finish. He also sent 16 copies of the *Rudolfine Tables* and 73 other assorted books. He would be stopping at the fall fair in Leipzig and wanted to have stock to sell. The stress of finishing the printing and the uncertainty of what faced him at court put him in a desperate frame of mind. As he rode out of town, his family thought it more likely to see the Day of Judgment than ever to see him alive again.

After the fair in Leipzig, he sent the wagoneer ahead to Regensburg and followed a few days later. On November 2, cold, tired, and saddle sore, he rode over the Stone Bridge into Regensburg on an old nag, which he sold upon his arrival for 11 florins. Traveling in the chilly autumn air had made him sick. At first, he shrugged it off as a nuisance, but then he grew worse. A high fever gripped him and he became delirious. A doctor was summoned, who bled him, but it did not help. Finally, men of God came to his bedside to console him.

He drifted in and out of consciousness for a few days, trying when he was lucid to express that he had done his best to bring the Protestants and the Catholics together. But the hateful Protestant pastor replied that that was like thinking that he could reconcile Christ with Satan. Finally, as he approached the end of his life, he was asked on what he pinned his hope for salvation. Kepler answered confidently, "Solely on the merit of our savior Jesus Christ, in which is founded all refuge, solace, and deliverance." He died at noon on November 15, 1630.

He was buried in the Protestant cemetery of St. Peter outside Regensburg's city wall two days later, after a funeral procession including some of the empire's most illustrious men, who had gathered in Regensburg for the meeting of the electors. Witnesses reported that, on that evening, fiery balls fell from heaven. We now recognize such meteors to be natural phenomena. In Kepler's time, however, when such displays were perceived as supernatural omens, it might have seemed that the heavens themselves were weeping for their interpreter.

The location of Johannes Kepler's final resting place is no longer known. The storms of the religious intolerance and war that buffeted his life did not let him rest peacefully even in death. Scarcely a few years later, Swedish forces besieged and captured Regensburg and then were expelled in turn by Bavarian and imperial troops. Whether by the city's defenders or attackers, the churchyard and Kepler's grave were eradicated in the process.

Our only record of Kepler's grave is a sketch of the gravestone made by a friend. It contained a description of his career as mathematician to three emperors, and proclaimed him foremost among astronomers. In addition, it carried an epitaph written by Kepler himself, which read:

> *I measured the heavens,*
> *Now the earth's shadows I measure,*
> *My mind was already in the heavens,*
> *Now the shadow of my body rests.*

The only record of Kepler's tombstone in Regensburg is this sketch by a friend.

Vindication

The sheer mathematical complexity of employing Kepler's laws of planetary motion and his unusual commitment to celestial physics ensured that the reception of his ideas would be problematic in the astronomical community of his time. In the end, it would be the tremendous increase in the accuracy of the prediction of planetary positions that would force astronomers to grapple with them. Only a handful of astronomers immediately recognized Kepler's accomplishment.

Toward the end of his life, Kepler foresaw a pair of upcoming celestial events that had never been witnessed before. His theory of Mercury predicted that Mercury would pass across the face of the sun on November 7, 1631. (Venus would likewise transit a month later, though it would not be visible in Europe.) The invention of the telescope and methods of using it to project an image of the sun onto a white screen had allowed astronomers to observe sunspots in the early 1610s. The same technology would allow them to observe Mercury in transit for the first time. Excited by this prospect, Kepler wanted to spread the news as widely as possible, so that observers throughout Europe could try to witness it. In 1629, he published an eight-page pamphlet entitled

De raris mirisque anni 1631 phaenomenis, Veneris puta Mercurii in Solem incursu, admonitio ad astronomos, rerumque coelestium studiosos (A Warning to Astronomers and Those Interested in Celestial Matters regarding the Rare and Amazing Phenomena of 1631, Namely, the Incursion of Venus and Mercury into the Sun) in which he predicted the phenomena and gave instructions for observing them. Alas, Kepler died before he could witness the extraordinary event he predicted.

Forewarned, astronomers set up telescopes to observe the transit of Mercury on November 7, 1631. Though Kepler's prediction was very slightly off, the transit occurred within 6 hours of the predicted time. "I have found him," exclaimed Pierre Gassendi in an open letter from France, "I have seen him where no one has ever seen him before!" Astronomers had to acknowledge that Kepler's planetary theory was at least 20 times more accurate than anyone else's.

Only toward the end of the 17th century, in the work of Isaac Newton, was the physical necessity of Kepler's three laws demonstrated. Newton succeeded in codifying the laws of mechanics and gravity and in using them to describe the dynamics of the solar system with unprecedented success. He showed how the motion of inertial bodies under the influence of gravity was necessarily described by Kepler's laws. Newtonian physics was entirely different in conception from Kepler's celestial physics, so it was inevitable that he dismissed Kepler's principles.

Though Kepler was never forgotten as an astronomer of genius and for a number of fundamental discoveries—the three important laws of planetary motion still bear his name—it was only when scholars began to focus their attention on the nature of scientific knowledge and the modes of thinking scientifically that Kepler's thought began to be examined in all its complexity. It can be said that it took the acquaintance with Albert Einstein's genius for scholars fully to appreciate his kindred intellect in Johannes Kepler.

CHRONOLOGY

December 27, 1571
Born in Weil der Stadt, Germany

1584–1588
Attends seminary school at Adelberg and Maulbronn

1589–1594
Attends the University of Tübingen, where he receives a
B.A. (by examination, 1588) and M.A. (1591); nearly com-
pletes three additional years of study in theology

April 1594
Arrives in Graz, Styria, to assume the position of mathematics teacher and district mathematician

1596–March 1597
Printing of the *Mysterium* cosmographicum in Tubingen

April 27, 1597
Marries Barbara Müller

September 28, 1598
Counter-Reformation begins in Styria; Protestant teachers
and preachers expelled from Graz; Kepler is allowed to
return after about a month

January–June 1600
Visits Tycho Brahe at Benatky Castle

September 30, 1600
Leaves Styria with his family and all their possessions
when all remaining Protestants are banished

October 24, 1601
Tycho Brahe dies; two days later, Kepler is named his suc-
cessor as imperial mathematician to Rudolf II in Prague

1604
Publishes the *Astronomia pars optica*

Around Easter, 1605
Discovers the elliptical form of Mars's orbit

1609
Astronomia nova finally published

March 1610
Galileo publishes the *Sidereus nuncius* containing his tele-scopic discoveries; Kepler responds, publishing the *Dissertatio cum nunceo sidereo* in Prague in May

Summer 1611
Kepler publishes *Dioptrice,* containing explanation of the telescope

July 3, 1611
Barbara Kepler dies

January 20, 1612
Holy Roman Emperor Rudolf II dies; Archduke Matthias succeeds him

May 1612
Begins work as mathematician to the Estates of Upper Austria in Linz

October 30, 1613
Marries Susanna Reuttinger

July 1615
Publishes *Nova stereometria doliorum vinariorum* in Linz

Fall 1617
Publishes the first volume of *Epitome astronomiae Coperni-canae* in Linz

Fall 1617–early 1618
Returns to Württemberg with his mother, but her court case is delayed

May 15, 1618
Discovers his third law of planetary motion

May 23, 1618
"Defenestration of Prague"; Thirty Years War begins

1619

Harmonice mundi libri V published in Linz

March 20, 1619

Holy Roman Emperor Matthias dies; Archduke Ferdinand
II suceeds him 5 months later

Early 1620

Second volume of *Epitome astronomiae Copernicanae* published in Linz

August 7, 1620–August 1621

Katharina Kepler arrested for witchcraft; Johannes Kepler
returns to Württemberg to assist in her defense

Fall 1621

Final volume of the *Epitome astronomiae Copernicanae* published in Frankfurt

October 1625

Counter-Reformation begins in Upper Austria

November 1626

Kepler and his family leave Linz

December 1626-September 1627

Rudolfine Tables printed in Ulm

July 1628

Kepler arrives in Sagan to become personal mathematician to General Wallenstein; Counter-Reformation in
Sagan begins four months later

November 15, 1630

Dies while visiting a meeting of imperial electors in
Regensburg

Works by Kepler in English translation

Epitome of Copernican Astronomy, Bks. IV and V, & *Harmonies of the World*, Bk. V. Trans. Charles Glenn Wallis. 1952. Reprint, New York: Prometheus Books, 1995.

The Harmony of the World. Trans. E. J. Aiton, A. M. Duncan, and J. V. Field. Philadelphia: American Philosophical Society, 1997.

Kepler's Conversation with Galileo's Sidereal Messenger. Trans. Edward Rosen. New York: Johnson Reprint Corp., 1965.

Kepler's Somnium: The Dream or Posthumous Work on Lunar Astronomy. Trans. Edward Rosen. Madison: University of Wisconsin Press, 1967.

Mysterium cosmographicum: The Secret of the Universe. Trans. A. M. Duncan. New York: Abaris Books, 1981.

New Astronomy. Trans. William H. Donahue. Cambridge: Cambridge University Press, 1992.

The Six-Cornered Snowflake. Trans. Colin Hardie. Oxford: Clarendon Press, 1966.

Works about Kepler

Baumgartner, Carola. *Johannes Kepler: Life and Letters*. New York: Philosophical Library, 1951.

Caspar, Max. *Kepler*. Trans. C. Doris Hellman. Introduction and References by Owen Gingerich. Bibliographical Citations by Owen Gingerich and Alain Segonds. 1948. New York: Dover, 1993.

Field, J. V. *Kepler's Geometrical Cosmology*. Chicago: University of Chicago Press, 1988.

―――. "A Lutheran Astrologer: Johannes Kepler." *Archive for History of Exact Sciences* 31 (1984): 189-272.

Gingerich, Owen. *The Eye of Heaven: Ptolemy, Copernicus, Kepler*. New York: American Institute of Physics, 1993.

―――. "Kepler, Johannes." In *Dictionary of Scientific Biography*, ed. Charles Coulston Gillispie, vol. 7, pp. 289-312. New York: Scribners, 1973.

Holton, Gerald. "Kepler's Universe: Its Physics and Metaphysics." *American Journal of Physics* 24 (1956): 340-351. Reprinted in

Gerald Holton, *Thematic Origins of Scientific Thought: Kepler to Einstein*, 53-74. Revised ed., Cambridge: Harvard University Press, 1988.

Jardine, Nicholas. *The Birth of History and Philosophy of Science: Kepler's* A Defence of Tycho against Ursus *with Essays on Its Provenance and Significance.* Cambridge: Cambridge University Press, 1984.

Koestler, Arthur. *The Sleepwalkers: A History of Man's Changing Vision of the Universe.* New York: Macmillan, 1959.

Koyré, Alexandre. *The Astronomical Revolution: Copernicus— Kepler—Borelli.* Trans. R. E. W. Maddison. 1973. Reprint, New York: Dover, 1992.

Kozamthadam, Job. *The Discovery of Kepler's Laws: The Interaction of Science, Philosophy, and Religion.* Notre Dame, Ind.: University of Notre Dame Press, 1994.

Rosen, Edward. *Three Imperial Mathematicians: Kepler Trapped between Tycho Brahe and Ursus.* New York: Abaris Books, 1986.

Stephenson, Bruce. *Kepler's Physical Astronomy.* 1987. Reprint, Princeton: Princeton University Press, 1994.

————. *The Music of the Spheres: Kepler's Harmonic Astronomy.* Princeton: Princeton University Press, 1994.

Wilson, Curtis. "How Did Kepler Discover His First Two Laws?" *Scientific American* 236 (1972): 92-106.

Related Reading

Hoskin, Michael, ed. *The Cambridge Illustrated History of Astronomy.* Cambridge: Cambridge University Press, 1997.

Thoren, Victor E. *The Lord of Uraniborg: A Biography of Tycho Brahe.* Cambridge: Cambridge University Press, 1990.

Taton, René, and Curtis Wilson, eds. *Planetary Astronomy from the Renaissance to the Rise of Astrophysics, Part A: Tycho Brahe to Newton.* Cambridge: Cambridge University Press, 1989.

Westfall, Richard S. *The Construction of Modern Science: Mechanisms and Mechanics.* Cambridge: Cambridge University Press, 1977.

AUTHORS

James R. Voelkel is an historian of science whose research has centered on Johannes Kepler and Tycho Brahe. He is a graduate of Williams College, Cambridge University, and Indiana University, where he received a Ph.D. in History of Science. He is currently Capabilities Manager of the History of Recent Science and Technology web project located at the Dibner Institute for the History of Science and Technology in Cambridge, Massachusetts. He has taught astronomy and history of science at Williams College, Harvard University, and the Johns Hopkins University.

Owen Gingerich is a senior astronomer at the Smithsonian Astrophysical Observatory and Professor of Astronomy and of the History of Science at Harvard University. He has served as vice president of the American Philosophical Society and as chairman of the U.S. National Committee of the International Astronomical Union. The author of more than 400 articles and reviews, Professor Gingerich is also the author of *The Great Copernicus Chase and Other Adventures in Astronomical History* and *The Eye of Heaven: Ptolemy, Copernicus, Kepler.* The International Astronomical Union's Minor Planet Bureau has named Asteroid 2658 "Gingerich" in his honor.

PENGUIN BOOKS

THE ROAD TO WELLVILLE

T. C. Boyle is the author of *Drop City*, *A Friend of the Earth*, *Riven Rock*, *The Tortilla Curtain*, *The Road to Wellville*, *East Is East*, *World's End* (winner of the PEN/Faulkner Award), *Budding Prospects*, *Water Music*, and six collections of stories. In 1999, he was the recipient of the PEN/Malamud Award for Excellence in Short Fiction. His stories appear regularly in major American magazines, including *The New Yorker*, *GQ*, *Esquire*, and *Playboy*. He lives near Santa Barbara, California. T. C. Boyle's Web site is www.tcboyle.com.

The
Road to
Wellville

T. Coraghessan Boyle

PENGUIN BOOKS

PENGUIN BOOKS
Published by the Penguin Group
Penguin Putnam Inc., 375 Hudson Street,
New York, New York 10014, U.S.A.
Penguin Books Ltd, 80 Strand, London WC2R 0RL, England
Penguin Books Australia Ltd, 250 Camberwell Road,
Camberwell, Victoria 3124, Australia
Penguin Books Canada Ltd, 10 Alcorn Avenue,
Toronto, Ontario, Canada M4V 3B2
Penguin Books India (P) Ltd, 11 Community Centre,
Panchsheel Park, New Delhi – 110 017, India
Penguin Books (N.Z.) Ltd, Cnr Rosedale and Airborne Roads,
Albany, Auckland, New Zealand
Penguin Books (South Africa) (Pty) Ltd, 24 Sturdee Avenue,
Rosebank, Johannesburg 2196, South Africa

Published in the United States of America by Viking Penguin,
a division of Penguin Books USA Inc., 1993
Published in Penguin Books 1994

13 15 17 19 20 18 16 14 12

A signed first edition of this book has been privately printed by
The Franklin Library.

THE LIBRARY OF CONGRESS HAS CATALOGUED THE HARDCOVER AS FOLLOWS:
Boyle, T. Coraghessan.
Road to Wellville: a novel/T. Coraghessan Boyle
p.   cm.
ISBN 0 670-84334-2 (hc.)
ISBN 0 14 01.6718 8 (pbk.)
I. Title.
PS3552.O932R63   1992
813'.54—dc20   92–50731

Printed in the United States of America
Set in Goudy Old Style
Designed by Brian Mulligan

B31388

Rosemary Post

1923–1981

Acknowledgments

Two texts were indispensable in inspiring and informing this novel—*Cornflake Crusade*, by Gerald Carson, and *The Nuts Among the Berries*, by Ronald M. Deutsch—and I am indebted to their authors. I would also like to thank Kevin McCarey, James Kaufman, Janet Griffin, Gordon Dale, and the staff of the Charles Willard Memorial Library in Battle Creek, Michigan, for their assistance.

Contents

Contents

Life is a temporary victory over the causes which induce death.

—Sylvester Graham, *A Lecture on Epidemic Diseases*

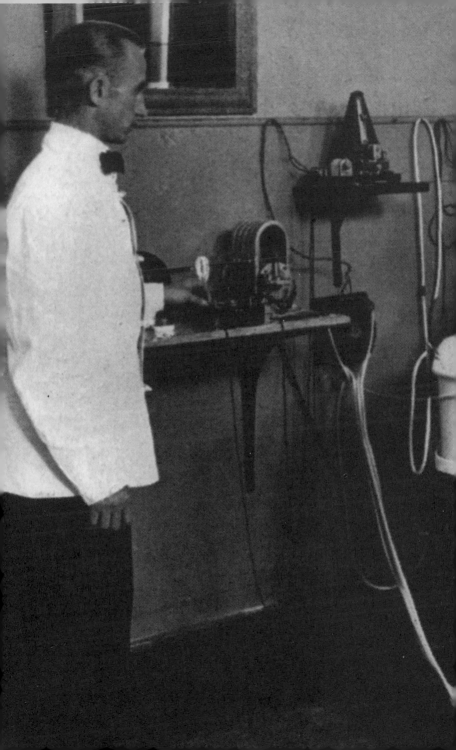

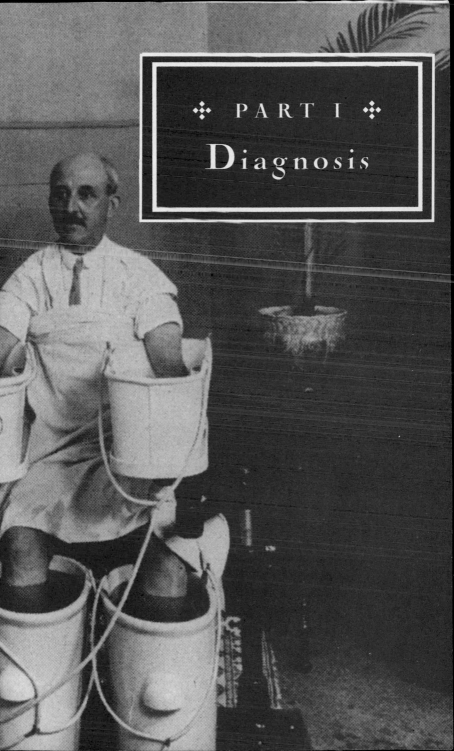

❖ PART I ❖

Diagnosis

Of Steak

and

Sin

❧

D r. John Harvey Kellogg, inventor of the corn flake and peanut butter, not to mention caramel-cereal coffee, Bromose, Nuttolene and some seventy-five other gastrically correct foods, paused to level his gaze on the heavyset woman in the front row. He was having difficulty believing what he'd just heard. As was the audience, judging from the gasp that arose after she'd raised her hand, stood shakily and demanded to know what was so sinful about a good porterhouse steak—it had done for the pioneers, hadn't it? And for her father and his father before him?

The Doctor pushed reflectively at the crisp white frames of his spectacles. To all outward appearances he was a paradigm of concentration, a scientist formulating his response, but in fact he was desperately trying to summon her name—who was she, now? He knew her, didn't he? That nose, those eyes . . . he knew them all, knew them by name, a matter of pride . . . and then, in a snap, it came to him: Tindermarsh. Mrs. Violet. Complaint, obesity. Underlying cause, autointoxication. *Tindermarsh. Of course.* He couldn't help feeling a little self-congratulatory flush of pride—nearly a thousand patients and he could call up any one of them as plainly as if he had their charts spread out before him. . . . But enough of that—the audience was stirring, a monolithic force, one great naked psyche awaiting the hand to clothe it. Dr. Kellogg cleared his throat.

"My dear Mrs. Tindermarsh, I do thank you for your question," he began, hardly able to restrain his dainty feet from breaking into dance even as the perfect riposte sprang to his lips, "but I wonder how many of those flesh-abusing pioneers lived past the age of forty?" (A murmur from the audience as the collective image of a skeletal man in coonskin cap, dead of salt pork and flapjacks, rose before their eyes.) "And how many of them, your own reverend forebears not excepted, went to bed at night and had a minute's sleep that wasn't racked with dyspepsia and the nightmare of carnal decay?" He paused to let that horrible thought sink in. "I say to you, Mrs. Tindermarsh, and to the rest of you ladies and gentlemen of the audience, and I say it with all my heart"—pause, two beats—"a steak is every bit as deadly as a gun. Worse. At least if one points a gun at one's head and pulls the trigger, the end comes with merciful swiftness, but a steak—ah, the exquisite and unremitting agonies of the flesh eater, his colon clogged with its putrefactive load, the blood settling in his gut, the carnivore's rage building in his brittle heart—a steak kills day by day, minute by minute, through the martyrdom of a lifetime."

He had them now—he could see the fear and revulsion in their eyes, the grim set of their jaws as they each inwardly totted up the steaks and sausages, the chops and pullets and geese consumed over the course of the greedy, oblivious years. "But don't take my word for it," he said, waving his arms expansively, "let's be scientific about it. After all, the Sanitarium stands as a monument to biologic living and scientific analysis, a veritable University of Health. Let's just perform a little experiment here—right here, on the spur of the moment." He ducked away from the spotlight and called out in a suddenly stentorian voice: "Frank? Dr. Frank Linniman?"

A flurry from the rear of the auditorium, movement, the craning of three hundred necks, and all at once the summoned assistant was striding briskly up the aisle, his chin thrust forward, his carriage flawless. The audience took one look at him and knew that here was a man who would unflinchingly throw himself over a cliff if his Chief required it of him. He came to a halt before the podium and gazed up into the brilliant light. "Yes, Doctor?"

"Do you know the Post Tavern? The finest hostelry in Battle Creek—or, for that matter, anywhere else in this grand state of Michigan?" This was nothing, a bit of stagemanship, and the Doctor had been through it a dozen times before, yet still the image of Charlie Post, blandly handsome, effortlessly tall, a very Judas of a man, rose up before him like an assassin's blade, and it ever so slightly soured the moment for him.

"I know it, Doctor."

Dr. Kellogg was a diminutive man himself. It wasn't so much that he was short, he liked to say—it was just that his legs weren't long enough. Sit him in a chair and he was as tall as the next fellow. Of course, as he'd grown into his fifties, he'd expanded a bit on the horizontal plane, but that was all right—it gave him a glow of portly health and authority, an effect he enhanced by dressing entirely in white. Tonight, as always, he was a marvel of whiteness, a Santa Claus of health, from his flawless white high-button shoes to the cusp of his Vandyke and the fine pale tenacious hair that clung to his scalp. He paused a moment to take a sip from his water glass and rinse the taste of Charlie Post from his mouth.

Setting the glass back down, he glanced up briefly and saw that the audience was hanging on his every gesture; half a dozen of them were actually gaping. He gave them a sagacious look and then focused on his assistant. "Frank, I want you to go to the chef there—a chef of international renown, I'm told, an epicure Mr. Post has imported from Paris, a Monsieur Delarain, isn't it?—and I want you to purchase the finest steak he has available and bring it back here, to this very stage, for our inspection."

A tentative ripple of laughter, the scrape of chair legs.

"Well, go, Frank—fly. What are you waiting for?"

"A steak, sir?" Frank knew the routine, God bless him, as sturdy a straight man as you could hope to find.

"Not just a steak, Frank—the finest steak money can buy."

Frank's face was an open book. He was guileless, as baffled as the audience, his only desire to gratify his Chief. "I'll be back in a twinkling," he announced, and he was already turning away, already poised to dash up the aisle, when the Doctor spoke again.

"And Frank," he said, drawing it out, "Frank, would you do me one other great favor?"

Silence. Not a breath expelled anywhere in the house.

"Would you stop at the livery stable and pick up a sample of another sort—for comparison, that is?" The Doctor chuckled amiably, avuncular, warm, the very avatar of geniality and good sense. "I'm referring to a bit of, well, horse excretus"—stunned laughter, picking up now, gales of it, so lusty the sequel could barely be heard—"about four hundred forty-eight grams, to be precise . . . or the size of a good sixteen-ounce steak."

❖   ❖   ❖

It was a typical Monday night at the Battle Creek Sanitarium, bastion of right thinking, vegetarianism and self-improvement, citadel of temperance and dress reform, and, not coincidentally, the single healthiest spot on the planet. The women were uncorseted, the men slack in their suspenders, both sexes quietly percolating over the toxin-free load of dinner in an atmosphere cleansed of tobacco, alcohol, corned beef, mutton chops and the coffee jitters. Stomachs full, minds at rest, they were gathered in the Grand Parlor to hear their Chief instruct them on matters relating to physical well-being and its happy concomitant, longevity. They might have been at Baden or Worishofen or Saratoga, but instead they were assembled here in the icebox of south-central Michigan—and paying a handsome price for the privilege—because there was no place on the map to equal it.

In the thirty-one years of his directorship, Dr. Kellogg had transformed the San, as it was affectionately known, from an Adventist boarding house specializing in Graham bread and water cures to the "Temple of Health" it had now become, a place celebrated from coast to coast— and across the great wide weltering Atlantic to London, Paris, Heidelberg and beyond. Twenty-eight hundred patients annually passed through its portals, and one thousand employees, including twenty full-time physicians and three hundred nurses and bath attendants, saw to their needs. Six stories high, with a gleaming lobby half the size of a football field, with four hundred rooms and treatment facilities for a thousand, with elevators, central heating and cooling, indoor swimming pools and a whole range of therapeutic diversions and wholesome entertainments, the San was the sine qua non of the cure business—luxury hotel, hospital and spa all rolled into one.

And the impresario, the overseer, the presiding genius behind it all, was John Harvey Kellogg. Preaching dietary restraint and the simple life, he eased overweight housewives and dyspeptic businessmen along the path to enlightenment and recovery. Severe cases—the cancerous, the moribund, the mentally unbalanced and the disfigured—were rejected. The San's patients tended to be of a certain class, and they really had no interest in sitting across the dining table from the plebeian or the pedestrian or those who had the bad grace to be truly and dangerously ill. No, they came to the San to see and be seen; to mingle with the celebrated, the rich and the preposterously rich; to think positively, eat wisely and subdue their afflictions with a good long pious round of pampering, abstention and rest.

At this juncture, in the fall of 1907, the San numbered among its guests such luminaries as Admiral Nieblock of the U.S. Naval Academy, Upton and Meta Sinclair, Horace B. Fletcher, and Tiepolo Cappucini, the great Italian tenor, as well as a smattering of state and national legislators, captains of industry, entertainers and assorted dukes, contessas and baronets. On the horizon were visits by Henry Ford, Harvey Firestone, Thomas Edison, Admiral Richard M. Byrd and the voluminous William Howard Taft. Dr. Kellogg was no fool, and he extracted as much benefit as he could from these dignataries, in terms of both promotional service and raw cash donations. He knew, too, that a diet of Protose fillets, beet tops and nut savory broth, combined with a prohibition on artificial stimulants and long unbroken stretches of ruminative time, might prove a bit, well, dull to the high-livers and men and women of action among his patients. And so he kept them busy, with a regimen of sports, exercise, rest and treatment, and he kept them entertained, too. There were concerts, lectures, sleigh rides, grand marches and sing-alongs. The Jubilee Singers might appear one night and George W. Leitch, twenty years in India and with his stereopticon slides in hand, the next. Or it would be "Professor" Sammy Siegel, hot off the vaudeville circuit, milking the strings of his mandolin, or the Tozer Twins and their trained dachshunds. And on Monday nights, without fail, the Chief himself took possession of the podium and held it for two and a half rapid-fire hours, enlightening his charges, edifying them and, as much as possible, scaring them half to death.

In the fifteen minutes it took Frank Linniman to trot down to the Post Tavern and back, the Doctor fielded two more questions. The first was from a gentleman in the rear (Mr. Abernathy, wasn't it? Gout, consumption and nerves?) who wanted to know of the dangers of tight-lacing among fashionable females who unnaturally constricted their midsections to achieve the "wedding ring" waist. The Doctor repeated the question for the benefit of those up front who might not have heard, and then, after stroking the white silk of his beard a moment, shot an admonitory forefinger into the air. "My dear sir, I can tell you without exaggeration that if the number of deaths recorded annually as a result of just such frivolous tight-lacing were properly recorded, you would be truly appalled. As a medical intern at Bellevue, I had occasion to be present for the autopsy of one such unfortunate woman—a woman, I might add, not yet out of her twenties. In any case, we found to our astonishment that her organs had been totally disarranged, the liver pushed up into the lungs and the intestines so effectively blocked they might just as well have been stoppered with a cork." He shook his fine head wearily and let out a sigh that could be heard in the back row. "A pity," he said, his voice cast low. "I tell you, it brought tears to my eyes."

The second question was from a tall and very striking young woman in the fifth row, whose skin, unfortunately, had a faint greenish cast to it. (Muntz, Miss Ida; greensickness, autointoxication.) She rose, visibly excited at the thought of all those curious eyes upon her, and cleared her throat. "Doctor," she asked in a plaintive, demure voice, "could you please give us your opinion of cigarette smoking, as practiced in private, of course, among young ladies of today?"

Dr. Kellogg furrowed his brows. He was furious, incensed, a tower of righteous strength and indignation. He paused to let his gaze fall upon the recidivist cigar and cigarette smokers among the audience. "Madame—or should I say Mademoiselle? Mademoiselle Muntz, I have only this to say, and it applies equally to both sexes. Tobacco"—and here the Doctor let a long shudder run through him—"tobacco destroys the sex glands."

Someone gasped. Miss Muntz sank into her seat, stricken. The Doctor held his stony gaze. "And that," he said, "is a medically proven fact."

It was at this moment that Dr. Linniman dashed through the rear door, an air of breathless urgency about him, two identical packages wrapped in white butcher's paper held out before him in offering.

"Ah," the Doctor exclaimed, pushing at his spectacles, "Dr. Linniman." And then he lifted his head to address the audience at large. "And now, to return, if we may, to Mrs. Tindermarsh's query regarding porterhouse steak and its value as a food source—" He broke off here to lean forward and give Dr. Linniman, who now stood before him, these further instructions: "Frank, would you examine the scales, please, weigh the respective samples and prepare slides of a precisely equal portion of each? Thank you."

A murmur from the audience. A few titters, a spatter of applause.

"Ladies and gentlemen, I am about to provide you with a pair of demonstrations that should, I would fervently hope, forever turn you away from such a disgusting and unnatural food as this. I say 'disgusting' because of its high bacterial content—a content I will show to be equal to or greater than that of barnyard ordure—and I say 'unnatural' because this flesh food is an innovation and corruption of modern man, whose ancestors have been proven by such eminent researchers as Von Freiling in Germany and Du Pomme of the Pasteur Institute to be exclusively frugivorous. And, too, I will assert that such foods are in fact 'sinful,' as Mrs. Tindermarsh would have it, not only in the sin occasioned by the taking of the lives of our fellow creatures—and I would think that the piteous bleats of those blameless herds led to slaughter would ring in the ears of any flesh eater the moment his head hits the pillow at night—but in the very greatest sin of all, and that is, of course, in polluting the temple of the human body."

The audience was hushed now, sitting rapt and motionless in the orthopedically correct chairs the Doctor had himself designed. Someone—was that Mr. Praetz, of Cleveland?—suppressed a cough.

"Frank?" The doctor swiveled round briskly to where Dr. Linniman had joined him at the rear of the small stage. "Are we ready?"

A plain deal table stood just behind him; on it, conspicuously displayed, were the beefsteak from the Post Tavern and the grainy pungent sample from the livery stable. Between these two exhibits, Dr. Linniman had set up a matching pair of microscopes and a small naked incandescent bulb for illumination. "Yes, sir," he answered. "All ready."

"Good." Turning once more to the audience, Dr. Kellogg flashed a toothy smile and rubbed his hands together with relish. "Now, we'll need a disinterested party as observer—do I have any volunteers? No? How about you, Miss Muntz?"

A little gasp, a titter, and there, in the fifth row, was Miss Muntz, coloring prettily.

"Don't be shy, Miss Muntz—this is all in the interest of science."

There were murmurs of encouragement, and in the next moment Miss Ida Muntz was clutching the sides of her skirts and making her way up the aisle, where she daintily mounted the three steps to the podium.

"Now, Miss Muntz," the Doctor began, and he momentarily lost his train of thought as he saw how she towered over him—she was pretty, yes, and she gave them something to look at, greensickness and all, but he should have thought to choose someone with a little less legbone, for God's sake. He fumbled a moment, uncharacteristically, and repeated himself: "Miss Muntz. Miss Muntz, I would like you to examine the slides beneath these identical microscopes and describe to us what you see, remembering that only Dr. Linniman knows which of these specimens is Mrs. Tindermarsh's beefsteak and which the, well"—laughter from the audience—"the waste product of an animal very much like the one sacrificed for the venal tastes of the gourmands at the Post Tavern."

The moment was exquisite: the girl bent prettily over the microscope, the men leaning forward in their seats for a better look, the women smiling secret smiles, the Doctor, as ever, conscious of his control, his benevolence, his wisdom—shepherd to his flock. "And would you describe for us what you see in the first exhibit, my dear?"

"Um, it's black—or no, now I see . . ."

"Yes?"

"Tiny things. Moving. Like, like bits of straw or rice—only alive."

"Good, very good, Miss Muntz. Those are bacteria"—the Doctor turned to face the audience now—"and they are truncated, like bits of rice, as you say, because they are unfriendly bacteria, the B. *welchii*, B. *coli* and *Proteus vulgaris* we so often find in the stool of our incoming patients here at the Sanitarium. And could you accurately count the bacteria for us, Miss Muntz?"

She turned her head now, looking up at him out of a bright crystalline eye, and gave a little cry of surprise. "Oh, no, Doctor—there are so many hundreds and hundreds of them."

"And now, Miss Muntz, would you do us the great favor of examining the sample beneath the second microscope?"

A flutter of skirts, a quick reassuring touch-up of the coiffure and millinery, and Miss Muntz was bent over the second microscope.

"Would you describe what you see now, Miss Muntz?"

"Yes, Doctor, it's . . . it's much the same thing—"

The audience breathed out, a ripple that became a tidal wave.

"And could you count the bacteria in this sample?"

"Oh, no, Doctor—"

"But would you say that there are fewer or more than in the first sample?"

Her eye still affixed to the aperture of the lens, Miss Muntz tugged unconsciously at a loose strand of hair and let her voice drop reflectively. "This one is, is more cluttered. A lot more."

"Would you say there were half as many more in this sample?"

"Oh, yes," Miss Muntz breathed, taking her eye from the lens and straightening up to face the Doctor and the crowd ranged myopically behind him. "Yes, at least, Doctor—at least half as many more. . . ."

"Very good. And now, Dr. Linniman, would you please reveal to the audience the identity of each of these slides?"

Frank's face was perfectly composed—wonderful, wonderful, thought the Doctor, a rush of triumph building in him. *How he loved this life!* "The first slide—"

"Yes?"

"—this is the sample from the livery stable."

At this, the audience erupted. There were hoots of laughter, cries of surprise and wonderment, and finally a sustained applause that echoed through the Grand Parlor like the steady wash of sea on shingle. It was a long moment before the Doctor, beaming and with both hands uplifted, was able to calm them. "I urge you," he called out above the dying clamor, "to step up individually once we're done here tonight, and confirm for yourselves Miss Muntz's observations. And thank you, Miss Muntz—you may step down now—and thank you, Dr. Linniman."

A moment drifted by, the crowd still abuzz, as Dr. Linniman helped the young lady from the stage, saw her to her seat and himself found a place in the front row. The Doctor could feel the pulse of the audience declining ever so slightly from the peak to which he'd brought it, and he knew now that they were vulnerable, putty in his hands: it was time for the pièce de résistance. "Ladies and gentlemen," he cried, "I thank you for your attention. I'll let you draw your own conclusions from what you've just seen," he added slyly, "but we have a problem here . . . what to do with Mr. Post's porterhouse steak." He held up a hand to silence the incipient laughter. "I propose a second small illustration of the Sanitarium's principles. . . ." Dr. Kellogg again looked pointedly to the rear of the auditorium. Those in front began to crane their necks. "Is Dr. Distaso ready?"

A gruff, French-accented bark of assent rose from the back of the room, and there was Dr. Distaso, the distinguished bacteriologist Dr. Kellogg had lured away from the Pasteur Institute in Paris, leading his ward for the evening up the aisle. This was an ancient, foul-smelling and fouler-tempered chimpanzee by the name of Lillian, an animal the Doctor had acquired from a circus some years earlier and kept around the San for just such a moment as this. When the audience caught sight of Lillian, who was usually confined to a cage in one of the back laboratories, there was a universal cry of approbation. Several of them actually got to their feet for a better look, and a pair of matrons in one of the middle rows clapped their hands like schoolgirls. The Doctor focused on one man in particular (Jennings, Bigelow; chronic flatulence, partial loss of hearing), who was laughing so hard his eyes were damp and his face seemed swollen to twice its size. Amidst the pandemonium, Dr. Kellogg took Lillian's leash from Dr. Distaso and led her up onto the stage, where, knowing her routine as well as Frank Linniman knew his, she clambered atop a stool in the far corner and gave the Doctor her undivided attention. Raising his hands high above his head, Dr. Kellogg called for quiet.

It took them even longer to settle down this time, but when they'd quieted somewhat, the Doctor raised his voice and gave a quick little speech about the evils of meat and how contrary to man's nature it was to consume it. "By way of illustration," he said, "I am going to give our simian cousin here—Lillian, that is, and she certainly doesn't resemble anyone on my side of the family"—a pause for laughter—"I'm going to give her a choice between Mr. Post's finest beefsteak and the contents of this bag," and he drew a brown paper bag out from behind the podium. "Let's see which she prefers."

The Doctor backed away from the podium and slipped on a pair of gloves that had been laid out for him on the table. He then hefted the dripping slab of meat, held it out briefly for all to see, and casually tossed it to Lillian. The chimp was adept. She snatched it from the air in a spidery hand and brought it to her nose, uttering a low coughing sound and folding her lips back over her teeth. The audience stirred, poked one another, hummed with laughter. Perplexed, Lillian touched the tip of her tongue to the surface of the meat, made a face of gargoylelike disdain, and then suddenly, and rather violently, flung the thing back at the Doctor, who caught it neatly. Setting the steak down, he extracted a banana from the bag. With a cry of "Voilà!" he threw it to the chimp, who immediately peeled and ate it. "Hoo-hoo," she murmured, turning her chocolate eyes on him with a look of pure and abiding love.

Dr. Kellogg tossed her another, and all at once the audience was on its feet, cheering, whistling, faces animated; ills, aches, twinges and conniptions all but forgotten. The applause was thunderous. Dr. Kellogg bowed deeply, and as Lillian greedily plunged the second banana into the rictus of her mouth and his patients cheered mightily, he waved his way out the door and into the hallway, floating on the exhilaration of the moment.

❖   ❖   ❖

Outside, amongst the potted palms and bathed in the gentle glow of the electric lamps, stood his secretary, Poultney Dab. Dab had been waiting patiently, a sheaf of papers clutched awkwardly in one hand, a briefcase in the other.

"Hear them, Poult? We taught them a thing or two tonight they won't soon forget, eh?" The doctor was already hurrying up the hall with his short brisk strides, throwing the words back over his shoulder at Dab's large and anxious face. "See that Lillian gets an extra ration tonight and that the new man, what's his name, Murphy? changes her litter—he's been remiss about that—and I'll need a second copy of the trustees' report, as I think I told you, and oh, yes, there's been a complaint of cooking odors on the fifth floor—Mrs. Crouder's room, five-nineteen, I believe—and I want you to have Sturman look into it, and be prepared to take dictation in my office at eleven P.M. sharp, will you?"

Dab was a short large man with an unfortunate waddle; the more he hurried after his Chief, the more pronounced it became. "Dr. Kellogg," he was saying, his voice harsh and breathless, and there seemed to be some sort of urgency stuck in the craw of it, "Dr. Kellogg—"

The Doctor pulled up short in the middle of the wide gleaming corridor that stretched five hundred thirty feet from the Grand Parlor to the lobby, the corridor set in the spotless Italian marble he'd chosen himself, and spun round to face his secretary. Over Dab's shoulder he could see the people filing out of the Grand Parlor, a parade of the distinguished, the celebrated and the wealthy. A group of nurses passed by, beautiful girls all, smiling shyly. "Evening, Doctor," they murmured. "Evening, girls," he replied grandly. "And now, Poult, what in God's name is it that's got you so worked up?"

But the doctor didn't have to wait for his secretary's response: there it was, slouching indolently against the wall not ten feet away; there it

14

was, staring him in the face. All at once his mood shattered like a windowpane. He could feel the rage take hold of him. "How dare you!" he choked, storming up to the ragged figure propped against the wall. "Haven't I told you—"

But the figure moved and spoke and cut him off. The words seemed to come from deep inside him even as the sparkling audience flowed through the doors of the Grand Parlor and made their way in a knot toward them; the words spat themselves out like a curse, twisted by the unshaven lips, forced from the stinking rags and the feverish eyes: "Hello, Father. Aren't you going to introduce me?"

Chapter 2

Scavengers
of the
Sea

❧

I gnoring the dainty little three-pronged fork, Charlie Ossining lifted the oyster to his mouth, tipped the shell forward and with a quick practiced pursing of the lips, allowed it to become one with himself. Before him, atop a bed of crushed ice, lay eleven others, glistening with the juice of life. He lingered over the second, garnishing it with a dash of cocktail sauce and a squeeze of lemon before sending it off to bed with its brother, the moment settling round him in a warm gastric glow as he took a leisurely sip of his Pommery & Greno '96, and contemplated the snug green neck of the bottle peeking out from its icy cradle. This was living, all right, he thought, patting his lips with a swath of snowy linen and letting his gaze fall idly over the glittering depths of the car.

Outside, the scenery beat by the windows, as cold and cheerless as an oyster's gullet—did oysters have gullets? he wondered briefly before downing another—but here, in the softly lit grip of the diner, it was all mahogany and crystal. Amazing, really. You'd hardly think they were rocketing along at nearly forty miles an hour—the car barely trembled, the champagne clinging to the rim of the glass even as the potted palm swayed serenely over the table. He could feel the vibration of the rails, of course, but it was nothing, a distant throb, as if threads of silk were pulling him gently through the bleak countryside.

He was halfway through the plate of oysters—six shells denuded, six to go—when the Negro waiter pranced up the aisle, a pair of menus clutched to his chest, a cadaverous-looking couple following in his wake. Casting a quick look round him, Charlie saw to his dismay that his was the only table for four occupied by a single diner, and saw further that they were headed straight for him. So much for solitary pleasures.

" 'Scuse me, sir," the Negro said, dipping his head in extenuation, and then he drew out the chair opposite Charlie for the lady (thirtyish, too pale, too thin, nice eyes, a three-tiered hat built up like the Tower of Pisa with artificial fruit, lace, ribbon, assorted gewgaws and a pale little dead bird with glass eyes perched atop a wire twig) and the chair beside her for the man (too much nose, unruly hair, dressed up like a prince on his way to the opera). Charlie took an immediate dislike to them, but then he softened a bit, always willing to make concessions for the rich.

"Good evening," Charlie offered. He was wearing a blue serge suit himself—a bit linty, maybe, but his pink-and-white-striped shirt had been worn only three or four times, and his cuffs and collar were new from the shop that morning.

The woman smiled—nice teeth, too. And lips. "Evening," the man murmured, handing the wine list back to the waiter as if it were a bit of offal and turning the menu face down without even glancing at it. He fixed Charlie with an ever-so-slightly cross-eyed gaze, held it perhaps a beat too long, and then broke into a grin. Suddenly, a fleshless hand, chased by a bony wrist, shot out across the table, and Charlie, startled, took it in his own. "Will Lightbody," the man said, his voice booming out now in an excess of enthusiasm.

Charlie spoke his own name, disengaged his hand, and turned to the woman.

"Mr. Ossining," Will pronounced, and there was an odd hollowness to his voice, as if he were speaking from the bottom of a well, "I'd like you to meet my wife, Eleanor."

The towering hat trembled beneath its excrescences, a pair of sharp mocking eyes took hold of Charlie's like pincers, and Eleanor Lightbody was murmuring a standard greeting. A moment of silence followed,

Eleanor glancing down at her menu, Will grinning inappropriately, nakedly, a thirty-year-old schoolboy with a new plaything. Charlie began to wonder if he wasn't a bit unbalanced.

"Oysters," Will said suddenly. Eleanor lifted her eyes from the menu. Charlie glanced at the half-dozen shellfish remaining on his plate and then looked up into Will's horse-toothed grin. "Yes. Bluepoints. And they're delicious, really sweet . . . would you care to try one?"

The grin vanished. Will's lower lip seemed to tremble. He glanced out the window. It was Eleanor who broke the silence this time. "It's his stomach," she said.

His stomach. Charlie hesitated, wondering at the appropriate response. Sympathy? Surprise? A spirited defense of the digestive properties of oysters? He gazed wistfully on the plate of shellfish—the air had to be cleared before he communed with another, that much was apparent. "Dyspepsia?" he wondered aloud.

"I haven't slept in three weeks," Will announced. He was fidgeting with the corners of the menu, and his leg had begun to thump nervously beneath the table. Without benefit of the grin, his face had grown longer and narrower, his eyes had retreated into his skull, and there were two pronounced caverns beneath his cheekbones. He looked ready for the grave.

"Really? You don't say?" Charlie glanced from husband to wife and back again. She had stunning eyes, she did, but the mocking gleam was gone from them now, vanished like her husband's grin. "Three weeks?"

Will shook his head sadly. "Afraid so. I lie there in bed staring at the ceiling and my stomach is like a steam engine, like a boiler, and pretty soon I start seeing all these visions in the dark. . . ." He leaned forward. "Pies, oranges, beefsteaks—and every one of them with legs and arms, dancing round the room and mocking me. Do you know what I mean?"

The waiter reappeared at that moment, hovering over the table with his order pad and sparing Charlie the awkwardness of a reply. "May I take your order, sir? Madame?"

Night was settling in beyond the windows, a descent of the dead gray sky over the dead gray landscape, shadows deepening, trees falling away into oblivion, the river running black. Charlie was suddenly aware of his reflection staring back at him—he saw a hungry man in a linty blue suit hunkered over a plate of oysters. Taking advantage of the momentary distraction, he hastily slid an oyster down his throat, emptied his glass and filled it again, the cold neck of the bottle as satisfying to the hand as anything he'd ever held.

"The potage," Eleanor was saying, "it *is* leek, isn't it?"

"Yes, madame."

"No beef or chicken stock—" Her voice took on an admonitory tone the waiter was quick to recognize.

"Oh, no, ma'am—veggehle stock only."

"Yes. All right. And none of the entrées is acceptable—would you bring me some vegetables, please? I don't suppose you have crudités?"

The waiter looked uncomfortable. He shifted from one foot to the other. His white jacket was so bright it seemed to glow. "We have all the very finest here, ma'am, I can assure you of that. . . ." He faltered. "I will inquire of the chef." And then, after gazing searchingly at the floor a moment, he added, "We do have a fine cucumber salad tonight."

Eleanor heaved a sigh. "All right, then—the cucumber salad. And a glass of water." As she leaned forward to hand the waiter the menu, she seemed to think of something else. "Oh," she said, "and a bowl of bran. To sprinkle over the salad."

"Bran?" The waiter looked confused. "I'll be sure to inquire of the chef, ma'am."

She made a little puffing noise with her lips. "Oh, never mind," she said. "Just the soup and the salad."

Looking relieved, the waiter accepted the menu and bent forward, attentively gazing into Will Lightbody's upturned face. "And for the gentleman?"

As Charlie took up another oyster, he couldn't help noticing the look of panic settling into his fellow diner's ever-so-faintly crossed eyes. Will waved his hand carelessly, as if he hadn't come to eat at all, as if this weren't the dining car of the Twentieth Century Limited, the world's premier train, boasting the finest cuisine and finest service known to man. "Oh, nothing for me. A bit of toast, maybe."

"Toast, sir?"

"Toast."

There was a silence as the waiter contemplated this request. This was an era of vigorous and accomplished eating, of twelve-course meals, of soups, sauces and gravies, of three meats and a fish course, not to mention a cascade of wines—sherries, clarets, ports, Zinfandel and Niersteiner—and a succession of oleaginous desserts. The kitchen was groaning with rib roasts, broiled geese and slabs of venison, the cooks were furiously shucking oysters and poaching sturgeon, waiters staggered up and down the aisle beneath the burden of their laden trays, and here was Will Lightbody ordering toast. The silence held and Charlie was aware in that moment of the distant ticking of the rails. At the next table a woman swathed in furs gave a silvery little laugh in response to something her companion—an old man with gargantuan mustaches—was saying in a muted rumble.

"And, uh, how would the gentleman like that?"

Charlie's new acquaintance seemed distracted. "Like what?"

"The gentleman's toast, sir."

"Oh, yes. Toasted, please." Will glanced uneasily at his wife. "And with a bowl of broth," he added in a single breath, as if afraid the tongue would be snatched from his mouth before he could get the words out.

"No broth," Eleanor countered just as quickly, and there was no arguing with the tone of that voice: the waiter penciled out "broth" as expeditiously as he'd penciled it in. "Full of creatine," she added, giving Charlie a look he couldn't quite fathom.

"Will that be all?" the waiter asked, clasping his hands before him as if in prayer and giving an obsequious little nod of his head.

Will glanced up sharply. "Yes, yes. That's all."

The waiter retreated, the woman at the next table laughed again, and the night deepened a further degree, so that the diners could no longer see the countryside rushing past them. Charlie ducked his head to receive another oyster.

"Scavengers of the sea," Will said suddenly.

Eleanor smiled, a faint compressing of the lips. Her eyes were keen again.

"Beg pardon?" Charlie returned, lifting the wine glass to his lips even as the soft pulp of the oyster met his teeth and found its way down his throat to join its companions.

"Oysters," Will said, turning to his wife. "Right, darling? Isn't that what your Dr. Kellogg calls them?"

There was a joke here somewhere—Charlie could see it in her eyes —and he seemed to be the brunt of it. She tilted her head slightly, so that the glassy dumbstruck eyes of the bird atop her hat flashed luridly in the light. "Yes, Will darling," she said, all the while staring at Charlie, "but he's only speaking the truth. Oysters *are* unclean, after all. They live in muck and filth and they feed on it. And oyster juice, he insists, is nothing more or less than urine."

Charlie glanced down at the three sorry bivalves remaining on his plate. "Urine?"

Her smile was widening. "Piss," she said, "to use the vernacular. As in 'making water'?"

Will was grinning at him again, too, his eyes swallowed up in a filigree of wrinkles and laugh lines; he looked like a gargoyle leering from its perch. "I wouldn't want to eat a scavenger, would you?"

Charlie could feel his hackles rising. "Actually—" he began, but Eleanor cut him off.

"Dr. Kellogg took a sample from this very train, did you know that?" she said, wagging a gloved finger for emphasis. "Had it shipped on to Battle Creek from the terminus at Chicago and analyzed it in the laboratories at the San. . . ." She paused for emphasis. "And he found the juice of each of those oysters to be almost identical to a teaspoon of, well, *human* urine."

Charlie had been about to defend his oysters—urine or no, they were about as perfect a way to begin an evening, or end one, as he could imagine—but a new note had entered the conversation and he jumped on it. "Battle Creek? Did you say 'Battle Creek'?"

Eleanor nodded. Will bobbed his head.

"But that's my destination—Battle Creek. I'm on my way there now. Once we get to Chicago, I connect with the Michigan Central Line." He loved the sound of that, *Michigan Central Line*—it made him feel worldly, well-traveled, an important man doing important things. Never mind that he'd never been west of the Jersey Palisades or ever before had anything to do with an overnight train other than to watch it roar out of the station, packed to the windows with its rich cargo.

He wanted to elaborate, the whole business of timetables and porters and connections wonderfully exotic to him, but he couldn't go on. The Lightbodys had burst out in a simultaneous peal of laughter, Eleanor actually clapping her hands together like a girl at a party. "But that's marvelous," she gasped. "What a wonderful coincidence."

"You too?" Charlie surmised.

"Yes," Will said, and his grin faded a degree or two, "we're on our way to the Sanitarium—for the cure." He hesitated, and the bleakness returned to his face: he was hunted, he was starved, he was condemned before his time. "I've—I've never been," he confessed, "but Eleanor—"

"This will be my third visit," she announced, reaching up prettily to adjust her hat. "I'm afraid I've become one of those 'Battle Freaks' you read of in the papers."

Charlie couldn't help giving her a quick once-over: the slim arms and dainty hands, the white arch of her throat above the choke collar set with a studded pin, the swell of her chest. And what was wrong with her? She seemed fine—a bit drawn and pale, maybe, but nothing a week in the country wouldn't cure. The husband was a man of sticks —he looked as if he could use all the help he could get—but the wife, the wife intrigued him. He was framing the question in his mind, wondering just how to put it, when the waiter materialized with two glasses of water and set them down with a flourish in front of the Lightbodys. "Is the gentleman finish?" the waiter murmured, making a feint toward the remaining oysters.

Charlie looked into Eleanor's mocking eyes and then at Will, who gave him a doleful sidelong glance. He waved his hand and the oysters vanished.

"Tell me, Mr. Ossining," Will said, "if I may inquire—what brings you to Battle Creek? Convalescence? Business? Pleasure?"

Charlie had been a bit off his mark since the Lightbodys had joined him—these people were odd, there was no doubt about it—but he understood only too well that oddness was the prerogative of the rich and that it was his job and mission to exploit it as best he could. He felt a sudden surge of the old confidence. "Business," he announced. "The breakfast-food business. I've got a card right here"—and he was digging in his vest pocket—"ah, here it is." He handed the card to Will, who even as he took it was rooting around in his dinner jacket for a card of his own.

"Which one is it, Mr. Ossining?" Eleanor was leaning forward to peer at the card clutched in her husband's hand. "Cero-Fruto? Tryabita? Force? Vim?"

Charlie obliged her with a second card—he was inordinately proud of his cards—which he laid out on the table before her:

> **THE PER-FO CO., INC , OF BATTLE CREEK**
>
> *The "Perfect Food," Predigested, Peptonized and
> Celery Impregnated. Perks Up Tired Blood and
> Exonerates the Bowels.*
>
> Charles P. Ossining, Esq.
> President-in-Chief

"How impressive," Eleanor murmured, and Charlie couldn't tell if she meant it or not.

"Very," Will agreed.

"I—and you'll forgive my saying so, I hope—I wouldn't have thought you'd be an advocate of scientific eating, Mr. Ossining," Eleanor said. "And this phrase—'exonerates the bowels'—this is one of Dr. Kellogg's obiter dicta. Though he uses it in the reflexive, insisting that the bowels must exonerate them*selves.*"

Charlie felt the blood in his face. He took a sip of wine to mask his agitation. "Yes," he said finally, "or, actually, I don't know. I read it in a magazine."

But by now Eleanor's cucumber salad had arrived, and Will's toast—two slices of dry white bread, cut neatly on the diagonal and with the crust removed. Expertly rotating his tray, the waiter set Charlie's second course before him—a covered white china dish exuding steam. With a waiterly flourish, he removed the lid to reveal the creamy hot liquid within: oyster stew.

Will regarded his toast morosely. He seemed to have forgotten his own card, which he'd finally managed to fish out of his pocket and held now between thumb and forefinger as he gazed down at the crisp brown butterless toast on the plate before him. Suddenly his eyes lit and he glanced up quickly at Charlie. "And how long have you been in business, Mr. Ossining?"

Charlie had been probing the chowder with a spoon, hoping to disguise the rippled anatomy of the scavengers of the deep as they poked here and there through the creamy chop of potato, onion and carrot. (All right—so what if he liked oysters? Was that a crime? How was he to know that eating an oyster was like drinking a teaspoon of his own urine?) Eleanor was busy with her salad, studiously inundating it with flakes of something or other she'd produced from a brown paper bag. "Oh," Charlie said, surprised by the question, "well, uh, in fact, I mean, the fact is, we've just founded the company."

Will raised his eyebrows.

"That is"—poking at the oysters as if they were his sworn enemies—"we *are* founding it, uh, tomorrow afternoon."

"I see," Will said. His lips were pinched, two stingy flaps of flesh in a fleshless face. "You say 'we'—you have partners in this enterprise?"

The image of Goodloe Bender, in his flashy suit and buffed shoes, rose briefly before Charlie's eyes. Bender would be waiting for him in Battle Creek, the equipment purchased, work force hired, orders taken. In six months they'd be millionaires. "Yes." He smiled.

Eleanor fork-cut a morsel of cucumber and looked up. "Have you been fully capitalized as yet, if I may ask?"

"Yes, oh yes. Of course." At that moment, Charlie couldn't have been any more conscious of the billfold lying flat against his breast if it had swollen to the size of a suitcase. In it was eight hundred forty-nine dollars cash—more than he'd ever seen at one time before in his life— and a check drawn on the account of Mrs. Amelia Hookstratten, of Peterskill, New York, in the amount of three thousand dollars. "Our biggest investor is a very prominent socialite from Westchester County—"

"Westchester?" Again Will's voice leapt out at him and the transmogrifying grin illuminated his face. "But that's where we're from— certainly you know Peterskill?"

24

And now it was Charlie's turn. "Now this *is* a coincidence. It is. It really is. Our investor—I mean, our principal investor—is a Peterskillian herself. Do you know a Mrs. Hookstratten?"

The heavens opened; trumpets blew; cries of wonder and astonishment silenced the dialogue at the next table over, and half the others in the car as well. "Amelia Hookstratten?" Will exclaimed. "Do we know her?" He exchanged a complicitous look with his wife, who'd paused over her salad, her eyes suddenly bright.

Charlie grinned crazily. The elderly man with the mustaches stared unabashedly at them. The rails clicked faintly below.

"Why," Will boomed in his hollow voice, "she's my parents' closest—my mother's very best friend in all the world. Do we know her?" And his laugh turned to a high choking whinny.

Charlie was feeling good all of a sudden, very good, capital. On the other side of his card, the side the Lightbodys had yet to examine, was a modest announcement and a post-box address in Manhattan: "A small block of stock can be had by the right sort of investor." It wasn't a thing to pursue just then, but, of course, the start-up costs of Per-Fo were going to be substantial—or so Bender kept insisting—and they needed all the investors they could get.

He finished the bottle of wine, all the while smiling on his new acquaintances, these wonderful and wealthy people—he could smell the money on them the way a weasel smells out a hen, oh yes indeed—these wonderful people, the Lightbodys, of Peterskill, New York. Peterskill. The place was a gold mine—maybe they should start a cereal factory there. There was one in Buffalo, wasn't there? He was about to toast their health—the dregs of his champagne against their plain abstemious water—when the waiter approached again, tray balanced nimbly over one shoulder, and set down the first of Charlie's meat dishes as if it were a gift from the Sultan of Morocco: porterhouse steak, medium rare and awash in a sea of its own rich and bloody juices.

Chapter 3

Sears'
White Star
Liquor Cure

❧

L ate that night, long after the last dish had been washed and the ovens shut down, long after the club car had been cleared and the last weary porter fallen off into oblivion, Will Lightbody lay in his berth in the darkened compartment and watched the stubble fields of eastern Ohio drift past the window. Eleanor, at her own insistence, had taken a separate compartment, though it adjoined his. They slept together at home still—that is, they slept in the same bed, an ancient four-poster Will's great-grandmother had brought with her from Bournemouth, a big dark fortress of a bed that could sleep six abreast with room to spare for a dog or two. But since Eleanor had lost the baby and his stomach had gone into receivership, there wasn't much physical contact between them. He'd protested at first, but she pleaded her delicate condition—and his. *Besides,* she'd added, *once we get to the San there'll be no time—and no reason—for any of that sort of business.* Dr. Kellogg, it seemed, didn't approve of sex either.

Will closed his eyes. He'd hoped that the gentle rocking of the train would put him to sleep, an infant rocked in his cradle, but it was no use. He'd lain awake for hours now, so exhausted that even falling asleep seemed like too much of an effort. It was his stomach, of course. The pain was fiery and intense, painting the edges of his insomnia with a

26

molten brush. And at the root of it, deep down there somewhere, was the toast. Innocuous, dry, twice-toasted and bland. But there it was, searing away at his insides till he thought he'd swallowed a beaker of acid, pushing itself up his throat to ignite his tonsils even as it drove down deep to assault the other end, too. No wonder Eleanor wouldn't sleep with him, the air filled with pestilential odors, his body racked with convulsions, the bedclothes twisted up like a hangman's noose. . . . God in heaven, what he wouldn't give for a few moments' peace. . . .

To sleep—just for an hour. And to eat something, anything, and have it pass through him as it should, quietly, decently, unconsciously, instead of searing his insides with all these peristaltic rumblings and outpourings of gas. He'd looked at those oysters Charlie Ossining had been eating, at the chowder and the steak, and he'd felt something clench in his jaws and the juices begin to run—and what he wouldn't give to be able to sit down to a meal like that. But no, it was toast, and even that was poison. Dr. Brillinger, his mother's physician and a man as respected around Peterskill as Chauncey Depew himself, had told him it was just a stomach upset—indigestion—and prescribed ipecac, Hostetter's Celebrated Stomach Bitters, Warner's Safe Cure and Castoria. Like a fool, he tried them all, dousing himself with stomachics after every pickle and sausage till he couldn't taste a thing but the alcohol that floated the stuff. Before he knew it, it was the alcohol he craved, and for a good long while—it was when Eleanor went away to the San the first time—he found himself spending more and more time at Mapes' or Ben's Elbow, taking beer with his whiskey and the occasional pickled egg to stave off the hunger pains. That was the beginning of the end.

When Eleanor came home, ten pounds heavier and preaching a new religion of vegetarianism and "scientific eating," she found him bleary-eyed and besotted with drink. The dog barely knew him, the servants were terrified, he hadn't changed his clothes in a week, and he had a bottle of Old Crow sequestered in every room of the house. She fed him pureed lima beans, nut butter on Graham bread and creamed parsnips, but it made no impact on him. She had his father come round to speak to him, arranged chance meetings with Reverend Tanner of the Episcopal church and Willa Munson Craighead of the Woman's Christian Temperance Union—all to no avail. His gullet cried out for booze, and six nights a week Sam Lent brought him home sprawled out drunk in the back of his hackney cab.

That was when Eleanor, in her desperation, first noticed the advertisement in, the Sears Roebuck catalogue. SEARS' WHITE STAR LIQUOR CURE, the ad proclaimed in big block letters, and then, below it: *House-wives, are you tired of spending the night alone in an empty house while your spouse ruins his digestion and throws away good money at the local saloon? Try Sears' White Star Liquor Cure—just 5 drops a night in your drinking husband's coffee and he will roam no more.* All of a sudden Will began to find himself dropping off in the armchair each evening after his rice surprise, Granose biscuits and lichee nuts. Ten, twelve, sometimes thirteen or fourteen hours later, he would awaken in bed, all the rough edges of his mind buffed smooth.

He was working for his father then, keeping charge of the accounts at the Water Street factory and ostensibly learning enough of the business to one day take it over, but now he found himself so muddled he rarely got to the office before ten. His father's reaction should have been a dead giveaway—normally the old man would chew his feathers off if he was anything other than a quarter of an hour *early* (Got to set an example for the men, Will), but he never said a word. And when Will woke each morning, so fuzzy he barely knew his own name, Eleanor always contrived to be there with as hearty a breakfast as the Kellogg regime would allow, and he was eating it, actually eating it, before he was fully conscious. And then he was dressed, and at the office, and before he knew it, it was six o'clock and he was home again, stealing a nip at the Old Crow and then sitting down to his lentil-and-tomato soup and grilled eggplant with soya sauce, and then he was in the armchair with his coffee and nodding off again.

It took him three months to discover the deception, and only then because he'd happened to thumb through the Sears catalogue one bleak rainy Sunday afternoon while his wife was holding a meeting of the Peterskill Ladies' Biologic Living Society in the next room. The ad got him thinking. While Eleanor was preaching the virtues of pure food and the simple life to a gaggle of her reform-minded friends, Mrs. Amelia Hookstratten among them, she was drugging her own husband. Sears' White Star Liquor Cure, six bottles of which he discovered that afternoon in the back of a drawer in the kitchen, turned out to be nothing more than a tincture of opium.

Well, he was outraged. Outraged and disappointed. His own wife, his own father. Standing there in the kitchen, listening to Eleanor's perky tones as she went on about the lazy colon and the evils of salt pork and kippers, he felt the rage steal over him and he almost—almost, but not quite—destroyed the little opaque coffee-colored bottles right then and there. Instead, he put the bottles back and waited for his supper and his evening coffee.

In the parlor that evening, a fire in the hearth, Dick the wirehaired terrier stretched out beside him, Will Lightbody made an effort and left his coffee untouched. It was no easy effort, because by now he'd become habituated to those five nightly drops of Sears' White Star Liquor Cure and he had to fight off the sight and aroma of that coffee as if it were the devil's own poison. But resist it he did, and when Eleanor breezed into the room half an hour later with her needlework, she actually started when she saw him sitting there conscious and staring into the fire.

"But Will," she said, "aren't you going to drink your coffee?"

This was the woman he loved, the woman he'd married the month he graduated Columbia with his baccalaureate, the woman whose every look and movement stirred him in a way he couldn't describe (but had tried to, time and again, to his classmates, to the rare Barnard girl he asked to the theater or a concert, and to the tarts and working girls he discovered in the blind pigs and outside the vaudeville houses). This was the woman, and she'd tried to poison him.

"No coffee," he said, rising from the chair. For the first time in months his brain was clear. He knew who he was, where he was, what he was doing and why. "I'm going down to Mapes'," he said levelly, "for a good steak and a glass of whiskey. No, five glasses of whiskey—one for each drop of Sears' White Star Liquor Cure."

Then the tears came. And with the tears, the recriminations. He'd never seen her so wrought up—even Dick, scratching his hindquarters in confusion and looking back dolefully over his shoulder, had to leave the room. "I never meant to harm you," she sobbed, "but I was at the end of my rope, and, and you'd changed so—you were like a stranger, a drunk, a seedy drunk in our own house." She straightened her shoulders and looked him in the eye. "It ran against all my principles," she said, recovering herself a little, "and you know I don't believe in drugs or foreign substances of any kind—Dr. Kellogg would throw the whole apothecary of this country right out the window, and I believe he's right, I do, but—"

But she'd drugged him. For his own good. And with the complicity, as it turned out, of both his parents, the cook and Dr. Brillinger. Their reconciliation was fine and tumultuous. She'd been gone three months in Battle Creek, and he'd been gone in his alcoholic and narcotic haze for the next three, and they came together that night with what he liked to think was real hunger—he still believed fervently that that was the night she got pregnant.

Fine. But one small problem remained: he was desperate to get at those six little bottles of Sears' White Star Liquor Cure. No: "desperate" wasn't strong enough a word—he was compelled, obsessed, mad with the need and craving for it. And, of course, when he went straight from her arms to the kitchen drawer for it, it was gone, all six bottles of it. That night his fevers began. His skin swelled till he could feel whole armies marching beneath it, then it shrank again till he thought it would asphyxiate him; his stomach dwindled to the size of a walnut and then sprang open like an umbrella in his throat; his feet became blocks of ice, his hands curling irons. He fell to the floor in the midnight kitchen and crawled on his hands and knees, retching and gagging, through the dining room and out into the parlor, where he startled Dick, upset the coal scuttle and scratched the skin of his arms till it bled like a roast wrapped in butcher's paper.

In the morning, on the table beside his empty bed (in which he somehow found himself), stood a little opaque blue bottle with a beautiful blue label emblazoned with that single all-encompassing, all-wonderful, redemptive and salvatory Sears' White Star. He didn't stop to think: brown bottle, blue bottle—what difference did it make? In the next instant he had the cork out and the bottle to his lips . . . but what was this? It tasted . . . different somehow. Different, but not bad. Not by any means. He drained half the bottle before he paused to study the label: SEARS' WHITE STAR NARCOTIC CURE, it read. And below it, in fine print: *Housewives, are you tired of spending the night all but alone while your spouse ruins his digestion and throws away good money in a narcotic-induced stupor in your own living room? Try Sears' White Star Narcotic Cure—just 5 drops a night in your nodding husband's coffee and he will be as bright and alert as a squirrel.* The irony wasn't lost on him. But what did he care? His stomach was shot, his life a shambles, he had cravings he couldn't control and a wife who grew more distant by the day. All right, he thought, all right, and he could already feel the narcotic cure working in his veins, and he drained the rest of the bottle.

Later that day, he had the druggist analyze the second bottle he found—he knew there'd be a second and a third and a fourth, ad infinitum—in the drawer of his wife's vanity. The narcotic cure tested out at about eighty-four proof, or two percent less than the Old Crow. He went back to his Old Crow, which, after all, was more reliable and, ounce for ounce, about a tenth the cost. Still, all this had had a profound effect on him, and with Eleanor's pregnancy, his life began to take on new meaning. He developed a renewed enthusiasm for his work, he spent less time at Mapes' and Ben's Elbow, and, after a while, he began to phase out the Old Crow and try his best to eat scientifically. And he might have made it, too, if his stomach hadn't collapsed on him.

It was an afternoon in late spring, still crisp but infused with a hint of the warmth to come, and he left the plant early, stopped in at Offenbacher's to pick up a bottle of Coca-Cola, two packs of Wrigley's gum and Eleanor's favorite—ginger ale, in the big green bottle—and started home early to surprise her. He walked up Division Street, the package tucked neatly under his arm, and turned in at the private lane that led to the grand three-story red-brick house his father had built for them. The dogwood was in bloom, pink and white, and the air was fragrant. He felt in that moment that all was right with the world, and with Eleanor and him, and with his son and heir to come. Bounding up the stairs, he saw the house in a new light, the way a child might, a little boy in a Buster Brown outfit whose father took him to feed the ducks in the park and to watch the trains thunder into the station. "Eleanor?" he called. "Elea-nor!"

He found her in the bedroom, packing, the maid—a pinched-up girl of eighteen with all the animation of a block of stone—at her side. "What are you doing?" he demanded. "Planning a trip? In your condition?"

She was. And there was nothing to discuss. She was going back to Battle Creek, to the Sanitarium, and she was going to stay there till the baby was born.

"But why?" he blurted, and it was then that he felt the first hot intimation of it buried like a sword in his deepest gut, burning, burning. "Why not here? We have a new hospital and, and the finest—"

"Hygiene," she said. "Scientific eating, biologic living—it's a whole different atmosphere there. You wouldn't know. You wouldn't believe it. I want my baby—our baby—to have the best. Don't you?"

He did. Of course he did.

The next day she was gone. So was his stomach. It hit him, full force, as he saw her off at Grand Central, a pain so hideous, so unbearable, so all-encompassing, it dropped him to his knees. How he made his way to the Hudson Line and got himself home he would never know; for the next week he lay in bed, and nothing, not Dr. Brillinger, not a hamburger sandwich from Mapes', not the Old Crow or the Sears' White Star Cure could help him.

He wrote her every day. And she wrote back—long enthusiastic letters full of terms like "autointoxication," "dextrinized starch" and "sinusoidal current." Four months dragged by and he was all but an invalid. He couldn't eat, couldn't drink, could barely raise himself from the bed. He lost twenty pounds, twenty-five; he stopped going in to work. Twice he thought to visit her, but she discouraged him. Both times. By wire. It would be too much on her nerves, she claimed. He knew she was suffering from neurasthenia, and if her nerves were in a jangle, what did he think that would do for the baby—the baby they'd already named Alfred, after his father? No, he was to be patient. She'd wire when the time came, and then, then he should fly to the San, and plan on staying awhile.

The wire came on a sweltering day in early September:

BATTLE CREEK MICH SEPT 4 1907

MR WILLIAM FITZROY LIGHTBODY

PARSONAGE LANE

PETERSKILL NY

DARLING. STOP. BABY GIRL. STOP. SIX POUNDS, THREE OUNCES. STOP. COME BY NEXT TRAIN. STOP.

ELEANOR

He was on his way, actually standing at the Peterskill station, his bags piled round his feet, Battle Creek—till this moment as impossible a destination as Sarawak or Mongolia—awaiting him at the end of the line, when his father's car pulled up on the cobblestones out front. Will's father was a big man, thick where Will was thin, and he had the stoic fleshy face of a butcher or baker. As the driver held the door open for the old man, Will, hurrying across the platform, caught his first glimpse of that face—funereal, dead and buried in its ruts and creases—and he knew what was coming. Knew it even before his father embraced him stiffly and handed him the second telegram.

The baby girl was dead. In the night. No one knew how. Or why. Eleanor was recuperating. She would be home in two weeks.

Stop.

And so here he was, seven weeks later, the cold grip of winter lying heavy over the land, his stomach shot, Eleanor a wreck, his baby girl dead, hurtling down the rails for Battle Creek and the cure. He lay there through the night and into the sleepless morning, and he changed trains in Chicago and sat propped up with an unread book in his lap while Eleanor embroidered beside him. He saw hills, naked trees, the same stubble fields he'd seen in New York, Pennsylvania, Ohio, Indiana and Illinois. Three weeks and a day without sleep. He laid his head back, closed his eyes and tried to doze . . . and then the brakes shrieked, the train slowed as if tugged gently backward on an infinitely supple cord of India rubber, and they were there. Eleanor was chirping something at him. Will didn't hear her. He was staring up into the blocky brownstone arches of the Battle Creek station and the sign that reared like prophecy against the sky above it:

BETTER YOURSELF IN BATTLE CREEK

Chapter 4

Father to All,
Father to
None

ᐅᖮᐊ

F *ather. Hello, Father.*
      He'd give him *Father*—he'd give him a swift kick in the hind
      end, is what he'd do. God, he was disgusting. Nineteen years
old and he looked sixty. Filthy, fetid, a sleeper in doorways and alleys
like his mother before him. And wasn't that meat on his breath? Meat?
It was, of course it was, and it turned the Doctor's stomach.

   And his posture. His posture alone was enough to send John Harvey
Kellogg through the roof—the concave chest, the drooping shoulders
and slack jaw, the pigeon toes and knock knees—and that sick sly
hangdog look even now creeping into his crapulous eyes. How many
times had he admonished him to stand up straight like a human being
instead of some infernal prancing ape? How many? And now look at
him. Look at him!

   The audience was coming up the hallway, Bigelow Jennings and Mrs.
Tindermarsh at the front of the pack, trying to catch his eye, and Dab
all the while wrestling with his high-pitched squeal of a voice: "Not
here, Doctor, not here where everyone can see."

   People were beginning to take notice of them now, staff members
and patients alike, some self-consciously averting their gaze, others
openly gaping at this freak, this avatar of filth and degeneracy sprung
up like a toadstool between their Chief and his secretary. It was mad-

dening. It was. For a long moment the Doctor stood frozen there in the middle of the wide gleaming terrazzo floor, the man of decision, crusader for the clean and the correct, brought to a grinding standstill. "George," he said under his breath, and he spoke the name almost involuntarily, almost as if he couldn't bear to individualize this lump of dejection before him.

George said nothing. He merely slouched there, ragged and twisted, ugly as a turnip, and grinned to show off his yellowed teeth and rotten gums.

It was too much. The boy was a walking, talking nightmare, the breathing refutation and antithesis of everything Dr. Kellogg and the Sanitarium stood for, an insult, a provocation, a slap in the face. Suddenly, before he knew what he was doing, the Doctor lashed out and snatched him by the arm, and in the next instant they were moving swiftly up the hallway toward the lobby, George hanging back sulkily, the Doctor's grip like iron. "Come out of this, George, come out of this *now*," the Doctor hissed.

"I want money," George spat, showing his teeth again, and the Doctor tugged at his arm as if at the leash of a willful dog.

Through the lobby, the Doctor said to himself, and into my office in the far corridor, a hundred and twenty steps to safety. They'll think he's a charity case, that's all, and then he'll be gone, out the door and into the night. "Money," he muttered, tossing it back at him out of the corner of his mouth. "You've had all the money you'll ever get from me."

George was striding along beside him now, a full-grown man, longer of leg, and for all his lousy posture a good head taller than the Doctor. "We'll see about that," he sneered.

They were just emerging from the corridor and entering the grand expanse of the lobby, with its careening bellhops, its benches and palms, the crush of luggage and new arrivals. Groups of patients lounged about, contentedly sipping milk and peach nectar from long-stemmed glasses; nurses bent over hypochondriacal matrons in wheelchairs; a murmur of voices whispered of the stock market, the theater, Caruso and Farrar, and the newest motorcars from Ford and Olds. There was Dr. Baculum with that Pittsburgh woman, wife of the steel magnate, what was her name?—Wallford? Walters? Walldorp?—and Admiral Nieblock at the telegraph cubicle with the Crouder woman, a blur of nurses, Meta Sinclair. Dr. Kellogg moved purposively through the room, nodding, waving, nothing in the world the matter, a bit of a hurry, that was all, some poor unfortunate at his elbow, and of course he knew they didn't want to see this side of things, but the Sanitarium *was* a charitable institution, after all, and their Chief was a saint, they had to understand that, a veritable saint.

Halfway across—fifty people at least crowding round the desk, the staircase, lining the benches and flowing in and out of the Palm Garden at the rear—George suddenly jerked his arm from the Doctor's grasp and came to a halt. "One hundred dollars, Dad, Pater, Pa—one hundred dollars or I scream my lungs out right here and now."

Fifty pairs of eyes were on them, the Doctor all grins and smiles, throwing kisses, winking, waving, nodding, everything under control. One sharp glance at his son: "In my office. We'll discuss it there."

Dab crowded them. George wouldn't budge. "SHALL I," he suddenly barked, his voice a ragged tear in the genteel fabric of the room before it dropped again to a whisper, "Shall I raise my voice?"

No one got the better of John Harvey Kellogg, no one. He was master of all he surveyed, Chief, king, confessor and patriarch to his thousands of dyspeptic patients and the forty-two children he and Ella had adopted over the years. There were the Charlie Posts of the world, to be sure, there was his brother, Will, who'd bought the corn-flake concession out from under his nose, there were the Phelpses and the Macfaddens and all the rest of them, and maybe they won the skirmishes, yet John Harvey Kellogg won the wars. Always. But the situation was delicate, he understood that, and he fought down his anger. "March down that corridor and into my office this minute," he said in a harsh whisper, "and it's yours."

George stood there half a beat longer, whiskers bristling, malice dancing in his loamy eyes. Then he dropped his arms and collapsed his shoulders. "It's a deal," he said.

Suddenly the three of them were moving again, the audience from the Grand Parlor just now spilling into the lobby behind them, the Doctor firing looks right, left and over his shoulder, practically scampering on his truncated legs and driving George before him with a firm and unwavering hand. He was almost there, almost out of it, almost safe, when a peremptory female voice took hold of him like a grappling hook. "Dr. Kellogg!" the voice rang out, and he was caught. Feet faltering, a weary automatic smile pressed to his lips, he wheeled round to find an impeccably draped female form engulfed in a maelstrom of luggage. Beside her and two paces to the rear rose the towering sticklike wraith of a long-nosed young man with flat feet and posture so egregious he might just as well have had curvature of the spine. "Doctor," she chirped, "Dr. Kellogg, what a pleasure to see you again," and his hand vanished in the grip of her black kid glove.

The party had halted in the middle of the room, Dab arrested in mid-waddle, George drooping like a frost-burned plant, the Doctor pulled up short. "Why," he gasped, beaming, beaming, the genial host and courtly physician, "if it isn't Mrs., Mrs.—?"

"Lightbody," she returned, "Eleanor. And this," indicating the gaunt, broken-down figure beside her, "this is my husband, Will."

An awkward pause. Though George had faded back a step, the Doctor couldn't get the smell of him out of his nostrils, a sick working stench of mold and fermentation, of grease, bodily functions and filth. He smelled like a garbage scow. Worse: a meat wagon. "Lightbody, of course," the Doctor exclaimed. "And how is your, uh, condition? Neurasthenia, isn't it? And autointoxication? Yes? Combating both, I trust. Winning the battle of biologic living, eh?"

He made as if to withdraw his hand, but Eleanor held him fast. "I know we're supposed to think positively, Doctor, and I know you're going to do wonders for him, for both of us, but I'll tell you—I must tell you," and here Eleanor's voice dropped as she leaned confidentially toward the Doctor, "my husband is a very sick man."

"Well, yes," the Doctor said, "of course, of course he is," and suddenly he was his old self, a magneto of energy, sparks flying from his fingertips, the grand leonine head wagging majestically on his shoulders. "You've come to the right place, young man," he said, disengaging himself from the wife to pump Will Lightbody's limp and skeletal hand.

All around them the room glowed with a calm eupeptic health. Life, promise and progress burgeoned in every corner, from the gaggle of milk-sipping millionaires lounging against the Corinthian columns to the tranquil uncorseted grandes dames, marchesas and housewives gliding in and out of the Palm Garden. The banana tree, in all its exotic glory, could be seen through the high arched portal, rising up from a thatch of palm, succulent and orchid in defiance of latitude and season alike, centerpiece of the Doctor's own private jungle.

Ignoring George—he could just cool his heels a minute—the Doctor turned to his secretary. "Mr. Dab, I want you to fetch a wheelchair for this gentleman and have Dr. Linniman see to him this evening. And the very best of your attendants—Murphy, find Murphy, will you? And Graves. I want Mr. Lightbody to have every comfort," he went on, expansive, sagacious, the intrepid man of healing for whom no case was beyond hope, no colon too clogged, no stomach too sour, "and I'll want to examine him personally first thing in the morning."

Eleanor fixed him with a look of surprise. The husband fidgeted. "Personally?" she echoed. A rare gift had been dropped in her lap, a boon from the gods. "But Doctor, that's too kind of you . . . we know how very busy you are, and—"

"You've suffered a great loss," the Doctor began hesitantly, almost in the way of a fortuneteller or swami, but then his memory—that ironclad infallible airtight faculty that had held him in good stead all these many years—began to coil round the facts of the case. *Lightbody, Eleanor. Caucasian, female. Twenty . . . twenty-eight years of age. Peterskill, New York. Neurasthenia, autointoxication, loss of child.* Yes, yes, that was it. "Nothing can rectify that, I know, and you have—and will always have—my deepest regret and sympathy, both of you. But you must go on, and scientific eating and rest and fresh air will restore you, just as surely as it's restored hundreds upon hundreds before you. You'll see." He paused, gazing into the wife's eyes, deciding something. "And I'll be supervising your case personally, too, my dear, of course I will."

A geyser of excitement seemed to shoot through her. Her lips trembled and her cheeks flushed; for a moment, the Doctor was afraid she was going to drop to her knees. "Oh, Doctor, Doctor," she cried, and it was a chant, a prayer, a hosanna of thanksgiving and joy.

He waved his hand: it was nothing. And now he turned to the husband. "And I can see that you're suffering, young man—I can see it in

the sallowness of your skin, in the whites of your eyes, and, and—"
Here he suddenly reached out, took hold of Will Lightbody by the lips
and forced his fingers into his mouth like a horse trader. "Yes, yes, say
'ah' . . . the coated tongue, I knew it! As severe a case of autointoxication
as I've ever seen. . . ."

Will's face sank. Eleanor looked stricken.

"But it's nothing we can't deal with here, I assure you," the Doctor
was quick to add. "Of course, I can't say for certain till you've been
properly and thoroughly examined, but I hold out every hope—" He
broke off suddenly. Where was George? He gave Dab a sharp glance,
made accidental eye contact with half a dozen patients—Hello, hello
—and twisted round completely before he spotted him. Suddenly his
jaw clenched. There was George, Hildah's boy, ragged and stinking, a
tramp, a bum in toe-sprung shoes, all the way across the room at the
elbow of J. Henry Osborne, Jr., the bicycle king, cadging change.
"George!" the Doctor cried out, and the whole room turned to him.

He was mortified. This was a place of healing, of peace and tran-
quillity, where the halls echoed with the soothing strains of the Battle
Creek Sanitarium String Quartet and no one spoke above a whisper.
And here he was, shouting like an Italian in a tenement.

In the next instant, Dab was scurrying across the marble floor, and
a pair of attendants, big men, sinewy, with rocklike chests and intransigent shoulders, were converging on the Doctor's errant son. Distracted,
the prophylactic smile frozen to his face, the Doctor bowed curtly to
the Lightbodys—"Charity case," he murmured, "nothing to be alarmed
about"—and hustled off in the direction of the far corridor, waving a
hand over his head to direct the attendants like an overwrought general
deploying his troops.

In his office, settled behind the great mahogany barge of his desk, the
bill of his eyeshade pulled down low, the Doctor was another man. He
was in command again, in control, everything was in its place and all
was right with the world. Except for George, that is. Not in the least
contrite, he sat there across from his adoptive father, slumped in his

chair, the omnipresent sneer ironed into his face. Behind George, sandwiched between the framed portraits of Socrates and Elie Metchnikoff, Dab stood against the wall doing his best imitation of a henchman, arms folded, shoulders squared, chin thrust forward. The two attendants waited just outside the door.

The Doctor pushed himself back from the desk and, never fully at ease unless he was in motion, began to pace the carpet. For all his talk of biologic living and the simple life, he drove himself relentlessly, working from 4:00 A.M. to midnight, seven days a week. Sleep? The Doctor disdained it—who had time for sleep? He traveled to Algeria, Italy and Mexico, to Paris, London and Lisbon, he addressed the Northern Nut Growers Association and the National Milk Congress, lectured his patients, dictated his books (*Plain Facts about Sexual Life*, *Man, the Masterpiece*, *The Crippled Colon*, and *The Itinerary of a Breakfast*, among others), oversaw the administration of the San, organized the Race Betterment Society and the Health Efficiency League of America, served as president of the American Medical Missionary College and half a dozen other organizations, and still managed to knock off as many as twenty-five gastrointestinal operations a day. If he couldn't find all the time he'd like for Ella, who'd become deaf and increasingly feeble, or for his forty-two children, who could blame him?

"George," he said, still pacing, his head down, "I'm disappointed in you. No, I may as well be frank: I'm disgusted by your behavior. Disgusted. I took you in. Rescued you. Why, your mother was nothing but a common, a common—"

"Go ahead and say it—a whore. She was a whore."

"You know I don't like to hear that language, George."

George's spine was bent like a strand of wire. He slipped lower and lower, until he seemed to be absorbed in the fabric of the chair. He made a pyramid of his grubby fingers and smiled a bemused smile. He said nothing.

The Doctor paced. Light glinted from the smoked celluloid of his eyeshade. The eyeshade was a fixture of the Doctor's office attire—it masked the expression in his eyes, and he wore it when dictating, giving instructions to his staff, conducting distasteful interviews such as this one. Pacing, he allowed himself to heave a sigh fruity with disgust.

"You've become a thorn in my side, George, and I just don't understand it. I educated you, gave you everything—"

George's laugh, sharp as the slap of a wave against the bow of a freighter, cut him off. "And just what did you give me? Five minutes of your time? A pat on the back? The thrilling opportunity to be your unpaid house servant?" George was aroused now, his eyes engorged, his head bobbing like a pullet's. "My life's a shit pile, that's all. A shit pile."

John Harvey Kellogg swung round on him in that instant, his lips twisted beneath the shadow that fell over his face. "You ingrate," he choked. "You, you guttersnipe with your filthy mouth. You meat eater. How can you dare—" But he couldn't go on. It was bad for his heart, for his nerves, for his digestion. George was the biggest mistake he'd ever made in his life, no doubt about it. And though he didn't like to admit it, he knew in his heart he had only himself to blame. Hubris, that's what it was.

Thirteen years ago, after a lecture in Chicago, he'd sat down to a vegetarian supper with Drs. Johannes Schloh, Mortimer Carpenter and Ben Childress of the Good Samaritans' Pediatric Hospital, and found himself embroiled in a debate over child rearing. Carpenter and his colleagues claimed it was all in the parentage—"A bad seed gives rise to a weed, John, to be short and sweet"—but Dr. Kellogg, with his messianic belief in the perfectibility of the human race, insisted otherwise. Conditions made the man, he asserted, wagging a finger for emphasis, and any child of the ghetto, any poor unfortunate from the stockyards or the shantytowns that stood awash in sewage behind them, would grow into as valuable and decent a young person as any if only he were given the opportunity. "Give me the worst case you can find," he said, "the single most deprived child in all of Chicago, and I'll take him in and raise him as my own son, just as I've raised the others, and I guarantee you he'll turn out a model citizen. I know he will, gentlemen. I know it."

Well, he was wrong.

They found George—he was known only as "Hildah's boy" then, with neither Christian nor family name attached to him—sitting beside the corpse of his mother in an unheated shack out back of a South Side slum. The police were unable to determine how long the mother had been dead—the cold weather had helped preserve her—but the marks at her throat and the contusions about her face suggested that her death was not the result of natural causes. No one knew how long the boy had been sitting there, nor what horrors he'd witnessed—he was six years old, wrapped against the cold in a scrap of old carpet, and he hadn't yet learned to speak. All around him, scattered like bones, were the stubs of candles he'd chewed to fight down his hunger.

The Doctor took him in, named him after Ella's uncle and gave him his own surname to go along with it. There were eighteen other children in the house at the time, including four Mexican boys the doctor had found abandoned during his trip to Guadalajara and Mexico City, three girls orphaned when their mother died at the San and a mulatto boy who'd been found wandering the streets of Grand Rapids with second-degree burns on his chest, his thighs and the soles of his feet. The Doctor's house, or the Residence, as it was called, had been built the year before, and it had been designed to accommodate a crowd. There were twenty rooms in all, including separate quarters for Dr. Kellogg and his wife (no matter how forbearing he might have been, there were times when he simply needed to escape that cacophony of piping voices), an office, a library, several bathrooms, a stenographer's room (he never knew when the urge to dictate a book would strike him), a small laboratory and a gymnasium for the children.

The children slept in dormitories according to their ages and sexes, they were attended to and educated by San nurses and staffers, and they were provided with all the plain unvarnished accoutrements of La Vie Simple, from calisthenics in the morning to beet soufflé, okra soup and three-ounce portions of baked Cornlet in the evening. They were expected to work, of course—John Harvey Kellogg was a firm believer in the twin principles that work is a great character builder and that no one gets anything for nothing. The younger children were assigned chores in the household, the yard and the garden, while the elder were encouraged to work at the San after school hours.

And they throve. All of them. Two of the Mexican children—the Rodriguez boys—became doctors in their own right, and half a dozen of the girls became nurses. They spoke well, kept their quarters neat and always looked presentable. The Doctor was proud of them—they were as much his achievement, his creation, as the corn flake and the electric blanket, and they were a credit to Battle Creek, to the Sanitarium and to the great progressive democratic country that gave rise to them. All of them, that was, except George.

From the beginning, he'd been sullen and withdrawn, the sort of boy who would as soon bite off the tip of his finger as crack a smile. He wouldn't—or couldn't—speak; he tore pages from his books, defaced his desk in the schoolroom, dismantled the gymnasium equipment and fought grimly and incessantly with the other children. Undersized, always dirty despite the vigilance with which the Doctor pursued personal sanitation, his eyes clouded with hurt and anger, he was a small tornado of disorder and grief.

Dr. Kellogg decided on a course of what in later years would become known as behavior modification. He began with the problem of George's slovenliness. Each day the boy would come in from outdoors and drop his jacket on the floor in the back hallway, while all the other children, even little Rebecca Biehn, aged four, would hang theirs on the hooks provided for that purpose in their rooms. A small thing. But one, the Doctor felt, that lay at the foundation of all the rest.

When George came in from school the following afternoon—it was a month to the day since the Doctor had taken him in—John Harvey Kellogg was waiting for him. Never mind that the Doctor had pressing business at the Sanitarium, never mind that he'd rescheduled a slate of operations and a staff meeting and put off answering his voluminous correspondence: the boy's education—*this* boy's education—was about to commence. Two of the San's girls led the younger children through the back hallway and up the stairs to their quarters, and the children followed docilely—and responsibly—behind. There was no shoving; no elevation of voices; no skipping, scampering, trotting, leaping or running. And no jackets were removed until the children were upstairs and the hooks to receive them in reach—that was the rule. George, as usual, brought up the rear.

If the children were surprised to see the Doctor seated there on a bench in the corner at such an unwonted hour of the day, they didn't show it. A few of the younger ones—little Rebecca, in particular—

gave him a shy glance, but they knew better than to be too demonstrative in the presence of their patriarch and provider. The Doctor didn't like noise. They all understood that.

George had his head down. He always had his head down, as if the ground itself were more fascinating than the great wide world about him, and this disturbed the Doctor, not only because it was a reflection of the boy's attitude but because it made for such unacceptable posture. Head down, George didn't see his adoptive parent sitting there in the shadows, and, sure enough, as carelessly as if he were a dressed-up ape in the forest, he shrugged out of his jacket and let it fall to the floor behind him.

"George," the Doctor called out in a voice of authority, "George Kellogg."

The boy had his foot on the bottom stair. The other children, under the guidance of their nurses, with whom Dr. Kellogg had conferred earlier, went straight up the stairs and into their rooms. George paused, contemplated his elevated foot for a long moment and then slowly tilted his head and lifted his eyes to the Doctor's.

"That's it," the Doctor said, trying to soften his expression. The boy *was* responding to the English language, after all, and what's more, the Doctor reminded himself, he'd been through God knew what manner of filth and depravity. Gesturing with both hands, the Doctor beckoned the boy to him. "Come over here, George," he coaxed, "come on. I won't bite you."

The boy's eyes fell again to the floor. He hung his head, shuffled his feet, slouched like a whipped dog—all of that, yes, but he did come, and he did seem to understand.

The Doctor wasn't very demonstrative physically— a quirk of his, one he didn't even recognize. It was just that deep down he didn't really see the need for much physical contact between human beings, beyond the business handshake or the husbandly peck at the wifely cheek, of course. Contact was unavoidable, he knew that, but it was also the means by which disease was spread. The upshot was that when George had crossed the room and stood there before him, the Doctor was reluctant to take him in his arms and explain to him his transgression. Instead, he rose from his seat, fussed with his hands a moment and

45

looked down at the crown of the small boy's head. "George," he began, "I do wish you would speak to me, to Mrs. Kellogg, to your nurses and your brothers and sisters. I know you understand the spoken language, and you'll learn to write it as well, and I know that you appreciate— or will come to appreciate—the rules of this household." Pause. "Now, you've been told countless times about your jacket."

George made no move to agree with this proposition. He stood there, staring at his feet, as motionless, and for all the world as insentient, as a post.

"I'm not going to punish you, George," the Doctor went on. "I know you're new here and I know too that you've gone through a great deal, but I am going to give you an exercise—let's call it an exercise in recalling one's duties and responsibilities."

George was lifeless, mute, unattached to the world and its currents of animation.

"Come with me," the Doctor said, and he slipped on his gloves before taking the boy's hand, instructing him to pick up the jacket and leading him up the stairs and into the dormitory to stand before the naked hook that was to receive it. "And now, George," he said, "I want you to spend the next twenty-four hours, aside from taking your rest tonight, of course, and your meals tomorrow, in just one task. I want you to put on your jacket, come in the door, go through the back hallway and up the stairs to this room; I then want you to remove your jacket, hang it on the hook, and begin the process all over again. George, I want you to do nothing but take off, hang up and put that jacket back on again, if you do it a thousand times. Do you understand me?"

The boy, head bowed, said nothing.

The Doctor glanced up sharply at Hannah Martin, one of the children's nurses, who now appeared at the head of the stairs. "Hannah, you'll be in charge of supervising George. He will enter the house, close the door, march up the stairs, remove his jacket and hang it on its hook, and he will continue doing so until bedtime tonight, and then he will recommence the process when he wakes in the morning. And he will continue with the exercise until this time tomorrow." The Doctor consulted his pocket watch. "Four P.M." He looked up. "Am I understood?"

Hannah nodded.

The following evening, when the Doctor arrived home for dinner, a hundred things crowding his mind, he was surprised to see the stooped and shrunken form of George shuffling along the back hallway in his jacket. He paused to watch as the boy slowly mounted the stairs, each step a nearly insurmountable obstacle, and then he followed him as he reached the top, made his way down the upper hallway, turned into the dormitory, and, like an automaton, removed his jacket, hung it on the hook, allowed it to rest there a moment, and then slipped it back on again. It was past seven in the evening. The other children had had their supper, and Hannah was supervising the younger ones in their nightly calisthenics in the gymnasium, while the older children were busy with their chores and lessons. But for the Doctor and George, the dormitory was deserted.

When the boy had shrugged back into his jacket and turned to retrace his steps, the Doctor spoke. "George," he said, "you can stop now. I meant only for you to go until four. I think you've learned your lesson. Now hang up your jacket and run along with the other children and get your exercise."

But George didn't hang up his jacket. He didn't run along either. He simply shuffled out of the room, studying his feet, proceeded down the stairs, out the door and then back in again, mounting the stairs to remove his jacket and hang it on the hook for a moment before shrugging back into it and repeating the process all over again.

Twice more the Doctor spoke to the boy, but George ignored him. John Harvey Kellogg might have been a hole in the wall, a lamp, a coat tree, a wraith wound in its invisible cerements. The boy's feet hit the stairs, shuffled along the planks. All right, the Doctor thought. All right. If he wants to be stubborn about it, let him. After all, the Doctor had better things to do—sit down to supper, for one thing, and then it was back to the San to take care of the work he'd put off the previous afternoon. The boy would tire. It was inevitable.

But George didn't tire. He kept at it, day after day, night after night—he neither ate nor slept that anyone could see, and no plea, no remonstrance could turn him from his obsessive task. In the door, up the stairs, down the hallway to the naked hook, and then back again.

The friction of the boy's feet began to wear a path in the floorboards, his shoes split, the jacket came loose at the seams. A week passed. Two. No one had seen him take nourishment, use the bathroom, sleep. In the door, up the stairs, down the hallway to the naked hook. The doctor awoke in the night and far off, through the tomblike silence of that vast and shadowy house, he heard the shuffling tread of miniature feet: *sh-shh, sh-shh, sh-shh.* It maddened him. It irritated him. It cost him sleep. Finally, in his exasperation, after George had been at it for two and a half weeks and the whole house had been thrown into an uproar, the Doctor jerked back the bedcovers one night and stormed out the door, marched past his wife's room, turned right down the front stairway and entered the children's quarters at the rear of the house.

The corridor was dim, palely lit by the moonlight spilling through the windows. He paused. Listened. He could hear his heart pounding in his ears—but nothing else. Nothing. Not a sound. And then, like a knife thrust, came the shriek of the door on its hinges, and there before him, ceaselessly shuffling, was the ghost of a tiny figure, locked in its compulsive labor: in the door, up the stairs, down the hallway to the naked hook. "George!" the Doctor bellowed. "Damn you, George —I say stop it. Stop this now!"

His words had no effect. He stood in the boy's way, blocking his path, but it was nothing to George. The tiny feet shuffled through two supernumerary steps, and the obstruction was behind him. It came to the Doctor then that if he stood there all night long, if he stood there until spring arrived and the trees burst into bloom and the bluebirds nested and a thousand abdomens went unplumbed by his surgical tools and healing fingers, George would continue to step round him, word-lessly, endlessly, as if the Doctor were nothing more than a statue carved of stone. And it was that thought, the thought of the boy's blindness and stupidity and stubborn ingratitude, that put the good Doctor over the line.

He was in his early forties then, and for all his short stature, he was among the healthiest and most physically fit men alive. In a single bound he was at the head of the stairs, and then he had the boy in his hands, the feel of flesh on flesh, and he was wringing the sticklike arms as if they were sopping towels. Grunting with the effort, he tore the jacket from the boy's shoulders, tore it to pieces, and then, in the pale light of the moon in the still and shadowy hall, he slapped that unyielding little wedge of a face till his hand was raw. When he was done, when he'd spent himself, he turned his back on the boy and went to bed. For the first time in a week, he slept, slept like an innocent.

In the morning, George, in his new jacket, was at school with the other children. According to Hannah, he'd slept in his bed, which he'd made up as soon as he awoke, and then he'd bathed, brushed his teeth, used the toilet and eaten his meals as he was expected to. There was no more shuffling in the hallway, no more the eternal whisper of those diminutive feet in their worn and diminutive shoes, no more the bowed head and the reproachful face. Dr. Kellogg felt a pang of regret when he thought of the violence to which he'd been driven—had Hannah noticed any marks on the child?—but he shrugged it off. He was a busy man. Busy? He was a juggler with a hundred Indian clubs in the air at once— and he hurried off to the San to take hold again of the world.

The day was a whirl, as hectic as any he could remember. He had an acrimonious meeting with Sister Ellen White and half a dozen of the Adventist Elders, who then still controlled the San; he worked furiously in the lab to get his vegetable-milk formula to taste like anything other than the almond-and-peanut paste it was; he saw to his patients; he repaired the electric-light cabinet-bath in the Ladies' Gymnasium (faulty wiring); and he gave his regular Monday-night Question Box lecture on the subject of self-abuse and the atrophied testicle. When he got home, it was past midnight and the house was quiet. He was tired but exhilarated, already thinking about the coming day's work, about the potential of the soya bean and Japanese seaweed, about the universal dynamometer, the pneumograph, the orthopedic chair and a way of bonneting windows to channel healthful winter air to the bundled and sleeping patient—all the raveling links of the infinite shining chain of inspiration that propelled his brain through day and night. He felt good, it seemed, for the first time in weeks.

Crossing the back hallway to fetch a journal from the library—a new number of *Vegetationsbilder* he meant to look into—he stumbled upon something at the base of the stairs, something that wrapped itself like a hand round his shoe. It took him a moment, bending to the thing like a paleontologist reaching out for a bone in the dirt, and even then his fingers had to interpret the material for him.

A jacket. A child's jacket.

Yes, and then there was the first time George spoke. Eight months he'd lived with them, eight months of eating their food, attending their school, wearing the clothes and sleeping in the bed they'd provided, and in all that time not a word had passed his lips. The Doctor examined the boy himself and called in his colleagues in consultation, and they found nothing: George's vocal apparatus was as normal as William Jennings Bryan's. Why he refused to speak was anyone's guess. The Doctor chalked it up to obstinacy, pure and simple.

One night, as he was sitting at the piano in one of his rare moments of relaxation, playing a better-than-passable rendition of "After the Ball" for little Rebecca, the doctor felt a sudden jab in his lower back. Startled—no one interrupted John Harvey Kellogg when he was relaxing—he stiffened his fingers over the keys and turned from the waist as the last chord hung suspended in the air. George stood directly behind him, the blunt stub of a pencil clutched in his hand. The doctor stared at him in surprise, and George, though he rarely made eye contact with his adoptive father, stared back. After a moment, the Doctor asked him if he wanted anything, expecting the usual dumb show in reply. But George surprised him. He cleared his throat and let a tight little smile creep across his lips. "Yes, Father," he said, and his voice was flawless, strong and composed, "yes, I do want something: you haven't got a nickel for me, have you?"

George. Hildah's boy. They should have left him in the shack where they found him, should have left him to starve and wither till the light faded from his eyes and the gums drew back from his lips. It was a terrible thing for a man of healing to think, but there it was. George had been nothing but trouble since the Doctor had first laid eyes on him, and now here he was back yet again, and this time it wasn't merely a nickel he wanted, either. "A hundred dollars?" the Doctor repeated.

George's eyes were cold. Dab swallowed audibly at the very mention of the figure. "That's right," George grunted. "One hundred dollars and I'll be out of your hair." He paused and that venomous little smile, the smile he'd employed at the piano bench all those years ago, came back to him. "I get the sense, Father Kellogg, that I'm an embarrassment to you, and think how that hurts me. Don't you want me here to entertain your patients? I can give them a terrific show."

John Harvey Kellogg was not a man to give up a dollar casually. In fact, he was widely known for his frugality, one of his commanding virtues. He'd built the San into the great institution it was largely on the basis of free or minimally paid labor—in the early days, his staff was composed almost exclusively of Seventh Day Adventist volunteers, and now that he'd wrested control of the place from the church, he staffed it nearly as cheaply with students from the Sanitarium-affiliated college, who were required to work in its kitchens, baths and gymnasiums in order to matriculate. And he pinched his customers, too. In summer, for instance, he prescribed the very healthful exercise of woodcutting for his male patients, thereby assuring himself of a plentiful supply of fuel with which to stoke the San's furnaces in winter. He stopped his pacing to turn to George a second time. "It's blackmail," he said.

George made a face. He ran a dirty hand through his hair and the doctor made a mental note to fumigate the carpet and chair when he'd got rid of him. "Blackmail? I'm offended, Father, I really am."

"Twenty-five dollars," John Harvey Kellogg said, "on condition that I never have to lay eyes on you again."

"One hundred dollars," George repeated, "and I'll think about it."

"*Think* about it?" the Doctor spat back at him, and he could feel himself slipping, just as he had on that shadowy night so many years ago. "You'll *think* about it? Ha! I can have you thrown out of here this minute."

George began to gather himself up now. He let his eyes wander over the framed portraits that decorated the walls—Luther Burbank, John Wesley, Thomas "Old Parr" Parr, the Englishman who'd reputedly lived to the incommensurable age of a hundred and fifty-two. "A big boast, Father. And I don't doubt that you can live up to it, what with your henchmen stationed outside the door, but, you know, I've been thinking how much I like Battle Creek. I really do. I've missed it in all my wanderings."

"Fifty dollars. That's my final offer."

"I've come here to better myself, Father, like everyone else. Just imagine me, bettering myself, out there on the public street right dead smack in front of your doorway. Imagine that."

Self-control. The Doctor was a model of self-control, he was, and he clenched his fists and set his jaw. Never let them see your emotions, he knew that, and he knew when to cut his losses—he would win in the end, he never doubted it. George, Charlie Post, Bernarr Macfadden, Ellen White and her Adventist lynch mob: he would outlast them all. He stood there a moment, stock-still on the edge of the carpet, and then he shot his cuffs and reached up to adjust his visor. "All right, Dab," he said with a sigh that seemed to drain his lungs, "draw a hundred dollars from the treasurer."

Chapter 5

The
Civilized
Bowel

∾❦∾

Will Lightbody fell into the wheelchair as if he'd been dropped from a great height—say, from a spot just to the left of the chandelier. His knees had suddenly lost their elasticity, his calves gone slack, and there he was, in the wheelchair, staring up at the ceiling like an octogenarian with egg in his lap. The Doctor—Dr. Kellogg, the Chief, the great and famous healer in the white spats and matching goatee—had disappeared, hustling off down the hallway till he receded in the distance like a scrap of paper blown by the wind. He'd been cordial enough—Will couldn't fault him there—but he'd seemed distracted, frazzled, not at all the solid and immovable rock he'd expected.

Not that it mattered. Not anymore. Not in the face of that cursory but terrifying examination. The great man had stuck his fingers in Will's mouth, though he was so short—another surprise—that he had to go up on tiptoe to insert them, and Will had seen the look of alarm in his eyes. It was a look that penetrated to the core of Will's being, a look that prefigured the coffin and the funeral wreath, and suddenly Will had felt as sick and weak as he'd ever felt in his life. He felt rotten. Light-headed. Doomed. And his stomach—there it was, as palpable as the hands before his face—his stomach clenched as if he'd caught a whiff of the grave.

"As severe a case of autointoxication as I've ever seen," the Doctor pronounced.

The words hit home like a storm of bullets. Will tottered, actually tottered, and then the wheelchair was there and he lost all conscious control of his muscles just as surely as if he'd drunk down a pint of Old Crow in a single gulp. He was frightened. His heart beat like a hammer in his chest. The ceiling seemed to fall in on him and then recede again.

"Eleanor!" a voice cried out, and the sound of it, hearty and bold, smooth as a surge of water over the buffed blue stones of a stream, brought him out of himself. The muscles of his neck tightened, the cords and sinews did their work, and all at once the ceiling was a memory and he was staring into the boyish eyes, cleft chin and brilliant naked teeth of Dr. Frank Linniman. "But you've lost weight," Dr. Linniman chided, clutching Eleanor's gloved hand and practically twirling her like a ballerina.

Eleanor called him "Frank." Not "Doctor," not even "Dr. Linniman." Just "Frank." "Yes, Frank, I know it, I know it, but it's just about impossible to eat scientifically in Peterskill, New York"—the way she pronounced the name of their hometown, she might just as well have been describing some huddle of huts in the Congo—"and Cook, though she's a dear, just can't seem to get the hang of Dr. and Mrs. Kellogg's recipes." Eleanor was glowing, her color high, her eyes struck with the light of the chandelier. She made a little moue, shrugged one shoulder, dipped her head ever so slightly to set the artificial bird atop her hat in motion. "I tell you, Frank," she breathed, "it's just heaven to be back here again."

In that moment, Will's fear of his own mortality was replaced by another emotion, one more often associated with the youthful and vigorous: jealousy. This was his wife, after all, the woman he loved, the woman who had borne his baby girl in tragedy, the woman whose breasts he'd held in his hands and whose curves and intimate places he knew like no other, or used to know . . . yes, and here she was fawning all over this, this *doctor* with his starched white suit and sunny grin. Good God, he looked more like a baseball player than a medical man, more like a brawling ham-fisted catcher or lumbering first baseman. Will cleared his throat. "Will Lightbody," he said, or tried to say, but un-fortunately all that came out was an incoherent croak.

"Oh," Eleanor gasped, a hand to her bosom, and in that moment the little group that was gathered round Will—his wife, the bellhop, the attendant at his back and Dr. Linniman—seemed to converge, the whole world and universe radiating out from that little gasp. "Forgive me," Eleanor went on, "but Frank, Dr. Linniman, I'd like you to meet my husband." And then, in a rush of breath: "He's a very sick man."

Suddenly, Frank Linniman's earnest face was hanging over Will's and his big friendly mitt of a healing hand was pumping Will's limp scrap of wrinkle and bone as if he were trying to draw water from a well. "Never fear," the physician was saying, conversant with the usual plat-itudes, "you've come to the right place. We'll have you scaling moun-tains in no time."

And then the hand was withdrawn, orders were given, the luggage vanished (and with it, Eleanor) and Will was being propelled across the lobby by an attendant as brawny, fit and eudaemonically sound as Frank Linniman himself. The wheels moved noiselessly, effortlessly, and the faces of his fellow patients—as jolly and robust a group as he'd ever seen—floated past him, barely curious. To them, Will was just one more sick man in a wheelchair.

But what they didn't know, what Will wanted to cry out to them, was that he'd never in his life been in a wheelchair before. Wheelchairs were for Civil War veterans, amputees, invalids, the superannuated, the infirm, they were for withered crones and doddering old pensioners with one foot in the grave. He thought of Philo Strang, the oldest living human in Peterskill, a blasted relic of a man who'd lost both his legs at Sharpsville when he was forty-two and had sunned himself outside his son's tobacco emporium in his rusting homemade wheelchair ever since, his eyes gone, hearing shot, clumps of yellow hair sprouting from his ears and nostrils and a dangle of phlegm caught in his beard. Well, now they had something in common, old Philo Strang and he, though Will was barely thirty-two and had been as spry as the next man a year ago.

Spry. He'd been spry, that's what he wanted to tell them.

Yet what did it matter? Now he was in a wheelchair. Now he was helpless. Old before his time. Used up, cast aside, hung out to dry. Gliding across the lobby through the hum of conversation and muted laughter that bubbled up round him as if the whole thing were some social affair, some cotillion or ball, Will felt a yawning cavern of self-pity open up inside him: surely he was the sickest man alive.

The silver wheels eased to a stop at the mouth of the elevator and Will felt himself swung gently round as the attendant expertly rotated the chair and drew it backward. The sensation was oddly familiar, a feeling of airiness and effortless suspension that wasn't altogether unpleasant, and Will realized that he'd gone from an old man to an infant in that moment, from Old Philo Strang with the snot in his beard to a babe in a perambulator. "Good evening, sir," the elevator man said, beaming at him out of a missionary face, "you look all tuckered," and he clucked his tongue. "Floor, Ralph?" he inquired of the attendant.

The attendant's voice spoke behind Will as if in some trick of ventriloquism: "Five."

"Oh," murmured the elevator man, winking an eye, "very nice, you're going to enjoy it, sir. Best air in the place, and a lovely view, too." He paused, sighed, reached for the grate. "Rail travel," he said, shaking his head. "Poor man looks all tuckered, Ralph."

At that moment, just as he was about to pull the grate across, a nurse slipped in to join them. Will was in a funk and delirium, and he didn't take any notice of her at first, but as they ascended, defying gravity, she turned to him with a smile of evangelic intensity. For all his exhaustion and despair, for all his pain and ruination, Will couldn't help feeling the force of that smile. He looked up. "Mr. Lightbody?" she inquired.

Will nodded.

"I'm Nurse Graves," she said, and her voice was a tiny puff of breath, as if she were unused to speaking above a whisper. "Welcome to the University of Health. I'll be your personal attendant throughout your stay here, and I'm going to do everything in my power to make the time both pleasant and physiologically sound for you." The smile held, perfect, confident, soothing. This was the smile the first cave woman had used on the first cave man, a wonder of a smile, a novelty and an invention. Who'd ever thought of smiling before this nurse came into the world? "But you must be tired," she said, and the smile faded ever so slightly to underscore the concern and sympathy of her words.

Will wanted to answer in the affirmative. He wanted to be undressed and put to bed like the antediluvian infant he'd become, wanted the surcease of the liquor and narcotic cures, wanted to drop dead on the spot and get it over with. *Yes,* he was going to say, *yes, tired to the marrow of my bones,* but the elevator man beat him to it: "Rail travel, Irene," he said, heaving another sigh. "It's as like to torture as anything they did in the Inquisition, let me tell you."

"Well," she said in her hushed, breathy tones, "I don't doubt it for a minute, though I've never been farther than Detroit myself," and she cocked her head alertly as the fourth floor rolled by beyond the grate. She stood there like a monument, like an advertisement for biologic living, breathing cleanly and deeply, chin held high, her spine so erect you could drop a plumb bob from it. And her uniform: it was an unbroken field of white, from the hem of her skirt to the cap perched atop the pinned-up mass of her hair, and it was perfectly—and naturally—contoured to the shape of her body, which was free of the corsets and stays the Chief railed against. Even in his fog, Will couldn't help admiring the fit of that uniform. And from his vantage point in the wheelchair, just behind and below her, he could make out the blades of her squared shoulders, the swept-up hairs at the back of her neck and the delicate little shells of her ears. He fixated on those ears. In that moment they seemed the most precious things he'd ever known. Little jewels. Little monkey ears. He wanted to kiss them.

"But Mr. Lightbody is at the very end of his journey now," she added, turning from the waist to beam that smile at him, "and we're here to receive him and comfort him and make him well again."

Will didn't mean to stare, but he couldn't seem to help himself. Something had come over him, a quickening in his groin, a heat he hadn't felt in months. Sick man that he was, bundle of bones and extruded nerves, he looked up into that smile, studied those ears and more, much more—that rump, those ankles, the bosom presented in profile—and all of a sudden he saw Nurse Graves spread out on his bed in all the glory of her naked and pliant flesh, and he, Will Lightbody, mounting her like a hairy-hocked satyr. Breasts, he thought. Vagina. What was happening to him?

"I haven't slept in twenty-two days," he croaked.

Nurse Graves held his eyes. She was young, very young, no more than a girl, really. "You'll sleep tonight," she said. "That's what I'm here for."

The elevator man announced the fifth floor, the grate drew back, and in the next moment Will found himself passing down a brightly lit hallway, Nurse Graves at his side, Ralph providing locomotion. There seemed to be quite a crowd in the corridor, seeing that it was nearly ten-thirty on a Monday night in November—nurses, attendants and bellhops hustling to and fro, men and women in evening clothes sauntering along as if they'd just come back from the theater, patients in robes lingering at the doors of their rooms and chatting in low tones. *Grand,* one robed and turbaned woman said to another, *simply grand.* But for the white flash of the attendants' uniforms, Will would have thought he was at the Plaza or the Waldorf.

And then an odd thing happened. Just as Nurse Graves pushed open the door to his room and Ralph swiveled the chair round to enter, Will had the strange feeling that he was being watched. Nearly devoid of volition at this point, he let his head loll against the leather padding of the chair and gazed up to see a young female peering at him curiously from an open door across the hallway. She was tall, striking, well formed, and the salacious thoughts began to flood his head again . . . but then the flood ceased as suddenly as it had begun: there was something wrong with her. Desperately wrong. Her skin—it had the color of bread mold. And her lips . . . they were dead, blackened, two little eggplants fastened beneath her nose as a morbid joke. Sick. She was sick. This was no hotel. He tried a sort of wry grin, commiserative and sad, but she only gave him a blank look and shut the door.

"There, now," Nurse Graves said as they entered the room, "isn't this cheery?"

Will took it in at a glance: Oriental carpet, drapes, a sturdy mahogany bed, matching armoire, private bath. He tried to respond, tried to seem interested, but he was sick to the very core. "Breasts," he said. "Vagina."

Nurse Graves's smile fluttered briefly, a hundred-watt bulb flickering between connection and extinction. "Beg pardon?"

Ralph's voice, blissful with enthusiasm: "He says it's very nice. But don't try to talk, Mr. Lightbody, not in your condition, please."

Nurse Graves—Irene, hadn't the elevator man called her Irene?—instructed Ralph to lift Will from the chair and lay him out on the bed. Will didn't protest. Ralph thrust one arm under Will's knees, wrapped his shoulders up in the other, hoisted him from the chair without so much as a grunt of effort and lowered him to the bed. There, Will found himself supported in a sitting position as two pairs of hands removed his jacket, tie, shirt and collar, and then his shoes, socks and trousers, until he sat before them in his underwear, too far gone to worry about modesty. No woman, save for his mother and Eleanor, had ever seen him in his flannels—and no man, for that matter. And here were Ralph (he didn't even know his last name) and Nurse Graves standing over him in his underwear as if it were the most natural thing in the world. Perversely, his groin began to stir again. He sank into the bed and closed his eyes.

He heard the rattle of a tray, the whisper of the chair's wheels. Nurse Graves—Irene—was going to put him to sleep. He wished her luck. He did. He hadn't slept in twenty-two days—had barely eaten or moved his bowels or even drawn breath, for that matter. It was Eleanor, of course. As soon as she'd announced that they were going to the San, both of them, for an indefinite stay, he began to lie awake through the eternal nights, his stomach churning with fear. Fear of what? He didn't know. But the Sanitarium was a club from which he'd been excluded, a club that had taken his wife, his baby girl and his stomach, and it loomed nightmarishly through the dark hours of the night. He longed for the oblivion of the Sears' White Star Liquor Cure, opium dreams edged in red and pink and opening on nothingness. *Then* he would sleep, oh yes indeed. But he fought the urge, fought it like a man on the brink of extinction—which is exactly what he was. And so he hadn't slept. Not at all. Not a wink. Every time he closed his eyes he was immediately swept down his own esophagus and into his stomach, where he lodged like an undigested lump of food—chops, fried potatoes, tumblers of whiskey and oysters with human faces gamboling and cavorting round him as he churned in his own juices. He wished her well, Nurse Graves, but how could she hope to accomplish what Sears and Eleanor and the Old Crow could barely manage?

There was the sound of water being drawn in the bath, and then Ralph's hands were on him again, unbuttoning his long johns. "There, now," Ralph murmured, "just lift your arm up." Will flashed open his eyes. Nurse Graves, her back turned, seemed preoccupied with a tray of instruments. "Right leg, that's a boy, now your left," Ralph coached, peeling the garment from Will's ankles and feet, and suddenly Will was naked, fully naked, in the presence of strangers. The stirring in his groin died stillborn. He was mortified. And what if she should turn round? What then?

Ralph, white-smocked, sure-handed, square-jawed Ralph, produced a swath of linen, a flap of white cloth the size of a dinner napkin and supported by a thin band at the waist. Nothing more than a diaper, really. Will took the garment from Ralph's outstretched hand, slipped his feet through the leg holes and hurriedly pulled the thing up over his loins.

"All set?" Nurse Graves chirped, swinging round on them in that instant as if she were clairvoyant. Will gazed up at her in helplessness and surrender. "Good," she puffed, rubbing her hands together. "We'll have you fast asleep in no time at all. Ralph, would you help Mr. Lightbody into the bathroom?"

Will gave her a startled look.

"Neutral bath and colon wash," she said, her voice as light as the air itself.

"Colon wash?" Will could only gasp out the words as he staggered to his feet and Ralph took hold of him and assisted his plodding steps across the floor.

"An enema," Nurse Graves said. "Hot paraffin, soap and tepid water. You haven't been thoroughly examined yet—we'll put you through a series of tests tomorrow—but the Chief and Dr. Linniman have both diagnosed you as suffering from autointoxication, among other things. In effect, Mr. Lightbody, you've been poisoning your own system. We find it's very common among meat eaters."

They were in the bathroom now, and Will was perched on the edge of the toilet in his pristine diaper. Ralph nodded his head and ducked out the door. "But I don't eat meat—or not anymore," Will protested. My wife won't let me. It's been nothing but Graham gems, parsnips and tomato toast for the last six months."

Nurse Graves was watching him closely. The apparatus—a sort of syringe, with a big distended ball of India rubber at its base—lay cradled in her arms like a sacred object. "That's very admirable, Mr. Lightbody; it's a very good start. But you must realize that all those years of abuse have severely taxed your system. I'm not a doctor, and I know you haven't been thoroughly examined yet, but if you're like the thousands of patients who come here from all over the world, I'd say your intestines are absolutely putrid with disease and germs—unfriendly germs."

It was seventy-two degrees in that bathroom, a temperature Dr. Kellogg maintained throughout the San, winter and summer, seventy-two degrees, and yet Will felt a chill go through him. "Unfriendly?"

Her hand was on his back, hot as a little nugget against his bare skin. "Bend forward now, Mr. Lightbody, yes, just a touch, that's right." He felt her probing at the diaper, felt it slip down round his hips. "Yes," she breathed cheerfully, "there are so many types of bacteria—people don't realize that—and so many of them are a natural and necessary part of the human organism—particularly in the alimentary canal." She paused, probing, probing. "We need to rout the bad ones so that the beneficial can . . . flourish. . . ."

Her hands. The warm bulb of the apparatus. What was he doing? What was going on? "Eleanor," he blurted. "My wife. Where's Eleanor?"

"Hush," Irene whispered. "She's fine. She's on the second floor, room two-twelve, no doubt undergoing this very same procedure . . . to flush her system, relax her."

Will was stunned. "Then she, she won't be staying here, with me?"

The nurse's voice caressed his ear, soothing, soft, as much a part of him as the secret voice that spoke inside his head. "Oh, no. The Chief keeps couples separate here. For therapeutic reasons, of course. Our patients need quiet, rest—any sort of sexual stimulation could be fatal."

Sexual stimulation. Why did those two words suddenly sound so momentous?

"Relax," she whispered, and all at once Will felt the hot fluid surprise of it, his insides flooding as if a dam had burst, as if all the tropical rivers of the world were suddenly flowing through him, irrigating him, flushing, cleansing, churning away at his deepest nooks and recesses in a tumultuous cathartic rush. It was the most mortifying and exquisite moment of his life.

That night he slept like a baby.

In the morning, after his wake-up enema, a sitz bath and a dry-friction massage administered by a mannish-looking nurse who was as mechanical as Irene Graves had been tender, Will, under his own power, hobbled down the corridor and took the elevator to the dining room for breakfast. When this second nurse—Nurse Bloethal—had produced the colonic apparatus, Will had protested. It had been disturbing enough to have the lovely and delicate Nurse Graves administer the treatment, but this woman—well, he felt it would be impossible. "But I just had one last night," he said, a hint of nasality creeping into his voice as he took a defensive posture on the bed and self-consciously adjusted his cotton robe. Nurse Bloethal, fortyish, arms like hams, hams like sacks of grain, with a squarish face and a smile full of crooked teeth, burst out with a laugh. "You'll forgive my saying so, Mr. Lightbody, but you've got a lot to learn."

She was referring, as Will would discover, to the Chief's obsession with interior as well as exterior cleanliness. Dr. Kellogg, tidy son of a broom maker, not only believed in a diet rich in bulk and roughage to encourage the bowels to exonerate themselves, but he was a strict adherent to the five-enema-a-day regimen as well. The inspiration for this mode of treatment had struck him some years earlier during a visit to Africa. He'd had the leisure there to study a troop of apes living in a tumble of blanched rock and sere trees at an oasis outside of Oran. The doctor studied them for a week, sometimes up to sixteen hours a day, hoping to gain some insight into the hominoid diet from these gregarious and frugivorous primates. What he discovered, so obvious, really, and yet till this point so easily overlooked, was that the apes moved their bowels almost continuously. Practically every mouthful they took was accompanied by a complementary evacuation.

Simple. Natural. The way it was meant to be. None of that tribe suffered from constipation, autointoxication, obesity, neurosis, hypohydrochloria or hysteria. But man did. Because man had civilized his bowel, house-trained it, as it were. Man could not, in the course of daily life, go about eliminating his wastes at will—society simply wouldn't be able to function, and the mess . . . well, the Doctor felt, better not to think about the mess. At any rate, through his observation of the Oran apes, Dr. Kellogg hit upon one of his greatest discoveries: the need, the necessity, the imperative of assisting the bowel mechanically to undo the damage wrought upon it by civilization. Hence, five enemas a day, minimum. Hence, Will on the toilet and Nurse Bloethal with the already familiar apparatus.

Will was met at the dining-room door by a motherly little woman with an enormous bosom and tiny recessed eyes so blue they looked artificial. She wore a prim white cap perched atop an explosion of hair the color of cornstarch. "Mr . . . ?" she inquired, the Battle Creek Sanitarium smile frozen into her features.

Tall, self-conscious, smarting from his recent encounter in the bathroom and broiling in the depths of his gut, Will gave her a curt glance. "Lightbody," he said in his hollow booming tones. A few of the diners in the vast room before him looked up from their plates.

"Yes, of course," the woman returned, "I've got you right here on my list. 'Lightbody, William Fitzroy.' " She paused to squint up at him for reinforcement. Will nodded. "It says here that until your examination is completed, you're to be put on a low-protein, laxative, nontoxic diet. But, oh, do forgive me"—and here she held out her hand—"I'm Mrs. Stover, the head dietician. I'll be overseeing your diet during your stay with us, under the direction of your physician, of course. Now, if you'll look out into the dining room a moment, you'll see a number of girls in white caps like mine. Do you see them? There, there's a girl, Marcella Johnson, she's one of mine. If you need any help or advice in choosing your dishes scientifically, please just flag one of us down, won't you?"

Will took her hand, released it, and promised that he would. He made as if to move on, but Mrs. Stover lingered there in the entrance-way, blocking Will's path to the comestibles as other patients sauntered casually by her and were seated in that grand and quietly seething room. Will didn't care much about eating—he couldn't remember the last time he'd experienced hunger or when he'd last eaten anything that didn't set his digestive tract aflame—but he wasn't particularly keen on stand-ing there all morning like an idiot while several hundred cud-chewing diners studied him surreptitiously. "Yes?" he asked. "Is there anything more?"

"One thing only." Mrs. Stover stoked up her smile a degree. So much cheer, Will thought bitterly. And for what? They were all of them hurtling toward their graves, scientific living or no. "Where would you care to sit? We do try to accommodate our guests as to seating arrange-ments, though not everyone gets an opportunity to sit next to a Horace Fletcher or an Admiral Nieblock, of course."

Will shrugged. "With my wife, I guess."

Mrs. Stover's smile contracted till it was just the template of a smile pressed into her dry and faintly reproachful lips. She looked hurt, of-fended. "Oh, no," she crooned, "you wouldn't want to do that, would you? Don't you think you might prefer to mingle, to meet some of your fellow guests?"

Will thought not.

Mrs. Stover looked crestfallen. She began to speak in a rush, barely pausing for breath. "I'll try my very best, for dinner, that is, but I'm afraid—well, I'm afraid I've already seated Eleanor, Mrs. Lightbody—such a charming woman, you're a very lucky man—and her table, number sixty, is full at the moment. You're quite certain you wouldn't prefer to sit with someone else?"

"Do I have a choice?"

Mrs. Stover studied the floor a moment before answering, and when she answered, her smile fluttered and her voice couldn't seem to hold its note. "No," she said, "I'm afraid not."

The waitress, a robust young thing who suggested Nurse Graves in the color of her hair and the set of her ears, led him into the huge palmy room with its skylights and twin colonnades. Will tried to hold himself erect, conscious of his fellow patients' scrutiny, but he felt unstable and weak and his shoulders seemed unnaturally affected by the tug of gravity. He saw a mass of bent heads, a hundred bald spots, mustaches, beards, the rats and fluffs of the women's monumental coiffures, the flash of silverware and the serene but constant movement of the host of waitresses in their dark dresses and white aprons. A murmur of conversation bubbled up round him: laughter, repartee, a smatter of economics and politics—he distinctly heard Teddy Roosevelt's name as he passed a table of six mustachioed gentlemen, none of whom seemed in imminent danger of starvation. He saw, in fact, that all the tables were set for six—no doubt the Chief had determined this to be the optimal number for conviviality and physiologic dining, not to mention superior digestion. A phrase popped into Will's head—"The Peristaltic Optimum"—and he had to smile despite himself.

He craned his neck to look for Eleanor, but she was nowhere to be seen in that sea of scientifically feeding heads, and when the waitress stopped abruptly at a table in the far corner, he wasn't quite as alert as he might have been. For a moment he lost control of his feet, which were narrow but overlong, and he suddenly found himself pitching forward in a spastic sprawl just as the waitress pulled back a chair for him. *The embarrassment,* he was thinking, *oh, the embarrassment,* when at the last moment he shot out an arm to clutch at the rigid spine of the chair and managed to rake himself around, swivel his hips and collapse heavily across the seat—but not before barking both shins and cracking his kneecap with a sudden sharp sound that echoed through the room like a gunshot.

"Are you all right, sir?" The waitress looked stricken.

All right? Was he all right? The immediate and shooting pain of shin and patella was nothing, kindling to the inferno raging in his gut. He wanted to bay at the moon, claw at himself, get down on all fours and tear out his innards like a poisoned dog. All right? He'd never be all right.

Tears of anguish in his eyes, he looked up into the startled faces ranged round the table before him and found himself staring into the chartreuse eyes and high green cheekbones of the girl he'd noticed in the hallway the previous night. Seeing her there flustered him, and he glanced down at his hands, into which the waitress, with a thousand apologies, inserted a menu.

"A bit eager today, aren't we?" a voice spoke in his ear. The voice belonged to an Englishman, sixty or so, with a white tonsure and teeth like a mule's. He was sitting to Will's immediate right. "Champing at the bit, eh? I know the feeling. All of this simple living builds an appetite, and there's no arguing that."

Will agreed with him, wholeheartedly, his eyes affixed to the menu.

"Endymion Hart-Jones," the Englishman's voice announced after a pause, and Will at first thought he was recommending a dish—but no, he was introducing himself.

Will had grown up in a proper household and gone to proper schools. He knew how to behave in society. In fact, he was normally gregarious, barely containable—but to say he was out of sorts would be an understatement. He locked eyes with the Englishman. "Will Lightbody," he said in his rain-barrel tones.

The Englishman introduced the others, Will nodding at each in turn. The heavyset woman to Will's immediate left was Mrs. Tindermarsh, of Indianapolis; beside her, a dwarfish man with a tiny pointed beard and bulbous head, a Professor Stepanovich of the Academy of Astronomical Sciences, in Saint Petersburg, Russia; at the far end of the table, Miss Muntz, the greenish girl, from Poughkeepsie, New York; and beside her, Homer Praetz, the industrialist, from Cleveland.

"The Nut Lisbon Steak with Creamed Gluten Gravy is absolutely divine," Mrs. Tindermarsh offered without a trace of irony.

Will could only blink at her. He could feel the presence of the waitress—or was it one of Mrs. Stover's dieticians?—hovering at his elbow as he tried to make sense of the menu:

BREAKFAST
Tuesday, November 12, 1907

		Prot.	Fats	Carb.	Oz.	Portion
SOUPS	Bean Tapioca	2.17	0.4	8.9	4½	½
	Brown	0.54	0.2	5.24	4½	¼
	Peas Consommé	7.1	5.2	8.6	4½	1
ENTRÉES	Nut Lisbon Steak	22.89	34.47	16.8	2	1¼
	Protose Patties	18.6	21.85	9.15	2	1
	Nuttolene & Jelly	12.0	22.0	26.0	2½	1½

		Prot.	Fats	Carb.	Oz.	Portion
VEGETABLES	Corn Pulp	3.7	2.9	23.2	2½	¾
	Stewed Tomatoes	1.4	0.5	4.7	2½	¼
	Creamed Celery	1.9	11.9	4.6	4¼	¾
BREADS	Bran Biscuit (2)	21.0	31.0	73.0	1	1¼
	Graham Bread (1)	10.0	4.0	61.0	1	¼
	Granose Biscuit (2)	7.0	1.0	42.0	1	¾
	Rice Biscuit (2)	8.5	0.9	96.6	1	1
FRUITS	Stewed Pears	0.7	1.1	23.3	4	1
	Sliced Banana w/ Beaten Meltose	2.6	2.0	106.3	4	1½
	Prune Fritters	3.4	10.5	24.0	3	1¼
CEREALS	Gluten Mush	3.2	0.3	14.68	5½	1
	Graham Grits	2.1	0.3	14.9	5½	1
	Granuto	19.1	5.0	91.8	1¼	2
	Corn Flakes	10.8	1.4	91.3	¾	¼
	Granose Flakes	13.4	1.0	83.8	¾	¾
BEVERAGES	Kaffir Tea	1.0	1.0	8.0	4	1/10
	Sanitas Koko	13.0	89.0	23.0	5	2¼
	Kumyss	3.3	5.6	6.3	5	¾
	Hot Malted Nuts	36.0	96.0	68.0	1¼	2
	Milk	23.0	67.0	35.0	6	1¼
DESSERTS	Squash Pie	4.27	22.7	36.5	5½	3½
	Indian Trifle	3.64	9.4	23.3	3	1

"Do you feel up to an entrée today, Mr. Lightbody?"

Will gazed up into the broad honest faces of the table waitress and dietician, buxom girls and young, radiating health, wisdom and the secret knowledge of diet and health to which their Chief and idol had made them privy.

"My name is Evangeline," said the taller of the two, "and I'll be your dietary advisor during your stay with us. And this"—indicating the second girl—"is Hortense. She'll be your waitress. Now, if I might explain the menu to you, sir." She cleared her throat. "I hope you'll notice the numbers printed beside each food item. . . ."

Will clutched the menu as if it were a rope suspended over a pit of crocodiles. His fellow diners had fallen silent, absorbed in his deliberations: this wasn't merely eating, this was science.

"Well," she went on, "these numbers, when summed up, will give you the total calories consumed—simply add the figures in the first, second and third columns and put down the sums at the foot of the respective columns. Mark each item eaten, sign the bill of fare, and hand it to your physician—for each meal, each day. It's really quite simple."

"Yes," Will agreed, his eyes jumping from the dietician's to those of Miss Muntz and the others, "yes, I suppose it is."

"Well, then," Evangeline said brightly, "may I repeat my original question: Do you feel up to an entrée this morning? Either the Nuttolene and jelly or the Protose patties would be very therapeutic for a man in your condition."

Will ran a hand through his hair. His stomach began to announce itself, an old adversary backed into a corner but not about to give up without a fight. "Uh, well," Will fumbled, "uh, I think I'll just have the toast. And water. A glass of water."

"Toast?" the girls harmonized, a look of shock and incredulity on their faces. "But surely—" began the taller one, and then she trailed off. "We can get you your toast, of course, if that's what you like, sir, but I'd recommend a serving of the corn pulp, the brown soup and prune fritters to go with it. At the very least. I can appreciate that you're not yet up to digesting a large meal, but I do advise you to eat generously and flush your system of its poisons."

At this point, the Englishman got into it: "That's right, old boy, flush the system. You'll be getting your flora changed, too, I'll wager"—and here, inexplicably, the whole table burst into laughter—"and it's never too early to give the little blighters a hand."

Will's face reddened. Flora? What on earth was he talking about? And the menu. That was nonsense, too. Nuttolene, Protose patties, Meltose and gluten and all the rest of it—Eleanor's concoctions, as unlike food as anything he'd ever had in his mouth. His jaw hardened. He fastened on the eyes of the waitress. "Toast," Will repeated in a firm tone. "Dry. And that will be all, thank you."

Suddenly meek, the girls melted away from him. When he turned back to the table, he found himself staring into Miss Muntz's startled yellow eyes, until she turned abruptly to the bulbous Russian and began talking of the weather—terribly cold for this time of year, wasn't it? The Englishman had suddenly become absorbed in studying his shirt cuffs, and Mrs. Tindermarsh gazed out the windows into intermediate space. Homer Praetz, he noticed, was carefully chewing a bit of something that looked vaguely organic. It was then, in that moment of relative calm, that Will again thought of Eleanor. Where was she? Why hadn't she come to the table to wish him a good morning? Was this the Kellogg method—to drive a wedge between husband and wife? To segregate them? Well, he'd be damned if he'd sit here and eat his toast without her.

He was just rising from the table when the waitress reappeared with his toast and a glass of kumyss for Mrs. Tindermarsh. Reluctantly, Will sank back into his chair, all the while looking over his shoulder for a glimpse of Eleanor. She was nowhere to be seen. Other women were, though—hundreds of them, ranging in age from fifteen to eighty, every last one of them dressed in the latest styles (as modified by their Chief, of course) and enjoying a healthy, bubbly, convivial meal. Their chatter was electric, all-pervasive, the buzz of a field of insects droning toward the intersection of afternoon and evening. Will bowed his head and morosely lifted the toast to his mouth.

No sooner had he taken a bite than his stomach began to rumble— or not just rumble, but growl and spit like a caged animal poked with a stick. "Down, boy!" the Englishman exclaimed, playing to the table with a show of his horsey teeth. Miss Muntz put a pretty green hand to her mouth and tittered. Will gave them a sick grin and munched his toast.

Just as he was transporting a second spear of scorched bread to his mouth, his stomach rumbling like Vesuvius and his coated tongue swelling in his throat, he felt a pressure on his shoulder and turned to find himself gazing up into a great shrewd globe of a face that hung over him like a Chinese lantern. The face belonged to a rubicund, snowy-haired man built on the Chief's mold—that is, stocky, foreshortened and expansive round the middle. The man had his hand on Will's shoulder. His look of sagacity almost immediately turned to one of consternation, and he began emitting a moist clucking sound. "No, no, no, no, no," he said, wagging a finger for emphasis, "you've got it all wrong."

Will was baffled. Did he know this man? He studied the blistering blue eyes, the firm jowls, the hair leached of all color dancing round the great pumpkin of his head . . . come to think of it, he did look vaguely familiar. . . .

"Chew," the man said, and he made a command of it. "Chew!" he cried, his voice corkscrewing upward. "Masticate! Fletcherize!" And he removed his hand from Will's shoulder to point to the ten-foot banner draped across the wall just under the entranceway at the far end of the room. The banner, in bold black letters three feet high, echoed the stocky little man's exhortation:

FLETCHERIZE!

Understanding began to dawn on Will. This was none other than Horace B. Fletcher himself, standing there before him in all his mandibular glory. Will knew him—of course he did. Was there a man, woman or child in America who didn't? Fletcher was the naturopathic genius who'd revealed to the world the single most fundamental principle of good health, diet and digestion: mastication. Thorough mastication. Fletcher maintained (and Dr. Kellogg concurred with all his heart) that the nearest thing to a panacea for gastric ills and nutritional disorders was the total digestion of food in the mouth. And he wasn't content merely to chew each morsel of food once for each of the thirty-two teeth in the human mouth, though he'd admit that it was a good start; rather, you were to chew a given bit of food fifty, sixty or seventy times even, until it dissolved in the mouth, the "food gate" opened and the mouthful was gone. With a shout of acclamation, the entire alimentary community had heralded this simple but momentous discovery. And now here was this celebrated figure, this hero of the oral cavity, standing before Will in the midst of this dining room crowded with luminaries, this great man coaching him in the intricacies of masticating a scrap of toast. Despite himself, Will was impressed.

He chewed slowly and thoughtfully, chewed as he'd never chewed before, the fluid mentorial tones of Horace B. Fletcher counting off the strokes in his ear: ". . . ten, eleven, twelve—that's it—thirteen, fourteen, yes, yes." And even in the depths of his concentration, Will felt the touch of the Great Masticator's strong square fingers as they gently wrapped themselves round the nape of his neck and forced his head down in the proper Fletcherizing position. Will chewed. And chewed. At the count of twenty, he felt a sharp pain in one of his lower rear molars; at twenty-five, his tongue went numb; at thirty, the toast was paste; at thirty-five, it was water; at forty, his jaw began to ache, and the toast was saliva. And then, miraculously, it was gone.

The whole table watched this operation in silence. When it was completed, and Will cautiously lifted his head, the Great Masticator gave him a congratulatory slap on the back, winked one sharp blue eye and sauntered off with an air of satisfaction. Will saw that Mrs. Tindermarsh was beaming at him—they all were, the whole table. For a moment, he thought they were going to burst into applause. He couldn't imagine how the simple act of grinding up a bit of toast could give them such a thrill, but it pleased him nonetheless, and he smiled shyly as he bent forward to repeat the performance.

It was not to be. For at that moment the thread of a single voice disengaged itself for just an instant from the general hubbub—a voice he knew as well as his own—and he jerked round in his chair as if electrified. *Eleanor.* And then he was on his feet, the chair thrust back from him as he scanned the crowd for a glimpse of her. Her voice came to him again, this time as it rose to cap off a witticism and trail away in the musical little laugh he'd already begun to miss. *Eleanor.* The feeding heads dipped and rose, waitresses waited, dietary advisors dispensed dietary advice. Will felt frightened suddenly, frightened and sick. "Eleanor!" he cried like a stricken calf. "Eleanor!"

He saw her in that moment, rising startled from a table not thirty feet away, the dark silk of her hair piled atop her head, her quick green eyes fixing him with a look of shock and admonition. *Not here,* that look warned him, *not now.* He saw the faces of her breakfast companions gaping up at him, a distinguished company, a brilliant company, no doubt. And who was that beside her, the napkin folded surgically in his lap? Who was that with the flaxen hair and the adamantine jaw? Who with the perfect teeth and the subtle, healing hands?

Not here, not now.

Will didn't care. He was already lurching toward her, the fist in his stomach beating at him as if to force a way out—he didn't want to be here, didn't want to be in Battle Creek, didn't want to be in a place where his wife was lost to him and people had to tell him how to chew his toast. He didn't know what he was doing—it had been ten hours since he'd seen her last, ten hours, that was all, and here he was awash in loss and self-pity. "Eleanor!" he cried.

They were all watching him, every anointed, spoon-fed, Fletcherizing one of them, and suddenly he didn't care. He blundered into a chair occupied by an immovable fat man, ricocheted off him and felt the strength fall away from his legs. Still, he staggered on, thinking nothing, thinking to embrace her, claim her, right there in the middle of the room.

Eleanor stood poised at the table, and she didn't look startled or even angry anymore. No: she looked embarrassed, only that.

Chapter 6

The Biggest Little
City in the
U.S.A.

❀

Charlie Ossining was a little late.

Not that the train had delayed him—it was right on sched-ule, rolling into Battle Creek's Main Street depot on the stroke of the hour, brakes crying out, steam rising in plumes, the town lit like an ornament beyond windows fogged with the rich exhalations of drum-mers, real-estate men and breakfast-food magnates. Leaning forward to peer out the window, Charlie felt his stomach contract with excitement, and he caught a brief taste of his supper—tongue sandwich and pickles—in the back of his throat. This was it: Battle Creek. The Mother Lode. He looked up into the big, gently swaying sign the local boosters had erected and felt it spoke directly to him. He *would* better himself, he knew it, just as he knew that Mrs. Hookstratten's $3,849—make that $3,846.55, after tips to the porter and waiter and drinks and sand-wiches in the club car—was nothing more than the first nugget prized from the mountain he was destined to conquer. This was his opportunity and this was the place. Battle Creek, the Biggest Little City in the U.S.A., Cereal Bowl of the World, Foodtown. "Right on time," a man in a bowler hat and overcoat murmured in his ear, and in the next moment he was disembarking into the thrilling cold of the star-hung Midwestern night.

The platform was a confusion of businessmen, health seekers, hawkers, cabbies, porters, newsboys, shine boys, boys who didn't appear to have any recognizable purpose, and they all seemed to want to go in the same direction at the same time. Charlie stood there bewildered in the middle of the throng, clutching his imitation-alligator-skin grip to his chest and keeping one eye out for the Negro with his trunk and the other for Bender. "Cyrus!" a woman cried beside him. "Yoo-hoo, Cyrus! Over here!" Charlie watched as the anonymous passengers found themselves in the animated faces and outstretched arms of those who'd come out to wait in the cold for them, and he felt more uncertain than ever, fretting about his trunk and the size of the tip he would be expected to press on the porter and where he was going to spend the night. He couldn't help feeling a stab of regret as the man in the bowler rushed past him and threw himself into the arms of a neat little woman in bonnet and muff while a boy of six or so clung to his legs, piping "Daddy! Daddy!" And where was Bender? All his anticipation seemed to sour in that moment, and he had a sudden longing to be back again in the cozy confines of the club car.

It was then that he noticed the Lightbody woman. She was descending from the near car like royalty, electric in her furs, the conductor fluttering round her gloved hand as if she'd just touched down from the clouds. Behind her, his head floating in the void like a balloon on a string, was her gawk of a husband, closely followed by a trio of porters straining under a burden of bags, satchels, hatboxes and Saratoga trunks—all in matching monogrammed leather. *A small block of stock can be had by the right sort of investor*, Charlie was thinking, and found that he was staring directly into Eleanor Lightbody's saturate eyes. He smiled, lifted his hat in greeting. She returned the salutation with a little dip of her chin and a smile of her own, and then her husband staggered between them like a blind man, like an ambulatory corpse, the porters closed in the gap, and they were gone. Charlie watched the little group wend its way through the already thinning crowd, then pass through the waiting room and out to the street beyond, where an automobile rolled up to the curb to receive them.

"Hey, mister." Charlie felt a tug at his sleeve and turned to find one of the superfluous boys gazing up at him expectantly from beneath the brim of a porkpie cap. The boy was about fourteen, sleepy-eyed and heavyset, and he slouched in his overcoat and galoshes like the old man he would one day become. A group of his compeers—seven or eight of them—stood a few paces off, watching intently.

Bender, Charlie thought. Bender must have sent him. "Oh, hello," he murmured, leaning down to him. "Are you from Mr. Bender?"

Something awoke and shook itself briefly in the depths of the boy's dully glinting eyes. He swiped the toe of one boot over the other and let out a long whistling breath that hung round his face in a pale cloud. "I don't think so," he said. "I, uh, just wanted to know if you were interested in an investment opportunity, a chance to be part of the newest and best Battle Creek breakfast food yet, at just fifty cents a share. What I'm talking about, mister," and here he produced a printed prospectus from inside the folds of his overcoat and lowered his voice as if disclosing a closely guarded secret, "is Push."

Charlie didn't know how to react. Was the kid serious? Or was this just a prank the local boys played on unsuspecting travelers? It was the sort of thing he might have done himself a few years back. "Push?" he repeated, distracted in that moment by the shriek of the train's brakes as it lurched forward a few feet and then halted again—where was that damned porter?

"Yes, sir, mister, that's it: *Push*. The newest and best Battle Creek breakfast food yet, and only fifty cents a—"

"Aaaaah, don't listen to him." A second boy was at his side now, taller, rangier, with a face splashed with freckles and ears that stood straight out from his head. "It's Grano-Fruto you want, just ninety cents a share to get in on America's favorite breakfast food—"

But he was interrupted by another, crowing for Vita-Malta and waving a prospectus in Charlie's face, while yet another shouted, "Twenty-five cents a share, twenty-five cents a share," as the whole band of them surged round him hopefully.

Charlie was late, and it was just beginning to dawn on him. He'd known there were a number of cereal companies here—Post had made his first million by 1901, and there were the Kelloggs, of course—but this was ridiculous. For the first time, as the boys cried out the names of their brands in breathy cracking voices and waved their offerings in the air, he began to doubt Bender. The uncertainty must have shown in his face, because the boys redoubled their efforts, scrabbling at him till he began to fear for his wallet, his grip, the fabric of his coat. "Beat it," he snarled, "all of you—just beat it."

The boys fell away from him like dead leaves, but then they regrouped and started after a new prospect, shrilly touting their wares: "Pep! Push! Vim!" Impatient, angry, shaken, Charlie set down his valise and paused to light a cigarette. But there was the Negro with his trunk, standing at the far end of the platform and looking as unconcerned as if he were curling up next to the stove in the waiting room for a good nap. "Hello!" Charlie cried, waving an arm over his head. "Down here!"

No response. Damn it. The man might just as well have been deaf, dumb and blind. "You, porter!" he shouted, but he was tired suddenly, very tired. Tired of traveling, tired of worrying over Mrs. Hookstratten's $3,846.55, tired of lazy porters and incompetent waiters, tired, already, of Battle Creek. He felt the exhaustion seeping into his limbs like gas into a coal mine, and as he wearily hefted his grip and started up the platform, he was just waiting for it to explode and shatter him into a thousand limp and volitionless pieces.

He hadn't gone five steps when he felt a hand on his arm.

The hand belonged to a man about his own age—twenty-four, twenty-five, maybe—and it exerted a pressure that was both apologetic and insinuating. "Excuse me, friend," the man said, "have you got a match?"

Charlie did have a match, and he set down his grip, squinting through the smoke of his cigarette, to produce it. As he held the flame to the freshly cut tip of the stranger's cigar, he couldn't help noticing his clothes—the tightly cut woolen suit in an up-to-the-minute brown-and-gray plaid beneath a fleece-lined overcoat, the pink-and-white striped shirt identical to Charlie's own, the elegant gray fedora that perched atop the crown of his head as gracefully as if he'd been born wearing it. Charlie was surprised. Here he was in the hinterlands, and the first man he ran into could have been one of the sports lounging round the theaters on Broadway or the amusement park on Coney Island—somehow he'd never expected westerners to dress so smartly. He'd expected hicks, rubes, cowboys.

The man exhaled with satisfaction. "Thank you," he said, "very much obliged." And then he held out his hand. "Harry Delahoussaye," he said. "Glad to make your acquaintance."

Charlie shook hands and introduced himself, and he looked up in that moment to see the porter yawn and consult his pocket watch. "I'm sorry," Charlie said, "I've got—"

"Oh, no problem," Delahoussaye returned, "I understand. Business, business, business, eh?"

Yes, that was it: *business*. Charlie was here on business. Big business. He felt flattered, felt important, felt like the President-in-Chief of the Per-Fo Company. He wondered if he should give the man a card.

"I could see it in your clothes, in your bearing," Delahoussaye said. "Just in from the city, eh? Philadelphia? Chicago? New York?"

"New York," Charlie whispered, and the words were like a balm on his lips, soothing, protective, words that bespoke his intimate connection with that great city and all its glamour and riches.

"I knew it. I just knew it." And then, before Charlie realized it, Delahoussaye's hand was on his elbow again. "Listen, a man like you, a man of business, you must be interested in an opportunity when it comes your way, am I right?"

A gust picked up at the end of the platform and threw a handful of cinders in Charlie's face. He saw the light now—this was a pitch, another pitch. The understanding saddened him, devastated him, took a stake and drove it right through the heart of the shrunken little ball of optimism he still carried with him.

"What I'm talking about, Charlie, is *Push*, the newest and best Battle Creek breakfast food yet—and just a dollar twenty-five cents a share. A man like you, though—you'd want a block of stock, I'm sure, and I can accommodate you, no problem. What can I put you down for? You'll be doing yourself a favor, believe me."

Without a word, Charlie bent for his grip and started up the platform. "Hey," Delahoussaye shouted at his back, "I can get you Vita-Malta at seventy-five—"

Charlie was short with the porter. He tipped him a penny and dragged the trunk himself through the waiting room and out to the cold, gaslit street. By now, the crowd had dispersed, and Charlie was left alone at

the curb—even the few horse-drawn cabs had plodded on up the street.
There was an interurban trolley, but Charlie had no idea where he was
going—Bender was at the Post Tavern Hotel, that was all he knew. He
was about to ask directions of an old man with rheumy eyes and a
tobacco-stained beard, when for the third time since he'd stepped down
off the train, he felt a tug at his sleeve.

It was too much. It was. What did they take him for—a rube? A
half-wit? A dupe? He whirled round angrily on yet another kid, jerking
his arm away in the process. "Beat it," he said, and his voice was bottled
up with the rage in his throat.

The boy held his ground. He was in short pants still, and his lips
trembled with the cold. Twin streams of snot depended from his nostrils.
"You Charlie Ossining?" he asked in the smallest rupture of a voice.

Charlie nodded wearily. He breathed out a sigh of resignation. So
this was Bender's emissary, this was his welcome, this was his grand
entrance into the Biggest Little City in the U.S.A.

"Mr. Bender says you're to come along with me," the boy squeaked,
reaching out a raw little bunch of knuckles to take the valise from
Charlie's grasp.

Relieved—at least Bender hadn't forgotten him—Charlie softened
and handed over the valise, but when he gave the street a quick
scan and saw neither car nor carriage, the anger boiled up in him again.
"And what about my trunk?"

The boy looked down at his shoes. His voice was a whisper in a closet
on the far side of the street. "Don't think I can manage it myself, sir."

They walked twenty blocks in a howling wind, the boy hunched and
snuffling, Charlie staggering like an inebriate beneath the weight of his
trunk. He'd managed to heave the thing up onto the unsteady platform
of his bowed back, and he held it in position by exercising his tailbone
as a stop and gripping the handles over his shoulders with two numb
clawlike hands. They hadn't gone a block and a half before he felt the
tin-reinforced frame of the trunk digging through his overcoat, jacket,

78

vest and shirt to gouge, with knifelike precision, at his spine and hips. "Where you taking me, kid—the North Pole?" he gasped.

The boy shuffled along, head down, the bottom of the imitation-alligator-skin grip dragging along the crust of ice hardened into the slats of the wooden sidewalk. "It's not far," he called in his piteous bleat of a voice, the tatters of his breath streaming behind him.

Not far? Ten blocks later they were still trudging along, every nerve in Charlie's body alive to the torturous pains shooting through his limbs and playing up and down his spine like Saint Elmo's fire. His feet were dead things, blocks of ice, stone, glacial debris, his nose a memory, his fingers forever twisted into hooks. The lights of the city were behind them, the sidewalks had given way to furrows of frozen mud, and the houses had begun to trail off. "Goddamnit," he muttered, dropping the trunk to the ground with a distant cold thud and fighting to arch his back against all sense and habit. "You, boy!" he roared into the night, "where the devil you taking me?"

The boy was like a mule on a treadmill, fixated, senseless, the sticks of his legs plodding on automatically in their torn stockings and disheveled knee pants. He swung his head round reluctantly, slowing but not yet stopping. "Just a little ways more," he piped. "Up there, ahead—see them lights?"

It was a distance of some blocks, and the street ahead of them was dark on either side, but there was a powerful, pervasive glow of electric light ahead of them, as if they were coming into another town altogether. Had they walked all the way to Ypsilanti? It sure felt like it. "What's that?" he asked, pulling the collar tight against his throat.

The boy had stopped now, ten paces ahead of him. "That's the White City."

The White City. Even Charlie, newly arrived, had heard of the White City, had dreamed of it, even. This was the home of Postum and Grape-Nuts, the hub of C. W. Post's empire, a manufacturing enterprise and residential community so pristine and enlightened it had been named after the glorious "White City" of the 1893 Chicago World's Columbian Exposition. For a long moment, though he ached in every fiber and the hyperborean wind drove at him relentlessly, Charlie stood there in awe of that distant electric glow. Here was an inspiration, and it made the petty annoyances of his journey seem like nothing. Was there an enterprising man or boy in America who didn't know the story of C. W. Post's rise from feeble health and poverty to the very first rank of American industrialists? Here was a man who'd come to Battle Creek in ruins, barely able to walk, who'd worked in the Sanitarium kitchens to pay for his treatment while his wife sewed suspenders by the piece in her unheated garret. *Yes: and six years later he was a millionaire.*

"Come on, mister," the boy whined. "I'm freezing."

"Yeah, sure," Charlie said, distracted. "But I thought the Post Tavern was in town. It's out here, then? By the factory?"

The boy was already moving. "Not goin' to the Post Tavern," he called over his shoulder. "Mr. Bender told me to take you to Mrs. Eyvindsdottir's."

"Where?"

❖   ❖   ❖

Mrs. Eyvindsdottir's rooming house was within sight of the White City itself, and it was clean, spartan and depressing. Charlie and the boy stood shivering in the coolish hallway, Charlie counting out another three dollars and a quarter from Mrs. Hookstratten's hoard while the boy wiped his nose on his sleeve and half a dozen sallow, hopeless-looking men huddled round the faintest glimmer of a fire in the parlor. Mrs. Eyvindsdottir beamed at them. She was a square-shouldered woman with a faint blond mustache who always managed to look as if she'd just received an unexpected gift, and whose English was all but impenetrable—at least as far as Charlie was concerned. She went up and down the scale like a diva doing her warming-up exercises as Charlie counted out the money, and he could only give her a blank look until one of the other boarders—a bald-headed man in a red-checked muffler—got up from his chair by the fire and translated: "One week in advance, due and payable on Saturday, breakfast at seven, dinner at one, supper at six-thirty, late boarders to fend for themselves." When the bargain was formalized and Mrs. Eyvindsdottir had deposited Mrs. Hookstratten's three dollars and twenty-five cents in the folds of her apron, she heaved herself up a flight of protesting stairs to show Charlie to his room.

The room wasn't much. It called to mind the root cellar on the Hookstratten estate, though it was barely half the size. Cramped beneath the pitch of the roof, thoroughly refrigerated, gloomy, damp and deathly still, the room needed only a few heaps of potatoes and a basket of rutabagas to complete the picture. A much-scrubbed kerosene lamp provided light—and, apparently, all the heat he was likely to get. There was no radiator, no fireplace, no stove. The narrow bed was wedged into the corner beside a washstand and worn porcelain basin; three unvarnished pegs driven into the wall served as closet and wardrobe. The only decoration was a tiny turgid oil painting depicting the midnight sun hanging over the fjords of Norway.

"No window?" Charlie wondered aloud, attempting to ease the trunk down on the bare floorboards with a minimum of damage.

Mrs. Eyvindsdottir yodeled something in response as the boy edged warily into the room and set Charlie's imitation-alligator skin grip in the corner.

"Beg pardon?" Charlie said, straightening up gingerly. The muscles of his lower back, long dormant, announced themselves: they were on fire, meat pounded raw and tossed into a vat of sizzling lard.

"She says, 'Mr. Bagwell's got it,' " the bald man said, poking his head in the door and attempting a smile. He was amazing, really, totally hairless, like some fantastic creature in a sideshow—he didn't even seem to have any eyebrows. "That's me," he added, by way of clarification. He pointed to the front wall of Charlie's room, a cheap partition left open where the ceiling slanted up into the attic. "I've got the window in my room, and I'm sorry about that, but I had to wait two and a half years for Mr. Bjornson to pass on before I could get it."

All right, Charlie thought, all right. Bender's economizing—so much the better. They'd need every penny to make Per-Fo fly—and fly it would, the cappers and the hucksters and the fast-talking boys at the depot notwithstanding. Mrs. Eyvindsdottir's was a far cry from a private compartment on the Twentieth Century Limited, with oysters and duck and even caviar available for the asking, but he was willing to tighten his belt for a while, no problem there—if C. W. Post could do it, so could he. "Thank you, ma'am," he said, ushering Mrs. Eyvindsdottir out the door, along with her interpreter, "and you too, sir—I'm very much obliged."

When he'd shut the door and turned round, wondering what to do next, he found himself staring into the blunted eyes of Bender's pathetic little messenger. "Well," he said, and he couldn't help it if his tone was a bit sharper than he'd intended, "and what do you want?"

The boy hung his head. "I'm sorry, sir, but Mr. Bender says you're to give me a dime . . . and he wanted me to take you to see him at the Post Tavern, no matter how late—".

The Post Tavern: yes, of course. Charlie was going to live like Peary among the Eskimos in a barren back room at Mrs. Eyvindsdottir's while Bender lived it up at the best hotel in town. Yes, sure. What else would he expect?

"—because, he says, the banks are closed for the night and he thought . . . well, he says you ought to put the stockholders' money in the safe there. For safekeeping. That's what he says. That, and you're to give me a dime."

❖   ❖   ❖

Nine-thirty at night, the wind had shifted round demonically to blow in his face again, and Charlie Ossining was plodding back up the long dark street to town, retracing his steps. The boy kept half a pace ahead of him, as if it were a point of honor, and there was no sound but the crunch of their footsteps and the hoarse wind-shocked rasp of their breath. At one point, the interurban sailed on past them, lit like heaven, but the boy made no attempt to flag it down, and when Charlie angrily questioned him, the boy looked away and murmured, "Mr. Bender said to walk. Both ways."

By the time they reached the hotel, Charlie was seething. If someone had tossed an effigy of Bender in his path, he would have booted it on down the street and cheerfully set it ablaze. Here he'd had to haul his own trunk twenty blocks in an arctic wind and in the company of a skinny, snot-nosed, down-at-heels runt of a kid in tattered short pants and a jacket that looked as if it had been fetched out of the rubbish, and then tramp the twenty blocks back again for an audience with the almighty Bender—and Bender hadn't even stuck his nose out the door in all that time. No, he couldn't even have bothered to meet him at the station and say, *Hello, Charlie, welcome to town, and by the way, I'll be sticking you out in the middle of nowhere in a three-dollar-and-twenty-five-cent boarding house while I soak my feet and order up another plate of bluepoints from room service.*

The fact that the hotel was imposing—really first-class—didn't help his mood any, either. Charlie could hardly believe it. Six stories high, a full block long, its banks of windows confidently glowing against the bleak Midwestern night, it was impressive, modern, very grand, the equal of anything he'd seen in New York—or anywhere else.

He'd passed through the porte cochère and the doorman had stepped forward to swing open the door for him before he missed the boy. He stopped to glance round him, and the doorman gave him a look. But in that moment he spotted the boy—out on the street still, lurking in the shadows, his shoulders fallen in on themselves. "What's the matter?" Charlie called, backtracking to where the boy stood hunched in the street.

"Nothing."

"You're not coming in?"

The boy wiped his nose on his sleeve. "I go in the service entrance," he murmured, "when Mr. Bender wants me. Anyway, I got school tomorrow."

School. Charlie felt a weight settle on him. Here he'd been bellyaching all night and this skinny-legged kid had waited out in the cold for him at the depot and then tramped all over creation just to see that he didn't get lost. What was he—nine, ten years old? *School. He had to go to school.* Charlie realized he didn't even know his name. "Listen," he said, glancing over his shoulder at the brightly lit entrance to the hotel, "I appreciate your help tonight, I really do . . . you know, I don't even know your name—"

"Ernest," the kid said. "Ernest O'Reilly."

"An Irishman, huh? Well, listen, Ernest O'Reilly, thanks a lot. You come round again—maybe Mr. Bender and I'll have some errands for you. We're starting up a breakfast-food company and I'm sure we're going to need a dependable errand boy."

Ernest O'Reilly said nothing to this. He stood there, hunched against the wind, a dogged expression on his face. "Mr. Bender said you'd give me a dime," he repeated.

Charlie had forgotten—after all that, the kid probably thought he was going to stiff him. Embarrassed, Charlie dug out his change purse. "Here," he said, feeling magnanimous suddenly, "here's fifteen cents."

Snatching the money and jamming it into his pocket, Ernest O'Reilly gave him a look suspended midway between gratitude and contempt. "Big spender," he piped, and then he was gone in a flash of spindly legs.

The transaction left a sour taste in Charlie's mouth—the little ingrate: what did he expect?—and as he inquired at the desk for Mr. Goodloe H. Bender, he could feel the indignation rising in his throat. "Mr. Bender?" the desk clerk repeated, as if Charlie had been speaking in a foreign language. The clerk looked him up and down a moment, the hollows of his cheeks drawn in cool appraisal, and then he turned away abruptly to conduct a brief hushed telephone conference. After a moment he set the earpiece back on its hook as if it were a precious jewel and shifted round to face Charlie. "Mr. Bender is occupied at the moment. Would you take a seat, please?"

Charlie was weary, bone weary. It seemed as if he'd been traveling forever. But still, in that moment, he could barely restrain himself from reaching out and seizing the man by the collar. *You chicken-necked little twit*, he was thinking, *in six months' time I'll buy and sell the likes of you a hundred times over.* He held the clerk's eyes till the man looked away, then stalked across the lobby and threw himself down on a red velvet settee in the corner. A long shiver ran through him, and he hugged his shoulders and stamped his feet on the carpet. After a moment, he began working at the buttons of his coat with stiff and aching fingers.

The lobby was quiet at this hour—it was past ten now, and the last travelers would long since have settled in. Charlie sat there, fiddling with his buttons, consulting his watch, yawning despite himself in the luxurious enveloping warmth. The place was certainly plush, that was for sure. Tapestries on the walls, oil paintings, chandeliers, that hushed air of elegance and ease hanging over the rooms as if they were suspended in time. It was what the rich craved, he supposed—the suspension of the whole temporal order of things, absolution from the cares and worries of plebeians like himself. That's what money was for.

And C. W. Post understood it better than anyone. He'd come to town with nothing, nothing—not fifty cents to invest—and he'd realized all of this. Of course, he didn't spend much time in Battle Creek anymore—he was all over the world, conquering one market after another, building a whole city in Texas, influencing votes and policies in Washington, making them eat Grape-Nuts and Elijah's Manna in England and France and Germany—but when he was in town, he lived here, in the Post Tavern Hotel. Charlie had heard he had a whole floor to himself, a magnificent suite of rooms with every amenity . . . and the clerks must jump out of their skins when he walks in the door, *Yes, Mr. Post, sir, yes, sir, yes, yes, yes.* . . .

Charlie must have dozed. He couldn't seem to recall seeing the bellhop move across the room to lean solicitously over him and place two gloved fingers gently on his shoulder. "What?" he gasped, starting.

"Mr. Bender will see you now," the bellhop returned, speaking in the whisper they all seemed to affect, as if using a normal tone of voice would somehow crack the pillars, shatter the chandeliers, bring the whole opulent edifice crashing to the ground. "Would you come with me, please, sir?"

Charlie followed the bellhop across the lobby and down a hallway that apparently connected to the rear street-entrance of the hotel, all the while focusing wearily on the man's pinched, squared-up shoulders and the pale depression at the nape of his neck. The bellhop stopped outside a long comfortable room fitted in Flemish oak, with a built-in buffet, stained-glass panels and an arrangement of heavy dark tables and chairs. A wrought-iron sign hung over the door: "The Wee Nippy," it proclaimed.

As Charlie entered, he saw Bender rising from one of the tables with a group of prosperous-looking men, most of whom wore sheepish looks, as if they'd made a pact against their better judgment and already regretted it. The table was littered with empty beer schooners, whiskey glasses, napkins, ashtrays, a decimated platter of sandwiches—and two decks of well-thumbed cards. Smoke rose from the gentlemen's cigars. There was a muted murmur of conversation. But if three or four of the men looked vaguely uneasy, Bender himself was the picture of rugged confidence, optimism, triumph, even. He had hold of one man's hand in a firm politician's grip, all the while gathering up a wad of greenbacks from the table with his free hand and raising his voice in a jocular, hail-fellow-well-met roar. *Poker.* All at once Charlie understood. *Bender had kept him waiting over a poker game.*

In that moment, Bender spotted him, and his expression wavered ever so slightly, as if he'd been awakened in the middle of a dream, as if for an instant he didn't recognize his partner, come all the way from New York with the wherewithal to make Per-Fo fly, but he covered himself admirably. "Charlie!" he boomed, sweeping across the room on his stupendous feet, a tottering, sweating, plum-faced tornado of a man, huge, ventricular, his fractured soapstone eyes leaping madly out of his head, arms spread wide for the crushing embrace. In the instant before they closed, Charlie noticed that he'd dyed his beard to contrast with the white fluff atop his head, and not only that, but he'd taken to parting it aristocratically in the middle of his chin, too. He looked like a general home from the wars, looked like a senator, a banker, a captain of industry.

As they embraced there in the glittering taproom, as Charlie felt the power in the older man's arms and took in the rich intoxicating odor of lilac water, Cuban tobacco and fine Scotch whiskey that enveloped him like a succubus, he couldn't help feeling relieved, proud even: this dynamo, this titan, this earthshaking figure of a man was his partner. He was in a daze as Bender introduced him round to the company (noses, mustaches, beards: he couldn't catch a single name), but it didn't seem to matter—the party was breaking up anyway. Bender bellowed his goodbyes, the others shrugged into jackets and overcoats, the smoke began to dissipate. And then, resplendent in checked trousers, sky-blue jacket with matching vest and yellow high-button shoes buffed till they threw back the light like twin dancing mirrors, Bender led him grandly through the corridors, out into the lobby and across the carpet to the elevator.

By the time Charlie managed to recover himself, Bender was ushering him into his fourth-floor room—or, rather, suite of rooms. Bender had a sitting room, with electric lamps and a rolltop desk in the corner; a bedroom visible through an open door to the left and lit invitingly by a single amber-shaded Tiffany lamp; and a glittering tile-and-porcelain bathroom that was itself bigger than Charlie's crawl space at Mrs. Eyvindsdottir's. As Bender crossed the room to the sideboard and poured them each a snifter of brandy from a cut-glass decanter, Charlie eased himself down on the wine-colored sofa and saw with amazement that the amenities here even included a telephone. *Bender had his own telephone. In his sitting room.* The convenience of it, the luxury—it was a revelation. It stunned him. It was almost beyond his comprehension. Sure, Mrs. Hookstratten had a phone, in her eighteen-room mansion overlooking Lounsbury Pond. And he supposed the Lightbodys and people like that had them, also, but a telephone in your own room? It was too much.

"So, so, so, my friend," Bender cried, whirling round on him and tottering across the room with the drinks, "and how was your trip? First-class all the way, eh? A little taste of the good life never hurt anybody—and it's just the beginning, Charlie, just the beginning."

Bender didn't wait for a reply.

"I would have been there to meet you, of course I would, you know that, but these people you've just been introduced to—Bookbinder, Stellrecht and the rest—well, they're the princes of this town, princes, and you've got to cultivate people like that, you've just got to. Know what I mean?" Bender had planted himself on the arm of the sofa, his wild smoke-colored eyes tugging at Charlie's as if they were connected by invisible wires. He lifted the snifter to his nostrils and inhaled. "Good stuff, Charlie. The best. Otard Dupuy '78."

Charlie had never been tireder in his life. He sipped the fiery liquor and watched Bender swell before his eyes. "Yes, very good," he murmured, and attempted a smile.

"Yes, well," Bender boomed, leaping to his feet and pacing up and down the length of the room, alternately sniffing at his drink and pulling at the ends of his beard, "I'm pleased that you like it. After all, your patron—or should I say patroness?—is paying for it, the whole kit and caboodle . . . and by the way, you've got the check, I presume?" He paused now, caught in the midst of a gigantic stride, to give his full attention to the framing of the question—and to its answer. "And the cash?"

All of a sudden, Charlie came to life, fully alert for the first time since he'd left the train. He heard the faint whisper of a cart moving past the door, the gurgle of a distant toilet, a murmur of voices. *The check. The cash.* Bender didn't care about him, didn't care about Per-Fo, didn't care about anyone or anything—all he cared about was Mrs. Hookstratten's money. He'd already had the first thousand of it, a check Mrs. Hookstratten had written and signed over in her own parlor on a glorious sunstruck October afternoon not five weeks ago—and where was that money? Tied up in Otard Dupuy and Havana cigars? Charlie wanted to ask, to press the issue, but it was late, he was exhausted, and he didn't know where to begin. "Listen, Goodloe—"

" 'Good,' Charlie. Just call me 'Good,' for short. Let my enemies call me 'Goodloe'—or 'Mr. Bender.' "

"I, uh, just wondered—about the factory. And the paper for the cartons. You wrote that you were making progress . . . ?"

"Well, we've had a problem there." Bender was pacing again, shooting his cuffs, toying with the heavy signet ring he wore on his right index finger. "We had the old Malta-Vita plant all tied up, two big flight ovens included, good as new—"

"Malta-Vita? You mean they're out of business?" Charlie felt a chill go through him.

"Pffffft." Bender waved a hand in the air, as if shooing away a fly. "They've been gone nearly four years, Charlie. Undercapitalized, over-paid, and the product wasn't worth a blue damn. Wheat flakes. Ha! The money's in corn, Charlie, that's where it is. Look at Kellogg—now *he* knows his cereal."

"But—but I was offered stock in it just tonight. I barely got off the train and this gang of ragtag kids was all over me as if I was some kind of mark or something."

Bender drained his cognac and turned his back to pour another. "You're thinking of Vita-Malta, Charlie, Vita-Malta. They just started up in the old Map-L Flakes factory out on the Marshall Road, oh, seven, eight months ago." He swung round, the snifter dwarfed in his big meaty hand, and pointed a rhetorical finger. "And they're shipping six carloads a *day* out of here now, Charlie. *Six carloads a day.*"

Charlie's mind floated away on the wonder of it: six carloads a day. That was good news. The best news he'd had since he dropped down off the train like a stone into the most hellish night of his life. If Vita-Malta could do it, so could Per-Fo. Charlie was grinning—he couldn't help himself. "So what sort of problem did you run into? With the factory, I mean?"

Bender's laugh shook the room. "Worried, Charlie? You look worried. You do. Trust me. Trust Goodloe H. Bender to steer you right—and your Mrs. Hookstratten, too. Don't I know this business? Don't I?" He perched himself on the arm of the sofa again, took a brief pull at the snifter. "It's nothing," he said. "The son of a bitch that's got title to the place wants too much for it now he sees somebody's interested, and I was running short and didn't really have the spondulics to put down, if you know what I mean—"

"Running short?" The fear was back. Charlie saw the future open up before him like a black hole. Suddenly he was on his feet. "You can't mean you've—?" He couldn't get the words out; they choked him, stuck in his throat. "You mean you *spent* it all, the whole of our start-up money? Already?"

Bender's face went rigid. "I don't like your tone, Charlie. I don't like it at all." He jerked his chin truculently, lifting three stout fingers to his throat to adjust his bow tie. Charlie fixated on that bow tie—it was bright yellow, made of silk, and it clung to Bender's collar like a mounted butterfly. "Are you questioning my integrity? If you are, you're in trouble, my friend. Deep trouble. No man questions the integrity of Goodloe H. Bender. No man."

Charlie looked away. He was tired, that was all. Tired.

"Listen, Charlie. You don't just snap your fingers and start up a business like Per-Fo overnight." Bender's tone was softer now, each syllable a fluffed little feather pillow tucked under Charlie's weary head. He was soothing, reassuring, the voice of reason and conciliation. "It takes capital, Charlie. Money to grease the wheels. You see those gentlemen down there tonight? Well, we played a friendly little game of cards—that's how they see it, anyway. But to my mind, it's business. Stellrecht owns eight paper mills in this state—eight of them—and Bookbinder used to be C. W. Post's chief engineer before Vim lured him away. Need I say more?

"And, yes, I know you're feeling put upon because I wasn't there to greet you and because I can't show you through the brand-spanking-new Per-Fo factory with its scores of tidy workers and the wainscoted office for its President-in-Chief with the little brass nameplate on the door, and I know I've stuck you out there in a dreary boarding house while I'm curled up here in the lap of luxury, but you've got to have business sense." He paused to put some gravel in his voice. "Who do you think in this town is going to give us the time of day if I don't stay in the best hotel they've got and put on a show for them? You ever think of that?"

Charlie hadn't thought of it. He fell back into the sofa and studied the carpet. He felt cheap, felt like a turncoat, a carper and a caviler, the weak cog, a negative thinker in a positive enterprise. He was ashamed of himself.

Bender leaned over him and wrapped an arm round his shoulder. "Now, Charlie, I asked you a question: You did bring the money, didn't you?"

❖   ❖   ❖

Later, much later—so late the streetcars had long since stopped running and the hack drivers and their nags were peacefully ruminating in bed and stable, respectively—Charlie Ossining staggered up the stairs at Mrs. Eyvindsdottir's, fumbled into his room and threw himself on the bed. Woozy with Bender's brandy, chilled to the marrow, stiff and aching in the long muscles of his legs from his cumulative hike of sixty blocks, he lay there facedown on the mattress, too exhausted even to remove his overcoat. For a moment he thought he was back on the train again, the bed swaying beneath him, the sound of the phantom rails ticking in his ears, and then he was home, in the gatehouse at Mrs. Hookstratten's, surrounded by his boyhood things and the familiar polished maple posts of his bedroom furniture. Sleep came like an avalanche.

At some point in the night—ten minutes later, an hour, two?—he woke in the chill darkness to the fruity rasping sound of a cough, *hack, hack, hack,* and for a moment he didn't know where he was. Instinctively, he clutched at his wallet: *Mrs. Hookstratten's money.* But then he remembered. He was at Mrs. Eyvindsdottir's rooming house in Battle Creek, in the middle of the first night of his new life, the life that would make him a millionaire and the equal of anybody, and that was Mr. Bagwell coughing his guts out on the other side of the partition, and it was so cold that the water in his washbasin was no longer water but a solid brick of ice. The money was safe. Three thousand eight hundred forty-three dollars and fifteen cents, minus the five dollars Bender had given him for living expenses, was finally beyond the reach of accident, theft or loss, nestled in the two-ton safe at the Post Tavern Hotel. It was a relief to be rid of it, and a relief finally to be here, at the very start of something, something big.

But the cold spoke to him—he might just as well have been laid out in his tomb for all the heat of the place—and he shrugged out of his clothes and under the bedcovers, pulling the comforter up over his head to take advantage of the sole heat source: his own breath. As he lay there shivering, shifting about in the bed and alive to every nuance of Bagwell's terminally irritating cough, he couldn't seem to get comfortable. Even after he'd warmed up enough to stop shivering for minutes at a time and Bagwell's coughs had turned to ragged intermittent snores, Charlie couldn't seem to get back to sleep. It was the mattress. It seemed to be filled with corncobs—or, no, some sort of paper stuffing, newsprint or ticker tape. He tried his left side, his right, his back, his stomach, tried the fetal position, the crouch, the spread-eagle. Nothing worked. He lay there in the dark, exasperated, as tired as any man could be. Finally, annoyed out of all patience, he lurched up in bed, fumbled for a match and lit the wick of the kerosene lamp.

The room bloomed with light. Shadows lurked in the corners. There were cracks in the plaster and the wallpaper was faded. Bagwell ripped through logs on the other side of the wall. With a curse, Charlie sprang from the bed and began a vigorous rearrangement of the mattress, lifting it off the frame and working the ticking till it undulated like waves at sea. But still the stuffing wouldn't settle—it kept bunching up like a sack of mail. Puzzled, furious, confounded—not to mention half inebriated still—he took his penknife to the seam at the base of the mattress, loosening the threads with the idea of inserting an arm and rearranging the stuffing.

Ah, yes: it was paper, all right. Paper. He seized a fistful of it in disgust and pulled it through the rent in the ticking.

A nasty little surprise awaited him, the last in a string that stretched back to the moment he'd stepped down off the train. This wasn't merely paper. No, it was very high quality paper, almost as supple as a banknote and embossed with the rich blue-green figure of a sheaf of wheat. Across the nexus of the bound stalks, printed in bold black characters, was this legend:

ONE SHARE, PREFERRED STOCK
THE MALTA-VITA BREAKFAST FOOD CO., LTD.
BATTLE CREEK, MICHIGAN

Chapter 7

Symptomitis

❀

After the ceiling came toppling down and the floor fell out from under him, Will Lightbody found himself back out in the corridor under the watchful and distinctly disapproving gaze of Mrs. Stover. Eleanor had ducked his embrace in the middle of that quietly seething dining room—and rightly so: what had he been thinking?—and then escorted him all the way up the central aisle, beneath the hortatory banner and through the Grecian portals of the pompous, overblown entrance. She stood before him now, her lips drawn so tight they seemed to be segmented, each little pursed line a division in itself. She was angry. As angry as he'd ever seen her.

"I just won't have this, Will," she said, biting off each word cleanly and then spitting it out again. Her pupils were shrunk to pinpricks and a petulant little furrow was drawn neatly between her eyebrows.

A moment ago, in the dining room, overcome by gastric distress and emotional confusion, he'd seemed to be on the verge of blacking out. It never occurred to him that a diet of unbuttered toast and artesian water might not exactly meet the full range of his nutritional needs, or that he was three-quarters starved and fully emaciated and the light-headedness and peristaltic agony he experienced might be linked to inanition, pure and simple. No: it had to be more complicated than that. This was the Progressive Era, after all, and "reform" was the catchword of the day. Will was sick because his way of life was sick. He would become well when he reformed his eating habits and submitted himself to the regimen prescribed by Dr. John Harvey Kellogg and the high muckamucks of health. Or so they told him.

At any rate, Eleanor did not fall into his arms, a familiar wooziness stole over him, and he felt his eyes rush up into the cover of his upper lids. Somehow, Mrs. Stover was there, short but strong of shoulder and capacious of bosom, and then one of her equally buxom nutritional girls—a strapping girl, corn-flake-fed and yogurt-toned—and finally, a male attendant. The scene was abbreviated, and Will, tenderly supported in the arms of strangers and shepherded by his wife, escaped the dining room. Now, in the relative privacy of the corridor, Eleanor wanted an apology. She wanted contrition, promises, protestations and expostulations; she wanted to drive the first post of the fence that would keep them apart.

The words were on his lips—*I'm sorry*—but he couldn't say them. The more he thought about it, and the more he looked into the furious shrinking hard green nuggets of her eyes, the more he felt his own innocence. All he'd wanted was a little reassurance. An embrace from his own wife. He was a sick man and he was new to all of this and it overwhelmed him. Perhaps he'd chosen the wrong place, perhaps such an embrace was a thing to be indulged behind closed doors and not in the midst of a dutifully masticating assembly, but still, shouldn't she be the least bit aware of his frame of mind, of his needs? "I don't like this place, Eleanor," he said finally. "I haven't been here a full day yet and I've been subjected to all kinds of indignities, from your Dr. Kellogg sticking his fingers in my mouth to a Nurse Bloethal plying the other end of me with her tubes and bottles and I don't know what-all—" He stopped there, short of mentioning Nurse Graves. Nurse Graves, and what had happened between them in the privacy of his own bathroom, was something he knew instinctively he should keep to himself.

Eleanor held her ground. Mrs. Stover, just out of earshot, seemed poised to rush to her aid. "Don't you spoil it for me, Will Lightbody," she warned, her voice dropping to a fiery whisper. "Don't you start in with your self-pitying sermons and your, your—" She seemed stricken all of a sudden. Her eyes had dilated, opened up like morning flowers, and there were tears in them. Tears.

Will felt ashamed of himself. He felt like a barbarian, an apostate— and yet he couldn't help deriving a small shred of satisfaction from the stance he was taking, though he couldn't have said why.

Eleanor's handkerchief had appeared. She dabbed at her eyes as a pair of white-clad attendants hurried down the hall and the fattest woman Will had ever seen staggered past them and into the dining room. He'd seen a woman nearly as fat once—at the Ringling Bros. Circus—and he was thinking about that, lost in a fantasy of bearded women, roaring cats and dancing pachyderms, when Eleanor, her voice soft and hesitant, spoke again. "I don't know how to make you understand. It's just that this is the only place where I think I'm truly happy anymore . . . and after the baby . . . I just don't know, Will. If I ever have a hope of getting well again, it'll be here, among my friends and mentors. This is where I've learned to live the right way, Will, the *only* way." She paused, holding him with her eyes. "And look at yourself. This is the place for you, too, Will, the only place I know of."

He heard the conciliation in her tone, heard the plea, but he couldn't help himself. "Outside the pages of the Sears Roebuck catalogue, you mean. And who was that at breakfast you were so concerned about? Dr. Linniman, wasn't it? *Frank?* And do the physicians dine with their patients now—is that part of the program?"

"I won't discuss this with you. I won't." Her eyes were sharp again, metallic, the flashing iridescent green of a pair of hovering dragonflies. "Dr. Frank Linniman happens to be one of this country's great healers, schooled at the elbow of Dr. Kellogg himself, and he's done more good for me than anyone in this world . . . since Mother died, anyway. If it wasn't for him, I don't think I'd have the strength to get out of bed in the morning." She looked off down the corridor. "He was here for me when I lost my daughter, the only one."

"The only one?" Will couldn't believe what he was hearing. "I was in Peterskill, eating my stomach up with worry and waiting for your telegram. What did you expect me to do—appear at your bedside like the Ghost of Christmas Past? It was you who told me to stay away."

"No, no, no," she said, her voice rising in inflection as she put her hands up to cover her ears. Mrs. Stover made a feint toward them but Will leveled a murderous look on her and she checked herself. "I won't argue, Will, I can't—I'm a sick woman."

"I'm a sick man."

"I'm sicker."

"Than me? You've got to be joking."

"I *am* sicker. Far sicker. You know that."

"I don't know it. It's always 'me, me, me'—how do you think *I* feel?"

But Will didn't get his answer. Eleanor turned her back on him. Just swung around and stalked up the hallway, his question—his pathetic, self-justifying cri de coeur of a question—hanging unanswered in the air. He watched her shoulders retreating from him, watched her angry stride and the purposeful rise and fall of her feet, watched her until she rounded the corner and disappeared.

"Mr. Lightbody?"

A voice spoke at his shoulder, a familiar voice, mellifluous, breathy and sweet. The voice of Nurse Graves. Will turned to her in a daze.

She looked good, fresh-spanked with health and color, the glow of an uncomplicated morning settling into her eyes and the parabola of her smiling lips. This wasn't the Battle Creek Sanitarium smile; this was genuine, artless, sincere; this was the smile of resurrection and salvation. Nurse Bloethal vanished from his mind. Dr. Linniman evaporated. Even Eleanor receded into the background. Will felt his own big-toothed smile blazing back at her and he fought to control the sudden tic in his left cheek. "Nurse Graves," he said, dipping his head, "good morning to you."

"Good morning," she returned, holding her smile and looking him candidly in the eye. It was a look that surprised him, made him feel naked.

Sick as he was, Will couldn't help wondering what that look was all about. It expressed a whole lot more than a cool, detached, nursely concern, didn't it? Or was he fooling himself? He remembered the touch of her as she put him to bed, the heat of her skin against his, and he stole a glance at her little feet in their white official shoes, saw how the thin cotton skirt clung to her hips and flat young abdomen. Oysters. What was wrong with oysters?

"Well," she said, "are you ready?"

"Ready?"

Was that a giggle that escaped her? No, of course not. But she showed him her gums, smiling so tightly he was afraid she might begin to ooze something sticky and sweet. "Are you being facetious with me, Mr. Lightbody?"

"Oh, no," Will insisted, "not at all." He was grinning, too.

She cocked her head to one side, as if to get a better look at him, and she let out a sigh. "It's time for your examination—or have you forgotten already?"

Ten minutes later, after exchanging banalities with the elevator man and taking advantage of the close confines of the compartment to inhale the heady, faintly antiseptic aroma of Nurse Graves's pinned-up hair, Will found himself seated in a back-gouging physiologic chair in the temperature-controlled office of Dr. Frank Linniman. The office was located on the first floor, in the Neurological Department, and its windows gave onto the frozen lawn of the deer park Dr. Kellogg had provided for the edification of his patients. (The power of suggestion: What decent, rational man or woman could continue to crave meat in the face of these gentle, sleek, blameless creatures?) Will attempted to lean back in the chair, but it had been designed by Dr. Kellogg to discourage lounging—lounging was the first step on the road to deleterious posture and bankrupt health. The chair was a sort of torture device, actually, its hard oaken slats bellying out to push the sitter's lower spine into his rib cage and force his shoulders back as if he were strapped to a barrel.

Will writhed in the chair, consulted his pocket watch, studied the phrenological charts on the walls and the row of yellowed skulls that lined the upper shelf of the bookcase in grim testimony to the fate of those who turned their backs on the principles of biologic living. And where was Dr. Linniman? Lingering over his bran and Meltose, no doubt, dispensing advice, roaming the dining room to insinuate himself beside married women and coach them in the intimate details of salivation, mastication and the proper use of the throat muscles. And what was that smell? Will couldn't pin it down, but the office seemed saturated with some musty essence, as if it were the repository of thousand-year-old eggs from China or mold scraped from the recesses of an Egyptian sarcophagus. He felt his stomach turn.

"Ah! Mr. Lightbody!" Frank Linniman suddenly appeared from behind a paneled door at the rear of the office, exploding into the room as if he'd just burst through the wall. Two strides brought him up to where Will sat immobilized on the rack of the physiologic chair. Dr. Linniman hovered over the chair a moment, beaming, bright, rippling with vegetarian energy and the brawn of high animal spirits, and then he eased himself down familiarly on the corner of his desk and focused his rinsed-out eyes on his patient. "And how are we this morning? Slept well? Kept some food down?"

Will heard the hollow boom of his own voice tolling in reply. He was very well, thank you. Or, no: what was he saying? He was unwell. Ill. Desperately ill. He'd slept, yes—for the first time in three weeks— and he'd eaten a bite of toast. It was his stomach, that was the problem.

Dr. Linniman absorbed this information without comment. He shifted his left buttock on the edge of the desk and clasped his knee with two meaty hands, stretching himself like an animal in its cage. On the wall behind him, opposite the bookcase with its row of antique skulls, was an arrangement of photographs Will had somehow, to this moment, overlooked. Each of them featured Dr. Frank Linniman in an athletic pose: with tennis racket, putter, baseball bat and lacrosse stick; astride a horse, clinging to the end of a rope with his teeth.

Frank. Eleanor had called him Frank.

"Well, and so," Linniman suddenly cried, bouncing down from his perch in a burst of motion that startled his patient, "this is the big day, eh? The day we turn your life around. Examination time."

For the next half-hour Will sat there on the unforgiving chair and allowed himself to be poked, prodded, pinched, pushed and tapped while Dr. Linniman scribbled in a notepad and put detailed questions to him regarding his bodily functions, history and genealogy. Will answered as patiently as he could, but he resented it. He hated physicals. They left him feeling inadequate, incompetent, violated. Or, worse yet, moribund. Dr. Brillinger had gone through the same routine, pushing and poking at him in his own bedroom in Peterskill, peering into his ears and down his throat, rapping his knees, lifting his arm and letting it drop again—only to confess himself stumped. He reminded Will that he was just a humble general practitioner and didn't fully appreciate the ins and outs of the antitoxic diet, naturopathy, heliotherapy, the sinusoidal current and all the rest of the newest advances in medical science. What Will needed, he felt, and it was the merest coincidence that Eleanor concurred wholeheartedly with his prescription, was an extended stay at one of the great sanitoria. There he could be examined by the best and ablest men of the time. There he could get answers.

Yes. And here he was, at the great, all-heralded and overpriced Battle Creek Sanitarium, and all he'd gotten so far was questions. How long? How often? What color? When? And how does this feel? This? Your father? Mother? Grandparents? Great-grandparents? Consumption? Smallpox? Yellow fever?

Will did the best he could. For half an hour he sat there answering this objectionable man's indelicate questions, his stomach burning, joints aching, eyeballs aflame, until he could take it no longer. He cut Frank Linniman off in the middle of a question concerning the color and texture of his last stool. "Enough questions," Will barked. "What's wrong with me?"

Dr. Linniman looked offended. His eyebrows—so pale as to be almost invisible—lifted in surprise. "Mr. Lightbody," he began, dropping his eyes to the notepad a moment before coming back at him with a professionally admonitory stare, "I'm in no position to make a diagnosis at this juncture. This is just the beginning. Why, we'll need blood tests and count, urine and fecal analysis, you've got to go to the X-Ray Fluoroscopic Room, the Colon Department, we've got to have specialists examine your teeth, eyes, tonsils and tongue, we need to see how much acetone you're exhaling and what your intestinal fluids look like. We won't have the full picture until this evening, at the earliest." He paused, squared his jaw, tugged at his tie. "I could make an educated guess, of course, judging from the color of your skin, the condition of your tongue, your general puniness and malaise. . . ."

That sinking, doomed feeling came over Will again, but he fought it. Puniness? Malaise? Who was this self-serving, conceited, pompous, lantern-jawed hyena to be pronouncing judgment on him?

"Actually," Linniman went on, lecturing now, "we see any number of cases like yours—but I wouldn't want to jump to conclusions. Nervous exhaustion. Coffee Neuralgia. Hyperhydrochloria. Autointoxication, certainly. But the Chief has already made that diagnosis." He nodded his blond head sagely, smacked his lips, gently closed the notebook. "We'll do the tests. You never know what might turn up."

Will was going under, drowning, spinning down the drain of a vast sink of doom. "What about my wife?" he snarled, coming up out of the chair suddenly, fighting it with everything he had in him. "What about Eleanor?"

❖   ❖   ❖

Nurse Graves was waiting for him in the hallway. The tile dully gleamed, patients drifted by in wheelchairs, a throng of nurses and attendants shouldered their way along the corridor. *Coffee Neuralgia. Hyperhydrochloria. Autointoxication.* It was medical jargon, voodoo, all but meaningless, and he wouldn't let it affect him. So what if he drank three or four cups of coffee a day—was it hemlock? Strychnine? Still, as Nurse Graves smiled and chattered and led him up the hallway to the X-Ray Fluoroscopic Room, Will couldn't seem to shake the spell of Frank Linniman's pronouncements: the tests were barely under way and already there was a name—there were *names*—for what was wrong with him.

His stomach had begun to groan and he couldn't seem to stop his legs from jittering as Nurse Graves ushered him into a sedate waiting room with framed landscapes on the walls and Turkish carpets underfoot. He stood there awkwardly in the center of the room as Nurse Graves handed his charts to a brisk little doctor with an Oriental slant to his eyes, center-parted hair and a monocle, and he couldn't help feeling a small stab of disappointment when she left him with a whispered promise to return in twenty-five minutes. What did he expect? Will asked himself as he chose a seat in the corner beneath one of the ubiquitous palms—she had better things to do than sit and hold his hand all day. She must have other patients, certainly; a family; time off for breakfast, dinner, good behavior; she must have a life of her own outside these healing walls.

Four men and two women shared the waiting room with him, each of them, like him, seated in one of the Chief's torturous chairs. They were surprisingly young—thirties and forties, anyway—and they looked as healthy as anyone you'd see on the street. Outwardly, that is. Who knew what miseries racked their insides or what pernicious shadows would show up on the fluorescent screen in the back room? After a brief struggle, Will gave up any pretense of making himself comfortable—anything would have been better than that chair: stretching out supine on the floor, dangling from the ceiling in a sling, being keelhauled by picaroons off the Barbary Coast—and he hunched awkwardly over his knees, skimming the Battle Creek *Morning Enquirer* for news of calvings and farm accidents.

Ten minutes faded from his life before he exchanged the *Enquirer* for a copy of Dr. Kellogg's house organ, *The Battle Creek Idea*. There on the front page, sandwiched between an article extolling the virtues of the San by a grizzled robber baron from San Francisco and a chatty piece on the Contessa Spalancare's Florentine villa, was a box listing the new arrivals. His and Eleanor's names leapt out at him from the page, given form and moment in printer's ink: *Mr. and Mrs. William Fitzroy Lightbody, of Peterskill, New York*. He crossed his legs, grunted. They might have been in separate rooms on separate floors, but at least they were still linked here, in black and white, in the great Doctor's newsletter.

An attendant came to the door of the inner sanctum and called out a name—"Mrs. Pratt?"—and one of the women rose nimbly from her seat and crossed the room. Will watched her furtively. She couldn't have been more than thirty, well dressed, no sign of a limp, humpback, bloated joints, pockmarks or ulcers, and she'd already mastered the Battle Creek carriage, so far as he could see—her squared shoulders and concave spine could have been used as a mold for the physiologic chair. And what was wrong with her? Something internal, he supposed, something hidden beneath the folds of her clothing . . . and the thought of that, her clothing and what lay beneath it, stirred him till he felt his penis stiffen.

God, he was randy. And how could that be, a man in his condition? First it was Miss Muntz, then Nurse Graves, and now this total stranger, this poor afflicted woman, and here he was having licentious thoughts about her, here he was sitting in the waiting room of the X-Ray Fluoroscopic Room of the Battle Creek Sanitarium with an erection. He thought of the weeds the gardener cut every summer at the Peterskill house—severed, desiccated, their vital juices gone and the best of them culled, used up, discarded, so much trash to be burned, and still they managed to burst into seed, white fluff floating on the breeze till it looked like an August snowstorm. Maybe that's what it was. Maybe he was dying and his body was desperately trying to disperse its seed, the organism mad to procreate and pass on its lineaments before it was too late, without a thought for the bonds of matrimony or the appropriateness of the receptacle. It was downright Darwinian. Deny him his daughter and the hoary voices of his ancestors cry out in priapic urgency; threaten him with extinction, with a childless grave, and he goes stiff in his pants at the mere sight of a woman. . . . He realized in that moment he was staring, and he dropped his eyes to the newsletter. *Mr. and Mrs. William Fitzroy Lightbody:* where was Eleanor when he needed her?

"Mr. Lightbody?" The attendant stood at the door, a little man, balding, sallow, no healthier-looking than anyone else in the room, but with the Battle Creek Sanitarium smile stamped on his face as surely as if he'd come off an assembly line. "Will you step this way, please?"

The remainder of the morning gave testimony to the advanced estate of the diagnostic sciences. Will stood before the X-ray machine and breathed in and out for the Oriental doctor—a Dr. Tomoda, the first Japanese Will had ever seen in the flesh—and his sallow, shrunken assistant. "You are not breathe too deep much," Dr. Tomoda informed him, squinting severely behind the glittering disc of his monocle. "Must fill lung." To demonstrate, he had the attendant stand before the machine and huff and puff mightily so that Will could watch the glowing bones of his rib cage swell and shrink on the fluoroscopic screen as his lungs took on their burden of air and expelled it again. It was amazing, really, like a magic trick, as if tiny rods of light had been inserted in the man's skeleton. "This," Dr. Tomoda solemnly intoned, "is the way how you must seize the air with your lung." The attendant, looking enervated—no doubt from the stress of having his bones illuminated for the edification of every shallow-breathing patient who came along —smiled weakly.

Will's next stop was the Ear, Nose and Throat Department, where a doctor with a bristling, linty beard carefully peered into Will's cranial cavities while delivering a running monologue reprising each stroke of each hole of golf he'd played the previous summer. Will drifted off in reverie to a description of a particularly knotty par three with a dogleg to the right, thinking back to his boyhood, when examinations were as clear-cut as right and wrong, when he was as healthy and lively as a cricket and the answer was a sum, a verb tense, a date or a place. But this exam was different. The answers were recondite, beyond his apprehension or control; they were coursing through his veins, hidden in his bones, his organs, seething in his gut. There was no right or wrong—only good news or bad.

After twenty minutes or so, the ear, nose and throat man put down his instruments. Will learned, for the third time since he'd reached the San, that his tongue was coated (though with what and how it affected his health remained a mystery), and as the doctor showed him to the door the man advised him to eat right and take up some form of outdoor exercise—a sport, perhaps, one that might involve some walking and perhaps the swinging of clubs and irons.

Nurse Graves led him next to the Dynamometer Room, where he waited his turn on one of several devices meant to gauge muscular capacity. A pair of cheerful, bulging young men in tights instructed Will to tug on various levers, bend over, stand on one leg, fasten leather straps to his brow, elbow, abdomen and knee, and generally fight against the resistance provided by the steely immovable apparatus. His efforts were measured on a dial set in a glass housing, and though Will was assured that the device had been created by the almighty Chief for precise and vital diagnostic purposes, the whole operation bore a suspicious resemblance to the sledge hammer and gong at the county fair.

As the morning wore on, Will gave blood, endured an unpleasant introduction to both the gastroscope and rectoscope, breathed into a vial of clear liquid to determine the amount of acetone in his breath and walked a treadmill like a blinded horse while a fussy little doctor with a huge watch auscultated his chest and scribbled notations on a printed form bearing the imprimatur of John Harvey Kellogg. At one o'clock, Nurse Graves left him in the care of a frigidly smiling Mrs. Stover at the entrance to the dining room, and Will sat again with Hart-Jones, Miss Muntz et al., mournfully spooning up a bite or two of the Rice à la Carolina the nutritional girls forced on him, and nibbling at a slice of Graham bread, toasted. If Eleanor was present, he didn't see her, though after his bout with the Universal Dynamometer, he really didn't have the strength to turn his head and look.

But the good Dr. Kellogg, in his wisdom and benevolence, saw the need for rest, and had already prescribed, on this day of relentless examination, an hour's nap. That sounded fine to Will—but there was a catch. The nap was to be conducted outside, on the veranda, in the bracing atmosphere of a sunless and hellishly cold November afternoon. And why? Because Dr. Kellogg believed in the curative powers of nature and couldn't overemphasize the necessity of breathing the air of the great outdoors, summer and winter alike. Nurse Graves provided Will with a hot-water bag, and then, with the help of a male attendant— was that Ralph?—swaddled him so tightly and in so many layers of woolen blankets he thought the weight would crush him, placed a nightcap on his head and wheeled him out onto the veranda, where he was lifted into an Adirondack chair and positioned so that he was facing the sun—or, rather, the spot in the firmament the sun might have occupied if it hadn't gone south for the winter.

Will gazed up at the leaden sky. A dull gray bird hurled itself across the horizon. The arctic air stiffened the little hairs lining Will's thoroughly examined nostrils, shocked his lungs, brought a distant but palpable ache to the thin layer of flesh that clung to his cheekbones. On either side of him, as far as he could see, stretched a phalanx of similarly cocooned patients, as alike as infants in swaddling clothes. He wondered if they felt as ridiculous as he did, a grown man, a rational adult, lying out on a flagstone veranda in a Michigan winter as if he were on a beach in the south of France. Below him, on the yellowed, rock-hard lawn, a pair of the Doctor's deer nosed at a bale of hay. Despite himself, Will began to feel drowsy.

It was then that he became aware of a small disembodied voice speaking to him from out of the gray void. "Hello," the voice piped, "lovely afternoon, isn't it?"

It wasn't easy, bound up in those blankets, but with an effort Will managed to wrench his neck round and focus on the figure to his right. He discovered a nightcap identical to his own, a protruding, deeply rutted nose and a pair of purplish eyelids, unfurled. "Over here," the voice called, appending a giggle, "to your left."

Will brought his head round again, a sudden glacial blast attacking his exposed chin and sending icy jets down his collar, and found himself staring into the yellowish broth of Miss Muntz's eyes. At least he presumed that those eyes belonged to Miss Muntz—he'd never experienced eyes of quite that color before, like chicken soup after it's thickened on the stove overnight, and they were, after all, framing a decidedly greenish nose. "Miss Muntz?" he ventured.

She responded with a second, more prolonged giggle. "Don't you find this cozy?" she asked, after a pause, her voice thin, the breath streaming from her bruised-looking lips and chartreuse nostrils.

Cozy? His idea of cozy was a seat in the inglenook of a tavern, a plate of meat and potatoes and a glass of ale before him, and the stomach to digest it with. But he didn't want to be uncivil, and he remembered the shape and bearing of Miss Muntz, for all her greenish cast, and the look she'd given him in the corridor the night before. *Her room is only two doors down*, he thought, and that sexual tingle raced through him again. "Yes," he said finally, regretting the fact that Mrs. Stover had twice now seated him at the far end of the table from Miss Muntz and that Hart-Jones, the braying ass, had so dominated the prandial conversation that Will hadn't been able to speak two words to her.

Miss Muntz's face seemed suddenly ecstatic, her eyes burning, a secret smile pressed to her lips, and she let out a sigh of cosmic contentment as she threw back her head and let her gaze roam over the sky, the naked trees, the deer on the lawn below them. After a moment, during which a stiff breeze off the icy black waters of Lake Michigan shook the veranda and sent a scrap of paper rocketing over the wall, she murmured, "Aren't they darling?"

"The deer?"

"Yes. So graceful, so much a part of the world of nature we insist on brutalizing with our guns and nets and fences, our roads and brick houses, so . . . so *right.*"

Will agreed with her, wholeheartedly, though he couldn't help seeing them as agents of the Chief's propaganda, and the very thought of a venison steak, streaming juices and served up with a sprinkle of thyme and pan-broiled carrots and onions, started him salivating. "Darling, yes they are," he heard himself answer, but now that they'd broken discursive ground, he couldn't keep his thoughts from drifting toward the morbid: What was wrong with her? What was greensickness, exactly? Was it fatal? Catching? He knew they weren't supposed to discuss symptoms—the Chief had strictures against it, negative thinking and all that—but his curiosity got the better of him. He cleared his throat and took a breath so bracing he could feel it all the way down to the tip of his tailbone. "Uh, Miss Muntz," he began, "if you don't mind my asking, just out of curiosity, I was wondering what a young girl like you would, uh, require from an institution like this—I mean, I hope I'm not being rude, but what's ailing you, anyway?"

There was a moment of silence. Miss Muntz turned to him finally, and he saw that the ecstasy had gone from her face, sopped up in her greenish pores like ink in a fountain pen. "We're not supposed to discuss symptoms, you know, though I forgive you because you're new. And because I like your eyes. And your nose."

This information gave him a little frisson: she liked his eyes and nose. He was a married man, of course, and, what's more, a married man deeply in love with his wife, and no woman's blandishments could really touch him . . . but still, there it was, a little thrill of pleasure.

"Dr. Kellogg calls it 'symptomitis.' The last thing he wants is for his patients to sit around like a bunch of old hens, trading complaints."

"True enough. But because you like my eyes and nose, and because,

Miss Muntz, though I've just got to know you, I have to confess I'm very concerned—without you at the table I'd be at the mercy of Mrs. Tindermarsh and that blathering Englishman—well, not to be too forward, but won't you put my fears to rest? It's not anything"—had he gone too far?—"not anything too grave, is it?" Will could feel the cold air numbing his gums as he gave her his best smile—suddenly it had become vitally important, crucial, that she tell him. They were two suffering confused put-upon souls trading confidences, that was all—and where was the harm in that? "It's my stomach," Will offered. "That's why I'm here. I can't eat, can't sleep. It feels like there's a hundred little coal miners in there having a torchlight parade."

A pretty viridescent hand had worked itself out of the cocoon of Miss Muntz's blankets. She put it to her lips to suppress yet another giggle—was the simile so amusing? Or his suffering? Will reddened—he'd tried to be sincere with her, hadn't he?

"I have greensickness," she announced suddenly, and looked away. "It's an anemia. 'Chlorosis' is the official name for it. Dr. Kellogg says I'm a very severe case, but his prognosis is for full recovery—if I stay on the antitoxic diet, of course."

"God," Will said, "don't you hate that food? I mean, corn pulp and Protose fillets?"

Miss Muntz gave a little sniff. "If it's going to make me well again, I'll eat anything. Besides, I've learned that it was meat that was poisoning me all these years. My mother is absolutely—well, with her it's salt pork for breakfast, beefsteak for dinner and a chicken, kidneys, chops or the like for luncheon. Little wonder I'm anemic."

Will was considering this, the specter of a loving mother unwittingly poisoning her own flesh and blood, when Nurse Graves appeared to change his hot-water bag and see how he was doing. "Get your rest now," she admonished in quick little puffs of breath as she slipped the hot rubber reservoir down under the blankets, "you've got your afternoon enema at two-thirty, and then it's off to the Colon Department, the Shadowgram Room and the Anthropometric Department. And then"—she held back a moment, as if announcing a visit with the crowned heads of Europe—"the Chief will see you."

Chapter 8

Changing
the
Flora

❀

I t was late in the afternoon, the windows gone opaque with the dark glue of night, a reflective calm settling over the corridors of the San as patients and attendants alike made preparations for the evening meal—the hour when, in another, happier venue, people would be gathering for cocktails. Will sat alone on a bench in the Palm Garden, breathing in the oppressive humidity and tropical funk of the place and listening to the Battle Creek Sanitarium String Quartet (four stiff-backed gentlemen sporting symmetrically pointed beards) dutifully sawing its way through something by Schumann. Or at least he thought it was Schumann. There was that fluid sadness, that precise Teutonic rush of joy. Schumann. Sure. He looked round him and yawned. He was exhausted, weak and profoundly bored, sitting there amongst the old ladies in their wheelchairs like the invalid he'd become, checking his watch, suppressing a ripple of gas as the three bites of Rice à la Carolina came back to haunt him. Where was she? What was keeping her?

Just when he'd given up, when he'd closed his eyes on the Adagio and let his thoughts drift over the cobbled hilly sunstruck streets of Peterskill to a distant Fourth of July parade, Eleanor on his arm, lunch in a hamper, the band striking up a foot-thumping Sousa march, he felt a touch at his elbow. It was Nurse Graves, she of the soft brown eyes and artful hands, come to fetch him off into the great Doctor's presence, where he would learn his fate, once and for all.

"You poor thing," she puffed, helping him to his feet, "you must be exhausted. It seems such a shame to interrupt your little catnap—"

"I wasn't napping," Will protested, giving her a loose-lipped grin. "I was just thinking, that's all. Meditating."

"Yes, of course," she breathed as they passed through the archway and into the lobby, her normally brisk pace attuned to the slow tread of his invalid's shuffle, "I always do my best thinking while snoring, too. And don't try to deny it—you were snoring in there. You see: one day in the San, one step in the direction of living the physiologic life, and already you're nodding off like a baby—you, who hadn't slept in over three weeks."

They were passing down the corridor to the right, now, the lights all ablaze, the odd patient returning from a last-minute blood count or colon check while physicians closed up their offices and headed home in full physiologic stride. Will couldn't help admitting the truth of what she was saying—he had slept, at least there was that. Maybe there was something to the Sanitarium system, after all—maybe, just maybe, he *would* begin to recover his health, with or without Eleanor at his side. The thought of that—of being able to stand up straight again, to walk in the woods, take an interest in life, drink a cocktail, smoke a cigarette, stuff himself like anyone else and relax on the toilet afterward—gave him a rush of hope. "Leave any man in front of that orchestra and he'll be unconscious inside of thirty seconds," Will boomed, bantering now, almost gleeful, on his way to see the healer with this angel of mercy at his arm. "If I'd only known, I would have hired them to serenade me in my parlor every night around eleven, a warm glass of milk in one hand, a bad novel in the other."

Nurse Graves's pure, cleansing laugh rang out in the hallway, infectious, bringing smiles to the faces of passing nurses and physicians and thrilling Will till he felt like the wittiest man alive, and she was still laughing as she knocked on the heavy polished oak door of Dr. Kellogg's office. Will recognized the harried overweight man who answered the door as Dr. Kellogg's amanuensis, and beyond him he saw an expansive, high-ceilinged office so brightly lit and sterile it might have been an operating theater. The only relief, aside from the radiator pipes, was provided by the unbroken band of portraits that lined the three visible walls just above the wainscoting. The effect was unsettling. Greek philosophers, celebrated vegetarians, medical heroes and captains of industry alike fixed the poor squirming patient with a stony and unforgiving gaze. These good and famous men—Lord Byron, Isaac Newton, Ben Franklin, Abe Lincoln, Plato, Joseph Lister, Sylvester Graham—all of them seemed to be staring down at him in accusation, crying out to him to give up his sinful carnivorous ways and follow the path of vegetarian righteousness.

"Mr. Lightbody?" the secretary inquired. He dabbed at his brow with a damp handkerchief as if he were staggering around in the middle of the Arabian Desert, though the temperature outside was fifteen above and the interior climate held at a steady seventy-two degrees Fahrenheit, just as the Chief ordained.

"Yes," Nurse Graves answered for him. "Mr. Lightbody is here for his five-forty-five appointment with Dr. Kellogg."

"Won't you come in, please, and have a seat?" the secretary returned, wiping his glasses now, as if his own internal climate had left them dripping with moisture. "Dr. Kellogg is expecting you."

But Will couldn't move. He stood there on the threshold, uncertain, his heart hammering at his ribs (*now, now* he would find out everything, for better or worse, and the thought paralyzed him), gaping at the big mahogany desk in the center of the room as if it were a sacrificial altar. The gleaming surface of the desk held three objects only: a lamp on one side, an inkwell on the other and, in the center, a single file, thick with lab reports. Strangely, though, Dr. Kellogg himself was nowhere to be seen—if he was in the room, he must have been hiding under the desk.

"Go ahead, Mr. Lightbody," Nurse Graves was saying, as the secretary urged him forward with a peculiar rolling motion of his pudgy hands, murmuring some excuse about the Doctor's previous appointment, when a quick excitable voice cried out at his back, "Ah! It's Mr. Lightbody, isn't it, if I'm not mistaken?"

Dr. Kellogg, all in white, bustled through the door, ducking round

Will like a child in a game of tag, a basket of fruit slung under one arm, a stack of books in the other. In a single brisk motion, he dropped the books into his secretary's nervous arms and swung round on Will and his nurse with the basket of fruit. "Nurse Graves, a piece of fruit? Mr. Lightbody? Dab?"

The basket was of woven straw, like something out of *Mother Goose*, and it was filled with apples, pears, out-of-season oranges, bananas, kumquats, tangerines and a single glowing cherry-red pomegranate. Nurse Graves selected a tangerine, neat in its ball of loose waxy orange skin, and Dab chose a banana, struggling to reach a hand forward without losing his grip on the Doctor's tomes. Will, still framed in the doorway, reached awkwardly for the pomegranate, thinking not so much of eating it as simply holding it, fondling it, anything to mollify the bustling imperious little man before him.

"But Doctor," Dab began hesitantly, "do you think . . . in light of—?"

"Of course—what am I thinking?" the Doctor cried, snatching back the basket as if the fruit were poisoned, as if he'd been offering toadstools and nightshade, as if the mere touch of it would kill. In the next moment he was at the desk, still on his feet, the basket of fruit perched out of reach on the bookcase behind him, Will's file in hand. He glanced up sharply, a quick-blooded clear-eyed little bird alert to the faintest stirring in the grass. "Forgive me, Mr. Lightbody—don't stand there as if you're afraid of me; I won't bite; come in, come in—but I've been making the rounds of the place, handing out fruit to my patients (best snack the Good Lord ever provided, antitoxic, antiscorbutic, full of roughage, the pomegranate in particular, miraculous fruit, that), and I lost my head for a minute there. No fruit for you, sir. Not yet. No, no, no, not at all. That will never do."

Will took a seat facing the desk, that curious lightness tugging at his head as if it were filled with helium, his stomach curdling in apprehension. Dab turned to fuss with the Doctor's books, inserting each into the gap reserved for it on the bookcase. Nurse Graves stood at the door, the tangerine cradled like an offering in her clasped hands, awaiting further instructions. The Doctor was pacing, munching on a glossy green-skinned apple and paging through Will's file—or what Will took to be his file. He saw that a smoked-celluloid eyeshade had appeared, as if magically, over the Doctor's brow, muting the reflective sheen of his lenses.

"Nurse Graves," the Doctor said, still pacing, head down, his voice starting up like the accelerating rumble of an automobile at the first catch of the crank, "that will be all, thank you. I've arranged for Nurse Bloethal to take over here for the rest of the evening."

Nurse Graves closed the door behind her with a soft deferential click and was gone, physiologic carriage, pretty ears, nurturing hands and all. Will felt lost suddenly, as he had when he was a boy on a shopping trip to New York and he lost hold of his mother's hand in the pitching, jostling crowd.

"All right, Mr. Lightbody," the Doctor said suddenly, fanning the file on the edge of the desk for emphasis, "I'll be frank with you: you're a very sick man. Your tests verify all the symptoms described by Dr. Combe in his masterly study of intestinal autointoxication, just as I suspected. The drawn features, sad expression, dry hair"—here Will reached reflexively for his scalp—"sunken eyes, coated tongue, emaciated chest, brittle nails . . ." The frenetic little man paused to snatch up Will's hand, inspect the nails briefly and drop it again, before continuing. "Not to mention palpitations of the heart, neurasthenic dislocation, low blood pressure, formless stools, prurigo, eczema and boils. You haven't experienced any memory loss, have you? Especially for proper names?"

Will was stunned. Boils? Neurasthenic dislocation? "Well, I—"

"Casual acquaintances, that sort of thing? Place-names, cities, states, rivers? Quick, tell me now, what's the capital of Paraguay?"

"Paraguay? Uh, that would be, uh—it's not Buenos Aires, is it?"

"Delaware? Sweden? Louisiana? What major river system divides Brazil?"

The Doctor was leaning over his desk now, a smug knowing look on his face, all his suspicions confirmed. Dab, the sweating secretary, had finished with the books and was taking notes in a leather-bound notepad, alternately writing and swiping at his forehead with his handkerchief, which had begun to bloom with ink stains. The banana the Doctor had given him was tucked carelessly in his breast pocket, bright as a boutonniere against the blackish blue of his suit. "The Amazon," Will said. "And the capital of Louisiana is, uh, New Orleans—am I right? And what else did you ask me?"

"Your wife is a wonderful woman," the Doctor said suddenly, apropos of nothing. "You're a very lucky man."

Will fidgeted in his chair, *palpitations of the heart, sunken eyes, brittle nails,* not knowing quite how to respond. Somehow, he sensed, this was not the time to bring up the question of their separate rooms and the seating arrangements in the dining hall.

"She's ill, too, I'm sorry to say, her nervous system entirely exhausted . . . but she's been pursuing biologic living with all her heart, and I'm confident she's well along the path to recovery—this is, after all, her third stay with us here. But her neurasthenia—and yours, too—is merely a symptom, an outward sign, of the deeper problem, and that is, of course, the poisoning of your own system with putrefactive, anaerobic bacteria. That's at the root of it all."

"But Doctor, how can *I* be suffering from neurasthenia?" Will protested. Did he have everything, every disease in the book? What about brain cancer? Cholera? Beriberi? "I thought—I mean, it was my impression that this was a woman's problem—"

Dr. Kellogg held up a healthy puckered white palm. "Tut, tut, Mr. Lightbody, I'm surprised at you. I am. As Begany and Grünweiss have shown, this pernicious malady strikes across the board, regardless of age or sex. Our own president suffered from it as a youth."

The image of T.R., with his stiff mustache and stern spectacles, standing over the carcass of a two-thousand-pound bison on the plains of the Wild West, leapt into Will's head. Teddy Roosevelt? The fire breather of San Juan Hill? The square-jawed, the vigorous, the manly? Trust buster and big-game hunter? Teddy, neurasthenic?

"There's no shame attached to it," the Doctor observed. "Some people are just higher keyed than others, too sensitive and thoughtful for their own good, too intellectual, poetical, too urbane and aesthetically minded—if it weren't for my own rigorous physiologic routine and the lessons of the simple life, I don't doubt that I myself would be a fellow sufferer. But enough of that." Dr. Kellogg leaned forward on the desk now, his arms rigid, the high arching moral brow of Abraham Lincoln looming behind him on the wall. "I bring up Mrs. Lightbody—Eleanor—for a reason."

Will was reeling. His throat was dry—it felt as if someone had taken a bottle brush to it and then packed it with hot sand—and the imp that dwelled in his gut poked a burning finger into the lining of his stomach. What next?

The stern little white-clad healer held Will with a stare that would have done a schoolmaster proud. "Again, to be perfectly frank with you, I must say that I bring up the subject of your wife's health because I need to emphasize how much restraint you're going to have to show with regard to your natural urges. Any connubial relations would, in my opinion, do irreparable harm to her, to you both."

The sweat glistened on Dab's bald, swollen-looking head. He was writing furiously, not daring to look up. Will felt himself redden. "Is this why you stuck us on separate floors? Is this why I can't so much as even sit down to a meal with my own wife?"

"Once again, in all candor," the Doctor went on, ignoring him, his voice leaping out in the way of the orator catching hold of his subject, "I must ask how often you've engaged in intimate physical relations with your wife during this period of your illness—and hers."

Will's right foot began to tap, rattling away under the desk as if it had suddenly come loose from his body. He looked away from the Doctor's cold unblinking gaze and found himself contemplating the craggy sexless visage of Thomas "Old Parr" Parr, dead of longevity at a hundred and fifty-two. "Well," he began, fumbling for composure, feeling like a criminal, a wife abuser, a veritable sop of venality, "we used to . . . come together, maybe once every, oh, week"—he glanced up furtively to see the good Doctor wince—"or less, sometimes less, a lot less, but then she, she became—"

"*Enceinte*," the Doctor supplied.

"Yes. And we, we . . ." Suddenly an image of his daughter rose up before him, the daughter he never saw or held or took to the soda fountain for an ice cream, an idealized vision of a little girl in pigtails, the flash of a bonnet and basket, a field of flowers nodding in the sun, and he broke down. "But she *died*," he choked, "died before I could even see her, just see her once—"

Silently, on catlike feet, the Doctor glided round the desk to stand rigid over Will, mechanically offering the crisp pressed linen of his handkerchief. "It's all right," he said, his voice a pitcher of sympathy, "I understand. The sad fact of human existence is that we must engage in these dangerous practices—dangerous for wife and husband alike, what with the excitation of the nervous system, the loss of life-giving fluids, the shock to the constitutions of both partners—we must engage in them, I say, to replenish the species. It's our lot in life. But don't blame yourself, Mr. Lightbody—I've seen worse, far worse. Men who indulged their appetites nightly—in one case every night without fail for over twenty years. That man was a beast of the jungle. He buried three wives."

There was a long moment of silence. Dab was still writing furiously—Will could hear the scratch of his pen against the faint ticking of the steam in the pipes and the odd muted sound from the corridor—but he'd turned away, as if the subject were too painful to bear. After a while, the Doctor moved quietly back to his own side of the desk, and for the first time during their interview, he took a seat. "The world is a busy place, Mr. Lightbody," he began, and he made a little pyramid of his fingers; the apple, casually gnawed, lolled at his elbow. "The streets are full of orphans. My wife and I have adopted all our children, and we're proud of it. I preach abstinence, sir, strict abstinence. Certainly while you're under our care and in your very tentative condition, but for the future, too . . . we *can* control our appetites, we *can*. God gave us that."

Thoughtfully massaging the back of his neck, the Doctor shuffled through the file. Without looking up, and in his clinically insinuating way, he dug a little deeper in the dirt. "Cravings for spirits? Opiates? You've conquered those problems?"

Will could barely speak. He was mortified, deeply ashamed of his body, with its furtive wants and secretions, ashamed of the terrible lewd thoughts that had crowded his mind throughout the day, ashamed ever to look Nurse Graves in the eye again. "Yes," he gulped, almost choking on the single simple little syllable.

"Good." The Doctor glanced up from beneath the eyeshade. "Now, we're going to change your intestinal flora, that's the first thing. You are aware, aren't you, that over one hundred sixty different types of bacteria inhabit the human digestive tract?"

Will nodded feebly. Yes. Or, no. No, he wasn't.

"Each of these separate species forms its own peculiar products and byproducts, many of which are highly toxic. The two main classes of these bacteria, the aerobes and anaerobes, as described by Tissier and others—you are aware of Tissier's work? No matter. At any rate, the aerobes are generally beneficial—vital to us, in fact, and they produce harmless acids for the most part—but the anaerobes, those bacteria we find in flesh foods, are pathologic and putrefactive. They are pernicious, Mr. Lightbody, and they are your scourge."

The Doctor was on his feet again. He took a bite of the apple, which by now had gone brown round the indentations left by his teeth. Chewing, pacing, stroking the white wisps of his hair, he suddenly pulled up short and whirled round on Will. "Have you ever studied the life habits of the Bulgarians, Mr. Lightbody? Not the city folk, but the shepherds and wood gatherers of the Balkans and the Rhodope range?"

Will hadn't.

"Well, as Metchnikoff has discovered, they are surprisingly long-lived. Not so long-lived as Old Parr, perhaps, but, then, he's the happy exception, isn't he? Still, as a whole, and Massal and Metchnikoff have subjected the proposition to rigorous statistical analysis, these rugged mountaineering Bulgarians outlive everyone on our grand and various little planet. And do you know why?"

The diminutive Doctor wasn't asking for an answer; Will, recovering from his shame, understood as much. He pushed himself up in the chair so that he could feel the stab of its orthopedic ribs in his kidneys and managed to produce a deep interrogatory grunt.

"Yogurt."

"Yogurt?"

"Yogurt." The Doctor was beaming, his stingy lips pressed into a thin, triumphant smile. "This is the key. Because yogurt, Mr. Lightbody, which comprises the bulk of the Bulgarian diet, contains the amicable bacterium *Lactobacillus bulgaricus*, which will drive out the wild bacteria, the pathogenic, poison-forming B. *welchii* and *Proteus vulgaris* implanted in the exhausted system—in *your* exhausted system, sir—by the putre-factive action of flesh foods. As Sir Arbuthnot Lane says, 'The colon is a common sink.' We must change that flora."

Will's critical faculties seemed to have been eroded by the torrent of information and odd sensation he'd experienced over the course of the past twenty-four bewildering hours. He was defeated, insensate, a mass of protoplasm occupying the iron seat of a physiologic chair in a high-vaulted little room in a great big brick building in Battle Creek, Michigan. He didn't know whether to laugh or cry.

The Doctor turned abruptly to his secretary. "Dab: the regimen and dietary for Mr. Lightbody, please."

Sweating and puffing, banana protruding from his pocket, collar pinching at his throat, Dab heaved himself across the room and handed two closely typed sheets to the Doctor, avoiding eye contact with Will. "Ah, yes. Yes, yes," Dr. Kellogg murmured, swinging back around. "We're going to start you out, for the first three days, on psyllium seeds and hijiki. The psyllium, which you will take as if it were a medication—this is a prescription, sir, and I'm afraid I will brook no deviation from it and no nonsense with the dieticians in the dining hall—the psyllium, as I say, is hygroscopic; that is, it absorbs water and will expand in your stomach, scouring you out as it passes through you just as surely as if a tiny army of janitors were down there equipped with tiny scrub brushes. The same with the hijiki, a Japanese seaweed intro-duced to me by Dr. Tomoda, of the Imperial School of Medicine in Kyoto. Perfectly indigestible. Like eating a broom—but that broom will sweep you clean, Mr. Lightbody, sweep you clean. Then we put you on the milk diet."

Will was confused. Yogurt, milk, seaweed: what about food? "The milk diet?"

"Oh, yes: I'm sorry. The yogurt, for the most part, will be entering you from the posterior end, in a sort of two-pronged assault, as it were." The Doctor paused to acknowledge his joke with a soft, reflective chuckle. Dutifully, Dab joined him, but in the secretary's throat the chuckle turned to a snicker and then a sort of throttled wheeze that had no trace of humor in it at all. "That's where Nurse Bloethal comes

in," the Doctor continued. "Twice a day, in addition to your postprandial enemas, you'll be getting a colonic injection of whey and *Lactobacillus bulgaricus*—that is, the yogurt bacterium, collected in Bulgaria
expressly for the Sanitarium and available only here. In time, we will
eradicate the harmful bacteria from your colon and repopulate it with
a bloom of health-giving flora, so that you can properly digest your food.
Stick to the dietary, stick to the exercise regimen, and your stomach
problems will be a thing of the past. Three months, Mr. Lightbody. In
three months' time, sir, you'll be a new man."

The interview was ending. The fact alone perked Will up. Added to
that was this glimmer of hope, this shining vision of the sanitized colon
and the quiescent stomach. He rose from the chair and ventured a joke
of his own. "Three months and I'll be on the Road to Wellville, eh?"

The words were barely out of his mouth when Will realized he'd made
a mistake. A pall fell over the room. The Doctor went rigid; Dab dropped
his eyes and edged off into the corner. "What?" Will said, straining
against his grin of embarrassment. "Did I say something wrong?"

A terrible, crippled moment limped by. "We don't speak cant here,
sir," the Doctor finally said, his mouth drawn up tight. "Not in this
institution. Cheap slogan-mongering, that's all it is. An attempt by an
individual who, who—"

For the first time in their brief acquaintance, the Doctor seemed at
a loss for words. And his color—the pink glow of blessed flesh, of
carefree, daisy-tripping health, had been supplanted by an ugly reddening, the angry bruised shade of a sausage about to burst in the pan. All
at once it came to Will: *The Road to Wellville.* This wasn't one of the
Doctor's slogans, not at all—it was C. W. Post's. Each twenty-five-cent
package of that burnt-weed powder he sold as a coffee substitute contained a tub-thumping, positive-thinking, self-congratulatory pamphlet
reprising the uplifting story of how "The Captain" had got himself well
and made his fortune. And what was the title of that pamphlet? What
was the catchword it had put on the lips of every man, woman and
child in America?

Will had made a faux pas. But how could you blame him? Until
Eleanor had come under the spell of the good Doctor, the whole lot of
raw-fooders, oat-bran nuts, antivivisectionists, Indian fakirs, nudists and

the like had seemed indistinguishable to him, fish out of the same barrel. "C. W. Post," Will offered.

The Doctor was aflame, all his burners lit. He tore the eyeshade from his head and flung it down on the table like a gauntlet. "We do not mention that name in this institution," he thundered, hammering at each word as if he were driving nails. "Ever."

Will felt he should apologize—he was innocent, he didn't mean any harm, he was confused, that was all—but he never got the chance. In the next instant the Doctor jerked his neck angrily round and shouted for Nurse Bloethal.

A door at the rear of the office opened, and the nurse lumbered into the room, graceless, big-armed, her hair pressed to her head like wire strands beneath the nurse's cap. She was smiling, but there was no hint of Nurse Graves's ingenuousness or even Mrs. Stover's artificiality in that smile; no, Nurse Bloethal's smile was hard and self-satisfied, with the smallest suggestion of something harder still. "Yes, Doctor?"

Dr. Kellogg had reined in his anger as quickly as it had come up on him. His voice was steady, matter-of-fact. "Mr. Lightbody is ready for the treatment. He'll be taking the full gallonage, followed by the whey-*Lactobacillus* culture. You're to escort him to the dining room afterward—and emphasize to Mrs. Stover, though she'll have the dietary program by now, that he's on the laxative diet through Friday."

The moment of release had come, though it wasn't quite what Will had been prepared for. He'd been expecting Nurse Graves, the gentle ministrations, the warm flesh, and here was her antithesis. "Uh, Dr. Kellogg, thank you, thank you very much for your help," Will fumbled.

Again the white palm. "It's nothing. We just want you to be well again."

"Doctor?"

"Yes?"

"I'm not sure—that is, I don't understand your instructions to the nurse . . . uh, I'm to go where?"

The Doctor looked up sharply, and Will sensed a tension in him that had nothing to do with the unfortunate Post reference—perhaps he resented looking up at anyone. His eyes were clear, cold, the unwavering eyes of the scientist. "Nurse Bloethal will be taking you to the baths.

The manual colonic, in your case, hasn't really been as effective as we'd like. We have two mechanized systems, very efficient, able to force up to fifteen gallons into the colon in a matter of seconds—to ensure proper evacuation."

Proper evacuation?

Two beats. The steam ticked in the pipes, Dab wiped his forehead. "Don't worry, Nurse Bloethal will show you the ropes."

Chapter 9

Per-Fo

ॐ

Charlie Ossining's first meal in Battle Creek, his first meal as the in-situ President-in-Chief of the Per-Fo Company, Inc., consisted of a bowl of tepid fish broth and a handful of stale soda crackers. He ate standing up, hunched over the bowl like a beggar on a street corner, his buttocks pressed to Mrs. Eyvindsdottir's kitchen stove in the vain hope of deriving some faint degree of warmth from its anemic embers. It was past two in the afternoon, and the other boarders, the bronchial Bagwell presumably among them, had already breakfasted and dined. Mrs. Eyvindsdottir stood at the drainboard, cleaning fish with a worn, fiercely honed blade. "Yust this once," she warned in her patient but barely intelligible gargle of a dialect, "I feed you late. But no more. Is this correct?"

Charlie nodded, barely able to stomach the broth, strewn as it was with pike bones and bits of scale, fin and other unidentifiable debris. He'd always been a good eater and he was ravenous after the night he'd gone through, but the broth had an unfortunate aftertaste of muddy bottoms and pondweed, and the sight and smell of the fish on the drainboard didn't improve matters any. Mrs. Eyvindsdottir's knife flashed as she deftly worked the blade up under the gill slits of two huge slack yellow-green pike, removed their heads and dropped them into a gleaming pot. Charlie caught a glimpse of blood-rich gill and the flat cold gaze of an extinguished eye and had to look away. He set the bowl down on the stove.

"Nice fish," the landlady observed, nodding proudly to the basket in the corner where some eight or ten of them, each as long as a man's leg and rigid with ice, bristled against the wall. Charlie didn't yet realize it, but he would see those pike, in various guises, every day for the next week, breakfast, lunch and dinner. Mrs. Eyvindsdottir was a widow, plump and economical, and a trapper who lived on Gull Lake and was particularly enamored of her charms—one Bjork Bjorksson by name— kept her supplied with mountains of fish and game. One week it would be pike; the next, muskrat, beaver, lynx or groundhog. No, Charlie didn't know it, but he would come to rue the day Bjork Bjorksson had entered the landlady's life, and his entire gastrointestinal system would seize up at the adjective "nice," as applied to any furred, finned or feathered creature. At this juncture, though, he was naive enough to agree. "Yes, nice," he grunted.

He spent the remainder of the afternoon trying to track down Bender. The presiding genius and pro-tem treasurer of the Per-Fo Company had left a rather cryptic message for Charlie at the desk of the Post Tavern Hotel: *Gone Goguac Boat Clb. Luncheon w/Stellrecht in matter of paper Per-Fo boxes. Meet 11:00 A.M. tomorrow for examine factory site, cnr Verona Wattles. Yrs., W/Bst Wshs & Sincest Regds, Good.* For a long moment Charlie stood there at the gleaming marble counter, reading the message over. He was mortified to think that he'd overslept and missed this luncheon, but then it was unclear whether he'd been invited or not—had Bender said anything about it the previous night? He couldn't remember. Too tired. And drunk. But if he wasn't invited, he damn well should have been—and he could feel the irritation rising in him. He was President-in-Chief of the blessed company, after all, and wherever and whatever the Goguac Boat Club was, he had a pretty strong suspicion that lunch there was bound to be an improvement over Mrs. Eyvindsdottir's room-chilled fish broth.

Well. And what to do? Perhaps it was a late luncheon and he could still make it, or maybe they were lingering over sherry and cigars in the smoking room. He pictured a rustic lodge with a high beamed ceiling and a great roaring blaze in the fieldstone fireplace, waiters in white jackets ducking respectfully in and out of the room, Bender and Stell-recht talking of paper in low fraternal tones. They wanted it stiff, didn't they? Paperboard. And how did it come—reams, rolls? *They're shipping six carloads a day out of here, Charlie, six carloads a day.* Charlie didn't know the first thing about the breakfast-food business, and he'd be the first to admit it—but how was he ever going to learn if Bender excluded him from even the most routine of business meetings? Or, worse: if he overslept and excluded himself?

Inquiring at the desk, Charlie discovered that a streetcar line ran out to Goguac Lake, a resort area south of the city, but to his chagrin he learned that it ran only in summer. Having footed it all the way from Mrs. Eyvindsdottir's in a subarctic gale over sidewalks that were like a bobsled run, he decided to invest in a hack and spare himself any further risk of pneumonia or a broken leg. And he didn't have to feel guilty about it, either—he was an executive, wasn't he? Chief Executive, at that. If Bender felt obligated to put on a show with Mrs. Hookstratten's money, then why shouldn't he? "Goguac Boat Club," he pronounced grandly to the driver, sinking into the seat like a bored prince.

The cabbie was a tired-looking gnome of a man, wizened and white-haired, hunched over a tireder-looking nag from which a nimbus of steam rose steadily in the cold of the street. He turned round in his seat. "You don't want to go there," he said, reflectively dredging his throat and hawking a glistening ball of mucus into the street. They were sitting beneath the elaborate sheltered bridge that connected the second floor of the Post Tavern Hotel to the Post Building across the street. The hotel doorman, rigid as a cigar-store Indian, was watching them intently.

Maybe it was the doorman, or the weather, or the cuisine, or maybe he was still on edge over the awesome responsibility of safeguarding Mrs. Hookstratten's investment, but there was no excess of civility in Char-lie's reply. "Goguac Boat Club," he repeated, grinding his teeth for em-phasis.

The cabbie never moved a muscle. Beyond the curve of his shoulders and the ridge of his hat the sky was a dead thing, cheerless and bleak. Was it always this cold here? Charlie wondered, and he had a vision of C. W. Post on the French Riviera, in Italy, in Post City, Texas, the sun baking the earth till it cracked like a stone in a furnace. After a moment the man leaned over to hawk up another ball of sputum. He wiped his mouth on his sleeve, and without bothering to turn his head, he muttered, "Where to?"

"Are you deaf?" Charlie couldn't help raising his voice. "Goguac Boat Club. Get moving, man, will you? I'm on urgent business."

The driver turned halfway round, presenting his profile. "You don't want to go there," he repeated, and Charlie was half a second from slamming his way angrily out of the cab when the little man elaborated, "—nobody out there this time of year. All froze up. Or mostly froze, I guess. Haven't been out there myself since, oh, September, I guess it was."

"But the Boat Club—there's a luncheon there today."

"Luncheon, hell. There's nothing out there but a boathouse—and it's all closed up for the winter. Who'd want to take a scull out in weather like this? Coldest it's been this early in maybe twenty years." The cabbie removed his hat a moment to adjust his scarf and collar, revealing a pink swatch of naked scalp in the process. "Unless maybe it's Stellrecht."

"Yes, Stellrecht," Charlie cried. "Stellrecht—that's who it is. I'm supposed to meet him there, at the Boat Club, him and my, my"—what would you call Bender?—"my business associate." And before he knew what he was saying, it was out of his mouth: "We need paper."

Now the cabbie turned round full and gave him a look. He lifted a dirty finger to one eye and winked it shut, gently working over the mucus in his throat with a soft frictive sound, almost as if he were purring. "You and everybody else," he said. "But let me guess—you're starting up a breakfast-food business, am I right?"

It was a crisp twenty-minute ride out to Goguac Lake, a ride that began amidst the prosperous urban canyons of Battle Creek, on cobblestone streets crisscrossed with telephone wires and streetcar cables and lined with three- and four-story brick buildings, and ended on a bleak country lane that gave onto a forbidding black expanse of water that might just as well have been an unnamed lake in the Yukon Territory for all the signs of life on its shores. The lake hadn't frozen over yet, not completely, and the open water had a nasty rolling chop to it that spoke of glancing doom and the grappling hook. This wasn't West-chester, with its placid ponds and cud-chewing cows; this was the West, and the sight of Goguac Lake, in all its primitive indifference, brought that home to Charlie Ossining in a way that no amount of scenery viewed from the windows of the Twentieth Century Limited could ever have. It was a grim place, no doubt about it. He knew he'd made a mistake the minute he set eyes upon it, but he was too stubborn to admit defeat—besides which, it was going to cost him at least fifty cents one way or the other, and he figured he might just as well get his money's worth. So when the driver pulled up the reins and turned round as if to say 'I told you so,' Charlie merely mouthed the words: "*The Boat Club.*"

There was no lodge. There were no waiters, no diners; there was no fire, no food, no warmth. The Goguac Boat Club consisted of a long white clapboard building that might have been a warehouse or a feed store if it weren't set out over the water. Charlie persisted in climbing out of the cab and trying the door. (And God, it was cold. Cold enough even under the canvas bonnet of the cab, but out here it was murderous.) There were no windows in the building and the door was padlocked. Charlie gave the door a brief hopeless rap with his knuckles while the driver regarded him scornfully and produced wad after wad of mucus, as if he were trying to turn his lungs inside out. He spat, briefly, three or four times, then looked up and said, "Where to now, fella?"

Good question. If Bender wasn't here—and clearly no one in his right mind would be, unless he was a wolf skinner or lumberjack—then where was he? And why the subterfuge? Huddled in the cab, Charlie extracted Bender's note from his coat pocket and reread it. There it was, in plain English: *Gone Goguac Boat Clb. Luncheon w/ Stellrecht.* And then it occurred to him—maybe, just maybe, the Goguac Boat Club held its luncheon somewhere other than on the frozen inhospitable body-and-brain-numbing shores of the lake itself. Somewhere in Battle Creek, for instance. Some conscientiously heated tavern, restaurant, lodge or meeting hall. The cabbie spat, produced a filthy handkerchief, blew his nose and spat again. Charlie sat there, feeling like an idiot. But then his eyes fell on the second part of Bender's message—the address of the factory site, at Verona Wattles, wherever that was. The day didn't have to be a total waste. He could go there now, see it for himself, get a head start on things. "Listen, driver," he called, poking his head out the window. "You know this place, Verona Wattles?"

The driver sat hunched over his lap. The horse dropped a load and shuddered. There was no sound but for the wind sitting in the trees and the slap of the waves against the bare teeth of the shore. "I know Verona Avenue," the driver said finally, without turning round. "I know Wattles Lane. It's going to cost you another two bits, on top of what you already owe me."

No matter how much he rationalized or how much he resented Bender's extravagance, Charlie didn't like to part with money—Mrs. Hookstratten's money, in particular. Yes, he told himself, he was cold and cynical and ruthless and calculating, a tycoon in the making who was born to fleece the rich, but Mrs. Hookstratten had been good to him and he truly wanted to see her get a fair return on her investment— while he himself coincidentally made his own fortune, of course. On the other hand, he was anxious to do something, anything, eager to get the company going and watch the profits roll in. He wouldn't accomplish a thing by going back to Mrs. Eyvindsdottir's and sucking on fish bones, that was for sure. He raised his voice above the wind. "Drive on," he said.

Dusk was setting in by the time they reached the old Malta-Vita plant at the corner of Verona Avenue and Wattles Lane. The company had enjoyed a brief but spectacular success some six years earlier, improving on Dr. Kellogg's Granose Flakes by sweetening them with barley-malt syrup and obtaining a patent on the new product. A pair of out-of-town promoters, men not unlike Goodloe H. Bender and Charles P. Ossining, lured Dr. Kellogg's former bakery foreman away from the Sanitarium Food Company, spent the lion's share of their capital on advertising and soon had five big traveling ovens operating day and night. (The ovens, each three stories high, worked on the Ferris-wheel principle, circulating the wheat flakes till they were toasted to a dry, crisp, toothsome perfection.) The public was ready for them. Tired of oatmeal, sick of grits, bilious with salt pork, pone and flapjacks and crammed to the maw with Malta-Vita advertising, they saw that the new product was convenient, nutritious, scientific, physiologic, hygienic and downright simple: just open the package, pour, add milk and eat. Success came like an acclamation. The newly minted tycoons started up a second factory in Toronto; they shipped crate after crate of their crisp and uniform wheat flakes, wagonloads, freight cars jammed to the rooftops with them, and they shipped them to Mexico, France, Germany, Norway and Czecho-Slovakia. But then the original promoters sold out— handsomely—and the product deteriorated. Kellogg's man went elsewhere, seduced by an offer he couldn't refuse, and something went wrong in the processing plant. The flakes molded. Went rancid. Rotted on the shelves and in the bowl. And Grape-Nuts, Golden Manna, Norka Oats, Tryabita, Cero-Fruto, Egg-O-See and some forty others rushed in to fill the breach.

And Charlie Ossining? He was just a little late.

Charlie got out of the cab and walked tentatively round the ruins of the factory, stunned at the havoc a few short years could wreak. The building had been impressive once, a mighty fortress, brick walls and a vaulting roof, but it was a shambles now. There'd been a fire, that much was evident from the street, fingers of carbon clutching at the windows, the roof collapsed in a scatter of blackened timbers. In falling, one of the beams had torn a V-shaped gap in the rear wall, and you looked out past the brick and into the wintry snarl of trees beyond. The doors were gone, too, and the windows stood naked, the panes long since shattered, the woodwork either reduced to ash or prized up for salvage. It was no habitation, but people had sheltered here over the course of the fading months and years—vagrants, itinerant workers, factory hands short of housing during the boom years of '02 and '03—and they'd left the detritus of their lives behind. There was the usual litter of patent-medicine bottles, cans, boxes, bones, shreds of weathered newsprint and magazines, but there were more personal things, too—a washboard, a bureau with the top staved in and the drawers missing, a boot, a sock, a scrap of gingham. And beneath it all, a fine glittering carpet of broken glass.

The waste of it, that's what got to him. It was like that poem he'd had to recite in school about the stone head buried in the sand. That's what this place was like—a stone head buried in the sand. There was no hope for it. None. Charlie felt his stomach drop. His breath came quick and shallow, and despite the chill blast of the wind he was perspiring under the arms, beneath the brim of his hat, and a single cold wet finger traced the ridge of his spine. Suddenly he was afraid for Mrs. Hookstratten, afraid for himself. This was the place Bender had chosen? This was the place where Per-Fo was supposed to fly? It was cursed, jinxed, a killing floor of failure and despair. He began to doubt Bender's judgment, his sanity, even.

His first instinct was to turn around right there and go back to Bender and tell him to forget it, they'd be better off building from scratch, but the morbid fascination of the archaeologist was on him and he kicked his way through the debris to the big open back room to have a look at the ovens. A bird—or was it a bat?—shot across the room and out into the gathering dark as he came through the open doorway, and something—rats?—stirred in the far corner. Then it was quiet. Eerily still.

Two of the great three-story ovens remained, rising up out of the ruins and into the sky, rusted, battered, strewn with swallow's nests and the crushed dark leavings of half a dozen autumns, but powerfully suggestive for all that. For a long moment he stood there in awe of the machinery before him, and in that moment he *was* an archaeologist, a treasure hunter come upon the undreamed-of temple, the rare find, the jewel. He was stunned. This was the source, the fount; this was where all those cereal flakes had come from, all those nuggets, all that cash, the cars and carriages, the libraries, the wine cellars and billiard tables—and it was what he wanted, all of it, his own billiard table especially. And a library, too, of course, not that he'd ever read much more than dime novels, Nick Carter, Frank Reade, Big-Foot Wallace and that sort of thing, but just to have it, all those leather-bound books with their gilded spines, the brandy in a cut-glass decanter, Otard Dupuy '78. That's what gentlemen had, the tycoons and the millionaires and the breakfast-food magnates—he'd bet his eyeteeth C. W. Post had the whole lot of it, billiard tables, London suits, libraries, limousines, stables and a thousand other things Charlie couldn't even conceive of. And these were the machines that made it possible—the Federal Mint in Washington couldn't have awed him any more.

It was while he was standing there in the midst of the rubble, gazing up at the big traveling ovens and trying to picture them in operation, burnished and new, dropping a shower of rich golden flakes, that the stirring in the corner started up again, a rasping, scratching sound that became a distinct rustle and then a crash accompanied by muffled curses. Charlie was not alone. He glanced over his shoulder and through a pair of neatly aligned door frames to where the cabbie sat hunched in his seat, and then back to the corner, behind the far oven, where a figure, cursing and kicking at the litter around him, began to emerge from the gloom. "Hello?" Charlie called. And then, stupidly, "Is anybody there?"

The figure hesitated—it was a man, Charlie saw now, a man dressed in a ragged torn greatcoat and an old silk top hat with the crown punched out so that it looked like a section of stovepipe fitted to his head. A beggar. A bum. Charlie's hand went reflexively to his wallet, and then he remembered that Mrs. Hookstratten's money was no longer a concern—and he relaxed. The man's voice came back at him, gloomy, hoarse, threatening: "Who the hell wants to know?"

The bum advanced on him, his eyes muddied with drink, a glistening spatter of vomit trailing down the front of his coat. His hair was tangled, dark, festooned with bits of leaf mold and a fine filigree of lint and cobweb, as if he'd been mopping floors with it. He stank like a sewer rat.

Charlie wasn't intimidated. He could go toe-to-toe with anybody, and there were plenty of times he'd had to—at St. Basil's Academy, where he was the youngest boy, courtesy of his parents' indifference and Mrs. Hookstratten's generosity, and afterward in the taverns and back rooms of Peterskill, Tarrytown, Croton and Ossining. Charlie was no stranger to the pugilistic arts—and besides, if anybody had a right to be out here in this dismal, godforsaken place, it was the Chief Executive of the company that was negotiating to buy it. He stood his ground.

The bum approached to within five paces and then stopped suddenly and looked round him a moment, as if he'd forgotten something. Then his eyes came up, sharp and quick, the drunkenness a cloud burned off by something hotter, more intense, sharper than Charlie would have imagined. "You think I'm a bum, don't you?" the man said. "The sort that begs change and sleeps in doorways? Am I right?"

"Listen, friend," Charlie hissed, and he folded his arms and set his jaw, "I don't give a damn who you are or where you sleep, and I didn't ask for any introductions, either."

A curtain of greasy hair fell across the man's face as he leaned forward to spit, and he was unsteady on his feet. Charlie was ready to knock him down, if that was what he wanted. But the bum was oblivious. He flicked his hair back with a jerk of his neck and gave Charlie a smile. The smile was private, mad, a reflex of the lips above the rotten skirts of the teeth, but Charlie saw in that moment that the man was young, younger than he. "No, you listen to me," the bum said, his breath going up in smoke. "You wouldn't think I had a hundred dollars cash on me, would you? Currency? Notes redeemable on the United States Treasury? Well, you bet I have. A hundred dollars—or damn near it, minus something for a whiskey or two." The wind came up then, a gust that tore through the windows, spun twice round the little amphitheater and rocketed away again. "I could book a room at the Post Tavern if I had a mind to, first-class all the way, you know that?"

Charlie was bored suddenly. Let the poor idiot sleep in his hovel, who cared? The place meant nothing to him. Maybe it was interesting to imagine what it might once have been, but clearly this wasn't what they were looking for. And he'd tell Bender as much, too. They'd just have to find more investors, that was all. He turned away abruptly and began to pick his way through the rubble and back out to the street.

"Hey, mister," the bum called at his back, but Charlie kept walking. "Mister, I'm talking to you."

Charlie paused at the front entrance to dig out a cigarette and light it. He turned to look back to where the man stood in semidarkness, his bearded face working. "It's the breakfast-food business, isn't it?" he called. "That's what you're doing out here in this shit pile in your shined-up shoes and your new overcoat—breakfast food. Am I right?"

Charlie didn't bother to answer. He drew on the cigarette and realized he was hungry. What he wanted was a steak. And some oysters—Battle Freaks, pure-foodists and health nuts be damned. He considered the prospects at Mrs. Eyvindsdottir's—Norwegian fish-head soup or some such slop—and wondered where he could get a good hamburger sand-wich without paying an arm and a leg for it.

The bum was still ranting. "I can see it on you," he spat, his voice cracked and ragged, "that tinhorn-millionaire look, just like my uncle. Or worse, my would-be father, the holy man of the temple himself. You know him, you know my father?"

Charlie didn't know his father, and he didn't care to, either. He flicked away the butt of his cigarette, turned his back and ambled across the litter-strewn yard to the cold leather seat of the hack.

"Where to now, Diamond Jim?" the driver asked.

He should have gotten out and walked to save the money, but he was tired, irritated, profoundly depressed over the ruin of the factory, the mattress stuffed with worthless stock certificates, the scramble of boys at the station—Christ, even the bums on the street were gibbering about breakfast food—and he decided he had to see Bender, right then, right away, no matter the cost. The uneasiness he'd felt all day settled into his stomach like a lump of cold cereal, like oatmeal scraped from the bottom of the pot, and he thought he was going to vomit. If so many had come before them and failed, what chance did they have? What chance of raising money, buying equipment and ad space, paying workers? He'd been a fool, he saw that now, eating his oysters and sipping champagne on the train, playacting at being a swell—did he think the money was going to fall into his lap? Where was the grain going to come from? Who was going to stuff the boxes? Who was going to buy them? *Bender. He had to see Bender.* "Take me to the Post Tavern," he said, and his voice was so weak he had to repeat himself before the driver heard him.

The streetlamps were softly glowing and the shop windows lit by the time they pulled up in front of the hotel, where a pair of motorcars and half a dozen carriages were taking on and discharging passengers. There was an early-evening bustle to the streets, couples walking arm-in-arm, people darting in and out of the shops, workers heading home to supper, and despite his misgivings, Charlie saw that the city did have its charms. It was prosperous, that was for sure. People had money—cereal money—and they meant to spend it. He made a mental note to stroll around and survey the various grocers to see what brands they were stocking—after he saw Bender, of course, and got something to eat. He was digging into his pocket when the cabbie turned round and said, "That'll be eighty-five cents—unless maybe you want to go back out to the Boat Club."

"Eighty-five cents? Are you crazy? You said fifty cents to the lake and two bits to the factory—"

"And ten cents back."

Charlie could feel the frustration rising in him, all the driver's little gibes and taunts come home to roost in that frigid moment. "But you didn't . . . I assumed—"

"Assumed, shit," the driver growled, working the mucus in his throat and rolling it back and forth across his palate before letting it go in the street, "what do I look like, a charity worker?"

Charlie was about to counter this, violently, the words already on his lips, when he looked up and found himself staring into the watchful face of the doorman. The man wore a smug, superior look, as if he knew to the penny what every man who entered the Post Tavern Hotel was worth, and he caught Charlie's eye as he leaned forward in his crisp uniform to open the door of the carriage ahead of them. Charlie was suddenly embarrassed. Here he was, President-in-Chief of the Per-Fo Company, and he was haggling over a dime on the front steps of the best hotel in town. A dime. When just yesterday he'd waltzed up those very steps with nearly four thousand dollars in his pocket. The doorman helped a woman out of the hack in front of them and turned to Charlie's cab. "Can you make change, at least," Charlie muttered, handing the driver a two-and-a-half-dollar gold piece. At that moment, the door swung open as if under its own power and Charlie backed out into the street, preparing to straighten up on receiving his change and nod a stiff, icy greeting to the doorman.

"Well, my goodness," came a voice at his back, "if it isn't Mr. Ossining!"

He didn't jump, but it was all he could do not to flinch as he turned to look into the mocking green eyes of Eleanor Lightbody. She was wearing a fur coat—a different one altogether from the one she'd worn at the station the previous evening—and she was in the company of a fit-looking man with fair hair and a boyish face, the sort that goes into middle age and beyond looking as if he'd just broken the tape at a track meet. Charlie tried to compose himself. Here was a potential investor, he told himself, not to mention a woman who seemed to offer him more each time he laid eyes on her.

"Ah," he returned, striking a casual note, the breakfast-food magnate returning in a coach from overseeing his dominion, "Mrs. Lightbody— Eleanor—what a pleasure." He was uncomfortably aware of the doorman at his side, and of the driver, hunched like a gargoyle over the seat of the hack and poking through a filthy coin purse with clumsy mittened fingers.

Eleanor held him a moment with her eyes, the whole group frozen as if in a portrait—*The Arrival of the Tycoon*, or some such nonsense— and then she turned to introduce the young athlete at her side. "Mr. Ossining, I'd like to present my physician, Frank Linniman. Frank, Mr. Ossining."

Charlie took the man's hand in a firm grip. "It's 'Charlie,' please," he said. "And Mrs. Lightbody," shifting his gaze back to her perpetually amused little mouth and mocking eyes—what was so funny?—"I hope you'll call me 'Charlie,' too. And I hope you won't mind my calling you 'Eleanor.' After all, we survived the Twentieth Century Limited together, not to mention the Michigan Central Line." He let an urbane laugh escape him, as if rail travel were a constant and unavoidable nuisance.

"Yes, of course," Eleanor murmured, but she didn't join him in a conspiratorial chuckle, as he'd hoped. She turned to her companion instead (she had hold of his arm, Charlie noticed) and let her voice ring out in a coy little trill, "Mr. Ossining is the president of a breakfast-food company, Frank—"

"Oh?" Frank didn't seem particularly impressed.

At that moment the driver entered the conversation. "Listen, Diamond Jim," he called, wiping his nose on the underside of his sleeve and leaning forward to leer at the whole group, "I'll have to give you pennies and nickels, I don't seem to have a whole lot of two-bit pieces—"

Charlie waved him off. "Keep it," he said. "Keep the change."

The man was incredulous. "But that's—?"

"Keep it," Charlie repeated.

"And what was the name of your company, Mr. Ossining?" Eleanor asked, taking her hand from the doctor's arm to reach up and adjust her hat. " 'Perfect Flakes' or 'Perfect Food' or something like that?"

"Per-Fo," Charlie murmured, heartsick over the dollar and sixty-five cents he'd just thrown away as if he were J. P. Morgan himself, and wanting only to get out of this, disappear, crawl into his den at Mrs. Eyvindsdottir's and lick his wounds. But a voice whispered in his head, *An investor, here's an investor,* and he stood his ground as the hack rattled off and the doorman returned to his station.

"Yes, Per-Fo," Eleanor pronounced, "how forgetful of me. And have you managed to find a manufacturing plant, Mr. Ossining, for this peptonized marvel of a celery-impregnated food?" She was mocking him.

"As a matter of fact, no—I've just come from inspecting a very, uh, substantial plant, a terrific-looking place, with all the equipment intact—went out of business, you know—but I don't think it's for us. Not nearly the floor space we were hoping for." He was talking too fast, and he caught himself. "By the way, have I given you my card?"

Eleanor held up the palm of a black velvet glove. "Yes, Mr. Ossining, thank you—you were kind enough to present both my husband and me with cards at dinner the other night. You did get Will's card?"

Distracted, forgetful, her gawk of a husband had left his card under the butter dish. *William Fitzroy and Eleanor O. Lightbody, Parsonage Lane, Peterskill,* was all the information it conveyed, but Charlie had held on to it, treasured it, in fact, as the key to establishing future contact. He nodded.

"Well." The sharp green eyes, the pursed lips, a pronouncement of finality. "We must be going, though I've enjoyed so much seeing you again—Dr. Linniman has been kind enough to take me out for my evening constitutional, and we really must get back. He means to build my appetite, don't you, Frank?" A pause, a glance to the doctor and back again. "Are you stopping here, Mr. Ossining?"

Charlie shot a quick glance at the grand entrance, the show of the lights, the rigid doorman. "Yes, as a matter of fact, I am. A splendid place, really, every bit as classy—elegant, I mean—as the best of our New York hotels. And the service is quite adequate. There's no place like it in town, I'm told."

"Oh, there you're wrong," Eleanor said, and still she seemed to be sniping at him. "You haven't tried Dr. Kellogg's Sanitarium. But, then, you wouldn't need to, would you, a healthy specimen like yourself?"

Charlie laughed, covering his mouth in the way Mrs. Hookstratten had taught him. "Well," he said, "I don't know about that, but—"

She'd already turned to go. "Watch out for those oysters," she warned, calling out gaily over her shoulder, and then she was heading up the street, her arm in the doctor's. Charlie watched her till she turned the corner, then made his way up the steps and into the lobby of Bender's grand domain, suddenly feeling as weary as if he were carrying one of those three-story ovens on his shoulders.

Bender wasn't in. There was no message. Guilt-ridden over his heedless expenditure—this was only his first day and already he'd gone through half of what Bender had given him for the week—he lowered his head and walked the twenty frigid blocks to Mrs. Eyvindsdottir's. And as he sat down at the table with the full, wheezing, snuffling, whey-faced complement of his fellow boarders and spooned up the landlady's bland fish balls and hard-boiled pike, he found that he couldn't stop thinking about Eleanor Lightbody and the way her eyes lit on him as if he were so vastly amusing, as if he were a clown or a court jester set down on earth for her royal entertainment. It was like an itch, an ache, and he was still rubbing at it as he mounted the creaking stairs, threw himself onto the cold rumpled mattress and let the night overtake him.

In the morning, it was fried pike with eggs and horseradish butter and a kind of pancake that tasted of fish—pike, specifically—and then the long lonely walk to the Post Tavern. Bender wasn't in. There was no message. Irritated, impatient, wanting only to get on with it and feel useful, to do something, anything, Charlie found himself pacing the lobby, back and forth, until he began to draw looks. The desk clerk, the long-nosed, suck-cheeked simp he'd wanted to throttle two nights ago, was particularly watchful, jealous of every step across his precious carpets and unblemished floors. The doorman, too—though he seemed a touch more respectful now that he'd seen Charlie lay so princely a tip on the hack driver. Even a few of the guests—pampered, white-haired, holier-than-thou types—began to take notice of him. It wouldn't do for the President-in-Chief of Per-Fo to get the bum's rush through the front door of the best hotel in town, so Charlie sank into his collar and went back out into the chill morning. Around the corner he found a sandwich shop, where he invested ten cents of his dwindling resources in a cup of coffee and a ham-and-cheese sandwich—anything but fish—and he sat there, reading the previous afternoon's paper over again and nursing his coffee till his watch showed 10:40. Then he pulled on his gloves, squared the brim of his hat and started off for his meeting with Bender at the old Malta-Vita plant at the corner of Verona and Wattles.

The day was brisk, but not nearly as cold as the day before, and if his feet weren't aching from overuse he might almost have enjoyed the walk. The exercise calmed him, and by the time he reached Capital Avenue he began to feel hopeful again—Bender knew what he was doing, sure he did. There was no sense in getting upset over nothing. For the first time since he'd got off the train he came alive to the sights and sounds around him, almost as if he were awakening from a deep sleep. A carriage glided sedately down the street, and he could hear the creak of harness and spring beneath the gentle, almost reticent punch and slap of the horse's hooves; a pair of women in bonnets and shawls passed him on the sidewalk with a whisper of skirts; somewhere a dog barked in anticipation of its morning run. The whole scene was like something out of a novel—the streets swept clean, the houses freshly painted, the trees marching along in an ordered row: nothing could go wrong here. This was the middle of America, and it was staunch, virtuous, noble, monied. Charlie peered up at the fanciful turrets and spires of the houses, at the wraparound porches with their motionless gliders, at the stained-glass panels brilliant with light and the big bay windows that seemed to invite the passerby in, and he wondered what it would be like to live in such a house, to go out to work in the morning and come home in the evening to a trim little green-eyed wife . . . and here the image of Eleanor Lightbody settled into his head, airily superior, deriding him with her unattainability. The image stayed with him, all the way up Capital to Verona and all the way down Verona to Wattles Lane.

Charlie arrived at 11:00 A.M. on the dot, but Bender was nowhere to be seen. The ruins were as still and silent as an Etruscan tomb. There were no birds to give the walls life, no rats stirring in the corners—even the bum seemed to have moved on to greener pastures. Charlie walked round the place twice, poked about in the rubble, stood before the great three-story ovens and tried to conjure up some of the awe he'd felt the previous afternoon. He checked his watch reflexively, every minute or so, the ritual of seizing the chain, pulling it from his pocket and snapping it open like a tic. It was twenty past the hour, half past, twenty till. No Bender. After a while Charlie huddled in the back corner, out of the wind, and turned his face to the wan, cloud-tattered sun as it put in its brief appearance for the day. At 12:30, he gave it up and trudged back to the hotel.

His mood was black. If before he'd felt a surge of hope and the streets had seemed pristine and cheerful, now his heart was a cinder, the streets sterile and dead. Bender had cheated him, he was sure of it. He'd taken Mrs. Hookstratten's nest egg and skipped town, leaving Charlie holding the bag. By the time he reached the Post Tavern he was in a state. He shoved past the doorman without a glance and strode up to the desk, where the clerk was busy with a couple just off the train from Chicago. "We do have a top-floor suite, if you prefer," the clerk was saying. The wife stood primly at the husband's elbow, cocking her head like a bird on a wire, a so-pleased-to-be-here smile pressed to her lips. The bell captain, a big-shouldered man squeezed into a tight red wool uniform with epaulettes and braids, was stationed behind her, poised over the sprawl of the couple's luggage.

Charlie pushed past the little group and laid a hand on the desk. "Mr. Bender," he hissed.

The clerk looked at him as if Charlie were a clot of manure he'd just scraped from the bottom of his shoe. He could barely suppress the contempt in his voice. "One moment, please," he said.

Charlie's fist came down like a sledgehammer on the desk. "One moment be damned," he choked. "I want Bender. Fetch him this instant."

The lobby was a fabric of whispers, the whole royal edifice tottering over the detonation of his rage. The couple backed off a step. No one would look him in the eye. The desk clerk's upper lip was crumpled, his gaze stricken; he looked like a schoolboy unjustly singled out for punishment. Charlie was filled with a brutal elation: the poor fool looked as if he were about to burst into tears. "Bender," Charlie snarled, his tone as sharp as a slap in the face. "Now."

But he didn't get to see Bender. Nor did he get to see the clerk break down in nervous sobs or the hand-wringing couple dance a little reel to their impotence and agitation. No. Because at that moment he felt himself seized as if by a monumental pair of pincers, as the bell captain, a former wrestler, put a full nelson on him and, with the aid of the doorman, wrenched him across the lobby, out the door and down the steps, dumping him unceremoniously amidst the horse droppings in the street. The two men, bell captain and doorman, titans both, stood silently over him, arms folded, only wishing that he would make an attempt to get back up the steps and into the hotel so that they could take him out in the alley and deal with him properly. Charlie lay there, his shoulder twisted and a bright vibrant glowing pain settling into the base of his neck, and cursed them weakly. After a moment the doorman stepped forward, and in a thoughtful, almost tender way, kicked him twice in the ribs.

Charlie just wanted to lie there in the street, the force of the humiliation a thousand times worse than any pain they could ever have hoped to inflict on him. But people were watching and he knew that the police would be bending over him any minute now, and he knew, too, just how sympathetically the police were likely to treat the reputed President-in-Chief of the Per-Fo Company after glancing at his torn trouser leg and the smears of horseshit on his coat. So he sucked in his ribs, pushed himself up as if nothing in the world were the matter—my goodness, had he slipped on a patch of ice?—bent for his hat and limped up the street with as much dignity as he could muster under the circumstances.

But he was raging inside. Revenge, that was all he could think of—finding that ape of a bell captain in a saloon one night or alone on a dark street, looking up the address of that wooden-faced doorman and surprising him over his soup, just blow in the door and give him a good crack at his own kitchen table. That's what he would do, and he was the man to do it, too. And Bender. Goddamn him. Goddamn the day he'd ever laid eyes on the miserable son of a bitch. He'd cut him up good, he would, just let him get his hands on the bastard. He was walking blindly, muttering to himself, neither knowing nor caring where he went, up one street and down another, walking to cool the rage in his heart. And the despair. Per-Fo. What a joke. Bender was a confidence man, that was all, and he'd reeled in Charlie like a fish. And Mrs. Hookstratten; what would he tell Mrs. Hookstratten?

When finally he looked up to take his bearings, he found that he'd landed practically on the doorstep of Battle Creek's grandest edifice, the rock on which the whole town was built: the Sanitarium itself. He stood across the street from it, on the walk of a busy city block, and the very solidity and massiveness of the place shook him out of his funk. So this was where the Eleanor Lightbodys of the world went to salve their little hurts and palpitations, this was where the corn flake was born and a thousand speculators had struck gold. The place was something, all right, he had to admit it—and she was right, it could have swallowed the Post Tavern three times over.

He was standing there, lost in reverie, in awe, when a familiar piping voice spoke at his elbow: "Hey."

He swung round on Ernest O'Reilly, Bender's pitiful little messenger boy. "Hey," he returned, and there was no animation in the greeting. "What are you doing out here, Ernest O'Reilly—shouldn't you be in school?"

The boy was tiny, shriveled, pathetic, a little homunculus preserved in a jar. He shrugged, looked away. "Nothin'. Business, that's all."

Business. Of course. Charlie leapt at him. "Where is he?"

Ernest O'Reilly was a sack of rags, lighter than air, hopeless. "You're hurting me," he said in his tremulous little flute of a voice, and there was no outrage in it, no protest, just a sad familiar acquiescence.

"Bender," Charlie repeated, and he tightened his grip. "Where is he?"

The boy jerked his neck to indicate the building behind them. It was a place with which Charlie was destined to become intimately familiar in the months that lay ahead, but his first view of it was inauspicious. He saw an awning, a bank of windows, a door. And beyond the windows, tables, chairs, people hunched over plates and cutlery: a restaurant. Like a hundred others. The sign over the door proclaimed "The Red Onion," and beneath it, in hand-painted letters, white on a barn-red background, there was this further inscription: *Tired of Bran & Sprouts? Try Our Famous Steaks, Chops & Fries & Our Detroit Special Hamburger Sandwich.*

Inside, the place smelled incorrigibly of grease, stale beer, sweat, cheap cigars and the gut-clenching ambrosia of a good sixteen-ounce steak in the pan on a bed of onions. Bender was sitting alone at a table in back, a half-empty pitcher of beer at his elbow, the remains of a T-bone steak settling into the plate before him. "Bender," Charlie barked, crossing the black-and-white tile floor in half a dozen strides, faces looking up in alarm from cutlets, chops, sausages, split chickens and wieners, and then, lowering his voice to a pained rumble, "where in hell were you?"

Bender rose from his seat with an answering roar, tumbling out of the chair like some great sea lion going into battle on the California beaches, crying "Charles, my boy," over and over, as if he were glad to see him. "Have a seat, have a seat"—he was repeating himself, saying everything twice, and Charlie saw that beneath the bluff exterior, he was agitated. "Pull up a chair, pull up a chair, sit down, sit down, my boy, my fine—my very fine—boy and business partner."

Charlie wouldn't sit. Bender hadn't answered him yet, and he was reluctant to surrender the high moral ground. "Where the hell *were* you?" he repeated. "We had an appointment, didn't we? At eleven A.M.? Do you know I waited around that broken-down factory freezing my damn bones for over an hour and a half?"

"Sit down, Charlie, you're making a scene," Bender hissed, and he was in command again, his face serene, unperturbed, sunk back into the mask it customarily wore. They sat down together. Bender reached over to pour Charlie a glass of beer. "Have you eaten yet?" he asked. "Hungry?" And without waiting for a reply he turned portentously in his seat and hailed the waiter in the fruity rich commanding voice he used on the public like some old Shakespearean faker. When he turned back round he drew a cigar from his breast pocket, clipped the end and leaned forward to light it off the tallowy candle puddled in a dish in the center of the table.

"Well?" Charlie demanded. "I'm waiting for an explanation. Listen, Goodloe, if we're going to be partners we've got to get a few things straight here, like—"

Bender cut him off. "Charlie, Charlie, Charlie," he crooned, massive, paternal, dredging up all the authority of his years and his bulk and his legendary successes (*I was a millionaire and busted flat two times over before I was thirty*, he'd told Charlie any number of times). "I apologize, I do. To tell the truth, the whole thing slipped my mind." And here he held up a hand to forestall any further protest. "The factory's small potatoes, Charlie. Something's come up. Something worth any twenty burned-out cereal factories."

At that moment the waiter sidled up to them, obsequious, squirming, dog-whipped, a man reduced to his rump-kissing essence. "Yes, Mr. Bender?" he breathed, and everybody in town seemed to know Goodloe H. Bender, the once and future tycoon. "May I bring you anything else?"

Bender kept him waiting as he drew the cigar from the crevice of his bearded lips and exhaled a cloud of smoke redolent of cane, frangipani, the steaming rains of the tropics. "Yes, as a matter of fact. Bring this gentleman the Delmonico steak, rare, smothered in mushrooms and onions, and serve him up a plate of your best fried potatoes and some soup and half a roasted chicken, will you? Looks like he hasn't eaten since he got off the train two days ago."

The waiter vanished. Bender leaned back in his chair like a sultan, pleased with himself, the rich blue tobacco haze wreathing his head like a crown. Charlie felt his heart slip. How could he have doubted a man like this? Bender was born to inherit the earth, to eat off silver salvers and drink from golden goblets, there was no doubt about it. "So what is it? What's come up?" Despite himself, he could barely contain his excitement.

The big smile, the self-congratulatory pause. "Nothing more than this: we're going to get rich at a rate six times faster than we were yesterday, that's all. Oh yeah—and we're changing the name of the company."

"Changing the name?" Charlie clutched involuntarily at the leather card-case in his breast pocket—how he loved those cards. "But why?"

"Just a minor change, Charlie, no big deal. We're just going to add another name to the full appellation, that's all." Again the pause, lingering and dramatic. Worlds collided, ships went down in the time it took Bender to flick the ash from his cigar. "Are you ready? 'Kellogg's Per-Fo Company, Incorporated,' that's what we're going to call it."

"Kellogg's? What are you talking about? We can't just—"

But at that moment the front door swung open and in walked the man Bender had been waiting for. He was clean-shaven and he'd had a haircut and somebody had buried the vomit-stained overcoat and gotten him a new suit of clothes, but Charlie recognized him in an instant. He staggered a bit as he came up to the table, and Charlie, bewildered, took Bender's lead and rose to greet him. "Ah, George," Bender purred as he took the man's hand in his fleshy embrace, "good of you to come. Capital." And, turning to Charlie: "I'd like you to meet my associate, Mr. Charles P. Ossining, Esquire."

The muddy eyes, the yellowed stumps of the teeth, and not the vaguest glimmer of recognition.

"And Charlie, dear old, good old, fine old Charlie," Bender crowed, flush with geniality, an arm round each of them, "Charlie, I'd like you to meet George Kellogg."

Chapter 10

A

Thankful

Bird

❦

Two weeks before Thanksgiving, that holiday of universal glut, Will detected a subtle change in the atmosphere of the dining hall. It was during the morning meal—or, rather, during the period he occupied at table watching Mrs. Tindermarsh gobble her chopped-beet-and-split-rail salad while Hart-Jones roared like an ass over his soft-boiled eggs and Miss Muntz took neat little bites of her leg of Protose, or whatever it was. He wasn't eating, himself. This was the second of his three days on the laxative diet, and he swallowed the rubbery psyllium seeds and cardboardlike hijiki as if he were taking so many pills; for beverage, he enjoyed a glass of water. At any rate, the ambience of the place seemed different somehow, almost festive, the buzz of conversation more animated, the titters and bursts of laughter more convivial and frequent. Something was afoot.

A bit sore from his prebreakfast bout with Nurse Bloethal and her irrigating machine, Will gave a stiff nod of welcome to his tablemates as he eased himself down and unfolded the napkin in his lap. There was no need to bother with the menu—he'd barely gotten the napkin settled when one of the dietary girls appeared with his plate of shriveled dark seaweed and bitter seeds, which had all the appeal of a bowl of wood shavings and lint. Professor Stepanovich gave him a shy look of commiseration, then went back to digging at his corn flakes; the others, even Homer Praetz, a man not given to levity, wore tight little smiles, as if they could barely contain themselves. "What is it?" Will demanded, and despite himself he could feel a silly grin tugging at the corners of his mouth. "Am I missing something?"

Miss Muntz, his lovely greenish friend who'd been swaddled beside him on the veranda for the past three afternoons now, let a little calliope toot of a laugh escape her. Homer Praetz put a hand to his mouth and harmonized in a reedy falsetto. "Haven't you noticed——?" she began, and broke down in a trill of schoolgirlish giggles.

"What she means, Mr. Lightbody," Mrs. Tindermarsh added, and she was in on it, too, "is that the hall seems a bit rustic today, wouldn't you say?"

"The barnyard invades the healing pen!" Hart-Jones crowed, waving a spoon slick with egg yolk and showing his blunt yellow horse's teeth.

Put on his mark, Will scanned the room. He saw the usual horde of feeding faces, the celebrated, the rich, the dyspeptic and nervous. Pillars rose to the ceiling; waitresses flowed though the aisles in an unrippled stream. He saw Eleanor's table and noticed, with a little stab of alarm, that she wasn't there—nor was Linniman. Maybe she'd eaten earlier— or overslept. Or maybe Dr. Kellogg had her on an early-morning enema- and-exercise regimen . . . but where was Linniman, the grinning one, that paragon of health and mesmerizer of married women, that breakfast eater? Will had learned that he was a bachelor, and the knowledge depressed him still further—no trim physiologic wife awaited the lusty doctor at home, no patter of running feet answered the rattle of his key in the door. All the more reason he should give free rein to his unbridled bacheloric libido and hunger after other men's wives.

But no, Will was probably just imagining things. So what if Linniman was cordial—exceptionally cordial—to his wife? That was his job, wasn't it? And besides, Will felt secure in Eleanor—she might poison him, but she'd never forsake him, never even think about it, never. Would she? They'd made up their differences—it was nothing, really, they agreed; it was just that they were both ill and under a good deal of strain, what with the change of scene and regimen and the long en- ervating journey. She'd come to his room the previous evening, sweet in a simple white shirtwaist and black skirt, to see how he was. She wound up staying for over an hour, sitting at his bedside and reading to him from Helen Keller's *The Story of My Life*, and when she got up to leave she bent over him, took his face in her hands and gave him a prolonged and very promising kiss.

"Oh, Mr. Lightbody, really," Miss Muntz laughed from the other end of the table, "don't tell me you haven't noticed it yet?" And then she was up out of her seat and sweeping round the table with a rustle of skirts to hover over him and point out this marvel, this wonder, this new cynosure of the dining hall.

Will saw it then, caught up in the aura of her perfume and tingling with the awareness of her proximity, and he couldn't help himself: he burst out with a laugh. How could he have missed it? There it was, the talk of the room, right there in front of his eyes, thrumming to itself in a wood-slat cage set up on a table in the corner. A turkey. A fat, wattled, feathery, preening bird staring out at the diners from the thicket of its glittery dull eyes. Above it, another of the Doctor's didactic banners:

A THANKFUL BIRD

And why was it thankful? Because two weeks hence the full complement of nearly a thousand San guests would be dining on Nuttolene steaks, thank you, with mock giblets and gluten-soya gravy to go with their turnips, mashed potatoes and cranberry sauce. Will had to hand it to Kellogg: he never missed a trick.

"Isn't it hilarious?" Miss Muntz breathed in his ear, her face radiant in its greenish glow.

It was as if a weight had been lifted from Will's shoulders: it *was* hilarious, yes, it was. And more, much more. Here was this noble bird, this avatar of winged flight and oven-browned skin, this provider of drumstick and wing, white meat and dark, their fellow creature who had every right to his life, liberty and pursuit of wattled happiness, here it was strutting about its pen and eating the same nuts and grains they were, spared forever the butcher's block and the fatal drop of the cleaver. This was what it was all about, the vegetarian ethos, a new kind of spirituality and moral bonding, and Will saw it pecking there before him, felt it deep in the pit of his stomach. At least he believed he felt it. Of course—and even in his moment of rapture the thought occurred to him—it might only have been a psyllium seed, expanding in its secret nook.

After breakfast, Nurse Graves escorted Will to the Men's Gymnasium for a session of Swedish Manual Movements and laughing exercises, followed by Vibrotherapy and a half-hour immersion in the sinusoidal bath. The Swedish Manual Movements, as developed a hundred years earlier by Ling, of Sweden, after reading an ancient Chinese text in French translation, consisted primarily of jumping and clapping in various contorted and unnatural attitudes, so far as Will could see. A hundred men of all ages and conditions took part en masse, while the chief therapist—a Swede with a prominent forehead and huge lumpish bread-loaf muscles—exhorted them. For the laughing exercises, designed not only to improve the patient's mood but to allow him to breathe more deeply and naturally, the same group reconvened in the same gymnasium to watch a pair of mimes in blackface take pratfalls while the stocky tenor, Tiepolo Cappucini, led them all in a tortured session of operatic laughter. Purged, half-starved and disoriented, his limbs numb from the Swedish movements and his gut leaden with seaweed, Will didn't find it all that funny. But he pranced and jogged up and down and shook his lean buttocks along with his fellow sufferers, with the old men in suspenders, the obese and the emaciated, the outwardly healthy and the visibly decrepit, and before he knew it he was laughing uncontrollably, desperately, without reason or cause, laughing like a lunatic rattling the bars of his cage.

Vibrotherapy came almost as a relief. This, the attendant explained to Will and a splinter group of half a dozen men similarly exhausted by the effort of laughing, was a passive exercise. The idea was to sit on a chair or stool or lie on a table fitted out with an electrical motor that caused the entire apparatus to quake, shiver and lurch like a buggy with broken springs hurtling down a washboard road. Will heard a brief lecture on each of the three forms of vibration—percutient, lateral and centrifugal—and learned how Vigoroux, Granville, Schiff and Boudet had found them effective in either increasing or diminishing nervous sensibility, according to the case at hand, after which he was strapped into a chair bolted to an iron plate and shaken like a Christmas eggnog for the next three-quarters of an hour. And that wouldn't have been so bad, really, but for the man in the chair bolted directly behind his, a grunter and tooth grinder of the first magnitude who kept butting the back of his head against the headrest of Will's chair. Or the man to his left, who blathered incessantly in a high clonic squeal about the vicissitudes of the stock market. Once that was over, Will was introduced to the special vibrators for the hands, arms and feet, as well as the vibrating stool, the vibrating table and the vibrating cot. By the time he left the Vibrotherapy Department, the walls, curtains and lamps had begun to vibrate, too, and it took him a good five minutes of pacing up and down the corridor with Nurse Graves before the world stopped trembling beneath his feet.

His final stop that morning, prior to being bundled up like a newborn infant and deposited by Nurse Graves on the frozen flagstones of the veranda, was the Electrical Department. Here, patients were subjected to varying degrees of electrical shock as a way of either stimulating or depressing groups of nerves and muscles—each according to his symptoms and needs, of course. Will was scheduled for the hot glove, followed by half an hour in the sinusoidal bath. He wasn't looking forward to either. For one thing, he was feeling cranky and tired, having been subjected to enough abuse for one day. For another, he didn't like the sound of the first treatment—the hot glove—and he'd always had an aversion to public baths and swimming pools, all that exposed flesh; apelike men with hairy shoulders and fur growing in clumps on their thighs, calves, between their toes; women like squashed melons in their lumpy bathing costumes. During their courtship and the first few years of their marriage, Will and Eleanor had bathed in the Hudson on those blistering, eternally blue days of July and August, but they'd always managed to find a spot to themselves—on the Brinckerhoff estate or his father's place or some such private enclave. At school, of course, there had been no escaping the public bath, and Will had been one among a throng of naked boys during his eight years at the Crowley Preparatory School for Boys in New Milford, Connecticut. But he hadn't liked it. And he wasn't in school anymore. And he resented having to remove his clothing in the presence of strangers—or for that matter, having to endure the sight of strangers removing their clothing in his presence, or appearing in public in any state of dress short of what would be considered good and proper attire for an evening at Sherry's or Delmonico's.

But the Electrical Department surprised him. There was no sign of the mob of bearded, hirsute characters in loincloths of which he'd had one brief horrifying glance when Ralph had taken him on a tour of the place and pushed open the doors to the men's swimming pool. Nor were there any strangers, male or female, lounging about in deshabille. The attendant, dressed in a suit, shirt, collar and tie like anyone else, took him into a private booth, bade him remove his shirt and directed him to lie prone on a padded table beneath a crisp white sheet. The hot glove, which was supposed to excite the muscles of his lower back (and, when he turned over, his much-abused abdomen), actually felt good. The shocks it administered were minimal, and the warmth was soothing. Afterward, he was instructed to dress himself but for his jacket, and roll up his sleeves and trousers so that he could immerse his forearms and lower legs in the elevated buckets of water that comprised the sinusoidal bath.

He complied passively. And the whole thing would have been at least tolerable if it hadn't been for the presence of a second patient, not exactly a stranger, but a man to whom Will had said so little he might just as well have been: Homer Praetz. They were seated side by side, Will and the industrial giant, in identical chairs that had been tricked out with four white galvanized buckets and the electrical wires that provided the healing charge. Homer Praetz had evidently just come from the pool or one of the more vulgar baths, as his hair was wet and he was wearing an enormous blue cotton bathrobe. "Lightbody, isn't it?" he'd cried, taking Will's hand in a moist and flabby grip. "Getting a bit of the old sinusoidal, eh?" And then he'd lowered his voice: "Can't say that I like this part of it, myself. Feels like ants crawling up and down my legs. And my privates, that's what kills me. Hurts a bit, too—nothing much, but enough to make you wince from time to time."

He heaved a sigh and threw off his robe to reveal a tumultuous puckered belly hung with twisted black hairs, and then he stalked round the room in his loincloth two or three times as if to show it off properly before easing himself into the chair beside Will. Casually, as if he were dipping a shirt in a washtub, he lifted first one blocky pale dead-looking foot into its receptacle, and then the other. "Anything for a cure, eh?", he whispered, giving Will a wink.

But Will didn't have a chance to respond. He could feel it in that instant, the attendant in his dark proper suit throwing the switch, the Chief's big generator whirling round somewhere in the depths of the building, and this tiny little jolt nibbling at him, biting, pinching, kneading, and it wasn't like ants at all—no, Will thought, closing his eyes on the whole strange business, it was like fish, fish in a pond, a school of hungry fishes pecking at each little etiolated hair up and down the length of his weary limbs till he felt he was being eaten alive.

On Saturday, the day of Will's emancipation from the laxative diet, the Chief had arranged for a formal "New Arrivals Banquet," a regular feature of the Social Department, which was intended to introduce the newcomers to a select group of a hundred or so of the more distinguished patients. Will and Eleanor had been asked to attend—together, arm in arm, just like husband and wife, like lovers, like cohabitors of the proud brick house his father had built for them on Parsonage Lane—and Eleanor had been cajoled into preparing a brief speech about her work in organizing the Peterskill Ladies' Biologic Living Society. Will was elated. Not only for the opportunity to spend some time with his wife —and show her off, in all her rare beauty and sophistication, to the ailing millionaires—but because, at long last, the psyllium seeds and the seaweed were behind him.

Of course, it wasn't all sunshine and roses—there was still the matter of the new diet to contend with. The milk diet, that is. The diet that commenced after his morning enema with exactly four ounces of pure white whole milk from the immaculate Sanitarium Dairy, where the cows were vacuum-cleaned twice a day to prevent even the remotest possibility of a speck of dander or bovine hair winding up in the finished product. The diet that prescribed an identical four-ounce glass of milk every fifteen minutes during the waking hours, and every hour on the hour throughout the night, to continue for as long as Drs. Linniman and Kellogg deemed necessary. The trouble was, Will had never much liked milk. Not even as a child. And for the past fifteen years or so the only use he'd had for it was in the odd milk punch or to lighten his morning coffee—if he put away three quarts a year it would have surprised him. And now he was soaked with it. Blotted, drenched, saturated. Now it would be milk, milk, milk, till it came out his pores and he dreamed of nothing but good pasture and pendulous dugs. Still, even in the context of that grim dietary, there was some cause for hope: Dr. Kellogg—ever genial, ever twinkling, ever coruscating with health and positive thought—had hinted at a change, somewhere down the road, and if conditions warranted, to the grape diet.

The banquet was held on the fourth floor, in a lofty meeting room just across the corridor from the main dining hall. The room was tricked out with the same sort of intercolumnar palms and exclamatory banners (THE BATTLE CREEK IDEA!) as the main hall, but here the tables were longer, seating twenty and more, and a podium had been installed on a dais against the far wall. Eleanor wore a green silk dress to bring out her eyes, with an ivory tatted collar and reticule to match. She was beautiful in her fluid, long-necked way, like some exotic bird, and Will had to admit that the Sanitarium was doing her good—if you didn't know, you'd never have guessed there was anything at all the matter with her. As he did every night, though it was only to bolt seeds or sip milk, Will dressed in a snowy shirtfront and a fine old-fashioned black tailcoat.

They were seated near the head of one of the long tables, which was already occupied by a party that included Mrs. Tindermarsh, Admiral Nieblock of the Naval Academy, Upton Sinclair, the novelist and reformer, and the Great Masticator himself, Horace B. Fletcher. The lighting was muted, with little shaded lamps set at intervals along the walls and candelabra on the tables. Will looked approvingly on the carnations, the glittering silver and crystal, and he restrained the urge to dig into a bowl of salted almonds that had been set out along with celery, olives and bran in sugar bowls to whet the guests' appetites. For the first time in as long as he could remember he felt a twinge of hunger, but the Doctor's voice spoke in his head—*No almonds for you, sir, no celery or bran even, not yet, not yet*—and he folded his hands and waited patiently for the first of his supernumerary servings of milk.

The meal itself—the meal the others were allowed to eat, that is— was haute San all the way, from the semimiraculous hothouse-grown-sliced-tomato-garnished-with-everything hors d'oeuvre to the vegetable meat loaf, sweet peppers stuffed with cream cheese, brick ice cream and after-dinner Health Koko. Will found the woman seated to his left (a Mrs. Prendergast, of Hackensack, New Jersey) to be perfectly charming, in addition to being a dog lover, and he regaled her in his echolalic tones with stories of Dick the wirehaired terrier and his various feats and doggy pranks. The man across from him was all right, too—a big red-faced Scotch-tweed character with a bad heart who seemed fixated on the subject of General Castro, the truculent Latin American dictator, but was perfectly happy to give a point-by-point analysis of Army's chances in the forthcoming Army-Navy game when Will abruptly changed the subject. And if there was a focal point at their end of the table, it had to be Eleanor. She shined, she really did, arching her neck and cocking her head to deliver one of her little verbal thrusts, or stopping cold in the middle of a sentence to give her auditors her best cross-eyed look of comic distress. Gardening, that's what it was. The fellow to her right—Will didn't catch his name—could talk of nothing but his estate and the improvements he'd made to it, the avenue of plane trees and the rhododendron arbor ad nauseam. Eleanor made mincemeat of him.

When it came time for the talk, the toastmistress, a lady doctor so salubrious she could have posed for the "Sweetheart of the Corn" portrait, raised her glass of prune juice and welcomed Will and Eleanor, Mrs. Tindermarsh and some dozen or so others to Battle Creek. "Here's to the thrill of an ice mitt in a cold gray dawn," she said, her glass held high, "to the tingle of that sinusoidal current up your spine and the rewards of a meatless life!" Next was a square block of a woman, the stone before it's been hewn, a woman so dense she made Mrs. Tindermarsh look petite. She was a missionary from Iceland, as it turned out, and she recited a Norwegian-dialect poem about stewed prunes and quick cold trips to the outhouse under a starveling moon. Then it was Eleanor's turn.

Will could feel his heart thumping as she ascended the dais and arranged her notes on the podium. He'd never been much at public speaking—had twice failed elocution, in fact—and he marveled at her self-possession as she stood there serenely and took the measure of all those strangers—dignitaries and bigwigs at that. She didn't even have to clear her throat or take a sip of water—she merely began, in a soft conversational tone that projected beautifully throughout the room. "I want to talk to you tonight, ladies and gentlemen, friends all, of my life before Battle Creek, of my own personal Dark Ages, when all my holy temples were besieged by the barbarian hordes of gluttony, flesh foods and sleepless nights. I was a lost soul. Twenty times a day I found myself in tears over things so trivial I'm almost ashamed to mention them—though I will, because I want you to understand just how very sick and lorn I was before I discovered Dr. Kellogg and La Vie Simple." She paused, her eyes huge, her mouth set in a pathetic, determined pout. "A torn postage stamp. The fine exquisite age lines in one of my Sèvres cups. A bird in a cage. The thought of a fen in the woods, dreary and forgotten, with the night closing round it like an apparition. A pen with a broken nib. Aigrettes. Apricots. The way the sun would slant through the parlor windows in late afternoon and strike the portrait of my mother in her best bonnet and gown. These, my friends, were the sorts of things that would set me off."

She went on in this vein for five minutes or so, and it was charming and frank and there wasn't a listener in the room unaffected by what she was saying, but she was speaking to the initiated, to a society of neurasthenics, and why in God's name was she being so sanctimonious about it? Will shifted uncomfortably in his seat, wondering when she would lighten things up with a flash of her satiric wit, or even clown a bit, as the Icelandic lady had, but he waited in vain. She dwelled on her symptoms and her sorrows in a way that smacked of symptomitis—but, then, Will supposed, that was part of the rhetorical strategy. Play their heartstrings for all it was worth, and then bring out the big guns in a thundering salvo in praise of the little goateed saint who made it all possible.

As proud as he was of her, he nonetheless found himself drifting a bit as she worked her way into the regenerate mode, but he snapped to attention when the appellation "my dear husband" dropped from her lips. Her "dear husband" was only now going through what she'd suffered in struggling toward the light, and the taste for meat, for liquor—even, she feared, for narcotic drugs—ran deep with him.

Will was mortified. She was looking him dead in the face, a soft compassionate glow illuminating her till she seemed to radiate like some saint in the Roman church, and every eye in the house was on him. He wanted to crawl under a chair, become a disciple of Father Kneipp in Worishofen and run barefoot through the snow, wanted to flog himself, wanted, more than anything, to smoke, swill whiskey, devour chops and steaks and gouty drumsticks in despite of them all. He shrank against the physiologic tines of his chair.

Eleanor went on to detail his excesses and the depth of despair to which he'd sunk even while supporting her in her struggle for wellness at the San. She told how she'd found him in his besotted state, his clothes spoiled, dog and servants alienated, the whole neighborhood in an uproar. And then she drew a breath so deep and piteous it was as if the entire congregation were breathing through her. "And it was me!" she cried suddenly, flinging her arms out in extenuation. "All me. I was the one to blame. In my selfishness, in my illness, in my passion to think positively and make myself well at all costs, I neglected my pillar, my partner, my husband. He was falling even as I took the first tottering steps toward recovery."

There was no sound in the room. No breath was expelled, no foot tapped, neither cough nor sniffle intruded on the awestruck silence that gripped the audience. "But that's not the end of the story, my dear friends and supporters, and those of you just now embarking on the adventure of biologic living. No, let me tell you that he sits here among us tonight." Pause, two beats. "Will? *Will?*" Was she addressing him? Was she pointing him out? Did she expect him to stand up and be welcomed into the flock? She was. And she did. "Will, stand up please, darling, won't you?"

His knees were rusted hinges, his legs as ponderous as anchor chains. Applause sounded round him, cries of "Bravo!" and "That's a boy!"

And then Eleanor was there, sweetly, sweetly, all in sweetness, and this time it was she who was embracing him.

Post-lecture, there were refreshments and the usual palaver. The hand pressers and well-wishers clustered six deep round Eleanor, while Will, shrinking into a corner, was assailed by a battery of total strangers who hemmed and hawed and shuffled and took him by the elbow and patted him on the back, offering up volumes of unsolicited advice, charitable thoughts and expressions of maternal concern. It was agonizing, and it lasted through three separate feedings of milk, a measurement of time that already seemed as regular and natural to Will as the chiming of the bells at St. Eustace's in Peterskill. When it was over, finally, when the last long sober well-meaning face had finished hanging over his with its concatenation of dreary advice and maunderings about Uncle Bill's drunks and Aunt Molly's furtive tippling, Will found himself alone with Eleanor, striding purposefully out the door and up the corridor.

But where were they going?

He could feel her glowing at his side, generating a current all her own, warmer than the sinusoidal bath, hotter than the hot glove. She was pleased with herself. Very pleased. She'd done her part for the San—she was a booster if ever there was one—and the audience had liked her, sincerely liked her. She was a success. The talk of the place. "Did you see how they crowded round me at the end? I could barely catch my breath. Will, oh, Will," she gushed, slipping her arm through his and leaning girlishly into him, "it was such an honor to stand up there before people like the Sinclairs—that was Meta there at the end of the table, the dark striking gypsy-looking woman? And of course Horace B. Fletcher. And did you see the funny little man in black broadcloth, looked as if he were attending a funeral? That was Almus Overstreet, the banker—and do you know what he said to me afterward, sweetest man in the world, really?"

Will held on to his wife's arm. He liked the feel of it, resting lightly in the crook of his own, her body moving in tandem with his, and suddenly he felt charged with the electricity running through her. "No, what did he say? Let me guess—he wants to make you a partner?" He couldn't restrain his laugh, and it was too loud, too exuberant, a bray almost, but he felt so good all of a sudden he couldn't help himself. "Or, no, he's going to send you out on the temperance circuit, advising wives how to resurrect their fallen husbands."

"Oh, don't be silly, Will. Though it's charming, and you're charming, and I'm so glad you're here." Pause, smile; her lips and teeth: God, how he loved her. "He told me it was the most moving speech he'd heard since John L. Sullivan had stood up at an Elks Lodge supper and described how drink had ruined him. And he said you were the luckiest man alive and he had no doubt—he'd bet half his fortune on it—that you'd recover with a wife like me to look after you. And wasn't that sweet, though of course he was just being polite. . . ."

They were at the elevator doors now, the loquacious day man having given way to an older, more reserved gentleman who looked a bit out of place in the tight-fitting parrot-green uniform he shared with the bell captain and his boys. "Polite or not, El," Will was saying as he handed his wife into the elevator, "he was right—I *am* the luckiest man alive. And I'm glad, I really am, that you thought to bring me here with you." He had a whole speech prepared, a sort of act of contrition he'd been silently rehearsing as she stood there at the lectern, an acknowledgment that he'd been difficult, recalcitrant even, a negative thinker, but that now, though perhaps she'd been a bit more personal than he would have liked in front of all those strangers, he'd begun to see the light. The words were on his lips, but he never got the chance to deliver them. "What floor?" the night man asked in a thick lugubrious tone, as if he were asking what plot they'd like to be buried in at the Oak Hill Cemetery, and Will was suddenly thrown into confusion.

Eleanor answered for him. "Two," she murmured.

"Yes, of course," Will whispered, giving her arm a squeeze, "I'll see you to your door." And then, as the elevator man stiffly drew the gate across, he dropped his voice still further and spoke against the warmth of her ear: "God, it's like courting all over again."

Eleanor said nothing to this, but she gave a look that took him by

155

surprise. It was a look he knew from some distant period in their lives, a time before Coffee Neuralgia, enervated nerves and her sad fruitless pregnancy. He felt his heart skip a beat.

He might have hesitated at the door, the Doctor's strictures worked into the grain of the wood, the brass of the doorknob, the paint on the walls, but he didn't. That look encouraged him and he wafted in behind her like a vernal breeze and swept her up in his gangling embrace before she could resist. He held her there against him, the green silk of her dress a whisper of friction against his dinner jacket, and he could feel the ache of her uncorseted and newly physiologic body beneath her skirts and petticoats and the last thinnest undergarment of all. He was desperate. He was trembling. He bent to kiss her.

"But Will . . ." Her voice was squeezed shut, the gasp of a pearl diver coming up for air. "Darling, dear, I need to . . . Frank—that is, Dr. Linniman—you see, he has me on the diuretic diet this week and I need to . . . need to . . . use the . . . bathroom. . . ."

Will was a tumble of apology, jumping back from her as if he'd burned himself at the stove, and suddenly he didn't know what to do with his hands, with his feet, with the whole tense bundle of leaks and wants and hurts that incorporated him. He waited in one of the Doctor's chairs, one knee crossed over the other, while waters flowed and burbled from behind the closed door and Eleanor made her secret ablutions.

"That was quite a speech, El," Will observed, addressing the null plane of the door, and he was talking just to hear himself. "A bit close to the bone, maybe—you barely mentioned the Peterskill Ladies' Biologic Living Society." From beyond the door, the sound of water, mysterious, enticing. "I was mortified, El. I was. I mean, in front of all those strangers . . ."

The door opened with a soft erotic click and Eleanor stepped lightly into the room. She was barefooted and she was wearing a nightgown; her hair was combed out and trailing down her shoulders in the way of some exotic witch or geisha. He knew that nightgown—pink flannel with a revelation of lace at the bodice and sleeves—and the recognition excited him. *My wife is in her nightgown,* he told himself, *and we're in the same room together.* Then he caught a glimpse of her ankles, brief, scintillating, white flesh and rippling movement, and he was up out of the chair.

She held him. They kissed. He felt the flutter of her tongue, the heat of her, and suddenly his hands came into play, roaming, massaging, re-exploring familiar territory. She took his arm and led him to the bed. "Hush, Will," she whispered, "don't fret now. My speech . . . it was for your own good. And the San's. Now come to me, Will. Take your jacket off."

He fumbled with his clothes, jerking at the cravat, the shirtfront, feeling light-headed and confused. "But, but . . . your condition," he protested, "Dr. Kellogg—"

She was watching him, her gaze steady, strong, without a flicker of vacillation. "I want a daughter, Will. Give me a daughter."

A daughter. Give me a daughter, Will. He was beside himself, trembling like one of the vibrotherapist's prize patients, and he fell on her—a bit awkwardly, perhaps, but with true passion and utter conviction.

Unfortunately, at that precise moment, a knock sounded at the door. A knock. They weren't at home, after all, nestled in the big dark canopied bed from across the sea while the servants busied themselves in distant regions of the house and the soft light of dusk pressed at the windows—no, they were inmates of the Battle Creek Sanitarium, where no less a figure than Dr. John Harvey Kellogg himself had strictly enjoined them from connubial relations, and there was a knock at the door. They froze. Guilty, panicked, discovered. Will was about to make a leap for the closet, when Eleanor, in a show of surprising strength, pushed him off her as if he were a heap of old rags. There was a moment of sustained tension—Would the intruder persist? Would he go away? Would the door handle turn with a click—and then, from out in the hallway, came the breathy clinical voice of reason and regimen: "Mr. Lightbody? Mr. Lightbody, are you in there?"

Nurse Graves.

Eleanor rose to answer the door, totally composed, regal, frosty—Eleanor, who a moment before had been passionate in his arms. "Yes?"

Nurse Graves stood in the doorway, a saucer balanced in one hand. The saucer supported a single truncated four-ounce glass, opaque with its burden of milk. "I'm very sorry to disturb you, ma'am," she breathed, barely audible, the color high in her cheeks, "but it's time for your husband's quarter-hour feeding. Of milk. And Mr. Lightbody"—looking beyond Eleanor now to where Will sat hunched on the bed in dinner jacket and undershirt—"you really should be preparing for bed. It's past ten. Quarter past. Sir."

Eleanor never moved a muscle. She listened to the nurse's speech in silence, and the soft trailing devolution of the younger woman's words seemed to fortify her composure. She was taller than Nurse Graves— Irene—by an inch or two, anyway, and she was slimmer, and her self-possession was unshakable. Of course, Eleanor was a woman of the world, thoroughly sophisticated, while Nurse Graves was a girl, an ingénue— firm, healthy, buxom, with a smile that was like the morning sun on a field of wheat, but an ingénue all the same. San or no San, Eleanor was in command here. "You may leave the milk with me, nurse. Mr. Lightbody is engaged at the moment, as you may have noticed. And while we appreciate your solicitude, I can't really say that we need to be followed around like children with a nanny." Eleanor never took her eyes from the younger woman's face. "That will be all, thank you."

But Nurse Graves surprised him. Instead of handing over the medicinal milk and bowing meekly out of the room, she stood firm. "I'm very sorry, and begging your pardon, ma'am, but Doctor's orders are that I should administer the feeding myself and observe the patient until the feeding is completed."

A long moment interposed itself, and Will thought of armies digging in, posting sentries, establishing lines of communication, shoring up defenses. Finally Eleanor let out an exasperated sigh. "All right," she said, "administer the feeding, observe the patient. Be my guest."

Nurse Graves entered the room in a brisk official way, her steps short and quick, her back rigid. Wordlessly, she bent over Will, handed him the saucer and waited while he drained his sixty-first glass of the day. And then, all business, she marched directly across the room with the empty glass balanced on its saucer, hesitating only at the door. Ignoring Eleanor, she addressed Will in her little itch of a voice—"I'll be waiting in your room, Mr. Lightbody"—and then she was gone, leaving the door gaping behind her.

Three quick steps and Eleanor set the door to with a shudder of lintel and jamb that made Will's ears ring. She was enraged, her eyes swollen, lips drawn tight. "Who does she think she is—your nursemaid? God, did you see the way she stood there and confronted me on my own doorstep? As if I couldn't be trusted to see that you drank your precious milk?"

"It's all right, Eleanor," Will crooned, rising from the bed to embrace her, to begin where they'd left off, "she's only doing her duty."

"Her duty?!" she cried, angrily shrugging him off. "Is it her duty to imply that your wife is incompetent? Untrustworthy?" Her face was small and hard, and she stood poised on the balls of her feet, half-crouched, a wrestler moving in for the takedown. Will backed up a step. "What's her name?" she suddenly demanded, and there was a keening, unsteady edge to her voice.

The words stuck in Will's throat. "Nurse Graves."

"Graves? All right. Thank you." She turned her back on him and strode to the writing desk in the corner, where she took up her pen and furiously scratched the name across a sheet of paper.

Will was sunk in misery. If they took Nurse Graves away from him he'd have nothing, nothing but an unbroken succession of days with their oceans of milk, the mystical pronouncements of Drs. K. and L., and the hard heavy hand of Nurse Bloethal. "She's very good, really," he murmured. "She is, El. Very attentive."

But Eleanor wasn't listening. She'd stepped into the bathroom, where Will could see her sprinkling something that looked suspiciously like flaked hijiki into an enormous tumbler of water she was filling from the tap. As she bent to the sink, the nightgown caught at her hips, revealing shape and definition and giving him another glimpse of her white, white ankles. Will couldn't help himself. He moved lightly across the floor, slipped into the bathroom and wrapped his arms round her. "El," he whispered, hoarse with passion, "let's go back to bed."

"Oh, Will," she sighed, "I'm too flustered now. I don't know what I was thinking, anyway—any of that business would be a terrible mistake for both of us. You know what Dr. Kellogg said." He was watching her eyes in the mirror, but he saw nothing there to encourage him. "Go back to your nurse, Will. Get well. Go to bed."

He heard her, but his blood was up and he couldn't stop now. Taking her by the hand, gently, gingerly, he led her back to the bed, reaching up to flick off the lamp on the night table as they eased down side by side on the rock-hard physiologic mattress. Darkness enveloped them like a blanket. The smallest sounds echoed through the room—the ticking of the clock on the bureau, the soft even suck of her breath. After a moment, a hint of light revealed itself at the edges of the curtains and in a single glowing band beneath the door. He turned to kiss her and got a mouthful of hair. "No, Will," she said, and her tone was firm. "My nerves simply can't take it."

"Please?" His voice was a squeak in the darkness, a child's plea, pathetic. "I'm better now, I am. And I need you." He was desperate, grasping at straws. "Our marriage vows, what about our marriage vows? And our daughter?"

Even as he spoke he knew he was doomed to failure. No argument could move Eleanor. Her father had spoiled her shamelessly and she'd done exactly as she'd pleased ever since Will had known her. And if once in a great while she seemed to give in, it was only because she'd decided it was to her advantage, a sort of bartering of concessions. No, she was a rock. She was adamantine. He might just as well give it up now and shuffle off to his solitary cell.

"Oh, all right, Will," she breathed in the darkness, and her acquiescence stunned him, electrified him, "but please hurry. Your milk's liable to get warm."

There was a whisper of flannel as she lay back and lifted the nightgown, her thighs palely glowing in the defeated light. Will tore at the buttons of his trousers—hurry, hurry—and jerked at his long johns. A moment—there—and again he fell on her. But there was something wrong. He couldn't seem to . . . it was . . . there was nothing there. Thunderstruck, he reached down to examine himself and found that he was limp—*limp*, after that barrage of unclean thoughts and all that unseemly stiffening in the crotch, *limp*, now that the hour had finally come.

Eleanor's voice spoke out of the void. "Come on, Will. My nerves. Get it over with."

He tried to concentrate, tried to think of Nurse Graves and the woman in the waiting room, but it was no use. He was a wreck, a hulk, a burned-out husk of a man. Even this, the most elemental human act, was beyond him now. He went cold with fear. He was a sick man, sick unto death.

"Will?"

He drew back from her, fishing in the gloom for his clothes.

"Will?"

"I—I think you're right, El. We can't do this. Not now. We're too ill, both of us, we're—"

"Will, stop it now. Don't be foolish. Come to me." She sat up and in the dim light he could see her holding her arms out to him. "Will." Her tone sharper now. *"Come. To. Me."*

But Will had sprung to his feet, jumping into his clothes as if he were escaping a burning house, tearing open the door and hobbling barefooted into the hall, shoes and shirtfront dangling from his fingertips. "Will," she called at his back, imperious, demanding, shriller and shriller, "Will, Will, *Will!"*

❖   ❖   ❖

He didn't know how long he wandered the halls, shambling along hopelessly, an inmate forever, an invalid, not a man but a eunuch, a castrato, a stud put out to pasture. His mind closed numbly around the sad truth of it, and for the first time in his life he began to question the value of going on with it all. What was the sense? There was nothing left to him now.

He drifted aimlessly, thinking only to duck into a doorway or behind a palm when a nurse or attendant happened by. They were sure to be looking for him by now—Nurse Graves would have sent out the alarm. He'd missed the last of his diurnal feedings, not to mention his bedtime enema, and even if Nurse Graves had gone home, the night nurse, who roughly shook him awake each hour for his nocturnal dose, would be wondering over the empty bed. He hid for a while in the Palm Garden, feeling like a child playing at hide-and-seek, and when the San settled down into the deep caverns of the night, he began moving again, haunting the hallways, the obscure corners, the back rooms. It was then that he thought of the turkey, that thankful bird roosting in its cage in a corner of the dining hall. He pictured it gargling and clucking to itself, folded in its feathery dreams, oblivious to the naked cheat of life. A thankful bird. Yes. And what did Will have to be thankful for?

It was late, and his reason had begun to slip. The turkey loomed up before him like a bugbear, symbol and embodiment of all the false promises the San made, all the bland reassurances and deadly assessments. The turkey was thankful and he was not. Suddenly he wanted to see it writhe. He wanted it to know pain, wanted to seize its leathery wattles and twist them from its stupid narrow bulb of a thankful head —he wanted to throttle it, pluck it, tear the wings from its body and the feet from its legs. Unconsciously, as if a force were pulling him, he found his way to the stairwell, and then he was climbing, a sleepwalker, a zombie (but not such a zombie that he didn't avoid the elevator— no, that would never do: they'd be expecting him there). It was six flights up. By the time he reached the top floor he was wheezing, choking for breath, and the sweat trailed down the back of his neck.

He spent the next several minutes recovering himself in the shadowy arena of the stairwell. An absolute unbroken silence had fallen over the San, and he pictured Miss Muntz asleep in her room; the Doctor in his Residence, breathing properly and rigorously even in sleep; Linniman snoring lustily in his bachelor's quarters; Eleanor settled finally into a light, cranky, dreamless sleep. The upper floor was deserted at this hour: no patients, no physicians, no nurses, no attendants. Will stepped out into the corridor and made his way along the wall to the grandiose entrance of the dining room, half expecting to see Mrs. Stover stationed there like a three-headed dog. But even Mrs. Stover had to sleep sometime. No one was there. Will stood before the door for a long moment before he took hold of the handle, pulled it open a crack and slipped inside.

The room seemed even vaster in the half-light seeping through the windows from the streetlamps that dotted the grounds. Solemn pillars, spectral palms: it was like some cavernous mausoleum. Overhead he could make out the bold black letters of Horace B. Fletcher's injunction and, in the far corner, the pale vacancy of the proclamation that hung over the turkey's pen. The tables, he saw, were set for breakfast. There was no sound from the thankful bird.

But what was he thinking, what was he doing? He felt like a thief, a murderer—he'd upheld the law all his life, and now here he was, about to commit mayhem. That innocent bird, that blameless life. But then he thought of the Doctor, smug and infallible, with his ready slogans and his easy, pink-cheeked health and all the rest, and the seductive irony of the deed overwhelmed him. A thankful bird throttled in its cage. Would they sweep it aside at first light and slip it out to the dustbin? Would the Doctor hustle in an imposter? How would he explain the empty cage, death in the place of life? Will squared his jaw and stalked across the room with the remorseless tread of the executioner, and there it was, the cage, right before him, its ghostly pale slats like pickets against the deeper gloom within.

He saw nothing, heard nothing. Where was the damn thing? Would it cry out as he flung open the door, as his fingers locked round its thankful throat? He had to be careful. If anyone should discover him . . . He could see the Doctor's severest face, the firm set of the goatee, the shrewd unforgiving little eyes. *And just what do you think you're doing with my turkey, sir?* His hand was on the latch—and how to work it? A bolt. Here, under his fingers. He slid it across. Nothing. The turkey stench rose to his nostrils, harsh, penetrating, ammoniac, the smell of the barnyard, manured fields, the dank working mold of the darkest corner of the darkest cellar. And then it materialized, a black heap of feathers on the floor of the cage, refuse already, a sack of nothing. He took a breath and reached for it.

No gobble, no cluck, no gasp of surprise: the thing was inert. Cold. Bloodless. Slack. Dumbstruck, Will closed his hand round its naked feet and yanked it from the cage in a dark moil of feathers and dust. With an effort, he held it up before him in the weak light. The big bird's neck hung limp, the wings were skewed. Will felt a chill run through him. Dangling, eternally thankful, the thing twisted round like a hanged man finding his center of gravity at the end of a rope.

Dead. Already dead.

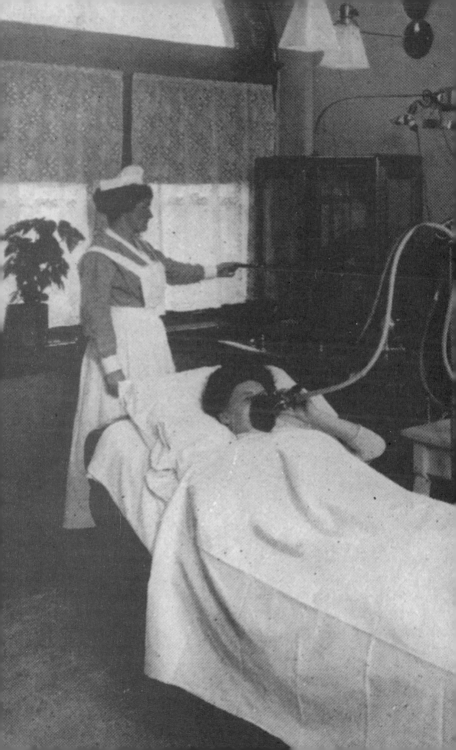

PART II
Therapeusis

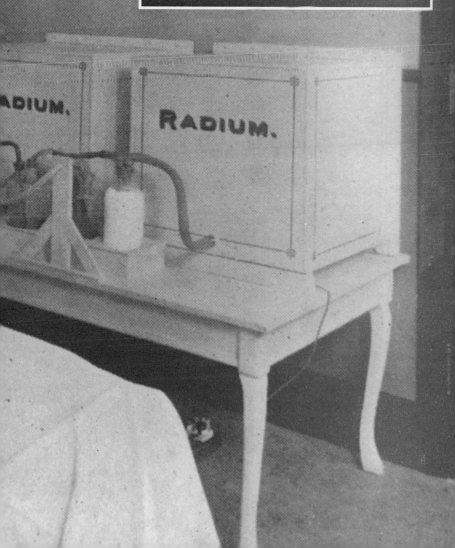

Chapter 1

'Tis
the
Season

❧

As Christmas approached, the San was transformed. The halls were decked with ground pine and holly, a twenty-foot tree appeared in the lobby, everywhere you turned there was a spangle of tinsel, crepe paper and mistletoe. Dr. Kellogg had always made good and provident use of the holidays, from Groundhog Day to the Fourth of July, doing his utmost to co-opt the spirit of the day and turn it into a triumph of health advocacy, but at Christmas he outdid himself. He kept his staff busy arranging sleigh rides, sing-alongs, gift grab bags and the like (an occupied patient is never a restive one, he always said), while the Sanitarium Orchestra incessantly worked over selections from Bach, Handel and Monteverdi, and "Professor" Sammy Siegel wandered the dining room with a triangle and pennywhistle, rendering versions of "Jingle Bells," "Silent Night" and the "Dance of the Sugar Plum Fairy" that were by turns comical and touching. The nurses seemed to have an extra spring in their step, doctors and busboys passed each other in the hallway whistling Yuletide ditties, and even the moodiest of patients couldn't help brightening just a bit. It was all part and parcel of the Battle Creek Experience.

But despite the holiday cheer and the prospect of distributing anti-scorbutic treats from his cornucopian basket while dressed as the true and original Saint Nick, a part he'd always relished, to John Harvey

Kellogg it seemed a cold season. He was in a funk. A hole. A pit. A depression so deep that if he were his own physician he would have prescribed the physiologic life and the full slate of the neurasthenic's regime, but of course that was the paradox—he already lived the physiologic life to the hilt and yet it seemed, ever so imperceptibly, to be letting him down. But maybe he was just tired. Maybe that was it.

As he sat quietly in his office, spooning up a bit of yogurt and arranging his notes for the evening's Question Box lecture, he tried to pinpoint the source of his malaise. It was George, he supposed, the latest in a string of imitators, schemers, gate-crashers, leeches, bunco artists and pretenders, not only to the fruits of the Kellogg genius but to his very name itself. He felt like a fierce old king besieged by rebellious underlings, like Laocoön in the grip of the serpents: throw off one coil and another springs up to replace it. Why couldn't they leave a man alone?

From the beginning they'd tried to tear him down, horn in, profit where they had no right. No sooner had he invented caramel-cereal coffee than there was Charlie Post to pirate the recipe, make a shipload of money from tawdry advertising, buy out half the town, including the morning newspaper, and make his life a living hell. No sooner had he invented the corn flake than a howling pack of scoundrels descended on the town, bribed his employees and started up rival concerns in every shanty that had two doors and a window to it—and his brother Will was the worst offender of the lot. The Doctor was still seething about that. The breach between them that winter was like the Grand Canyon, the Pacific Ocean, and still growing. To think he'd trusted him, to think he'd been naive enough to imagine that blood was thicker than water —well, he'd learned a lesson there, that was for sure. But it still hurt. Hurt like a tooth being pulled—the same tooth, a hundred days in a row.

The Doctor had rescued his younger brother from obscurity and made him bookkeeper, fund-raiser, chief factotum and majordomo of the San, but Will wasn't satisfied. Or grateful. He wanted to go head-to-head with Post, marketing the Doctor's Sanitas Corn Flakes like some infernal vegetable compound or snake oil, but John Harvey Kellogg had put his foot down. No sir. No way at all. He was more concerned with his standing as a physician and surgeon than he was with huckstering products. Besides, the medical community frowned on that sort of thing, cheap advertising, money grubbing and all the rest—it had taken him thirty years to distance himself from the swamis, nudists, antivivisectionists and snake charmers, and he wasn't about to go back now.

And so, for a consideration, he'd let Will have the right to his patent in order to set up an independent company, the Battle Creek Toasted Corn Flake Company (which Will was already calling *Kellogg's* Toasted Corn Flake Company), with the provision that the Doctor himself retain the controlling interest, as director and majority stockholder. It seemed like a good deal. The Doctor got $35,000 in cash and better than fifty percent of the stock—and, most important, he was able to make money without sullying himself with the machinations of commerce or having to answer inconvenient questions about the tax-exempt status of the San and its enterprises. But Will turned on him. His own brother. Turned on him as if he were a stranger, an enemy, a two-headed snake in the road.

And the irony of it was that Will had taken one of the Doctor's proudest virtues—his thrift—and turned it against him. For in lieu of salary increases during the past year, the Doctor had issued small blocks of stock to his physicians and staff, as a way of saving himself some ready cash and benefiting his employees with a sort of enforced savings. Fine. So much the better. But Will—and here the Doctor could feel his heart squeeze like a sponge wrung dry—Will got hold of a go-getting St. Louis insurance man, raised some capital, and went round surreptitiously buying up all those shares at something like half their value till he had a controlling interest. Coldly, slyly, like the backstabber he was, he'd waited till they'd sat down to a board meeting, peered out from beneath the brim of the peasant's cap he always insisted on wearing, and growled, "You'll make no more decisions in *this* company, John."

It was maddening. Sickening. A real true testimony to the venality and depravity of human nature—and he didn't just blame Will; he blamed his doctors, too, for selling out. They'd paid the price, though, ten times over. Half a dozen were already gone, and he had his sights set on turning over another little group, too, just as soon as he could find superior replacements.

Yes. And as if that weren't bad enough, there was the Sanitarium business. While John Harvey Kellogg couldn't take credit for inventing that—there had been some fifty spas and water cures operating in the U.S. alone when he'd taken over the Western Health Reform Institute in 1876—he could certainly claim full and undiluted credit for turning the foundering Adventist enterprise from a twenty-bed clapboard dungeon with a handful of rheumatic patients into one of the greatest and most modern surgical hospitals in the world—and turning a nice profit in the process. And what was his reward? No sooner had he done it, no sooner had he single-handedly established the Battle Creek System and made Battle Creek, Michigan, the health mecca of the world, than a dozen imitators, Post and the Phelps brothers among them, sprang up to challenge him. Post's La Vita Inn was nothing more than a factory adjunct now, a place where they stored old rotary ovens and malt tubs, or so the Doctor's spies told him. And the Phelpses, operating on the despicable and cynical principle of reversing everything the Doctor stood for—they served meat, beer, spirits; they even had a smoking room—had gone under in less than two years' time. But the building was still there, just across the street from the San, and the Doctor had to look at it every day of his life. "The world's biggest fieldstone building," as they touted it, had been picked up at auction by Charlie Post and leased to Bernarr Macfadden, a harebrained, posturing, bare-chested, dumbbell-thumping parody of a health professional, who'd christened the place "The Macfadden Health Home" and used it as a front to push his own breakfast food, Strengtho. God, how it rankled.

But it got worse. On the heels of the health prospectors came the confidence men, gypsies, root peddlers and all the rest. A man calling himself Frank J. Kellogg—the "Anti-Fat" Kellogg—showed up one day with a birth certificate validating his right to the name and an alcohol-laced formula for the swill he passed off as "Kellogg's Safe Fat Reducer." The Doctor's attorneys told him there wasn't a thing he could do about it.

And now there was this business with George. Not content with the hundred dollars he'd extorted in November, he was back with a new scheme. Earlier in the day—and this was what was getting the Doctor down, this was the source of his funk, George, George yet again—the boy had appeared in his office with two men. The Doctor had just come out of surgery and he was settling down to a quick lunch at his desk, simultaneously dictating some two dozen letters and consulting with Murphy, Lillian's keeper, over the chimp's sudden loss of appetite, when there was a knock at the door. The knock itself was unusual: the entire staff and all but the very most important patients knew not to intrude on the Doctor unannounced; only in the direst emergency was he to be disturbed. Dab got up from his stenograph to answer the door, and there they were, an unholy alliance if ever the Doctor had seen one.

George was a surprise. He was clean-shaven, dressed in nearly presentable clothes, including a pair of boots that were merely scuffed and not yet toe-sprung and down-at-the-heel, and he looked as if he'd actually found his way in and out of a bathtub at some point in the past week. The man to his right was a big blustery older fellow, somewhere in his middle sixties, the Doctor guessed, with a ridiculous beard and a vest made of some sheeny material in a solid gold color. The other one, nearly as young as George and dressed in a cheap but vulgarly fashionable way, had the easy good looks and artificial swagger of the apprentice confidence man. No one moved. No one said a word. George broke out in a smile.

It took the Doctor a full five seconds to react, running the emotional gamut from surprise to bewilderment to outrage. Dab blanched. Murphy, a sinuous, bony contortionist of a man whose face seemed composed entirely of eyebrow and nose, writhed deferentially in his seat. "What is the meaning of this?" the Doctor sputtered.

"Begging your pardon, *Father*," George said, edging into the room with his escort, "I know I really should have applied for an audience with all the other supplicants, but I felt, well, I felt you'd want to see me."

"*Want* to see you?" The Doctor was incredulous. "See you about what?" The boy infuriated him with his oily grin and the familiar, unctuous way he made his little pronouncements.

"We have business."

The older man, the one with the dyed beard and coruscating vest, made as if to speak, but the Doctor cut him off. Glaring at each of them in succession, an erupting volcano of physiologic fury, Dr. Kellogg spat out his words as if they were about to ignite in his mouth: "I have no business with you. Not now. Not ever."

The little group stood uncertainly just inside the door. George rubbed his hands together as if to warm them. His grin was unnatural, hateful, a display of cankered gums and yellowed teeth that was enough to turn the Doctor's stomach. Finally, he said, "Ah, but Father, there I think you're mistaken."

What followed was one of the sorriest spectacles the Doctor had ever witnessed. Though he waved them impatiently out the door, Dab and Murphy providing enforcement, such as it was, and though he kept them stewing out there in the hallway a good forty-five minutes, it was clear that they had no intention of leaving. Of course, he could have had them forcibly ejected from the premises, but then he ran the risk of having George create a scene. No, he decided, he would have to see them—and listen to them—though it galled him. He took his time with the letters and his advice to Murphy (which was, essentially, to beef up Lillian's rations with Protose scraps from the kitchen and scour her bowels with psyllium and hijiki), then finally rose from his desk with a sigh and threw back the door to admit the interlopers.

Murphy made a quick exit, his eyebrows crawling like caterpillars across his face, and Dab took up a defensive posture behind his Chief. George's smile was gone now, and the trio looked all business as they marched in the door to the strains of "What Child Is This?" echoing down the corridor.

The Doctor didn't offer them a seat. "All right, what is it?" he snapped, the smoked eyeshade pulled down over his brow like the visor of a helmet.

The older one started in right away, words pouring out of him like the gas from a fermenting tub. He was Mr. Goodloe H. Bender, Esquire, and he was pleased to present his colleagues, a Mr. Something-or-Other—the Doctor was too irritated at this point to concentrate on trivialities—and, of course, the good and celebrated Doctor's own son, George. "Quite a boy, George," Bender gassed, "a veritable fountain of business acumen and penetrating wisdom. You must be proud of him." Was Dr. Kellogg aware that George had joined them in a business venture? No? Well, and here Bender gassed on at such length about breakfast foods and carloads of dent corn and factory space and the like that the Doctor found his eyes clouding with rage.

Again, he cut him off. "Sir," he snapped, "may I remind you that I am a busy man? How in God's name can you imagine that any of this concerns me?"

A conspiratorial glance passed between the older man and his cohort. George's grin reappeared and it flickered briefly across the lips of the others. "But Doctor," Bender boomed, "you haven't even asked the name of our little concern. . . ."

John Harvey Kellogg gritted his teeth. He had three meetings yet to attend, two hours of patient consultations, his evening lecture to prepare and the typescript of his paper "Nuts May Save the Race" to proofread. All this, and here he was, stalled in his own office, listening to this egregious ass raving on about nothing. "To repeat, sir, since you seem to be hard of hearing—or penetration—I am a busy man and I have no time whatever for—"

"*Kellogg's,*" Bender pronounced, "Kellogg's Per-Fo Company, Incorporated, of Battle Creek, Michigan. What do you think of that? Catchy, isn't it?"

The Doctor had begun pacing behind the desk, but now he pulled up short. "All right," he demanded, "out with it. What do you want?"

This seemed to be the other one's cue. He took a step forward, attempted a nervous smile, worked the brim of the hat in his hand. "We were just interested to know if you'd be interested in backing the company, that is, we can offer you a block of stock, if you're interested—"

"At a bargain price," Bender chimed in. "I really don't expect that our little company would affect you to any great degree or cause any, uh, shall we say, *confusion* among the general public. . . ." Here he paused to smack his lips thoughtfully, as if contemplating all those breakfast bowls set out on all those tables across America, an endless plane of polished wood, oilcloth and linen. "But, of course, if your, uh, *investment* were generous enough, there might be no need to begin manufacturing at all, if you see what I mean—"

The pitch had been delivered, the strong-arm applied. Dr. Kellogg knew precisely what the odious, blustering, big-bellied and decidely unphysiologic man before him meant, and now he could claim the high moral ground and let his wrath rain down like lightning from the heavens. "Oh, yes," he said, his voice dropping low to lull them into a false sense of security, "yes, I know just what you're talking about—saving me some embarrassment, hey?"

Bender and the younger man nodded eagerly. George gave him a malicious, black-eyed stare, the cocky grin still set immovably in place.

"Keeping my good name unsmirched?"

Again the nod, and now the older man appended a wink, as if some unspoken bargain had been concluded.

"Extortion?" the Doctor continued, his voice rising. "Threats? Blackmail?" He was roaring suddenly, and he slammed his fist down on the desk. "Violations of every principle of human decency and contempt for the law? Am I right, gentlemen?"

Startled, the little group had involuntarily backed up a step. George's smirk was gone. The younger man looked frightened. Only Bender seemed unperturbed, leveling a knowing look on the fuming little Doctor.

The Doctor had picked up the telephone. His tone was curt, professional, and he kept his eyes locked on Bender's as he spoke into the mouthpiece. "Schroeder? This is Dr. Kellogg. There's been an emergency in my office. I want five orderlies here at once." He set down the earpiece as if it were a loaded gun, spread his hands wide and leaned forward on the desk. Beneath the eyeshade, sparks of light glinted from his spectacles. When he spoke again, his voice was measured and calm. "You'll take your cheap threats elsewhere, gentlemen—and I use the term loosely. I'd suggest my brother Will for starters. He's been there before you, boys, and appropriated my name all for himself. 'None Genuine Without This Signature.' Ha! I say it doesn't amount to a pile of cold manure. My attorneys will deal with him, and with you, too."

No one said a word. The silence was absolute, but for the thump of rapidly approaching footsteps coming up the corridor. The Doctor pointed a finger at his errant son. "As for you, George, your little schemes may have worked in the past—and more than once—but I'm through with you. Try to embarrass me, even think for one minute about sitting out there in the street with your tin cup or harassing my patients in any way, and I'll have Chief Farrington throw you into the Marshall jail so fast you won't know what hit you."

George muttered an obscenity, and then there was an impatient booming knock behind them and five husky young men, in Sanitarium white, filed in the door. The Doctor shifted his gaze to Bender. "And you, sir, are nothing more to me than an odious inconvenience, as if I'd stepped in something in the street. If I ever lay eyes on you again I won't hesitate to scrape that something off on the curb—do you get my meaning?"

Bender began to bluster—his pride was hurt, and the Doctor would be sorry and so on—but Dr. Kellogg waved his hand and his orderlies hustled them out of the office, down the hallway and through the heavy oak doors at the north end of the building. The Doctor watched from the window as the recalcitrant little group was ushered off the premises and into the public street. There was a degree of shoving involved, and the younger man lost his hat, but Dr. Kellogg was able finally to observe them in full and disordered retreat. Blackmail him: the idea of it. Did they think he was born yesterday?

The Doctor had felt a little surge of triumph—he'd love to be there to see Will's face when they descended on him—but it quickly dissipated, and he spent the rest of the afternoon brooding over George's perfidy. Why did the boy hate him so? Where had he gone wrong? He'd tried to be charitable, tried to be a good father, and he'd treated George no differently from the others. Look how well the Rodriguez boys had turned out, and little Nathaniel Himes, the mulatto, and Lucy DuPlage, who never failed to send him a gift on his birthday and came all the way from Boston each summer just to sit and chat with Ella and help with the chores. He went through the afternoon in a haze, turning over the past in his mind, sifting through the debris, trying to recall even a glimmer of brightness—had George ever shown the least bit of gratitude?

No, he hadn't. Never so much as a murmur of apology or whisper of thanks. It was sad, the Doctor thought, shoving himself up from the desk and consulting his watch—he was expected in the Grand Parlor in less than ten minutes—it was sad, and it made him feel impotent, as if the failure were somehow his. The empty bowl, sticky with yogurt and crumbs of bran, sat on the desk beside his notes, and as he gazed into it an ineffable weariness stole over him. For perhaps the first time in his life he didn't feel up to lecturing, and the knowledge ignited a little spark of alarm in him. Here he was, the messiah of health, a pillar of strength, a man who prided himself on his devotion and indefatigability, and he didn't feel like mounting the podium—and who would spread the gospel, who would improve the race, if he faltered?

Damn that George, anyway. He was a curse, a walking curse. Even now, as the audience gathered to hear him, the Doctor couldn't shake the image of the boy, an image that shrank back over the years to the first full winter he'd spent in the bosom of the Kellogg family. He was seven that year. Seven years old—a sweet and winning age in children, a time suspended between reason and innocence, a time when they first come fully alive to the sacrament of life and its multifarious joys. Most children, that is; George was different. George hadn't changed at all as far as the Doctor could see. Shuffling, shambling, head down, he slouched round the house like a little deaf-mute, neither speaking nor responding when spoken to. Almost a year had passed since he'd come to them and he was as obstinate and inexpressive as ever. And if the lesson of the jacket had proved his obstinacy, his mulishness, his disregard for reason and human sympathy, the coming of Christmas—and the Doctor recalled it vividly—had deepened it, burnished the hate and rebellion in him till it glowed like a precious stone.

There were twenty children in the house that Christmas, ranging in age from three to eighteen. The Rodriguez boys, already fluent in English, were making top grades at the local school; Lucy DuPlage, then twelve, was showing a real vocation for the piano; Nathaniel Himes, fully recovered from his burns, excelled in carpentry, chess and floor waxing; and Rebecca Biehn, always one of the Doctor's favorites, had, at five, the most angelic little soprano voice anyone had ever heard. Some nights, before he turned in, the Doctor would tiptoe into the dormitory to listen to the gentle rise and fall of their breathing and catch a glimpse of their untroubled faces as they lay wrapped in their dreams, and the experience soothed him more profoundly than any sedative the pharmacists and pill worshipers could ever hope to concoct. In all, it was a good group of children, a deserving and grateful group who appreciated to the depths of their hearts what Dr. Kellogg and his wife had done for them. And as Christmas approached, though his schedule was as cluttered as ever, the Doctor determined that they should have their reward.

To begin with, there were the little treats they received at Sunday school after performing their parts in the Christmas pageant—hard candy and the like. John Harvey Kellogg disapproved of the candy—sucrose was no substitute for fructose, and, of course, there wasn't a grain of roughage in the whole peppermint-flavored sack of the stuff—but he indulged the children and let them do what they would with their teachers' gifts. In addition, the Doctor and his wife planned to place a handful of English walnuts, an apple, an orange and a bar of sweetened biffiki in each of the children's stockings, and a jumping jack or rag doll under the tree for the younger ones. The older children, those seven and up, would receive articles of clothing appropriate to their age and stature. And, of course, for Christmas dinner the household staff would serve the children a special meal in their dining hall, a meal replete with a goose fashioned from Protose and gelatin, hazelnut dressing, Mexican tortillas in honor of the Rodriguez and Diaz boys, broiled Nuttolene, a salad of head lettuce and grapefruit with French dressing, and, for dessert, soya-bean pie with whipped cream.

On the day before Christmas, after counseling with a score of patients and seeing to final arrangements for the San holiday, the Doctor managed to slip away to the church for the latter portion of the children's program. He joined Ella, who was already dozing, in the first pew, settling down between her and his sister Clara just as Nathaniel Himes rose to recite "Jes' Before Christmas I'm As Good As I Can Be." Nathaniel acquitted himself well, the audience chuckling appreciatively at the contrast between the boy's sober vow and his urchin's expression, and the Doctor flushed with pride. He breathed deeply of the scents of pine and red Life Buoy soap, and looked round him with satisfaction. The children, about half of whom were the Doctor's wards, were fresh-scrubbed and glowing, the church was cozy and pleasantly decorated, and outside a fine feathery snow drifted gently down to enfold the streets in the silence of the ages. All was right with the world. The Doctor relaxed.

Jonella McGimpsie, fifteen and already developing into an almost embarrassingly well-endowed young woman, rose to recite "Annie and Willie's Prayer." Dr. Kellogg leaned forward in anticipation. He was a sentimentalist at heart, and he wasn't afraid to admit it—in its proper place, of course—and he'd always found the poem deeply affecting. As Jonella's adolescent voice rose and fell, the familiar story began to cast its spell over him: Annie and Willie's father, wrapped up in his own problems, was a man blind to the spirit of the season, and on hearing his children talk of Father Christmas and the gifts they hoped to receive, he scolded them and sent them to bed. Later, passing by their room, he heard them praying for him and was so touched he rushed out to the shops just before they closed and bought everything he could lay his hands on. Jonella was in fine form, never hesitating, charging the homely stanzas with drama and pathos, and when she reached the part where the children discover their gifts, the Doctor found himself filled right up to the back of the throat with emotion.

It was then that the interruption began. A rude noise—the passing of intestinal gas, or its counterfeit—began to punctuate each of the poor girl's lines. The audience hushed. She stumbled, went on bravely, but the noise persisted.

Dr. Kellogg was incensed. He sat bolt upright on the hard wooden bench, scanning the faces of the participants—some forty-three children in all—to detect the source of this outrageous and profane display. Adolfo Rodriguez's gaze darted angrily amongst his brothers and sisters and classmates; Lucy DuPlage looked as if she might burst into tears; Rory McAuliffe was white as a corpse. Only George—the smallest child on the stage but for Rebecca Biehn and one of the four-year-olds—was unaffected. He stared straight ahead, as if in a trance, unmoving, unblinking. Jonella had come to the final stanza, and still the rude noise tore at her composure. It was George, it had to be. Was he rubbing his palms together? Working his biceps against the damp places under his arms? Was it a trick of ventriloquism? To sit there and endure it was almost more than the Doctor could bear—it was all he could do to keep from crying out in his rage.

" 'Blind father,' " Jonella declaimed, her voice quavering, " 'who caused thy stern heart to relent' " (*brrrupt! brrrupt!*)/" 'And the hasty words spoken so soon to repent?/'Twas the Being who bade thee steal softly upstairs' " (*brrrupt! brrrupt!*)/" 'And made thee His agent to answer their prayers.' " (*Brrrupt!*)

Never in his life had the Doctor been so humiliated. His stomach was wrung like a rag in the wash, his heart rapping at his rib cage—to think of the embarrassment, his own children, and in public yet! He couldn't hear the hymns and carols that followed, couldn't see the streets for the yellow slush, snapped at Ella and ordered Clara out of the sled as if she were a servant. At home, he lined up the children, all twenty of them, and began an inquisition that would have made Torquemada blanch. There would be no Christmas, he roared, no presents, no special dinner, no privileges for any of them for a month, unless the guilty party stepped forward. And he knew who it was. He knew already—and there was no use trying to blame it on their brothers or sisters or the townschildren—and that person should quail not only before the Doctor and poor Jonella, but before the God that had fashioned him and whose holy house he had defiled. Well?

The children were mute. No one stepped forward.

"Arms outstretched!" the Doctor roared. Forty arms rushed up in a wave, held shoulder-high and parallel to the floor. "You will stand here, all of your arms held in just this posture, until the malefactor steps forward—and I don't care if it takes all night, till New Year's, Easter, Decoration Day! Do you understand me?"

Little Rebecca Biehn began to snuffle. Her tiny arms, plump with baby fat, were already trembling. George, just behind her, was expressionless. "Hannah Martin!" the Doctor cried, and the children's nurse appeared, eyes downcast. "You will supervise." Then John Harvey Kellogg turned his back on the children and sequestered himself in his private quarters.

Twenty minutes later there came a tentative knock at the door of his study, where he'd retired with a sheaf of Sanitarium documents and a cup of negus (alcohol-free, of course). It was Hannah Martin. Beside her, unable to hold the Doctor's gaze, stood Adolfo Rodriguez, then fourteen years old. "Yes?" the Doctor said.

Hannah Martin ducked her head in extenuation, swallowed hard and whispered so softly that the Doctor, even with his keen auditory powers, could barely hear her. "Adolfo has confessed."

Dr. Kellogg was thunderstruck. It took him a moment, but then he understood: Adolfo, brave boy, stalwart boy, principled, noble and sacrificial boy, was taking the onus on himself. "I am sorry, sir," the boy said, "but I must confess."

"Come here," the Doctor commanded.

Adolfo, his back ramrod straight, crossed the room like a little soldier. He halted five feet from the Doctor's desk. "Closer," the Doctor said.

Adolfo obeyed, edging up to within a foot of the gleaming, polished surface.

"All right," Dr. Kellogg said, "I know perfectly well what you're about, Adolfo, and I'm proud of you. But you would never under any circumstances lie to me, would you? A falsehood from you would hurt me more than a hundred vile little performances like the one this afternoon—do you understand me?"

The boy hung his head.

"You are not the guilty party, are you, son?"

The response was barely audible. "No."

"Just as I thought." The Doctor was on his feet now, hardly able to contain himself. He picked up a protractor and set it down again. "And who was it, then? And remember, you are not to try to protect anyone, no matter whom, if it will lead you to obscure the truth. This is the lesson of the moment, and a lesson for life. Now—who was it? And speak up like a man."

The burden was lifted. Adolfo raised his tan Aztecan eyes to the Doctor's and tried to contain the faintest tic of a smile. "George," he said. "It was George, sir."

Without another word the Doctor stalked past the boy, across the vestibule and into the children's hall. The children were still at attention, their arms held out tentatively before them. "George," the Doctor roared, "George Kellogg, step forward this instant!"

But George wasn't there. "Where is he?" the Doctor thundered, beside himself with rage—and a fine Christmas Eve this was turning out to be—but the others didn't know. They hadn't noticed him slip away. Genuinely. Truly. They hadn't.

He instructed them to drop their arms, which they did with a groan of relief, and then he informed them that he wanted George standing before him within five minutes. "Search him out," he cried. "And then we'll have our Christmas. I won't let one malingering, malicious, ill-behaved child ruin it for the rest of us. Now search him out!"

With a shout, the children disbanded and tore across the floor like a pack of hounds. They searched the pantry, under the beds, in the recesses of the closets and the basement, looked in chests and wardrobes, searched the carriage house, the barn—even, with their patriarch's permission, the Doctor's private quarters. No George. It was five in the evening, dark, the children wanting their dinner and the joy of the season, the whole world awaiting the coming of its Savior, and George was nowhere to be found. Reluctantly, the Doctor telephoned the police chief, Dab and half a dozen of his most trustworthy aides. The boy must be out in the storm somewhere, and though a voice told him it was just as well to let him go, he couldn't—there would be a scandal, he'd look like a fool. Bill Farrington and the others were instructed to keep things quiet, but to mount a search: the boy hadn't taken his jacket, and he could freeze before morning found him.

The night wore on. There were songs before the fire, punch and bran cakes for the children. The Doctor sat at the piano and went through his repertoire of Christmas carols for the older children, and Ella and Clara sang a duet of some of Schumann's settings of poems by Heine and Eichendorff. Spirits were high, the little ones went off to bed dazzled, the snow mounted at the windows—and yet still, in everyone's mind, there was the image of George, stunted, rail-thin, big-headed and angry, alone with the elements. Chief Farrington telephoned at eleven to say that they'd found no trace of him and were calling off the search. At twelve, his stomach in knots—damn the boy, anyway—Dr. Kellogg climbed wearily into bed.

In the morning, after exchanging gifts over breakfast with his wife and sister and her husband, the Doctor and his party strolled across the house to the children's wing to watch the children dig into their stockings and open their presents. There'd been a message earlier from Chief Farrington—no sign of George; could the Doctor provide an article of the boy's clothing for Michael Doyle's bloodhounds?—but the Doctor had filed it away in one of the back drawers of his mind, determined that nothing should spoil the holiday and his pleasure in the children. All things considered, he was feeling buoyant—chipper, even—as he stepped into the children's parlor, with its glittering tree and the mantel festooned with stockings.

Dressed for church, their faces shining in anticipation of their gifts and treats, the children were a vision. The Doctor greeted them individually, wished them a merry Christmas, and bade them look to their stockings. As one, they started for the mantel, orderly, hushed, never forgetting their posture or the Doctor's respect for peace and quiet, and they tugged down their stockings with subdued squeals of joy. The Doctor was smiling. Ella was smiling. Hannah Martin, Clara and her husband, Hiland, were smiling. It was a special moment, shot through with an emotion as tangible and warm as a hot-water bag slipped between the sheets on a frigid night. But oddly, as the children examined their stockings, the little chirps of joy and surprise turned leaden—there was a murmur of disbelief, and their faces fell, older and younger children alike.

What was it? The Doctor moved forward, puzzled, nineteen pale oval faces fixed on his, and he saw little Rebecca Biehn burst into tears as she clutched the hijiki bar in one hand and turned her stocking inside out with the other: it was empty. They were all empty—no nuts, no apples, no oranges. Only the hijiki had been left behind.

George. The name burned like acid in the Doctor's brain. He stood there immobilized, his face gone hard, all the joy washed from the day like soil in the gutter. And to think he'd been worried, to think he'd lost sleep over the boy's welfare, over the night, the cold, the storm, and all the while George had been holed up someplace in the house like a bloated little rat. "Find him" was all he could say.

"Who?" Ella replied, her voice plunging into a well of silence broken only by the bitter sniffling of Rebecca and her little brothers and sisters. His wife's face was transformed by the look of confusion that would, in a few short years, settle permanently there. "Find who?"

The Doctor's impulse was to root out the little ingrate in that instant,

The Doctor's impulse was to root out the little ingrate in that instant, tear up the floorboards, break through the walls, anything, but he caught himself. The children must have their Christmas—he would be playing into the boy's hands otherwise. He sent out to the San for a supply of nuts, oranges, apples and bran cakes, supervised the opening of the gifts and accepted his own present from the children—a monogrammed fountain pen—with grace and composure. But all the while he kept seeing George's pinched little face before him, the keen black pits of his degenerate eyes, the mocking curve of the lip, and he determined to take the house apart brick by brick if necessary until he uncovered him.

It wasn't necessary.

Cramden, the stableman, was waiting for him as he stepped out into the snow for the ride to church. "The boy youse're all looking for, Dr. Kellogg, sir—he's in the root cellar, back in the far corner behind the taters and rutabagers. I seen him there myself, not ten minutes ago, when I was down to fetch a couple dried apples for Bosco and Maisie —and I hope you won't mind, but I thought the poor horses deserve their holiday, too."

The Doctor made no response. All he said was "Hold the sled," and then, dressed in his finest suit of clothes, in his gloves and overcoat and buffed black patent-leather boots, he made his way along the narrow path the kitchen help had trodden to the root cellar, pulled back the half-sized door and stuck his head in. "George," he called. "George Kellogg—are you in there?"

The root cellar was a cramped and incommodious plank-roofed cave dug out of the ground and sloping sharply downward, home to spider, mealybug and daddy longlegs. It smelled of the earth and its dry cold secrets, and it never failed to remind Dr. Kellogg of his preference for the aspiring vegetables, which absorb the healthful rays of the sun, over the gouty, unsanitary relics that lay round him here in dusty heaps. Straightening up, he knocked his head against the door frame, and his hat—brand-new, made of silk, and a good grand seven and a half inches tall—tumbled forward into the dirt. "George!" he roared, snatching the hat up out of the filth and beating it against his thigh. "Answer me!"

Blinded by the dazzle of the snow, he could see nothing at first. But there was a movement in the far corner, the rustle of a pilfering stinking little human rodent that should have been left to starve in the slums of Chicago. Hunching his shoulders, the Doctor edged forward. "George?"

It took him a moment, but then his eyes adjusted to the dim light and he saw the fuscous mounds of potatoes, rutabagas, turnips, carrots shrunken like the fingers of the dead. Amidst them, his puny limbs mocked with shivers, his teeth chattering and nose running snot, lay George, atop a mound of orange peels, apple cores and nutshells. He looked dazed, bewildered, as if he were still crouching beside the corpse of his mother in that bleak and barren tenement. His black cold eyes fixed on the Doctor without the least hint of recognition. He coughed.

"George," the Doctor demanded, furious still, furious at the tricks of nature, at himself, at this little wad of misery before him, "George, come out of there now and take your punishment."

The boy didn't move. But that yellow-toothed smirk sprang to his lips. "Father," he said. "Merry Christmas."

Chapter 2

The
Baser
Appetites

An expectant hush fell over the crowd gathered in the Grand Parlor for the evening's lecture. The palms stood firm in the sockets of their earthenware pots, here and there a patient on the psyllium diet fought down the urge to visit the restroom, and the milk-glutted tycoons were as alert suddenly as turkey cocks spying out a fleck of glitter in the barnyard dust. Dr. Kellogg had just delivered his thunderbolt—there was a couple sitting amongst them, he announced, apprentices to the physiologic regime, who had engaged in marital relations against his express injunction and who would henceforth have to suffer the consequences—and now he paused, his spectacles ablaze with light, to let this startling information have its effect. Three hundred pairs of eyes were riveted on his plump white surgical hands as he poured a glass of water from the pitcher on the lectern. Three hundred pairs of eyes watched as he held the glass up to the light as if to say, *Here, here is all the human animal needs to satisfy its appetites, aqua pura and a handful of roots and nuts,* and three hundred pairs of eyes followed the glass to his lips and the fine physiologic rise and fall of his Adam's apple as he emptied it.

If to this point the Doctor had felt uninspired, no one knew it—and yet they'd all been waiting for this moment. The lecture had been provocative, stimulating and informative, yes, but they missed his patented stunts and the talk had lacked a certain titillation, the frisson they'd come to expect. Till now, that is.

He'd begun, nearly an hour earlier, by responding to half a dozen inquiries patients had dropped in the Question Box during the course of the past week, expatiating on the link between brain work and dyspepsia and the use of the frigid bath as a means of hardening oneself against the common cold, while taking time out to lament the sad fact that the American foot, like American teeth and the American man and woman in general, was undergoing a process of deterioration. And to prove the latter point, he'd adduced the case of the Filipino foot, in which the great toe is so much longer than the others and so far separated from them that it renders real service in grasping and clinging—so, too, the Japanese foot. Why, he had personally known Japanese who could walk unshod across tile roofs severals stories from the ground, weave, write, and even, in one case, play the violin with their bare feet alone. Like all his audiences, this one was eager, partisan, crying out for initiation into the secrets of health and vigor, and they'd listened raptly, though the Doctor knew he really wasn't on his mark. But then he spied the Lightbodys in the fifth row, and he began to discover the real subject of the evening, and the old fire began to stoke his furnaces once again.

It was Nurse Graves who'd informed him of the occasion on which Mr. Lightbody had vented his lust on his enervated and all-but-prostrate wife—nearly two weeks ago now, around the time the Thanksgiving bird had turned up dead. But the Doctor had been away on business to Sioux City, Minneapolis and St. Louis, addressing gatherings of the Western Cracked Wheat Association, the National Cheese Congress and the American Soybean Association (of which he was a founding member), and he hadn't yet had an opportunity to consult with the couple individually and ascertain the severity of their lapse. Certainly the evidence was against them. Mr. Lightbody had, as best anyone could determine, spent the night in Mrs. Lightbody's room, and while of course no one could say what went on behind closed doors, it certainly looked suspicious—especially to one who knew human nature as thoroughly as the Doctor did. Perhaps the husband had simply sat up with the wife or slept—merely slept—beside her. Still, all excuses aside, it was an outrage, and no matter the culpability, the Doctor, already wound up by his little confrontation with George and his confederates, was determined to let them writhe a bit one way or the other.

"I do not mention this transgression lightly, ladies and gentlemen," he said, setting the empty glass down and leveling his sternest gaze on the audience, "but rather as an example to you all and a strict admonition to avoid the greatest risk to life and health I can imagine."

He was warming up now, his brain choked with a logjam of medical terms, horrifying statistics, the names of eminent physicians and arresting conditions, his arms twitching with their inchoate gestures, feet breaking away—and all of a sudden he was out from behind the lectern, standing bold and upright among the good but misguided people who had gathered to hear him. "Even the youngest, healthiest and most vigorous among us are, my friends, subject to the debilitating effects of sexual excess, I'm sorry to say. But I shudder to think of the consequences when the systems of both partners are already depleted—as the systems of this particular couple most certainly were—by the twin shocks of autointoxication and neurasthenic prostration." And now his voice reached out on the tendrils of their attention, demanding, proclaiming, laying down the law: "There is a hygiene to be observed in marriage, ladies and gentlemen, and that hygiene is no more to be disregarded than forgoing a bath or failing to change one's linen."

There was a stir among the audience. Several of the men—was that Homer Praetz?—looked away from his steely gaze.

"And let me ask you this—why do you suppose our gynecologists' offices are so crowded with worn and exhausted women in this our supposedly civilized society? Because husbands abuse the marital bond, that's why. The popular view seems to be that any indulgence of the passions is made permissible by the marriage ceremony. No view could be more erroneous."

The little Doctor strode amongst them like a colossus, now whirling, now pointing a declamatory finger, locking eyes with one abashed husband after another. As he spoke, warming to the subject, denouncing the baser appetites and the priapic urge, the women in the audience seemed to come quietly to life, like so many flowers blooming in a hothouse. Miss Muntz was wrapped in a greenish glow and her eyes seemed to devour her face; Mrs. Tindermarsh wore the tiniest smirk of recognition, though her acquaintance with the matters at hand would almost certainly have been memorial at this juncture; Nurse Graves, standing demurely with a group of nurses in the rear, held herself with virginal rectitude. Even Eleanor Lightbody, who should have been ashamed of herself, seemed preternaturally alive to his words. Regal, unabashed, she offered up every least particle of her attention.

"We have no room in the University of Health for satyrs and fleshpots, libertines and sybarites, any more than we have room for abusers of the whiskey bottle, the tobacco pouch and the frying pan. Let me quote no less an authority than Jeremy Taylor in this, ladies and gentlemen—and I might add that I most heartily concur with every word. 'It is a common belief,' Taylor says, 'that a man and woman, because they are legally united in marriage, are privileged to the unbridled exercise of amativeness. This is wrong. Nature, in the exercise of her laws, recognizes no human enactments, and is as prompt to punish any infringement of her laws in those who are legally married, as in those out of bonds.' "

Dr. Kellogg paused to scan the audience; there wasn't a single man or woman in that room who wasn't perched at the edge of his or her chair. He cleared his throat. "I'd like to add my own italics here, ladies and gentlemen, seekers after health and right living, because Mr. Taylor hits the nail directly on the head: 'Excessive indulgence between the married produces as great and lasting evil effects as in the single man and woman, and is nothing more or less than *legalized prostitution.*' I repeat, ladies and gentlemen, *'legalized prostitution.*' "

There was a gasp from one of the younger patients—*Froeble,* wasn't it? *Annaliese; age fourteen, Chapel Hill, North Carolina; Bright's disease, diabetes, autointoxication, obesity.* That gasp gave the Doctor pause: perhaps this sort of truth telling was too unsettling for young ears? But he dismissed the notion as quickly as it came to him—she would learn the harsh truths soon enough at the hands of some libidinous brute of a husband; better she should be girded in physiologic armor when the time came.

Waving his arms like a dervish, spinning on his diminutive feet, he worked his way back to the little stage and mounted to the podium. "Yessss," he hissed in a long constricted rush of breath, "and what is the effect of such failure to control the carnal appetites? What is the danger to which I've alluded so many times tonight, the sad fate that awaits married couples who seem to think that connection can be repeated as regularly and almost as often as their meals?"

There was no response. They were as silent as stones, but he had them, had them by their noses—he could see it in the alert looks, the sidelong glances, the bowed heads and nervously tapping fingers and feet.

"Well, then: what would be the effect of pouring gasoline into an engine that had known only water? Most men—most decent men, at any rate—and all respectable women have lived a continent life till marriage, and then suddenly they are thrust into a tumult of nervous excitation which literally combusts their nervous systems and in the process destroys their digestion and bankrupts the emunctories. For the man, at least, giving up as he does so many emissions of life-giving fluid, it is ruin, absolute ruin."

Miss Muntz shifted in her seat, gave the Doctor a brief mortified glance and looked quickly away. Mrs. Tindermarsh was a living statue, but for that hint of a smirk. Several of the men, Will Lightbody and J. Henry Osborne, Jr., the bicycle king, among them, looked uneasy, unwell even.

"But for the woman"—and here Dr. Kellogg's voice became saturated with pity—"being of feebler constitution and hence less able to bear these terrible shocks, the result runs the gamut from mild hysteria and nervous exhaustion to cancer, marasmus and death. Little wonder that Midulet characterizes our era as 'The Age of Womb Diseases.'" And then, shaking his head piteously, dredging his glistening brow back and forth like a pendulum drifting between heartbreak and surcease, he drew himself up to deliver the ultimate blow. "Finally, my friends, my patients, my fellow travelers in the quest for a life free of disease and impairment, I ask you this: how many women among us tonight can say, 'I have never been well since the night of my marriage'? Think about it, ladies and gentlemen. Think and act."

He brought his hands together, as if in prayer, dipped his head. "I thank you."

And then the applause started up, startled, shocked, an applause surprised by itself but growing increasingly firmer, steadier, more thankful and heartfelt, an offering to the one man who would stand amongst them and speak the painful but unvarnished truth. Dr. Kellogg bowed his head in humble acknowledgment. A full minute elapsed before there was any diminution in their enthusiasm, and then, as the applause began finally to die down and the Doctor gathered up his notes, a hand shot up in the front row and a voice called out over the clamor: "A question, Dr. Kellogg—will you take a question from the audience?"

The request had a calming effect, and the applause fell away to a spatter and then it ceased altogether. The Doctor focused on a man in his early twenties with something of an effete air about him. He wore a thin black mustache, waxed at the ends, and an artist's plume of hair at the point of his chin. He lowered his arm languidly and rose to put the question—but who was he, now? John Harvey Kellogg knew, he knew them all. Let's see: Crampton? Cruthers? Crowley? No, no. *Krinck*, that was it. *John Hampton Krinck, Jr.; Hyde Park, New York; morphia addiction, venereal disease, autointoxication.* Oh, yes. A libertine of the first stripe, a reader of the plays of Shaw and that tripe of Dreiser's. "Yes, Mr. Krinck?" the Doctor said, bracing himself for a challenge.

Young Krinck stood there a moment, his shoulders slumped forward as if they'd been molded of butter, a sick sly rebellious look sunk into his sensualist's face. His voice was blown through a reed, nasal and nasty. "I'm very sorry, Doctor, but don't you seem to be advocating extinction for the race? If sexual connection is to be avoided at all cost, even within the bonds of marriage, then what hope is there for us, outside of virgin birth?"

This provoked a titter—certainly the impudent young mooncalf meant it as a provocation, a sick joke, the sort of thing George might have conceived or enjoyed—but no one in that crowd dared so much as a smile. The Doctor was angry. This addict, this pampered, snot-nosed sponge of craven desires and self-indulgence, this notorious black sheep who was a disgrace to one of the wealthiest and most respected families in New York, dared to twit him? Ha! He could crush him, demolish him with a single phrase—but no, that wasn't the physiologic way. This was a learning experience—for all concerned, even Mr. Krinck. Demonstrating a lofty restraint, the Doctor held the young man's gaze a moment, perfectly straight-faced, before glancing up to play to the audience. "Virgin birth, did you say? Well, as a scientist, I hardly find it feasible"—pause for the appreciative chuckle—"but as a moralist and physician, I couldn't wish for anything more."

As usual, Dab was waiting for him in the corridor, and as usual, the secretary was in a huffing, puffing, sweat-running dither about something or other. Whatever it was, the Doctor didn't want to hear about it. He was coasting on the glory of the moment, and he felt his heart sink as Dab came thumping up to him, wringing his hands and sputtering inarticulately—*Not now,* he was thinking, *not today*—but he allowed his secretary to fall into stride beside him and paused just long enough to growl, "All right, Poult, let's have it—what's the problem?"

But there wasn't just a single problem—the problems, plural and multifarious, each swelled to crisis proportions and each required his immediate attention. First, there was George. Apparently agitated over the Doctor's earlier dismissal of him, the boy had made use of the intervening hours to get himself violently and shamefully drunk, and he was now crouched in the middle of the public street just opposite the San's main entrance, hurling epithets at the crème de la crème of health-reform society as they climbed into their conveyances in the San's circular drive. "He's calling them 'gizzardites' and 'chaff chewers,' Doctor, and the bellman reports that he actually threw a projectile at one of the patients."

They were striding up the hallway toward the main lobby, Christmas glitter spangling the walls, the genteel clamor of the lobby opening up around them. The Doctor fixed his eyes straight ahead, struggling to control himself. Every word out of Dab's mouth was a straight pin jammed into his nerve endings—he had to rest, he had to; no mere mortal could cope with all this. "Projectile?" he said, striding along furiously, nodding curtly at this doctor or that.

"Uh, actually, Chief," Dab gasped, doing his best to keep up, "it was a corn-flake box—one of your brother's—and it was stuffed with, uh, well, *corncobs,* sir. *Used* cobs, sir, if you catch my meaning."

John Harvey Kellogg stopped dead in his tracks. A patient in a wheel-chair simpered at him—Mrs.? Mrs.? Oh, *who gives a damn!*—and he ignored her. "Used?" he repeated.

Dab studied his hands. "He must have got, uh, into a, uh, latrine somewhere, and, uh, and then—"

The Doctor drew in a breath so sharp it might have been his last. "God!" he cried. "Damn that boy, damn him, damn him a thousand times!" Twenty heads turned and as quickly turned away again. The Doctor was in motion now, marching across the lobby like an infan-tryman with fixed bayonet. As he entered the far corridor, striding angrily for his office, he stopped and whirled suddenly on his secretary. "Lock him up," he said. "Call Farrington and have him thrown in jail. But keep it quiet, understand?" Then he turned on his heels and spun into the office.

Dab was right behind him.

There was more. The furnace had failed in the San's hothouses and the tomatoes, okra, mango trees and chrysanthemums were freezing; a Mr. Smotkine of Sedro Woolley, Washington, had broken a tooth on a piece of the Doctor's patented zwieback and was threatening a lawsuit; and Lillian the chimp had locked Murphy in her cage, ripped Dr. Dis-taso's pant leg from cuff to crotch and was now loose and running amuck in the experimental kitchens . . . and then there was the situation with the Christmas goose.

In all his life, through all the crises he'd faced, even the mysterious fire that had left the San in ashes just five years ago, the Doctor had never felt himself so close to the breaking point. It was too much. Too, too much. He'd attained the sanctuary of his desk, and he stood behind it now, the eyeshade clamped firmly in place. "Situation?" he repeated, and he heard the quaver in his own voice. "What situation?"

"Sir?"

"The goose. What's wrong with the goose?"

"It looks a bit peaked, Doctor. And it won't eat. Murphy seems to feel it's caught cold, and we wouldn't want a repetition of the problem with the Thanksgiving turkey, at least I felt you wouldn't, and I thought you ought to know."

Just what he needed. The Thanksgiving bird had been a major embarrassment, the dining room already half filled with dutifully Fletch-erizing patients when one of the nurses discovered the corpse—and how to explain that one to his physiologic novices? If he couldn't even keep a turkey alive, what did that say for Grandma and Aunt Emmeline? As a distraction, he'd brought the Christmas goose in ahead of schedule and arrayed it in the same spot, under a banner that read: IS HIS GOOSE COOKED? NOT AT THE BATTLE CREEK SANITARIUM. What a debacle. Next thing he knew, one of the patients would turn up dead. "All right, all right!" he barked suddenly, and he felt his stomach take a decidedly unphysiologic dip. His hands were trembling, actually trembling, as if he were some sort of coffee fiend or something. It was the moment of truth.

The Doctor was equal to it. Who else? He fought down the negative thoughts that had threatened to drown him all day, reached deep within him and somehow managed to summon the strength to fight back, as he always did, indomitable, indefatigable, positive-thinking and right-living, the one man among the millions of the world to prosecute this crusade and see it through to the end. He was a reformer, a titan, a tower of strength. All at once he was in command again, pacing the room like a panther, firing out orders, his voice powerful, clear, decisive: "Wrap the goose in a blanket and give her a yogurt-whey enema—clearly a case of anserine autointoxication; find a locksmith to release Murphy from the cage and get Barker out of bed and into that power plant, *tout de suite*—and have them mist all the plants so they'll freeze hard on the surface, thereby preserving their vital parts; George to jail, as I said; offer Mr. Smotkine—odd name, that: is it Bohemian? Polish?—at any rate, offer Mr. Smotkine a year's free supply of Health Koko and Sanitas Wheat Flakes if he'll reconsider pressing his suit; and as for Lillian, well, I'll take care of her myself. Understood?"

Dab was scribbling vigorously across the surface of his notepad, mur-muring, "Yes, yes, of course," and nodding his chins in unison—*he really should get the man to try radium emanation as a means of reducing; he was hardly an advertisement for the Sanitarium bill of fare*—when the Doctor looked up to see the gaunt, lust-haunted form of Will Lightbody framed in the open doorway. Lightbody was alone. He stood there, looking uncertain, the naked slabs of his hands dangling at his sides, his sickly pale mortified features floating up out of the cheery backdrop of the hallway like the bad spot on an otherwise perfect piece of fruit. "Dr. Kellogg?" he boomed in his sepulchral tones, "do you have a minute?" He glanced at Dab and back again. "I need, I mean I want very much to discuss something with you—in private. About your lecture, I mean . . . but if this isn't a convenient time . . ."

Now here was something else. Just as he was mobilizing his forces, just as he was calling up his inner resources to combat strange chances and put his nemeses to the sword, the Doctor found himself confronted with yet another disappointment. The man was a walking cadaver, a hound of venery, and he'd directly and flagrantly contravened his physician's orders—and now he'd come crawling back. Dr. Kellogg felt something harden in him. He shooed Dab out of the office—"I'll see to Lillian directly," he called to the secretary's retreating form, "keep everyone away from the kitchens"—and then he instructed Will to shut the door behind him and take a seat. The Doctor remained standing. "Yes, Mr. Lightbody? And what seems to be the problem?"

The man looked uneasy. He shifted in his seat, cleared his throat, produced a handkerchief and thoughtfully evacuated first one nostril, then the other.

The Doctor regarded him with a steely gaze. "I'm very sorry, sir, but I must advise you that I haven't more than sixty seconds to consult with you at this juncture—several minor emergencies have arisen. You say, sir, that my lecture affected you. Have you not perhaps guessed the identity of the couple to whom I was referring?"

Lightbody gave him a blank look.

"Come, come, man," the Doctor exploded, "don't play innocent with me. I happen to know for a fact that on the night of November sixteen, overcome with your sick lusts, you inflicted yourself on your invalid wife, thereby risking her life—her *life*, I say—just as surely as if you'd held a knife to her throat. And you. Look at you. Your vital fluids depleted, your digestion ruined, the rotten scrawl of death written all over you."

Ashen, the long bones of his legs chattering, Will Lightbody got unsteadily to his feet. "What are you saying?" he gasped. "I, I knew I was unwell, but I'm doing my best—it's hardly fatal, is it, my condition?"

The Doctor grudged him even this—it was time to crack the whip. "It can be—it most certainly *will* be—if you don't stop this nonsense."

"Nonsense? But I haven't—I deny it. I certainly did not 'inflict' myself on my wife, and I resent your tone and your implication. . . ." He broke off in confusion, shifting his weight from foot to foot, his clothes hanging from him as if from a peg in the closet. "Or, well, maybe I did lose track of things there," he admitted, his voice rattling in his throat, "you know how things are, between man and wife, that is—but there was no excitation of the nervous system, no consummation." He faltered, tugged at his fingers, licked his lips. The cast in his eye gave him the look of a shying horse. When he spoke again, it was in a whisper. "That's what I wanted to talk to you about."

The chimp was amuck, the goose dying, George being carted off to jail, the heating plant in chaos and yet another lawsuit pending, and still the Doctor stood there. He'd heard some shameful revelations in his time, seen men—and women—at their worst, and he braced himself. "Go on," he said, softening his tone.

"I don't know what to say," Lightbody murmured, hanging his head. "I was a slave to the baser appetites, I did come to Eleanor with marital, uh, relations in mind, I did turn a deaf ear on your warnings, and I hope you'll forgive me and know that I'll never, not until we're . . . what I mean to say is, I failed."

The Doctor was disgusted. It was just as he'd suspected—and the fool had missed his milk feedings all that night, too. How in God's name did they expect to get well if they couldn't follow instructions—even when under direct supervision? "Failed?" he repeated.

The great gangling sack of self-abuse and adolescent lusts that stood there before him flushed crimson even to the tips of his ears. He couldn't look the Doctor in the eye. "I wasn't a man," he whispered.

"You mean you were impotent?"

Will Lightbody winced at the term. He nodded.

Dr. Kellogg couldn't restrain a snort of contempt. "I don't doubt that you would be," he cried suddenly, tugging at the brim of the eyeshade. "How could you hope for anything different? What would ever possess a man in your condition to put it to a test, anyway? Don't you understand the gravity of this situation? Are you a child in a nursery, sir?"

The patient had no response. A silent moment reverberated in eternity. Finally the Doctor spoke. "I'm happy for you, sir. Your own body revolted at what you were about to subject it to. If you were incapable of saving yourself—and sparing your wife—you should get down on your knees and thank the heavens that nature intervened. You say you're impotent? I say congratulations."

Without another word, John Harvey Kellogg swept by the man, exited the room and hurried off down the hallway. If he'd been a bit hard on him, so much the worse—the patient had to be made to understand that the physician could take him only so far; after that, it was his own responsibility to control the animal urges that were digging him an early grave. The Doctor took a corridor to the right and then headed down the stairwell, taking the steps two at a time. He quickened his pace as he pictured the damage Lillian could do to the equipment, his gleaming pots, cookers and retorts, not to mention the food she would almost certainly foul. He'd been working with the macadamia nut, trying to come up with a nutritious nut butter, like his peanut concoction, that would give the right-thinking consumers of America yet another sandwich option to replace the beef and pork on which they glutted themselves like beasts in the Alaskan wild, and the last thing he needed was chimp dander in the mix.

As he came round the corner to the kitchen, the little group of staffers and dietary girls that had been standing timorously at the door opened up to admit him. Someone had jammed a wedge under the door from the outside in order to prevent Lillian's escape, and the Doctor bent briskly to remove it before cracking the door and peering in.

"She's been hooting to herself in there, Chief," someone murmured at his back.

"Yessir, and making one hellacious godawful racket with the pots and pans and kitchen things." This from Abraham Lincoln Washington, the man the Doctor employed to sweep the kitchen floors. "Dr. Distaso, he try to stop her but she went and torn his pants right off him—I'd be careful, Doctor. She's in a mood."

Dr. Kellogg ignored them. This was the moment he'd been born for, the time to take charge, to put on the mantle of the Chief and act when others could only stand round and wring their hands. He thrust back the door boldly and stepped into the room.

Nothing. Not a sound. The keen blue eyes took in the damage at a glance—smashed lights, overturned counters, a faucet wrenched from its receptacle and spewing water—and the unflagging abacus of the Doctor's thrifty mind translated it into dollars and cents. "Lillian!" he called, his voice clamping round the silence like an iron collar. "Lillian, come here this instant! Bad girl. Bad." It was then that the stench rose to his nostrils, a dark foul primitive odor that spoke of Africa at its darkest: she'd loosed her bowels. Everywhere. Her scat fouled the counters, the floors, even the walls, a pure expression of the uncivilized bowel at its most uninhibited. He moved forward, wary, sly, glancing right and left, above and behind, his feet reverting to the slow silent shuffle of the hunter. He heard something then, the whisper of a movement, and glanced up sharply to his left: nothing. "Lillian?"

Catlike, the Doctor tiptoed across the floor to the great cast-iron vat of macadamia butter—he had nearly a hundred pounds of the stuff, beaten smooth and thickened with cornstarch, and he'd planned to try it out on some of the patients at breakfast. At first glance it looked all right, and he felt a flood of relief—the nuts had come all the way from the Sandwich Islands, and at a price that made him shudder to contemplate. But then he looked again and saw the stain; his nose told him what it was.

At that moment, as if proud of her handiwork, Lillian appeared, slowly separating herself from the shadows cast by the mixing vats. She was no more than fifteen feet away. The Doctor froze, impaled on the bitter spear of defeat that had pricked at him all the day long. She was grinning, black rubber lips folded back from long sepia teeth, and in that moment she looked just like George.

Chapter 3

Cold
in the
Middle

❄

A thick wet snow was falling as Will Lightbody left the San and made his way briskly down Washington Avenue. It had rained the day before and then frozen during the night, and now, at the end of a long gray December afternoon, it had begun to snow. Of course, none of this affected the inmates of the San, basking as they were in seventy-two-degree temperatures amid hibiscus and palm or wrapped in half a ton of blankets on the veranda for a preprandial snooze, but for Will it was an adventure. Stooped, thin as a bent wire, his throat wrapped in a woolen scarf and his hands thrust deep in his pockets, he kicked through the slush in his galoshes like a boy let out of school early.

To this point, he'd left the grounds of the Sanitarium exactly twice in the six weeks of his residency—to walk into town with Eleanor one bright cold afternoon so she could pick up some items at the stationer's, and to participate in an open sleigh ride arranged by Nurse Graves as a Christmas amenity for three of her select patients. The walk into town was one of the few good things he'd experienced since he'd arrived. It was a simple joy, a revelation, the aroma of wood smoke on the air, children playing at tag, the sky leaping back to its farthest ethereal reaches—life as it was meant to be lived, a real life, not some dreary limbo of laughing exercises and sinusoidal current. Unfortunately,

Eleanor couldn't linger—she had to be back within the hour for her salt-mush rub and colon massage—and the outing was all too short. But just to have left those pristine corridors with their neutral smell and eternal lights, just to have escaped the scrutiny of all those correct and sanctimonious biologic livers, if even for an hour, had made Will feel like a man reborn.

So, too, the excursion with Nurse Graves.

Will was pleased, truly pleased, to have been included, considering the way Irene had treated him since the night she'd traced him to Eleanor's room, a night Will would just as soon forget on all counts. From the way she acted, you would have thought he was a child molester or a bigamist or something. Cold, rigid, mechanical, she went about her duties in silence, and as the days marched on Will seemed to see more and more of Nurse Bloethal and less and less of Irene—and there was nothing he could do or say to sway her. One evening, during his eight-o'clock feeding, he took the glass from her hands, and instead of draining it at once, set it down deliberately on the night table. Irene was agitated. He could see it in the way she set her mouth and narrowed her eyes in rebuke—first the business with his wife and now this, putting the milk aside as if to toy with her and make a mockery of his Doctor's orders. "Nurse Graves—Irene—what's the matter?" he pleaded, and because he knew the answer, because he knew how much it meant to her and how all the evidence was stacked against him, he couldn't help reddening.

She turned away, made some unnecessary adjustment to the ventilation hood at the window. She wouldn't answer him. He watched her a moment as she moved about the room, her back to him, the dress clinging to her hips and buttocks in a way that stirred him miraculously despite his ruined stomach, his failure with Eleanor and the milk that saturated his pores and soaked his brain till he could hardly think. Her elbows flew as she tidied up and he admired them, admired the plumpness of her upper arms and the quiet strength of her shoulders. "Irene," he choked, fumbling for his words, "listen to me . . . appearances can be deceiving—nothing happened between Eleanor and me, nothing at all. I swear it."

She swung round then, and the look she gave him was like the flat edge of a sword. "If a patient under my care doesn't *want* to get well," she began, and her voice trembled with the effort to control it, "then there's nothing I can do. Nothing. And yet when all is said and done, the failure devolves on me. I don't want your, your *decline* on my conscience. . . ." She looked away. Will could hear a gurney creaking by in the hallway, India-rubber wheels on the hard Italian floor. "I . . . I care too much for you," she said finally, her voice reduced to a thin hesitant whisper, and then she was gone, and he was left for the first time to drink his milk in solitude, unobserved.

She'd softened gradually—to hold a grudge, even in matters of therapeusis and medical principle, just wasn't in her nature—and by the time she came for him and bundled him into the sleigh out front of the San amidst a burst of flurries and a medley of carols from the Sanitarium Glee Club, they were on their old footing again. The day was blustery and cold and the wind burned his lungs and chafed his nose and ears, but he was fully alive to the world around him. The smell of the horses (had he ever smelled anything so life-affirming, so potent!), the sight of the sparrows huddled like pensioners in the wind-whipped branches of elm and oak, the music of the sleigh bells and the exhilaration of the icy air crashing about his ears—it was a feast for the senses. And, too, he had to admit he was relieved to discover that the other two specially favored patients were women—a Countess Masha Tetranova, who, though she hailed from Petersburg, claimed never to have heard of Professor Stepanovich, and Mrs. Solomon Teitelbaum, the young wife of a lard manufacturer from Brooklyn. He was relieved because he'd been expecting men, men for whom Nurse Graves would presumably have performed the same intimate therapeutic rituals she'd performed for him, and he'd expected to be annoyed by having to share her attention. Was he jealous? He was. And what did that mean? He didn't want to ask.

At any rate, they spent a good part of the afternoon dashing through the countryside, the sleigh bells beating rhythm to the muted *clop* of the horses' hooves, a fine frosting of snow escaping the runners and settling over blankets, mittens, scarves, fur collars and hats. Their destination—a surprise—was the farm of Nurse Graves's parents, some six miles to the east of town. They left the Marshall Road, crossed a one-lane bridge made of split logs and discovered a neat fieldstone house with a snow-dusted roof of blue-gray slate set amidst a grid of stone fences and ancient-looking outbuildings. An avenue of pine and fir skirted a fair-sized pond—glassy with ice at this season—and brought them up to the doorstep, where a pair of Border collies awaited them with rich liquid eyes. The Countess remarked that the place was "perfectly charming," but her tone said otherwise; as for Mrs. Teitelbaum, she'd never before been outside the city—any city—and her features were pinched with uncertainty.

Will had no sympathy for them. He was charmed, purely and ingenuously. He stroked the dogs' ears, admired the wreath of holly on the door, went faint at the first ambrosial whiff of Mrs. Graves's pfeffernüsse cookies (but alas, no cookies for him—he was still on the milk diet, and Irene had brought along sixteen neat little four-ounce bottles, each sealed with wax, to take him through the afternoon). There were sisters and brothers, eight of them in all, ranging in age from less than a year to seventeen, and Will gave each of them a coin and looked into their faces like an anthropologist, wondering at the marvelous repetition of the features that had been given such glorious expression in their eldest sister. There was a characteristic set to the jaw among the Graves tribe, a look of quiet determination, gumption even, that hearkened back to their Potawatomi-fighting ancestors, but it was tempered by an ever-so-faint upturning at the corners of the mouth that gave them all the air of just having heard a good joke. Their ears were perfect, like Irene's; their eyes fathomless and uniformly brown; their hair its own indeterminate color, neither blond nor brunette. Will studied the parents, too, and saw that Nurse Graves had borrowed her slice of a nose from her father, and her arms, shoulders, lips, teeth and smile from her mother (not to mention a whole lot more still discernible in the ruins of Mrs. Graves's generous figure).

The afternoon progressed. The fire leapt at the fender; there were songs; the Countess Tetranova accepted a glass of cider as if it were strained offal; Leila Teitelbaum shrank into the corner until Irene's mother drew her out on the subject of molten lard; the smell of roasting chestnuts basted the air; Will sang, sledded and bobbed for apples with the children; and the dogs, cats, a pet raccoon and the pulsing current of brothers and sisters kept up a continuous but joyful din through the shank of the afternoon. Will enjoyed himself thoroughly. So thoroughly, in fact, that for minutes at a time he forgot he was an invalid (though Nurse Graves reminded him, every quarter of an hour, by uncapping yet another four-ounce bottle of milk, while his bladder sent him out the kitchen door to the outhouse in a periodic scurry). But it was amazing. His stomach was quiescent; his prurigo, eczema and boils had dried up; his heart was nonpalpitant and his tongue uncoated. He felt better than he had in months, in years. He felt human, felt youthful, felt like a man who had never known the despair of a ruined gut, a limp organ or a turkey laid low by the hand of fate.

As darkness fell, Tetranova and Teitelbaum made their way precipitately to the sled, but Will could barely tear himself away. The dogs licked his hands, the children kissed him, Mrs. Graves wrapped up a dozen cookies against the day of his recovery. And on the way home, slicing through the night that wedded earth and sky so completely he couldn't tell if the runners had left the ground or not, Will settled himself luxuriously beneath the rugs and furs and heavy blankets, and though he knew it was improper, though she was his nurse and he a married man, he slipped his arm round Irene's shoulder and held it there till the lights of the Sanitarium rose up out of the cold streets to engulf them.

And now he was out again. In the air. On his own. Heading down Washington Avenue with his billfold clutched tight, the snow brushing his cheeks and lashes with soft wings, every scent of the earth as new as if he'd just uncorked the bottle that contained them. There were two days to Christmas, and he was on his way to the local jeweler's to see if he might not find something there to please Eleanor. That was his conscious purpose. But deep in the exfoliate layers of his mind, there lay a second thought, a thought he couldn't approach too directly for fear of chasing it out into the open: he was thinking of getting something for Irene, too. Nothing too significant, of course, nothing she might tend to take in the wrong way—no rings or lockets or anything like that. A brooch maybe, or a pendant. Something for her hair, a necklace, a bracelet. Just a token, that was all. A little thing that would say *Thank you for the care. The service, that is. The personal attention.* He didn't see anything wrong in that. He always gave a little something to the postman, the maids, the delivery boy from Offenbacher's—Christmas was the season of giving, wasn't it?

As he was crossing Champion, the air seemed suddenly to congeal and a single electrifying odor rose up out of nowhere to drive all else before it and stop him dead in his tracks. Apprehension was instantaneous: this was the natural pure unapologetic aroma of meat sizzling in the pan—a hamburger, to be specific—and it was emanating from the restaurant on the corner. *The Red Onion*, read the sign out front, and Will recognized the place as the iniquitous den in which the San's gizzardites and yogurt gobblers took refuge when they could tolerate the Kellogg regime no longer. The Doctor had spies there, Will had heard, and it was said that he'd once dismissed a physician who'd been caught red-handed in the back room with a double order of short ribs in tomato sauce. Will couldn't remember ever having smelled anything as keenly, even as a boy, and he stood there transfixed in the middle of the road, wondering at this dominance of the olfactory sense. Was it some sort of organic reaction to the deadening of his senses through those eternal mucousy feedings of milk?

It was. It had to be. But oh, what a smell!

And now his stomach asserted itself for the first time in a good long while, and he had a sudden epiphanic vision of himself at a comfortable table with a checked tablecloth, a bottle of beer at his elbow, the waiter setting down a plate of fried potatoes and a hamburger sandwich with a garnish of onion and a dill pickle fresh from the barrel. The vision was so palpable that he'd actually begun to reach for the plate when a man in a hack brought him back to reality. Will looked up into whiskers, teeth, heard the shriek of wheels and the thunder of hooves. "Get out of the street, you goddamned moron!" the man hollered, and then he was gone, the hack swaying indignantly up the road.

Will crossed to the sidewalk, his eyes fixed on the window of the restaurant—he saw a man in side-whiskers lifting a fork to his mouth, movement, a waiter in mustaches, apron and suspenders—but he continued on past. *No*, he told himself, and he was a man of steel, *no*. He was making real progress—Drs. Linniman and Kellogg had promised a switch to the grape diet for Christmas if everything went well—and he couldn't risk throwing it all away on a single impulse, no matter how enthralling. Was he insane? Lunatic? Mad? Was he willing to measure his life against a hamburger sandwich? The answer rattled around like a loose bearing inside his head: *Almost, almost.*

He passed a buttermilk shop on West Michigan and didn't look twice—he'd had enough dairy to last him six lifetimes—but the Christmas display of fruits, nuts and candies in the window of Whalen's Grocery slowed him down, and Tuckerman's Meat Market, with its rubbernecked geese and broad-beamed hams, brought him to a halt. A ham, he thought, and what a terrific gift that would make . . . but for whom? He no longer knew a soul in the world who'd want it. Except for his father or Ben Settember down at Ben's Elbow—and they were so far away, through space, time and disposition, as to be on another planet in another galaxy. How far he'd come. And how far—how interminably, exhaustingly, impossibly far—he had yet to go.

But enough of that. It was Christmas, and nothing could suppress his delight in the season. His pace was jaunty, the bowler winking low over one eye, the tails of his scarf flying behind him in the breeze. To the denizens of Battle Creek he was a remarkable sight, all prancing shank and flapping elbow, a great gangling mantis given human form and marching through the icebound streets like a parade of one. He tipped his hat to the ladies, called out Christmas greetings to men and boys alike, and despite himself, he allowed the notion of a gift for Irene to work its way to the very top of his list of charitable intentions.

The jeweler's—Casaubon's, by all accounts the best in town—was right where Homer Praetz had said it would be, on McCamly, just across the street from the Post Tavern Hotel, another den of iniquity. Will paused a moment at the jeweler's door, craning his neck to study the great looming brick-and-granite building behind him, where no doubt the backsliders and the blissfully ignorant were even then digging into legs of mutton, beefsteaks and pork loins, and washing all that delicate indigestible flesh down with schooners of beer and shots of good malt whiskey. With a sigh, he turned his back on it and entered the shop to the soothing mercantile tinkle of the bell over the door.

In an instant, Will was transported. Warmth embraced him. A murmur of voices whispered in sacerdotal tones of stones and settings, of

Vever, Gaillard and Lalique. A pretty girl, trying on an opal ring at the near end of a long gleaming display case, glanced up at him and smiled. In a kind of reverie, Will felt the coat fall from his shoulders, discovered the luxury of a plush chair interposed between his lean buttocks and the nullity of intermediate space, opened his hands to receive a steaming redolent cup of the finest *chocolat chaud* from Paris, allowed the shop owner himself to present him with the full pageant of reigning jewels and their habiliments of gold and silver and champlevé enamel. He bought too much and he paid too much for what he bought. But it didn't matter. Not a whit. Patrick Henry Casaubon was the soul of hospitality and his shop a pasha's palace, and together they gave him a welcome respite from the antiseptic and the physiologically correct.

Will sipped chocolate like a turncoat, an outlaw, and he nodded an imperial yes or no at this glittering object or that. And when he left, when he girded himself against the cold and started back up the cheerily lit streets for the San, he took with him an opulent necklace of Ceylon sapphires and rose diamonds for Eleanor, and a starburst brooch of seed pearls and one little unostentatious and absolutely forgivable diamond for Irene. Two small elegant velvet-lined packages. They were nestled in his breast pocket, palpable and satisfying, a barely discernible bulge against the rich fabric of his coat, as he strode up the hill to the San. He felt lighter than air all of a sudden, as if he'd shrugged off some heavy burden, and he couldn't help himself, he couldn't—though people looked at him as if he were drunk or mad or floating along behind a full sail of Sears' White Star Liquor Cure, he burst into song:

> Now Christmas is come,
> Let us beat up the drum,
> And call all our neighbors together,
> And when they appear,
> Let us make them such cheer,
> As will keep out the wind and the weather.

His voice rose up, hollow as the wind in a drainpipe, tuneless, flat, hopelessly unmelodic, but infectious for all that. First one dog took it up in a crazed stuttering high-pitched yowl that irrevocably shattered the compact of the night, and then another and another, until up and down the length of Washington Avenue, the whole neighborhood was singing with him.

❖   ❖   ❖

But the mood wouldn't hold. How could it? How could that damnable purgatory of brick and stone and marble sustain any measure of joy that wasn't connected directly to the bowels?

She wouldn't take the brooch. Nurse Graves, that is. Irene. "I'm very sorry, Mr. Lightbody," she breathed, and Will's room was still as a mortuary, no hint of sound from the radiator, the water pipes, the hallway or the room next door, "but we're not permitted to accept gratuities from the patients. It's strictly forbidden."

Will was stunned. "Forbidden? To accept a gift, a Christmas token given selflessly and in commemoration of the season?" He was outraged. "By whom? Forbidden by whom?"

The light of the postulant shone in her eyes as she pronounced the name: "Dr. Kellogg."

"Dr. Kellogg," Will repeated, and his emphasis was entirely different. "Dr. Kellogg. Is he governor? President? God? Does he have to dictate every last thing that goes on here, from our bowel movements to our emotions?" Will was stretched out on the bed, in robe and nightgown, his thin ankles crossed in front of him. He sat up now, his voice tight with anger. "And what about me? What about my right to express my, my affection and gratitude to my fellow man—and woman. To people, I mean, people I consider friends?"

There it was, he'd said it: *friends*. The term lay there before them like the trunk of a toppled tree, the bigger, more complicated terms— *gratitude, affection*—tangled in its branches. Nurse Graves chose to ignore it. "When we're hired," she said, reaching up to adjust a cap that was already set flawlessly in place, "we sign a pledge to the Sanitarium in which we vow to uphold its principles and to refrain from fraternizing with the patients outside the confines of our duties."

Fraternizing. Her tone infuriated him. Dry, cold, impersonal—she might have been quoting from a medical text. And here he'd just quaffed his final four ounces of milk for the day, without argument, just to please her; here he was, filled with gratitude and the pure unblemished spirit of giving, and she called it *fraternizing*. He watched her preparing his bedtime enema, making a show of heating the paraffin over a burner and filling the reservoir with painstaking precision so she wouldn't have to contemplate the velvet-lined box on the nightstand with its bow of red ribbon and the personally inscribed card attached. "But that's ridiculous," he protested. "I'm the patient, you're the nurse, sure—but we're people, too, aren't we?"

No answer.

"Aren't we?"

She murmured a reluctant "yes" as she bustled across the floor to the bathroom and ran some water in the sink. He studied her through the open door, the swell of her shoulders, firm, compact, tendons leaping as she worked the faucets, her legs, the neat squared heels of her shoes. Then she was back, looking flushed but determined.

"Well, won't you even open it then? Won't you have a look—even if you can't accept it? I picked it out myself. For you. Thinking of you."

A mocking smile crossed her lips. "Given selflessly, eh?" she said. "And have you also selflessly chosen little tokens of gratitude for Nurse Bloethal and Mrs. Stover? For Ralph? . . . Mr. Lightbody, I think you're deluding yourself—"

"Can't you call me 'Will'?"

The apparatus was in her hands, slick, hot, catharsis in an India-rubber bulb. She shifted it nervously from one hand to the other. A pin glinted in her hair. "No," she said, "I can't."

"Because Dr. Kellogg wouldn't approve?" Will sat up abruptly, his blind feet seeking the carpet slippers on the cold germ-free glaze of the floor. "The man who sees all, hears all, knows all?"

"Because it's not right. Because it's against the rules."

"The rules." Will was on his feet now, gaunt and towering, the robe hanging from him like a deflated sail flapping at the mast. "Whose rules? What rules? You don't really believe all this bunkum, do you? This, this holier-than-thou dietary crap, the enema treatments, the mud packs, the sensory deprivation? What's it going to get us—another six months of eating mush or grapes or psyllium seeds? Another year? We

die anyway, all of us, even the exalted Dr. Kellogg—isn't that the truth?"

Irene looked as if she'd been slapped. Her face was hard, outraged, stung to a whiteness that alarmed him. But when she spoke, her voice was calm and controlled. "Yes," she said, "I most certainly do believe it. Every word, every treatment, every principle. With all my heart—and my brain, too, thank you. You're a sick man," she added. "You don't know what you're saying."

"I do," Will insisted, but he was flagging. "I just don't think your Dr. Kellogg is God, that's all, and I don't think he has the right to control your life—or anybody else's."

But the argument was already over. She was serene now, gazing up at him like an ecstatic, a crusader, a Mohammedan on the eve of the jihad. "There's a God in heaven, Mr. Lightbody, and I believe in Him in a way I suspect you never will, a God who cares for our immortal essence, but there's a god in every one of us, too, and the holy temple of that god is the human body, and if it takes a man like Dr. Kellogg to bring that truth home to us, then he's a part of the godhead, too." Her voice was airy, her eyes distant and unfocused. "When I think of what he's done for mankind—for the alimentary canal alone—I have to say, yes, he is a god, my god, and he should be yours, too." She turned to him with an accusatory look, her eyes burning with the fire of righteousness. "And after all he's done for you, you should be ashamed of yourself, ashamed to the very core."

Will was defeated. The brooch was nothing. He couldn't even look at the box. Perhaps it was frustration, disappointment, despair, but what he did next shocked even him—he lurched forward and took her clumsily in his arms, Nurse Graves, Irene, took her in his arms like a lover and bent his lips to hers. He kissed her, held her, squeezed her to him until he felt something warm and wet on his chest and she was breaking away from him and the naked bulb of black wet rubber lay on the floor between them like some sort of ghastly birth.

"Mr. Lightbody—" The breath escaped her. She backed up a step. "This is . . . I don't—"

"Will," he said. She'd kissed him, kissed him back.

"Mr. Lightbody, I—"

"Will."

"Will . . . Mr. Lightbody . . . I'm too confused, I'm sorry, I—I can't do this. Not tonight."

Not tonight? Can't do it tonight? But that meant—? His heart whirled like a turbine. If not tonight, then some other night—yes—and he needed no grape diets or sinusoidal currents to arouse him now, he was ready, straining at the fabric, lifting the tent of his nightgown as if this were the moment and this the center ring.

But she was looking past him, staring down at the enema bag deflated on the floor. "I can't," she repeated, and she wouldn't look at him, wouldn't look at the brooch on the night table, wouldn't look at his feet, his hands, the stake driven into his groin, his sick hungry eyes. "Nurse Bloethal," she whispered, and her voice had gone distant. "I'll have to get Nurse Bloethal."

And so it was Nurse Bloethal, she of the callous hands and iron grip, and his erection—his glorious, life-affirming, rejuvenant erection—came to naught. And if Irene believed in her gods and applied the syringe like a sacrament, Nurse Bloethal used it like the jackal of death.

❖   ❖   ❖

In the morning, it was Nurse Bloethal again, and it was Nurse Bloethal before lunch and after. And where was Irene? She wasn't feeling well. Nothing serious? he hoped. No, just a touch of indigestion.

Indigestion. And wasn't that ironic? Will's own stomach was acting up again, too. He'd achieved a kind of truce there for a while, the seaweed and psyllium having done their work as advertised, the steady analgesic flow of milk inundating that hypersensitive organ until it was dead to all sensation. Despite himself, he'd begun to feel guardedly optimistic. But now, suddenly, on the eve of his graduation to the grape diet, Will's stomach was a cauldron of acid all over again. He could taste it in the back of his throat, on his palate, his lips, his tongue: the acid of rejection, the acid of anger and despair. He'd awakened with an erection, dreaming of Irene's lips, her body pressed to his, the wonder of her soft untrammeled breasts, and his first thought was of Eleanor. It was an unclean thought, a selfish and lustful thought, but there it was.

The clock on the bureau read 5:05; the night-light glowed softly. Will pushed back the hood of his outdoor respirator, shivered into his robe and slippers, and crept out into the sterile reaches of the San's halls. If he'd been furtive on the night of the turkey, now he positively slunk along the silent corridors, guilty on a host of counts, not the least of which was his present intention of forcing himself on his ailing wife. *Give me a daughter, Will,* she'd whispered. Well, now he was ready, and all frailty, all suffering, all notions of restraint and appeals to reason were as nothing in the face of that momentous fact.

Down three flights and into a corridor identical to the one he'd just left. Bright lights. Cold floors. Room 212. Knocking—just a tap—eyes right, eyes left, no one, not even a nurse in sight. "Eleanor? Are you in there?" Hand on the doorknob, belching back an attack of gas, twist of the wrist, the room gently aglow. "Eleanor? It's me, Will."

Nothing. Not a whisper. He slipped into the room like a thief, pulling the door softly closed behind him. Eleanor was not in her bed. Ten past five in the morning, and his wife was not in her bed. His first wild thought came like an arrow, whoosh, and it bored into his brain: *Linniman.* But no. The bed had been slept in, pillow rumpled, bedclothes in a heap. Ten past five in the morning: where on earth could she be? The bathroom gave him no clue: toothbrush, face powder, rouge, a damp towel and a silk dressing gown he recognized from happier days. Back into the room again, poking through the bureau drawers: underthings—they electrified him—scarves, gloves, hatpins. On the nightstand, two books, bound in leather and with gilt titles: *Nature's Own Book,* by Mrs. Asenath Nicholson, which seemed mostly to be about carrots and parsnips, and *Freikorper Kultur,* by one Gerhardt Kuntz, which espoused sunbathing in the nude. Will lingered over this latter, paging through endless disquisitions on light, air and the health-giving properties of meadows and beaches to find a single riveting description of a group of heliophiles of both sexes romping round a spring in the Black Forest. It was five-thirty when he looked up from the book, and he was more inflamed than ever.

The whole affair would have ended there if he hadn't accidentally dislodged a typewritten sheet of paper from the night table on setting the book back down. It was a "Rehabilitative Schedule" for Mrs. Eleanor Lightbody, and it began at 5:00 A.M. with a colon wash, sitz bath and massage in the women's baths, followed by calisthenics and Indian-club toss in the gymnasium. At 5:30 she was to have a "Silesian mud pack," whatever that was, and take twenty minutes of deep-breathing exercise on the upper veranda.

The upper veranda. Will was out the door and down the hall before the schedule hit the table.

Unfortunately, the veranda was deserted but for an unrecognizable figure wrapped like an Eskimo against the lingering night. The figure hovered near the far railing, high above the sleeping rooftops of Battle Creek, and it seemed to be grunting or crying out in agony, its burdened arms flapping helplessly, legs leaden beneath a bulky wrap of blankets. Will was about to turn away, disappointed, when something in the tenor of those grunts spoke to him. "Eleanor?" he whispered, drawing his robe tight at the collar.

Eleanor—if this was Eleanor—didn't respond. "Eight—uh, uh, *phaw!*" grunted a feminine voice, and a cowl hid her face. She bent at the waist, flailed her arms. "Nine—uh, uh, *phaw!* Ten—uh, uh, *phaw!*"

"Eleanor?"

The hooded figure turned to him then and showed him a face that wasn't his wife's, a death mask of a face, horrific, immobilized, features clenched like a fist. He took a lively step backward, startled, and the hollows of the eyes, luminous against the dark vise-grip of the mask, seized him. "Will?" The lumpen figure spoke his name, mouth fallen open in a rictus of surprise. "What in God's name—?"

It was all right—the spell was broken. This wasn't a messenger from beyond the grave, it wasn't the Grim Reaper or an escaped lunatic—it was only Eleanor, his wife, his love, basted in Silesian mud and indulging in a little deep breathing on the frozen flagstones of the veranda two hours before breakfast and in the dead black of the night. Eleanor, it was only Eleanor. With recognition came confidence, and with confidence, ardor. He glided forward in his slippers and tried to take her in his arms, but the layers of blankets impeded him. Clutching at what he took to be an arm, he sputtered, "I-I came to see how you were—"

"At five-thirty in the morning?"

"I missed you. It *is* Christmas Eve, after all. Or the morning of Christmas Eve."

(This was a sore point between them. Will had wanted to go home for Christmas, home to the house on Parsonage Lane and their friends and family, but Eleanor refused. She couldn't leave now, right in the middle of her treatment—nor could he. What was he thinking? But it would only be for a week, two weeks at most, he'd countered. No, she said, no. He could go if he wanted—though in his condition it was tantamount to throwing his life away—but she wasn't budging. Did he think she was suicidal? He didn't, of course he didn't, and he'd mumbled something apologetic and gone off, chastened, to his room. And so they'd stayed, though the fall season at the San was over and the halls grew more deserted by the day, stayed to eat Nuttolene giblets and artificial goose among strangers in the bleak forbidding ice-shrouded wastes of south-central Michigan.)

Eleanor didn't respond. "Eleven—uh, uh, *phaw!*" she gasped. "Twelve—uh, uh, *phaw!*; Thirteen—"

Will was freezing. A shiver racked his body so violently it was as if he'd been lifted by the nape of his neck and shaken, vertebra by vertebra, to the tip of his tailbone. "I just wanted to say I have a present for you, something nice, something you're going to love—wait till you see it."

"—uh, uh, *phaw!*" She bent over now to adjust her padding and Will saw that an electric cord trailed away from her backside, looped round half a dozen vacant Adirondack chairs and found its way to an outlet just inside the door. "That's sweet of you, Will," she murmured, hot breath steaming from invisible nostrils, and she cracked her mask to give him a smile. "I have something for you, too."

"Your cord is tangled," Will said, though it wasn't, and he used the distraction as a pretext for moving into her and clinging ardently to her cocoon of blankets. He dropped his voice to a passionate whisper. "And I have a little something with me now, too, if you want to come back to my room and try it on for size. . . ."

"Don't be ridiculous, Will—we'll exchange gifts tonight, as we'd agreed, at Frank's party for Dr. Kellogg."

This rankled him—"*Frank's* party for Dr. Kellogg"—but he ignored it and clung to her blankets all the more fervently. He was cold. His robe was nothing. A predawn wind whistled over the rooftops to sit in his ears. The tip of his nose was insensate. "No, no," he whispered, and he couldn't seem to stop his teeth from chattering, "th-that's not what I mean—you-you-you said you wanted me-me to give you a d-daughter, don't you remember? And I, I was—well, n-now I'm ready. Can't you f-feel me? I'm ready to give her to you. Right now. This m-minute." He gazed passionately into her mud-rimmed eyes. "C-come to my room."

"You can't be serious?" She broke away from him, the cold morning air hissing through her nostrils. "Marital relations are strictly forbidden here, you know that." And then she laughed and shook her head. "Will Lightbody, you're impossible. Impossible. Talk of the most inappropriate time— and what are you doing out here in your robe and slippers anyway? Are you mad? You'll catch your death."

Will was already backing toward the door, his member flaccid and drawn up into his body against the cold, shoulders cradled in his quaking arms. "M-merry Christmas," he said, and sneezed, "—Eleanor."

But she didn't hear him. She was crouching, bending from the waist and straightening up again, over and over. He could hear her counting as he closed the heavy door to the hallway: "Fourteen—uh, uh, *phaw!* Fifteen—uh, uh, *phaw!*"

❖   ❖   ❖

The rest of the morning was consumed in routine. At seven, Nurse Bloethal welcomed him to the day with his morning enema and escorted him to the dining room for the first two feedings of his final seventeen hours on the milk diet. The word had come down from on high: all signs were favorable and Will was to proceed to grapes on Christmas Day. The news was thrilling, wonderful, a kind of earthly miracle. At the stroke of midnight, on the commencement of the day that commemorated the birth of his spiritual savior, Will's corporeal savior would allow him the great boon of solid food. Grapes. Grapes bountiful, grapes delectable, grapes medicinal. As Will had come to understand it, the grape diet represented the third rung on the alimentary ladder to recovery, and it prescribed an unlimited quantity of those fleshy, spherical, sweet and sustaining fruits—the golden muscat, the royal Concord, the humble Thompsons and fat red Tokays—freighted in from some distant and still vernal corner of the world and peeled lovingly, one by one, by Mrs. Stover's nimble-fingered dietary girls. Will was looking forward to it. Grapes had their limitations, and he'd never consumed more than a bunch or two in a good year, but anything was better than milk. At least you could chew them.

After breakfast, Nurse Bloethal led him to the Men's Gymnasium for his daily calisthenics under the hortatory direction of the big-armed Swede, after which he forced himself through a lackluster session of laughing exercises and settled into the tremulous oblivion of the Vibrotherapy Department. All this, over time, had become a monumental bore. Far from developing a positive outlook, Will found himself growing increasingly depressed as he twisted his grallatorial limbs and shook his nugatory buttocks with the rest of his fellow sufferers—it was the same thing, day in, day out, a purgatory of the unwise and the unwell. About the only things he had to look forward to were Nurse Graves (and she was indisposed today, frightened half to death by a simple little human gesture of affection) and his visit to the Electrical Department, which had become one of the few high points of his daily routine.

He couldn't say why, really. Perhaps it was the initial surprise of that first day, when he discovered that the sinusoidal bath didn't involve public disrobing, public waters, body hair and the display of portions of the male anatomy that were best left under wraps. There was a neatness and civility to it that appealed to him. Roll up your cuffs and sleeves and feel the salutary prickle of electricity on your skin while remaining otherwise fully and decently dressed. Will had no idea whether the treatment did him a lick of good or not, but he found it relaxing and, if not actually enjoyable, then at least something less than an ongoing torture.

On this particular day, he was paired again with Homer Praetz, the industrial magnate. Over the course of the past weeks, through their meals and sinusoidal fellowship, Will had come to know the man somewhat better. Tireless, driven, dynamic, fleshy, Homer Praetz seemed cut from the same mold as Will's father, though Praetz was younger, much younger, one of those men who settles so thoroughly into his role, it's impossible to guess his age—he could have been anywhere from thirty to fifty. He was king of the machine-tool industry in Cleveland, having managed in a few short years to increase his initial investment a hundredfold while simultaneously driving his competitors to ruin; unfortunately, he'd defeated his stomach and undermined his heart in the process.

Praetz had warmed to Will in the dining hall, shoveling up great glutinous masses of Rice à la Carolina and Indian trifle while Will stuck to his ascetic servings of milk, and in the absence of Mrs. Tindermarsh and Hart-Jones, both of whom had gone home for the holidays, had begun to make a species of higher conversation at the table. And as he warmed to Will, so the feeling became mutual, and Will had become more animated, joking with Professor Srepanovich over the collapsing rings of Saturn and flirting, as much as he dared, with Miss Muntz. What's more, Praetz's schedule had been changed, so that he now appeared in the Electrical Department before his steam bath rather than after, thus sparing Will the unsettling sight of his tumultuous nakedness. On the days when their schedules coincided, they would sit there side by side in their sinusoidal chairs, feet elevated, hands immersed, chatting away like a pair of bankers at the shoeshine parlor. It was a conceit Will could live with.

"Well, well, well, Lightbody," Praetz chuckled as he sat heavily and began removing his shoes and socks, "and a happy Christmas to you— I understand you'll be eating solid food like the rest of us come tomorrow, hey?"

Alfred Woodbine, the impeccably dressed attendant, with his crisp bow tie, immaculate collar and pomaded hair, was helping Will into the chair beside Praetz's. Will smiled. He looked from Homer to Alfred and back again. "You know, it's been so long, I think I've forgotten what teeth are for."

"Don't I know it, Will," Praetz sighed, dropping his shoes to the floor and massaging his massive feet as tenderly as if he were caressing the cheek of a lover. "Dr. Kellogg likes to humble you, take you right back to the beginning till you're nothing more than a squalling little red-faced baby clawing for the teat . . . I suppose it's some sort of psychological effect he's after, he ought to know, God bless him, what with all the lives he's saved—isn't that right, Alfred?" But before Alfred had a chance to agree, Praetz let out a hoot of laughter.

Will was grinning. "What? What is it?"

"Oh, I was just thinking. . . ." Praetz was leaning forward now, his face swollen with hilarity. "I mean, now that you're teething, what's on the menu? Mush? Corn pulp? Or is it grapes?" His smile was sly, his eyes bursting in their sockets. "It's grapes, isn't it? Am I right?"

Will didn't mind the ribbing. It was a rite of passage, a Battle Creek tradition, and he was secretly pleased to be matriculating to the next phase of treatment. "Yes," he admitted, "grapes. But I can't help wishing it was lobster." This was funny, very funny, and the tile walls reverberated with his whoop of laughter.

"Don't you listen now, Alfred—you didn't hear that, did you?" Praetz worked his mouth as if there were something caught between his teeth, trying unsuccessfully to suppress the laugh that rushed through his nostrils in a high-pitched whinny.

The attendant shook his head and compressed his lips, but his eyes gave him away. He was feeling it, too, the zaniness, the hilarity, the holiday spirit that lifted them all free of their shackles and made them as giddy as children rushing the tree at first light. Will whooped.

Homer Praetz eased himself back in the sinusoidal chair and slapped his knee. "Next thing you know, Will, the Chief'll graduate you to Protose fillets and you'll be hot as a farm boy on his first date."

The breath caught in Will's throat. He glanced up at Alfred, who was bending over him to fold his sleeves back, and blushed.

"Don't blush, Lightbody," Homer crowed, plunking his feet into the big white galvanized buckets before him, "come on now, you fox, I've seen the way you work Miss Muntz at the table—ah-ah, don't deny it—and I wouldn't say a word but that I've been through it myself. Good Christ, when they brought me in here back in October I could barely find the strength to get up out of the chair, and as for women, well, my wife was the loneliest woman on earth"—here he leaned forward and winked—"if you know what I mean."

Will knew. He knew all too well. Closing his eyes, he thought of Eleanor, Irene, Ida Muntz, the anonymous woman in the waiting room, and let out a sigh. He really didn't feel comfortable discussing private matters, particularly in the hearing of Alfred, who for all he knew could be one of the Doctor's spies, but what Homer was saying spoke directly to him: *he'd been through it, too.* The knowledge made him feel better —it was all part and parcel of the Battle Creek way, and he appreciated the confidence, he did. Cracking his eyes lazily to see if Alfred had flicked on the current—his hand was on the switch—Will gave a grunt of assent. "I know, Homer," he said, and his voice was drowsy, "I know what you mean." He let his eyes fall shut again.

He heard Homer's voice come back at him, thin as hammered wire —"She's lonely no more"—and waited for the familiar pinch and nibble of the current as it took his limbs in its delicate little rows of teeth and then released them again. There was a faint vibration, a sort of rattle, as of spoon and cup, and his mind settled into its groove. It took him a moment before he realized that nothing was happening.

"You going to turn it on, Alfred?" he murmured, and in that instant he understood that something was amiss, that the rattling he'd been vaguely aware of for the past ten seconds was growing louder, steadier, the insistent chatter of a pair of drumsticks, a windup toy gone berserk. His eyes flashed open. Time seemed to have frozen. There was Alfred, impeccable still and still at the switch. But he was moving, jerking his limbs and shuffling his feet as if he'd suddenly been transported to a hoedown at the county fair, and his hand was flapping, fishlike, at the wall panel, which in turn was rattling and trembling so, the palm in the corner had begun to wave its fronds in sympathetic response. Bewildered, Will turned to Praetz. But Homer was in on it, too, his features seized up, eyes riveted, limbs kicking out as if the chair were a bucking bronco and he a Wild West cowboy, and that was odd and unexpected, yes, but what was that red froth on his lips and, and that *substance*, that pink and wet thing clinging to his collar like a second tie?

His tongue, Will, his tongue.

That was it. Comprehension seized him like a pair of hot tongs and he was up and out of the chair in a bound, water sloshing, Alfred dancing, Homer Praetz's eyes like hard-boiled eggs, the shelf rattling, the current sizzling. *Don't touch that switch!* Panic put the flame to his heart. *Run!* screamed a voice in his head, but he fought it down. No.

No. No. And then he was moving, no time to think, feet grabbing for purchase on the slick floor, shoulder down: he hit Alfred in the chest, just under his flailing arms, and broke the connection.

In the next moment they were on the floor in a tangle of limbs, a fugitive smell of urine emanating from Alfred's impeccable trousers, and Alfred was breathing, gagging, bringing something up . . . and then, behind them, a sudden violent crash, the wet heavy slap of water, the tumbling tubs: Homer Praetz took the sinusoidal chair down with him, down into the bear hug of outraged gravity. Will saw him there, sprawled horribly in the ruins, the big white slabs of his feet still jerking, and knew that no amount of restraint, no degree of physiologic living or rigor of scientific eating could bring him back again.

❖   ❖   ❖

One P.M. on the day before Christmas, the sky like an untended grave, and Will Lightbody, hastily dressed and still trembling, was heading down Washington Avenue for the second time that week. He wasn't humming Christmas ditties and he wasn't thinking of gifts. Eleanor was off somewhere at a skating party—or so he'd been told—and Irene was indisposed. He watched his feet and thought nothing, nothing at all.

When he got to the corner of Washington and Champion he stepped out into the street without turning his head and made straight for the Red Onion. *Tired of Bran & Sprouts?* the sign out front asked. He was. Mortally tired. The door swung open as if greased, the waiter dipped his bald gleaming head, the smells hit him like a memory of Paradise before the Fall. He was shown to a table by the window, checked cloth, guttering candle. The waiter hovered at his elbow. "Whiskey," Will said, and his voice sounded strange in his own ears. "Make it a double. And a beer chaser."

"Yes, sir," the waiter said. "Double whiskey and a beer. Any preference as to brand?"

Will shook his head.

"Yes, sir. All right. And will you be wanting anything to eat?"

"Eat?" Will repeated, as if he'd never heard the term before. He gazed round him at the shadowy interior, the fire leaping over its coals, the mistletoe and pine and the beery joyous faces gathered along the bar. "A hamburger sandwich," he said finally.

"Hamburger sandwich," the waiter tolled, scribbling the order in his notepad. "And how do you want that?"

"I'm sorry?" Will said.

"How do you want it cooked?"

Will took a moment, the waiter poised over him with his mustaches, his gleaming brow, the fixed, faintly inebriate stare of his eyes. "Oh, I don't know," Will said vaguely, waving a hand in the air, "rare, I guess. Or, no, not just rare—cold in the middle."

❖ Chapter 4 ❖

The
Advertising
Game

⚜

It was getting dark by the time Charlie Ossining drifted into the Red Onion. He'd spent the past two hours drinking hot rum punch at the party Bender had hosted for Stellrecht the paper manufacturer and a smattering of grocers, buyers, grain suppliers and newspapermen, along with the odd representative of the local carriage aristocracy ("Potential investors, Charlie, potential investors," Bender reminded him), and he was feeling good. Feeling warm and optimistic and aglow with the spirit of the season. Bender had opened the bar at the Wee Nippy and draped banners proclaiming "Kellogg's Per-Fo—The Perfect Food!" and "The Newest Health Food From Kellogg!" round the room, which seemed a bit reckless—subversive, even—in the Post Tavern, but a whole host of people showed up to gobble little meatballs on a stick and pickled herring on soda crackers. Charlie had shaken hands and quaffed punch and talked up Per-Fo till he began to believe in it all over again.

"Advertising!" Bender had roared that morning as they watched the barman hang the bright red-and-white banners from the beams. "You can't sell a product without advertising!"

Charlie reminded him that they didn't yet have a product.

Bender was undaunted. "Create the demand, Charlie, and the product will follow, as sure as summer follows the spring."

It had been six weeks since Charlie had arrived with Mrs. Hookstratten's check, and they were no closer to their goal than they had the first day. They'd been rebuffed by both Kelloggs—Will Kellogg wouldn't even let them in the gate at his Toasted Corn Flake Company and he'd had his lawyers on them before the sun went down—and factory space was impossible to come by at any price. Suitable factory space, that is. There were any number of rat-infested ruins like the Malta-Vita plant for lease, sale, barter or trade, but Charlie didn't seem to have the special vision it took to picture them in operation, and since George had come along, Bender hadn't expressed the slightest interest in any of them. "We'll build, Charlie," he shouted, waving sheafs of blueprints in the air, "everything new and spanking clean from the ground floor up. To hell with these depressing, burned-out heaps of rubble—what do we need them for, eh? We've got George Kellogg behind us now!"

Yes. Well, sure. And though he didn't want to be a naysayer, Charlie couldn't help wondering what good it had done them. As far as he could see, the only thing the use of the Kellogg name had accomplished thus far was to arouse the considerable ire of the breakfast-food brothers and provoke a pair of lawsuits for trademark infringement—which in turn had necessitated the immediate outlay of a precious portion of Mrs. Hookstratten's dwindling investment to defray legal expenses (though to Bender this was nothing, nothing at all, merely the cost of doing business). And as for George himself, though Charlie had found a room for him at Mrs. Eyvindsdottir's when another of the decrepit inmates had gone on to meet his Maker, he was unavailable—unfindable, even—at any given moment. His bed was unslept in, the clothing they'd bought him scattered round the room and his own piss-drunk person lying sprawled in the alley behind the dry-goods store or folded up on a cot in the Marshall jail. Twice now Charlie had had to hire a cab, drive the twenty-four miles round-trip to Marshall and bail him out— and why there was no jail in Battle Creek was another mystery. The first time the judge had let him off, but the second time—George had been drunk and disorderly—he'd given him ten days. So they had George Kellogg behind them—and what did it get them but the cost of renting a room he didn't use and providing meals he didn't eat while their distinguished associate did hard labor on the county roads?

But tonight, all that was behind him. The party had reinvigorated him, got his enthusiasm up all over again. Bender knew what he was doing. All Charlie had to do was watch him working some local rube in the corner and he could feel the money sprouting between his fingertips; and the Kellogg thing might have seemed crazy, but Bender would find the angle to make it work, just as surely as Ford would build his automobiles and Rockefeller suck oil from the ground. Besides, it was Christmas, and the walk to the Red Onion would invigorate any man's soul, church bells tolling, children caroling, strangers crying out greetings, a candle glowing in every window and a wreath on every door. Charlie stepped in the door and half a dozen men called out his name.

He had a drink at the bar with John Krinck, one of the young San patients who slipped out now and again to do some tippling on the sly, and he traded Sanitarium jokes with the bartender and had one on the house. Then Harry Delahoussaye came in and stood drinks for the bar. (Charlie had long since forgiven the man for trying to hustle him the night he arrived—it was nothing personal, after all.) Charlie returned the favor. By the time he spotted the slouch-shouldered, loose-limbed figure of Will Lightbody slumped over a table by the window, he was as full of cheer as a man short of delirium could be. On an impulse, he decided he'd wish his late traveling companion the best of the season, and he ambled over to the table with a beer in one hand and a plate of pickled eggs in the other.

"Will!" Charlie cried, slapping him on the back in an excess of enthusiasm, "it's me, Charlie Ossining! Remember? On the train?"

Will Lightbody looked up from a table littered with spattered plates and scraps of bone, with dirty glasses, pots of ketchup, wadded-up napkins, fish bones, half-eaten fries, an ashtray buried in cigar stubs. His eyes seemed to have gone loose in his head, the misaligned one rolling round in its socket like a marble on a Chinese-checkers board. He looked haunted, juiceless, withered like last year's apple gone dry in the cellar. If this was what the Sanitarium did to you, Charlie wouldn't wish it on his worst enemy.

"Remember?" Charlie repeated lamely.

Raising a glass of dark amber whiskey to his lips, Will Lightbody began to grin, and his grin spread until he had to concentrate on it and lost his grip on the glass. Whiskey trickled down his chin and sank into his collar, which was unfastened and already stained with ketchup, mustard and steak sauce. "Sure I remember," he boomed, but his words were slurred and his eyes unsteady. "Charlie Ossining. Sure. Amelia Hookstratten, right?"

"Right." Charlie brightened. As inebriated as the man was, Charlie still knew the value of a good connection. "I saw you here and thought I'd wish you many happy returns of the season, Christmas, I mean—"

"Happy returns," Will slurred, and his voice seemed to reach out to every corner of the room as if it had tentacles. Heads turned at the bar. The waiter—Charlie knew him by name, Frank Loquatto—looked embarrassed. "Sure. Yeah. Happy returns. Whyn't you join me? Have a drink on me, huh? Yeah, Charlie Ossining. Let's drink to the birth of Christ." He turned his head and gestured for the waiter. "Another round here," he boomed, "and you can clear away some of this, some of this, this . . . clutter, yes, all right? And so"—turning back to Charlie, who'd set down his pickled eggs and pulled out a chair—"Charlie Ossining, how the hell are you? How's the breakfast-food business—breakfast food, right? Yes? Well, how is it?"

Charlie told him it was good, told him it was terrific, thriving. "Kellogg's in on it now, George Kellogg—he's the son of the Kelloggs, you know?"

Will Lightbody had lifted one of Charlie's eggs to his lips. He set it down, carefully, as if it were still in its shell and yet to be cooked. His eyes focused—that is, the recalcitrant one, the one with the cast, came back into orbit. "The name's anathema to me. Kellogg"—he spat out the syllables—"he's a fake, a sham, a charlatan, he's a wife stealer and a fraud and a . . ." He trailed off, waving a long lax hand in disgust. "He's a murderer," he said finally.

Charlie didn't know quite how to take this, so he let it go by. "Yeah, well, there's a lot of money there—and a lot of people would disagree with you. My partner, Goodloe H. Bender, he claims the Kellogg name alone is worth its weight in—"

"Dead before my eyes, dead as this, this egg—"

"Worth its weight in gold," Charlie said, overriding the interruption.

"God knows how many millions that name is worth—it's all in the advertising, did you know that?"

Will knew. He dipped his head and stroked the bridge of his nose in mute appreciation of the power of advertising. "Homer Praetz," he said, and then threw his head back to drain his glass.

Charlie liked the guy, he did. He might have come across like some kind of idiot prince on the train, but here he was, drinking them down like anybody else. Suddenly he wanted to do something for him, give him something, a token, a gift. Inspiration came like a fist between the eyes: "How about a plate of oysters? On me. We'll share them."

"Scavengers," Will began, but he broke off to pound his breastbone and lean forward to dribble something into his drink. His voice was pinched when it came back to him: "Of. The. Sea."

"Yes, I know," Charlie laughed. "So you and your wife informed me. But there's nothing sweeter, not the sweetest fish that swims the ocean, not the fattest shrimp or juiciest lobster—am I right?"

Will paused a moment, as if considering degrees of sweetness. Then he began to bob his head as if it were caught on something, as if it were made of wood and somebody else was pulling the strings. A grin split his face. "Nothing sweeter," he agreed, and in that instant his bony arm shot into the air and he snapped his fingers at poor glowering Frank Loquatto.

Over the oysters, Charlie found their conversation leaping from one thing to another, from Mrs. Lightbody's preferences in food and undergarments (she wore no corset and kept her camisoles simple and transparent to the health-giving rays of the sun) to somebody named Homer Praetz (Will kept harping on him, something about sinuses and baths) to Peterskill, life in New York, motorcars and Mrs. Hookstratten. After the waiter had cleared the plate away and freshened their drinks, Charlie steered the conversation back to the breakfast-food business in general, and to Per-Fo in particular. "We're going great guns, Will," he said, lighting up a cigarette and soaking in the smoke with a great deep sigh of pleasure, "but to be frank with you, we're expanding our original design and we're a bit, well, undercapitalized at the moment. I mean, this is the opportunity of a lifetime for the right investor. . . ."

I don't know if you're interested, but I can offer you a block of stock, Will—right here on the spot. If you want."

The man across the table from him looked as if he could barely carry the weight of his head. If half an hour earlier it seemed to be supported on invisible strings, now the strings had been severed. Will's head wobbled. His hands shook. His eyes roamed the room at random. "You need money?" he said all of a sudden, as if the idea had just penetrated to his brain. "I'll give you money"—he was fumbling in his coat pocket—"no problem, happy to help out a, a, friend. How much do you want?"

For all he'd had to drink, for all his goodwill and casual nature, Charlie sat riveted in his seat. He watched Will flip open a checkbook, spread it on the table and smooth out the leaves, watched as he called cavalierly for a pen and took it from Frank Loquatto's hand without so much as glancing up at him. "I; uh, well, anything you'd care to invest, of course—my partners and I would be delighted—you could, I mean if you want, you could—"

Will Lightbody was writing. Charlie watched the bony knuckles ride up and down the astonishing, wonderful, insuperable loops and dips of three inspired words: *One thousand dollars.* Will tore the check from the register, sat back and scribbled *Pay to the Order of Charles Ossining* across the top.

Someone was singing at the bar, off-key, *We three kings of Orient are, gold, frankincense and myrrh,* and another voice joined in, sonorous and exalted. Charlie took the check in a daze, folded it once and tucked it in his breast pocket without daring to look at it lest he break the spell. Lucky. He'd always been lucky.

Will Lightbody belched. It was a long protracted belch, and when he was finished with it he held up a single scrawny big-knuckled finger. "Charlie?" he said, and his voice was too loud, too hollow, a depthless quavering shiver of a voice that seemed on the verge of breaking.

Charlie froze. Was he going to ask for his check back? Was that it? His throat constricted. He shifted in his chair. "Yeah? What is it, Will?"

"You know any place where we can get a real drink?"

Charlie awoke to the gray void of an indeterminate hour, huddled in his bedclothes on his mattress stuffed with useless stock certificates. The muffled sounds of subdued gaiety drifted up to him from between the cracks in the floorboards, and he had a fuzzy vision of Mrs. Eyvindsdottir and her rinsed-out boarders celebrating the day with Norwegian mulled wine, or a fruitcake that might have been put to better use as roofing material. He emptied his bladder in the pot in the corner, noting with a clinical detachment that the liquid draining from him was exactly the color of that which he'd put in, and then he took his very tender head and tentative limbs over to the mirror for a cold shave. His brain was a bit clouded—he remembered taking Will to Bathrick's for a drink, and then to a back-room place on Calhoun—but from the moment he'd opened his eyes he was aware of the check. Of the fact of it. Of its existence. Of its presence in the room with him, looming large, a Christmas offering for Per-Fo tucked away in the inside pocket of his jacket. He glanced up from the mirror to where the jacket dangled from its peg, and he began to whistle. A thousand dollars. Not bad for a single night's work. Wait till he told Bender.

But wait: why tell Bender at all? The check was made out to him, wasn't it—to Charles Ossining? Who would be the wiser if he—but no, he couldn't just take the poor fool's money like that, could he? For one thing, it was illegal—false pretenses, fraud, theft even. And it was seed money, money that would grow a hundred times over—he knew that and knew he had to be patient. But he could hold it back from Bender, hold it in reserve, that is, squirrel it away for the moment the Per-Fo factory opened its doors and they needed a little extra for greasing the wheels, for advertising or paying off their suppliers or carton manufacturers or whatever—hell, for throwing a party. A thousand dollars. He could hardly believe it. It would take his father two years to earn that much at Mrs. Hookstratten's, opening and closing the big wrought-iron gates every time the Oldsmobile went in or out. . . .

He couldn't help himself. He set down the razor and crossed the room to throw back the flap of his jacket and dig out the check—just to admire it, gloat over it, stroke it in the way a red Indian might stroke a favorite scalp or a millionaire his bankbook. His fingers closed on it —and it was there, it was no dream—the feel of the crisp, single-folded sheet of paper like the feel of ready money, and then he was scanning the rich, spare, resonant command scrawled across the face of the thing: *Pay to the Order of Charles Ossining, One thousand dollars, The Old National and the Merchants Bank, Battle Creek, Michigan.* The elation rose in him, his heartbeat took off on a pair of flapping wings, and he was half a breath away from springing back from the wall and dancing round the room with Will Lightbody's check for his sole partner when he noticed something odd: there was no signature at the bottom of the check. Nothing. Not a mark.

The wings plummeted. His stomach clenched. *The idiot had forgotten to sign it!* And he, Charlie Ossining, was twice an idiot for not examining the thing on the spot—what would it have taken to say casually, "Oh, Will, by the way, I'm afraid you've forgotten to sign it here—ha-ha— no problem, no problem at all—another drink?" But now—he slammed his fist into the wall and watched a vein sprout in the plaster, capillaries and all—now he'd have to go up there to the Sanitarium, with all those bloated ducks and bran munchers gawking at him, and broach the subject to Lightbody over a bowl of celery soup. And what if he didn't want to sign? What if he didn't remember or had changed his mind or excused himself because he was drunk and didn't know what he was doing? What if the wife was there? Or old man Kellogg?

No matter: there was no time to waste. He stepped into the pants of his blue serge suit, slapping haphazardly at the eternal flecks of lint, dug a semidecent collar and a pair of cuffs from his suitcase, buttoned up his yellow shoes and hurried down the stairway, shrugging into his greatcoat on the fly. He caught a quick glimpse of Mrs. Eyvindsdottir, Bagwell and some of the others sitting round the table mournfully masticating goat's cheese burned into rounds of toast and a "nice" haunch of muskrat or groundhog or whatever it was her intrepid inamorato had managed to pull out of his traps that week, and then he was out the door. Walking. Walking yet again. The interurban wasn't running because of the holiday, and the hacks, if there were any, would have been clustered round the Post Tavern at the other end of town.

It took him twenty minutes to reach the grounds of the San, and his ears were stinging and his toes dead by the time he entered the gleaming, cavernous lobby. There wasn't much activity—nothing like his first visit, when he'd had to cool his heels outside the old man's office with George and Bender. A whole parade of people had trooped by them that day, nurses, doctors, women in the kinds of dresses you'd see in the magazines, beautiful women and women not so beautiful, bodybuilders, lacto-ovo vegetarians, a squadron of millionaires in beards and bathrobes (Bender claimed to have recognized half a dozen of them—"It's not the clothes that make the man, Charlie, it's the way they carry themselves, fore and aft, remember that—fore and aft"). But today was Christmas day, and the place was pretty quiet. Just as well. Charlie didn't relish the idea of running into the Doctor or one of the apes who'd hustled him out the door and into the street after his last, ill-fated visit.

He was concentrating on the man at the desk, trying to act casual, ignoring the inquisitive stares of the bellhops in green and the white flash of an orderly he spied out of the corner of his eye, striding purposefully, as if he were at home, as if he belonged here, and he came within a deuce of bowling over a little stick of a woman in a wheelchair with her plaster-bound leg stuck out in front of her like a battering ram. Profuse apologies, tip of the hat, bow to the waist, and a merry Christmas to you, too, ma'am, and all the while he was scanning the place for Kellogg, ready to shrink under the hand at his collar, the boot applied to his backside. He straightened himself up, stared down the nearest bellhop and crossed to the desk without incident.

The man behind the desk had the pinched face and bright fawning eyes of a lapdog. He stood there as if he'd been nailed to the floor, his back as stiff as an ironing board. "Merry Christmas," he said, and his smile was saccharine, oozing, insipid, "welcome to the University of Health. And how may I be of assistance?"

Charlie asked for Will Lightbody.

"Lightbody, Lightbody," the man murmured, scanning the register, "ah, here it is—room five-seventeen. Shall I ring him for you?"

Charlie glanced round him. There was a codger with a cane at the base of the staircase, a pair of old ladies positioned like statues in the jungle room, no orderlies, no doctors, no Kellogg: this was easy. "Yeah, sure—would you do that?"

The clerk picked up the telephone and asked for five-one-seven. He froze his smile on Charlie while the call went through the switchboard, and then he was asking for Mr. Lightbody in a stilted syrupy voice that seemed to drip out of him as if he'd sprung a leak. There was a pause for the reply and Charlie watched the man's face change—the artificial smile fell away, the lip dropped, and he let out a low gasp of surprise. "No, you don't mean it?" he said. "Really? For how long?" Another pause. Charlie could feel his heart going. Finally the man hung up the phone and turned to him. "I'm sorry," he said, "I've just spoken to Mr. Lightbody's nurse and she says he's indisposed—quite ill, actually. It seems he's taken a sudden turn for the worse. Are you a . . . relative?"

"Me? Oh, no. No, no. I'm a business associate—acquaintance, that is. Did the nurse happen to indicate how long it will be? Until he can see people, I mean?"

The lapdog eyes came to rest on him with a melting, watery gaze. The clerk took a moment, working a ministerial gravity into his tone. "We can't know that, I'm afraid. Until we get a diagnosis—well, we can't even know if . . ." He broke off. "It seems it's fairly critical. I'm sorry."

A tic started up under Charlie's left eye, beating time with his racing pulse, one thousand dollars, one thousand dollars, Per-Fo stalled, the check a worthless scrap of paper. How could it be? Lightbody hadn't looked so bad, had he? Or maybe he did look bad, terrible even, sallow, sunken, ready for the grave, but he acted fine. Ate everything in sight. Roared and hooted and drank like an Irishman at a funeral. Charlie didn't know what to say. It was over, done, finis, time to give it up and trudge on back to the boarding house, but he couldn't move. His hands gripped the edge of the desk as if it were made of tar, the check seemed to burn through his shirt and into his skin, his feet refused to move.

"I'm sorry," the clerk repeated. "Deeply sorry, sir. But there's always hope—and remember, your friend couldn't find himself in a holier temple of healing."

It was then that another voice intruded on Charlie's consciousness, a bright sarcastic chirp of a voice that sang in his ear like a playground taunt: "Why if it isn't Mr. Charles P. Ossining, the breakfast-food dynamo!"

He spun round on Eleanor Lightbody, resplendent in green velvet, her hair swept up above a pair of crimson earrings and a necklace of bright gemstones clasped round her white, white throat. She was giving him that infuriating little purse-lipped smile, the one that seemed to invite the world to bend over and kiss her feet. Or her posterior.

"And what brings you to our little citadel of health?"

The check was in his pocket, her husband fading, Per-Fo still on the ground. But Charlie had self-possession—he was born with it—and he had charm and looks and a smile all his own. He took a deep breath. "Well, well, well, Eleanor—and how are you?" He showed her his teeth. "Just inquiring after a friend . . . but don't you look the perfect vision of the season?"

It was the right thing to say. "Oh, this?" she murmured, resting a hand on the front of her dress. "Yes, they do tell me I look festive in green."

"Brings out your eyes." Charlie looked into those eyes as he spoke, glanced away as if he were suddenly interested in the dowager descending the staircase, and came back to them again. He dropped his smile. He was earnest suddenly, serious, a sponge of pity and sympathy. "I hear your husband took a turn for the worse."

Now her smile was gone, too, a stricken look settling in around her nose and upper lip. (He saw that her nostrils were faintly reddened—had she been crying?) He felt for Will in that moment—poor sap—and for himself and the worthless check, too, and he couldn't help feeling for Eleanor, imagining her widowed, rich as a peacock in a nest of feathers and needing support, the support of a younger man, someone to brighten up her days, someone she could pamper and spoil and take to bed at night. . . .

Her voice was soft. "I'm afraid so," she said.

There was movement around them. The dowager turned the corner and disappeared in the foliage of the jungle, a nurse flickered by, the desk clerk turned his dripping eyes on a middle-aged man in tweeds who'd suddenly materialized at the desk. The telephone rang. Baggage arrived. An attendant wheeled a cart of covered dishes into the elevator. Even on Christmas day, the business of healing went on.

"Is it—is it serious?" Charlie asked.

"Everything is serious," she said, arms akimbo, eyes boring into him, her dress lifting a fraction of an inch to show off a pair of bright red patent-leather shoes. "The world is serious. Life is serious. But listen, it's Christmas day, my husband is"—her hand fell like the drop of a guillotine—"indisposed, and it's rude of me to keep you standing here in the lobby as if you were some sort of notions peddler or door-to-door salesman or something, forgive me, please." And here she arched her eyebrows and gave him the old familiar look of bemusement. "Have you eaten, Mr. Ossining?"

He'd been wondering if he should broach the matter of the check, but in that moment he decided against it. Here they were, chatting like old friends, the queen come down off her pedestal, Charlie rising to his station like the magnate he was destined to become. The check would only sully things, put them back on their old footing. He showed her his teeth again. "Why, no. No, I haven't."

"Will you join me for dinner, then?"

Charlie was at a loss. The smile faltered. "You mean—here?"

"Of course," she laughed, and her laugh conspired with him, warm and chummy, the sort of laugh he'd hoped for when he ran across her on the steps of the Post Tavern. "Dining scientifically won't kill you, Mr. Ossining—not if you try it just once. But I warn you, be careful —you never know what it might lead to."

The dining room was grandiose, dwarfing anything Bender's Post Tavern had to offer, a big open columned room that might have been a Roman bath or the training quarters for the gladiators—bears, lions, bulls and all. Palms sprouted from the floor every ten paces, chandeliers glittered, a sea of elegantly set tables swept the buffed marble floors all the way to the great gray windows that looked out over the Biggest Little City in the U.S.A. The room was impressive—it was meant to be, in a showy, pompous way—but except for the odd table here or there, it was largely deserted; aside from Eleanor and Charlie, there were maybe fifty people in the place. "It's the Christmas holiday," Eleanor said, as a brisk little woman with a big front showed them to their table and pulled out chairs for them. "Most of the patients have gone home. Or they're dining privately."

Charlie unfurled his napkin and laid it across his lap. "And what about you?"

"Oh, I'm much too ill to travel. I'm the classic neurasthenic, I'm afraid—or so Dr. Linniman tells me. Too sensitive by half, too thin-skinned, too wrapped up in things, too involved in the evolutions of this sad old world. The slightest thing will set me off—rain on the windowpane, an old woman crossing the street, my own kitchen. It's all dietary, of course." She laughed. "And Will. *He* wanted to go home. To Peterskill. The dreariest town on earth. And look at him now."

Charlie wanted to pursue the issue—yes, let's look at him; what was wrong with him anyway?—but a girl dressed in blue and white with a little white cap perched like a folded napkin atop her head was hovering over them. "Hello, Mrs. Lightbody. Good afternoon, sir. And a happy Christmas to you both. May I get you something to drink?" she asked, handing each of them a menu.

"Water, thank you, Priscilla," Eleanor said, and Charlie watched the earrings play against the swell of her jawbone as she dipped her head to the menu. He fought down an urge to lean over and take one of those earrings in his mouth.

"And you, sir?"

"Whiskey and soda," he murmured, before he realized what he was doing. Eleanor put a hand to her lips to suppress a giggle; her eyes took hold of him as they had that first night on the train, probing like needles, digging in, sizing him up in a quick shrewd glance.

The waitress was scandalized. For a moment she was speechless. But then, her smile wavering, and pronouncing each word as if she were reading from a text, she treated him to a curt little lecture. "I'm very sorry, sir, very sorry indeed, but this is a temple of right living—and right thinking—and we do not serve injurious spirits here. In fact, sir, we feel very strongly that such poisons must and will be banned and prohibited in any civilized society."

Charlie threw up his hands in mock surrender. "All right, mea culpa, I'm sorry, forgive me." Eleanor laughed. The girl tried out her smile again but couldn't hold it.

"Let me help you," Eleanor said, leaning over the table to lay a hand on his wrist and pull the face of the menu gently toward her. "Here," she said, "down near the bottom: *Beverages*. The Doctor is offering Kaffir Tea, Health Koko, Kumyss, Hot Malted Nuts, Milk, of course, and a Christmas Special Eggnogg—with Orange-Cranberry Flake and Cinnamon Flavorings. I'd take the kumyss if I were you."

Her hand lingered on his wrist. He could smell her perfume. He felt dizzy suddenly and recalled that he hadn't eaten since the night before—and at that only a hamburger sandwich that was like a wave-tossed raft in a typhoon of booze. His head ached. He felt queasy. "Kumyss?"

Eleanor let go of him, arched her back against the chair. "You'll love it. Believe me."

The waitress left them and Charlie found that he was staring into Eleanor's eyes. He'd read somewhere that green eyes were the sign of a passionate nature—or was it brown eyes? No matter: he'd been living like a eunuch at Mrs. Eyvindsdottir's, and Eleanor's presence excited him. "Yes, well," he said, "I'm sure you wouldn't steer me wrong. But we were talking about your husband, about Will—what happened? What's the matter with him?"

Her mouth tightened. She toyed with her silverware. After a moment, she asked, "Have you seen him lately?"

"No," Charlie lied.

She sighed. "He *was* improving—immeasurably. Everybody said so. He was to go on the grape diet today."

Charlie lifted his eyebrows.

"His first solid food. Doctor Kellogg had him on a bulk dietary at first, to flush his system—don't smirk, Mr. Ossining, and don't presume to make light of a sphere of human knowledge of which you are entirely ignorant, and you a breakfast-food man. . . . Well, at any rate, he'd been on the milk dietary ever since, in an effort to revitalize his intestinal flora and improve his digestion, and today he was to graduate to grapes."

At that moment, a spindle-thin, hook-nosed man dressed in the bells and motley of an elf or jester burst through the doors at the far end of the room, strumming a mandolin. He was playing a Sousa melody— "Bonnie Annie Laurie"—and, as one, the diners clapped their hands and laughed. Eleanor turned her head and smiled, and her smile was pure and uncomplicated. Charlie smiled too. He couldn't help himself—he felt giddy just to be in her presence, let alone dining with her intimately, like husband and wife. She was three or four years older than he, and a married woman to boot. But she was class, pure class. When Per-Fo flew, when he was a tycoon and a force to be reckoned with, with his own car and tailored suits and his billiard table, this was the sort of woman he envisioned at his side. Just this. Exactly. "Yes?" he prompted. "And what happened?"

She furrowed her brow, all trace of amusement gone. "Will had a lapse. Last night. Something terrible happened—in the sinusoidal baths—some sort of accident. I'm still not clear on the details, but it set him off. You see"—leaning forward, lowering her voice in confidence—"my husband has an addictive nature."

The jester swept round the room, playing carols now and singing in a high, pinched, nasal whine that brought tears to the eyes of the old lady at the next table over. A handful of people began to clap out the rhythm and sing along.

Eleanor was still there, still leaning toward him. "First it was meat, then liquor, and finally, though I don't like to think about it, opium. It's ruined him, it has. This is his last chance, I really believe that, Mr. Ossining." She looked up at him for sympathy, confirmation, hope.

Charlie gave her all that and more, putting on his best I-understand-I-appreciate-and-I-sympathize-to-the-depths-of-my-soul look, but he was elated. So that was it—Lightbody was hung over. Hung over. Charlie was hung over himself and none the worse for it, beyond the usual headache and a little sinking in the stomach. God, these bran munchers were a bunch of self-dramatizing idiots. Hung over. You'd have thought he'd been stabbed in the guts or worked over by a couple of stevedores, you'd have thought he had stomach cancer or paralysis. What horseshit. He was thinking he'd come back in a couple of days with the check and maybe a pint of Old Overholt, loosen the guy up, when the waitress appeared with a glass of water for Eleanor and the kumyss—a frothy, whitish-looking concoction—and set them on the table. "Are you ready to order?" she asked.

"Yes, of course," Eleanor murmured. "If you don't mind, Mr. Ossining, may I order for us both—since I'm familiar with the Anti-Toxic Diet?"

A grunt and a nod of the head from Charlie. Sure, why not? He could always pick up something at the Red Onion on the way home.

Eleanor ordered, the names of the dishes falling from her lips as if she'd invented them on the spur of the moment in a mad culinary improvisation, and then the waitress was gone, and Eleanor was asking him about Per-Fo. "I'm curious," she said. "Have you begun actual production yet? I mean, it must be difficult with so many competitors—"

Charlie gave her the usual spiel in response, careful not to linger over the terminology she'd caught him up on before. He talked about the rush of new investors to the company—a pure fabrication—and about his partner's determination to build a new factory for a new product instead of their contenting themselves with taking over the facilities of one of the concerns that had wound up in bankruptcy court.

"And how do you propose to avoid a similar fate?" she asked, coy with him still, still mocking, but somehow sincere, too. He felt that their relationship had changed, that she'd given ground. She was content to be there with him in that moment, the mandolinist yodeling out his inanities and the artificial goose stewing in its own artificial juices, the room shrunk to the size of a single table, to him and her. Her precious doctor was nowhere to be seen, her husband huddled over a bedpan: she was glad for the company.

"By offering a superior product," he said, "and advertising it. Advertising is the key. It's the modern way." He was gesturing broadly, warming to the subject, regurgitating Bender's lessons. "You've got to create a demand—no matter how good the product is, no matter what its merits and deserts, it'll die stillborn if the public isn't educated to it. Did you know that C. W. Post spent a million dollars on advertising alone in the past year? A million dollars!"

Eleanor's hands were folded on the table before her, the wedding ring prominent in the nest of her fingers. She was perfectly motionless, watching him as a naturalist might watch some exotic species at work in the wild, that faint mocking smile on her lips.

"What?" he said. "What is it?"

A pause. "You haven't touched your kumyss."

He hadn't. He'd forgotten all about it. There it was, frosting the glass with a mucus-colored foam that reminded him of the tide line along the Hudson. He picked up the glass and took a swallow.

The taste was rank, and he damn near brought it up again. The stuff was rotten, literally, whatever it was. It smelled like a wet dog and tasted of rancid butter, cider mold, dirt. "What—?" He choked it back. "What is this stuff, anyway?"

Her eyes were bright. "Fermented mare's milk originally. But the Chief uses the bovine variety here."

Charlie just looked at her.

"Cow's milk. Fermented. To produce the lactobacillus culture your poor abused alimentary system needs to repair the damage you've done to it. If it isn't already too late. *Oysters*," she said scornfully. "Beefsteak. Pommery and Greno. You've been poisoning yourself all your life, Mr. Ossining, just as surely as if you'd taken a drop of arsenic in your coffee every morning—and that's not to mention the poison of the coffee itself.

"Go ahead," she urged. "Finish it. It won't kill you."

And so, for the sake of Eleanor Lightbody, for the sake of her husband, the check in his pocket, and the future of Per-Fo, Charlie Ossining tipped back his head and let the foul glutinous liquid fill his throat till it nearly choked him. And then came the meal itself: Protose goose stuffed with hijiki-hazelnut dressing, soya-gluten gravy, Nuttolene-and-apple salad, Cranberry Surprise, and vegetable-oyster fritters. Eleanor ate lightly. Charlie forced himself. When he was full up to the ears with it, whatever it was, when he felt that the next bite would be like an ice pick thrust into his solar plexus, the waitress materialized with the dessert menu. He protested; Eleanor insisted. The waitress brought them two servings of kumyss cake, with a generous garnish of kumyss ice cream.

It was over the kumyss cake that Eleanor told him how unhappy she was. How depressed. How low and defeated. Dr. Linniman, the golden boy he'd seen her with on the street, was gone, off attending a conference in New York and not expected back for two weeks. And Will was a wreck. He'd missed Frank's (Linniman's, that is) Christmas-farewell party the night before, off on the carouse she'd mentioned earlier. How could she be happy with a man like that? A man who preferred cheap drink and vulgar companions to his own wife? A man who couldn't resist a hamburger sandwich though it would kill him? She'd tried so hard, she had. And now she just felt hopeless.

Charlie murmured the usual blandishments through the course of this pathetic recitation, clucking his tongue over the specter of the vulgar companions, commiserating over the horrors of meat. He was embarrassed. He didn't know what to say. But he relished the moment, relished every quiver of the lip and dab at the eye.

She'd never believed in divorce, she told him—for better or worse, till death do you part—but Will was dragging her down. She had her own health to consider—she was a very sick woman, she was. Must she sacrifice herself for him, throw herself on his funeral pyre like one of those fanatical Hindu women in India? Was that part of the marriage vow?

No, Charlie shook his head, uh-uh, no.

She laughed suddenly, a bitter fractured laugh, full of self-pity and a misery too deep for words—the misery of the rich, the misery of the pampered and spoiled. He leaned forward, his face suitably doleful. "But I shouldn't burden you with all this, Mr. Ossining—Charles. You have your own problems, I'm sure. And really, we hardly know one another—"

"Yes," he said. "Or, no. No, I don't feel that at all, Eleanor. We're friends, aren't we? Everyone needs a shoulder to cry on sometimes." Clichés, that's what the moment called for, platitudes and bromides. "That's what friends are for." He was about to launch into a speech on the subject of friendship and its deeper implications (he wanted her, wanted her in every way, from her signature on the check to the feel of her skin against his, her naked breasts, her tongue, her lips, her hair) but he never got the opportunity. At that moment, just as he was fighting down the aftertaste of the worst meal of his life and trying to organize his thoughts, he felt a hand on his shoulder. In the instant of his turning round he saw Eleanor's face light up with joy, and then he was gazing up into the cottony white beard and bespectacled eyes of Santa Claus himself.

Short, potbellied, with the canny look of the Yankee trader drawn tight round the corners of his mouth and the fanatic's gleam in his eye, the Santa Claus of Health stood there before them in the red velvet trappings and high Dutch boots of the Santa Claus of Legend. "Ho-ho," Dr. Kellogg announced, and you could see he was relishing the role, "and have you been good little men and women this year? Abstaining from pork, beef, mutton and venison? From beer and booze, tobacco and coffee? Ho-ho! Of course you have, of course!" and he threw down his sack and extracted a pair of bristling yellow pineapples. And one for you, my dear," he crowed, handing Eleanor a pineapple as if it were the last and choicest jewel of King Solomon's hoard, and then he turned back to Charlie. "And for you, sir."

Charlie took the thing, stunned, and cradled it in both hands. Everyone in the room was watching them. Even the mandolinist had fallen silent.

"Ho-ho," Kellogg said, and he was about to turn away, about to dance on over to the next table, when he paused. "Don't I know you, sir?" he said.

Charlie tried to look like someone else, a gizzardite, a bran muncher, a visitor from Cleveland. "No," he mumbled, "I don't think so."

"Oh, I think I do, I think I do!" the Doctor cried, twirling round with an exaggerated dip of his shoulders and an antic shuffle of his boots. "Santa knows everyone in the San, all his guests, great and small. . . ." The place erupted in laughter. He leaned forward with a wink. "Help me out, now, help me out. Mr. Hodgkins, isn't it, of Dayton? No? Well, sir, tell me this—you're not one of my patients then, are you?"

"No, I—"

"A visitor?"

"Well, I—"

"Ho-ho, ho-ho! I knew it, I knew it!"

It was Eleanor who unwittingly came to the rescue. She was laughing—heartily, disingenuously, laughing like a girl in pigtails in the front row at a Punch-and-Judy show. "Doctor," she gasped, breaking off in a little trill of giggles and countervailing hiccoughs, "Doctor, let me introduce"—she broke off again—"introduce a friend from New York, Charles—"

"Tarrytown, actually," Charlie blurted, hoping to deflect attention from the name, lest it should turn the tumblers in the little man's brain and lead to a scene unpleasant in the extreme.

"—Ossining," Eleanor said.

But Kellogg wasn't listening. Lit by the madcap possibilities of his role, he cried, "Yes, yes, Mr. Tarrytown-Ossining!" playing to the house, and everyone was laughing, genial, vegetable-fed, free of vices and glowing with health—everyone in the place, from waitresses to grandes dames to the dishwashers, who stood at the kitchen door in awe. "A pleasure, sir, a pleasure," the Doctor hooted, and in the next instant he was bounding across the room to a roar of approval, and Charlie was left cradling his pineapple like an anarchist with a bomb that hadn't gone off.

Chapter 5

Kellogg's Kink

❧

W ill had been hung over before—in fact, given the slow spiritual death of his managerial position at his father's plant, combined with Eleanor's descent into the morass of vegetarianism, neurasthenia, frigidity and quackery, he'd been crapulous the better part of the past five years. But never like this. This was different, a scourge that assaulted him from both ends, as if he'd drunk hydrochloric acid instead of whiskey, eaten iron filings in place of beef, bun and pickle. He vomited for two days, a thin sour mash tinged red with blood. A watery gruel cascaded from the other end, and it was red, too. His fingertips tingled, his feet were blocks of ice, his tongue sprouted a new coat. He lay there on the rack of his physiologic bed, praying for equilibrium, and when he caught his breath to hold the pain in place for ten seconds at a time, he was sure he'd swallowed a long snaking strand of molten wire.

He didn't know how he'd got back to the San or how he'd found his bed and crashed through the wall of consciousness into oblivion. All he knew was the next morning, Christmas morning, and the old pain, recidivist, glowering, reborn like an avenging demon: all he knew was the toilet and the sink. That first day, he had only two visitors—Nurse Bloethal and Eleanor. Gauging his condition at a glance, Nurse Bloethal mercifully set aside her hot wax and whey culture and canceled his morning regimen of Swedish Manual Movements, laughing exercises and the sinusoidal bath. If she knew anything of Homer Praetz and the previous day's events, she didn't let on. Will vomited and shat and trembled. He said nothing of having left the San, of Charlie Ossining, pickled eggs or the Red Onion, though the nurse could count up the milk feedings he'd missed and make her own nearest guess.

Eleanor appeared at nine, irate and red about the ears and nostrils. Where had he been? She'd looked all over for him before giving it up and going off to Frank's party on her own—or with Mrs. Rumstedt, rather, for appearance's sake. But Will didn't seem to care much for appearances, did he? Her own husband! And on Christmas Eve, no less! Well? And where had he been?

"I'm sick," he croaked. Outside the window it was as gray as the grave, the very clouds fallen from the sky to press down on the earth as if there were no intermediate plane, no trees, no buildings, no life.

Eleanor stalked across the room and flung her handbag down on the table. She was dressed in green and red, festive for the season. "I'm sick, too," she cried as the handbag found its mark with the harsh killing thump of the blackjack or cudgel. "Sick to death of this, this *attitude* of yours. And where were you? Answer me!"

Where was he? Where had he been? Even as she asked, even as she demanded an answer, a vivid, if disjointed, series of images flashed across his brain, careening helter-skelter from the stark puckered white soles of Homer Praetz's feet to the amber glow of the whiskey in its glass and the purse of Charlie Ossining's lips as he sucked an oyster from its shell. Homer Praetz, he thought, Homer Praetz. It had started there, he was sure of it. Or was it with Irene and the way she'd turned her back on him and his gratitude alike? "Homer Praetz," he mumbled, hugging his shoulders and turning his head aside on the pillow. "He, he died."

Eleanor was standing over him now, hands on hips. There was a crease between her eyes, a vertical gouge that appeared when she was angry. "You've been drinking," she accused. "That's it, isn't it? After all I've done for you, after all Frank and Dr. Kellogg and these selfless nurses and dieticians and I-don't-know-who-all have done to help you, you alone, what do you do? You go *drinking*"—she threw the word at him, bloated with disgust—"guzzling whiskey and beer and gin like some degenerate in the street, falling right back into your old habits as if the whole thing were some sort of joke. What were you thinking, what was it—'I'll just have a little nip for the holiday'? Huh? Was that it? Some Christmas cheer?" She didn't give him a chance to deny it, to plead, remonstrate, even open his mouth. "Will Lightbody, you answer me. And don't you dare lie to me, don't you dare!"

Will confessed. He was a fool to have admitted anything, but there it was.

Eleanor couldn't keep still. She raged, stormed, expostulated, preached, lectured, exploded in tears and, at one point, in a wild electric excess of frustration and hate, pounded his frail quivering bones beneath the blankets with the balled-up nuggets of her physiologic fists. Christmas day, in his sickbed, and the green velvet blows rained down on him. "I'm through with you, Will Lightbody. I give up, I really do. I wash my hands of you."

She'd turned and snatched up her purse and was on her way out the door when Will struggled to his elbows and called out to her, pleading his case. "Homer Praetz," he repeated. "It was Homer Praetz. Yesterday. In the sinusoidal bath . . . I'm sorry, I'm so sorry." He broke down then, rough chesty sobs caught in the thick sour phlegm of his binge, and he felt himself open up till he was a thousand feet tall and as empty as a drainpipe through every last inch of it, weeping for himself, for Eleanor, for Nurse Graves, for the whole sad doomed and deluded human race. "He's dead, I'm telling you, he's dead."

Eleanor had stopped at the door, and she was standing there stock-still and alive in every sense, like a deer surprised along the road. She clutched the Yule-red purse to her green dress, and, like a deer, she seemed ready to bolt. "Dead?"

Will hoisted himself to a sitting position and his hair fell across his face. He closed his eyes, shoved his hair back with an automatic gesture, and nodded.

"But Will, darling"—her voice softer now—"I'm so sorry to hear it. He was the machine-tool man, from Cleveland?" She went on without waiting for confirmation. "But really, you mustn't take these things so hard . . . yes, I know you've got a hypersensitive nature, like my own, that's what attracted me to you in the first place, and I love you to be compassionate and full of fellow feeling and all that, but Will, you've got to realize that when one comes late to the biologic life, as your Mr. Praetz did, there can be no guaranteeing that six months or a year of right living can reverse the effects of all those years of debauch and dietary suicide—"

It wasn't what Will wanted to hear. If Praetz was gone, what hope was there for him? Besides, he didn't need lectures, he needed sympathy, and her complacent wrongheaded vegetarian righteousness infuriated him. "He didn't just shut his eyes and pass away in his sleep," Will boomed out, cutting her off in the middle of her cautionary harangue. "He was killed, murdered, done in by your Dr. Kellogg and his 'Battle Creek Method,' just as surely as if the goateed little fraud had pulled the switch himself."

The crease had returned to Eleanor's brow. Now he'd done it, now he'd assailed the temple itself. Her eyes leapt at him; she squared her shoulders impatiently. "How dare you call—? What in God's name are you talking about?"

"Electrocution, loosing of the bowels, frying of the flesh. Death, I'm talking about death." He looked away in disgust, kneaded his aching temples. "It could have been me."

Eleanor hadn't moved. She stood there at the door, exasperated, angry all over again. "You're still drunk, aren't you?" she accused.

Miserable, Will just stared at her. He felt his jaws tighten, and he wondered how he'd ever come to love, court and marry this demanding, intransigent, cold-hearted woman—couldn't she ever see his point of view, even once? "I'm not drunk," he said. "Though I wish to God I was. Do you understand, Eleanor? The man was electrocuted in your damned sinusoidal bath—electrocuted, fried, just like some convict, some maniac at Sing Sing. Alfred would have been gone, too, but I, I broke the connection . . . thank God."

But she wouldn't have it. "You can't be serious," she insisted, and the crease grew deeper, deeper, till he thought it would split her face. "I'm quite sure that Dr. Kellogg would never allow—"

"He's dead, Eleanor. I saw it all. With my own two eyes."

She didn't know what to say. He had her, he could see that. She stood there a moment longer, clouds pressing at the windows, Christmas laying a gloomy, unredemptive hand over the San and all its goods and chattels and carefully appointed environs, until finally she snapped, "Yes, all right, perhaps he is dead, then—but that's no excuse for you to drink yourself into a coma, now is it?" There was the sharp tattoo of her heels on the floor, the door jerked open, and she was gone.

❖   ❖   ❖

The following day it was Dr. Kellogg's turn.

It was past four in the afternoon when he showed up unannounced, having just come from surgery. He was brisk, excitable, and he wore a mask of high patriarchal dudgeon. His panting secretary followed him into the room, hands clasped before him, eyes downcast, a priest at an execution. "Now, sir," the Doctor cried, thrusting his hand into Will's mouth to peer at his tongue, thumping at Will's chest as if it were a half-empty keg of sauterne and snatching up his wrist to feel for his pulse, "now, sir, suppose you just tell me what's the matter."

Will said nothing. His mind was clear, and he was seething. Snake oil. Voodoo. He might just as well have gone to a witch doctor in a grass hut. The whole thing, from the vibrating chairs to the salt-mush rub to the sinusoidal bath—it was quackery, plain and simple. And this little charlatan was the root and cause of it all. Will was seething, yes, but he was afraid, too—terrified. He was in rough shape, and he knew it. There were no grapes in his future, that much was apparent, and though he didn't feel like eating anything, though he felt as bad as he ever had in his life, he was back to psyllium seeds and hijiki, back to square one. He gazed up into those steely blue eyes and had a premonition that sent a shudder through him: he was going to die in this bed, die in the Sanitarium, die under the healer's hand and be laid to rest out back with the other failures, with Homer Praetz and the woman with consumption and the limp cold thankful bird. "Help me," he croaked.

"Hmp!" the Doctor snorted. "Help you, hey?" He was up from the bed already, pacing, stroking his beard, wriggling his shoulders and arms and shaking off his fingers as if he'd just stepped out of the shower. He removed his glasses without breaking stride, breathed on the lenses, produced a spotless handkerchief with which to wipe them, then pivoted and started back across the room again. "I can't help you if you won't help yourself." He paused, slipped back into his spectacles, eyes cold in their frigid white frames. "I'm told you've flagrantly contravened your doctors' orders—mine and Dr. Linniman's both."

Will looked away. He could feel his heart pounding in his throat, his temples, his fingertips.

"Don't you look away from me, sir. I say, you've contravened my orders, risked your life, plunged into some sick reckless debauch. Meat was taken, so I hear. Alcoholic spirits. Pickles, relish, ketchup. Was there black coffee, too? Good Lord, I'm surprised you didn't oxidize your insides with Coca-Cola while you were at it. Well? Answer me, sir. What do you have to say for yourself?"

Will had turned back to him on command. The humorless eyes pinned him to the pillow. The man was unforgiving, merciless, as persistent and inhuman as the Furies themselves. He decided to lie. "No," he said, giving some dimension to his voice, "it's not true."

The Doctor drew himself up short, froze on the spot, every muscle in his body gone rigid; his look was murderous. "Don't lie to me, sir," he snarled, "I won't have it. Do you take me for a fool? An idiot? Even if I didn't have a pair of eyes at the Red Onion—yes, the Red Onion —I'd have to be blind not to see it in the wreck you've made of yourself. Meat!" he cried suddenly. "Slaughter! Red flesh and blood!" He was trembling, the rapier of his beard stabbing at the air as if he were driving invisible opponents before him.

But in that moment, Will could feel a matching anger rising in himself. Who was this little martinet to be lecturing him as if he were in knee pants still? The inventor of the sinusoidal bath? The murderer of Homer Praetz? "What of it?" he said.

" 'What of it?' " the Doctor howled. "Dab? Dab? Do you hear this? The man lies there bankrupt on what could very well prove to be his deathbed, self-poisoned, ruined—absolutely ruined—by his own vices, and he throws it back at me. 'What of it?' he says. Indeed. Well, sir" —turning back to Will now—"why don't you allow me to get you a good dose of chloral or strychnine and put an end to it properly, hey? Hey?"

The secretary was bright with blood, flushed, fat, steaming. He looked as if he'd been dipped in the scalding tub at a slaughterhouse. And the Doctor—that pale etiolated little mushroom of a man—was nearly as red. Puffed up. Bloated with rage and moral indignation. Will studied them, two overheated zealots snarling over the bone of their dogma, and it hardened him. Though he was sick with weakness and guilt, though the reference to his deathbed had chilled him to the marrow, he decided to take the offensive. "Yes, all right, and if I'm on my deathbed why don't you tell me about Homer Praetz—come on, confess it—tell me how your precious treatment redeemed him."

A blister, swelling and swelling till it bursts—that was Dr. Kellogg. He was blind, he was deaf, he was a god on a cloud: the name of Homer Praetz had never been uttered. Such impudence didn't merit response. "Nurse Bloethal!" he roared, and the door fell open, Will catching a glimpse of an ashen Irene Graves peering anxiously in at him as Nurse Bloethal strode through the doorway in all her rugged glory. "Take this, this"—the Doctor lowered his voice to a hiss—"this *meat eater* to the Colon Department and put him on the enema machine until further notice. Do you understand me?"

Nurse Bloethal jumped. "Yes, Doctor," she barked, and for a moment Will thought she was going to salute him.

"Yes," the Doctor said meditatively, speaking to himself now even as he stared Will in the eye, "we'll scour him out yet."

Later that night—it must have been eight or so, the windows black, a hush fallen over the depopulated hallways of the San, bedpans tucked away and enema bags rinsed—Will had another visitor. After a violent irrigation at the hands of Nurse Bloethal, who'd clucked her tongue and scolded him the whole while, he'd taken his meal (such as it was) alone in his room. When the knock came, he was lying there in his agony, staring at the ceiling, the familiar slack-tide taste of seaweed on his palate, seeds expanding in his gut, his bowels washed as clean as the bed of an Alpine stream. The lamp at his bedside was lit, and it focused a sickly yellow light on the hollows of his cheeks and the high ridge of his nose. A pitcher of water stood on the night table, a single glass beside it. The *Atlantic Monthly*, in its plain brown cover, lay forgotten at the foot of the bed, along with a spine-sprung copy of *Camping and Tramping with Roosevelt* and the *Harper's* Christmas number. "Come in," he called weakly.

The door cracked open and a disembodied face peered round the edge of it. A wink. A grin. And then Charlie Ossining was in the room, the door easing shut behind him. "Hello, Will," he whispered, tiptoeing across the floor to the chair in the corner, which he seized by its physiologic slats and eased up to the bed. "You're looking—" his voice dropped off as he settled himself in the chair and produced a paper sack from his coat pocket. "I was going to say you're looking grand, but I'd be a liar if I did. You look awful, friend, plain awful."

Will barely glanced up, but he was glad to see him. The last two days had been hellish, a continuum of cranial ache and abdominal pain broken only by the odd visit from a frosty Eleanor, a sadistic Kellogg and a rough-and-ready Nurse Bloethal. Irene, no longer 'indisposed,' was keeping a low profile: he'd seen her only sporadically during the eternal hours of his relapse. In short, he was hurting and he was bored. Bored witless.

Charlie Ossining gave him a knowing look. "Hung over, huh?" he said. "We made a night of it, didn't we? Hell, I felt like I'd been run down by the 5:05 myself—and dragged half a mile in the bargain." He let out a laugh.

The room fell quiet. Charlie was studying him. A question had been put to Will: was he hung over? It was a naive and hopeful question, and he could see the concern on his friend's face—a hangover was something he could relate to, something quotidian and explicable, a complaint from which the sufferer could logically be expected to recover. How tell him the truth? How tell him he was doomed, condemned, sentenced to die of a balky bowel and hypersensitive nature?

But Charlie didn't wait for an answer. His eyes roamed the room, settling finally on the copy of the Burroughs book. "I see you've been reading about the president and his bears," he said. "Rich, isn't it?"

Rich, yes. Will concurred.

Charlie shrugged. "I don't know," he said, brandishing the brown paper bag, "this whole rugged-individualist business is just a bit much for me, Jack London and all that. I like city stories, men and women in society, that sort of thing. Racy stuff, too. What's his name, Dreiser? You read him? That book about the hometown girl without a scruple in the world? Just like real life. Women." He tossed his eyebrows for emphasis, then casually withdrew a pint of whiskey from the bag, broke the seal with a twist of his wrist and worked the cork out of the bottle. "You know, I saw that Olga Nethersole in *Sappho* before they closed it down a few years back. You want to talk about racy, whew! That was it. Boy oh boy."

Will's eyes were fixed on the bottle, liquid gold, sleep and forgetfulness, booze. He sat up.

Charlie reached for the glass on the night table. "Join me?" he said. "Just a little nip to kill the pain, eh?" He was pouring. Will watched the golden liquid rise in the glass: two fingers, three, four. "I don't know what ails you"—a significant look here—"but I'll bet this'll go a long way toward curing it." He handed Will the glass, touched the bottle to it in salutation and then tipped back the bottle and drank.

Frail, throbbing, his stomach plunging like a runaway elevator, sweat standing out on his brow, Will clutched the glass as if he were afraid it would slip through his fingers. His watched his friend's larynx rise and fall as he lowered the level in the bottle by an inch, and all he wanted to do in that moment was drink. There was no more pain, no more fear, no more tyranny of the elect—there was just the glass in his hand and the bright warm complexion of honey it took on in the glow of the lamp. He held the glass up to the light. Now it was pale as air, now dense as smoke. He lifted it to his nose and smelled all the blossoms of the field, smelled the burnt-oak barrel, the mash, the electric fumes themselves. Out of the corner of his eye, he saw that Charlie was watching him. He didn't need any urging. As if in a trance, he lifted the glass to his lips and drained it in three swallows.

"Hits the spot, eh?" Charlie breathed, trying to settle himself in the Doctor's orthopedic chair. "Christ," he swore, twisting his neck and peering over his shoulder to examine the ribs of it, "where'd they get this thing—out of the king of Spain's torture chamber?"

Suddenly Will was laughing. And as Charlie made a show of getting up out of the chair as if it were on fire, turning it round and finally lifting a leg over the seat to mount it backward, he laughed even harder, laughed till there were tears in his eyes and he felt his chest tighten. "Kellogg's—" he choked, "the Great Healer's idea of comfort."

Charlie was laughing with him, a deep belly laugh that ended in a series of hoots and stutters. He leaned forward to refill Will's glass. "Here's to Kellogg and his gizzardite chair," he proposed, holding the bottle aloft, and they drank again, and they laughed so hard the liquor nearly came back up. After a while, Charlie's look grew serious. "I think this place is killing you, Will—and I don't care what Eleanor says, no disrespect intended. It's not natural, eating nuts and sprouts and what-not. A man needs meat, tobacco, booze. If it's all so hurtful, then how'd we get here today? Hell, old Adam would have keeled over before he could start on the rest of us."

Will had reached a state of equilibrium. Somewhere in his brain a warning bell was going off, but he ignored it. After two days of misery and humiliation, he'd attained tranquillity, and all because of Charlie and the ambrosia that comes packaged in a flat little bottle. "Charlie," he said, and his voice was thick, "you ought to be my doctor, damn it all—and I mean it. You've got more common sense than our little Napoleon here any day—and all his doctors and nurses and dieticians combined. '*All* things in moderation,' right? *All* things." He gestured vaguely. "Give me another little snort of that, will you?"

Charlie poured. Will drank. The room, which just half an hour earlier had seemed like a mausoleum, was alive now with color and texture. There was hope in the paint on the walls; promise in the grain of the wood; life, spirit and energy in the way the lamps threw their shadows against the chest of drawers. There was no better friend, no better man, than Charlie Ossining.

"Will?"

Charlie was addressing him. "Will?" he repeated, and Will looked up from his reverie. Charlie was leaning forward, so close their foreheads were nearly touching, and now he had a warm grip on the back of Will's neck, pulling them together in a football huddle. Will could smell the other man's breath, warm, intoxicating. His face blurred. "Do you remember the other night, Christmas Eve?"

"Sure I do," Will said, "sure. The Red Onion. Hamburger sandwich. Blind Pig. Best thing in the world for me."

Charlie was still there, still huddling with him—as close as anybody could get. It was strange. But right, somehow. There was an aura about it, an intensity, a kind of man-to-man fervor that no woman could know. Will thought of the grassy field, cleats, the canvas ball and the smooth solid ashen bat.

"That's right," Charlie said, and now he was the coach himself, "and do you remember this?" He let go of Will and sat back. He seemed to be holding a slip of paper in his hand—a banknote? No, a check. A very familiar-looking check . . .

"Is it mine?"

"Uh-huh." Charlie gave him a sage look. "The other night, out of the bigness of your heart, Will—and because you're blessed with the kind of business sense that can't resist a sure thing—you became one of our stockholders, one of Per-Fo's select few."

"Yes," Will agreed. "Of course, of course." He was in a daze. How that whiskey worked its magic, hot in his stomach and cold in his brain—and why couldn't Kellogg put some of that on the table?

"You forgot to sign it."

"What?" Will took the check from him and examined it under the lamplight. Sure enough, he'd forgotten his John Hancock. He was embarrassed suddenly. What must Charlie think of him? He gave a little laugh and his voice went hollow again. "Don't think I'm in my dotage yet, Charlie—forgive me, will you? It's just this damned place"—he waved a hand to take in everything, from the enema bag lying on the counter in the corner to the wheelchair behind the door and the four floors beneath and the one above. "Of course," he added with a conspiratorial chuckle, "I was in my cups, too, you know. Remember?"

Charlie's laugh was high and sharp. He slapped his knee, then leaned forward and refilled the glass. Will fumbled through the drawer of the night table, came up with his Waterman and signed the check with a flourish.

Charlie thanked him and Will said it was nothing. They sat there in the afterglow of the moment, both satisfied, their troubles behind them. After a while Will ventured to ask how much he'd invested—with a laugh he admitted that he hadn't thought to look at the amount. "Oh," Charlie said, and he returned Will's laugh with a deep chuckle of his own, "it may not seem like a lot to you, but to us at Per-Fo, just starting up as we are, it's really generous, and I thank you from the bottom of my heart, and my partners thank you, too." A pause. Shrug of the shoulders. The voice drops. "A thousand."

A thousand. The tiniest coil of doubt gripped Will in his innermost gut, but he lifted the glass to his lips and quieted it. "I'm pleased," he said, but his lips caught on the *p* and sounded a *b* in its place. Charlie didn't seem to mind. He was beaming at Will, rocking back on the legs of the chair and giving him a look of pure gratitude and unadulterated joy.

"Well," Charlie said, rising from the chair, "it's getting late, Will, and I've got to be going—I really do—and I wish you could join me down at the Onion, but listen, keep the rest of the bottle and take a judicious sip now and again to wash down all those bean sprouts, all right?" He was standing in the middle of of the room, just where Eleanor had stood, his smile locked in place. "All right?" he repeated.

And it would have been all right—everything would have been all right, from the glow in Will's stomach to the laxness of his limbs and the fine feeling that existed between them—if Dr. Kellogg, the little white dynamo himself, hadn't chosen that moment to blast through the door like some hurling, whirling meteorological event, words of caution, praise, hope and command on his lips. "—sticks to the dietary regimen," he was saying, his secretary at his heels, "rest and a good regular cleansing, hourly now, hourly, up to the point of the procedure—" and then he stopped short. For the second time since Will had known him, the saint of health was at a loss for words. "What?" he said, glancing from Will to Charlie and back again. "Who—?"

"Good night, Will," Charlie said quickly, "I hope you feel better," and he made a move for the door.

"You!" the Doctor suddenly cried, flinging the door shut behind him and pressing himself up against it to bar Charlie's exit. "I know you, sir, I know you now—the cheapest kind of scoundrel!"

"Now wait a minute—" Will began, but the Doctor cut him off.

"Not a word from you, sir," the little man fumed, pointing an admonitory finger. "Dab"—and his eyes fastened on Charlie's—"telephone for Rice and Burleigh. I want them here this instant."

It was a tableau vivant: Will in his bed, Charlie backed up against the wall, the Doctor at the door and Dab beside him. Then the secretary broke the spell by lumbering across the room to the telephone and calling for the orderlies. There was a silence while Dab's voice rose in agitation, and then the Doctor uttered a single word, harsh with astonishment: "Whiskey!"

The bottle of Old Overholt stood there on the night table, incontrovertible, the half-filled glass beside it. Will exchanged a glance with Charlie, and in the next moment the Doctor was in action, catlike in his quickness, springing across the room to seize glass and bottle and smash them over the edge of the table so that the floor exploded with jewels of glass and the jagged neck of the bottle, gripped tight, blossomed in the bulb of his fist. "Here," he said, his voice pitched high, fighting for control as he sliced at the air inches from Will's shrinking face, "cut your own throat with it—or would you prefer a surgeon's touch?"

No one moved. Dab looked as if he were about to faint. Charlie's eyes were lit with excitement, a rough insouciant look settling into his features. Will's head felt as if it were floating free of his body.

The sequel was brief. The orderlies arrived and escorted Charlie from the San; he took with him the Doctor's warning not to set foot on the grounds again under penalty of criminal prosecution. A nurse swept up the glass. The Doctor paced back and forth. Will hung his head. Finally, when the nurse had left and the Doctor had had time to compose himself, he ordered Dab out of the room, shut the door quietly, pulled the chair up to the bed and perched himself on the edge of it. "Mr. Lightbody," he began, and Will could feel the tension in the air as the Doctor struggled to maintain his composure, "as long as you are under my care—and leaving it at this juncture would be purely suicidal, though you don't seem to give two hoots about your own life—you do want to live, don't you, sir?"

Will nodded.

"As I say, so long as you are under my care, you will not leave this institution for any purpose and you will not be allowed any visitation privileges whatever, save for the visits of a select group of your fellow patients—should your condition allow it. For the time being, however, I am limiting you to this room, the dining hall, the gymnasium and the baths. You remain on the laxative diet and you recommence your full exercise regimen the first thing tomorrow morning. Is that clear?"

It was. Will had been caught red-handed and the fight was gone from him.

The Doctor gazed at him as if he were a speck of something curious under the microscope. There was a silence. "You know of Sir Arbuthnot Lane?" he said finally. "No? I didn't expect that you would." He studied his nails a moment, then glanced up sharply. "Well, sir, he happens to be one of the most eminent physicians in the world, attached now to the Royal College of Surgeons, London, and he has perfected a surgical technique to improve motility and correct the often fatal consequences of autointoxication. To amateurs, the operation—an abdominal section to remove a portion of the lower intestine where stasis routinely occurs—is known as the 'Lane's Kink' surgery. Surely you've heard of it?"

Will could only blink at him. He was drunk still, drunk as a loon, but all the elation had gone out of him. He didn't like the turn the conversation was taking. He was frightened suddenly, and the fiery fist in his stomach took hold of him with a jerk.

"No matter," the Doctor said, and he held up his hands to admire the nails again. The nails were smooth, perfect, the fingers lithe and expressive: a surgeon's fingers. "I've located my own 'kink,' as it were," he said musingly, "though no one has taken to calling it 'Kellogg's Kink' yet, to my knowledge, but they will, they will . . . and my technique has relieved scores of severely autointoxicated and even moribund patients from the symptoms that afflict you. What I'm saying, sir," and the Doctor got to his feet and leveled a long, keen-eyed, almost loving gaze on him, "is that I've scheduled you for surgery just after the New Year."

He leaned over then and reached for the lamp, a serene self-satisfied smile on his lips, and pulled the switch. "Sleep tight," he said.

Chapter 6

From
Humble
Beginnings

◈◈

I t was a basement. Fieldstone and mortar, earthen floor, a smell like the cork in a bottle of wine gone bad on the shelf. There was a clutter of the usual junk—a sagging perambulator, rusted garden tools, a coal scuttle with a broken handle. The dirt was pulverized, grainy, ancient—dust—and the mummified corpse of a mouse lay in a drift of it in the center of the room, a pathetic wrinkle of naked hands and feet. Charlie had to duck his head and compress his shoulders like a hunchback to avoid knocking himself unconscious on the low-hanging beams. He kicked the dead mouse aside in disgust and looked up to where Bender and Bookbinder stood at the top of the steps, framed against a bleak January sky.

"It's a basement," Charlie said.

"It's cheap." Bender huddled in his greatcoat against the wind, his top hat glued to his head, silk scarf wrapped tight round his throat. George crouched on the bottom step, half in, half out of the cellar, a dazed and drunken look on his face. There was a swollen yellowish contusion over his left eye from when he'd fallen—or been pushed— in the street.

Charlie struck a match and lit one of the candles they'd brought with them. He set it atop a stack of split wood in the far corner and made a slow ambling inspection of the place. It was big, he'd say that for it, but the ceiling couldn't have been any higher than five feet eight inches, and the place was cold, filthy, a sink of neglect. He heard footsteps overhead, a shuffle and thump, repeated over and over, as if someone were dragging sacks of potatoes across the floor. "Who lives upstairs?" he asked, and he could see his breath hanging in the dank close air.

"Bart's mother," Bender returned, indicating Bookbinder with a nod. "It's her place."

She's afflicted, poor woman," Bookbinder put in. "The last stroke took the use of her left side and we've had to go and hire a Swede to look after her."

But Charlie wasn't listening. He was thinking of Mrs. Hookstratten —his "Auntie Amelia"—and the faith she reposed in him. Not to mention its tangible expression in cash and check. At Bender's urging, he'd written her a series of letters describing the immaculate new Per-Fo factory headquarters and he'd enumerated an entirely fictitious list of prominent investors. He'd waxed eloquent about the clean and thrifty Midwestern work force, men and women alike, and the newly designed Per-Fo boxes, and the real and enduring mission of Per-Fo itself, which was, of course, to provide the good people of America with a predigested, peptonized, celery-impregnated miracle of a ready-to-eat vegetarian breakfast food—in short, to save the American stomach. His letters ran to twenty and thirty pages, and he found, at least for the hour or so in which he was engaged in their composition, that the fiction grew actual in his mind so that he saw the factory floor in its idealized version, saw the desk in his office behind the smoked-glass door, knew and admired and encouraged the workers—particularly the girls, who wore tight skirts and deferred to him as he inspected the line, murmuring "Good afternoon, Mr. Ossining," one after another, and one after another turning away with a blush.

The letters had been effective. They'd got an additional twenty-five hundred dollars from the Hookstratten treasury. Twenty-five hundred dollars that Bender had turned toward the production of one thousand dummy cartons, and which had brought them, with a wagonload of used retorts, mixing tubs and rollers and a big new Sears wood-fired oven-range, to this dungeon on the outskirts of the Biggest Little City in the U.S.A. The cartons, designed by Bender himself, were quite the thing, actually—he had to hand it to Bender there. Red, white and blue, with a representation of two cherubic children and their prim and yet somehow randy-looking mother sitting round a kitchen table in the absence of the breadwinner of the house, it bore the title KELLOGG'S PER-FO, THE PERFECT FOOD across the top. There was a line beneath it about the celery and the rest of it, then the illustration, centered, and at the bottom of the box, in red block letters, a legend paraphrased from no less an authority than C. W. Post himself: MAKES ACTIVE BLOOD. (It was Postum that made red blood, and they couldn't trespass there, though Bender loved the ring of it.) The whole business was repeated on the reverse, but the picture was smaller and a paragraph of health-conscious gibberish had been added to appeal to the Eleanor Lightbodys and Amelia Hookstrattens of the world.

"The floor's filthy," Charlie said, "nothing but dust. No matter what we mix up down here it's going to taste like dirt."

Bender had descended a step and was peering into the cheerless cold vault of the cellar. "We'll get a rug," he said. "Half a dozen of them. And the oven'll heat the place, isn't that right, Bart?"

C. W. Post's ex-foreman grunted his assent. "I've seen concerns start up as humble as this," he said, speaking through his nose and shifting a pair of undersized, startled-looking eyes around the room. "The Doctor's first factory, for one. And his brother started out in a shack two years ago, and look at him now."

"Of course," Bender added in a considered tone, "we'll have to rely on candle power for the nonce—there's no electric coming out this far yet—but remember, Charlie, all we need at this juncture is a sample, enough to fill those thousand boxes, and we're off to the races from there."

George, who'd found himself a seat on the edge of a staved-in crate in the corner, gave a snort of contempt. "The dog races, maybe."

Bender ignored him. "Charlie? What do you think?"

What did he think? He thought it was dismal, poor as piss, thought it was a sham and a crime and it broke his heart. But it was a beginning. And it was better than chasing Bender all over town, better than brooding in his icebox of a room at Mrs. Eyvindsdottir's or drinking himself into George's habitual state at the Onion. He shrugged. "It'll do," he said finally. "But just for now. Just till we've come up with something to fill those boxes and get started. Then I want a real factory—and I don't care who knows it."

Bender just nodded and smiled. His plan, as Charlie understood it, was to use the sample boxes as advertising tools in a select few Mid-western cities—along with hoardings, newspaper announcements and the like. Brash as ever, he assured Charlie that he'd use those sample boxes as bait to reel in the fish with a host of advance orders—fifty percent down, cash or check, on writing the order. And *that* money would put them into full production—in a regular four-walled factory—and generate a whole lot more to spend on advertising. What he didn't tell Charlie was that he expected Will Kellogg to step in and buy them out long before they reached that point.

Charlie buttoned up his coat and pulled on his gloves. "Okay, George," he said with a sigh, "I guess we better get the wagon unloaded."

❖   ❖   ❖

Two days later, they were in business.

True to his word, Bender had provided carpeting—half a dozen foul-smelling rugs of painted canvas and a few oily and discolored straw mats that reeked of mildew. The smell could have been improved on, but at least the things covered the floor and kept the dust down. Bookbinder had erected a tent outside in the frozen yard to house the three wagon-loads of choice dent corn Bender had managed to divert from Will Kellogg's Toasted Corn Flake Company in a move worthy of any of Sherlock Holmes's adversaries for pure deviousness. Charlie, who'd led a pretty soft life the past few years, in and out of taverns and pool halls, apprenticing at the hustler's trade, spent the first day splitting wood for the oven. He stood there in the barren yard, all his digits gone dead with the cold, lifting the axe and bringing it down, over and over again, while Bartholomew Bookbinder put a hole in the basement wall for the stovepipe and his invalid mother sat at the second-story window gazing out serenely on the commotion as if it were as usual to the progress of her days as a trip to the outhouse. George was supposed to be helping with the wood, but he was present in body only. Bookbinder had to throw a blanket over him to keep him from freezing to death.

By the morning of the second day the stove was hot as a griddle and began to roast all sorts of foul and noxious odors out of the rugs, walls, ceiling and joists. It was the smell of history, rank and immemorial. Charlie choked on it. He was experiencing the pain of the athlete on the first day of training, the soreness of the galley slave freshly shackled to his oars. His back was like raw dough, without substance or fiber, his shoulders, elbows and forearms shot through with quibbling aches and argumentative cricks, pangs and spasms. He'd spent the night curled up next to George on the rug beside the stove—there was no sense in trudging all the way across town to Mrs. Eyvindsdottir's—and he ate whatever Bookbinder was able to scare up. Which wasn't much. Salt pork and flapjacks, with a weak tepid unsugared tea to wash it down, dinner and breakfast both. It wasn't exactly the sort of life—or bill of fare—he'd pictured for the President-in-Chief of the Per-Fo Company, Inc., but he was stirred in spite of himself. Now, finally, and at long last, he was going to be initiated into the mysteries of the flaking process.

Per-Fo, as it turned out, was going to be a product nearly indistin-guishable from any of the other flaked cereals on the market. Its unique-ness would derive from its special flavorings and the impression its blizzard of advertisements made on the public, but in all other respects it would be no different from Kellogg's Toasted Corn Flakes or C. W. Post's newly introduced Post Toasties. Its manufacturers (Charlie, Bender and Bookbinder, who in return for his expertise had been hand-somely rewarded from Mrs. Hookstratten's reserves and promised a stake in the company) would adhere to the conventional flaking process pi-oneered by Dr. Kellogg thirteen years earlier, when he produced his first wheat flake, and perfected by that same culinary wizard in his 1902 recipe for toasted corn flakes.

First, the corn kernels had to be milled to separate the horny outer shell and oleaginous germ from the starch-laden grits (too much germ and the flakes would go rancid on the shelves, as had been the fate of the now-defunct Korn Krisp product). The kernels were steamed until they cracked open, after which hull and germ were removed and the grits further steamed in rotary cookers—at which point flavorings were added—salt, sugar and malt most commonly. The grits were then dried and cooked again and allowed to stand and mellow in order to develop flavor and the ability to flake properly (this last step a serendipitous discovery of Dr. Kellogg, who, after forcing batch after batch through the process without success, was called away and inadvertently let a tub of grits turn moldy; the moldy grits flaked up beautifully). After tempering, the twice-cooked grits were rolled into flakes under the crushing pressures generated by a series of water-cooled rollers, and finally they were toasted. That was it. The whole process, beginning to end. All Per-Fo had to do to capture its share of the market was incorporate a little celery flavoring and vary the proportion of malt extract to achieve a slightly different taste (very slightly—no reason to fool with success).

By midafternoon of the second day, Charlie found himself in charge of a pair of hog-scalding tubs full of cooling grits that Bookbinder was "impregnating" with malt extract, salt from a shaker and a secret bile-green fluid derived from boiling down a bunch of celery to its essence, leaves and all, while at the same time he was expected to help George and a hired man hand-turn a set of laundry wringers to produce the flakes. Three big iron kettles steamed the next batch on the stove, while the preceding batch toasted on a tray in the oven. The basement was chaotic, George hauling in wood and stoking the fire, Charlie darting between stove and cooling tub, Bookbinder shouting out his nasal orders like a general under siege. A slick mash of cooked corn accreted underfoot, the rumble of roller and milling tray defined the internal weather, steam shrouded the air till the basement was indistinguishable from a Turkish bath. And the finished product—greenish flakes, burned at the edges or not, depending on the vigilance of the baker, i.e., Charlie—mounted in a series of peach baskets set against the far wall.

The pace was so frantic, Charlie didn't have time to think about what he was doing—he was just glad to be doing something. And when Bookbinder ordered him out to split more wood, he obeyed without question, and when the cart pulled up with the flattened pasteboard boxes, he went right at unloading them without a moment's hesitation. So it went for the better part of the next two days and nights.

It was around nightfall on the fourth day that Bender turned up to sample the finished product. Of course, Charlie had tried the odd flake from this batch or that, and Bookbinder had varied the formula periodically in search of the best-tasting and crispest flake, but no one had as yet sat down with a bowl, a spoon and a pitcher of milk to pass judgment. The batches had been numbered and labeled, and there were now twenty-seven overbrimming peach baskets stacked up against the stone wall, the contents of each differing in some essential way. Some contained flakes that held too much oil and were already turning; others were so crisp they'd achieved the color and texture of soot scraped from the walls of a fireplace. Still others had been peptonized (predigested through the action of Bookbinder's special pepsin mixture, which was designed to make the product easier on the American stomach), and one batch festered like pus and smelled so bad they had to store it outside beneath a denuded elm at the far end of the yard. The carpets were thick with a congealed mush, and there was a steady drip of condensation from the joists of the floor above.

"Well, well, progress, progress!" Bender cried, doffing his hat and bowing his way into their dungeon. He was beaming, and he went into a spiel about how he'd already taken advance orders for five hundred cartons—just on the design of the package alone. His face changed when a big brownish drip of bilge water drooled from the ceiling to stain his white silk scarf, but he murmured something about "difficult conditions" and refreshed his smile. Then he clapped his hands together in their pearl-gray kid gloves and roared, "Hell, boys, let's knock off and go upstairs for a taste test."

Upstairs they went. Bender led the way, outdoors into the cold star-hung night, up the back steps and into old Mrs. Bookbinder's lantern-lit kitchen with its dry sink and Puritan-brand icebox. George chugged at a bottle of something and slammed his shoulder into the door frame on the way in; the hired man—Hayes was his name, just Hayes—was next, followed by Charlie and, finally, Bookbinder. The kitchen table was a big oaken affair covered with a greasy oilcloth. Old Mrs. Bookbinder, twisted like a root, sat grinning on a stool in the corner. "I'll be yer judge," she cried in a voice that was three-quarters whistle, like a parrot's, and showed them a set of gray and toothless gums. "If I kin chew it, you know you're on to somethin'."

The table was set for six: six stoneware bowls, six tin spoons, six napkins of graying cloth. They sat without ceremony, exhausted, dazed, glad to be away from that close and unnatural space that lay somewhere below them like one of the nine circles of hell. Bender had arranged samples from the four most promising bins in serving bowls, which stood now on the sideboard. The first was labeled *Batch #13C, Pep., Cel. Imp., 2 oz. salt, 6 ext. malt*. Its contents, Charlie saw as Bookbinder solemnly scooped up a bowl for each of them, resembled shavings of green wood with fluted edges. Bender made a joke about saying grace, George snarled something unintelligible, the milk went round, the spoons were dipped.

There was a silence. Outside, a light icy rain had begun to fall, and it tapped in an insinuating way at the windows. George was the first to give up the pretense. With an excruciating rumble of palate, sinus and esophagus, he brought up a wad of Per-Fo #13C and spat it into the palm of his hand. "Christ Jesus!" he gasped, and a spasm passed over his body, "I'm poisoned!" In the next moment he had the bottle pressed to his lips as a palliative, and each of the taste testers, old Mrs. Bookbinder foremost among them, quietly spat out his or her mouthful into napkin, bowl or palm. Noises of relief, surprise, sorrow, panic, disgust circulated round the table. Bookbinder gravely rose, collected the bowls and scraped them, one after another, into the slops bucket for the pigs. Then it was on to batch #21A.

The lamps glared. The rain fell. The night was long. All four sample batches were passed on with varying degrees of revulsion, and when Bookbinder descended into the basement to recover samples from the next-most-promising bins, no one gave him the slightest word of encouragement. It was five samples this time, and the spoons moved sluggishly in the depths of the bowls. In the end, the hogs got the whole lot, all twenty-seven batches of the first run of Kellogg's Per-Fo, and the saddest thing was, even they wouldn't eat it.

If Charlie was disappointed, he didn't let it get him down. This was a minor setback, a hitch in their progress, and he never doubted that

Bender would work things out. Perhaps he didn't have quite as much confidence in Bookbinder—the word was he'd been lured away from Post Foods by another concern, now bankrupt, and that he'd taken a real bundle out of it, but who could say?—yet it wasn't the end of the world. If Bookbinder couldn't get Per-Fo to shape up into something appealing—or even edible—well, they'd have to chalk up the loss to experience and get someone who could. It was a setback. A disappointment. But there was always a way.

At twenty-five, Charlie Ossining was essentially an optimist. And why wouldn't he be? The Fates had smiled on him, and he'd walked in sunshine the better part of his life. Born Charles Peter McGahee in the town of Ossining-on-Hudson to Irish-immigrant parents who occupied themselves more strenuously with the uncorking of a whiskey bottle than with the means of obtaining such trifles as bread and meat and a roof over their heads, he might have been consigned to the dung heap and suffered through the usual grim and deprived childhood. But he wasn't. The tutelary gods, in the form of his benefactress, Mrs. Amelia Dowst Hookstratten, prevailed. His father, Cullum, largely through glossal endurance and the strength of a fevered, overactive imagination, had persuaded the widow Hookstratten to take him on as gatekeeper, man-about-the-place and majordomo of her Tarrytown estate, in addition to engaging Charlie's mother, Mary, as cook and parlormaid. Charlie was a boy of four at the time, precocious, winning, with the wide-open eyes and ready-made grin of the born confidence man (or pastor, tycoon or senator, for that matter).

From the start, Mrs. Hookstratten had taken a consuming interest in the boy, dressing him in the fine calfskin shoes and English tweed jackets her own son (then in his midtwenties and a power on the New York Stock Exchange) had worn in his youth. The boy delighted her. He made her feel necessary again, young at heart, essential; he lent credence to her mornings and regularity to her afternoons. Most of all, he helped her to fill the void left by the death of her husband.

She took Charlie's schooling in hand, too—though she was as democratic as the next person, she couldn't help feeling that the village school was the resort of the uncouth, the foreign and the ruffianly. Accordingly, Charlie spent his grammar-school years at Mrs. Partridge's

School for Young Gentlemen in Briarcliff Manor, where he learned comportment, Latin and music, as well as the three Rs, and spent his later years at St. Basil's, in Garrison. When Mrs. Hookstratten moved to a more commodious place just south of Peterskill, she did it in order to better display her plumage, of course, rising to her station on the strength of her late husband's investments as managed by her pencil-sharp son, but also—though she'd admit it to no one, not even herself—to be closer to Charlie; that is, if he wanted to come home for the occasional weekend. And it was for Charlie, too, that she brought Cullum and Mary with her, though Charlie's father was by this time so far gone in his drink that he couldn't even be relied upon to open the gate when the occasion demanded it, and Charlie's mother had developed a host of mysterious ailments, from a ringing in her ears to palpitations of the phalanges, that rendered her all but useless as cook, maid, pot scrubber or linen changer.

Yes, Charlie had had all the advantages, but as so often happens under such circumstances, he rejected them. Not outright, of course, but in the long run, in a growing repudiation of the expectations society had for him and a corresponding fascination with the life of those who live outside those expectations, who live by their wits, instincts, poise and balance. It was while he was at St. Basil's that this new way of looking at things first dawned on him. He was fifteen at the time, expert with his fists, a good runner, an indifferent athlete, a mediocre scholar. Intellectual pursuits held no interest for him. The quizzes, the tests, the essays, the committing of facts to memory and words to paper were torture to him, forced labor, the work of the underclass and the imprisoned—it wasn't even paid work, that's what got him. Mrs. Hookstratten had to pay *them*—Dr. Van Osburgh and the rest—to torment him with names and dates and numbers, with plane geometry and ancient history. Charlie wanted out. He dreamed of running off and setting up on his own; of being a power in business, any business; of acquiring the tangible accoutrements—the house, the carriage, the billiard table—that would tell the world he was no mere gatekeeper's son. And what did St. Basil's Academy have to do with any of that?

One night, thumbing through an issue of *Scribner's* because he couldn't stand the thought of memorizing the names and dates of all the regents

of England from Edward of Wessex and Ethelred II to Victoria, he came
across an advertisement that caught his eye:

BE BRILLIANT AND EMINENT! Brainworkers. Everybody. The new
physiological discovery—MEMORY RESTORATIVE TABLETS quickly
and permanently increase the memory two to tenfold and greatly
augment intellectual power; difficult studies, etc., easily mastered; truly marvelous, highly endorsed. Price, $1.00 post-paid.
Send for circular. MEMORY TABLET CO., 114 Fifth Ave., New
York.

Here was an easy out. A miracle. Suddenly he saw his way to becoming
the top scholar in the place, spoon-feeding Mrs. Hookstratten and grad-
uating to his real life in business or finance or something—and all
without a lick of effort. He snuck a look over his shoulder to see if his
roommate, Wapner, was watching, tore the page from the magazine,
folded it carefully and secreted it in his pocket.

Charlie invested a dollar and sent for the tablets. He took one the
day they arrived, but it didn't seem to help much with his Latin para-
digms, on which he received a grade of F. The following day he took
two, thinking the increased dosage would fix the lines of Portia's speech
on the quality of mercy indelibly in his head, but when he got up to
recite in class, all he could remember was the phrase "twice blessed."
It stuck there, like a broken tooth in a gearbox, until the class dissolved
in laughter and the master told him to sit down. He tried three pills,
four, five, took them on an empty stomach, after meals, before bed,
first thing in the morning. He went through six dollars and three hundred
tablets before he understood that he'd been taken. The pills were useless,
worthless, no more effective than chewing bark from the trees or grass
from the playing field.

Here he was, sharpest of the sharp, looking for an easy way around
the demands of St. Basil's, looking for a way to circumvent the system,
and he'd wound up throwing away his spending money for the term on
a sham, a hoax, a confidence game even the dullest and weakest of the
boys would never have fallen for. He'd been sucked in because he was
vulnerable, because he had a need, a weakness, the gull's hope. It was

a lesson. A lesson more valuable than anything Mr. Petrussi or Dr. Van Osburgh ever taught him. And who was the man who'd dreamed up the idea of the memory tablets to begin with, who'd placed the ad and watched the money pour in from a legion of dupes and half-wits that stretched from coast to coast? Who was he? There was real genius. There was the man they should be studying.

When Charlie left school in his junior year, Mrs. Hookstratten was disappointed. He didn't return home, didn't write or send word or explanation. He just packed his bag one night, caught a ride into Peterskill with the milk wagon and began the study of billiards in earnest. After a week he showed up hungry at the gatehouse. His father lamented in a red-eyed, sloppy-mouthed way; his mother groaned about her pains and conniptions; Mrs. Hookstratten pleaded with him. But to no avail. By the time he was seventeen he was living on his own, in a rented room over a dry-goods store in Tarrytown, earning an uncertain living at cards, dice and pool. He drank, but never in the way of his father, and he found women to comfort and amuse him but he made no attachments. It wasn't until he'd matured a bit and began to grow impatient with his two-bit hustles, with the taverns and the fistfights and the women who thought that "youse" was the plural form of the pronoun, that he came back to the Hookstratten fold. And then it was only because he'd met Bender, and because he had a goal and a vision— because he had Per-Fo.

A week after the dismal failure of their efforts in the Bookbinder basement, Bender sent Ernest O'Reilly to Mrs. Eyvindsdottir's to fetch Charlie to the Post Tavern Hotel. Charlie went in the service entrance and up the back stairs, as he customarily did now to avoid the doorman and bell captain (though he hadn't forgotten he owed them a little debt, which he intended to pay back, with interest, someday). Bender was lordly in a red silk dressing gown and his nose was flushed from any number of medicinal doses of Otard Dupuy. Single-minded and devoted to his goal, Charlie had long since ceased to concern himself over the disparity between his and his partner's living styles. Bender was Bender, and that was all there was to it. There would be plenty of luxury to spare when Per-Fo flew.

"Charlie, Charlie, my boy, my boy," Bender cried, doubling up his words and crossing the room to crush Charlie in his volcanic tycoon's embrace. He fell back, redolent of cognac, and indicated a chair with a princely sweep of his arm. "Sit down," he said, "there's something I want to discuss with you."

Charlie sat. Did he want a cognac? Sure. Cigar? No thanks.

Charlie revolved the snifter in his hands. "Well, okay," he said, and he'd been cooling his heels at Mrs. Eyvindsdottir's for seven days now, reading dime novels and trying not to think about what his thrifty landlady might be stewing up in the big iron pot on the stove, going quietly crazy, "so what is it?"

Bender pulled his big feet up under the chair opposite and sank into its plush depths. "It's just this, Charlie," he said, scratching at the side of his nose and bringing his fractured gray eyes to rest on Charlie's. "It's obvious that we're encountering a bit of a problem with the formula for Per-Fo—I mean, I appreciate everybody's effort, I'm not saying that, but I just don't think we're going to be able to get it right out there in that old lady's basement."

Charlie started to protest, but Bender held up his hand.

"Look, Charlie, I know what you're going to say, we've laid out a considerable expense here, what with the dent corn, Batt's fee, the oven—but it's chicken feed, really, when you think of the millions we'll be taking in by this time next year. And we can reuse the oven and some of the tubs and whatnot, that's not a problem, and the whole thing, despite appearances to the contrary, was not a wasted effort." He paused, sniffed at his brandy. "At least we learned something."

"What? What did we learn?" Charlie was irritated. He'd broken his back to make that hog slop, and he'd put his heart into it, too. Sure, conditions weren't what he wanted, but it had been Bender who'd convinced him to go along with it in the first place—and at least he'd had the feeling that they were accomplishing something. After eight weeks of frustration, at least they were moving forward, at least they were *doing* something . . . and now Bender was telling him it was a waste of time, effort and money, but that they'd learned something. *Learned something.* Big deal.

"We learned I was wrong, Charlie. You were right. You were against that basement from the beginning. I thought we'd at least get the ball rolling there, settle on a formula and fill up our sample boxes—that's all we need, just those thousand boxes and it's off to the races. But it didn't work. We were too ambitious. We jumped in before we had factory space, equipment, proper ovens and retorts and mixing tubs. Peach baskets, for Christ's sake. No wonder it didn't turn out." He paused to let a little taste of brandy trickle down his throat. "No, Charlie, I was wrong."

Charlie wanted to remonstrate, wanted to go back to Bookbinder's and give it another try, but he'd never heard Bender admit that he was wrong before, even after Kellogg had summarily booted them off the Sanitarium grounds, and he held his peace to see what was coming.

"I guess you're wondering what the next step is, aren't you?" Bender said in a mellow, ruminative voice, a voice of assurance and quiet confidence, the voice of a man with an ace in the hole. Bender always had an ace in the hole. He sat back and stretched, the smoke from his cigar wafting lazily round him. Outside, beyond the elegant curtains and double-hung windows, it was another gray and relentless Michigan day. "Well, I'll tell you. I've got a plan, Charlie, and I don't know why I didn't think of it before . . . it would have saved us—*you*—a whole lot of expense and confusion. Anyway, everything's on track again, don't you worry."

There was a pause. Why didn't he get to the point?

"Listen, to get to the point, I want you, George and this fellow Hayes down at the loading dock of the Grand Trunk Railroad—you know it, on the east end of town?—at twelve midnight tonight."

"Midnight?"

Bender nodded. "Fourteen carloads of Will K.'s finest, crispest, genuine and guaranteed toasted corn flakes are going out of there first thing in the morning—and I've already fixed it with a man I know down at the train yard, so don't worry about a thing—"

"Don't worry? What are we going to do, steal them?"

Bender simply smiled. A rich paternal smile, the sort of smile a teacher might bestow on his prize student when the grades are handed out.

Charlie was incredulous. "You can't be serious?" he cried. What in Christ's name were they going to do with fourteen carloads of Kellogg's Toasted Corn Flakes? *Fourteen carloads.* Where would they hide them? How would they transport them? They'd need a hundred men, wagons, horses, lights, uniformed cops to direct traffic, for shitsake. . . . But as he watched Bender's face, the sly thick-lipped grin, the signal flare of a nose, the cracked gray eyes narrowing in amusement, he began to understand: they didn't need fourteen carloads of corn flakes, no, not at all . . . all they needed was one thousand boxes.

Chapter 7

Organized Rest
Without
Ennui

❧

I t was a brisk morning in early January, winds gusting at twenty-five miles an hour, the thermometer sluggish at minus eight degrees Fahrenheit, a black mass of cloud spreading across the sky like a stain in water. The hands of the big walnut clock in the parlor of the Res showed a quarter to seven, and the Doctor, already arrayed in his white worsted suit, sat in his armchair, white-shod feet neatly crossed on the ottoman before him, going over his schedule for the day and finishing up his remarks on the lazy colon for the forthcoming issue of *Good Health,* of which he was editor-in-chief. He'd been working since five, having begun the day half an hour prior to that with his morning enema, a cold bath and twenty minutes of deep knee bends and jumping jacks in his private gymnasium. Some of the older children were up and at their chores by now, and one of them—he'd been so absorbed in the tragedy of the lethargic colon he hadn't looked up to see which—had brought him his breakfast. This morning it was bran cakes saturated in pure golden butter from his buffed and vacuumed cows and honey from the San's hives, pea patties with fruit compote, one apple, one orange, one banana and a steaming hot mug of Sanitas Koko.

He ate with good appetite, as he always did, even when aggravated —and he'd been plenty aggravated lately, what with one thing and another, the circle ever tightening, the whole world waiting for him to stick his head in the noose so they could string him up and rifle his pockets. There was the business with George, a constant source of irritation—and that young scamp he was in league with, Charlie something-or-other, damnable, perfidious man. Liquor on the San's premises. It was outrageous. Well, he'd called Chief Farrington about that one, and if Mr. Charlie ever had the temerity to show his face around the San again, he would be sorry, good and sorry—John Harvey Kellogg and the statutes of Calhoun County and the great state of Michigan would see to that. But just thinking about that human garbage made his stomach broil over his bran cakes and honey. Yes. And then there was the staff at the San—they wanted a raise. A raise! As if it wasn't enough that they were medical missionaries, dietary messiahs, young men and women privileged to work at the very apex of their profession and acquire—gratis, and more power to them—the tools they would need to take that mission out into the world. And they wanted money on top of it—mere money! He shook his head over the irony of it, paging through his itinerary to see when he was scheduled to meet with them—ah, there: two o'clock—and his eyes happened to fall across his surgical schedule at the same time. Eight patients scheduled. All for repair of balky sphincters, or, as he would determine once he got in there, removal of what he'd already begun to think of as the "Kellogg's Kink" in the intestine. But what was this?

Lightbody, William F.

A line had been drawn through the name. Were they canceling on him this morning? The Doctor hadn't been apprised. He lifted his eyebrows in annoyance. The man was a special case—as recalcitrant and backsliding a patient as he'd ever seen—and one of the very sickest. Most definitely. But it was probably just a quirk in the scheduling—he couldn't operate on them all at once, after all. He'd get to him tomorrow or the next day or the day after that. It didn't really matter. Still, he made a mental note to consult Dab about it.

As he munched the apple and went back to his text, reworking a phrase here and there—changing "putrefying" to "putrid, foul and moribund"—he couldn't quite shrug off the button of irritation he'd pushed in his brain. George. Charlie whoever. The old goat of a confidence man with the dyed beard who'd put them up to it. McMickens, the orderly who'd been stirring up the staff with nonsense about wages and unionizing. Lightbody. The lectures. The papers. The petty details of running the San on a day-to-day basis—good God, they couldn't even see to the chimpanzee without him. Sometimes it all seemed to weigh him down, harass him till he felt his nerves had been rubbed as raw as a coffee fiend's.

Revolving the apple in his hand and sinking his strong white teeth into its perfect flesh, he couldn't help wistfully reflecting on his younger days at Bellevue—life had been so much less complicated then, and just as stimulating, maybe more so. Those were the days. No Georges, no sour employees or rampant chimps. No. It was just the medical texts then, just the cadavers, the lectures, the grateful healing patients. He'd lived frugally, too, and it hadn't hurt him. Not one iota. Over the course of two years he'd gained nearly seventeen pounds on a diet of oatmeal, apples, Graham bread and pure spring water—and at a cost of sixteen cents a day. Yes, he thought, finishing the apple with a sigh, those were the days. Still, there was no sense in reliving your yesterdays when there was so much to be done today. He'd been a private then in the great campaign to save the alimentary canal, to improve the race and spare the eternal herds from slaughter, and he was a general now—four stars' worth and aiming for five—and there was no one to stop him but himself. John Harvey Kellogg rose from the chair, stretched mightily, and called to one of the children to fetch his bicycle from the carriage house.

Dab arrived promptly at seven, accompanied by the new fellow, A. F. Bloese, a saturnine rigid little man with a boyish face (or a boy with a mannish face) who happened to be a master stenographer, typewriter and codifier of the lithe symbology of shorthand. A real find. Yes, sir. Dab provided contrast, bloated and puffing, wrapped like an Egyptian mummy in his scarves, overcoats, mittens, sweaters and cummerbunds. He was a shambles of a man, an embarrassment. The Doctor stood there in the vestibule of the Res, regarding him with a cold eye: the man had to be forced into the physiologic regime. For his own sake, and the sake of appearance, too. Here was the Doctor, avatar of the strenuous life, and he was shadowed everywhere he went by this sweating fleshpot, this, this—but enough of that. Time was wasting. "Morning, Poult," the Doctor said as he pulled on a pair of white gloves and slung the white scarf jauntily round his neck—no arctic claptrap and dragging coattails and the rest of it for him. Not unless the temperature dropped another twenty degrees and the wall of ice that had gouged out Lake Michigan came back again.

"Morning, Chief," Dab returned, already beginning to sweat.

"Bloese." The Doctor acknowledged the understudy with a curt nod.

"Sir," Bloese said. His carriage, the Doctor noted with satisfaction, was impeccable. His teeth, too. Bone structure. Even his hair, parted in the middle and neatly clipped round the ears.

"All right, men!" the Doctor cried, and they were out the door and into the blast of the electrifying wind. "To work, hey?" One of the children—little Calvin Smoke, wasn't it, the boy who'd been found living among the Nez Percé in a filthy tepee and subsisting on a diet of squirrel jerky and black-footed ferret?—stood patiently in the driveway, holding the bike. Yes, it was Calvin—of course it was. And what was wrong with his brain these days? He couldn't even recognize his own children now? It was frightening, deeply disturbing, but he brushed it off. "Thank you, son," the Doctor crooned, mounting the bicycle and hurtling off down the ice-crusted drive, Dab and Bloese quickstepping behind him.

"Poult," the Doctor cried over his shoulder, breath steaming, the petite white shoes pumping at the pedals, "we'll need to accomplish several things on the way to the San this morning, so get your pencil ready—and you, too, Bloese." And there he was, the blinding white dynamo, cutting a caper on his bike at the age of fifty-five and counting, the front wheel rising from the pavement as he dodged back at his jogging secretaries to give them a moment to prepare pencil and paper. Up the icy curb and down again, a figure eight, and he was back out in front of them, the words flying into the wind at a Kelloggian clip.

"First things first—about the notice for the San in the new issue of *Good Health*, and, by the way, I've made some corrections on the colon piece and it will have to be typed up the minute we get in—well, about the notice. I'm looking for a catchy phrase, nothing vulgar like that charlatan conjures up for his Toasties and Post-stickers and the rest—remember, gentlemen, this is not an advertisement, not at all, but a notice, and a notice by its nature has the dignity these hucksters wouldn't recognize if it bit them . . . at any rate, I've come up with this phrase, to run under the Battle Creek Sanitarium heading"—the bicycle careening, there's a dog, narrow miss, the Doctor glancing back over his shoulder at his blowing secretary and the wiry little man beside him, both scribbling furiously and thumping along the icy streets like refugees scrambling for the last train—"and it's a fine and effective phrase, plenty of dignity to it, but it feels somehow incomplete, as if"—dodging back again, the figure eight to split them—"well, I've got this far: 'The Battle Creek Sanitarium: Organized Rest.' "

Bloese didn't seem to be breathing hard —good man, that. Dab was pathetic, wheezing like a cart horse, and the Doctor had to keep circling back for him.

"You see what I mean?" the bicycling Doctor cried over his shoulder, weaving, weaving, "rest that isn't a bore, or something like that—we don't want to give the impression of a nursing home, not at all, that's the last thing we want . . . on the contrary, we want to emphasize the excitement of the Battle Creek"—there's a wagon, up on the left, look out now —"Sanitarium. Oh, and by the way, Poult—Poult?"

The Doctor let out an exasperated sigh. Dab was lagging now, half a block back, damned inefficient man; the Doctor swung sharply to his right and doubled back. "This Lightbody thing," he called out, running straight at Dab and swerving at the last minute, a bit of fun here, and why not? "—the man's been dropped from today's surgery. Any reason?"

Dab's ponderous legs carried him in a blind stagger up the bone-chilling street. He looked dazed. His breath was ragged. "No—no reason especially," he wheezed. "It's just that—that we—with the employees' meeting and all—we—"

The Doctor zoomed by him on the left. "All right, fine. But reschedule him. And advise Dr. Linniman. The man's a certified disaster—the sooner we get to him, the better."

Bloese came up on the right side then, moving along effortlessly, a born miler making for the tape. "Without ennui," he said, his voice cast low in deference and respect. At first the Doctor didn't quite catch on to what he was saying, but then it hit him: he'd completed the slogan. And beautifully. Of course, that was it: "The Battle Creek Sanitarium: Organized Rest Without Ennui." Perfect!

"Yes," the Doctor shouted, "that's it, Bloese, excellent!" And then he was doubling back again for Dab. "Have you got that, Poult? Yes? Good. And now, if we could begin dictation—I'll need to have a new version of the Battle Creek Sanitarium Platform for the Battle Creek Sanitarium book I've proposed—are you with me here, Poult? Good. All right. Then start: 'Number the First: Fundamental and Curative Principles. Nature alone can cure. The Power that creates is the Power that can heal. Physicians, nurses, medicines do not cure; they can merely direct and help the healing process. Patients, not diseases, are to be cured—by removing the causes of disease instead of the symptoms only. Number the Second: A Natural Dietary—"

When he was dictating, the Doctor was generally oblivious to the world around him. He was concentrating, peeling back the layers of his brain like a mental onion, digging for the deep stuff, the Kellogg essence, and the phenomenal world receded of necessity into the background. And so the woman with the perambulator had to be quick on her toes, and Bloese became an object, a tool moving at the required speed, and Dab—poor Dab—a duller tool, lagging behind. It took a good long moment—the course of a block, at least—before Dr. Kellogg began to understand that Bloese was trying to communicate something to him, something urgent and critical for all its inarticulacy. Man of decision, general to his troops, the Doctor doughtily applied the brakes.

Bloese halted beside him. He wasn't even winded, his hair was unmussed, he seemed unaffected by the cold. But there was something in his eyes that gave the Doctor pause, a look of desperation, wildness, fear. "Well, Bloese, what is it, man?" he demanded.

"It's Dab, sir." The secretary jerked his head in the direction from which they'd come. "He seems to have fallen."

It became clear in that instant. The Doctor's keen eyes took in the scene at a glance: the massive form of Dab, collapsed like a heap of rags in the street, the young woman with the perambulator bent over him, the trees reaching nakedly for the funeral stone of the sky. He was quick, Dr. Kellogg, nimble and quick—back down the street in a trice. But all his quickness aside, he was too late to do a thing for his fallen amanuensis.

The woman's face, Bloese's, Dab's. A carriage stopped. People had begun to emerge from their houses, crack their doors, stand on their porches and gaze out on the scene in fascination and dread. The little Doctor lifted his head from the secretary's chest, dropped the wrist he'd gathered between thumb and forefinger. Dab's features were locked in the vise-grip of death, mouth open, tongue prominent, eyes fixed in blind contemplation of the lowering sky. John Harvey Kellogg pushed himself up from the street, brusquely rubbing his palms together to remove any particulate matter that might have adhered to them. "Massive coronary arrest," he pronounced, and his eyes went hard suddenly, "—there's nothing we can do." There was a sound of shuffling feet, muted cries and whispers.

"Poor Dab, poor Poult," he went on after a moment, addressing the crowd gathering round them, and his voice rose as he began to appreciate the significance of the blow, the moment, the historical framework of the secretary's life and its meaning in the greater context. "Here lies a man, a good man, and a fine secretary, a man brought low in the prime of his life." He lifted his head then, made eye contact with each and every member of the stunned and white-faced crowd. "But for all that"—he shook his head sadly—"a man who ignored the dictates of the physiologic life."

There was a silence. No one said a word. The young mother tried to suppress a cry of general and specific grief. Finally the Doctor turned to Bloese. "I'm sorry, Bloese," he said, "and what was your given name again?"

"Aloysius, sir."

"Aloysius," he repeated, his voice somber, as if he were meditating on the deep significance of the name. "Aloysius"—and he reached out a hand to clap him on the shoulder—"you've got a long day ahead of you."

❖   ❖   ❖

He was not heartless, the good Doctor and Chief of the Battle Creek Sanitarium—far from it. An hour later, in his office, the eyeshade pulled down low, Dab's body laid out on a slab in the mortuary, he shed a quiet tear. He blamed himself, he did. How many times had he told himself he had to get the man on a proper regimen, simplify his life, fill him to the core of his essential self with the life-giving elixir of physiologic well-being? And yet he was angry, too. Damn that Dab. He was a slob, that was all. A slob. A face of eating, a disgrace. *Patients, not diseases, are to be cured.*

He was revolving the disaster in his mind—half the town had witnessed it, after all—when the phone rang. Without thinking, he picked it up.

"John?"

There it was, the voice of his own blood, country-inflected, porkpie-cap-wearing, horse-trading, skinflinting and backstabbing, the voice that had spoken to him from the bunk bed on a farm morning, the voice that had taken his orders with a yes and a sure and an I'll-do-it-if-it-kills-me, the voice of his brother, Will.

"Yes, I'm here."

"I know there's no love lost between us, John, so I'll get right to the point. It's this new breakfast food—"

The Doctor cut him off. "Breakfast food, my foot," he cried, "you've got what you want—my name, my hard work, my invention and the knife you twisted in my back, so don't you call here telling me about breakfast food."

Will was calm, always calm, born calm. "John" he said, "it's our name I'm talking about. They're calling it *Kellogg's* Per-Fo. You know of it?"

Kellogg's Per-Fo? What was this nonsense? What was he talking about? And then suddenly, cutting through the field of the Doctor's peevishness like a black knight with his halberd raised, was the image of George.

"John? You there?"

The Doctor's reply was a whisper, static on the line.

"It's your boy George—he's behind it and he's got legal use of the name, just like me, and I was born with it, whether you want to admit it or not—"

On the defensive now—George, Dab, McMickens, it was all too much, "Yes? And so? I wash my hands of the boy. Washed them. Years ago."

The level voice came right back at him, no irritation, no lift, just plain good sense. "It's an embarrassment, John. To my business, sure, but I expect you don't give a hoot about that—"

"Damn right, Will. You've never been righter."

"—but I expect you'll begin to reflect on what this is going to look like vis-à-vis your precious Sanitarium. This Per-Fo is nothing but a scheme, John. All they want is for us to buy them out and quiet them up. I've got my lawyers on it now—"

"*Your* lawyers. Sure. The same shysters you used to squeeze the toasted-flake concession away from the Sanitas brand, are they the ones? Blood-suckers, vampire bats and I don't know what-all—*your* lawyers. Ha!"

"I didn't call to wrangle, John. Our differences will be settled in a court of law—"

"You'll rue the day—"

"But this is an embarrassment to us both and, what's more, an injury to my business *and* yours. Now, he's your son, no matter what you say, and word will get out that the son of the Almighty Doctor on the Hill is a flimflam man, and how do you think that's going to sit with your precious bowel-plugged patients?"

The conversation ended there. Dr. Kellogg slammed down the ear-piece in a rage. Faces swam before his eyes—his brother's, Dab's in its final agony, George's, always George's. He pushed back the eyeshade and lowered his head to the desk.

❖   ❖   ❖

A good percentage of the staff was waiting for him in the Grand Parlor as he came through the door, Bloese at his side, and there wasn't a one he didn't recognize, not a one to whom he hadn't shown special kindness or given his personal attention. Nurses, bellhops, cooks, janitors, electricians, pot scrubbers, bottle washers and peanut-butter decanters, they were all there, two hundred and more, while the others, those who were loyal to him, to the institution and its philanthropic mission, kept away. He saw McMickens at the head of the queue as he made his way to the podium—a pasty-faced, flat-headed, dollop-nosed Irishman with coils of black ursine hair on the backs of his hands. What was it about these Irish, he thought irritably, never satisfied with their lot, always crying out for more like piglets at the teat? The man was a sorehead, a menace, and when the furor died down, the Doctor would quickly see to his dismissal.

The room fell silent as Dr. Kellogg stood at the podium and bowed his head. "My friends," he began, and he'd yet to look up, "my employees and fellow vegetarians. I have tragic news, news that will sadden every heart in this room." He looked up now, suddenly, and his eyes were clouded with tears. "One of your rank, one of the men most dear and indispensable to the workings of this great, unique and charitable endeavor in which we all, even the humblest and most recent hiree, are engaged together, has fallen. Yes, friends, my confrere and secretary, that great and good man, Poultney Dab, is dead."

Someone gasped. There was a murmur of voices, a confused muttering, suppressed coughs, followed by a stricken silence.

"It happened this morning, just this morning, and in the line of duty, too. Poultney Dab worked for this grand enterprise right up to the end, taking dictation even as he was taken from us and delivered to a far happier and a better place. His death was unexpected, but, then, what man's isn't? Or what woman's? Or child's, even? The Lord God, in His wisdom, has made us the imperfect vessels we are, subject to the whims and wants of the organism, sinners all, liable to fall."

There wasn't a murmur in the room. All eyes were riveted on the platform. The Doctor paused to remove his glasses and dab at his eyes with a handkerchief.

"Yes," the Doctor continued, his voice growing in dimension, lordly and dramatic, "Poultney Dab is fallen. Sacrificed. Dead before his time. And which one of us will be next?"

There was no response.

"We say that his death was unexpected, yes, but that's just a way of comforting ourselves, a litany, as it were. I say this to you: Poultney Dab's death *was* expected, apparent to us all, were we not blind, visible in the flare of his cheeks, the glaze of his eyes, the sallowness of his skin and the corpulence of his frame . . . for wasn't he one of the unlucky ones, one of the unregenerate, one of the millions of men, women and children in this country—yea, the *world*—who know not what they do to their own bodies, those priceless temples, tokens of God's faith in us? You all know the evils of improper diet, you all know the failings of the meat eater, the drunkard, the coffee fiend, and you all know how unforgiving Nature can and will be—I say this to you, my friends and employees, my *co-workers*, my fellow missionaries: he was a victim of autointoxication."

A single lamp burned at the far end of the room. The cold wind rattled the windowpanes and the clouds drove at the building as if it were an ark at sea. The Doctor raised his arms to the light, came up off the platform on his toes and shot his eyes at every face in the room.

"Yes!" he cried finally. "Autointoxication! And he a member of this staff, privy to the last word in enlightenment and reform. What of the others? What of the legions of the ignorant, laboring in darkness, their lives doomed to be cut short, brutally and without warning, in their season of fruitfulness? What of them?"

Again, he hung his head. When he raised it once more, the tears glistened on his cheeks. "And you speak"—here his voice cracked pitiably—"you speak of money. Of lucre. Of gain. You gather here, beneath the portals of this fortress of health reform, this bastion of truth, and you ask me to give you—*you*, who have your health and the wisdom and discipline to maintain it into the golden years of your productive and harmonious lives—to give you mere money." He threw up his hands. "Believe me, I would if I could. I know how little we're able to pay even the most experienced of you. I know the ascetic life of the first-year nurse, given nothing but the roof over her head, her uniform and the means of knowledge. But is such a life so untenable? Can any man put a price on knowledge—the knowledge that will save your lives and the lives of thousands upon thousands of others less fortunate than yourselves? You are missionaries—*I* am a missionary—and the whole of humankind is our mission. Can you put a price on that? Can you?"

The Doctor's voice rang out through the room. Fully half the audience was in tears, handkerchiefs waving like flags of surrender. A second-year nurse in the front row raised her face to him, her eyes soft, cheeks wet, a reverential glow illuminating her plain features. The Doctor cleared his throat and bathed the audience with his most compassionate gaze.

"I take nothing myself," he said, his voice pitched low. "Not a cent.

Nothing. You all know that. My time here—and you all know just how much of my time and energy I devote to this institution—is given freely, willingly, gladly, in the service of mankind. This is my life . . . and I trust, I fervently hope, it will be yours.

"I will not ask you to pray for your fallen comrade; Poultney Dab would not have had it so. If I knew his heart, and there's not a man or woman amongst us today who can better lay claim to that knowledge, he would have exhorted you to carry his name into battle like a regiment following its guidon; don't shed your tears for Poultney Dab, my friends, but sing out his name. Use it as a prick, a lance, the shining symbol of our holy united endeavor. . . ." And then the little man in white began to sing, his voice naked and grief-stricken, alone in the first bar but swelling, swelling with the full complement of all the kindred spirits in the room before he'd drawn a second breath:

Onward, Christian Soldiers,
Marching as to war,
With the cross of Jesus,
Going on before. . . .

And with that, he left the podium, his right arm raised high and beating time, the hymn ringing to the rafters, as he made his way through the sea of broken faces and grasping hands for the door.

❖   ❖   ❖

Night fell over the San. It was the night of the death of Poultney Dab, and Dr. Kellogg and his new secretary, A. F. Bloese, were working late. The Doctor had triumphed, as usual, but at what cost? His stomach was sour, his joints ached, his eyes were tired. There were just too many troubles, too many things pressing on him, too many hands reaching into his pockets. Despite the rigors of the physiologic life and the fortitude of mind and body it inspired, he was depressed. Tired. Overworked. And it was the deep black icebound nadir of the year.

Bloese, his features ironed with concentration, sat beneath the lamp at the typewriter, polishing up the Doctor's early dictation. The wind was still up and the Doctor, momentarily distracted, heard it come and crouch in the trees with the forlorn wail of a demon lover risen from the grave to take its own back again. He toyed with his pen. Pushed a pair of scissors up and down the length of the blotter. It was then that he thought of Florida. Miami Springs. The golden sun, the everlasting sun. Palms. Sea breezes. Sand. Miami Springs. And wouldn't it be nice to—?

There was a knock at the door.

Bloese's head snapped up like a guard dog's.

"I'm not in, Aloysius," the Doctor said.

Bloese rose and answered the door, holding the plane of oak rigidly to him and speaking through the crack. "The Doctor is not in," he repeated. "He's gone home for the day," he said, and then stepped swiftly out into the hallway, slamming the door behind him—but not before Dr. Kellogg caught the drift of the commotion outside. A voice was raised, a voice that grated on him like a harrow dragged the length of his body: it was the voice of Lionel Badger. Badger! He'd forgotten all about him. But, yes, come to mention it, he did seem to recall something in his calendar about Badger's coming to lecture and stay again—for God knew how long.

"I know he's in there," came the hoarse nag of Badger's voice.

"I assure you, sir—" Bloese countered.

The Doctor pictured Badger's great swollen head fringed with a red fluff the consistency of pubic hair, the bulging eyes, the grim set of the jaw. The last time he'd visited he'd had the temerity to take the Doctor to task for wearing shoes of animal hide—leather, that is—while he, Badger, wore rope sandals, winter and summer. Lionel Badger—he was a fanatic of the worst stripe, the nearest thing to a flagellant the Vegetarian Movement could lay claim to. The Doctor shrank from the thought of confronting him, humoring him or whatever: *Not now,* he prayed, *not tonight.* The voices disputed in the hallway, the wind rattled the panes, and now, more strongly, in all its greens and cerulean immensity, the vision of Miami Springs arose before him again. *Organized rest without ennui.*

It took him one minute. Sixty seconds, that was all. John Harvey Kellogg picked up the phone, asked for Nichols at the front desk.

"Nichols?" he inquired, keeping his voice low lest Badger overhear—the man's ears were keen as a rabbit's.

Properly unctuous, Nichols's voice came back at him. "Yes, sir, Dr. Kellogg?"

"Phone home, Nichols, and inform Mrs. Kellogg—and my sister, too—to pack their things, and a small bag for me."

"Sir?"

He'd gone off in a reverie for a moment, the sound of the surf whispering in his ears. "Oh, yes—and make a reservation for three, private sleeping compartment. . . . Yes, on the Michigan Central Line. . . . We'll be going through to Miami."

❖ Chapter 8 ❖

Groundhog Day

❧

T he weather was indifferent. One minute a tepid pale rinsed-
out sun would poke through the clouds to feebly illuminate the
grounds of the San, and the next, clouds would close over it,
big-bellied and truculent. It was anybody's guess as to whether Dr.
Kellogg's groundhog would see his own shadow and thus be startled back
into his burrow for another six weeks' sleep, but after enduring nearly
three months of gray cold changeless Battle Creek afternoons, Will
Lightbody, for one, was praying that it would be overcast just this one
last time. Not that he put much credence in such nonsense, but, then,
who could say? The creatures of the wild did seem to have an uncanny
way of predicting the weather—skunks and raccoons growing extra fur
between their toes at the approach of a severe winter, swallows building
their nests higher in advance of a rainy season, grubs and earthworms
digging deeper before a drought and so on. *The Farmers Almanac* depended on them.

Will watched from his window as the Doctor's tame deer roved across
the yard in little groups, the uncertain light now silvering their backs,
now blotting them, until they seemed to flicker like images on a moving-
picture screen. He thought back to the day he and Miss Muntz had lain
side by side on the veranda, wrapped like Eskimos and watching these
same deer at their hard work, pawing at the frozen ground for a tidbit

here and there. Miss Muntz, poor girl, had found them charming, but Will saw them then as he saw them now, as instruments of the Doctor's message, as propaganda. So, too, with the mangy chimp and the dispirited wolf the Doctor kept in a cage in the basement and fed exclusively on scraps of bread to illustrate the carnivore's docility when deprived of the kill. Or the white rabbits that bounced from bush to bush, happy in their pacifistic pursuits, and the Christmas goose, which had somehow managed to survive the Doctor's regimen and could be heard honking blissfully from a pool in the Palm Garden. And, of course, the celebrity of the day, the groundhog.

In honor of this rodent, Dr. Kellogg had built an enclosure on the south lawn of the San and proclaimed it "Groundhog Glen," a neat and unobtrusive hand-lettered sign identifying the place for the curious. It consisted of a four-foot-high fence of chicken wire, presumably sunk deep, a tumble of rock and a log or two for authenticity, and a concrete trough of drinking water, long frozen. The burrow itself had apparently been engineered by its occupant—a creature Will had never laid eyes upon, at that. When he'd arrived in November, the burrow was silent and unrevealing, cold dirt, black hole. As a boy he'd shot dozens of groundhogs at his grandfather's country place in Connecticut and hadn't thought much about it one way or the other. But this one had taken on a special, almost mystical significance, part and parcel, as it were, of the Doctor's newly announced scheme of "Organized Rest Without Ennui" (every least holiday an occasion, as well as a reminder to abide by and respect the rights of the animal kingdom). Despite himself, Will couldn't help feeling a real and compelling interest in seeing the deserted hole in the ground come to life. No matter what the trappings, it was a pledge of renewal, rebirth, the coming of the sun. And he was curious, too: how would the little white-clad impresario manage it? Was the ground electrically wired? Had he put an alarm clock in the hole? Or would one of the attendants simply dig the thing out?

The deer moved on. The sun stabbed through the clouds. Will put his fingertips to the window and belched softly, tasting milk, always milk. He felt his stomach clench suddenly, and it clenched around an idea, an apprehension that had been with him for days, off and on, minute to minute. The fact was that neither he nor Dr. Kellogg would be present for the groundhog's performance, scheduled, according to the San's house organ, for twelve noon, amid the usual Sanitarium hoopla, with a formal out-of-doors luncheon and a "Groundhog Ball and Cotillion" to follow. No, they would be engaged in an intimate prognostic performance of their own—at twelve sharp, Will was scheduled to go under the knife. .

He'd been spared for better than a month now, a month during which he'd consulted endlessly with Linniman and the beard-pulling, lip-tugging, inappropriately grinning and evasive staff of the Colon Department. The tests had been repeated, and then repeated again. Milk came back into the diet, psyllium and seaweed departed. There were no grapes. And there was no Dr. Kellogg. He'd disappeared, called off on urgent medical business to some distant place, from which he'd only recently returned, brown as a walnut served up in the crisp white napkin of his worsted suit.

During all that time—the entire month of January—Will's condition remained static. He didn't improve, he didn't worsen. His routine was unwavering, all the usual treatments redoubled (with the exception of the sinusoidal bath—Will drew the line there). He didn't take any sleigh rides, didn't visit the jeweler's, didn't stop at the Red Onion (every time he stepped out the door to take a stroll round the grounds he was shadowed to make sure he didn't fall prey to the temptation). His stomach was an acid pit, his stool nonexistent, the enemas ceaseless. All he wanted was to go home to Peterskill, to be away from the San and Dr. Kellogg and his fixation with the mouth and anus, but the whole institution rebelled at the thought. Doctors and nurses alike echoed Eleanor: it would be suicide. And as for Eleanor herself, she meant to stay another three months at least. Maybe longer.

And so, the knife. And so, the stomach that would not work and the intestines that would not flow were to be invaded, prodded, examined in their bloody wet lair, hefted, weighed, pronounced upon—and, if the Doctor, the Almighty Doctor, saw fit, excised, snipped, cut, mutilated. That was what Will Lightbody had to look forward to on the windy uncertain afternoon of Groundhog Day.

❖   ❖   ❖

Earlier, at breakfast (Drs. Linniman and Kellogg insisted that Will take his meals in the dining hall, even if it was only to lift a glass of milk to his lips in the company of his fellow seekers after the physiologic ideal or, in this case, to take nothing at all in preparation for surgery), Eleanor had joined him at the table. Will was elated. Here was his wife, this elegant showpiece in high lace collar and jewels, this adornment and inspiration, abandoning the brilliant company of her own select group to show her concern for him, her husband, as he faced the liability of surgery. When she took Professor Stepanovich's place (he was back in Russia, peering into his telescope, desperately attempting to restore the credibility of Saturn's rings), Will felt his eyes go glassy with tears of gratitude. "Eleanor," he said, flushing with pride, "what a surprise," and he introduced her to his tablemates, though, as it turned out, she knew them all already, through her social activities and her directorship of the Sanitarium Deep-Breathing Club.

For all of thirty seconds Eleanor was solicitous and tender, asking how he felt, reassuring him, wondering if there was anything she could do for him, but then she ordered breakfast, looked up and threw herself into the general conversation. Five minutes later, Will found himself growing irritated: she was ignoring him. In fact, she was excluding nearly the whole table—the braying Hart-Jones, Mrs. Tindermarsh, the shrinking Miss Muntz—in favor of the newcomer to Will's group, a big-headed loudmouth by the name of Badger. As he'd let them know, endlessly, Badger was President of the Vegetarian Society of America, and a Very Important and Influential Individual. It turned Will's stomach to see Eleanor playing up to him (and his stomach certainly didn't need any additional turning). This was just the sort of thing that was wrong with her—she had no sense of proportion.

They were discussing prominent vegetarians they knew in common, Badger holding forth, Eleanor name-dropping, Hart-Jones fluttering round the edges of the conversation with a stutter and whinny, hopelessly trying to pass for a wit. Will gazed out the window on the piercing sunshine and spongelike clouds of Groundhog Day, watching the treetops go from light to dark and back again, until he could stand it no longer. He turned to Mrs. Tindermarsh, who sat mountainously to his left, her hands folded over a plate as barren as his own. "You're not breakfasting this morning, Mrs. Tindermarsh?" he murmured, by way of saying something, anything, to distract himself from the inanities of the Eleanor-Badger dialogue.

Mrs. Tindermarsh stiffened. She unlocked her fingers, one by one, and spoke without lifting her head. "I'm having surgery today."

A spurt of panic shot through Will's veins—in his irritation with Eleanor he'd managed to forget for just a moment the terrible sentence that hung over his own head. "Me, too," he said in an unnatural voice, a voice that sailed too high, a squeak of a voice.

The great solid frieze of Mrs. Tindermarsh's head turned toward him and a kind of dim sympathetic interest lit her eyes. "Oh, really," she said without animation, "what a coincidence. I'm due at eleven-thirty—for the kink. I'm nervous, of course. But I can't help thinking it's for the best, for my . . . well," and she attempted a smile, "we can't be going on like this, can we? It does so smack of symptomitis."

Will nodded. Gave her a sick smile. "I'm at twelve," he said. "Same kink. Or so the Doctor thinks. He won't know, of course, until he's in there. . . ." His voice trailed off. He had a sudden image of the Doctor in his surgical mask poised over the incision—a hole, deep and black —and reaching in like a magician to pull out a groundhog by the ears. He shut his eyes and rubbed his temples, then reached for his water glass. Shakily.

"—knew the Alcotts personally," Badger was saying, "I was just a boy, of course, but I learned some invaluable lessons at Dove Cottage. . . ."

And Will knew he would go on to elucidate those lessons in excruciating detail, as he had at breakfast, lunch and dinner for the past month, finding virtue in tautology and inspiration in his own hoarse ragged bottomless nagging voice. The man wore rope sandals in winter and spurned wool, going about in a cotton shirt in freezing temperatures. And he conspicuously consumed nothing but coarse unleavened cottage bread made of Graham flour he'd brought with him, dried apples and pure unfiltered spring water imported from Concord, Massachusetts, where Bronson Alcott had made his home. The Kellogg diet, as he'd let them know innumerable times, didn't go far enough. Molasses, milk, butter, potatoes! He scorned them all. For his part, Will wished him the peace and solace of the grave, hoping against hope that he'd choke to death on his cardboard crusts.

Eleanor countered Badger's speech with something equally stupid, and Will, trembling now with the effort to contain himself, turned his attention to Miss Muntz, who sat to the left of Mrs. Tindermarsh. "And Miss Muntz," he said, making a stab at a smile, "may I ask how your drawings are progressing?"

Will didn't dare ask about her condition—or even how she was feeling. The tall and regal girl with the greenish complexion he'd known two months ago was now stooped and wrinkled, the skin fallen loose from her bones, hanging in pouches beneath her eyes, turning to scale at her ears. She was so pale she looked like a victim of one of Bram Stoker's monsters, sucked dry of blood, even her viridian glow faded to a faint dullish crème de menthe. But worst of all, and most horrifying, was her hair. It had gone gray, gray as a crone's, and had begun to fall out in clumps. He looked at her now and saw that her scalp shone under the lights of the chandelier like buffed leather.

She smiled. "Lovely, I think. Grand. I've done portraits of Dr. Kellogg and Mr. Hart-Jones. I'd love to do one of you—just a charcoal sketch, nothing elaborate. Will you sit for me one day?"

Sit for her? Of course he would. Of course. Will felt flattered and he unconsciously sat up a little straighter and forgot for another precious second the weight of the doom hanging over him.

Badger's voice, a natural irritant, caustic to the ears, suddenly intruded on them. "And I'm ashamed to see you wearing leather, Mrs. Lightbody," he rasped. "Ashamed and disappointed. Rarely have I met a woman so well informed about our cause, so devoted and dynamic. Really, though, you must come to terms with *every* aspect of the Vegetarian Ethos, neglecting nothing. Only then can you achieve a complete physiological harmony."

Will tuned him out. "I'd be delighted," he said to Miss Muntz. "After, well . . ." He hesitated. Would he be able to sit? Would he be drawing breath and occupying space? He had a vision of Miss Muntz leaning over him like the hag of death, pressing her cold fingers to the lifeless mask of his face. "I'm going in for surgery today."

"Oh, you, too?" she exclaimed. She seemed strangely excited. "You and Mrs. Tindermarsh on the same day. Well"—drawing a deep breath—"congratulations."

Will gave her a look of bewilderment.

"You'll get well soon, that's what I mean. Isn't that marvelous?" She clapped her hands girlishly, folded her fingers and nibbled thoughtfully at her pale green knuckles. In her decline, she'd taken to progressively more radical cures in a kind of desperate leap at health, and perhaps her values had become distorted. She was even then undergoing one of Dr. Kellogg's newest and—if you believed his self-puffery—most efficacious cures for chlorosis and a host of other conditions, from erysipelas and obesity to ingrown toenails: inhaling radium emanations. Radium, as Will understood it, was some sort of stone that gave off healing rays or vibrations. The Curies had discovered it, along with polonium, and won the 1903 Nobel Prize in Physics in acknowledgment of their achievement in isolating this miraculous substance. Dr. Kellogg had picked right up on it. A stone. A healing stone. It almost sounded pagan.

"Yes," Will agreed, uneasy with the conditions of Miss Muntz's radiant, liver-lipped smile. He was going under the knife, but he put a brave face on it and gave her back her smile. "That will be marvelous. Mrs. Tindermarsh and I will have to kick up our heels and lead the Cotillion. . . . But not this afternoon, I'm afraid. For Lincoln's Birthday—will that satisfy you, Miss Muntz?"

Miss Muntz smiled serenely, the vision of the square-shouldered Tindermarsh in Will's embrace briefly illuminating her ghastly yellow eyes. She was sick. Desperately sick. Will stood abruptly. "Eleanor," he announced, interrupting his wife in the middle of an anecdote about the time she'd arranged a speaking engagement for Lucy Page Gaston, the anti-tobacco crusader, at the Peterskill station, "we need to go now." He leveled a look of annoyance on Badger. "I undergo surgery in less than three hours."

Badger snorted, made some disparaging remark about Dr. Kellogg and his surgical skills, waved his hand in dismissal. Eleanor rose dutifully to join her husband. "It's been a pleasure talking with you, Lionel," she said, "and very enlightening, too."

"Likewise," growled the vegetarian prince, and he bit down hard on his cottage bread.

When the time came, it was Nurse Graves who prepared Will for surgery, and he thanked the Fates that it was she and not Nurse Bloethal, who, as it turned out, was busy irrigating yet another costive bowel with the aid of the Doctor's enema machine. Irene was brisk and beautiful, and though she tried to be as matter-of-fact and businesslike as possible, Will could see that she was concerned for him. Deeply concerned. Concerned above and beyond the call of duty and the normal limitations of the nurse-patient relationship. It was the way she moved and spoke, a certain breathlessness to her voice and an exaggeration of her small movements that betrayed her. She cared for him. She did. And though she hadn't accepted the brooch and though she'd been upset and angry with his lapses, they'd come to a rapprochement in the past weeks and seemed to be on their old footing again. It was an exhilarating thing to be back in her good graces, to see her smile, to joke with her, to participate with her in the team effort that bound them so intimately together—the struggle to salvage the broken heap of his body and soul.

She came for him at eleven o'clock and found him brooding at the window. They made small talk about the groundhog and whether he'd make the event, and then she took his temperature, auscultated him, attached the sphygmomanometer and noted the result on her chart. She gave him a potion to relax him—it felt curiously like the Sears' White Star Liquor Cure, a warmth that spread from his belly to his limbs, his fingers, the tip of his tongue—and then she helped him onto a gurney and Ralph, brawny dependable Ralph, wheeled him to the elevator and thence to surgery.

At a quarter to twelve he was lying in a private anteroom to the surgery, Nurse Graves at his side, waiting for Eleanor. Eleanor had her own morning routine to attend to, so she couldn't be with him through his long wait, but she'd promised to duck out early from her posture therapy session to be with him in his final moments. Irene's voice, soft as a breeze warmed by the sun, floated over him; she held his hand and caught him up on the doings of her brothers and sisters as a way of distracting him—little Philo had fallen through the ice on the pond and the hair froze to his head; Evangeline had blackened two nails on the butter churn; the dogs had trapped a fox in the barn. Will felt lazy, disembodied. Odd moments of his life drifted in and out of his head, and he saw himself as a whiplash of a boy, sound in mind and body, gorging himself on fried chicken on Decoration Day, bicycling through a grove of white birch, fishing under the bridge, stepping out the door on a morning transformed by snow. But then his stomach clenched again. He was going under the knife: that was the reality. The knife. He pictured Mrs. Tindermarsh, that monument of flesh, the sagging belly and drooping breasts, exposed and naked beneath Dr. Kellogg's probing scalpel, the scalpel that sliced, cut, burrowed. "Take me out of here," he croaked, and his own voice startled him. "Irene, take me back to my room, take me away—I don't—I can't—"

Nurse Graves hushed him. She talked, sang, hummed away his fears. The "Brahms Lullaby"? Yes, Brahms. She talked on and on, and as he lay there, his privates swaddled in a sterile towel, she soaped his abdomen and began to shave the little thicket of coiled hairs that flourished there out of sight of the sun. He was vaguely aware of Eleanor bustling into the room, her face hanging over his like a lamp, angry words between his wife and his nurse—*What do you think you're doing to my husband?* —and then Eleanor was gone, the gurney was in motion, the doors parted, and Dr. Kellogg was there, his hygienic beard tucked away beneath a surgical mask.

It was bright. Intolerably bright. He tried to turn his head away, but Ralph was there to hold him down. They fastened his ankles, wrists and elbows, people in masks, their eyes gleaming, soulless, and he was the sacrificial victim, laid out on an ancient slab. Then the mask came to his own face, black rubber, the smell of the ether, sick and sweet, so much richer than air . . . the Doctor's voice speaking to him out of the void, crooning, cajoling, comforting, *Don't struggle now, Mr. Light-body, it'll all be over soon, over soon, over soon . . . and you'll be well again . . . relax now, relax. . . .*

How could he resist that injection? He relaxed. Felt himself drifting. . . .

But then all of a sudden the Doctor's billy-goat beard sprang free of its restraints, bristling and naked, a leer transmogrified the sober face, the hairy hocks of the satyr kicked away the gown, and there was the Doctor's primitive tool, huge and red and swollen, a weapon in his hands, thrusting, thrusting. . . .

And then the scene faded, and all was dark.

Out on the south lawn, warmed by braziers of charcoal and steaming mugs of Sanitas Koko and Kaffir tea, a crowd of some three hundred patients, attendants and townspeople assembled lightheartedly for the main event of the day. There was an air of festivity about the gathering, fostered by the Sanitarium Marching Band, poised to play "Hail to the Chief" the moment the rodent showed its whiskered face and made its momentous choice, and by the smell of roasted chestnuts and broiled Protose that drifted over the scene. Children crowded the groundhog's demesne, their voices airy and bright, the thrill of recess jerking at their limbs and pulling cries of juvenile glee from their throats. They shouted and danced and tore after one another in elaborate games of tag and hide-and-seek. The adults looked on benignly, their own voices no less restrained, and they drank and ate and joked among themselves as if winter really were at an end.

Eleanor was there, standing between Lionel Badger and Frank Linniman. J. Henry Osborne, the Bicycle King, stood off by himself, a mug of cocoa in his hand. Ida Muntz, in a wheelchair, flanked Adela Beach Phillips, the archery champion, and Admiral and Mrs. Nieblock, near the rear of the crowd, were reduced to stitches over the antics of Horace B. Fletcher, who was turning somersaults on the lawn and wearing the expression of a groundhog in heat. The clock struck twelve.

At precisely that moment—and no one knew how the Doctor had managed to arrange it—there was a stirring at the hard frozen lip of the burrow. The laughter died, conversation ceased, a hush fell over the crowd. And there: wasn't that a handful of dirt pitched high in the air?

It was. And now a second clod and a third flew from the burrow. The crowd closed in. All eyes strained to see.

The thing appeared then—simply appeared—emerging from the burrow without ceremony. It was sleek, bottom-heavy, its nose slit, whiskers bright. Was this a groundhog? Was this what they looked like? The crowd held its breath as the rodent scratched at its ear with a vigorous hind paw and gazed up into the sky—and at that moment, as if it had been ordained, the clouds broke and a single narrow tube of light fell across the animal's glistening hide and threw its shadow on the dead yellow grass. That was all it took. The rodent fixed the crowd with eyes like hard black pellets, flung its head over its paws as if it had been electrified and vanished down the hole.

The clouds closed over the sky like a fist.

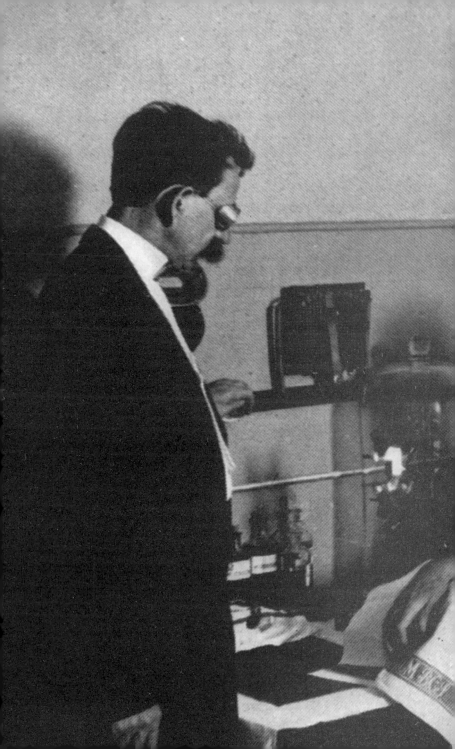

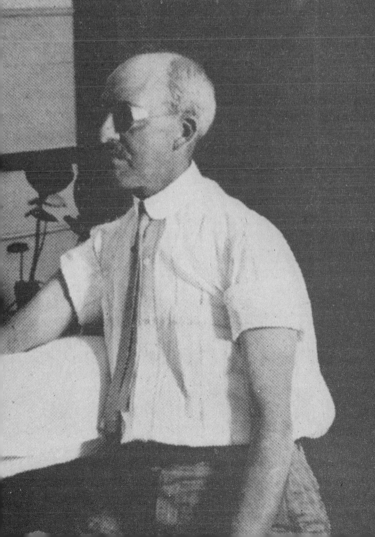

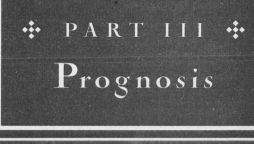

❖ PART III ❖
Prognosis

Chapter 1

Questions, Questions, Questions

❧❦

Spring came late to Battle Creek that year. Two and a half feet of snow fell during the first week of April, riming the catkins of the pussy willows, stupefying the spring peepers in their slippers of mud and providing Bjork Bjorksson with a windfall of baffled skunk, porcupine, beaver and opossum that blundered into his traps. Cows and goats were caught in pasture, sleighs hastily pulled out of storage; two farm wagons and a brand-new Model T Ford automobile collided on the slick Washington Street bridge. On the eighteenth, after a thaw that falsely encouraged the crocuses and snowbells, there was a hard freeze followed by an ice storm that turned the trees to crystal sculptures and the streets to one big interconnected hockey rink. The birds were late, too. The San's feeders were mobbed with sparrows and jays and the starlings that had just begun to colonize the area, but there was no sign of robin, bobolink or oriole. It was May before the skunk cabbage began to push up through the ooze of the swamps, before the rhubarb reddened the back corner of the garden and the spring peepers finally emerged and began abrading the edges of the night with their lovesick vibrato.

Like everyone else in Battle Creek, with the possible exception of Bjork Bjorksson and the odd tobogganist, John Harvey Kellogg was disappointed. He was ready to move on, to fight back ennui with picnic lunches, fishing expeditions, bathing alfresco and the crowning of the

Queen of the May. He'd dyed his beard black and donned a stovepipe hat for Abe Lincoln's birthday, appeared in toga and garland for the Ides of March, set loose a hundred white rabbits at Easter. All in good fun, sure, the entertainments of the season. But for a man who believed in the curative powers of light, the lingering frost was a sore trial. He had all the flowers he wanted, cultivated in the artificial environment of the San's hothouses, and he had his Palm Garden and electric-light boxes, but his Florida tan had long since faded and he'd begun to feel the enervation of the Laplander or the Eskimo, so long deprived of the real thing, Helios, the warm and nurturing sun of the vernal equinox.

On this particular night, a Monday early in May, he was preparing to address his constituency on the subject of the hidden evils of meat. No one had actually asked him to address the subject, nor had anyone deposited the requisite query in the question box during the previous week, but he didn't let that deter him. He'd found over the years that the patients' questions tended to be painfully specific—What do I do about a bunion on the great toe short of changing to a larger shoe size? Miss M.S.; Is a growth on one's neck, just below the right ear, in any way connected to a torpid liver? Mr. R.P.P., Esq.; Can strabismus in a child be corrected by the application of herbal compresses? Mrs. L.L.—and while he took pleasure in answering them and turning the discussion toward the larger picture, he felt no obligation to do so. If no one had submitted a question about the pork muscleworm or the *Taenia saginata*, the common tapeworm, and these happened to be uppermost in his mind, as they now were, well, then, he would speak to those parasites and their very real horrors. The question box was hardly meant to be democratic, after all—he, the physician, was there to tell his patients what they most needed to know. What they *wanted* to know was another thing altogether; sometimes it dovetailed neatly with his own requirements and sometimes it didn't. Tonight was one of the latter occasions. But he did have a demonstration planned for them, oh, yes indeed, one they would never forget.

Bloese called for him in his office at five minutes to eight and the Doctor made his way down the corridor, across the lobby and into the south wing, nodding, smiling and calling out greetings to his patients and staff every step of the way. There was a burst of applause as he

298

entered the Grand Parlor, a burst that rapidly grew in breadth and depth until it rose to the level of ovation as the full complement of the audience became aware of his presence. Modest and neat in one of his summer suits—white, of course, and why not push the season?—he held up his foreshortened arms and called for quiet.

"Welcome, ladies and gentlemen, distinguished guests all," he cried, pausing to clasp his hands together and gaze out on them with a look of saintly benevolence—they were his flock and no harm would come to them. Not for them the hardening of the arteries, the palpitations of the heart, the tumor, the ulcer, the jactitating hand and the faltering step. They were the elect, the chosen, the righteous, and they glowed in his presence.

"Well," he exclaimed, chopping it off abruptly. "In the great spirit of La Vie Simple, let's pitch right into tonight's subject, shall we?" A clearing of the throat, an adjustment of the white-rimmed spectacles. "Yes. We have a question"—unfolding a slip of paper—"from, uh, Mr. W.B.J., regarding the dangers of flesh foods. I quote: 'We have learned that the consumption of animal foods is dangerous in the highest degree; besides being unnatural and against all the laws of God and man, it gives rise to autointoxication and the many illnesses—often fatal if untreated—associated with it. Are there other hidden dangers resulting from flesh consumption, and, if so, what are they?' " The Doctor looked up from the slip of paper. "An excellent question, Mr. W.B.J.—I congratulate you.

"Well, now, aside from the shocking and deplorable conditions in the abattoirs of this country, which I believe I addressed from this podium two weeks ago—was it two or three weeks, Frank?" The Doctor paused, a look of benign consternation on his face, to put the question to Frank Linniman, who sat erect, with his legs neatly crossed, in the front row.

"Two weeks, Doctor," came the reply.

"Yes. Well. For those of you who weren't with us then, let me say that you might consult *The Jungle*, Mr. Upton Sinclair's excellent novel on the subject—and he was our guest here just this past fall, incidentally; a great privilege to have had him—and, of course, my own book on this issue, *Shall We Slay to Eat?*, published and disseminated by our presses here the year previous to Mr. Sinclair's laudable volume, and which is, by the way, available to you all, and at a very small cost, the whole of which helps to sustain this institution and its vital work. . . .

"Be that as it may, I needn't tonight regale you—or should I say horrify you—with tales of animal waste, feces, blood, urine and even vomit being pressed into sausage casings or tins of potted meat, or the practice of grinding up the flesh of tubercular animals—infectious tubercles and all, I might add, a sort of flavoring, as it were—to disguise the foul quality of the meat. . . . I can see at a glance the depth of revulsion you feel at the mere mention of these facts, which are a matter of record, and what civilized person wouldn't recoil from such a horror? Just try to imagine for a moment, won't you, the helpless terror-struck cries of the calves, lambs, piglets, chickens, ducklings and turkeys led to slaughter, the blood of their cousins, their sisters, brothers, the blood of their own progenitors reeking in their nostrils. . . ."

He held up his hands in a gesture of disavowal. "But it is not my intention tonight to enumerate these blasphemies against life and health, blasphemies that continue even as we sit here, that continue despite the efforts of Mr. Sinclair and Dr. Wiley and the Federal Food and Drug Administration and all of us who seek to pursue a sanitary, progressive, pure, kind and enlightened life—no, it is my intention to answer Mr. W.B.J.'s question, to tell you, in all its stomach-turning detail, of an evil far more insidious even." He let his eyes roam over the faces ranged round him, wave upon wave of them, running all the way back to the big oaken doors at the rear of the room and beyond—there must have been twenty or thirty people crowded into the hallway itself. "Tonight, ladies and gentlemen, I would like to tell you something of the parasites—the worms, if you will—that seethe in every morsel of flesh you might consciously or unconsciously have lifted to your lips over the course of a lifetime—prior, that is, to your conversion to biologic living."

It was a moment of delight for the diminutive Doctor, the moment he lived for, the moment when he had his audience right where he wanted them. There wasn't a murmur, a yawn, a sigh: his hold on them was absolute. "All right," he said, "let's take the trichina worm to begin with. *Trichinella spiralis*, to be precise. This scourge of man and animal alike—it's recently been discovered in animals as various as the American black bear and the African hippopotamus—owes its foul existence entirely to carnivorous practices, most particularly, among humans, to the consumption of the flesh of the pig. It is little wonder that the ancients of the Levant, Hebrew and Arab alike, banished this filthy beast from their tables. . . . Would that they had banished mutton and beef as well," he added with a wistful sigh.

"At any rate, pork which has been improperly dressed and inadequately cooked, when ingested, will free the trichina larvae from their capsules, or cysts, cysts in which they dwell for an indeterminate period—years, in many cases—in the muscular flesh of their host. Once that flesh is consumed, the larvae free themselves of their capsules and breed within the digestive system, each worm producing as many as a thousand offspring. The young worms bore through the intestinal walls and are carried in the blood to their final destination, the body's muscular fibers. And there they will lodge, encrusted in the rock-hard cysts they fabricate, until they are in turn eaten. Which in the case of the human being is unlikely, unless one finds oneself at the mercy of a tribe of South Sea cannibals. No: these cysts are permanent. There is no cure."

He paused, waited. What one of them wasn't recalling that distant strip of bacon, the chop, the loin? Half a dozen of the women actually squirmed in their seats.

"I cannot tell you," he went on, his voice somber now, "how much agony I've witnessed as a result of these parasites, all but powerless to help despite the physiologic tools the Almighty has put into my hands. Oh, the grinding shoulders and clacking knees, the infested respiratory muscles, riddled hearts! I had a patient once who came to me after years of heedless abuse—he was an Iowa farmer who had butchered a hog each and every autumn of his life. Well, this poor distressed individual couldn't lift his arms to shoulder level, so riddled was he with trichina cysts. It was heartbreaking. He would try to raise his arms, wincing against the terrible knifing pain. . . ." The Doctor broke off, overcome. His eyes clouded and he struggled with his voice. "I tell you truly, the sound of those cysts grating against bone and sinew alike will never leave me. Friends, it was like the sound of cracking walnuts. Just to lift his arms. Cracking walnuts. Can you for one minute appreciate the pain that must have racked that suffering frame?"

Silence, suitably appalled.

"Mercifully, my friends, he didn't have long to suffer—he was dead at the age of forty, the heart muscle itself invaded by these treacherous parasites, these worms, *worms*, ladies and gentlemen." He shook his head sadly. "And all because he had a taste for pork."

The Doctor went on to illustrate his point with a gimmick similar to the one he'd employed in the instance of Mrs. Tindermarsh's beefsteak. From an icebox located strategically behind him on the platform, he produced a pork shoulder from Tuckerman's Meat Market ("Guaranteed fresh today," he announced breezily), still wrapped in Tuckerman's crisp white paper and fastened with Tuckerman's twine. He instructed Frank Linniman to take three thin-cut samples of the meat and arrange them on slides under the microscopes lined up on the table at the rear of the platform. He then called for three volunteers from the audience to examine the slides, looking for the telltale coils in the striations of the muscular tissue.

John Hampton Krinck, the reprobate, backslider and nihilist, waved his hands energetically, but the Doctor ignored him. What the occasion demanded was a little feminine pulchritude, the well-turned ankle and athletic bosom. And here he missed Ida Muntz, and felt, for just a hairs-breadth of a second, a stab of uncertainty—he'd never have admitted her if he'd suspected just how severe her condition was. Greensickness. It was nothing. And yet she'd been one of his most pronounced failures, the very worst sort of advertisement. At the funeral, her parents— odious people, for all their money—had almost seemed to blame him, as if he hadn't done all he could to undo the years of carnivorous abuse they'd heaped upon her. And yet still he wondered: Had he given her too much of the radium? Not enough? Was the element all it was cracked up to be?

But there was no use in crying over spilt milk, and so he shrugged it off and chose Eleanor Lightbody—stunning woman, beautiful, really, but too thin: had she been starving herself?—and a young lady from Ho-Ho-Kus, New Jersey, who had to supply him with her name—an annoyance: and what was it with names lately; was his mind going now?—and Vivian DeLorbe, the actress from Broadway. All three found the unmistakable evidence, the evil little worms coiled like snails in their shells, just waiting to spring forth and invade the unsuspecting body. Miss DeLorbe even emitted a number of very satisfactory and highly theatrical expressions of disgust.

It was a charming performance, but nothing compared to what came next. Once the stage had been cleared and the audience had had a moment to reflect on the quality of the meat served up by Battle Creek's finest butcher and how that reflected on the quality of the meat served up elsewhere, the Doctor returned to the question of the pseudonymous W. B. J. and spoke at length of the tapeworm. He gave special attention to his description of the adult form and the hooks by which it attaches its scolex to the walls of the human intestine, and when he had suffi- ciently impressed his point on the audience, he asked Frank Linniman to circulate among them while cradling a jar in which a twenty-foot specimen had been preserved.

"I remember the patient well," the Doctor began, reminiscing as the tapeworm made its rounds in Dr. Linniman's capable hands. "He was a man of means, an attorney who'd risen to the top of his profession as a founding partner of one of New York's great law firms—there are few in this room, I'm sure, who will not have heard of it. I was an intern at Bellevue at the time, and the man expired suddenly and without warning, of complications arising from acute autointoxication—he was, from all accounts, a great frequenter of tavern and chophouse. During the autopsy, which I had the dubious honor of supervising, this little specimen turned up, perfectly preserved and still very much alive." There wasn't a face in the room, not even Krinck's, that hadn't gone white. "I just thought I'd share that little story with you," the Doctor went on, "in the event that any of you might be tempted at some point in your life to return to the carnivorous diet. Wiener, anyone? How about a nice rare pork chop?"

There was a flurry of questions, all delivered in hushed bloodless tones, concerning various preparations and types of meat—"Venison?" the Doctor cried at one point, "why, you might just as well swallow the tapeworm eggs themselves and have done with it!"—and an exhaustive comparison of individual symptoms to the effects of the organism at hand. At least a dozen questions began with the hypothetical "What if—?"

Dr. Kellogg was patient with them. After all, by exposing the short-comings of Tuckerman's select pork and showing them that hideous, faceless, hook-headed flatworm in the jar, he'd succeeded in his purpose—that is, to arouse and disgust them and harden their resolution to avoid meat and meat products forever. After half an hour or so, he took a few unrelated questions on heliotherapy, *Naturkultur* and nudism (he approved of it all, even nudism, so long as the sexes were rigidly segregated) and the physiological causes of yawning and the power of suggestion. Then, just when they were worn down emotionally, sapped, exhausted, fighting to maintain the proper physiologic posture in their orthopedic chairs, the Doctor brought on his showstopper.

The yawning question had given rise to an epidemic of that oral phenomenon, and Dr. Kellogg was just winding up his comments— "Bathing the face with cold water, drinking a glass of hot or cold water or some refreshing beverage will generally cause the disposition to yawn to disappear"—when Dr. Linniman, having disburdened himself of the pickled tapeworm, strolled casually into the room with Fauna, the timber wolf, on a leash.

The crowd immediately came to life. Fauna wasn't perhaps the crowd pleaser that Lillian the chimp was, but her appearance signaled one of the Doctor's stunts. Heads turned. The yawning ceased. A whisper of voices buzzed up and down the aisles. Dr. Kellogg beamed as Frank, with his fair hair and physiologic jaw, made his way up the aisle, the wolf padding docilely at his side. To the Doctor's keen eye, the animal's faults stood out in sharp relief—the uneven stride, the dysplastic hips, the dullness of the eyes and the discolored swath of hair along the underbelly where Murphy had neglected to powder her. The question of her diet had been the very devil from the beginning—the Doctor gave her peanuts and vegetable milk, Protose, cornmeal and wheat gluten, and he saw that her bowel was kept rigorously clean, but there was something lacking. On close inspection, the animal just didn't look healthy. Still—and he released a small grunt of satisfaction—no one would notice. No: all they saw was a magnificent creature, a big white vegetarian wolf, rescued from the wild as a pup and fed up to adulthood on Sanitarium fare.

Frank brought her up to the platform and handed her leash to the Doctor. The wolf, who knew her part as well as Lillian knew hers and was a whole lot more tractable to boot, gazed out calmly on the audience, as pure and rugged a symbol of nature as anything Jack London had to offer. She licked the Doctor's hand and then settled down on her haunches, as comfortable as a retriever sitting before the fire. The Doctor waited until Frank Linniman had descended from the stage and left the room, and then he began his commentary in an easy off-the-cuff manner.

"You all know Fauna," he said, laying a hand on the broad white head. "You've all seen her at play on the Sanitarium lawns, watched as she gamboled and cavorted with our deer and the conies we released at Easter. But one thing you've never seen is this animal's wolfish nature. For you forget, ladies and gentlemen, that Fauna is no lapdog, no collie or shepherd, but a wolf, of that ravening breed that has been a bane to humankind from time immemorial, a real live wild wolf recovered from the wastes of the Northwest, at the very remotest tip of Lake Superior. But would she harm a hair of my head? Of yours? Would she dream of falling on those placid and innocent does and rabbits?" He patted her, and again she licked his hand (he made a mental note to wash up the minute he left the podium). "No, my friends and fellow seekers after the biologic ideal, of course she wouldn't. And you all know the reason why—because she has never experienced nature red in tooth and claw, never killed, never once tasted meat. She was as yet unweaned when she was brought to us, and she has been fed exclusively on the foods that you and I customarily consume, a champion and exemplar of the vegetarian diet."

At that moment, the crowd at the entranceway parted and again Dr. Linniman entered the room. This time he was accompanied by a pair of husky attendants bearing a cage, from the depths of which issued a steady savage warning growl, a rumbling antiphon of rage and hate broken only by the odd snarling insuck of breath. There was danger in the room. The audience felt it, and it poked at their spines, got the ancestral juices flowing, elevated the short hairs at the napes of their necks. Fauna felt it, too. Her ears went erect and she let out a barely audible whimper, but the Doctor silenced her with a surreptitious kick.

When the cage was delivered to the platform, its occupant became visible to all: a second wolf, black as a dream in the deadest hour of the night, crouched against the bars, its eyes flaring yellow, knotted strings of saliva dangling from the white flash of its teeth. The Doctor had to raise his voice to be heard above it. "Calm yourselves, ladies and gentlemen. Believe me, this is a demonstration only. No harm will come to any of you." The audience was stirred up, not simply buzzing but distressed, exclamatory, cacophonous even. The Doctor had to clap his hands sharply to get their attention. "Ladies and gentlemen, calm yourselves," he repeated.

Though they quieted then, the Doctor held off. He merely stood there, the white wolf lying placidly at his feet, its counterpart tearing at the bars of its cage, giving the audience the benefit of a good long look at the tableau he'd arranged for them. Finally he spoke. "You've all had an opportunity in these last few minutes to observe the radical disparity in temperament between these two beasts, beasts of the same species, though judging from appearances you might find it hard to believe. The second wolf—that's a boy, yes, yes, growl for us now—as I say, the second wolf, until seven days ago, knew nothing but the reign of unholy terror that rules the forest day and night—and not just in some dimly imagined Western setting, but here in the fens and glades of Michigan. Yes, here. This specimen was brought to me by one Bjork Bjorksson, a local trapper, who caught him in a leg snare not twenty miles from where you now sit." Master of the moment, Dr. Kellogg paused to let this information have its effect. "And do any of you doubt, on the evidence, that *this* wolf means you no harm? Or that *this* wolf would roll playfully across our lawns with the young of our deer herd?"

As if on cue, the caged wolf raised the level of its growl a decibel or two. The Doctor's point was taken.

"And what is the difference between the two—the one fed on bloody chunks of raw meat torn piecemeal from its prey, the other on vegetable things? Would any man or woman amongst you care to experience the emotions of the beast in that cage? Yes? I don't hear you." Silence, but for the steady crosscut growl. "Well, just feed yourselves up on meat, then, on caffeine, bourbon whiskey and tobacco, and you'll know the rage in that heart. But let's have a demonstration, shall we? Frank? Frank, where are you?"

Frank Linniman, efficient and obliging as ever, was there to assist him, rising from a chair at the foot of the platform as if the Doctor were working him with levers. "Yes, Doctor?"

Perfect. Couldn't have been smoother if they'd rehearsed it. "May we have the other package from Tuckerman's Meat Market, please?"

And here, Frank mounted the platform, bent to the icebox and retrieved a second package wrapped in butcher's paper: inside was a prime beefsteak, marbled with fat and oozing blood, a steak not dissimilar to the Post Tavern issue of November's demonstration. But how many of them remembered back that far? The San had turned over at least half or more of its clientele since then—and if some few of them had been present, what did it matter? The more he impressed upon his audience the perils of meat eating, the more the Doctor was doing to save their lives—and the lives of their children and their children's children. Slipping on his gloves—this was the danger, this red and dripping time bomb, not the animal in the cage—the Doctor lifted the steak from its paper nest and laid it on the floor at Fauna's feet.

The wolf sniffed, sniffed again. Then she looked up helplessly at the shining Doctor, whimpered, and backed away as far as the leash would take her. "You see?" the Doctor cried, and he couldn't begin to count the number of solemnly nodding heads. "She will *not* eat this obscene and unnatural food, not by choice or preference—or even, at the risk of inflaming the Society for the Prevention of Cruelty to Animals, by compulsion." (What he didn't mention was that she had been trained, through negative reinforcement, to view meat as the prelude to a beating—just touch her tongue to it and she was whipped—or that her vegetarian diet had so weakened her, she wouldn't have had the strength to chew it in any case.)

Making a face, the Doctor bent to retrieve his lump of flesh, and after handing Fauna's leash to Frank Linniman, he crossed the stage and gingerly dangled the steak over the cage. As he'd approached, the growling rose in volume, but now suddenly it choked off entirely and for the first time since the caged wolf had entered the door, the room was silent. The silence held a second longer, and then the wolf lunged at the meat with a snarl and bolted it as if it hadn't eaten in a week. (Which it hadn't.) But was it thankful? Not a bit of it. The moment the beast's throat was clear it started in again, and, if anything, it was louder now, more ferocious and hateful. The Doctor made a feint for the cage and the animal threw itself at the bars, gagging on its rage. "Is that gratitude for you?" he asked, and one or two members of the audience gave an uneasy chuckle, but then he was bowing like an orchestra leader and with a nod and smile recognizing his co-performers, the white wolf and the black, and the applause rose up to engulf him: the show was over. Or so they thought. But the impresario of health, the preceptor of the stage and resuscitator of the race had one more surprise in store for them.

"I thank you all, ladies and gentlemen, for your attention tonight. The Question Box lecture has now come to an end, but I'll be back next week, same time and place, with my trusty assistant, Dr. Frank Linniman"—a spatter of applause—"to answer your health questions. And now, before you hurry off to tonight's reception in the Palm Garden, I'd like to leave you with this, a thought for the evening, as it were. . . ." He cleared his throat, adjusted his spectacles. "It's a poem I've written for the occasion of this lecture and demonstration. . . . I call it 'Methuselah':

No fish was he fed,
No blood did he shed.
And he knew when he had eaten enough.
And so it is plain
He'd had no cause to complain
Of steaks that were measly or tough.
Or bearded beef grimy,
Green, moldy and slimy,
Of cold-storage turkeys and putrid beefsteaks,
With millions of colon germs,
Hams full of trichina worms,
And sausages writhing with rheumatiz-aches.
Old Methuselah dined
On ambrosia and wined

On crystal-pure water from heaven-filled springs.
Flesh foods he eschewed,
Because, being shrewd,
He chose Paradise fare and not packing-house things.

The balding head shot up again and an antic smile played across the Doctor's face. "And how long did *he* live, my friends?"

Will Lightbody stood beneath the banana tree in the Palm Garden, a cup of Kaffir tea in one hand, a bran-nut health cookie in the other. The tea smelled and tasted like something you might use on the woodshed to discourage dry rot, and the cookie, though vaguely sweet, had the consistency of animal fodder. Still, Will was glad to be admitting this liquid and this food to his body—any liquid or any food, for that matter, so long as it didn't look, feel, smell or taste like milk or grapes, or contain, in even trace amounts, any milk or grape products. Actually, milk was a fading memory, though his throat still seized up at the thought of it—at the moment, it was the grape that was uppermost in his mind. He'd been on the grape diet until eight days ago, taking in nothing but grapes, grapes in all their varieties and guises, from Concord jelly on muscadine halves to Tokay pudding, black-currant stew and tall unending glasses of faintly cloudy thrice-strained Sanitarium-blessed grape juice. But no wine, of course. Not a drop of the only form in which grapes would ever again be acceptable to him, even if he should live to be twice as old as Methuselah.

Grapes. The very thought of them, of the way they popped individually between the teeth to release their pulpy, mucousy load, to the bitterness of their seeds, to the blatant bulbous sight of them, gathered to the vine like little cannonballs, dollops of lead, mucilage, poison, was enough to send him gagging for the toilet. Whenever he spotted some poor deluded soul picking away at a plate of peeled Perlettes in a forlorn corner of the dining room, he had to turn his head. He couldn't help himself. Toward the end he would awaken in the night, certain that he was in the grip of a thick ropy vine, leaves sprouting behind his ears, tendrils creeping down his throat to strangle him, and he'd find himself heaving up off the bed, gasping for breath. In the morning, he would sneak off to the toilet before Nurse Bloethal could catch him, and deposit whole strings of perfect little royal-purple spheres in the white porcelain basin.

But now he was drinking Kaffir tea and eating cookies. He hadn't gained any weight—had lost a good fifteen pounds, in fact—and he stood there in his dinner clothes like an animated coat rack. Beneath the starched white shirtfront, which was fastened with onyx studs and secured by his black satin cummerbund, he wore a summer undershirt, and beneath the undershirt, he wore a neat and tidy six-inch scar, a single railway spur running up the slope of his abdomen. This was Dr. Kellogg's handiwork. He'd done the cutting, the delving, the poking and removing, and he'd done the sewing, too. It was said among the patients that in idle moments, while traveling or dictating, the Doctor often practiced his sewing on articles of the children's clothing, keeping his eye sharp, his fingers nimble and his stitches tight. Will couldn't speak to that, but he couldn't complain, either: the wound had healed beautifully. Of course, as far as he could tell, the operation hadn't accomplished a thing. Oh, perhaps the fire in his gut had been damped a notch or two, like the flame under a kettle set on a gas range, but it was there still, burning, burning.

He had questions about that, of course, questions he'd like to bring up during one of the Chief's absurd lectures—really, the wolf in the cage had been too much, though he had to admit it was high entertainment—but he hadn't quite got up the nerve. And in private, consulting with Linniman or the bearded little saint himself, Will had learned not to complain, learned to fake recovery, in fact. It was either that or drown in milk and die of grapes. His father had told him to go ahead and stay for as long as it took—he'd long since found a replacement for him at the Water Street plant, and Will's position there had never been more than ceremonial in any case—and Eleanor, after six solid months, still showed no inclination to leave. And so here he was, in Battle Creek, at the Sanitarium, paying a monthly stipend to the Kellogg coffers that would have bankrupted any number of South American dependencies, and improving at a glacial rate. He figured that if he stayed on into the 1920s the flame might almost be extinguished (until he lit it again with booze, cigars, coffee and porterhouse steak—and there was no sense in living at all if you had to abjure those things forever), but he'd weigh less than he had at birth. It was a real conundrum, and he was brooding over it and working his tongue up behind his molars to dislodge a stubborn fragment of bran-nut cookie, when Eleanor entered the room in the company of Dr. Frank Linniman.

Eleanor had lingered in the Grand Parlor with a group of enthusiasts to exclaim over the Doctor's performance, and Will had left her to wait here alone under the saw-toothed fronds, dipping his boredom into the noxious tea like a crust of stale bread. She came up to him now with a swish of her skirts and emitting a sort of clucking, cooing sound that set his teeth on edge, and already she was gushing on about something—pottery shards, skull fragments, some sort of expedition she was planning with Frank, precious Frank, who stood smiling at her side. "Only for a morning and an afternoon," she gasped, looking up into his eyes and glancing away again, as if she already knew what she'd discover there and didn't find it worth examining. "Virginia Cranehill will be going, too. And perhaps Lionel."

"Expedition?" he echoed, but she'd already turned away, distracted by a bloated matron in yellow taffeta who just happened to have organized her own deep-breathing club in Milwaukee and would be the happiest thing alive if she could inveigle her way into Eleanor's group. A further flutter of skirts and they were gone. Will was left alone with Linniman. For lack of an alternative, he gave him a partial smile.

Linniman was studying him with a doctorly eye. "Feeling up to snuff lately?" he asked. "Taking to the new dietary?"

"Food, you mean?" Will said. "Yes. Sure. It's been proven advisable in the human diet, essential, even, hasn't it? By all those teams of health professionals and researchers, I mean."

Linniman wouldn't rise to the bait. He just smiled and nodded, his breathing easy, features composed, mind elsewhere. Will had a sudden urge to drive a fist into his physiologic gut and leave him writhing on the floor, but he resisted it. "What's this expedition Eleanor's talking about?"

"Oh, that." Linniman, who'd been watching someone across the room, came back to him. "My phrenological studies. So much has been done with the modern skull, but hardly anything at all with the ancient. We've just found an Indian site—pre-Potawatomi, by all indications—out in the Springfield area, to the west of town. Professor Gunderson —you've seen him here, the rachitic little man with the lame leg?—well, he's been staying with us to combat severe autointoxication, but he's an archaeologist by trade. He discovered the site. But he's offered me the opportunity to collect some of the skulls."

"And Eleanor?"

Linniman looked him right in the eye. "I won't say she's bored, but it's been a long winter. I've managed to interest her in my work—or hobby, I should say. My proper work is healing, of course."

"Of course," Will agreed.

"We're going to determine the intellectual capacities and affective propensities of these bygone Indians as a matter of curiosity—and we'll preserve the skulls in my collection, that goes without saying. It should be good for her. Fresh air, sunshine."

"She'll be digging, you say?"

"Oh, no, no." Linniman let out a tightly controlled little laugh. "Heavens, no. We've hired a pair of laborers to do the physical work —neither Professor Gunderson nor Eleanor is in any shape to take on that sort of strenuous activity—not yet, at any rate. Good God, man, you should know that. Do you think I would subject your wife to anything she wasn't fully prepared for?"

Will didn't like the sound of the terminology here: *subject your wife.* Subject his wife, indeed. He'd like to subject this grinning hyena to some strenuous activity, and it wouldn't be digging, either. He was rankled, he was irritated, but he let it go. What could he do about it? He could already feel the molten finger poking at the cookie in the frying pan of his stomach, and he wasn't inclined to physical violence in the best of times. Besides which, Eleanor would do exactly as she pleased, whether he liked it or not. She would go on her expedition, and Will would grit his teeth.

Of course, if he felt impotent in the current instance, that was the way of the San. Homer Praetz had been right: it was the Doctor's method to reduce you to dependency, to a second infancy, and if you wanted to get out of diapers you had to put up with his spoon-feeding, with his grapes and sinusoidal currents and his eternal glasses of milk, not to mention his asinine lectures and the rigid segregation of lawfully married couples. But as Will looked at Linniman standing there before him, sinewy and disdainful, symbol and bulwark of everything the San stood for, he felt a surge of independence: Will had a secret. And it had to do with just that—impotence. Not the psychological sort, the sort he'd just suffered at the hands of Eleanor and her dubious "expedition" in the company of three men, at least two of whom were bachelors, or the sort fostered by the pampering, cajoling and browbeating of the San's staff, but the very real physical impotence he'd inexplicably experienced on that cold November night when Eleanor had invited him to inseminate her.

It had alarmed him. Terrified him. Made him feel old and used up and deeply ashamed, too. The Great Healer had been no help—he'd thrown it right back in his face, taunted him with it, made him feel depraved and deluded even to think of exercising his marital urges. He had seemed glad that Will was incapable, exultant even. But Will wasn't glad. Though the condition seemed to come and go in the oddest way and at the oddest times, on the three or four occasions he'd gone back to Eleanor and she hadn't dismissed him out of hand, he'd had the same problem. He wondered if the whole thing wasn't connected in some way to his stomach.

"Care for a cup of Kaffir tea?" Linniman asked, looking for an excuse to move on.

"Thank you, no," Will said, waving the empty cup under Linniman's nose, "I've already had one. And one is plenty—too much, in fact. Way too much."

Linniman merely grunted. "Nice talking to you," he said, already ambling off in the direction of the refreshments.

What the fair-haired boy didn't know, or Dr. Kellogg, either, was that Will was striking out on his own. Intrepidly. Courageously. He'd had to overcome his aversion to Sears products and to electrotherapy to boot, but he was desperate, half a man, a eunuch, progenitor of no one and nothing, and one afternoon, browsing through the Sears catalogue in the San library, he'd come across an ad for the Heidelberg

Belt. The ad showed a mustachioed gentleman with a decidedly phys-iologic build, naked but for a pair of undershorts and the electric belt, which he wore just over his navel and which blossomed with bursts of miniature lightning bolts. The lightning bolts—potent, vital, totems of Thor, Zeus, Crazy Horse—were clustered round his front and hips, and, indeed, the product promised relief from "disorders of the nerves, stom-ach, liver and kidneys," but what caught Will's eye was a larger and more detailed representation of the belt at the bottom of the page. Here, one could plainly see the attachment—"the electric sack suspensory"—with its cup for the sexual organs. The same lightning bolts, though drawn more delicately so as not to alarm the potential purchaser, danced round the cup in radiant display.

Will studied the ad for an hour. *Don't suffer in silence,* he read, *don't endure in secret. $18.00 will buy our Giant Power 80-Gauge Current Gen-uine Heidelberg Electric Belt. $18.00 will bring you health and strength, superb manliness and youthful vigor.* Superb manliness and youthful vigor—it was what he wanted, no doubt about it. But the image of Homer Praetz rose up before him, the face distorted in death, the eyes like two poached eggs, the thin useless flap of the severed tongue pinned to his collar like a medal. That was electricity. That was a cure. But it wasn't so much the current as the medium that had contributed to that tragedy—the water, that is—and there would be no water involved with the Heidelberg Belt; it was hardly a bath apparatus, after all. Will would wear it to bed, removing it at dawn before Irene or Nurse Bloethal could catch sight of it. And it was good for the stomach, too—that's what the ad said: *The Heidelberg Belt, for disorders of the nerves, stomach, liver and kidneys, is worth all the drugs, chemicals, pills, tablets, washes, injections and other remedies put together*—and maybe, just maybe, he'd be killing two birds with one stone. It took him an hour, but in the end, Will decided to invest his eighteen dollars and sent for the belt.

And it was working, too—at least it seemed to be. At least when Nurse Graves was present, in any case. He hadn't yet tried it out on Eleanor—the thing had come only two weeks ago—but the very first morning, as Irene was administering his morning enema, he felt himself growing hard, embarrassingly so, hard as a steel rod, a baseball bat, a great stiff oak rooted deep in the earth. The moment was inappropriate and he must have colored with shame, but he couldn't help exulting, too. He wondered if Irene had noticed and, if she had, what she thought about it. She hadn't said a word, and he couldn't very well ask her— or could he? She'd kissed him, after all, deeply, practically melted in his arms, and she'd as much as admitted her affection for him. And what should come after the kiss, if not the caress, and then the act itself? He was ruminating on the situation, still planted beneath the banana tree, the empty cup clutched absently in his hand, when there was a visible stirring in the room—even the rubber plant seemed to stand up and take notice—and Dr. Kellogg, trailed by half a dozen luminaries and dogged by Lionel Badger, made his entrance.

Eleanor was one of the first to move toward them, as if by force of magnetic attraction, leaving the matron in taffeta to fend for herself. Will couldn't help smiling on seeing the Doctor, fresh from his triumph among the wolves and the worms, hounded by this rasping fanatic who seemed to have taken the higher moral ground in the contest of vegetarian wills. As the little Doctor called out his greetings, making his way from one smiling group to another, Will almost felt sorry for him. He might have built an empire, might have made health a religion and longevity a sacrament, but he still couldn't shake crackpots like Badger and competitors like Post, Macfadden and the Phelps brothers—and for all his treatments, for all his vibrating stools and salt-mush rubs and enemas, for all his oceans of herbal tea and mountains of Nuttose, he couldn't begin to compete with the Heidelberg Belt.

Will was distracted by the Countess Tetranova, who laid a hand on his arm, peered up myopically out of her vague Russian eyes and asked if he might get her a cup of Kaffir tea. She was a small woman, no bigger than a twelve-year-old boy, or constructed any differently, so far as the eye could see, and her features were invested with the pallor and the blandness of the steppe. Since their Christmas trip to Irene's family farm, she'd considered Will a great friend, often interrupting his progress through the San to allow him the privilege of fetching her one thing or another. Polite, eternally polite, Will had obeyed her without demur, but he wasn't enthusiastic about her friendship. She didn't appeal to him. She was no Miss Muntz, but, then, he had to remind himself that Miss Muntz was no more. If she could be said to exist at all, it was as a bald-headed corpse in a vault of dirt in Poughkeepsie, New York, food for worms, a collection of soup bones gone bad in the icebox. Will had attended the service for her in the Sanitarium chapel. It hadn't been well advertised—death, after all, was bad for business.

Will brought the Countess her tea and watched as she took half a dozen tentative little sips, dipping her head to the saucer like a sparrow at the birdbath. "A rich brew," she said, raising her chin to him, the cup balanced neatly on its saucer. "It never ceases to amaze me how Dr. Kellogg manages to make healthful things so appealing to the palate. Don't you agree?"

Will didn't agree—he violently disagreed, in fact. Boiled turpentine couldn't have tasted any worse. But it would have been rude to say so, and as the Countess seemed happy in her delusion, he got away with a noncommittal grunt. She didn't pursue the issue, but instead made some banal comment about the cut of Mrs. Tindermarsh's dress—"Charming, isn't it?"—and Will, dutiful and correct, uttered a banality in reply. It was just then that the little group surrounding the Doctor made its way up to them, the Great Healer playing the room like a politician on election eve, patting elbows, chucking chins, whispering confidences into waiting ears. Eleanor was at his left hand, Badger at his right. The Countess fawned; Will tried to look both healthy and pleased to see him.

"Countess," the Doctor purred, bowing deeply and taking her hand lightly in his, "a pleasure as always. And I expect that little problem we spoke of last week has corrected itself?"

The Countess was murmuring her gracious thanks, at length—yes, she was so much better now, just as he'd predicted, but she didn't want to be accused of symptomitis, so she'd just hold her peace—when the Doctor turned to Will. "And Lightbody," he breathed, eyeglasses throwing light, a foxy, self-satisfied look stamped into his face, "bearing up, I take it?"

Will's reply, sunnily delivered, was lost in the nagging rasp of a Badger tirade on the subject of a petition drive to close down a tannery in Michigan City, Indiana. Badger had been haranguing Eleanor, but now he insinuated himself between Will and the Doctor, grinding on about the stink of the hides, the barbarity of the whole concept—why not just go back to living in caves and get it over with?—and his breath, reeking of garlic—latest thing, keeps the blood flowing and the heart strong—seemed to choke the air from the room. Will could see that the Doctor was irritated, that he couldn't stand being upstaged, even for a minute—leonine, saintly, Chief of it all, he still didn't know quite what to do with the vegetable puritan at his side. Will enjoyed the flash of annoyance in the Doctor's eye, and he egged Badger on, asking a disingenuous question about the antivivisection rally in Cleveland, and as Badger took the thought up and chewed it over, the Doctor made as if to excuse himself.

He never got the chance.

All of a sudden, the murmur of polite chitchat that had held the room in its convivial grip fell away to nothing. There was one stunned interval of five seconds during which the only voice to be heard in the room, naked now and unconscious of its nakedness, was Badger's. All heads had turned to the rear exit, where the kumquat tree wrestled with a scattering of flowering vines and birds of paradise. There was a man there, medium height, unshaven, his hair wildly unkempt, his suit like cheesecloth, smudges of dirt on his visible flesh like deep blue bruises. He clutched a jumble of newspaper under one arm and worked a match-box in trembling hands. And why did he look so familiar? Where had Will seen him?

Before the murmur could resume, before anyone could say anything, the man—he might have been a boy, actually, still in his teen years; the dirt and dishevelment made it hard to judge—produced a match, crumpled a ball of newsprint, and set it afire. Someone cried out. The flaming ball of paper shot like a rocket over the heads of the crowd, the soft fanning *whoosh* of the flames sustaining it in its flight. But then the man lit another, and another, and the cry became general. An instant later, as the pyromaniac danced gleefully round the room flinging his missiles to the wind, pandemonium seized the crowd.

"George!" roared the Doctor, and the Doctor knew him, knew this mindless anarchist with his paper bombs, and now there was a nascent fire among the palm husks in the corner and the woman in yellow taffeta was suddenly fanning a quick bright little jewel of flame at her bodice. People were running. The smell of incineration startled the air. A man in a wheelchair, seated just to one side of the fish pond, collapsed without a word into the reedy murk. Exotic plants were trampled. The exits were clogged. "George!" the Doctor cried. "George!"

Will stood rooted to the spot. But he reached out a hand for Eleanor, pressed her to him. "My God," she gasped, her shoulders buried in his chest as women shrieked and Badger gaped and the Doctor, Linniman and a small army of attendants threw themselves into the fray, chasing the interloper like hounds, "what's happening?"

It was a good question. Will didn't know, didn't have the faintest idea. But judging from the look on the Doctor's face, he couldn't help suspecting that the Chief knew all about it.

Chapter 2

The Letter
and the
Note

P ressed close to his hammering heart, in the left breast pocket of the very suit in which he'd transported Mrs. Hookstratten's $3,849 from New York, Charlie Ossining carried the letter that had arrived at Mrs. Eyvindsdottir's two days earlier. He carried the letter where he could feel it against his flesh, wearing it in the way a monk might wear his hair shirt, in fear and trembling. From the moment it had come, his prospects, which had been dismal enough to begin with, suddenly became superfluous, a dream to be discarded, wadded up and tossed in the rubbish like the rag they used on the spittoons at the Red Onion. He took no notice of the sun, the budding trees, the daffodils, azaleas, dogwood, the greening lawns and pollen-drunk bees—it might just as well have been winter still. As far as he was concerned, it *was* winter, deepest winter—and what was he going to do?

He was going to Bender, for one thing. On foot. Head down, moving along with the brisk heedless stride of the soul in torment, and no, he wasn't wearing the sandwich board, and no, he didn't feel guilty about it, either. What sense did advertising make if the whole world was crashing down around your ears? Of course he'd gone to Bender the minute the letter arrived, and then again yesterday, and Bender had cooed and hummed and purred and given his assurances and his vows and patted Charlie's hand and poured out anaesthetic doses of Otard

Dupuy and reasoned and remonstrated with him—and what good had it done? None. Zero. Zilch. What was he going to tell Mrs. Hook-stratten? How could he face her? He was just rounding the corner at McCamly, brisk-legging it up the street, when he thought of the alternative: not to face her at all. To vanish. Skip town. *Poof:* the disappearing act. All he had to do was keep walking till he reached the depot, get on the train and ride till the sun exhausted itself.

But even as he thought of the coward's way out, he felt the sharp edge of the envelope stabbing through his shirt, and knew he couldn't do it, not to Mrs. Hookstratten. Not to her. Never. All of a sudden he jerked himself to a halt and tore the letter out of his pocket, poring over it for the hundredth time, hoping against all reason that its meaning and configuration had somehow changed.

They hadn't.

He stood there in the middle of the sidewalk, head sunk into his chest, shoulders slumped, reading, and his lips moved and his voice underscored the words in a sort of moan. People stepped around him. A woman in a hat as wide around as a wagon wheel gave him a look of alarm and the man in front of the cigar store, lounging in a rocker beside his carved Indian, gave him a good long unabashed stare. But what did Charlie care—was he an investor? Was she Mrs. Hookstratten? He read and moaned, spelling out the sentence of his doom yet one time more:

> Twin Oaks
> Lounsbury Pond
> Peterskill
> Monday, May 4, 1908

Dear Charles:

I hope this finds you well and our spanking new breakfast-food factory thriving (how I *do* love mahogany—it's the perfect choice for the offices; you've acquired exquisite taste somewhere along the line, and I can't help thinking your Auntie Hookstratten has had more than a little to do with it). But that Per-Fo flies! It's all very exciting.

But I anticipate myself: that's what I wanted to tell you. Good news, dearest boy. I'm coming to visit. Auntie Hookstratten, who used to bounce you on her knee, who used to make all your little hurts and troubles go away as if they'd never existed, is on the way. Yes! To Battle Creek!

Yes, Charles, it's true! And not just for a whistle-stop visit (is that what they call it?), but to stay and settle in. You see, I've been in touch with Eleanor Lightbody, from Peterskill (you do know her, don't you—charming woman), and she's convinced me of what I already knew in my heart but wouldn't admit—and what Dr. Brillinger has known for two years now . . .

Well, it's my nerves. It's as simple as that. Dr. Kellogg will be admitting me to the Sanitarium for tests a week from today, and though we can't know what we'll find or how long the cure will take, I've made arrangements to stay through the end of June, at the very least.

I'm terribly excited, darling! I'm thrilled and elated! Already, now that the decision has been made, I can feel myself growing better and calmer—and I just know that seeing you, and all you've accomplished, will be the crowning touch.

You have all my love.

Sincerely,
(Auntie) Amelia

Eleanor Lightbody, eh? He cursed her aloud for a meddling bitch, and the cigar-store man dropped his eyes, suddenly absorbed in contemplation. And what else had she told the old lady? That she'd seen the President-in-Chief of the Per-Fo Company on the street in a sandwich board, touting a nonexistent product like a door-to-door peddler, like a rag-and-bone man? *God*: he had to close his eyes and massage his temples over the memory.

It was Bender who'd set him up for that. After the absolute, utter and unqualified failure of the manufacturing attempt in the Bookbinder basement, Bender had disappeared on an extended sales trip, but so as to occupy his partner's time while he was away, he'd convinced Charlie that local advertising was the key to their success: if they could establish a presence in Battle Creek, Foodtown, U.S.A., they could do it any-

where. That was clout. Real clout. And how could they advertise—
really blanket the town—in the most economical way? Well, Charlie
wouldn't really be doing anything while Bender was out stumping his
samples all over God's Creation and breaking his back lining up accounts, would he?

And so, long before the weather turned, before the grizzled ice fell
back to the curbs and the snowfields turned to mud, before people felt
the urge to leave the coal-stoked warmth of their homes and businesses
to take a turn round the streets, Charlie Ossining was beating the
pavement sandwiched between two stiff new sheets of plywood that
read, front and back: PER-FO, THE NEWEST HEALTH TREAT FROM KELLOGG!
MAKES ACTIVE BLOOD! TRY A BOX TODAY! Of course, there were no boxes
to try, aside from the samples stuffed with Will Kellogg's genuine
article—and they were in Bender's possession, God only knew where.
Charlie protested, but Bender had assured him they'd be creating a
demand by withholding the product from the public—if you believed
Bender it was the greatest advertising gimmick since free samples. People
couldn't get it, right? he'd asked, putting on his rhetorical face. And
when people can't get a product, what do they do—they get frustrated,
right? Bender had held his smile a good long moment, his proposition
self-evident—even a simpleton could see that. When they got the stuff
on the shelves, he assured Charlie, there'd be riots in the aisles—why,
people would buy up three and four boxes at a time, just to have it, just
for insurance.

Charlie gave in. He walked the streets, a living billboard, a barker,
a shill, and he felt like an idiot. The first day, a blustery March afternoon,
dust, soot, fragments of leaf, paper and horse detritus leaping up into
the air in a thousand whirling cyclones, he ducked into an alley whenever he saw someone coming. But then he steeled himself—maybe
Bender was right, maybe they *were* creating a demand that would pay
out a hundred times over—and he kept at it, making an effort to fight
down his humiliation and show off his slogans to anyone and everyone
with eyes in his head and a working knowledge of the English language.
It wasn't a raging success. Children shied away from him, pedestrians
looked through him, shopkeepers turned the other way. Dogs, he didn't
bother with.

By the end of the week, though, the whole business had become second nature to him, and he was no more conscious of those two flaps of plywood than he might have been of his overcoat or shoes: the sandwich board was a part of him and he began to feel incomplete without it. When he got back to Mrs. Eyvindsdottir's in the evenings, his feet aching, hands gone dead from the cold, he slipped out of the straps and thought he would float away. It felt strange to mount the stairs to his room and not have to walk sideways, to eat sitting down and have nothing more than his own head to support on his shoulders, odd to stretch out on the bed and smoke a cigarette without his wooden frame to enclose him. The weeks passed in a blur, one day indistinguishable from the next. He was a drone, a drudge. He walked the streets of Battle Creek from first light to sundown, and never a thought passed through his head.

Until he ran into Eleanor, that is. It was a raw day, around the beginning of April, a thick misting rain making the air palpable, the streets all but deserted. Charlie was wet through to his long johns, his bowler shapeless and spongelike, strands of wet hair glued to his forehead and a persistent running drip cascading from the tip of his nose and trailing down the front plane of the sandwich board in a thin fan of tributaries. He was crouched beneath the awning out front of Sherwin's Grocery, trying to light a wet cigarette, when he glanced up and found himself staring into those cool appraising eyes for the first time since he'd sat across the table from them at Christmas.

"Mr. Ossining," Eleanor chirped, "is that really you? Yes? What a surprise to see you—wet enough for you?" She was gathered beneath a parasol along with a tall, rawboned man with sunken eyes and a fringe of vaguely reddish hair poking out from beneath the brim of his hat. He wasn't her doctor, and he wasn't her husband. Charlie had never laid eyes on him before.

"Eleanor." Charlie cleared his throat. The match sputtered, the cigarette dissolved in his hand. He wondered if she knew about the thousand dollars he'd got from her husband, speculated on her choice of the formal "Mr. Ossining" instead of "Charlie"—weren't they pals, bosom friends, dining companions and intimates?—and then recalled, all in an instant, that he was wearing a sandwich board. It wouldn't have been so bad if she'd been wearing a sandwich board, too, and the lumphead with her and the man stepping out of a cab on the far side of the street and everyone else in Battle Creek, the rest of America and Europe, but that wasn't the case. He, and he alone, was wearing a sandwich board, this gauche and awkward thing, this greedy silent shriek of a garment that had become so much a part of him it had taken him a full sixty seconds to recollect himself. His smile wavered. He swiped at his hair, beat the hat against his leg and, failing all else, tipped it in a mock-gallant salute as he settled it back on his sodden head. "It's been a while," he managed, as if it were the most natural thing in the world to make conversation in a sandwich board.

"I see you're wearing a sandwich board," Eleanor observed.

Charlie tried to look casual. "Yes," he said.

There was an awkward pause. Rain oozed from the awning. A cabriolet went up the street with a *shush*. Two feet from them, behind the big plate-glass window, a pyramid of Post Toasties boxes rose to the height of a man. Charlie felt foolish suddenly, deluded, no different from "Popcorn George," with his stale and crumpled bags of popcorn for sale or barter, or the cripple covered in whisk brooms who wandered the streets like a ghost. What was he doing? What was he thinking? Was C. W. Post tramping around in a sandwich board?

"It's one way to advertise," Eleanor offered, but she seemed dubious. He could feel her eyes sucking at him, bright green leeches draining the color from his face. "Oh"—and she gave a sudden little gasp—"but please forgive me," she said, and then she was introducing the lummox at her side, a man of unintegrated parts, the head too big for the shoulders, hands like flippers, the nose barely there and the teeth every-where. Badger, his name was Badger.

"You're in the breakfast-food business," Badger put in, and there was no melody to his voice, only rhythm. Dry, throaty, feral, it was like the sound a dog makes when it's crouched over a bone, only somehow he'd managed to strap words onto it. But he was astute, all right—and he could read. Yes, sir. No doubt about that.

The rain dripped. Charlie said nothing.

Badger didn't seem to notice. He was off on the subject of breakfast foods, of their value to society as a corrective and an example to the carnivores amongst us, and his voice rasped on till it was as dry as the wind raking a field of cornstalks. Charlie watched Eleanor as her companion gnashed away at his adjectives and adverbs—she never took her eyes from him, her expression fixed midway between worship and rapture—and he wondered what she saw in him. Was he some kind of Sanitarium savior? The gizzardite Messiah? He certainly looked the part—deranged, sallow, thin-wristed, his eyes lit with the fanatic's gleam. "Animal fodder, they call it," he said with a snort of contempt, "and so they think they can dismiss it as if, as if—" The umbrella seemed to collapse round his head then, and in the process of extricating himself and Eleanor, he lost his train of thought. He never did complete the metaphor.

"I couldn't agree more," Charlie interjected, seeing his opening—and his exit. "Breakfast food's the ticket, peptonized and celery-impregnated. Well. Eleanor"—he tipped the soggy hat again—"and Mr. Badger. It's been a pleasure." And then he waddled off into the rain, ungainly as a tortoise in his plywood shell, the flap, flap, flap of his slogans crying out behind him, MAKES ACTIVE BLOOD, MAKES ACTIVE BLOOD, MAKES ACTIVE BLOOD.

The next day he retired the sandwich board—at least until Bender got back. Standing there in the driving rain, looking ridiculous in front of Eleanor Lightbody while the true cereal tycoons sat warm and dry in their offices or on their yachts and had their lackeys build pyramids of boxes in grocers' windows, he'd had an epiphany of sorts. What it boiled down to was this: what was the use? At that point, Bender was scheduled to return within the week, and he'd written twice—from Gary, Indiana, and Galena, Illinois—to report that the orders were flowing in. Well, all right. In a week they'd have the capital to open a real factory, with a bona fide expert, not some worn-out yea-saying imposter like Book-binder, and then they'd be in business. Charlie figured he'd worry about advertising then, when they actually had something to sell. Let Bender wear the sandwich board if he was so keen on it.

Bender got back at the end of the week and re-established himself at the Post Tavern like Caesar returning from the Gallic wars. He had the best of everything, of course, and welcomed himself home with a lavish private dinner at the Wee Nippy, to which he invited Charlie and a dozen of the most suggestible local burghers, people he'd been courting since the fall. He gave a long speech before dinner—three-quarters oration, one-quarter pep talk—in which he outlined his plans for Per-Fo and dwelled on the significant sums he'd already taken in advance orders for the most revolutionary new breakfast food in the history of Battle Creek, and hence, America. And he let his close friends and associates, now gathered before him, know just how much their shares in this new enterprise could be expected to appreciate if only they got in on the ground floor.

Charlie had never seen his partner in better form. Bender railed and thundered against his competitors and the nay-sayers who dared claim that the breakfast-food market was glutted, against the timid and short-sighted who insisted on living in the last century, the sort who wouldn't have invested in Ford or Standard Oil, in streetcars and telephones. But he didn't simply rail. Oh, no: Bender was far too subtle for that. He was a master of the art of persuasion, a virtuoso of the sales pitch. Once he'd softened them up, once he saw the doubt come to roost in their eyes, he modulated his voice, sweet-talking, seducing—he even passed round his ledger showing some $32,000 in advance orders. By the time the guests had finished the bowls of Per-Fo he'd served as an appetizer (that is, Kellogg's Toasted Corn Flakes poured conspicuously from bright new Per-Fo cartons) and were digging into their lobster and steak, he had commitments from all but one of them and three fully executed checks already tucked neatly away in his wallet.

It was a glorious night for Charlie. A night of redemption, promise, hope, vindication. Thirty-two thousand dollars! And these new checks on top of that. It made Mrs. Hookstratten's contribution seem paltry by comparison—paltry, and safe. After all the months of doubt and frustration, the pounding of the streets, the solitary hours at Mrs. Eyvindsdottir's, the fish-head soup and the heartbreak of the Bookbinder basement, it was finally happening—at long last, Per-Fo was fully fledged. Charlie could have raised a statue to Bender that night, could have worshiped him with incense, candles, blood sacrifice.

But then nothing happened. Three weeks dragged by, Bender wrapped in inscrutability, Bender vague about the factory site, the builder, the plans. In Charlie's joy and delirium on the night of the dinner, he'd been so carried away he'd almost told his partner about the check from Will Lightbody, its proceeds accruing interest in an account under the name of Charles P. McGahee at the Central National Bank on the corner of Capital and Michigan. Almost, but not quite. Some kernel of apprehension, a last resisting pinch of caution, had held him back. Now that kernel had begun to bloat and swell, stewing in the bile of Bender's indifference, his dilatory tactics, his testudineous progress through the days. What was he doing? What was he waiting for? "All in time," he'd said. "All in good time. Have I steered you wrong yet?"

And then the letter had come, and Charlie's life was demolished.

The sun hung overhead, fat as a melon, splashing the street with light. Women in straw bonnets glided in and out of shops, neighbors called out giddily to one another, an old man on a bicycle wobbled up the street in a magic-lantern show of sun and shadow. Though it was morning still—quarter past eleven by Charlie's watch—it was warm, the warmest day of the year so far, but Charlie experienced it only as an irritation. By the time he turned the corner opposite the Post Tavern, he was breathing hard and his shirt was damp under the arms.

Since his strained relations with the hotel's underlings precluded his entering through the lobby, Charlie was in the habit of making his way along the alley behind the Wee Nippy and slipping in at the service entrance. That was his plan now. When he'd passed by the hotel altogether, he crossed the street, dodging vehicular traffic, a flock of pigeons scrabbling in the gutter and a piebald cat catching up on its sleep on the curb out front of the jeweler's. Cradling the letter in his pocket with the crook of his left arm, moving swiftly, agitated and preoccupied (what did he expect from Bender, anyway—some sort of delaying action, a sham factory fabricated overnight for Mrs. Hookstratten's benefit, a speech, miracles?), he didn't think to glance up to see if he'd been noticed until it was too late. He had. The doorman, implacable, immovable, eternally vigilant, was stationed in his usual spot, his eyes locked on Charlie's. Charlie looked away.

He felt the man's eyes on him as he mounted the sidewalk and hurried past the corner of the hotel and out of his range of vision. But as he passed the Wee Nippy's street entrance and the alley behind it, he thought to look back over his shoulder—and a good thing, too. The son of a bitch was there, standing at the corner, two hundred feet from his post, his arms folded across his chest, watching. Charlie kept going. It was ten minutes before he ventured back up the street, and this time the doorman was nowhere to be seen. Ducking down the alley, Charlie made for the service entrance, wondering if they could manage to dynamite the tracks along the Michigan Central Line or send Mrs. Hookstratten a phony telegram informing her that her sister had suddenly and unexpectedly passed away, and he was in the door and headed for the back stairs before he understood that the form in the chair propped against the rear wall and materializing now from the shadows was that of his old antagonist, the bell captain. The man occupied the chair like a side of beef, a slab of meat molded to bone. He was in his shirtsleeves and he was barefooted, the uniform draped over a peg on the wall behind him. He held a sandwich in one hand, and it was hard to tell where the sandwich ended and the hand began. "I'll be goddamned," he uttered in a low growl, and lurched up out of the chair with a quickness that was startling.

Charlie had fought bigger men. Or men as big, maybe. He wasn't afraid of anyone. But all he wanted at that moment was Bender, Bender with his soothing words, his sangfroid, his ability to take things as they come and wriggle out from under the boot heel of calamity—all he wanted was for Bender to tell him that everything was going to be all right, just one more time. He tipped his hat to the bell captain's engorged features, turned on his heels and went right back out the door and up the alley again.

Next he tried the entrance at the bar, but it was locked—the Wee Nippy wouldn't be open till four in the afternoon. Frustrated—he had to see Bender, he had to—he paced up and down the street, muttering to himself, gazing up at the high sunstruck plane of the hotel's windows and again attracting the attention of the doorman, who hunched his shoulders and made a fist of his face. It was then that he thought of Ernest O'Reilly.

Sure. Of course. He could send the boy up to Bender's room and slip him a note—they'd meet at the Red Onion for lunch and hash over this Hookstratten thing one more time. He could have telephoned, he supposed, but he really didn't want to have to deal with the snooty desk clerk and then hear that Bender's line was engaged or that he was unavailable or some such crap. No, Ernest O'Reilly was the ticket— but where was he? It was a school day, wasn't it? Charlie hadn't laid eyes on a schoolyard since he'd left St. Basil's and didn't have the faintest idea where the spawn of the breakfast-food industry's toasters, packers and bosses learned how to read and write, but he was instinctively moving in the right direction, hurrying, hurrying, and a few pointed inquiries led him to a three-story brick building on Green Street.

It was ten minutes of twelve. He stood there in the shade of a tree across from the schoolyard, feeling conspicuous. He lit a cigarette, shook out the match, checked his watch. An unearthly silence had fallen over the building and its environs, as if the place were enchanted. Nothing moved. He wondered if this was what a pervert felt like and checked his watch again. He began to feel sleepy.

And then a bell sounded and the schoolyard exploded in motion, accompanied by a mad ululating din that was like the charge of the Comanches. Suddenly children were everywhere, legs, arms, shouts, the scrape of shoes and the thump of balls, and they all looked alike. Charlie moved toward them, but they were like an army on the march and they surrounded him, engulfed him and hurried on by to other engagements and distant battles. The crowd had begun to thin and he was beginning to despair of finding Ernest O'Reilly, when he felt a tug at his arm, just as he had at the railway station on that night that seemed so long ago. "Hey," Ernest O'Reilly said.

Charlie saw that he hadn't put on any weight. There was a scab the size of a silver dollar under his right eye and a matching one on his bare elbow. His shirt, shoes and pants were too big for him. His eyes were watchful. "Hey," Charlie replied. "You want to make a dime?"

"Two bits," Ernest O'Reilly said.

"Fifteen cents."

"What do I have to do?"

Charlie waited round the corner while Ernest O'Reilly, his narrow shoulders slumped forward like an arrow in flight, darted in the rear entrance of the hotel. He was to go straight to Bender's room and give him the message—*Meet me at the Onion, 12:30, URGENT*, Charlie had scrawled on a slip of paper—and if Bender wasn't there, Ernest was to leave word at the desk. Five minutes of Charlie's life eroded there on the corner, then ten. It was going on fifteen minutes and Charlie's fingertips were beginning to ache from flipping open his watch and snapping it closed again, when the boy finally reappeared.

He wasn't alone. Charlie was thunderstruck to see both the doorman and the bell captain sustaining Ernest O'Reilly in the grip of their meaty bloated hands, one on each side of him, while the boy kicked away at the air as if he were running in place. Charlie's impressions were fleeting—the white flash of the boy's bare knees; an envelope fluttering in his hand; the look of intensity leaping into the eyes of bell captain and doorman as they spotted Charlie; sunshine, gay and incongruous —and then the scene began to drive itself. "Run!" Ernest O'Reilly piped, and in that moment he broke away from the two men and shot up the alley toward Charlie, the envelope held out before him like a baton. Charlie was in motion, too, though he was confused and indignant— what were they after him for? Sure, they were his sworn enemies, but he was out on the public street, wasn't he? Still, there they were and you couldn't deny them, coming up the alley on the boy's heels, surprisingly quick for such big men, and Charlie was starting off now, too, trying to gauge the distance to the envelope—a message from Bender?—and finesse the moment at which the apes would be upon him.

It didn't work. They weren't interested in the boy at all, as it turned out—or the envelope, either. No: it was Charlie they wanted. Sausage-faced, blowing, their boots pounding at the pavement like hammers, they overtook Ernest O'Reilly easily and left him in their wake—Charlie had no choice but to run, run for all he was worth. He bolted across the street, turned left down a block lined with shops and ducked into an alley to his right. There was a livery stable here, and the way was blocked by half a dozen carriages in various stages of disuse and repair. Charlie never hesitated. He dodged round a big red gelding, vaulted a hack with the top down and kept on going, pumping his knees and jolting his shoulders, running because he was being pursued.

And why? Why? What had he done? It was no time for deductive reasoning, the thundering footsteps of his pursuers ten paces behind him, but the terrible twisted seed of an explanation began to sprout in his brain: Bender. Something had happened to him. Something bad. Inadmissible. Something that would cut the insides out of Charlie, Per-Fo and Mrs. Hookstratten and hang them on a wire for the crows to pluck clean.

He kept running, an amalgam of rage and fear caught in the back of his throat, his eyes fixed on the obstacles ahead—the open door, the barrel, the cart. Midway through the next block he risked a glance over his shoulder and saw that the doorman had fallen out of the race. It was only him and the former wrestler now, and he could hear the big man's breath dragging at his lungs, torn ragged gasps that were like sobs, like an infant's puling cry, like weakness and collapse. Without warning, Charlie dug in his heels and swung round on the bigger man and in the next moment felt him melt into his fist: the bell captain went down like a corpse. He lay there wheezing in the dirt, and when he rolled over on his back, the eyes loose in his skull, Charlie saw Bender, only Bender. His feet did the rest. A kick for the Otard Dupuy, another for the telephone in the private sitting room, one for Bookbinder, one for the sample boxes and one final bruising sharp-toed boot for the hope raised and the hope denied. *He knew it, knew it all along!*

Voices cried out. There was a face at the end of the alley, two faces, a cluster. Charlie lurched off blindly and he ran another three blocks before he began to calm himself—*A phone*, he thought, *I've got to get to a phone*. Sweating, wild-eyed, his tie askew and his hat clamped down like a lid over his head, he lurched into a druggist's and asked to use the telephone. The old man behind the counter was glad to oblige. "Are you all right?" he asked, his face fractured with concern.

Charlie waved him off and asked the operator for the Post Tavern Hotel. There was a click, and then the effete whine of the desk clerk came back at him, wishing him a good afternoon. "Goodloe H. Bender," Charlie pronounced, and his heart was beating like a drum.

There was a pause. Static over the line. "I'm sorry, but Mr. Bender is no longer with us—may I ask who's calling?"

"That's not possible," Charlie heard himself say, and the drumbeat was in his throat, beneath his eyelids, paradiddling his scalp. "Mr. Goodloe H. Bender. Check again."

"Who is this calling?"

Mountains were toppling into the sea, lava erupting all around him. "Goddamnit, man, will you connect me or not?"

Another pause. The words were etched in acid: "Mr. Bender has . . . disappeared, shall we say, as the fourth-floor maid has only just discovered. His account here—a substantial sum, very substantial—has been left unsettled. Would I by any chance be speaking to his business partner?"

Charlie broke the connection.

When he found Ernest O'Reilly back at the schoolyard and Ernest handed him the envelope containing Bender's note, he already knew what it would say, already knew what had happened to the $32,000 in advance orders, to the checks from the local burghers and Mrs. Hookstratten's ill-advised investment in the breakfast-food business, already knew who was left holding the bag, culpable, foolish, had: Charles P. Ossining, Esq., President-in-Chief of the Per-Fo Company, Inc., Battle Creek. He could have read it off his business card. In shock, his fingers trembling as Ernest O'Reilly gazed up at him in wonder and a hundred jostling, hooting schoolchildren filed by on their way back to class, he slit open the envelope and unfolded the note inside. It was written in the block letters of a child, Bender's characteristic hand, as if he'd never learned to write in cursive, as if his sophistication were as spurious as his dyed whiskers:

CHARLIE, YOU WILL KNOW BY THIS THAT I AM GONE & THAT THERE IS NO REASON TO LOOK TO THE PER-FO ACCOUNT AT THE OLD NATIONAL & MERCHANTS—CONSIDER IT MY FEE IN YOUR EDUCATION. WITH ALL REGRETS AND BEST WISHES, YOURS, GOOD.

Charlie stared numbly at the words. He might just as well have been reading his own epitaph.

The evening was mild, hushed, the breath of some fragrant austral place hanging over the depot like a benediction. Shadows striped the tracks and the trees behind the station were cast in bronze. Somewhere a bell tolled the hour. Though people had begun to gather on the platform, their voices were pitched low, and the only sound that came to Charlie as he sat on a bench against the outside wall was the murmur of the swallows flitting in and out from beneath the eaves. The swallows didn't charm him. The softness of the evening and the play of light in the trees didn't uplift him or fill him with a reverence for the earth and the creation and the pure animal joy of being alive. Quite the contrary. He waited there for the whistle of Mrs. Hookstratten's train as he might have waited in his cell for the footsteps of his executioner.

For the past three nights he'd slept in his clothes, afraid to approach Mrs. Eyvindsdottir's till past midnight and slipping out the back way at the first hint of dawn. Suddenly it seemed as if half of America wanted a word with him. The very day after he'd made his escape from the bootlickers at the Post Tavern Hotel, the Per-Fo correspondence mysteriously began to turn up at Mrs. Eyvindsdottir's—and with it, as if it were almost coincidental, Bender's bill. (The bill, which not only included the last month's charges but carried a line of credit all the way back to October, was a sybaritic wallow, a blow-by-blow chronicle of excess and indulgence. On such and such a day, Bender had ordered shellfish in his room, or he'd descended to the Wee Nippy to entertain in state, risen to his suite with Coq au Vin, Tomcod Frit and Escalope de Veau à la Guennoise, plunged again to the main dining room with a jeroboam of Piper-Heidsieck and a plate of beluga caviar, sent out for three pairs of shoes and six shirtfronts, ordered a carriage, cut flowers, personalized linen.)

But the bill was the least of his worries—that, at any rate, was in Bender's name. What was disturbing, what kept Charlie from his bed, his room, his house, was the flood of angry letters from bilked grocers, hapless investors, irate realtors and concerned law-enforcement agencies from all over the Midwest and Northwest—all of which were addressed to Charles P. Ossining, President-in-Chief, The Per-Fo Company, Inc., Suite 414, The Post Tavern Hotel. Had Bender been posing as his partner while foisting off his phony boxes of Per-Fo and bilking widows out of their pensions? Could he stoop to such a thing? It certainly looked that way. Oh, yes indeed. And that was only the beginning—there were more immediate legal problems, too, all of which Bender had kept from him. It seemed that separate lawsuits had been filed in the Calhoun County Court to enjoin the production, sale or transport of "Kellogg's" Per-Fo and to sue for damages on the grounds of trademark infringement. There were also three letters from their own attorney, a Mr. Barton Noble of Woolhough Street, who wanted to discuss the matter of his account with them. Urgently.

Charlie was in shock. Had been for four days now. He should have known better—did know better—but Bender had strung him along just as he'd strung along the Post Tavern Hotel and everyone else he'd ever run across, paying out a sop on account now and then, bluffing, boasting, flimflamming and humbugging. Charlie was a fish. A chump. A sucker. He'd been hooked, landed, scaled, gutted, stuffed, roasted, chewed, digested and shat out. He thought he was on his way to becoming a tycoon—and now he was only a criminal. George Kellogg, a bum off the street, a drunk in rags, was curled up blissfully in his prepaid room at Mrs. Eyvindsdottir's, oblivious, while Charlie couldn't get within a hundred yards of the place—they had men out front waiting for him. Process servers. Bill collectors. Bone breakers.

If this was the low point of his life, sitting there helpless on the mute uncaring boards while the boys began to gather to hawk their worthless stocks and Harry Delahoussaye slunk out of the shadows at the far end of the platform, things were about to get a whole lot worse. For at that moment the great moving shadow of Mrs. Hookstratten's train came into sight, and he could hear it and feel it in the earth, a tremor rising up through the platform and into the soles of his feet, the rush of implacable power that set the big sign before him quaking on its hinges like some sadistic joke: BETTER YOURSELF IN BATTLE CREEK.

He stood then and the whistle blew and a harsh wind stung his face.

Chapter 3

Freikorper
Kultur

❦

T here wasn't much to see, really—a vague, horseshoe-shaped mound with a bite of raw earth taken out of it and a tumble of rock, fragments of unglazed pottery and what might or might not have been human remains. Eleanor didn't know quite what she'd expected—the skeletons of braves and squaws bound together in supernatural embrace, every bone perfectly articulated, as in the model Frank kept in his office, a favorite dog at their sides, maybe. Headdresses. Vases. Beads. Jewelry. Those pipe things with the feathers on them—what did they call them? Still, it was a pure joy just to be out here under the sun, drinking up the health-giving rays, lying back on a bed of wildflowers and watching the scroll of the sky roll ceaselessly back on itself.

She was of two minds with regard to the sun, and she'd brought her parasol along so as not to get too much of it all at once. She'd always been taught—and she'd felt it instinctively—that sun-braised cheeks, sallow skin and reddened hands were coarse and unsightly, the emblem of the foreigner and the day laborer. But Dr. Kellogg had taught her the vital importance of phototherapy and she'd spent an otherwise pallid winter invigorating her constitution beneath the healing rays of the electric-light bath, the photophore, the thermophore, the arc light and the quartz actinic lamp. If anything, her skin was fresher and more

335

supple than ever. She'd been blessed with a flawless complexion, the envy of the girls who'd gone to school with her, found husbands and settled down to homes and children in the crisply painted and turreted houses that garnished the undulating hills of Peterskill. And what were they doing now, those girls? May Boughton, Christine Peckworth, Lucy Strang? Obliviously poisoning their husbands and children with creatine, with putrefying flesh, with steaks, chops and roasts. Lucy, at least, should have known better. . . .

Peterskill. Her thoughts hovered there a moment, and she saw the yellow roses climbing the trellis outside her kitchen window, the honeysuckle spilling over the fence into the Van Tassels' yard, her father's soft wistful smile and the way he took up her hands as if they were buns warm from the oven . . . God, she hadn't written him in weeks. . . .

"Well, well, well, well—enjoying a bit of the old Sol, eh?"

Shading her eyes, she looked up into Lionel Badger's sun-dazzled face. He was wearing a Panama hat and a pair of canvas lederhosen with galluses of woven hemp, and he was grinning. He'd omitted a shirt and she ought to have been mildly shocked to see the flesh revealed beneath the hempen straps, the body hair, the striations of his rib cage, the white slash of a scar at his shoulder, but he'd removed his shirt twice in her presence in the past week and she was growing used to it. After all, he was only opening himself up to the sun, as per the Kellogg regime and his own persistent lights (anything the Doctor advocated, Lionel advocated to the power of ten). "Yes," she murmured languidly, the sun like a great warm golden spatula, pressing her back into the torporous, sensual earth. "But really, I've been about to get up and join Virginia for the past half-hour now."

Lionel laughed, no more than a tickle in the back of his throat, and he squatted beside her, his shadow swooping over her like a cold hand. "Truly, Eleanor," he said, and she could smell the garlic on his breath, potent and earthy, "you must open yourself up to the radiant energy of the sun, unbutton your blouse, roll up your sleeves, lift your skirt—"

She studied his face for signs of impropriety, but there were none. He was in earnest, proselytizing, a disseminator of the news, a prophet of health. "Actually," she breathed, coloring just a bit, "I've been trying. With the Women's Auxiliary of the Deep-Breathing Club—well, you know that we've been meeting out-of-doors these past two weeks, where we have privacy, of course, round the women's pool—"

There was a strange light in the health preceptor's eyes, as if he were picturing her there leading the women's group in a state of deshabille. "Yes?" he said. "And?"

She looked away. "Well, we've been experimenting—just as I understand the men do routinely—with freeing ourselves of our garments—"

"Yes!" he cried suddenly, clenching his fists and raising up his arms in a warrior's gesture of triumph, "that's it, that's it exactly! Dress reform, Eleanor—it starts with liberating the body from its artificial constraints, and I'm not just talking about whalebone corsets now, though the things are about as appropriate on a modern woman as the bones the cannibals in New Guinea stick through their noses—no, Eleanor, and you've perceived it all along, it goes much deeper." He held her eyes. "Do you know what I'm wearing underneath these shorts?"

She hadn't given it a thought, not in her wildest imaginings, but in that moment she knew.

His smile was huge and toothy and it lingered over her just a moment too long. "Are you familiar with *Freikorper Kultur*, Professor Kuntz's seminal work on the German Nudist Movement?"

And why was her pulse racing suddenly? She felt like a girl waiting to be asked to dance. "Yes, of course."

If he'd looked interested a moment earlier, he was positively transfixed now. Behind him, no more than a hundred feet away, Frank and Professor Gunderson directed a pair of workmen with shovels and pickaxes, and Virginia Cranehill, fortyish and stout, sat primly on a blanket beside a hamper of sandwiches from the Sanitarium kitchens. "Really? And what do you think of it?"

Still shielding her eyes, Eleanor pushed herself up on one elbow and plucked a stalk of grass to chew. "It's quite revolutionary," she said, without hesitation. "And logical. If one looks at mankind's beginnings, well, then, to be naked to the sun is the most sensible thing in the world. It's natural and pure. But society, unfortunately, has given us these odious costumes to wear—" and here, for emphasis, she plucked at the heavy folds of her skirt.

337

"But it's charming," Lionel protested, easing to his knees now and leaning closer. "I've meant to tell you all morning how perfectly charming you look today—the whole ensemble suits you, flatters you, and that wide-brimmed hat just seems to make your eyes melt away like twin pats of butter. . . ."

What could she say? She thanked him for the compliment.

"But I know what you mean," he went on, "—clothing is confining, fashion-driven, wasteful, downright silly in weather such as this. And I can't help imagining how equally charming you'd be without it—*au naturel*, as it were. Professor Kuntz would have you out of those clothes, bloomers and all, in half a minute." He leaned back on his heels, spread his arms wide to take in the light, the soft breeze, the wild landscape that fell back to the horizon around him. "And on a day like this! Why, no glade in Bavaria, no Black Forest crag or tumbling cascade could hope to match this—don't you agree?"

"Yes," Eleanor assented, nibbling at her stalk of grass, "but if we were practicing the local brand of *Freikorper Kultur* today, Lionel, I'd be deprived of your company—and Frank's and Professor Gunderson's— not to mention the edifying companionship of our two earth diggers over there. It would be just me and Virginia, and I can't imagine a duller outing, even if all the sunshine in the world were available."

"But not so, not so, my darling Eleanor. Perhaps the rather hidebound and puritanical director of the San would have the sexes separated, as if there were something to be ashamed of in revealing the human body, as if it were some sort of dung heap instead of the temple he's forever proclaiming it, but Gerhardt Kuntz, as you must know, mixes the sexes freely. And why not?"

Eleanor couldn't think of a single reason. She had read Kuntz's descriptions of naked gambols with her heart in her mouth, picturing the men as hairy-legged satyrs plunging into icy torrents and basking afterward on thrones of granite, while the women, their bodies shy and soft, their breasts released to the caress of gravity, sat beside them and made witty, giddy conversation. She'd known no man but Will, and she loved him, she did, but there was something else in her, too, something beating strong and secret in her veins, struggling to get out. She looked Lionel in the eye. "Why not?" she agreed.

Later, after they'd picnicked on Graham bread, peanut-butter-and-cucumber sandwiches and a bottle of Concord water that Lionel had brought along, they all sat in a circle on Virginia's blanket—Lionel on one side of Eleanor, Frank on the other, Professor Gunderson beside him and finally Virginia to complete the arrangement—and talked of archaeology, health, phrenology and nudism to the clank of pick and spade. On the last of these subjects, Frank was wary (though he clove to the Kellogg party line vis-à-vis sunlight and the untrammeled body), Virginia was enthusiastic and Professor Gunderson noncommittal. Lionel gave Eleanor a significant look as Frank waffled and the professor became suddenly occupied with his notes. Virginia went so far as to loosen the top button of her blouse, roll up her sleeves and fold back her skirt to expose the white-frosted hem of her bloomers (Eleanor remained fully and properly dressed—for her it would be all or nothing), and then it was on to archaeology and a sermon from the little professor about the mound-building tribe that had preceded the Potawatomi in these parts. Frank chimed in with his phrenological theories about Indians in general and these Indians specifically, and Eleanor couldn't help feeling he was getting to be something of a bore lately, a one-note virtuoso. It wasn't until later, when one of the workmen cried out in excitement and Frank and the professor bounded up to peer into the distant ginger-brown hole, that the conversation took a more interesting turn.

"Speaking of the untrammeled body, Lionel," Virginia breathed, edging in nearer to close the circle, "I want to thank you for sending me to Dr. Spitzvogel—I've never felt so good in all my life, though I don't mean to derogate the San's methods. They've done me a world of good, and I have no intention of leaving—but oh, Dr. Spitzvogel!" She rolled her eyes theatrically, a great cow of a woman, and then smiled at Eleanor.

Eleanor had heard of the physician in question. The whole business was very hush-hush and the mention of his name among the ladies of the San always brought on a shock of titters, suggestive looks and faraway stares. "I've heard of him, of course," Eleanor said, "but I didn't know that you—"

"For three weeks now," Virginia broke in.

Eleanor could feel Lionel's eyes on her. He was rarely silent for more than an inhalation at a time, and she could feel his silence like a palpable weight, brooding on her. She hadn't known he was involved, but she might have guessed. The treatment—it was called "Movement Therapy" and it was something especially attuned to women, that's all she knew—wasn't offered at the San. This Dr. Spitzvogel, an enigmatic figure whom no one seemed to admit knowing, had set up his offices in Battle Creek sometime in the fall. Eleanor searched Virginia's bright pregnant eyes. "And is it—the treatment, that is—is it valuable?" She was hoping for some sort of description.

"Very," Lionel offered. "Particularly for the hypersensitive nature, for the neurasthenic, Eleanor. I'm not your doctor"—here he threw up his hands and gave her another of his looks—"but I will say I've sent several women to Siegfried now, and I haven't heard a single complaint."

"I'll second that," Virginia said, ducking her head conspiratorially. "When I come out of that office I'm floating on the clouds, so relaxed that every pore of my body is just oozing—the last two times I was so in tune with my inner nature, the doctor himself had to help me into a cab. I was weak, Eleanor, practically melting."

Eleanor didn't understand. Why would you want to be weakened—wasn't the whole idea of physiologic living to strengthen oneself for the long life it guaranteed? "Weak?" she echoed.

"Relaxed, dear." Virginia exchanged a look with Lionel. It was a complicitous look, smug and chummy, and it irritated Eleanor.

"Listen, Eleanor." Lionel's voice was soft, persuasive; in the distance, the men peering into the hole in the earth exclaimed over something. "Dr. Kellogg's methods are first-rate, I won't argue that, but you know he doesn't take things far enough, doesn't value extremes. I say extreme cures for extreme conditions. No, now listen to me. This is nothing to be afraid of—for you, of all people, who have gone boldly where others fear to tread, a Vegetarian and Progressive leader among women—for you it would be a simple extension of what you've been doing all along. But it happens to lie outside the parameters of what Dr. Kellogg sees fit to rigidly impose on his patients—he's a great man, Eleanor, but he isn't God."

"I'll say," Virginia put in. She was close now, so close Eleanor could smell the peanut butter on her breath; mingled with Lionel's garlic, it was intoxicating.

Eleanor smiled and let a little laugh escape her, though her blood was racing. "You make it sound like such an ominous thing—you don't have to build it up so, Lionel, Virginia. You know I'm progressive." She paused. "What exactly does the treatment consist of?"

Virginia's eyes shot to Lionel's; Lionel turned to Eleanor. "It's very simple, really. The doctor gives you a loose-fitting garment, a shift really, and lays you on a padded table—"

"—in a very cozy room," Virginia added.

"Yes, of course. The atmosphere is one of perfect compose—it really has to be, that's the idea."

"And Dr. Spitzvogel has the warmest hands of any living being, warmer than the hot glove at the San, it's as if he radiates his own energy—"

Yes, Eleanor said to herself, but what does he *do*?

"Eleanor." Lionel flattened his voice. "I'll be frank with you—why shouldn't I? We're good friends, aren't we? And what's to be ashamed of where the human body is concerned?"

There was a shout from Frank in the distance. "Yes?" Eleanor said. "Go on."

"In German it's called '*Die Handhabung Therapeutik*.' "

"Manipulation Therapy," Virginia breathed.

"Well," Lionel said. "The doctor manipulates the womb—"

"And the breasts," Virginia put in, lingering over the sibilance of the word as if she couldn't let go of it.

"Yes," Lionel puffed, warming to the subject, "because this is the seat of the hysterical passions in the female anatomy and the key, many feel, to neurasthenic disorders. By manipulating the womb—"

"And the breasts," Virginia softly hissed.

"—and the breasts, the doctor is able to stimulate blood flow to these regions and release the negative humors that build up there, just as ptomaines and other poisons build up in the intestines in cases of autointoxication. It's the newest treatment—utterly safe—and all the rage on the Continent." Lionel gave her the full benefit of his caramel eyes. "Again, it's only because Dr. Kellogg—not to criticize, he's done me good and his ideas are on the right track—is so puritanical that he hasn't offered Siegfried Spitzvogel a place on the Sanitarium staff as yet. But it's not a problem: I can offer you an introduction."

They were watching her now, breathing shallowly, the perspiration standing out on both their faces. The sun was warm and Eleanor felt uncomfortable suddenly and saw that the backs of her hands had turned pink. She was about to say yes, of course she would try Dr. Spitzvogel's therapy—if this cow of a Virginia Cranehill could experience positive results, well, then, she could derive any measure of benefit from it herself—but Frank Linniman interrupted them.

He was standing over them, a smudge of soil on his white duck trousers and another on his cheek. "Look," he cried, "look what we've found!" Eleanor was vaguely aware of Professor Gunderson hunched behind him like a gargoyle, grinning till his face seemed split in half. Frank seemed to be offering them something, white stone shrouded in loam, but then she saw that it wasn't a stone at all.

"Four hundred years old, at least," Frank said, and his voice rode up and down its currents of emotion. "A female, we think. And look at this"—pointing with a blackened fingernail to the crevice where an ear might once have been, where a lover's fingers might have lingered in a long-ago caress—"do you see this? This organ behind the mastoid here at the base of the skull?"

Eleanor saw bleached bone, honeycombed with age, saw the vacant drop of the jaw, the punctured eyes, death compressed in a living hand. "Yes," she said, "yes, Frank: what is it?"

"Amativeness," he said. "This is her organ for amativeness. Do you see how developed it is compared to this for calculation? Or this for order? Or look here—see how small this plate is? This is spirituality." His finger roamed the naked globe of the skull, jabbing here and there like a lecturer's pointer.

"What does it mean?" Lionel asked, shifting his weight on the corner of the blanket.

Frank took his time, reveling in the moment. Behind him, butterflies fell through the air like scraps of colored paper and the two workmen, satisfied, leaned on their shovels. "It means lust," he said. "It means she held nothing back. It means she was a sink of sensuality." He shook his head. "These Indians," he said finally, "no wonder they never amounted to anything."

There was rain at the end of the week, on Friday, a warm seasonal rain that puckered on the pavement and dropped musically down the gutters. Eleanor had finished her daily regimen by four that afternoon and was dressing to go out when Will stopped by her room. "Hello, darling," he said, hesitating in the doorway, "I just dropped by to see how you were doing—you're not going out, are you? In this weather?"

She'd made up her face and was buttoning the cape of her cashmere mackintosh and making a final adjustment of her blue velvet toque in the mirror. Will's question, ingenuous as it seemed, contained a hint of criticism—was she blind? couldn't she see that it was raining?—and it irritated her. Especially now, especially today. Her nerves were in a flutter, and she felt light-headed, odd, almost as if her feet weren't touching the floor. For though she'd dressed in one of her smartest suits (the latest English cut, double-breasted, royal blue, with an exaggerated collar appliquéd in taffeta silk for contrast) and one of her best French satin blouses, she wore nothing beneath her slip and nothing to contain her breasts. The sensation was freakish and liberating at the same time, her nipples coming into random contact with the polished fabric, a coolness between her legs, but she felt it necessary to the experience—at four-fifteen she was meeting Lionel, who was escorting her to Dr. Spitzvogel's for her inaugural treatment, and she didn't want to be thought unprogressive. "Oh, I'm just going for a stroll," she said, watching Will's face in the mirror.

"A stroll? But it's raining out there, dear."

She turned round on him now, crossed the room and let him hold her elbows while she pecked a kiss at his cheek. "But you know how I love to walk in the rain—it's my artistic nature. I let my soul soar like the lark ascending."

Suddenly Will was beaming. "I know," he cried, "I'll go with you! I could use the exercise. But listen to me—I'd make Dr. Kellogg proud, wouldn't I?"

"No, Will," she said, suddenly flustered. "Or, yes, you would make Dr. Kellogg proud and I'm pleased to see you taking a more positive attitude toward physiologic living, but I mean I think I'd rather walk by myself—and please don't take that the wrong way. I just need to be alone with my inner self, that's all."

Will looked hurt. "You mean I can't even take a stroll with you anymore? Eleanor, what's happened to you? I've done everything you've asked—eaten grapes till they came out my ears, jumped up and down laughing with a bunch of overweight tycoons in the gymnasium, had the kink in my intestine snipped out like a wart. God, let's go home, can't we, El? Just go home?"

"We will," she murmured, drawing away from him, "all in good time."

"Oh, don't give me that, El—that's what you always say."

The fact was, she couldn't bear the idea of going back to Peterskill after the excitement of the San. What could she do there—play bridge, do church work, watch the grapevine snake its way through the trellis? She couldn't stay at the San forever. She knew that in some way she was prolonging the inevitable, forestalling her real life and avoiding her mother's grave and her father's desolation and the pink room with the bassinet at the top of the stairs that was meant for her daughter. But she was sick still, a very sick woman, and she couldn't leave yet. Not yet. "I mean it, Will," she said, "I promise you."

His face was like a big bruise. He looked as if he might break down and cry. When she reached out to comfort him, alarmed, he flung her hands away. "Don't," he said, harsh, bitter, put upon, "I don't need it. Go walk in the rain," he said, "let your soul soar." And then he turned and was gone.

She met Lionel in the lobby and went wordlessly into the cab waiting at the curb. It was stuffy and close inside and she was acutely conscious of his knee pressed against hers as he tried to arrange his legs in the tight compartment. "You're doing the right thing," he told her. "You'll thank me a thousand times over for this."

She wanted to be witty and gay, wanted to command the situation, but it just wasn't in her. She listened to the clatter of the horses' hooves on the wet pavement, watched the trees come at them over the driver's shoulders, smoothed a wrinkle in her glove. "I'm sure I will," she murmured.

Dr. Spitzvogel's offices were in his residence, a perfectly respectable-looking Tudor on the fashionable West Side, not far from Dr. Kellogg's own residence. Eleanor gave a glancing thought to her Chief and mentor—what would *he* think of what she was doing?—and felt like a traitor. But the look of Dr. Spitzvogel's home reassured her, as did Lionel's presence at her side—the President of the Vegetarian Society of America wouldn't very well lead her astray, would he? Besides, though Dr. Kellogg prided himself on keeping up with every medical advance in the world, from the doings at the Pasteur Institute to the Royal College of Surgeons, even he couldn't be expected to know everything. And so many other women at the San found Dr. Spitzvogel's innovations effective—and gratifying. What did she have to lose? Eleanor stepped out of the hack with an open mind, determined to give herself up wholly to the Spitzvogel regime, come what may, and make her judgments without prejudice, as befitted a forward-looking and progressive spirit.

The enigmatic physician turned out to be an ordinary enough man of medium height, with a dark slash of slicked-down hair, waxed mustaches and a monocle clenched in his right eye with what seemed an amazing effort of muscular control. His accent was thick, but had none of the harshness Eleanor associated with German speakers—he didn't talk so much as purr. He was dressed in tweeds and there was a faint smell of wood smoke and licorice about him. She liked him immediately.

Dr. Spitzvogel showed them into a sitting room done up in the Aesthetic style of the late seventies, replete with a gilded and ebonized floor screen in a Japanese pattern and a matching curio cabinet by the Herter brothers. They sat round a low table and chatted over bran wafers and a musky-scented herbal tea that tasted of exotic soils and faraway places, making small talk. After a while, Lionel got up and excused himself. Once the door had closed behind him, Dr. Spitzvogel took up a pad and pencil and questioned Eleanor regarding her condition—in general terms at first, but becoming progressively more probing and intimate as the dialogue advanced. She told him of her sudden rushes of emotion, how the sight of a three-tined fork or a tatted collar filled her with an unbearable overbrimming joy or corresponding sorrow, how she awoke trembling in the night and ran barefoot through the dew, told him of her mother's death and her husband's troubles and how she felt that beauty and truth and the pursuit of the physiologic life were the only things worth dedicating oneself to.

He understood her completely. "You poor woman," he murmured, pulling at his lip and gravely nodding the brilliantined bulb of his head as her litany of woes mounted. When he'd satisfied himself, he gave her a wink so broad and sympathetic it threatened to dislodge his monocle, and then stepped behind the screen. He emerged a moment later in the white jacket of the conventional physician, though the tweed trousers fell away incongruously beneath it, and Eleanor wondered that he would bother to change his jacket and not his pants. "Will you step this way, please?" he asked, placing a peculiar buzzing emphasis on his s's.

A door to the rear of the screen led to his offices proper, a pair of sedate, wainscoted rooms so softly lit it took a long moment before Eleanor's eyes adjusted. There was a desk, several straight-backed chairs, the usual physician's paraphernalia. Through the open doorway to the back room, she could dimly make out a padded examining table and the dull glint of the oil paintings that decorated the walls. Suddenly her heart was pounding. To say something, anything, she commented on the framed credentials displayed on the wall behind the desk, not a word of which was legible in this light. "You've had your training in Germany, I presume?" she said, gesturing at the display.

"Oh, yes," he buzzed, and then he was purring and buzzing at the same time, "at the Universität of Schleswig-Holstein and at Württemberg, too. But not in medicine, dear lady, which as you know is so constrained and narrow a field, but rather in the Philosophy of Physiological Systems, and, of course, Therapeutic Massage—*Die Handhabung Therapeutik*, in particular. But please, allow me," he purred, taking her lightly by the arm and escorting her into the back room.

Here the odor of licorice she'd recognized earlier was pervasive, as if the air itself had been spiced, and the room was noticeably warmer than the one that adjoined it. The only light derived from a pair of flickering sconces and there were no windows, not even a bit of stained glass to admit the light of day, and that was odd. And yet it lent an atmosphere of privacy and retreat to the place, a sense of security untouched by the rolling day, and it lulled her. The effect was instantaneous—she felt languid and her heart slipped back into its accustomed rhythm. In the meantime, Dr. Spitzvogel had crossed the room to pull open the wardrobe in the corner, and as she followed his movements she glanced up and the paintings above the wainscoting came into focus. They were pastoral settings mostly—stretches of lowering sky, sheep in their folds, nymphs, fauns, hovering cherubim, fairies melting into woodland shadow—and they added to the air of unreality that hung over the room. Unaccountably, the word "seraglio" fluttered in and out of her head. And what was she doing here?

"Please," Dr. Spitzvogel was saying, and he stood before her now, the sheen of his hair and mustaches gone dull in the candlelight, the ghost of a pale silken garment held out in offering. "You will remove your clothing and slip into this—the wardrobe is here for your convenience. And then, please to lay yourself on the table and relax, dream, think nothing but beautiful thoughts." He smiled—was he winking again or was this a trick of the light?—and then he was at the door. "I return presently, and then we will begin, *ja?*"

She changed hastily, afraid he'd come back before she finished, feeling a little foolish for having gone without underwear—she could have worn an iron corset for all anyone would have known. The garment the doctor had given her was open at the sides and she felt it against her bare skin as she'd felt the blouse, a sheet of sensation. She lay back on the padded table, her head on the pillow, eyes closed, and waited. It was no good. She was too tense. What would it be like? What would he do? She concentrated on relaxing her muscles, one by one, beginning with her toes and working her way up. By the time she reached her hips she was so relaxed, what with the heat and the incense and the languor of all those perennially bathing nymphs on the walls, that she didn't notice he was in the room with her till she felt his hands on her abdomen.

His hands simply lay there—there was no movement, no compression, no attempt at massage—and they were hot, fiery, just as Virginia had said. Eleanor kept her eyes closed, fought to remain still, calm. An eternity dragged by. Nothing happened. But then, as if magically, his hands had migrated to her breasts, her nipples, his hands like smooth river stones heated in the fire, and there was the faintest distant movement of his fingers.

Later, much later, so much later she didn't know if she'd been lying in that room for hours, days, weeks—if she'd been born there, melting into the padding, through the table, the floor—she became aware of his touch in a place where she'd never been touched before. So delicate, so painstaking, so exquisite in its patience and deep probing wisdom, this was a touch she could never have conjured or imagined. There was no question of resisting it. She sank beneath it, dreaming of those sylvan glades, of men and women alike gamboling through Bavarian meadows, as naked as God made them, and she felt herself moving, too, the gentlest friction of her hips against the leather padding, moving forward and downward and ever so therapeutically into that firm sure touch.

Chapter 4

Rigid Control
and Other
Matters

❧❦❧

Eleanor wasn't eating. Now that she'd switched her affiliation more or less permanently to Will's table, he had an opportunity to observe her at meals, and he was alarmed to see that she never did much more than stir the food with her fork, as if she were an artist mixing paint. She'd grown thinner, and that was alarming, too. Her cheekbones, always prominent, were stark against her eyes now, and the flesh fell away from them to the corners of her mouth with the harsh tympanic tension of hide stretched over a last. Her wrists were two pairs of thimbles bound together with a cord of skin and her eyes were haunted, growing bigger and more luminous by the day. One evening at dinner he noticed that she wasn't wearing her wedding ring, and he was mortified, but didn't mention it at the table with the others present. When he took her aside in the corridor and asked about it, she fished the diamond band from her purse and showed him why: it would no more fit her finger than it would a pencil.

"But what's the matter, El?" he asked her then. "You're here to gain weight, not lose it."

She shrugged, looked up at him sheepishly, and her eyes drank up her face. "I'm eating," she said.

"You're skin and bone."

"You should talk."

"All right, granted, but I've had stomach problems, you know that —and at least I'm eating solid food now, even if it is bran mush or wet pasteboard or whatever it is they serve up around here, but you're eating next to nothing, as far as I can see."

She was leaning into the wall, pouting, playing with her necklace. "I'm not hungry," she murmured and smiled past him, showing off the full complement of her even white teeth to an elegantly dressed couple passing by.

"Not hungry?" Will was incredulous. He was pained, outraged. "But you're the biologic liver, you're the vegetarian princess, you're the one who thinks mock oysters and Sanitas fricassee are the height of culinary art—"

She was already moving, her face composed, sweeping serenely along the hallway as if she hadn't heard a word he'd said. But she had. Because she stopped before she'd gone ten paces and swung round on him. "It's temporary, I assure you," she said. "I'm not feeling hungry right now, that's all. Can't you give me a moment's peace?"

Later that night, after shuffling round the halls in his slippers by way of exercise and trying, unsuccessfully, to get through the first page of *The Awakening of Helena Ritchie* (it was putting him to sleep), he confided in Irene. "I'm worried about Eleanor," he told her, lingering over his ablutions in the bathroom while she tidied up his room and turned back the bed for him. "She's not eating."

Irene appeared in the doorway. "Yes, I've noticed it myself," she said, watching as he dredged his molars with the toothbrush, "and I've seen this sort of thing before in other strong-willed women. Women like your wife, that is."

Will paused, removed the toothbrush from his mouth. "You've seen it before? What do you mean?" He gargled, talking around a froth of tooth powder before bending to rinse his mouth. If Eleanor had lost weight in recent weeks, Irene had gained it, rounding out gloriously where it counted most. She'd always been robust, but now she was fairly bursting at the seams, big-shouldered and -bosomed, her thighs standing out in vivid relief against the pale firm clutch of her uniform.

"It's not pathological, I don't think. She's not vomiting, is she? Purposely, I mean?"

"No, of course not. Or not that I know of."

Irene was on the far side of the room now, arranging things that had already been twice arranged, never really at ease alone with him in the room anymore—though the door was always left open for the sake of propriety, and in accordance with the Chief's mandate. Since that long-ago evening of the kiss, she'd shied away from physical contact with him, unless it was for strictly medical purposes—monitoring his condition, administering grape, lactobacillus and enema, nursing him through his postoperative trauma. They were friends, certainly—he felt more warmly toward her than ever—but there were no more gifts, no more kisses. He wished there were. "You know, Mr. Lightbody," she breathed, turning round as he entered the room, settled himself in the armchair and idly lifted *The Awakening of Helena Ritchie* from the table, "the physiologic life takes tremendous courage, a real effort of the will—"

He smiled. Crossed his legs. "Who should know better than I?"

Nurse Graves returned the smile, and it was a smile that acknowledged the magnitude of his own sacrifice in his personal war for physiologic equilibrium—he bore the battle scars on his abdomen, after all. "Of course you do," she said in her husky whisper of a voice, "it was just a rhetorical figure . . . but what I mean is that a very strong-willed person can sometimes take the struggle too far, from engaging in sound eudaemonic practices to the point of denying the body its essential needs. If one conquers the urge for meat, tobacco, alcohol, coffee, tea, pharmacopoeia of any kind, then perhaps the will clamps down even further, do you see?"

Will didn't see. Not at all. He'd given up a whole world and what had it gotten him? A partially ruined stomach instead of an utterly ruined one. And for what? To be able to eat corn pulp and gruel?

She tried a new tack. "Women are particularly suggestible. If dietary control can cure autointoxication and neurasthenia, as well as practically any other malady you can think of, then it follows—to the overreaching mind, that is—that the more rigid the control over the appetites, the more complete the cure."

Will lifted his eyes from the first paragraph of the novel, a paragraph he'd read over at least eight times in the course of the past hour without registering a word of it, and wondered aloud if this was what was wrong with Eleanor—and, if so, what was the cure?

Irene was moving briskly now—she had other patients to irrigate and put to bed, and in any case, she was no great friend of Eleanor, who'd tried to have her removed from all contact with Will until Will got wind of it and overruled her—and at first she didn't answer. Her brow was furrowed with concentration as she measured out the ingredients for the enema, and Will just sat back and admired her. He'd been feeling increasingly randy of late—in fact, he'd had to cut back his use of the Heidelberg Belt to three hours a night, rather than wearing it straight through till morning—and Nurse Graves excited him more than ever. Especially given the new lushness of her figure and the sad fact that Eleanor showed no interest in him whatever—all he had to do was poke his face in the door and she would put her hands to her temples and mutter, "Not now, Will, please—I'm a shattered woman."

Irene turned to him with the venerable tool and an official smile and he felt his bowels loosening at the sight of it. "I'll speak to her doctor," she said finally in her puffiest, breathiest, tiniest little scratch of a voice. "And now"—and the soft soothing whisper of the words made him tingle as if it were seltzer water and not blood percolating through his veins—"are you ready for your irrigation?"

Another meal.

Yet another.

And how many meals constituted a life, Will wondered, picking at his Protose hash and macaroni cutlets, how many four-and-a-half-ounce servings of mush, paste, gruel and boiled oats? Outside, it was a day of insistent beauty—the angels spoke on the breeze, every bud on every tree, shrub, flower and weed was firing perfume into the air, every bird singing—while here, in the dining hall, biologic living went on with a vengeance. Oh, it was elegant enough, well-to-do gentlemen with facial hair and English suits, ladies in the latest fashions from New York and Paris, a warm murmurous undercurrent of chitchat and higher discourse, but was it life, life as it was meant to be lived, raw and untamed and exhilarating, or just some glassed-under simulacrum? Will lifted the fork to his mouth, inserted a tasteless lump of roughage and sighed.

Eleanor sat to his left, insouciantly poking at a yogurt-drenched mound of fava beans and brightening only to the conversation. Mrs. Tindermarsh was seated beside her, and Badger in Miss Muntz's former spot. Hart-Jones, brick-faced and obtrusive as ever, sat at Will's right, and their new dining companion occupied Homer Praetz's old place. But that was all right by Will, that was just fine—Mrs. Hookstratten was like a letter from home. Better. She lived and breathed and spoke of the one place in the world he most wanted to be. She'd filled him in on everything from his father's health (vibrant) to the quality of the loaves at Shapiro's bakery (declining) to the status of the Peterskill Yacht Club's forthcoming season (ambitious). Peterskillian society had suffered in their absence, she assured him, but everyone was hoping for his and Eleanor's speedy recovery and return—at least in time for the theater season. The duration of her own stay was indefinite—she didn't like to be away from her flower beds—but, of course, Dr. Kellogg would be the final arbiter there.

She was telling him about a new shop that had opened on Division Street when Hart-Jones distracted her and she fell prey to the general conversation. Will let her go. Lost in a fugue of Peterskill, he stared down at his plate, fork poised over his water-lily salad, remembering how the late-afternoon sun would reach through the windows of the parlor in the house on Parsonage Lane, and how, in happier days, he would sit there in the golden shower of it and browse through *Collier's* or *The Saturday Evening Post* while the small comforting sounds of the household ticked round him and Dick the wirehaired terrier sat at his feet. And how was Dick holding up?, he wondered. The poor dog. Left in the company of servants, no one to rub his belly or throw a ball to him on the great rolling emerald tongue of the lawn.

"The Sinclairs?" Mrs. Hookstratten suddenly exclaimed, and Will came back to the moment to see her throw her hands up in a gesture of shock and amazement. "*They* were here? Truly?" She was a small woman—smaller than Will had remembered her—with shrewd slicing eyes and a complexion that was bathed in milk. She was sixty if she was a day, and there wasn't a line in her face. "Oh"—and she clasped her hands at her breast now—"I can hardly believe it. What was *she* like, Eleanor?"

There followed Eleanor's description of Meta Sinclair, a description that lauded her beauty at the same time that it undermined it, adjectives like "gypsyish," "Arabian" and "exotic" applied to her various features and body parts, while her wardrobe was simultaneously admired and dismissed.

"Well, you know, of course, what a scandal they caused in New Jersey," Mrs. Hookstratten confided, lowering her voice, "in that colony or commune or whatever they called it." This was gossip, high and delicious, and she set her fork down in her Nut Ragout to concentrate on it.

Hart-Jones, who knew nothing of the subject and wouldn't have recognized the novelist and his wife if they were sitting in his lap, broke in with a braying and typically asinine comment, but Badger cut him off in a voice of high dudgeon: "*I* was there at Helicon Home, and I can assure you, madame, that the experiment in communal living was a noble and progressive one."

Eleanor held her peace, but gave Badger a congratulatory little smile.

"But there were accusations of all sorts of improper goings-on there," Mrs. Hookstratten countered, "of sun worship, nudity, free love—"

Free love. The term hung over the table like a visible thing, palpable, shining. For a moment no one spoke and Will turned over in his mind all that he knew about the Sinclairs' experiment in communal living— which began and ended with what he'd read in the newspapers. It was a big story at the time. They'd purchased a rather grandiose property in Englewood, a former preparatory school, and set up a colony on Socialist principles, pooling the resources of their forty members—New Thoughtists, vegetarians, Single-Taxers, suffragettes, assorted college professors, muckrakers and Socialists of every stripe. The press made a big to-do over the issue of free love, to which Sinclair apparently subscribed, and titillated readers throughout the Hudson Valley and beyond with visions of midnight rendezvous and wives available for the asking. It was all very exciting in a voyeuristic way, but then the place mysteriously burned to the ground and that was the end of that. Until Will and Eleanor arrived at the San, that is, and saw Meta Sinclair wandering the halls like Ophelia, gliding along with a natural and unconscious grace, her bouquet of hair wild on her shoulders, her cat's eyes fixed on some glittering thing in the distance. Will tried to picture her—Mrs. Sinclair, Meta—in the arms of another man and relieved of the flowing gowns and wraps she favored, and felt himself going faint with the possibilities.

"Nonsense," Badger rasped. "Upton is a great and forward-thinking man—a vegetarian champion—and as respectable as anyone at this table. Yes, he was a heliophile—or, rather, Meta was, and he went along for her sake—but who isn't? I certainly am, and no less an authority than our own Dr. Kellogg is a vigorous supporter of sunbathing—and that means, by definition, with as little sartorial impediment as possible—and not just sunbathing but all other forms of light therapy as well. And is there anything even remotely scandalous about Dr. Kellogg?"

Mrs. Tindermarsh had gone pale. She was so agitated she couldn't lift her eyes to Badger's, addressing her plate instead. "But Mr. Badger," she said in a voice that seemed reluctant to leave her throat, "what of these accusations of, of free love? Certainly, in a civilized society—" She couldn't go on.

Badger was unflappable. "Free love shouldn't be seen in a pejorative light, not at all, Mrs. Tindermarsh. Indeed, its roots are purely feminist. Have you ever considered that conventional marriage"—and here the muddy eyes came to rest briefly on Will and then darted away again—"is a sort of prison—for the woman, that is? The man is free to indulge his whims, but if a woman should presume to take a lover, why, the president wouldn't be able to sleep at night."

Eleanor applauded this grand speech with a quick soaring laugh and Hart-Jones joined her, belatedly, with a bucolic guffaw all his own. "Women in chains!" he cried, choking on his own wit. "White slavery!"

Ignoring him, Badger went on: "Both the Sinclairs, whom, as I say, I know and admire as intimate friends and companions, happen to feel that one should go wherever love leads and that it is not love but jealousy which is the obscenity. Love gives all rights, and a true marriage, a forward-thinking marriage, takes none away."

Badger seemed to be studying Will as he said this, and all at once Will was irritated. What was the implication? That he was holding

Eleanor back? That he should share her around like breeding stock? "I beg to disagree," Will croaked, and the tenor of his voice seemed to startle the table. Before he knew what he was saying, he was launching a passionate plea for nuptial fidelity, for love offered up like a gift, whole and complete in the giver and receiver, but all the time, in a kind of panic, he was thinking of Irene.

"Cant," Badger pronounced, dismissing him with a wave of the hand. "Nothing but cant and platitudes."

Mrs. Tindermarsh sat rigid, her head bowed, as if she'd just sustained a crippling assault. Hart-Jones had lost interest—his powers of concentration ran no deeper than a gnat's—and returned to his food. Her eyes darting from one face to another, Mrs. Hookstratten sat back in her chair and brought a contemplative thumb to her chin. Will, in the meanwhile, felt personally affronted, felt like arguing the issue into the ground, felt like tearing off his jacket and hammering Badger till the smug little dirt-colored eyes went as cold as two marbles, but he never got the chance. Just then Eleanor gasped and put a hand to her mouth. "Oh, my God, Lionel—I'm late for my appointment," she cried, rising hastily from her chair. "Please excuse me," she murmured, turning to the table at large and covering herself with a smile as the men rose and the women tried on looks of mild surprise.

Eleanor was already backing away from the table, the smile stuck there on her face as if it wore pins on the underside. "Therapy, you know," she said, and tried to shrug and curtsy at the same time, like some sort of circus performer. "That's what we're here for."

And how did all this affect Will? His wife had fallen under Badger's spell and she was undergoing some sort of arcane treatment outside the Sanitarium—that much he gathered, though he'd yet to confront her with it—and she was exercising rigid control over her appetite. Will had never been much for rigid control—he was more inclined to grill up a steak and quaff a bottle of Sears' White Star Anything Cure—but he was exercising rigid control over himself just to keep from setting the San afire and catching the first train back to New York. And why was he doing it? For Eleanor's sake, that was why. Because he loved her.

But as he slipped surreptitiously into the cab behind hers on a sunstruck afternoon a week later, he couldn't help wondering if that love had already begun to discover its limits. He was spying on her. Following his own wife as if she were a criminal. He didn't stop to examine what he was doing, but it was a terrible thing and he knew it, and as the hack started off with a lurch and the startled trees of the drive went by in a blur, his stomach sank in on itself. "Where to?" the driver said, leaning into the window. He was wizened, white-haired, short as a man sawed in half, with a glob of a nose and two hard cynical eyes that shone like penny candy. Will, his gut cinched to the very last loop, told him to follow the hack in front of them, at which point the driver gave him a knowing look, turned his head to spit in the street and flicked his lash lightly across the horse's pounding buttocks.

They turned right on Washington and then left on Manchester. The houses grew bigger and finer as they traveled up the street, shadows galloping along ahead of them, the odd automobile pulled up at the curb or standing solitary in a shaded drive, as if on display. Another left on Jordan took them within sight of the roiled Kalamazoo River, and then Eleanor's cab was slowing in front of a mustard-colored Tudor with burnished brown beams and matching shutters. "Keep going," Will told the driver, and he shrank back against the canopy lest Eleanor see him, "but slowly, very slowly."

The driver obliged, and Will's cab crept by Eleanor's, which had come to a halt at the curb out front of the house. As they passed by, Will could see his wife in silhouette as she paid her driver, and then the driver emerged to open the door for her. Momentum pulled Will forward and he had to twist himself round in the seat and look over his shoulder to frame her in the back window as she made her way up the walk. "Slower," he hissed to the driver, and he saw the door of the house draw back and a man there, receding; a monocle, the pencil-stroke of a mustache, and that was it: she was gone.

Will had the driver turn round at the end of the block and make another pass. The cab slowed as they went by again and Will studied the house so intently he might have been looking through the walls, but it refused to become anything more than just a building—stone, mortar and plank. As the house fell away behind them, Will leaned forward and asked the driver if he knew who lived there.

Jostling in his seat, the little man considered the question a moment, spitting rhythmically over his shoulder three or four times in the process, as if the act were an aide-mémoire, and then, speaking into the breeze, he said: "A doctor."

"You know his name?"

Another flurry of throat clearing and expectorating, the head nodding and bobbing on its stalk of a neck, the horse jogging, streetlamps and tree trunks flicking past like pictures in a deck of cards. "Nope. All I know is I take your sick ladies from the Sanitary Hospital and then sometimes I pick 'em up again, depending, and, well . . ." (More hawking, the sleeve across the mouth, a quick flick of the lash.)

"Yes?"

"Well, I can't say what-all goes on in there, but the ladies? They seem a whole lot calmer on the way out than when I drop 'em—so it must work, whatever it is. No lack of 'em, either. Ladies, I mean."

Will mulled over this information as the cab proceeded up the street, but he didn't find much comfort in it. If this was just another one of Eleanor's "progressive" enthusiasms (the term "crackpot" occurred to him as being more appropriate), then it really wasn't anything to worry about. Could it be worse than the sinusoidal bath, after all? But what if it were truly dangerous, addictive, subversive? Just because the other ladies flocked to the treatment didn't legitimize it—they were all San habitués, veterans of every harebrained health adventure that came along, as susceptible as if they'd been bound, gagged and delivered to the doorstep. And who was this mysterious "doctor," anyway? And if he was legitimate, then why wasn't *he* at the San or one of its imitators? Worse: why should Eleanor keep the whole business a secret from her own husband? Fishy. Very fishy.

Absorbed in his thoughts, Will didn't notice that the driver had brought him back to the San until they turned into the circular drive. He looked up and there it was, looming grand and impregnable before him, the Temple of Quackery, an Idea and a Way made concrete, cut, hewn and stacked in stone. The wheels glided over the pavement, the sun scoured the windows, patients wandered the lawns, and Will, suspended in his carriage, had an unsettling revelation: he was coming home. No longer was he William Fitzroy Lightbody of Parsonage Lane, Peterskill, but an open checkbook, a card-carrying member of the Gizzardite Society of America, a votary at the shrine of rigid control. "Driver," he called, and there was an edge of panic in his voice, as if he'd just risen to the surface of a pond after being tangled in the weeds, "take me away from here."

He was answered by a deep-throated frictive command and a tautening of the reins. The wheels chopped to a halt, though there was another hack behind them and a high-crowned Buick automobile behind that. "Where to, friend?" the cabbie asked with a leer.

"I don't know. Anywhere. Take me downtown."

The driver let him off at the corner across from the Post Tavern and Will got out to stretch his legs and have a look around. Though the Doctor's spies no longer shadowed him (apparently they thought him harmless now that the offending kink had been removed), he didn't get downtown much and he really didn't know why. Maybe it was because he'd fallen into the San routine like a sleepwalker, all of society and its entertainments incorporated there in microcosm, or maybe it was just that the town held little interest for him if he couldn't dine out or stroll into a tavern, put his foot up on the brass rail and have a drink at the bar. But anyway, he was bored and the day was fine and all of Battle Creek was spread out before him like the petals of a flower opening to the sun.

He poked his head in a bookshop, bought a handful of soda crackers at the grocer's, watched two men in shirtsleeves dig a hole in the lawn out front of city hall and set a sapling in it. Later, it must have been around five, he sat on a bench and read an editorial by C. W. Post in the *Morning Enquirer*. It was while he was sitting there, wondering if Eleanor had finished with her treatment for the day and thinking he ought to walk back up to the San and see what sort of food substitute they were passing off as supper—not that he was hungry, but just for the comfort of the routine—that he glanced up from the paper and caught the eye of a man passing by on the sidewalk.

The man looked away and seemed to quicken his pace, but beneath the patchy whiskers, the smoked lenses and the superfluous overcoat there was something about him that looked familiar. This was no stranger, this was—"Charlie!" Will called out suddenly, as if the name had come to life on his tongue, "Charlie Ossining!"

Drawn up short, head turtled in the socket of his collapsed shoulders, Charlie looked like a scab fingered from the picket line. He looked tentative, nervous, worn down, his shoes scuffed, his body twisted in a defensive cringe. Lowering the shaded lenses, he peered back over his shoulder with a pair of eyes that had no expectation of pleasure—or even clemency—in them.

"Charlie!" Will repeated, and he was up off the bench now, shaking the limp hand that stuck out of the overcoat like a decoration. "How are you? How's Per-Fo going? Taking the world by storm, eh? Yes?"

Charlie gave him a tepid smile. Was that a mustache? It was so sparse you could count the individual hairs.

"By the way," Will went on, relieved to be talking to someone, anyone, "your Mrs. Hookstratten's been assigned to our table at the San, talks about you all the time—but you probably know that already." A pause. No encouragement from Charlie. Nothing. "Well. And so. It's good to see you."

"Likewise," Charlie mumbled, and his eyes were busy, reading the street in both directions, leaping from the bench to the trees behind it to the building at the corner.

"Eleanor's fine," Will said, tucking the newspaper under one arm and letting a fruity sigh escape him, "and I'm about the same, no better, no worse—you know how it is. You're looking"—Will was about to say "good," but amended it at the last moment—"different. Growing side-whiskers, are you? And a mustache? Very distinguished. I wore one—a mustache—when I was younger, did I ever tell you?"

"No, I don't think so," Charlie said, and he removed the colored spectacles, folded them up and tucked them away in his pocket. He looked less furtive now, more like the old Charlie, the boon companion and razor-sharp entrepreneur to whom Will had entrusted his check for a thousand dollars. "Mrs. Hookstratten," he said, as if he were just catching up with the conversation, but the name seemed to fall away from his lips and he faltered.

Something was wrong here, and Will couldn't quite fathom what it was. He gave Charlie a reassuring grin. The sun fell back a notch and the shade deepened. Birds flicked through the trees. They both turned to watch a man on a bicycle glide up the street.

"What I mean is, it's a real joy to have her here," Charlie said, but there was no joy in his face, "Mrs. Hookstratten, that is. Just like home. I'm arranging a tour of the Per-Fo factory for her."

"Oh? That sounds terrific. I'm sure she'll enjoy it. And where did you say the factory was located, just out of curiosity? I might like to have a visit someday myself, you know." Will gave a laugh, meant to imply that while it was his prerogative as a stockholder, there was no pressure involved—he wasn't fishing for an invitation. Or perhaps only partly.

"Raeburn Street."

"Raeburn? I don't think I'm familiar with—"

"It's on the east side of town—or on the south side, that is. Southeast." Charlie's eyes were busy again—up the street and down, over Will's shoulder, back to the building on the corner. "Listen, Will"—the old smile, the warm one—"I've got to run. Business, you know. But let's meet for lunch one day. Soon. All right? No whiskey, I promise."

Will laughed. "It's what I want more than anything, but we've got to control our appetites, right? Should I bring Eleanor? Amelia? We could make it a foursome."

"Yeah, sure," Charlie said, but there wasn't a whole lot of conviction in his voice.

"You know," Will said, keeping him—keeping him simply because he had nothing else to do in the world but crawl back to his cell at the San—"it's funny we never met in Peterskill, what with your being Mrs. Hookstratten's protégé, I mean. But of course she's my mother's friend primarily and Eleanor and I have our own circle of acquaintances. . . . How old did you say you were?"

It was a simple enough question, straightforward, direct, but Charlie seemed to be having difficulty with it. He retrieved the smoked spectacles from his pocket, wiped them on his sleeve and hooked them first over one ear and then over the other before answering. "I'll be twenty-six in July."

Twenty-six. There was a poignancy in that. A beauty and a sadness. Not so long ago Will had been twenty-six, a happy and a healthy man, happily married and with the sheen of immortality glowing round him like a second skin. All at once he was seized with the urge to take Charlie by the arm and lead him up the street to the Red Onion, to sit over shots of whiskey and tall sizzling beers and compare notes on their boyhoods in Peterskill, the concerts at the band shell in Depew Park, skating on the river, school, baseball, girls they'd known in common and maybe even courted or danced with, but he fought it down. "There's only five and a half years separating us," he murmured instead. "Or maybe six. Strange we never met—but I guess we traveled in different circles—"

"Yeah, I'm sure that's it. But listen, Will, I've really got to be going." Charlie seized his hand. "Good talking to you."

"And you."

Will stood there and watched till Charlie turned the corner and was gone, and then he made his way up the street toward the San. They'd be serving dinner soon, and while the prospect of the food didn't hold much interest for him, Eleanor would be there, and that was something. Though he had to share her with Linniman and Badger and Dr. Kellogg and half the matrons, Foodists and housewives in the place, though he'd followed her to the door of that mysterious house on Jordan Street like a cuckold and sat at her side like a trained monkey, she was his wife still, and he took what he could get.

Besides, he just loved the look on her face when she got back from her treatment.

Chapter 5

The
Per-Fo
Factory

There was nothing to do but lie.

The train was heaving into the station, the porters were jumping, the Push, Grano-Fruto and Vita-Malta boys jockeying for position with the people who'd come down to greet their friends and relations, and Mrs. Hookstratten—Auntie Amelia—was perched behind one of those shimmering windows, peering out on the town of vegetable legend with all the anticipation Charlie had felt on the night he'd arrived. How could he tell her that the whole thing was a bust, a dismal failure and worse? How could he explain that every last cent of her $6,500 investment in Per-Fo, along with the thousand dollars she'd laid out as start-up money, was gone, vanished down Bender's insatiable gullet like a stone dropped in a well? How could he admit that there were no happy workers whistling over crisp mountains of golden cereal flakes; that there was no office appointed in mahogany, no conveyor belt, no factory, no product; how could he tell her that the only thing Per-Fo had produced was lawsuits and injunctions?

He couldn't and he didn't. Somehow, when he rose up off that bench and stepped into the surging crowd, he found the strength to fight down the fear and loathing that ran through his veins like an infection. In that moment he made himself over. He felt the smile leap to his face, tasted the sweet syrup of the lies gathering on his tongue, saw the world come into focus as if for the first time. Nothing he'd experienced in his life could approach the cold-sweat tension of this moment, not the giddiest hustle, not the shakiest hand at cards or the luckiest kiss on the billiard table, not even the finessing of Will Lightbody—till now it had been easy. This was his baptism, this was his trial by fire.

In his jacket pocket, neatly folded in an oversized envelope, were the handsome blue-and-gold, and utterly worthless, Per-Fo stock certificates for Mrs. Hookstratten—the same issue he'd delivered to Will in exchange for his check—and in his right hand, tucked into the crook of his arm like a bouquet, was the last red-white-and-blue-striped sample box of the sham product itself. There was no going back now. There was no crying over Bender, no covering his flank—there was only this moment. Grinning, ecstatic, his eyes glowing and his back arched, he stood there on the platform like a suitor, and went forward to meet it.

Like Eleanor Lightbody before her, Mrs. Hookstratten descended from the train in a flurry of porters and baggage. She wore a traveling gown of some sheeny blue material, tightly corseted, a hat that shot feathers like sparks and a trailing fur stole. Brisk and small—she wasn't much taller than a child, though she was as solid as a fireplug—she sank into the snarl of activity and Charlie lost sight of her. He shouldered his way past a man with a trunk the size of a coffin, neatly sidestepped a pair of nuns walking arm in arm, and with a twist of his hips sent a Vita-Malta boy sprawling into the knees of a man hawking Dr. Pettibone's Health Tonic. "Auntie Amelia!" he cried, though the words stuck in his throat, and in the next moment he was embracing her.

"Charles, my Charles," she cooed, patting his shoulders in an explosion of perfume and powder, her grip surprisingly firm and tenacious. "And let me have a look at you," she demanded, standing back now at arm's length. Her eyes, magnified by the thick polished lenses, darted like fish in an aquarium, and then she pronounced him looking fit but a little thin. "And that suit," she added, clucking her tongue, "—it looks like you slept in it."

"Yes, well," he mumbled, at a loss suddenly, but holding his artificial smile (he *had* slept in it, three nights running), "business, you know. I hardly have time for anything but. And speaking of business"—with a flourish—"this is for you," and he handed her the last remaining box of Per-Fo in the world.

Her mouth dropped. Her eyes went soft. And as traveling salesmen, juvenile stock peddlers and grandparents from Ohio surged round her, she took the garish pasteboard container from him and pressed it to her bosom like rare treasure. Three porters, burdened with her baggage, looked on numbly, watching this ritual with the impassivity of Indian fakirs. "Charles," she gasped, struggling to summon breath sufficient to express the precipitous emotion of the moment, "oh, Charles, I'm so proud of you."

In the cab on the way to the Sanitarium, while Charlie tortured his brain to come up with an even faintly credible explanation as to why he couldn't help her in with her things, she elaborated. "I'm proud that you've chosen the field of health, Charles," she breathed, her eyes shining with excitement as the dusk settled in around them. "I mean, dedicating yourself to the general good, while coincidentally making your way in the world. Why, it's almost a crusade. Just think how many digestive systems Per-Fo will save from ruin. . . . I only wish your Morgans and your Rockefellers had such humanitarian aims. I'm afraid the majority of our boosters and go-getters think of nothing but money. It's a shame, really. A shame."

Charlie nodded, forcing an inarticulate rumble of agreement from his larynx. He was thinking of money himself at the moment, wondering if he could somehow manage to hold off the stroke of doom long enough to get more of it out of her—love, gratitude and the Eighth Commandment notwithstanding. If Bender had taught him anything, it was this: never let mere scruples stand in your way. Bender had taken something soft in Charlie, something weak and yielding, something human, and held it over the torch of his cynicism till it blackened and shrank and grew hard as an ingot.

"And how is Mr. Bender?" Mrs. Hookstratten wondered, patting his hand and leaning forward to peer out the window, drinking in this new and glorious environment like a pilgrim come to the shrine. "Such a sincere man. And with such vision."

Vision. Yes, he had vision, all right. Bender made the inventor of the memory tablets look like a blind man. Right from the beginning, from the moment Charlie had been introduced to him at the odd soirée at Mrs. Hookstratten's, a friend of a friend of someone in Philadelphia society, Bender had seen the entire jerry-built framework of Per-Fo rise up before him on rotten timbers, had seen all the suckers lined up out the door and across the countryside all the way to Battle Creek—and Charlie first in line—and he'd seen the day when the take would be sweet enough to pull the whole thing down. What Charlie wouldn't have given for a little of that vision.

"Charles?"

"Huh?"

She let out a laugh. "Has business got you that distracted? I was asking about your partner, Mr. Bender: How is he?"

"Fine," Charlie blurted. "Thriving. Couldn't be better. He's out of town at the moment, though," he added, feeling the ground slip out from under him. "In St. Louis—looking after our accounts."

"What a pity," Mrs. Hookstratten murmured as the carriage turned up Washington Avenue and the lights of the Sanitarium came into view, showy and audacious, a six-story electrical blaze that set the twilit night afire. "I'd so looked forward to seeing him again—but, then, I suppose he'll be back soon?"

"Soon? Oh, yes, sure—of course he will, of course. In a few days or so. Or a week. What I mean is, who can tell how long a sales trip will take—got to drum up business, you know. But he'll be back. He will."

If he was hedging, Mrs. Hookstratten didn't seem to notice. She'd spotted the San now and was emitting a low gurgle of appreciation and grasping blindly for Charlie's arm. "That's it, isn't it?" she cried, but didn't wait for an answer. "I've seen it so many times in pictures and on postcards. 'A goodly temple upon the hill'—and it is a temple, isn't it?" She was distracted in her excitement, thinking aloud about her glossitis, her shingles, her nervous itch ("I've scratched my arms and legs till I look like a skinned savage strapped to a totem pole or whatever you call those things"), and it gave Charlie a precious moment to work up an excuse for being unable to help her check in, find her room, arrange her things for her, stay to dinner, gossip, visit and tuck her in. The carriage swayed. The horses clopped. The lights grew closer.

"—and Dr. Kellogg," she was saying, "a saint on earth. I don't know how you were fortunate enough to become associated with such an illustrious family—was it *his* son or his brother's?"

She paused. The gap opened. Charlie fell into it. "*His* son," he said miserably. "The Doctor's."

"Didn't you say his name was George in one of your letters? George, wasn't it?"

"Yes," Charlie affirmed, and his voice had sunk low.

They were swinging into the circular drive in front of the San now and Mrs. Hookstratten was cooing and exclaiming like a tourist: "How grand!" and "Is that Italian marble?" In the midst of it, craning her neck, peering, ejaculating, she turned back to him and said, "George, yes, how I do look forward to meeting him—and to seeing his father again. Did I tell you that I first met Dr. Kellogg three years ago in Manhattan? Or was it four? Well, anyway, he was lecturing on food drunks, I remember it as if it were yesterday, Meg Rutherford and—but goodness, here we are."

There they were. The hack stopped and the driver was climbing down. The doorman from the San and a matching pair of bellhops descended on them like jackals. "Listen, Auntie, I have to tell you something—" Charlie began, tugging at his words as if they were stuck to his teeth.

"Oh, look! That's that perfectly adorable Mrs. Cormier I met on the train coming in from Chicago"—her head out the window now—"yoo-hoo, Winifred!"

"I, uh, I've got to go. I mean, I can't come in. I'd love to, I would, but I've got to get back. To the factory, the books—"

No one moved. The doorman, the bellhops, the cabbie—they might have been hewn of stone. Outside, the crickets seemed to choke off in unison and Winifred Cormier, a woman with a convex figure in a plain dress, halted at the door of the cab ahead of them, perplexed. Mrs. Hookstratten was staring at him in astonishment, the corners of her mouth working. "Can't come in?" she repeated. "But what do you mean?"

Charlie's smile was foolish, swollen, a bravura smile that didn't begin to cover his panic. "Work," he said lamely.

"Work? At this hour?"

Nouns dropped from his lips like succulent little fruits—"duty," "competition," "nose," "grindstone"—but they had no effect. Mrs. Hookstratten cut him off in the middle of a convoluted apology. "Do you mean to tell me that after I've come all this way and after all I've done for you since you were practically an infant in diapers—and for your parents, too, don't forget about them—that you don't want to see me? Can that be possible? Am I losing my hearing?"

"Auntie, I—"

"Don't 'Auntie' me. I want an answer, yes or no: are you coming in or not?"

"Please don't be upset, but I've got a business to run—you've been after me for years to get involved in something, find my way in life, and now I have—"

"Can you for just one minute imagine how utterly depleted I am, Charles? Can you? A woman in my condition, whole days and nights on the train, shoddy service, food that would choke a hog—"

Charlie hunched his shoulders. He looked up into the faces of the Sanitarium doorman and the bellboys in the kelly-green uniforms with the fig leaves embroidered over their hearts, and he took a gamble. "Yes. All right," he said, uncoiling himself from the seat to step down and offer his hand, "but just for a minute."

❖   ❖   ❖

Luck had been with him that night. The vast roiling life of the Sanitarium lobby, with its comings and goings, its glissade of wheelchairs, the dinner-jacket socializing and clubby chitchat round the milk bar or beneath the palm fronds, swept obliviously past him. No one so much as looked twice at him, and for his part, he saw no muscle-bound orderlies, no imperious little doctors and no Lightbodys, male or female. Better yet, Mrs. Hookstratten was distracted by the swirl of attention —they had her in a wheelchair, her baggage was already on the way to her room, and would she care for a lacto-ovo vegetarian snack?—and she let him off easy. For the moment. But just as he was leaving, the hat jerked down over his brow, the blood settling back into his veins, she snatched at his sleeve. "Tomorrow, Charles," she said, pulling his face down to hers. She was mollified, he could see that, but her eyes were like needles, pricking and probing at him. "Tomorrow—and I don't care how exhausted I am or how busy you are—I want you to myself. All to myself." She grazed his cheek with her own and made a kissing noise. "And the very first thing I want to do is see this marvel of a factory."

From the Sanitarium, Charlie went directly to the Red Onion, where he slammed through the door, hurled himself at the bar and had to throw back two whiskies with beer chasers just to clear his head. *Tomorrow.* What was he going to do? The options were narrowing fast. Of course, he could go to the bank in the morning, withdraw Will Lightbody's thousand dollars and vanish like Bender—close the whole business like a book and be gone and out of it. There'd be no one to answer to then, no games to play, no lawyers to forestall or Auntie Hookstrattens to placate . . . but then he'd be back where he started, condemned to the life of the small hustle and smaller expectation. A thousand dollars richer, sure, but that wouldn't last long—and he'd always be looking over his shoulder.

No. What he needed was capital, more capital. Per-Fo was dead—raped and murdered by that son of a bitch Bender—but that didn't mean Charlie had to lie down and die, too. He knew the breakfast-food business now, he did—all he needed was a new start, a new name. Christ, he could think of a hundred of them—*Zip, Flash, Fruto-Fruto, Flakies, Crunchies, Chewies.* . . . Yes, sure—and *Albatross, the Breakfast Food You Hang Round Your Neck.* He sighed. Ordered another whiskey. There had to be a way.

When he looked up again, Harry Delahoussaye was standing beside him, one foot propped on the brass rail, an elbow cocked on the bar. Delahoussaye was watching him, a slow grin settling into his face. He was as casually stylish as ever, in a new suit of some imported material and a checked silk tie. Charlie looked at him and saw himself, a little man trading on his charm and wit and going nowhere farther than the next oyster bar—for every C. W. Post or Will Kellogg there were a million Delahoussayes. "What do you hear, Charlie?" Delahoussaye said. "How's the breakfast-food business?"

Was it his imagination or was Delahoussaye shouting? "Shhh," Char-

T. Coraghessan Boyle

lie warned, taking him by the arm. He scanned the room nervously for off-duty hotel employees, lawyers, disgruntled investors. No one looked up. Conversation careened round them. The barman said something about a horse to the man on Charlie's left and turned to draw a beer.

"Not so good, huh?" Delahoussaye said, and his grin got wider, as if the whole thing were funny, as if it were a joke. "Come on, let me buy you a drink. What are you having?"

Charlie was having whiskey. Delahoussaye ordered; the barman wiped the gleaming surface of the bar, set down two shots and absently watched the men lift the glasses to their lips before shuffling off to attend to another customer. "I've had a few problems," Charlie admitted, setting down the empty glass, and now he was grinning, too, a show of bravado, "nothing I can't handle. How about you?"

Delahoussaye looked down at the bar, feigning modesty. "The train was grand tonight, really grand," he murmured, stroking his nose thoughtfully. "Didn't I see you down there, by the way?"

Charlie nodded.

"Sold seventy-five of Push and twenty-something of the Vita-Malta, though even the dead ones fresh off the train know it's sinking through the floor."

"What? Vita-Malta? But didn't they just open the factory last September?"

"They come and go, Charlie—you ought to know that as well as anybody." Charlie wondered what he'd heard, but Delahoussaye gave no sign one way or the other, just dropped his shoulders and lifted his eyebrows. "Lousy management—and the stuff tastes like the box it comes in."

"And Push? What about that? I hear they're selling it as fast as they can make it."

Delahoussaye paused to light a cigarette, regarding Charlie with a hooded look as he shook out the match and exhaled. "Yeah, sure— they're thriving. Smart, that's why. My cousin Garth's out there, you know—assistant to the foreman—and I'll tell you, they keep that place as spotless as your mother's kitchen. They've got a new plant now, too, and that helps. You know it? Out on South Union, across the tracks from Post?"

Charlie knew it—a brick building painted in green and red, the Push colors, that took up the better part of a block all by itself. He couldn't count the times he'd admired it—it was just what he'd envisioned for Per-Fo, something substantial, something to be proud of, the kind of building that said, *Here I am, come take me on.* But just then, the image of the Push plant glowing in his mind like a living photograph, something came over him. It was an idea, an inspiration, a scheme, and it struck him like a hard physical blow, like a slap to the head—he had to take a gulp of air and spread both hands out on the bar to steady himself. He turned to Delahoussaye, hoping the look in his eyes wouldn't give him away, and said, as casually as he could, "Your cousin, huh?"

The hardest part was stalling Mrs. Hookstratten. The rest of it was no stroll in the park, but at least it was straightforward, a matter of distributing Will Lightbody's money in the right places and in the right proportions. It took less than one hundred dollars of the Lightbody trust, doled out to Delahoussaye, his cousin, the night watchman and a select few others, to convert the Push plant into the Per-Fo factory for two furtive and illusory hours. The biggest share went to the sign painter, a hand-wringing artiste who couldn't bear to prostitute his talents on so ephemeral a work. In the end, he did manage to produce a reasonable facsimile, though he never stopped grumbling about it. KELLOGG'S PER-FO, the banner read in four-foot-high letters evenly spaced across an expanse of bedsheets sewed together end to end, and though it hadn't come cheap, Charlie couldn't complain: when tacked down tightly over the soaring Push billboard, it looked like the genuine article. Especially at night.

No: the trouble was with Mrs. Hookstratten. She was a woman who wasn't used to being denied. From the time she was a girl and sole heiress to the Van der Pluijm brickworks fortune to her later years as wife to Adolphus "Dolph" Hookstratten, the lion of Wall Street, and her subsequent viduity, she had gotten exactly what she wanted when she wanted. But Charlie couldn't gratify her for eight interminable days— it took that long to make his arrangements and wait through to the following Sunday, when the plant would be vacant. Push, like Post Foods and the Kellogg company, was running a twenty-four-hour-a-day operation, and the only time Charlie could manage his imposture was on the Lord's Day, when the ovens were quiescent and the packing line deserted.

Mrs. Hookstratten didn't understand. He telephoned her two or three times daily, ostensibly from his mahogany-lined office, but actually from the drugstore, or from the Chinese laundry, where the sound of the steam press lent an air of authenticity to the ruse. Why couldn't she call him? she wondered. Something wrong with the lines, he countered, outgoing calls only, and that was hell on business, as she could imagine, and he had the phone company working on it even as they spoke. But why hadn't any of the people at the San heard of Per-Fo and its benefits, and why wasn't it on the shelves at Offenbacher's, back in Peterskill? She'd looked and looked. That was why he was working so hard, he told her, static crackling in his ear, that was why, this week especially, he was having difficulty in getting away. But, she insisted, he *had* to get away, and there was no arguing with the tone of her voice. He had to squire her around town, soothe her nerves, help her acclimate herself to all that was strange and new—and, most particularly of all, he had to show her this factory she'd underwritten to the tune of a small fortune. "A small fortune, Charles," she'd repeated for emphasis.

She'd arrived on a Friday, and he managed to put her off till Monday, when he persuaded her to dine with him at a new vegetarian restaurant that had just opened downtown, rather than at the San (anything but the San). In the interim, he began growing side-whiskers and a mustache, took to wearing dark spectacles and found himself a room, no board, for a dollar and a half a week. The room was on the south side of the city, halfway to Goguac Lake, on an overgrown back street that looked as if it were still in the process of being carved from the wilderness. It was remote and quiet and he felt safe there, all things being equal. He sent Ernest O'Reilly to fetch his things from Mrs. Eyvindsdottir's, instructing him to use the back staircase and take a devious route both ways. It was mad, hopeless, and he was living on the edge of the precipice, he knew it, but there was no other way. This was the life of the man of vision, the man who dared all, the genius, the tycoon: risk nothing, gain nothing.

The Cafe Nonpareil ("Nutritious Food Without Slaughter") was a replica in miniature of the San dining hall, run by a zealous former patient who attributed her cure to the Doctor's recipes and a quasi-religious revelation in which an anthropomorphic lamb had appeared to her with a butcher's diagram stenciled on its hindquarters. The menu ran to things like Beet Tops Salade and Jerusalem Artichokes, Broiled Tender. Mrs. Hookstratten kept up an unrelenting stream of complaint throughout the meal, wondering how in heaven's name her own boy, whom she'd seen through the finest schools and staked in business, could treat her so shabbily, delivering her up into the hands of strangers and all but deserting her. "Don't tell me you can't find time for me, Charles, don't tell me," she huffed, picking at a glutinous ball of unhulled rice.

Charlie pleaded, charmed, lied. He used all his skills as an apprentice confidence man and professional dissembler to propitiate her, giving way on every point, issuing promises like paper money and weaving a fabric of lies so tight it could have sustained the political platform of a national party. On Friday he took her out again, and she nagged him inexorably—Where had he been? Couldn't he at least have phoned? Sent a note? She'd been here nearly a week now and he hadn't even seen her room yet. Didn't he care how she was doing or where they'd put her? Did her comfort mean nothing to him? Her health? Her nerves? Her itching? And what about the factory? She was beginning to believe it was built on air.

This time Charlie was ready for her. Finally. "How does Sunday sound, Auntie? It's the only day the workers are off, and believe me, you wouldn't want to set foot in the place with all the noise and confusion of the full-scale operation, not with your nerves—"

The light froze in her spectacles. She clutched the fork like a weapon and the diamond at her throat glared in its uncompromising purity. "What time?" she asked, her lips clamped round the question.

"Seven."

"Seven? But isn't that awfully early? I've got my Swedish Manual Movements to get through, you know—and morning services."

Charlie smiled with his whole face, his whole head, smiled till he could feel the skin at the back of his neck tugged up like a window shade. "Seven in the evening," he said.

Night fell deep and early that Sunday, accompanied by a steady sizzling rain that drove the earthworms up onto the sidewalks and obscured all the hard lines and recognizable features of Foodtown, U.S.A. To Charlie's mind, the weather was perfect. Once they got into the cab out front of the San, Mrs. Hookstratten couldn't have known whether they were traveling north, south, east or west, or if they'd risen up into the sky like one of the Wrights' airplanes. She was visibly excited. And though she didn't pause even for breath, her tone was less combative and he could feel her softening. Should he ask for five thousand? he wondered. Ten? He didn't want to shock her with the figure, but, then, he didn't want to underplay his hand, either.

They were met at the door by Delahoussaye's cousin, a bald-headed man in a cheap but respectable-looking suit and an ingratiating smile. Twenty dollars was a lot of money, but it bought Charlie an exhaustive tour of the facilities, from the flour-milling room to the roasting room to the packing line and the folding and stitching room, where the cartons were constructed (the cartons themselves had, of course, been conveniently mislocated, so as not to cause Mrs. Hookstratten any undue perplexity). It also bought—or, rather, rented—an oracle who could answer even the most recondite question with a thoroughness that would have exhausted a team of engineers. In fact, the cousin was so good, he had Charlie half convinced that this grand and immaculate plant was his after all, and Charlie resolved to tip him a dollar when they left.

The problem came when they reached the offices. Charlie had arranged for Per-Fo letterhead and a nameplate for the desk, and he'd been careful to sanitize the place of all signs of its true affiliation. Telephone, typewriter and blotter were stationed on the desk, along with a homely spill of pens, pencils and gum erasers. "And here,

Auntie," Charlie said, throwing open the door, "is my inner sanctum."

Mrs. Hookstratten's face fell. She bit her lip. Her eyes devoured the room and spat it out again.

"Auntie?" Charlie croaked, frantically scanning the place for the telltale trace of Push paraphernalia, the corpus delicti, the dead give-away. "Is there something the matter? Don't you like my office?"

The steely eyes, the unforgiving compress of the lips. Mrs. Hook-stratten could be tough—tough enough to drive whole armies howling before her. "But this isn't mahogany, Charles—even a child could see that." She shot a wilting look at the cousin, as if he were somehow responsible for duping her boy in this most essential of equations.

"Cherrywood, ma'am," the cousin said.

"Painted in a mahogany stain," Charlie put in, waving his fingertips as if he'd burned them. "Isn't that right, Garth?"

"That's right, sir."

But Mrs. Hookstratten wouldn't be placated. "It's criminal, is what it is," she puffed, "using a cheap domestic wood that doesn't have one-half—not one-half—the elegance and richness of mahogany, and here I'd been led to believe . . . but surely you were deceived, Charles? If it weren't mahogany and you knew it, you would have been the first to tell me, wouldn't you?"

Charlie exchanged a glance with the cousin. "Yes, Auntie, of course, but—"

"Well, then," and she bounced the flat of her hand off the desk as if to dismiss it, "it's a terrible, awful shame. If you can't distinguish your woods, as any child can, then I don't wonder you're having difficulties getting that breakfast food into Offenbacher's."

There was an awkward moment, during which Charlie put on a face of mock righteousness, expressing his outrage with the furnishers and their cheap deceptions, and then he humbled himself and said a prayer aloud, wishing only that his Auntie Hookstratten had been there from the beginning to see that he wasn't taken. And then he vowed, with the squarest set of his jaw, to have those furnishers back in to re-place the whole business—wainscoting and all—with genuine Malay mahogany. She sniffed her approval, and the moment passed. After bidding their farewells to the cousin, they gathered up their things and stepped out into the rain beneath the bright startling plane of the Per-Fo sign.

It was then, just as he was escaping unscathed, just as he was unfurling the umbrella and working up the courage to broach the subject of pressing needs and lagging investment, that a new and infinitely more dangerous threat arose. What would it have taken them to reach the cab without incident—twenty, thirty seconds? What if they'd lingered half a minute more to chat with Charlie's presumptive foreman or spent another five minutes in the granary, absorbing the sweet farinaceous odor of the drying corn? But no, they had to leave just then, just on the crux of that nasty fatal moment.

"Charlie!" a voice bawled from the drenching dark, "Charlie Ossining!"

The rain fell, the puddles grew, Mrs. Hookstratten huddled beneath the umbrella and looked round her, startled. Charlie froze.

"It's me, partner," the voice cried, and then it began to solidify round a form staggering out of the gloom, a ragged form, oddly familiar, creature of the crushed hat and vomitous overcoat, poised to deliver the death-blow to all Charlie's dwindling hopes. George Kellogg, in all his rancid glory, stood astride the walk before them.

"George," Charlie said, and gave a curt nod of dismissal. He tightened his grip on Mrs. Hookstratten's arm and tried to hurry her past the obstruction in the path, but George was too quick for him. Suddenly he was under the umbrella with them, his arm clapped round Charlie's shoulder, a miasma of earthy and human stinks enveloping them like a shroud in their fetid little pocket of the night.

"Saw the sign," George slurred. And then he stuck his face in Mrs. Hookstratten's and breathed, "Nice evening, ma'am."

"Look," Charlie said, trying to fight his way out from under George's arm while at the same time managing to keep a grip on the umbrella and Mrs. Hookstratten, "I haven't got time for this foolishness now—"

"Who *is* this horrid man?" Mrs. Hookstratten demanded. The rain beat at the fabric of the umbrella; it drooled from the eaves of the factory in a maudlin hypnotic dirge.

"I said get away, George," Charlie growled.

But George wouldn't let go. "Get away? Foolishness? Horrid man?" he echoed, sober suddenly. "I'm insulted, Charlie. Deeply hurt. Is that any way to talk to your closest business associate, the man who's lent his good and valuable name to all this, this"—he flapped his arm at the high-flung sign cut into the roof of the night behind them—"this enterprise?"

Mrs. Hookstratten hardened beside Charlie—he could feel her going rigid as the outrageousness of the situation grew on her. "What's he saying?" she demanded. "Who is this man?"

Charlie never got a chance to answer. George let go then, his features hammered in light, and removed his hat with a mock bow. "George Kellogg, at your service, madam. You wouldn't happen to have any spare change, would you?"

Chapter 6

A
Sword of
Fire

ଏ୨⊛୧ଏ

I t was a night for sleeping, the wind gentle in the trees, rain counting time on the shingles, the house held in the soft fluttering grip of its tics and rustlings. But for John Harvey Kellogg, sleep would not come. He lay there in his bed, stiff as a corpse, scrubbed inside and out and enfolded in the crisp white sheets and freshly laundered blankets as if he'd been sealed in an envelope, and willed himself to relax. He forced his eyes shut, listened to the house settle around him. It was so still and the rain so soft, he could hear the occasional muted snore from Ella's room across the hall, the faintest little slip of a sound that somehow filled him with sadness.

It was past two in the morning, and he needed sleep. Not in the way an ordinary man might, and not so much of it, either—but he needed it nonetheless. He routinely got by with four hours a night and had always regarded the whole notion of sleep with suspicion. It seemed wasteful, sinful, a squandering of precious resources, and he was always amazed to find that some people actually looked forward to it. But as a physician, he understood and appreciated the body's need for respite from the trials of waking life, and he was willing to give in to it once a day, as part of his regimen. Just as he wouldn't dream of going without his enemas or his Swedish Manual Movements or oat bran, so he wouldn't go without sleep, either—it was a vital component of the physiologic life. And usually, through force of will, he was able to get to sleep in an efficient and economical way. After a cup of Sanitas Koko or herbal tea and some quiet reading in the *Journal of the American Emunctory Society* or the *Hydrotherapy Newsletter*, he would slip into his white cambric pajamas with the silver J.H.K. monogram over the heart and drop off to sleep the moment he extinguished the light.

But not tonight. There were too many things on his mind. Though it was a Sunday, generally the most tranquil day of the week for him, what with the time he spent in reflection at church and the musical half-hour he enjoyed at the piano with one or another of the children, he was far from tranquil at the moment. Among other things, he was wrought up over the following evening's Question Box lecture. Not over the substance of it, that was never a problem: white sugar had been on his mind lately, a commodity as pernicious and enervating as bleached flour, and he would speak to that. No, the worry—the fear, actually—was over George. It had been two weeks since he'd made his criminal assault on the reception following the tapeworm lecture, and though he hadn't attempted anything in the interval, the Doctor was sure he was planning some new hatefulness. And what better time for the odious little ingrate to strike than when he was at the podium? That was how George's sinkhole of a mind worked.

They hadn't caught him that night—and woe to George if they had. If they'd caught him—and the Doctor's eyes snapped wide open at the thought—he didn't know if he would have been able to restrain himself, didn't know but that it would have been a repeat of that terrible night on the stairwell when George had first come to them. The boy had made a fool of him, set the curtains ablaze and scared the daylights out of a hundred patients whose nerves were in no condition to be tampered with. He'd very nearly ignited Mrs. Cornish's taffeta gown in the process, and in fact had given her a nasty second-degree burn on the left breast when one of the missiles had lodged in her cleavage. How he'd managed to escape was a mystery. After stampeding the patients with his pyro-maniacal display, he was somehow able to elude the Doctor, Frank Linniman and half a dozen attendants, no doubt slipping out one of the rear exits at the height of the confusion. He knew the building well—the Doctor had to give him credit for that.

But it was damnable. An outrage. This wasn't merely an embarrassment, this wasn't cadging change or shouting obscenities in the street; this was criminal assault, arson, attempted murder. Chief Farrington and his force of twelve deputies had been combing the streets for him ever since, poking through the tramp "jungle" under the South Jefferson Street bridge and roving as far afield as Kalamazoo, Olivet and Albion. George was going to prison this time, and no mercy was to be extended him, no mitigating circumstances taken into account. "Bill," the Doctor had told the constable, "I made a mistake with that boy, a grievous mistake, and I'm sorry to have to admit it. There's a taint in his blood, a sign of the degeneracy that's already overtaking the race, and I want him put away behind bars where he's not liable to hurt anybody else. You catch him, Bill," he added, and his voice was steady and cold, "and you do it quietly and quickly, and while you're at it, you just give a moment's reflection as to how much my support and goodwill have meant to you and the mayor over the years."

Farrington was no fool. He'd gotten the message, all right, no doubt about that, but it would be two weeks tomorrow night and George was still unaccounted for. And that was no small thing. The boy had made his intentions perfectly clear—it was all-out war on John Harvey Kellogg, the man whose only crimes were compassion, generosity and hope, the man who'd given him the clothes on his back, the roof over his head, the food in his mouth, an education, a name, a place in the world that was his for the taking. It was beyond fathoming, beyond human understanding. But at this point, the Doctor's patience was exhausted —all that mattered now was that the boy be stopped. He was a self-declared enemy, for whatever reason—or lack of reason—and the Doctor knew how to deal with enemies. George would never see the light of day again.

Yet what frightened him as he lay there rigid in his bed, what kept the sound of the rain from lulling him and the pillow from loosening the knotted muscles at the base of his skull, what kept his eyes stuck on the shifting, ghostly, half-visible pattern of the wallpaper, was the way the boy had delivered his message, the balls of newsprint flaring through the air like rockets, like the bright semaphore of doom. It paralyzed the Doctor even to think of it. Fire was his bête noire, the thing he feared above all else, the one thing he couldn't control. And George knew it. How old had he been—thirteen? fourteen?—when the fire had swept the San? Whatever his age, the lesson of it hadn't been lost on him. This was the way to strike out at the world, this was the way to humble his betters and twist the knife in his adoptive father's heart, this secret spark, this flame in the darkness, *this*.

Lying there in the chasm of the night, staring into nothing, the Doctor could see the San, his precious San, as it was on the day he rushed home from a lecture tour to find it in ruins—February 19, 1902. He would never forget that day, the most heartbreaking day of his life, and he would never forgive himself for having been absent at the critical moment. Fire had raced through the place the previous morning, taking the life of one patient and reducing the Sanitarium and all its equipment, its Experimental Kitchens and its vibrating stools, its heated tubs and physiologic chairs, to ashes. He could see the skeletal remains of the chimneys poking up out of the wreckage as if to mock him with their solidity, the fine white ash three feet deep and glowing with a satanic intensity, everything he'd built and struggled for and believed in eradicated in a single stroke. And he could see George's face as it was then, the clotted venom of the eyes, the slug of a mouth, the smirk, the grimace, the undisguised satisfaction that reddened the tips of his ears and made his head bob on the wilted stem of his neck.

The boy had loved that fire, loved what it had done to the Doctor and his idea of himself. Dr. Kellogg could remember George standing there on the verge of the blackened pit, his shoulders slumped, a private hateful smile on his lips, while the other children gasped and cried out and held each other as if they were about to fall off the edge of the world.

They never discovered the origin of that fire. Though it stank with suspicion. Reeked. Oh, yes. Oh, yes, indeed. The Doctor never thought of George at the time—and even now, after all that had transpired, he still didn't think the boy had had an active hand in it. He might have abetted it mentally, might have prayed for the conflagration and inwardly cheered as the top floor collapsed round the elevator shaft, but he wasn't yet devious enough to have conceived of the blaze itself. No, the finger pointed to Sister White and her Adventist vigilantes.

The prophetess and co-founder, with her husband, of the Sanitarium's predecessor, the Western Health Reform Institute, Sister Ellen White had in those years become the voice of the Adventist church, her frequent and remarkably specific visions shaping its policies as neatly as a last shaped the shoe to fit it. For the better part of a decade she'd been struggling with the Doctor over control of the San, but he'd always kept one step ahead of her. When she dunned him for contributions to the church's far-flung concerns—its shoddily managed and unprofitable sanitaria in places like Spokane, Peoria and Moline, its overseas missions and the print shops that spewed out its superabundant literature—the Doctor had the San declared nonsectarian and benevolent, ostensibly for tax purposes, and inserted a clause in its charter requiring that all its income be disbursed within the boundaries of the state of Michigan.

The move might have mollified the tax collector, but it didn't please Ellen White. She had a vision, conveyed to all the faithful from the pulpit, suggesting that God Himself wasn't pleased, either. The Sanitarium had become godless, she asserted, condoning "evolutionary" thinking and putting the greenback dollar above its mission of Christian charity. God's wrath had been aroused. What Sister White saw, twisting and slashing at the firmament over Battle Creek, was the coruscating sword of that wrath—a sword of fire.

It was a prophetic vision. In July of '98, a fire raked the Doctor's Sanitarium Health Food Company, and the following year a blaze of suspicious origin gutted the Sanitas Food Company plant, another of the Doctor's concerns. Then there was the Sanitarium fire, and while he was rebuilding (the Elders hadn't dreamed of the extent of his connections or the depth of his friends' pockets), he had to contend with a steady stream of warnings, prophecies and rumblings of further divine intervention, all channeled through Sister White's perfervid imagination. But this time he built of stone, though the San's stables, vacuumed cows and all, were mysteriously consumed by fire less than a year after the present structure went up. Never for a moment did John Harvey Kellogg doubt who was responsible.

Till now.

But no, and he shook his head unconsciously against the pillow, he didn't really think George capable of that, not at fourteen. No: it was

Ellen White. It had to be. She was the worst kind of rabble-rousing, evangelical charlatan, appealing to the most gullible and ignorant elements, and her followers, simple rural folk for the most part, would go to any lengths to see the word of God made concrete. Still, George had been a problem that year, no doubt about it—more of a problem than usual, his adolescence clinging to him as awkwardly as a shirt two sizes too small.

He wouldn't eat, for one thing. Just took it into his head that he wasn't going to eat anymore, and that was that. No reason, no explanation. He woke up one morning that fall, sat down at the table with the other children and refused to touch his food. This was the sort of thing the children's nurses were expected to deal with, and it might never have come to the Doctor's attention but for an unusual circumstance. Ordinarily, he and Ella took their meals in their own quarters, the Doctor's irregular schedule preventing him from dining with the children, which he was disinclined to do in any case, finding their habits —the twice-handled food, the furtive wipe of lip on sleeve, the unconscious dribble and the tendency of sauces to collect about the corners of the mouth—unsettling to his own digestion. But around this time—the fall of '01, that is, some months before the fire—the Doctor had been experimenting with several new food products, and had taken to strolling through the children's dining room at mealtimes to observe their reactions to them.

He was then in his couscous-kohlrabi phase, attempting to blend the semolina and the high-fiber vegetable into a mash that could, like the breakfast foods he'd pioneered, be twice-baked, desiccated and dextrinized, for easy digestion and prolonged shelf life. They'd tried it, reconstituted, as a porridge, but the kohlrabi infused the resulting mixture with an odd greenish tint and a taste of the earth that even the most pliant of the children had had difficulty with. For subsequent meals it was baked into wafers, stirred into a clear broth of reduced vegetables, ground up and sprinkled like bran on a lettuce salad, and congealed in an eggplant-chayote ratatouille. On this particular evening, at the Doctor's suggestion, the cook had rolled it into a Protose loaf to serve as an entrée, accompanied by a yogurt-piccalilli sauce.

When the Doctor entered the room, the children looked up as one and sang out, "Good evening, Father," before a gesture from him let them know they might return to their plates. He took a seat in the corner, unfolded a newspaper and made a show of studying it in order to put them at their ease. In reality, his spectacles twinkling in the light of the chandelier as he cocked his head ever so slightly this way or that, he was studying them, attuned to every least curl of the lip, every grimace and smile. He watched the hovering forks, the dutifully Fletcherizing jaws, the dip and rise of the Adam's apples. The older children—the Rodriguez boys, Lucy DuPlage and Nathaniel Himes—studiously maintained the approved dining posture and a commendable silence as they finished up their portions and waited patiently for the soup course—Saniterrapin—and the stewed gooseberries with Graham mush they would receive for dessert. The younger ones had some difficulty with their utensils and general deportment, as was to be expected, but their nurses were there to guide them, and, in general, they seemed pleased enough with the new dish.

George, alone among them, refused to eat. He merely sat rigid at his place, staring down at the table as if in a trance. When Hannah Martin, his nurse since he'd come to them at the age of six and perhaps the person closest to him in the world, bent to ask him what was the matter, he refused to answer. The Doctor, observing from behind his newspaper, felt a tic of annoyance start up in his left cheek: George, it was always George.

The boy's face was a hard little kernel of fury as Hannah Martin leaned over him, murmuring blandishments and words of encouragement. George wouldn't respond. He sat there like a dead thing, the balls of his fists clenched tight in his lap. After this had gone on for several minutes, the Doctor folded his newspaper in irritation and spoke up. "George?" he called out in his voice of authority, and the children looked up at him with their blameless faces, forks suspended over their plates. "What seems to be the matter?"

No reaction.

"George Kellogg," the Doctor intoned, resisting the urge to rise to his feet, "I'm speaking to you, George—now, what seems to be the problem?"

Hannah Martin straightened up and gave the Doctor a stricken look. "I, uh, I don't think he feels well, sir. . . ."

Dr. Kellogg silently cursed the boy for his unrelenting, puerile, pig-headed obstinacy. He was a negative thinker, born to it, and there was no changing him. But that was just where the danger lay: the attitude was subversive, contagious. Let him get away with an infraction, however minor, and the others would slip, too, and before long license would rule. The Doctor focused on the boy's simian ears, the wedge-shaped head with its fringe of irregularly cut hair (he'd apparently taken a scissors to it himself, defacing the perfectly good haircut he received twice a month from the Sanitarium barber), and couldn't suppress a flare of hatred. How had this human wreckage come into his life? How could the Fates be so cruel? Still seated, he directed his response to the nurse. "If he doesn't feel well, perhaps I should examine him? Or perhaps he simply needs a purgative."

Hannah Martin said nothing. George sat rigid. Collectively, the children held their breath.

Finally, with a sigh, the Doctor pushed himself up, set down the paper and walked the length of the table till he stood directly behind the boy. "Well, George," he said, laying his hand on the boy's shoulder as Hannah Martin lost her color and the children hovered on the edge of the moment, "what will it be? Calomel? Castor oil? Or are we going to stop this nonsense and eat up our food?"

George seemed to shrink into himself, the Doctor's touch eating through his skin like acid, all eyes fixed on him, the house fallen into a trough of absolute unbroken silence. Slowly, degree by slow degree, the pointed little chin rose till it reached the shoulder, and the black pits of the eyes confronted the Doctor's. "Food?" George spat. "You call this food?"

The Doctor was dumbstruck. He had to restrain his hand from lashing out, curling round that stunted little face with all the sudden outraged power of muscle, tendon and bone.

But George wasn't done yet, not by a long shot. "Meat and potatoes, that's what we want," he cried, the unformed voice gone suddenly shrill, and he turned his back on the Doctor as if he were negligible, throwing a fierce, giddy, triumphant look into the faces of his adoptive brothers and sisters. "Meat and potatoes!" he cried, taking up his fork and beating time on his plate, "meat and potatoes, meat and potatoes!"

The others looked on, stunned, their faces gone white, but for one child, a new boy from West Virginia, no more than five or six years old, towheaded and open-faced. He picked up his fork as if in a game and began to beat rhythm along with George, his tiny angelic voice crying out for "meat and potatoes, meat and potatoes."

No one would have faulted the Doctor for putting a quick and savage end to it, but he was not a violent man—would not be a violent man, would not be ruled by the bestial passions—and he held back. Hammered in brass, locked in place, his eyeglasses harsh with light, he stood there immovable till the towheaded boy grew sensible of him and choked off the chant in midphrase, till Hannah Martin reached for George's arm and the other children wilted under his gaze. Then, George's brazen taunt ringing in his ears as Hannah Martin fought to contain it, the Doctor turned on his heels, threw back his head and marched out of the room.

George. And that was George. For a full month and more he took absolutely nothing, so far as anyone could see—and the Doctor made certain he was watched day and night. He was made to sit at table with the other children and he was served precisely as they were. He wouldn't touch a thing. No matter what it was or how it was served. He sat numbly over his plate as egg dishes, vegetable foods, dairy, predigested grains and savory sauces passed in front of him, meal after meal, day after day. Never a robust child, he rapidly dwindled in the joints and the long muscles, and the flesh tightened round his skull. In her moments of lucidity, Ella pleaded with the boy, and every time Hannah Martin laid eyes on him, tears started up in her eyes. The Doctor was concerned, and guilt moved in the deeps of him like a stone rolled by the currents across the floor of a vast sea, but he wouldn't give in, wouldn't dream of it. George would either eat what he was given or die of inanition. And that was that.

The night closed around him in its faint calibrations, and finally, though it was past four and creeping toward dawn, Dr. Kellogg gave in to it. He felt himself slipping away, and George's face became his wife's, his dead father's, a nameless patient's, and he was almost there, almost asleep, when a sudden dull booming noise reverberated through the house like the drumroll of calamity. Bolt upright in bed, as awake as he'd ever been, he listened for it again—was it thunder, was that it? The rain fell with a steady sibilance, the sound of it like distant frying, like a thousand Yankee chefs bent over pans of salt pork and flapjacks with their stomachs of iron, and he strained to hear the fainter sound, the harsh rasping friction of the struck match blooming in the darkness.

It was then that he remembered the look on George's face the day he finally began to eat again, without explanation or apology, sitting down to a breakfast of taro gruel and gluten biscuits as if there were nothing to it, as if he'd eaten supper the night before and dinner before that and all the long succession of meals that dwindled into the past, so many pounds of flesh totted up on the ledger, so many bowel movements and micturitions. Flushed with excitement, biting her tongue, Hannah Martin had come to fetch the Doctor as he meditated over his notes and spooned up his own breakfast in his private quarters. She led him through the house to the children's wing and into the dining room, and there he was, George, working his spoon and reaching for his glass just like any other child. He never lifted his eyes when the Doctor entered the room—just sat there, neckless, fleshless, his bones like sticks at the bottom of a dried-up pond, and ate. He never lifted his eyes, but his face gave him away. Wasted, drawn, the eyes ponderous in their sockets, he wore the expression of a hero, a conqueror, a man—no longer a boy—whose point has been made.

One sleepless night couldn't really faze a physiologic marvel like John Harvey Kellogg, but round about three in the afternoon he did feel himself slowing down just a bit, as if there were an invisible tether attached to him. He was sitting at his desk in the afterglow of a particularly gratifying kinkectomy, taking a cup of hot beet juice for strength and working up a sketch of a new apparatus for suspending patients with circulatory problems by their heels, when there was a knock at the door. He couldn't suppress a look of annoyance, but Bloese bounded up like a hound from his desk in the corner, announcing, "That'll be your three-fifteen consultation—Mrs. Lightbody."

Clamping his eyeshade firmly in place, the Doctor rose to greet her as Bloese drew back from the door. *Consultation?* he was thinking, wondering when he'd last examined her and who had referred her and why, and he was in no way prepared for the sight which greeted him. It was Eleanor Lightbody standing there in the doorway, no mistake about it, but she was a ghost of herself, wan and emaciated, her eyes blunted and her clothes in need of taking in at the seams. The welcoming smile faded from the Doctor's face. Bloese dropped his eyes. How long had it been since he'd seen her, really seen her? A week? Two? A hot little pinprick of fear stabbed at the Doctor—was he going to lose another one?—but he covered himself by moving out from behind the desk to take her hand and offer her a seat.

Eleanor sat primly, thrillingly beautiful for all her loss of weight. Dr. Kellogg's keen diagnostic gaze never left her. Was it cancer? Marasmus? Tuberculosis? Or was it a balky sphincter, a plugged loop in the small intestine, a case for scalpel and clamp? Yes, now he remembered—it was Frank Linniman who'd expressed concern over her condition, but the Doctor hadn't really given it much credence. Eleanor Lightbody was one of his prize patients, one of the healthiest and most cooperative, well along the road to recovery and with the very brightest of prognoses. He glanced at her sharply cut cheekbones, the stab of her shoulder blades and the attenuated line of her tibia beneath her skirts and couldn't suppress a quick sharp whistle. "You've lost weight," he observed.

Her voice was muted. "Yes."

"Well," and he began to pace now, a panther of health measuring out the cage of his knowledge, "we'll have to put you on a new dietary, more taro, tapioca, nut milk and the like."

She gazed at him out of placid eyes. "Oh, no, Doctor," she murmured, and even her voice was listless, "you don't understand. I've been fasting."

"Fasting?"

"Yes." She produced a booklet from her purse. "I've been reading in Mr. Sinclair—*The Fasting Cure*—and thought . . . well, I thought I'd give it a try."

The Doctor shook his head. An admonitory finger rose from his fist as if by its own volition and he began to shake it at her. "Do you mean to tell me that you've been fasting without consulting me? But I'm speechless. You come to this institution and put yourself under my care and then you arbitrarily go off on a dietary program—a fast, no less— without so much as a by-your-leave?"

"But Dr. Kellogg," she protested, "it's only for twelve days—just as an experiment. Mr. Sinclair is so convincing, I just—well, I thought I'd give it a try. After all, what better way is there to control one's appetites than to deny them altogether?"

Secretly, the Doctor was relieved. She was fasting, that was all. No harm done. Start her off in the evening with some yogurt and warm milk and prescribe some starchy sauces for her vegetables, whole-grain bread and Italian spaghetti, and she'd be back to normal in a week. Still, he couldn't let the relief show in his face, couldn't allow her to think he would condone any instance of a patient's attempting to treat him or herself—there was no telling where that would lead. "That's not the point," he said.

Eleanor was paging through the book in her lap. "With all due respect, Dr. Kellogg—and I'm in no way making a comparison between you and Mr. Sinclair, who is after all only following your lead—I still have to say that I'm feeling better. These eleven days have given my system yet another way of cleansing itself—a sort of vacation for my bowels, as it were. . . ."

"I see." The Doctor was tight-lipped. He wanted to be generous and understanding, receptive to progressive views and new ideas, but all he felt was irritation. He put on his lecturer's face as a warrior might have plucked up a shield. "Fasting can be an invaluable tool in the complete physiologic regimen, of course," he said, "and though you must never forget that Mr. Sinclair is, after all, a layman, his notions do have some validity according to the most advanced medical thinking. You may be aware that I myself have addressed the question of fasting cures in my *Good Health* column."

Eleanor dipped her head in acknowledgment.

"Yes, well." He rubbed his hands together vigorously. "And may I see the book in question? I must confess that I'm not familiar with it."

"It's just in typescript, Doctor," Eleanor murmured, handing him the text. "It's not yet been published."

Settling himself casually on the edge of the desk, the Doctor thumbed through the book, until, in a section called "Some Notes on Fasting," his eyes came to rest on one particularly disturbing passage: *In the course of my search for health I have paid to physicians, druggists and sanatoriums not less than fifteen thousand dollars in the last six or eight years. In the last year, since I have learned about the fast, I have paid nothing at all.* Dangerous stuff. The worst kind of cant and pecksniffery. He shut the book with a firm clap of its covers and handed it back to her. "And where did you say you obtained this, Mrs. Lightbody?"

She colored, fumbled for her words. "I, uh, well, to tell the truth, I've been seeing another physician—I mean, one outside the Sanitarium. He gave it to me. Through Lionel, that is."

Now this was something new—a real blow and no mistaking it. An outside physician? Lionel? The Doctor gathered his brows. Bloese, bowed over his desk in the corner, winced. "I'm astonished," the Doctor said finally. "I really am. Mrs. Lightbody. Eleanor. This is one of the very gravest matters that has ever been laid before me in all my years as head of this institution. Don't you understand how dangerous it is to listen to such a chorus of voices, however well-intentioned? Worse, don't you realize how many ill-informed, ill-equipped and unscrupulous practitioners there are out there, each of them willing to prey upon the businessman with a bankrupt bowel or the housewife with shattered nerves? As well-meaning as they are, neither Lionel Badger nor Mr. Upton Sinclair is a physician and neither has any right to attempt to direct the medical program of any of my patients. It's an outrage, that's what it is—an outrage. How could you, of all people—?" He couldn't go on. Incomprehension had turned to rage and he was afraid of what he might say next.

Eleanor Lightbody stared at the floor. Her hair was a mass of curls, piled up high on her head like the plumage of some exotic bird. She was sad and beautiful, and all the more beautiful in her sadness. "I'm sorry," she murmured.

"Sorry?" he echoed, and he was pacing again, unable to sit still for a minute. "Sorry? For what? For whom? Don't be sorry for me, my dear lady—I live right and think right through every minute of every day. Be sorry for yourself—you're the one at risk here, you're the one racked by neurasthenia and the aftereffects of autointoxication, you're the one gambling all your progress and future happiness on a whim, a misapprehension." He stood over her now, trembling in the rush of his righteous anger, and she couldn't look him in the eye. "And who, might I ask, would this 'physician' be, this great genius to whom you've entrusted your health in utter abnegation of everything we seek to accomplish here? Who? Who is it?"

She spoke a name, but her voice was pitched so low he didn't catch it.

"Who?"

A sidelong and sorrowful gaze. There were tears in her eyes and the flanges of her nostrils were red. She sniffed and touched a handkerchief to her face. "Dr. Spitzvogel," she choked, and a tremor of emotion went through her.

"Spitzvogel? Never heard of him. And just what might his speciality be—if, as your physician and head of this institution, I might be so bold as to inquire?"

At first she wouldn't answer. She seemed to be turning it over in her mind, and the delay infuriated him—would she dare to keep it from him? But then she bit her lips and looked him directly in the eye. "Manipulation Therapy. *Die Handhabung Therapeutik.* He manipulates my, my"—she looked at Bloese, then shot a glance at the Doctor and finally dropped her eyes to the book in her lap—"my womb."

"Your *womb?*" The Doctor tore the eyeshade from his brow and slammed it down on the desk. He thought he'd heard it all, everything, every weakness, every peccadillo and scheme, every last breath of ignorance and depravity, but he was wrong. Astonishment punctuated his words: "He—manipulates—your—womb?"

There was a moment of silence, a silence so profound the Doctor fancied he could hear the blood rushing through his veins. Bloese was inanimate. No one breathed.

"Yes!" Eleanor suddenly cried, leaping to her feet, her voice raw with passion, with shame, with defiance. Her cheeks were wet, her limbs rigid. "Yes!" she repeated, the affirmation harsh as a battle cry, "and I've never felt better in my life!" And then she turned and ran for the door, flinging it shut behind her with a noise that was like the first premonitory rumble of a gathering storm.

The Doctor stared at the door in bewilderment, exchanged a look with Bloese and slowly began to shake his head. He was tired. God, he was tired.

Chapter 7

Goguac Lake

W ill couldn't stop whistling. He was ebullient, leggy, absolutely on fire with the finger-popping, toe-tapping melodies of the greatest bandmaster of them all, the nonpareil, the king, emperor and god of the march, John Philip Sousa. For the past hour he'd stood in the dappled shade of a Sanitarium elm and watched the Sanitarium Marching Band wheel across the Sanitarium lawn, legs snapping in physiologic precision, elbows rocking rhythmically, instruments seizing the light. They were rehearsing for the Chief's gala Decoration Day festivities, which would include picnicking on the South Lawn, a blackface minstrel show featuring "Professor" Sammy Siegel and half a dozen conscripted Sanitarium talents, several tableaux vivants starring Vivian DeLorbe and an original drama performed by members of the Sanitarium Deep-Breathing Club. Though he was homesick, though his wife was a stranger and his miseries multiplied like fruit flies on a blackened banana, Will couldn't resist Sousa. The air whistled through the gap in his front teeth like the shrill of an overheated teapot and a high thin rendition of "The Free Lunch Cadets" echoed through the San's corridors as he made his martial way up the hall to Dr. Kellogg's office.

Though he couldn't fathom the reason for the summons—the Doctor's stone-faced secretary had stopped by before breakfast to wonder if eleven A.M. would be all right—Will didn't let it faze him. After six months, he knew the routine—smile till your gums ache, look healthy and stupid, reveal nothing. Above all, ask no questions and expect no answers. If Will had ever wavered, if he'd ever come to hope that the little white-clad dictator's methods were worth anything at all, the loss of his kink, the estrangement of Eleanor and the unequivocal fate of Miss Muntz, Homer Praetz and the Doctor's own sweating amanuensis were enough to tip the balance permanently. He remained a patient, his condition static, but he was only biding his time in the desperate aching hope that Eleanor would come to her senses and they could go back home to Parsonage Lane and start their lives over. He labored under no illusions. None at all.

But on this particular day, Dr. Kellogg seemed almost glad to see him—and that was unusual, unusual in the extreme. Their relationship had settled into an unwavering pattern of stern admonishment on the Great Healer's part and contrition on Will's. Will had had liquor on the premises, he lusted after his own wife, he resisted the dietary and refused the sinusoidal bath, he was lackadaisical about his calisthenics and unenthusiastic with regard to his laughing exercises. He didn't chew his food properly or stand up straight. And what was this nonsense about refusing to strip for the swimming pool? The Doctor was disappointed in Will, and he made no bones about it—Will was a backslider, a negative thinker and a bad example to his fellow patients. And so it was something of a surprise when Bloese ushered Will into the office and Dr. Kellogg rose to greet him with a benevolent smile and a firm handshake. "Mr. Lightbody, Will—and how are you?"

Will shrugged. Flashed a smile. "Improving," he said.

"Yes, hmpf." The Doctor's antiseptic eyes roved up and down the length of him, as if searching out the lie. "Well, I'm very happy to hear that," he said finally, "and you can't deny that clean scientific living is having its effect, eh?"

Will didn't deny it.

"The new dietary all right?"

Since the withdrawal of the grapes, Will had been allowed to order from the regular menu, though his intake of things even remotely palatable—blueberry muffins, corn bread, pancakes—was tightly regulated by the dietary girls. He could have all the fake fish, counterfeit meat and corn pulp he wanted. Which was none. "Fine," he said. Already he could feel the spirit of Sousa draining from him.

The little Doctor was in motion now, gathering a sheaf of papers from the desk, removing his eyeshade and setting it carefully in the wooden tray reserved for it, his bald spot glistening in the spill of May sunshine that flooded the office till it glowed like a clerestory. "But it's not you I wanted to discuss," he said, giving Will a cagey look.

Confused, Will shuffled his feet awkwardly on the cold tile floor. "It's not?"

"But let's walk, shall we?" the Doctor cried, and he dodged round the desk and made for the door without waiting for a response, Bloese simultaneously herding Will forward with an exaggerated shooing motion. "I just can't see sitting behind a desk on such a glorious day, can you?"

Before he knew what was happening, Will was back out in the hallway, quickstepping to keep up with the brisk little man of healing, while Bloese, always in sympathy with his Chief, moved along effortlessly at his boss's side. They strode up the familiar hallway, the Doctor nodding to this patient or that, calling out a greeting or an expression of concern, the white tails of his jacket fluttering in his wake. He made for the exit at the north end of the building and for once he didn't seem to have anything to say—by the time they reached the door Will had begun to wonder if the Doctor had forgotten all about him. He was puzzled—*It's not you I wanted to discuss*—and not a little irritated, but Dr. Kellogg led and he followed.

Bloese held the door and in the next moment they were gripped by the bright fragrance of the day, flowers in bloom, the world on its track, the distant invigoration of Sousa still ringing on the air. "Well," the Doctor barked, swinging round on him after waving to a couple taking the air by the rhododendrons, "you've probably guessed what this is all about?"

Will didn't have a clue. But in a sudden flash of cognition that started just under his breastbone, shot like a Ping-Pong ball to his brain and ricocheted back to his tongue, he stammered, "El-Eleanor?"

"Yes, I'm afraid so," the Doctor clucked, nodding his head gravely.

The light caught his hair, infusing it with a sad medicinal dignity, and he stood firm in the grass, never shirking. Will went cold with fear. "But come, let's talk peripatetically," the Doctor said, brightening his voice a cautious degree, "—stimulate the circulatory system, stretch the legs, hey?" And then they were off, moving at an uneasy clip, the Doctor's hand clamped to Will's elbow as if he were guiding him through the motions of some ritualistic dance. They circumvented flower beds, passed patients on crutches and in wheelchairs, watched a pretty young nurse with pinned-up skirts sail by on a bicycle. "She's in serious trouble, I'm afraid," the Doctor said finally, turning his face to Will's.

Will couldn't help himself. He pulled back, jammed his heels into the turf. "What do you mean?" he croaked. "Are you saying that . . . that she's getting worse?"

The Doctor had halted now, too, though he kept pumping his legs and shifting his shoulders, marching in place. Bloese, steel-rimmed and silent, stood just behind them. "Good God, man," the Doctor suddenly cried, "are you blind? This is your own wife we're talking about here, sir—don't tell me you haven't noticed anything?"

"She's—well, she's lost weight, I know that, but I thought it was part of the program, her regimen—"

"Bah!" the Doctor spat, still pumping his legs and puffing and deflating his diaphragm with a great gulp and rush of crisp pure salubrious air. "No regimen of mine. Do you think I willfully starve my patients, sir?" He didn't wait for an answer. "She's on the fasting cure. All on her own. As if she were her own physician all of a sudden, as if she were the one who'd interned at Bellevue and put countless thousands on the path to health and well-being, as if all this"—he waved a hand to take in the buildings and grounds, the great incorporated healing plant that stretched as far as the eye could see in any direction—"as if all of this were a game, an illusion. And what do you say to that, sir—your own wife?"

Will didn't know what to say. Certainly Eleanor had come to Battle Creek to gain weight, not to lose it, but, then, given the general run of the food the Doctor offered, who could blame her for going on a hunger strike? "Is—is it serious?"

"Serious!" The little man seemed to implode, gasping in shock as if he'd somehow managed to suck in his own beard, and he spun round twice on the balls of his feet like a bantamweight dodging his opponent. "That's the least of it. It's far worse than you can imagine—at least the fasting cure has its merits, if prescribed and strictly supervised by a qualified physician, that is . . . but no, your wife seems to have gone off the deep end altogether." He paused, squinted, drew up the corners of his mouth. "She's consulting someone outside this institution."

All at once Will saw the stately Tudor, the man at the door, the mustaches and monocle. "Yes, I know," he murmured.

The admission seemed to freeze the Doctor. His mouth began to work, but nothing came out. Will watched as a sheen of sweat sprang up to wrap the physiologic brow in its grip. "*You know?*" the Doctor repeated.

High overhead a cloud melted into the sun. Will nodded.

"The man's a charlatan," Dr. Kellogg shouted. "A fraud. A menace. Calls himself a doctor—what's the man's name, Bloese?"

"Spitzvogel, Chief."

"Spitzvogel." The Doctor chewed over the name as if it had gone rotten in his mouth. Veins stood out on the eudaemonic temple, the all-seeing eyes blazed. "Do you know what he's doing to her, do you have any idea? Do you even give two hoots about what's going on with your own wife?"

Will was alarmed. It had to be something unsanitary, something sensual, a release of the primitive appetites—nothing short of that could get the Great Healer so worked up. "Yes, I do give two hoots," he said weakly. And then: "What is it? What's this man"—he could barely get the words out, gulping down the rest of sentence like a glass of water on a scorching day—"what's he doing to her?"

"Movement Therapy," the Doctor spat contemptuously, "*Die Hand-habung Therapeutik*," and he made it sound filthy, utterly depraved. "He manipulates her womb."

It took a moment for this to sink in—manipulates her womb? What in Christ's name did that mean? But then he began to think about that, Eleanor's womb, and its point of ingress, that private place that it was a husband's privilege, and only a husband's privilege, to . . . but no, it couldn't be. Will was appalled. He felt his face coloring.

"Your own wife," the Doctor repeated. "But that's what happens when patients play doctor, when they think they know better than the keenest medical minds of the age, when they presume to treat themselves, sir." There was something else in his face now, a shade of malice. He snapped his fingers: "Bloese!" Will was barely conscious as the secretary moved forward with the cloth satchel which Will only now and dimly realized he'd been carrying all along—he was underwater, deep down at the very bottom of the deepest pit in the deepest ocean, the weight crushing him, his lungs crying out for air, as Bloese reached into the satchel and produced a familiar apparatus, an electric belt, slightly used but still in excellent condition, and the genital suspensory that went with it.

The two men, Doctor and factotum, ramrods of righteousness, folded their arms and leveled a withering gaze on him. A moment went by, thin and niggardly, and the least paring of another. "Nurse Bloethal found this under your bed, sir," the Doctor said at last. "And what do you have to say for yourself?"

Will hung his head. All he could think of was Eleanor, Eleanor and Badger, Eleanor and this quack doctor, Eleanor and her womb.

Brandishing the Heidelberg Belt, the Doctor stepped closer and pinched his words for emphasis: "This is the curse of my profession," he hissed, "the very sort of thing that is even now putting your wife at risk. Self-doctoring. Lending an ear to every huckster and mountebank that comes along. Pandering to the sickest and weakest of the sensual appetites. Don't you know that this thing can kill you? Don't you realize how ill you are? Why, a man in your condition—" he broke off in astonishment. "Even a single discharge of seminal fluids could be fatal. But what really astounds me is that here you are secretly practicing to build up your reproductive organs and all the while your wife is in the very gravest danger because of them. I say develop your resolve, sir, not your genitals."

Though he couldn't quite follow the Doctor's logic, Will was mortified all the same, as deeply and thoroughly mortified as ever he'd been. He wanted to bolt, fly off crazily across the lawn, trample the flower beds, throw himself in the river and be done with it. He stared numbly into the blaze of the Doctor's spectacles.

But the Healer, as if divining his thoughts, had hold of him again, and his grip was like iron. "I can't do anything for her," he said, his voice pitched low, dead earnest. "I'm not her husband, only her physician. But I tell you this, sir, and I say it with all my heart: look to your wife."

Eleanor wasn't in her room. She wasn't in the Palm Garden, the parlor or the Ladies' Gymnasium. Will carried his loose joints up and down the stairs, rapped on the doors of a dozen rooms where she was known to visit with one or another of her lady friends, stalked Virginia Cranehill and Mrs. Zachary Cornish, the yellow-taffeta lady. No one had seen her. Heartsick and fuming, Will went up to dinner early, hoping to confront her there, and sat for two hours listening to Hart-Jones rhapsodize about the bird life of the Lake District, where, to the everlasting dismay of everyone within hearing distance, he'd been born and raised. Neither Badger nor Eleanor put in an appearance.

At three, Will skipped a session of medicine-ball tossing under the direction of the big-armed Swede, and instead dropped in on a dress rehearsal of *The Fatal Luncheon*, the Deep-Breathing Club's original drama. He took a seat in the cool afternoon shadows of the downstairs parlor, heart pounding in his ears, waiting for Eleanor to make her appearance. The play, co-authored by Eleanor and Mrs. Tindermarsh, seemed to be about a man with a ruined stomach struggling against the twin demons of alcohol and carnal abuse. Mrs. Tindermarsh, in overalls and greasepaint mustaches, portrayed the protagonist, stalking about the stage spouting lines like "O woe to this digestive tract and unquiet stomach that ever I saw chop or steak!" Eleanor was to play the female lead, the role of the long-suffering wife who contends against all hope to bring her deluded husband to see the redemptive light of physiologic living. Will's stomach contracted at the thought of it—the play was just one more knot in a string of humiliations stretching all the way back to the night he'd arrived and Dr. Kellogg had inspected his tongue as if he were a horse going to stud. He shrank into the shadows.

The play was difficult to follow and he was so wrought up in any case that even Wilde or Ibsen would have seemed a burden, but after half an hour or so he began to realize that Eleanor's part had been taken by another woman. The woman had been onstage since the outset, playing opposite Mrs. Tindermarsh, but Will had assumed she was a domestic or a distant relative, and now he understood that he was wrong. Eleanor wasn't here, either.

He rose abruptly in the dark and made his way up front, where he attempted to inquire after her but was roundly shushed from all quarters. Sinking nervously into a seat just under the stage, he bided his time till the rehearsal was over and then approached Mrs. Tindermarsh.

"Oh, Mr. Lightbody," she crowed, "—and what do you think of us? Will we make a hit?"

Faces had gathered round them, garish in their stage makeup. Will glanced up uneasily. "Oh, yes, of course," he boomed, his voice setting up a shiver in the glass decanter perched beside the fictive husband's armchair, "splendid, very moving—and true to life."

Eyes batted, mouths pursed. A squeal of voices started up behind the curtain, someone laughed at the rear of the stage. Will swiveled his neck and masked his eyes. "But where's Eleanor? I thought she was playing the wife?"

Mrs. Tindermarsh's gaze fled to the far corners of the room. She stroked her mustaches and came away with blackened fingertips. "Didn't she tell you?" she murmured, looking round for a towel. "She resigned two weeks ago—her treatments were just eating up all her time. Gloria Gephardt's taken her role, but it's a shame, it really is—your wife's such a natural actress."

He finally cornered Eleanor in her room late that night—she hadn't made a supper appearance, either, though Badger was there, the sot, blathering on about esculents and tubers and all the celebrated people he knew. She was in bed, reading, and when he surprised her—he didn't bother to knock—she looked up guiltily and slipped the book beneath her pillow. "Oh, Will," she murmured, her voice languid, artificial, fat with venality and deceit, "how are you?" She let out an abbreviated laugh. "We hardly get to see one another anymore, do we?"

Will wasn't about to be distracted by small talk. "I spoke with Dr. Kellogg," he said. He loomed over the bed, practically tottering, arms clenched rigidly at his sides.

"Oh? And what did he have to say?" Her nonchalance was infuriating. She was toying with him, pretending, putting on an act. "Come, give me a kiss."

Will stood rigid. "I don't want a kiss. I want to talk about Dr. Spitzvogel."

The name flashed across her face like a whiplash, but she never gave herself away. "Yes? And what about him?"

How could she be so brazen? The man was manipulating her womb and everyone knew it. "I've seen his house." It was all he could think to say.

"Will," and she was crooning now, her eyes fluid and rich, his own wife, "what's this all about? Is something troubling you? You're not jealous of my doctor, are you?" She laughed again, a little trill of private amusement. "Look at you—you've become the Battle Freak. Here I go to an outside physician and you act as if it's the end of the world. Really, Will," she said, and her laugh followed it up.

"Outside physician!" He threw it back at her. "He's no more a physician than I am."

Her eyes sharpened suddenly, and the familiar furrow appeared between her eyebrows. "How would you know?"

"Because Dr. Kellogg told me. Your Dr. Kellogg. The great and only. And he told me what this Spitzvogel is doing to you, too, in the name of 'treatment,' and it's shocking, Eleanor, and I, I think you owe me an explanation—no, I demand an explanation, and right now, right this minute. No more excuses, no more hiding behind this 'biologic living' nonsense—the man's manipulating your womb, isn't he? Well, isn't he?"

She'd gone pale beneath her tan. She was guilty, she'd been found out, but she never flinched and she never took her eyes from his. "Yes, he is. And what does that have to do with anything? It's a perfectly respectable and effective treatment for a condition like mine, and that's not all he does, not by a long shot—"

"Yes? And what else does he manipulate? Your breasts? Your bottom?"

The suddenness with which she sprang from the bed surprised him, and he stumbled back confusedly to avoid her. She was in her nightgown, a new one he'd never seen before, loose at the collar and provocative, but he didn't have a chance to admire it—she hit him across the face with the flat of her hand, twice, three times, till he took her wrists and held them. "Let me go, you son of a—let me go!" she shrieked, rocking in his arms, and he felt her elbow like a knife in his side, and then she was free. "Get out!" she cried, and he could hear movement in the hall.

"I won't," he panted, the rage building in him, pushing him beyond reason and control. He wanted to slap her back, pin her down, hurt her. "And I won't allow you to go on like this. No more quacks, no more Kelloggs or Spitzvogels or Badgers or any of them—I'm taking you home."

Her face was fierce, alive with flashing eyes and snapping teeth. "Ha!" she cried, and her voice twisted toward hysteria. "You think you own me? You think you're my lord and master? You think this is feudal times?"

She wasn't beautiful in that moment, wasn't tender, wasn't his wife. Eyes bulging, crouched like a wrestler, circling him in her rage, she was murderous and hateful. He felt the love go dead in him. "We'll let the law decide that," he said.

"The law?" she screamed, and there was a knock at the door now, a voice from the hallway—*Mrs. Lightbody, are you in there? Is everything all right?* "Threaten me with the law, will you, you weakling. . . . Get out!" she shrieked. "Get out or I'll call the orderlies—"

"No, I won't. Not unless you come with me. Now. Tonight."

The banging at the door. "Mrs. Lightbody?"

She looked at him evenly a moment, and then let herself go, her voice splitting a new register, gathering itself into a face of screaming. "Help!" she cried. "Help, help, help!"

Under the circumstances, who could blame a man for seeking consolation elsewhere?

Will accepted Nurse Graves's invitation to go boating on the afternoon before Decoration Day, and he didn't think twice about it. He was through with enemas and nut butter; through with cranks and quacks and the tyranny of fork, knife and spoon; through with Eleanor. She could have every private flap and wrinkle of her anatomy manipulated by the entire medical establishment of Germany for all he cared. And to prove it to himself he'd gone down to the Michigan Central depot and purchased a ticket to New York—a single ticket, for one passenger, one way only.

Standing there at the ticket window, he closed his eyes and pictured the old familiar house on Parsonage Lane, its rooms and halls and furniture, the horsehide sofa in the back parlor that was perfectly contoured to the mold of his back, the four-poster in the master bedroom with its curtains drawn to shut out the world, his bookshelves and reading lamp and the way the front hall took the morning sun and held it like a gift, and he didn't see Eleanor anywhere in the picture. He saw Dick the wirehaired terrier and Mrs. Dunphy, the housekeeper, he saw the gardener and the delivery boy from Offenbacher's . . . and who else? Who else did he see there? Nurse Graves, that's who he saw. Irene. In the kitchen, gazing out on the roses, in the pantry, the parlor, the bath—oh, the bath—and a plan came to him then, born of the moment and fully formed. He would get a divorce, that's what he would do, and Irene would climb with him into that high-vaulted connubial bed, soft where Eleanor was hard, sweet where she was bitter, and he would reach out to her and take her in his arms, and no belt, no diet, no theory or rationale would have a thing to do with what came next. . . .

It was a vision that stayed with him, that haunted and inspired him, and he walked around in a dream for the rest of the week. He saw Eleanor only at meals, and she didn't move him, not at all. Which was just as well, because she refused even to glance in his direction, let alone speak to him. She was coming off her fast and taking peach, apple and pear pulp, a spoon or two of pabulum and egg pastina, cautiously working her way up to breads and puddings and the rough-edged but cleansing bulk of the aspiring vegetables. Will watched her eat with the detachment of a scientist, and found that he didn't care one way or the other, didn't care whether she ate or starved, and he listened to her dialogue with Badger, Hart-Jones and the others as he might have listened to a language he couldn't place. On the third day after their falling out, Eleanor moved back to her old table, and she took Badger with her.

But Eleanor wasn't the issue, Eleanor wasn't what concerned him—it was Irene. Irene of the caressing voice and soothing hands, the farm girl, the nurse, the angel: *Irene.* She couldn't accept a gift—no, that was against the regulations—but flowers were different. They were like little bits and pieces of the sun, she cooed, and they were the gift of God—she could never refuse flowers. And so each morning that week Will walked all the way out to a poultry farm at the end of Washington Avenue, battling hay fever and gnats and the stink of chickens and the sun that bit into the back of his neck, just to purchase a bouquet for her. Lilies and gold alexanders, phlox and cinquefoil, he let the farmer's wife choose them, something new each day, and when Irene came in to take him to his eleven-o'clock vibrotherapy session, the flowers were there for her, in a vase on the night table. He didn't say anything about the ticket in his wallet or how he was leaving Eleanor and needed a nurse, a friend, a companion, a lover and soul mate to accompany him to New York and stay there with him and be his wife, not a word, not yet. He smiled and flattered her and told her she was prettier than any bouquet, and she looked at her hands and blushed. No, he would save the speeches for Sunday, in the boat, as they drifted out over the bosom of Goguac Lake, vernal breezes wafting off the shore, swans bobbing beside them like accomplices, and there would be no place to go, no appointments to keep or regimen to follow, no doctors or orderlies, no prying eyes.

Of course, as luck would have it, he discovered on Thursday that both the Countess Tetranova and Mrs. Solomon Teitelbaum were coming along, as per the Christmas expedition to the Graves homestead, and that took the wind out of his sails—or, rather, the oars out of his hands. The news—Irene let it drop casually as she was changing his bed—depressed him. Utterly. There was nothing special here, nothing romantic in the least—it was all in his head. For Irene it was merely charity work, a duty, just another therapeutic outing for a pitiful bunch of shut-ins and autointoxicatees, nothing more. Hurt, stricken, insulted to the core, Will brooded over his disappointment through the course of a long afternoon, his plans in ruins. Didn't she realize how he felt about her after all this time? Was she blind? Coy? Or was it shyness?

Whatever it was, Will wasn't about to give up so easily. By dinnertime, he'd already managed to speak with Mrs. Teitelbaum. He found her in the Palm Garden, pale as a peeled egg, reading a novel and struggling to relax in the clutch of an orthopedic chair. He allowed himself approximately one hundred and twenty seconds of small talk, then launched into a discussion of the insect life of the Goguac Lake region. They'd been talking about Mrs. Tindermarsh and her virile stage presence as the husband in *The Fatal Luncheon*, when Will shifted the subject. "She was bitten during rehearsal, you know," he said.

"Bitten?" Mrs. Teitelbaum looked confused.

"Oh, yes," Will assured her, shaking his head. "Just under the ear— it's so swollen they're afraid she might not be able to go on. One of those nasty biting flies from Goguac Lake—greenheads, I believe they call them. I hear they're positively swarming out there this time of year, clouds of them so thick you can barely see the water."

With the Countess, he chose the direct approach. "I want to be alone with her," he said.

They were in the corridor just outside the ladies' sudatorium, the odd patient moving languidly past them, the faint hiss of steam in the background. The Countess lifted an eyebrow. Will could see the pellet of gossip ricocheting in her eyes—the whole Sanitarium would know by Sunday. But, then, what did he care? He was already gone, and he'd never look back. Never.

"With your nurse?"

He really didn't want to go into it, and so he gave her what he hoped was a rakish look. "A man has his urges," he said.

She peered up at him from her little porcelain doll's face. "Especially when his wife is so ill, am I right? But then *you* must have made a remarkable recovery . . . Will," she purred, laying a tiny hand on his arm.

His instinct was to pull away, but he fought it. He was a lover, a Lothario, a man of the world. He gave her a lewd grin.

"Yes, I see," she said finally, giving his arm a squeeze. "You know, I've just remembered—I promised Amelia Hookstratten I'd help her plan for her luncheon. I really must do something about this memory of mine. . . . Mustn't I, Will?"

The day was perfect, high-crowned and glorious, no clouds to filter the sun, warm but not overpowering. There was a breeze—Will's straw boater sailed off his head and across the lawn the minute he stepped out the door to climb into the car Irene had arranged for them—and that was potentially worrisome, but, then, you couldn't have everything, could you? One of the San's bellhops fetched the hat back and Will kept it firmly in place with one hand as he helped Irene into the automobile—an Italian Zust donated by one of the San's patrons—which was, unfortunately, open to the elements. It was a struggle. Will never let go of his hat the whole way out to the lake, and the anxiety of it prevented him from enjoying himself or engaging in the witty banter and romantic innuendo he'd been looking forward to. In contrast, Irene, in a great wide-brimmed panama decorated with artificial flowers and silk butterflies, seemed perfectly at ease—never once did she touch her hand to *her* hat, no matter how stern the gust. The mysteries of the feminine, Will thought, his arm aching from holding *his* hat so long in one position. Or maybe it was just hatpins.

The sight of the lake cheered him. They wound through the trees and out to a public beach, where scores of people sat around on blankets picnicking, and children ran about raising a healthy din. The lake gave back the sunlight in rolling flashes and sudden incendiary sparks, pushing at the shore as if testing its limits, and there were a number of boats out on the surface despite the wind. Will saw sculls, rowboats and half a dozen sails, and way in the distance one of the steamboats that brought people to Picnic Island and Jennings' Landing. He was encouraged. Excited. Nothing could have kept him from those oars.

Unfortunately, the wind had combed through the fields all morning, explosive with its load of pollen, and that slowed him down a bit. His eyelids itched, he couldn't seem to stop sneezing and there was a spot over the bridge of his nose, just between the eyes, that throbbed as if it had been struck with a mallet. He was having a little difficulty breathing, too—a certain constriction of the windpipe—but these were the familiar symptoms that had dogged him, spring and fall, since boyhood. So what if he had flat feet, hay fever and a ruined stomach? Would it have stopped Roosevelt, Peary, Harry K. Thaw? This was his best chance and he wasn't about to let it get away from him on account of a runny nose and itchy eyes. Of course, there was the matter of the rowboat, too—he'd lain awake half the night trying to recall just exactly where one sat while rowing. Was it with the back facing forward or the front facing backward?

If he was tentative—there went his hat again, damn it, and he only just caught it this time—Irene seemed oblivious. She was utterly serene, a soft smile of anticipation on her lips, ready to yield herself up to the moment, spontaneous and free, ready for anything—Goguac Lake today and Peterskill tomorrow. What a woman. What a jewel of a woman. But she seemed to be saying something to him as he helped her from the car and fumbled to hand her her parasol without letting go of his hat. She had to repeat herself, the wind playing tricks with his ears: "Would you mind bringing the hamper along, Mr. Lightbody?"

The hamper. Yes, of course. And she was practical, too. Couldn't very well have a picnic without a wicker basket chock-full of Sanitarium goodies—bean-paste sandwiches, endive salad and Graham-grit cookies—and some fine foamy kumyss and grape juice to wash it all down. But what a beautiful dress, what a beautiful fit. He'd have to ask her about that. Lovely material. Really.

The driver, a scrawny antediluvian man with white hair and mustaches, was fussing over the hamper in the front seat. "I can manage it myself," Will said, taking it from him over his protestations, "no problem at all, really, thank you." Cradling the basket, Will stood there at attention while Irene gave the driver instructions to be back for them by five-thirty, adding, with a wink for Will, that she wouldn't want her prize patient to miss his dinner. And then they were off, down the path to the dock where the rental boats bobbed and jerked at their tethers like living things and the wind-driven waves threw foam at the shore. It was a rich and intimate moment, almost domestic, and he wanted to slip his arm through hers, the most natural thing in the world, but he found he didn't have an arm to spare, what with the hamper in one hand and the other clamped firmly to his head, so he let it pass. Regretfully.

The dockhand insisted on Will's getting into the boat first, something about counterbalancing the lady's weight, and Will, at a loss, crouched low over the edge of the dock and set a foot down in the rearing depths of the boat. As soon as his foot touched the planking the thing plunged away from him, only to fly back up as he planted his weight and snatched the other foot from the dock. There was an uneasy moment, poised between the wet and the dry, and just when he thought he'd achieved equilibrium, he felt himself going over backward and threw out both arms like a tightrope walker. Miraculously, he recovered himself, falling heavily athwart the seat as the waves, black-lipped and ugly, snapped and snarled beneath him. He was dry and unhurt and spared the embarrassment of an unplanned dip, but unfortunately the straw boater chose that moment to permanently part company with his head, sailing out over the chop like a discus and vanishing in a trough a hundred yards out. He hardly noticed. Bareheaded, his hair whipped by the breeze till it stung his eyes, he snatched frantically at the oars, thinking to steady the craft for Irene—and he might have succeeded, too, if he hadn't been facing in the wrong direction.

At any rate, he swung round at the dockhand's instigation and found himself facing Irene, who'd somehow managed to slip into her seat without setting up so much as a ripple. They were practically knee-to-knee, an arrangement he found both romantic and nautically satisfying. "Bracing, isn't it?" he said, showing her all his teeth, and then the dockhand pushed them off with a bamboo pole and they were out on the lake, boating.

It didn't go well at first, not at all how he'd envisioned it. He fought with the oars, which seemed somehow to have grown absurdly in length since the boat had left the dock, great long recalcitrant logs lost in the depths until suddenly and without warning they emerged to shower poor Nurse Graves with foam and flecks of pondweed. And he couldn't quite get them synchronized, either—he'd pull on one only to find the other lagging at the surface, and then when he went for that one the boat swung perversely the other way, pulling the first oar out of his hand.

They went round in circles for a good fifteen minutes before Will, with Irene's help and instruction, began to get the hang of it. By then, the wind had taken them and the shore was a distant memory.

But Irene was a good sport about it—he couldn't fault her there. She seemed watchful, content, full of some deep inner joy that filled him with hope—was she so happy just to be with him, was that it?—and she was patient with him even when the odd sneezing fit came over him and he had to drop the oars and press a handkerchief to his face. "You seem happy today," he said, the oars finally at rest, the boat drifting before the wind. "Happier than usual, I mean—not that you're not happy or that you don't look happy every day, I just mean that today, you, uh, well—" and he gave it up with a shrug. "You know what I mean."

She held her smile for a long moment, her face a perfect oval beneath the brim of her hat, a strand of hair caught in the corner of her mouth. "Yes," she said finally, in her whisper of a voice, appending a little sigh of contentment to the end of it. "You're very observant, Mr. Lightbody—or *Will*, I should say. It seems absurd to be so formal with you. You're my patient, sure—you always will be—but you're my friend, too. I've felt that for some time now, and on my lips you may be Mr. Lightbody, but in my heart"—she lowered her eyes—"you're Will."

Will couldn't help himself. Her words made his blood quicken and he knew that as long as he had her he'd never again need the Heidelberg Belt or Eleanor's encouragement or anything else. The boat sank beneath them, rocked back up again. A pair of geese skimmed the surface with a short sharp cry and settled down in a fan of spray. "It's very kind of you to say that, Irene—it means an awful lot to me," he said, and he could feel his heart pounding. This was it, this was the moment he'd been waiting for. "You're very sweet, you are, and you know how I feel about you, how I've felt since the beginning—"

She cut him off with a gesture. Their knees were touching. The wind took her hair. Her eyes glowed. He remembered the day they'd had their debate over Dr. Kellogg and his methods and the look of reverence and surrender that had come into her eyes at the mere mention of the man's name. That was how she looked now, but this time it wasn't Dr.

Kellogg who'd inspired her, oh no—but would she leave the San, could he ever convince her? He hadn't thought of that, it could be a real obstacle, and yet he knew he could win her over, he knew it—

But what was she saying?

"I wanted you to be the first to know."

The waves beat at the bow. Will felt his stomach sink. "Know what?"

She held it an instant, and there it was, the sun, the breeze, the glory of the sky that existed only to frame her, to show her off, envelop her in all her ripe rich beauty and the poignancy of the moment: "I'm getting married."

"Married?" The word burst from his lips in a verbal eructation, autonomous, barely formed. "What do you mean?" he asked stupidly.

She was holding up a finger now, the ring finger of her left hand, and he saw a ring in place there, a little thing with a minuscule stone, so small it was hardly there at all—but how could he have missed it? How could he have been so misguided? So stupid? So self-involved? Suddenly, in a flash, he saw it all as clearly as if it were written out for him: the childhood sweetheart, the yokel, the bumpkin, chickens scratching in the yard, her breasts pendulous with milk, feet splayed, figure ruined, her face seamed and rucked and creased till it looked like a dried-up mud puddle. . . . How could he have been so blind?

The pucker of the lips, a little moue. "His name's Tommy Reardon."

Will couldn't speak. Tommy Reardon. What had he been thinking, what was wrong with him? She was getting married. *Getting married.* And he'd never even suspected, never guessed she had a life outside the San . . . oh, the waste of it, the waste.

The boat rocked, the wind blew. What about *me*, he wanted to shout, what about Peterskill and my father and my stomach and Dick the wirehaired terrier? She was merciless, that's what she was, thoughtless, toying with him all along. He stared bitterly at her. What was she, anyway? An ignorant farm girl, too broad in the beam and too big in the chest, a woman who worshiped the little charlatan who'd ruined his life—and what did that say about her? She was a follower, a gizzardite, a nurse. But he'd loved her, he had—oh, how he'd loved her —and the hurt and bitterness twisted inside him. He covered his face with the handkerchief.

"Will?" she said gently, and he hated the sound of his own name on her lips—why couldn't she call him 'Mr. Lightbody'? He was a paying customer, wasn't he? "Will? Aren't you going to congratulate me?"

The question seemed to hover over him, as big and bloated as a balloon, and he never answered it. Suddenly he thought of Eleanor, Eleanor with her quack doctor, with Badger and Virginia Cranehill and all the rest, baptized in nudism, free love, vegetarian ecstasy, and a kind of panic seized him even as the fire roared back to life in his deepest gut. In that moment, that dismal hopeless itchy-eyed wave-driven abyss of a moment, he understood that he loved Eleanor more than anything in the world. Eleanor, only Eleanor.

Chapter 8

The Fatal Luncheon

❄❄❄

I t felt odd to be sitting in a darkened room at eleven-thirty in the morning watching a bunch of matrons parade around a stage spouting out health-food slogans. Extremely odd. And uncomfortable. For Charlie Ossining it was a form of torture one step removed from the application of hot irons to the soles of the feet. Couldn't they at least have gotten someone halfway attractive up there? Or under sixty, at any rate? Where was Eleanor Lightbody when they needed her? He wouldn't have minded seeing her up there under the lights, sashaying across the stage and declaiming her lines about putrid flesh and demon rum as if she meant them. These others were strictly amateurs—and not much to look at, either.

But here he was, in the Grand Parlor of the Sanitarium, in the very camp of the enemy, suffering, and all because Mrs. Hookstratten willed it. She sat beside him now, her spectacles shining, as absorbed as if she were watching Sarah Bernhardt and David Warfield go at it. She'd invited him for the day's festivities, beginning with the play and then a private luncheon, to be followed by the rest of the San's holiday program—marching bands, picnic supper, fireworks and he didn't know what else—and the invitation had been anything but casual. She'd insisted. Demanded. Required his presence. And he didn't dare demur, because she'd offered an inducement far sweeter than mere duty: money.

412

Hard cash. The wherewithal to save his neck and set him back on the road to financial well-being, prosperity, the making of his first million and more, much more. He was going to be a tycoon yet. Oh, yes. Oh, yes, indeed.

What it amounted to was this: Mrs. Hookstratten was doubling her investment. And why? Because she believed in him, because he was her boy, her own boy, and because he'd used all his powers of persuasion on her, talking till his larynx ached and the spittle went dry in his throat. *It's a wise investment, rock-solid,* he assured her the day after the tour of the spurious factory, *and I know you're already one of our biggest investors, but the fact is we need capital to expand.* He'd given her figures, invented but plausible, and explained how the giants like Kellogg and Post were squeezing him, and she was sympathetic and clearly reassured by the sight of the factory, but she held back, cautious and hesitant, and wouldn't give him a commitment. He kept after her. If he'd made himself scarce prior to the factory visit, now he was invariably at her side. They lunched and dined and breakfasted and he took her on rides in the country and walks in the park, all the while pleading his case. And now, finally, she'd come round: today, at the luncheon, she was to present him with a check for an additional seven thousand five hundred dollars.

Seven thousand five hundred dollars! The amount jolted him, made his blood rush—he'd hardly had the nerve to name a figure, and yet when it had come down to it, he found his lips moving. *How much do you need?* she'd asked. *Seven thousand five hundred dollars,* he'd answered without hesitation, naming a sum that was large but not impossible, hoping for half that and willing to bargain down if he had to—Bender had taught him well. Of course, the name "Per-Fo" had to go and the real manufacturing plant would be a good deal more modest than the fictive one, but he'd explain all that later. Much later.

For now, though, he was a guest of the Sanitarium once again. His whiskers had grown in and he was parting his hair in the center and wearing a pair of spectacles he didn't need fitted with lenses as clear as windowpanes, and he was confident—reasonably confident, anyway—that the little martinet who ran the place wouldn't recognize him. Still, as he watched the square-shouldered old lady in the greasepaint mustaches agonize over the fatal luncheon of the play's title—oysters and sparkling wine, ironically enough—he couldn't help stealing a glance over his shoulder from time to time.

If he felt vaguely uneasy, Mrs. Hookstratten was no comfort. She seemed strangely distant, as if there were a wall between them, and when she laughed at the rare comic interlude the play provided, the laugh seemed to catch in her throat. Then, too, when she'd greeted him that morning her smile had seemed unsteady and there was something about the way she held herself, the way she looked at him, that he didn't like. Was she suspicious? Had she by some ugly mischance driven past the factory and discovered its true colors? Had she been talking to people? There *was* the matter of George Kellogg—he'd nearly brought the whole thing down that night in the rain, piss drunk and stinking of it, cadging change and making pointed comments beneath the umbrella—but Charlie had explained all that to her, painstakingly and at length. (They'd been deceived by the fellow, that was all, taken in, swayed by his name and the philanthropic mission to which his father had devoted himself—until they discovered his weakness for the bottle. Well, he and his associates had discussed the matter and felt they simply couldn't condone that sort of behavior and they'd resolved to drop the Kellogg name—it would be "Per-Fo" hereafter, plain and simple. And didn't she prefer it that way? After all, the public would be depending on them to lead the way in scientific eating, to set an example, and, sad to say, there was no place for a tosspot in their ranks—honesty was the best policy, wasn't it?)

Still, there was something wrong. He could feel it in the air the way he might have felt a dip in the barometer before an electrical storm. He felt it as the blocky woman in the greasepaint mustaches collapsed into her plate, done in by oysters and drink, felt it as the audience clapped their approval and the actors took their bow and the hour of Mrs. Hookstratten's luncheon drew near. The square-shouldered woman descended from the stage and he offered his congratulations in a daze, all the while keeping his eyes on his benefactress, trying to read her, fathom her, pin it down: what was wrong here?

Nothing, he told himself, nothing at all. He had to get a grip on himself. He was just anxious because of the check, that was all. Mrs.

Hookstratten would never do anything to hurt him—no matter what she knew or what he'd done. He was her project, her great experiment, more a son to her than the one she'd given birth to. She wouldn't have invited him if she were suspicious, wouldn't have offered the check if anything had changed between them. Would she?

❖   ❖   ❖

They moved out into the corridor at a glacial pace, the men stiff as corpses, the women fluttering and cackling like the old hens they were. If Charlie hadn't already felt uneasy, the fact that no one in the crowd seemed to be less than twenty years older than he didn't help any. Still, he glad-handed this one and that, trying his level best to look as if he belonged, working the crowd as Bender might have done—you never knew. He didn't give a damn for the Sanitarium or anything about it, but these people were all food cranks, every last one of them, and if that wasn't a ready-made audience for Per-Fo (or whatever it was going to be called) he didn't know what was. And they had money. Money to invest.

He found himself discussing breakfast food as he moved up the hallway and into the lobby with this suddenly congenial group, all his vague fears dissolved in the growing awareness of what the connection could mean to him. And then he understood: this was the reason Auntie Hookstratten had arranged this little luncheon for him, of course it was, and if she seemed a bit distracted it was because she was anxious to see him make a good impression. He felt a sudden surge of affection for her. Where was she? There, at the head of the crowd, with the countess she'd introduced him to earlier, showing her guests into the Palm Garden, where the luncheon was to be held under the glass ceiling. She was good to him, yes she was, and he resolved to make it up to her.

The crowd bunched up at the entrance to the garden room, most heading for the elevators to dine upstairs, a select few moving in amongst the ferns and creepers to sit at the long, linen-covered table he could make out through the doorway. Charlie lingered a moment, making his farewells to this former group and chatting amiably with the latter, no hurry, everything moving along at a sedate and leisurely pace. It was while he was standing there pumping the suety hand of an elderly gentleman from Mississippi—"Cotton's my game, son; what's yours?" —that he spotted Eleanor Lightbody. She was standing at the foot of the grand staircase in a white muslin dress and a wide-brimmed straw hat decorated with artificial flowers. There was a woman at her side, similarly dressed, a picnic basket in her arms and a pair of binoculars dangling from her neck. They weren't moving, but were poised there at the banister, eyes ranging over the crowd as if they were waiting for someone. Charlie excused himself and made his way toward them.

"Eleanor," he said, coming up to her and taking her hand, all thought of sandwich boards and the humiliation of traipsing through the rain like an itinerant peddler banished in a stroke.

"Oh," she gasped, dropping her eyes, and it was as if he'd interrupted her at some private moment, "hello." She seemed confused, stripped for an instant of that self-possession that stirred and alienated him at the same time.

He felt awkward suddenly—was she going to snub him?—and he removed his hand from hers and hid it behind his back. "I was just here to see Mrs. Hookstratten—Auntie Amelia—and I thought I'd say hello. . . ."

"Oh, yes, of course—your luncheon."

He was surprised. "You know of it?"

Her eyes were cold, translucent, glass. "Of course—and I did so want to come, but I'm afraid I have a prior engagement. Virginia and I are going bird-watching. . . . Have you met Virginia?"

Eleanor's companion—she looked to be about forty, with sallow skin, a disproportionate bosom and a pair of hips that cut like scythes at the seams of her dress—held out her hand. Charlie took it.

"Virginia Cranehill," Eleanor said, "Charlie Ossining."

"The Per-Fo man," Virginia pronounced with a smirk, and Eleanor gave her a sharp look. "A pleasure."

"Likewise," Charlie said, and he wondered what was going on between them—and how did this woman know about him? Would Eleanor have told her? Mrs. Hookstratten? And what would they have said—judging from that smirk it wouldn't have been all that flattering. After all these months, Eleanor Lightbody was still making a joke of him. He felt a surge of resentment—and who was she to feel so superior? What had she ever accomplished—marrying a rich man? He would show her. He would show them all.

"Amelia tells me your new factory is really quite the thing," Eleanor said, the old mockery dancing in her eyes, "very modern and efficient. You must be pleased to have come so far so quickly."

There was no mistaking her tone and it chilled him suddenly. How much did she know? How much did any of them know? The uneasy feeling he'd had all morning tightened its grip on him. Something was wrong here, terribly wrong.

He glanced round him at the gilded trappings of the place, the men and women in their expensive clothes and polished accents, and suddenly he was angry. She was one of them and he was nothing to her, nothing more than a diversion, a toy. There was no romance in that Christmas dinner, no intimacy at all. She was rich and bored and her husband was incapacitated and half the society of the San had gone home for the holidays and so she'd fastened on him the way she might have picked up a lapdog or a penny dreadful. He was nothing, nothing at all.

"You're looking thin," he observed, throwing it back at her. "The dietary doesn't agree with you?"

No trace of amusement in those arctic eyes. He shot a glance at the entrance of the Palm Garden—the crowd was thinning. "I've been fasting," she said finally. "It's the latest cure. But we'll be eating today, won't we, Virginia?"

Virginia patted the basket and emitted a tight little nasal laugh.

Charlie didn't so much as glance at her. He held Eleanor with his gaze. "And your skin," he said. "Have you been out in the sun?"

He seemed to have struck a chord. Eleanor put a hand to her throat, an instinctive gesture, and he saw that the hand contrasted sharply with the high white collar of the dress. She was dark, dark as a gypsy. "Yes, of course," she said, and a crease of irritation had appeared between her eyes. "The sun's rays are purely natural and health-giving and we should drink them up whenever we can—and wear white clothing, as Dr. Kellogg does, to allow those health-giving rays to penetrate to the innermost flesh, the flesh that's never seen the light of day. It's a basic scientific truth, Mr. Ossining"—and now they were on a formal footing again, strangers—"one that I think even you should be aware of."

He wanted to say something cutting, something about washerwomen and grape pressers and how much they enjoyed the sun, too, but he didn't have the opportunity. At that moment, careening, brash and loud, Eleanor's companion of that rainy April afternoon descended on them—he of the overlarge head and nagging, fitful voice. "Eleanor, Virginia," the man rasped, taking them each by the hand in turn and completely ignoring Charlie, "are you ready?"

They were. They gathered themselves, tiny little steps in place, a twitch of the shoulders, a smoothing of the dress, a touch to the hat, women on the verge of movement. "You look charming," the big-headed man growled, turning his back to Charlie and reaching out an arm to shepherd them along, "perfectly charming. Both of you."

Charlie felt something go off inside of him. He wouldn't be treated this way, he wouldn't be ignored. He was President-in-Chief of the Per-Fo Company, whether it had flown or not, and he was on the brink of great things. "Nice to see you again, *Eleanor*," he said, putting all the venom he could into it.

The little group halted, arrested, and turned back to him, the big-headed man—Badger, wasn't that his name?—looking as if he'd just seen a clod of earth rise up before his eyes, shape itself into human form and speak. Virginia Cranehill ducked her chin defensively. Eleanor's jaw went hard. She looked round the room once, and then, without warning, she leaned into Charlie, took his elbow in a raptor's grip and swung him away from the others. "I know all about the thousand dollars," she hissed, and her breath was hot in his face. "You took advantage of my husband at his weakest, a poor sick man struggling for his very life—"

"It was a legitimate investment."

"In what?" Their faces were so close they might have been embracing. A man in Sanitarium white, arms folded across his chest, was quietly watching them from across the room. "An imaginary company? A sham, a fraud, an illusion? The Charles P. Ossining Pension Fund? Where's that 'investment' now, huh?" She was trembling. Her eyes dug at him. She tightened her grip on his arm and then flung it away from her as if it were something she'd picked up in the street. "There are laws, you know, for people like you."

He wanted to explain, wanted to reason with her, lie, win her over—against all odds he wanted her to like him, admire him, he did —but it was too late, he could see that, and it frightened him. If she saw through him so clearly, what of the others, what of Mrs. Hookstratten?

There was a touch at his arm, and his benefactress was there, standing at attention, her feet pressed neatly together. "Charles," she said, "Charles, dear," and her voice seemed to quaver as she exchanged a look with Eleanor, "come on in—everyone's waiting."

He turned to go, but Eleanor wasn't through, not quite yet. "And Charlie," she called, tucking her arm into Badger's and giving him a sour look over her shoulder, "if I don't see you again, enjoy your lunch."

✢   ✢   ✢

There were twenty guests in all, a glittering collection of brushed whiskers, brilliantined hair, hats, silks, diamond earrings and gold watch fobs, and they were already seated, setting up a muted buzz of polite conversation and having a go at the celery, crackerbread and bran cakes on the table before them. As Mrs. Hookstratten led Charlie into the room, they looked up as one from their butter knives and celery sticks, a feast of sharp penetrating eyes. Charlie shot a quick glance up and down the table, muttered an apology, and sank into the chair on Mrs. Hookstratten's right, the place of honor. A pair of Sanitarium girls in blue caps and starched skirts moved up and down the length of the table, pouring fruit juices and water from the Sanitarium springs. There were ferns everywhere, creepers, flowers, fronds, the jungle itself come to life in Michigan. Charlie gave the man across from him a nervous smile and self-consciously brushed at the lint clinging to the lapels of his cheap but serviceable blue serge suit.

And then there were the introductions. The man to Charlie's right was a judge from Detroit, and beside him was the thespian lady, Mrs. Tindermarsh, now relieved of her greasepaint and stage powder. Directly across from him was a Mr. Philpott, police chief from Baltimore, and Mrs. Philpott, a wizened little nugget of a woman with skin like old newsprint and a rubbery, exaggerated smile. To her left was a hulking red-faced man with pinned-back ears and a name Charlie didn't catch—he was with the Michigan Association of Correctional Institutions—and beyond him, which was about as far down as polite introductions would allow, was the diminutive Countess, blanketed in jewels and holding forth on the subject of bowel movements.

Charlie gave each of them a forthright smile and replied, to the inevitable question, that he was in the breakfast-food business—but what was that glimmer in their eyes as they asked, and why the preponderance of people associated with the law? Was it chance? Or was there something else going on here, something grim, nasty, final? But no. He was wound up tight, that was all. These were just decent, ordinary food cranks with jittery stomachs and clogged-up intestines who happened coincidentally to be in the field of law enforcement—he'd just have to avoid soliciting investments from them. In fact, he made a mental note of it.

The girls were bringing in the soup course and Charlie was engaged in a conversation with the Philpotts over the relative merits of the various breakfast foods, when he happened to glance down the table and catch the eye of a very familiar looking individual, a gangling, overdressed, ever-so-slightly cross-eyed individual with an untamed shock of hair fallen across his brow: none other than Will Lightbody himself. It was a jolt to see him there after the encounter with his wife—but how could Charlie have missed him? Charlie gave him an agitated wink—was he going to demand his investment back now, on top of everything else?—but Will gave no sign that he recognized him. He looked preoccupied, somber, a whole continent away. Charlie's first thought was to avoid him when the party broke up, but there was no sense in that—Mrs. Hookstratten would have invited him expressly because of the Peterskill connection. He would just have to put the best face on it he could.

They were well into the entrée—the usual boiled pasteboard and soggy greens—when Charlie had a second surprise. A shock, actually, of the first magnitude. Across from Will Lightbody, at the far end of the table and blocked from view till this moment by the grazing heads and busy hands of the intervening guests, was the erect and unmistakable figure of Bartholomew Bookbinder. *Bookbinder.* And what in God's name was he doing here? The answer, too horrible to phrase, rang like a tocsin through his veins and he turned to Mrs. Hookstratten in fear and bewilderment—"Auntie," he pleaded, "Auntie"—but she looked away from him and he saw her lip tremble. He had to get out of here, had to get out now—

It was too late.

At that moment, just as the guests were sucking thoughtfully at the last morsels of whatever it was they'd been served and the girls in the blue caps had begun to exchange the dinner settings for dessert plates, the little white general himself, the impresario, the Chief, the lord of the manor, strode through the door from the lobby accompanied by six of his white-clad lieutenants and a ferrety slope-shouldered man with a badge pinned to his shirt and a baton dangling casually from his right hand—and there was no doubting who he was. Charlie froze. There were two other exits—one leading to the Men's Gymnasium, the other to the Women's—and the orderlies quickly fanned out to cover both of them. Paralyzed, staring down at the table for fear of lifting his eyes, Charlie sat there hunched inside himself like a man being beaten with a stick. In that moment he saw himself stepping off the train, full of his pathetic naive hopes and dreams, saw himself in Bookbinder's basement, tramping the streets in his sandwich board, lifting a glass of Otard Dupuy with Bender in his high-flown suite of rooms at the Post Tavern Hotel. *And so it all comes down to this,* he thought. *It all comes down to this.*

"Good afternoon, my friends," the Doctor boomed, rubbing his hands together like a workman setting out his tools, and striding down the length of the table to the far end before pivoting and staring back up again. "I wish you all a very happy holiday and urge you to enjoy all the many festivities we've organized for the remainder of the day, including the sing-along and fireworks display this evening, and I want to thank you all for attending this little luncheon I've asked Mrs. Hookstratten to arrange, and hope you will find it instructive, as well as gratifying to the palate. And, oh yes, of course, I'd like to thank Mrs.

Hookstratten for her participation, which I know must have been difficult for her, in light of what will shortly be revealed. . . ."

There was a spatter of applause for Mrs. Hookstratten, but she barely acknowledged it. She bit her lip and clasped her hands before her. She wouldn't look at Charlie.

For his part, Charlie stared so hard at his plate he could have reproduced its every least line and fracture from memory. He didn't move a muscle. Couldn't. The smell of the place immobilized him, rank and tropical, the smell of decay, rot, fatality, of betrayal and the death of hope, and it clogged his nostrils till he could smell nothing else. He choked back a sob. He could barely breathe.

The Doctor whirled, pirouetted, danced on his toes—he was enjoying himself. He stopped opposite Charlie, framing the heavy shoulders and sagely nodding head of Philpott, the police chief from Baltimore, and made a pyramid of his fingers. "There is here among us," he announced, "a fraud and criminal of the very worst stripe, a man so heinous and without conscience that I've taken time out from my crowded schedule to arrange this gathering both to ensnare and expose him and to warn you all against him and his ilk."

He paused, never taking his eyes from Charlie. "This is a man who would violate every fundamental principle of human decency, who would defraud his own patron, the very woman—Mrs. Amelia Hookstratten —who took him up from poverty and low circumstances to dress and educate him and give him a start in life . . . a man who would think nothing of taking money under false pretenses from our own Mr. Lightbody, a model patient and as decent and trusting a fellow as there is, and this after weakening his resolve with alcoholic beverages smuggled into this institution in direct contravention of all we hold sacred . . . a man who, without a glimmer of moral awareness, would defraud a legion of poor honest hardworking grocers throughout the country, all but steal the staggering sum of thirty-five thousand dollars from the most steadfast citizens of this our decent little forward-looking town, our Battle Creek, and, worst of all, betray the public trust in our great and selfless mission to save the American stomach and ensure each and every one of us the full enjoyment of life and longevity to which we are entitled—and if that isn't murder, I don't know what is."

The Doctor drew himself up, his head swinging on its axis with its freight of grief, anger, heartache and denunciation. "I say to you, ladies and gentlemen, this is cynicism at its most pernicious, this is nay-saying and criminality, this, without exaggeration, is the greatest danger facing America today."

Charlie was dead, numb, all the receptors of sense and pain shut down to the threshold of endurance. He hung his head. He shrank. He prayed for it to end, longed for the clasp of the handcuffs, the clank of the iron door.

"Per Fo," the Doctor pronounced, and the once-cherished name, the name that had made Charlie proud, was the vilest curse on his accuser's lips. "*Kellogg's* Per-Fo. Have any of you heard of it? No? Well, it's a good thing. A blessing. Would that Mrs. Hookstratten, Mr. Lightbody and our own Mr. Bartholomew Bookbinder could say the same. Would that *I* could. Yes, I, even I. For this vicious venal individual, and I'll pronounce his name and be the first to point an accusing finger—Mr. Charles P. Ossining, sitting here before you in all his wretchedness— this man tried to enfold even me in his web of deception, shamelessly using the name of one of my unfortunate adoptive sons as a means of blackmailing me to 'invest' in his nonexistent breakfast-food company. I say it's outrageous, ladies and gentlemen. I say it is sick, twisted, perverted."

A murmur went up from the table, ugly and incriminating. Mrs. Hookstratten sobbed into her napkin. "Auntie," Charlie whispered, appealing to her against all hope, "help me, please, I didn't . . . I'm sorry, I'm so sorry—"

She lifted her face to him, and he barely recognized her. Her eyes were wet, nostrils pinched, her face a pit of age and misery, gone old in an instant. "The factory," she choked, and the whole table was riveted on them now, "your letters . . . how could you do that to me? Tell me what I've done to deserve this? Tell me?"

Charlie looked wildly round the table. "It wasn't me—it was Bender!" he cried. "Bender, Bender did it!"

The Doctor loomed over him now, suddenly interposed between him and Mrs. Hookstratten, as if to shield her with his body. "Your accomplice, sir, is now under custody in Detroit, or so Judge Behrens informs me, and will get everything that is coming to him," the Doctor observed dryly before raising his eyes to the company at large. The judge threw Charlie a malignant look, and his wife drew back her lip in a sneer.

"I am a humanitarian," the Doctor announced after a moment's reflection, and all the while he was patting Mrs. Hookstratten's erupting shoulders with a plump and consolatory hand, "and I do believe in rehabilitation and the ultimate perfectibility of man, and yet"—the swipe at the brow, the thunderous breath—"some things disgust me to the very core of my being. This man—and I won't waste much more of your valuable time on him, believe me—this man, Charles P. Ossining, is such a threat to all our good work, such a subverter and perverter of the dietary truths to which I have dedicated my life and all my energies, that I cannot find it in my heart to pity him—no, not for a second."

There was a silence—the Doctor was finished. Mrs. Hookstratten, the betrayer, melted into his healing embrace, her every breath torn with the ferocity of her sobs. Overhead, palm fronds knifed at the light and alien creepers dangled their nooses and coils. The guests sat motionless in their chairs. Charlie looked desperately from one face to another—it was Bender, couldn't they see that?—but there was nothing there but loathing and contempt.

"Bill," the Doctor called sternly into the silence, and the man with the badge stepped forward and Charlie felt himself lifted from the chair, felt the distant cold kiss of steel at his wrists and heard the snap of the handcuffs as if from some immeasurable distance, as if someone else were being shackled, someone else drubbed, humiliated and crushed in full public view. Dr. Kellogg stood at attention, his lips compressed in triumph. "Take charge of your prisoner," he said, "and see that he is prosecuted to the very fullest extent of the law."

Chapter 9

Fireworks

Will was depressed. Yet another holiday, and here he was, still at the San, still alientated from his wife, still aching, still alone. Eleanor had gone off bird-watching—that was a new one: *bird-watching*—with that cow of a woman, and no doubt Badger as well. The three of them were practically inseparable, though he couldn't begin to fathom what the attraction was. Badger was like a sliver driven under your nails and Virginia Cranehill was just plain coarse, that was all. *Bird-watching.* He wouldn't be surprised if they'd taken their doctor along, too, the womb manipulator. The man needed a day off just like anyone else—his fingers must have been exhausted, worn down to the nubs. Yes: ha-ha-ha. Jokes, pathetic jokes. That's what he'd been reduced to.

He lay there on his physiologic bed in his physiologic room on the fifth floor of the Sanitarium and stared at the physiologic ceiling. Somewhere beyond the windows, bands were playing, children cheering, women wrapping sandwiches and men gathering to chat, throw horseshoes, drink a beer in commemoration of the Union dead and the casualties of the Spanish war. There were flowers, butterflies, frisking dogs, the scent of sausages and quartered chickens and cherrystone clams grilling over open fires, the sound of the birds, the crickets, the feel of sun-warmed grass and the cold curve of the horseshoe in your hand. Here there were enemas and watercress sandwiches.

God, he was depressed. Nurse Graves—he wouldn't call her Irene anymore: what was the use?—was gone, off somewhere with her bumpkin fiancé, boating, bicycling, picnicking, lying on a blanket in a meadow. It was a form of torture to think about it, but he couldn't help himself. He pictured them holding each other in the dappled shadows, thinking up names for their children, counting chickens, cows, furrows plowed and furrows seeded, kissing, touching, whispering secret desires over the gentle pulsating hum of the insects. All that. He'd done it, too, more or less, when he and Eleanor had been in love, in a time before chewing lessons, Graham gems and lost daughters. Nurse Graves was living in that time now, savoring life, the caress of the sun and the slow sweet unfolding of the day, while he'd had to go alone to that deadening melodrama replete with the backsliding husband he recognized all too readily and then the horrific luncheon that followed hard on its heels.

And that was part of the weight on him, too—the luncheon had been hard to stomach, gripping and potent in a way that insipid play could never have hoped to be. He didn't like to see any man humiliated like that, no matter how much he might have deserved it. Kellogg had really made poor Charlie squirm, really seemed to enjoy letting the sanctimonious boom drop while the police chief waited in the wings with his truncheon and his handcuffs. And that was depressing, too. Charlie was a thief, a crook, a confidence man, and Will was a thousand dollars poorer. But it wasn't so much the loss of the money that stung him—it was the thought that Charlie had seen him as a mark all along, right from the beginning, from the moment he and Eleanor had sat down across the table from him on the train. That hurt. Really hurt. He'd liked Charlie, liked the easy way he laughed and the confidence he had in what he was doing, liked the fact that he was a normal average regular meat-eating beer-drinking cigarette-smoking human being and not some Sanitarium monk. Aside from Homer Praetz and Miss Muntz, whose current condition he'd almost begun to envy, Charlie was about the only friend he'd had. Or thought he'd had.

He was chewing over these sour reflections when Nurse Bloethal appeared at the door, grimly efficient, the makings of his postprandial enema in hand. "Resting up for the evening's festivities, I see," she observed, big and brisk in her cork-soled shoes. She passed over the bed like a dark cloud, already in the bathroom opening the tap. "Half the others're out there on the lawn watching the Tozer Twins and waiting for the band to start up, but you're the wise one—no sense in risking everything for a few minutes' pleasure, hey?"

He wasn't listening. He was thinking about the chain of events that had brought him to this moment with this woman in this room, about how he'd become a party to it, how he'd lost his volition, his spine, his basic human right to control his own body and its functions. He felt like a whore, a concubine of the Sanitarium, Dr. Kellogg's plaything This nurse—look at her—she was a nattering fool, idiotic, rough and uncouth and beneath him in every way and he hated her and all she stood for, and here he was, for the thousandth time, about to roll over and submit while she performed a filthy and degrading act on his most intimate person. What was he? What had become of him?

Ah: he had a weapon, though, and it could defeat them all—Bloethals, Fletchers, Linnimans and Kelloggs alike. A train ticket. His means of egress and passage, the sword of his liberation. And he'd use it, use it today, but for one thing, and that thing sat on his chest like the great wheel of rock they had used to crush transgressors in the Middle Ages, *peine forte et dure:* the ticket was no good to him. Not now. Not anymore. Not since Goguac Lake. He wasn't going anywhere unless Eleanor was going with him. And what was the likelihood of that?

"All right then, Mr. Lightbody, there's a good fellow, if you'll just step in here a moment," Nurse Bloethal was saying, standing in the doorway to the bath like some beast transposed from the bottom of a bog, the enema bottle clutched in one meaty hand, the other idly scratching at some unmentionable portion of her anatomy. That was the situation, Nurse Bloethal beckoning and Will supine on the bed, crushed under the weight of his depression, when the telephone rang. Sharp and peremptory, the signal propelled Will from his bed to warn off the nurse with a yelp of admonition: "Don't touch it—I'm expecting a call!"

And he was. Though he didn't like it and it went against his grain and he felt ashamed to have arranged it this way, he was expecting a call. From the driver of the Sanitarium car that had taken Eleanor and Virginia "bird-watching." "Hello?" he gasped into the mouthpiece.

The voice on the other end came back to him with a clarity and volume that made it more immediate than Nurse Bloethal's—and she was standing right there, waiting, an impatient frown on her face. "The party you inquired about?"

Will was breathless. He turned his back on the nurse and crouched low over the receiver. "Yes?"

"Well, it was the two ladies we originally discussed, and they was joined by a man right out on the Sanitarium steps, a ginger-haired gentleman that never give his voice a rest the whole way out there—"

"Where? Where did they go?"

"Well, let me tell you, that wasn't the whole party—there was one more."

One more. Will felt the thrust of those two curt syllables in the place where it hurt him most, and he unconsciously stroked the scar on his abdomen. He knew what was coming, knew it as surely as if he were turning the pages of a book.

"Another gentleman, some kind of foreigner. Wore a monocle and walked like he had a stick up his ass, if you'll excuse the expression. Picked him up at a private residence on Jordan."

Will could feel the nurse's eyes on him and he clutched at the back of his neck as if to ward them off—"Mr. Lightbody, it's ready," she droned—and he turned partially to her and felt the words erupt from him: "Just a minute! Just a damn minute!"

"Where are they?" he snapped at the telephone.

"You know the Kalamazoo road? About five miles out of town heading west? They had me drop them off there by the milepost and I watched 'em making out across the fields—that'll be the Onderdonk place— heading down to the river, I guess. They had a picnic basket and all like that, so I guess that's what they're up to—and a lovely fine day for it."

Will broke the connection without responding. The Onderdonk place, yes, all right. He was up from the chair, the blood beating in his ears, checking his pockets, reaching for his hat and jacket, when Nurse Bloethal hove back into sight. He was frantic, desperate, eaten up with urgency, and she was there on the horizon, big as a ship, a movable mountain, one hundred and eighty pounds of physiologic impedimenta. "I said it's ready," she repeated.

"Not now," Will cried, shrugging into his jacket, "it's an emergency," and he made for the door.

Nurse Bloethal wasn't having any of it. She stood in the doorway, blocking his way, arms folded across her chest, an adamant, there-will-be-no-exceptions-to-the-rules look ironed into her face.

Will drew himself up. He was rushing with adrenaline, trembling, outraged. "Out of my way!" he boomed.

Her fingers tightened round the neck of the enema bag. Her eyes were flat, blunt, without sheen or sympathy. "I'm sorry," she said.

She was a woman, all appearances to the contrary, frail vessel, a representative of that weaker sex which any gentleman was bound to serve and protect as a matter of course, but for all that, there was no civility or restraint in what came next. "And so am I!" Will suddenly roared, putting all his weight into the stiff extended arm that burst the enema sack in an explosion of hot paraffin, water and whey, and sent her teetering into the corner like a bowling pin struck right on the mark. He wasn't there to witness her bottom-heavy collapse, but he heard the thump and rattle of it, heard the rending and the splintering and the sudden sharp crunch of the ceramic vase on the bureau as he ducked off down the hall, flaying his shins and his shanks into a loping stoop-shouldered run, dodging wheelchairs and tycoons in carpet slippers, and it was all he could do to keep from shouting out Eleanor's name.

There was the lobby, the sunstruck steps, the circular drive, the cab. "The Kalamazoo road!" he thundered at the cabbie, slamming the door so hard the carriage shuddered on its springs, and he was wrought up, frenzied, murderous. The cab ride didn't soothe him any. The horse seemed to be having trouble standing upright, let alone moving forward, and the driver—the same obstinate little gnome he'd had the last time he'd spied on his wife—was unmoved and unhurried, no matter how much money Will thrust at him. "We'll get there when we get there," he said, hawking up a ball of phlegm for emphasis. "Keep your shirt on."

Will did manage to keep his shirt on, though he sweated through it and into the lining of his tweed jacket and repeatedly dabbed at his brow beneath the crown of his trilby with a handkerchief that was wet through by the time they reached their destination—he always kept his shirt on, and his jacket, collar, tie and waistcoat, too. He was a gentleman, after all, even in extremis.

When finally the cab did roll to a halt, the fact didn't register on Will right away, what with the heat and his anxiety. The driver never said a word. At some seemingly random point in the interminable ride, the little man checked the horse, and they were no longer moving—if they could be said to have been moving to begin with. Will sat there a moment, stunned—he didn't know what he meant to do, but he was rushing headlong toward it, seething, goaded on by the image of Badger and that monocled faceless quack of a womb-manipulating wife-massaging doctor—until the driver finally spoke up. "You gonna sit there all day, friend?" he asked, spitting with great care and precision into the dust between the horse's hind legs. "Correct me if I'm wrong, but ain't you the one that was in such a hurry?"

Will ignored him. He stepped down from the cab and into the soft dark earth on the shoulder of the road, straightened his collar and tie, and paid the fare. He saw open fields, a line of trees, rolling hills raked with a wild pelage of dark motionless vegetation—there was nothing to distinguish this place from any other along the road. "This it?" he asked, and his eyes were feverish and he felt a sneeze coming on.

The driver pointed to the side of the road, a little man on a high perch. At first Will saw nothing in the tangle of tall grass and wildflowers that rose up out of the dirt nearly to his knees, but there it was, the milestone, a flat face of rock all but obscured by the vegetation:

KALAMAZOO, 20 / BATTLE CREEK, 5

"You'll wait for me?" Will asked, looking out over the fields and then squinting back up into the driver's eyes.

"Sure I will," the little man said out of a face compressed like a lemon in a squeezer, "sure I will, friend."

Will gave him a halfhearted wave, mounted the fence and started off across the field, annoyed by the way the weeds tugged at his trousers and filled his cuffs with dander and duff. He sneezed four times in quick succession, but he fished out the damp handkerchief, blew his nose stealthily and kept going. He hadn't gone a hundred yards before he was startled by a noise behind him and turned to see the hack swing round with a rattle of harness and start slowly up the road for Battle Creek. He looked at it stupidly for a long moment, as if he'd never seen a hack before, listening to the protest of the springs, watching it sway gracefully over a rut, and then he felt a surge of hatred so violent he could gladly have pulled that half-formed runt of a driver from his seat and choked him till the tongue swelled in his throat and his face went black—if only he could get his hands on him. He wanted to shout out, but he forced down the urge for fear of giving himself away—for all he knew, Eleanor and the others could be lounging on a blanket just beyond the line of trees. Helpless, he just stood there and watched the hack recede in the distance.

All right, what did he care how he got back—or even if he got back at all? What did it matter? Eleanor was all that mattered—and she was out there somewhere in the bushes with Badger and the womb manipulator. Mouth dry, heart racing, the next sneeze pricking at his sinuses, Will forged on. Grasshoppers took wing before him, butterflies scattered. A meadowlark rushed him and then folded away into the sky. Head down, trying to control his breathing and ward off the effects of the sun and the miasma of pollen that hung over the place like an arresting cloud, he scanned the clover and timothy for any sign that he was on the right track—and what if this wasn't the field at all? What if they'd crossed the road on the other side? He stopped to wipe the sweat from his face, looking round him in a daze, his ears attuned to the smallest sounds. All was silence.

When he reached the line of trees—pines, planted as a windbreak —he found what he'd been looking for. Someone had passed this way recently, no doubt about it. There was a distinct path—or two paths —where the long grass had been flattened, and the gate at the juncture of the rough timber fences had been left open. Here was the evidence, physical and real, deceit in a swath of grass—bird-watching, sure—and it exhilarated and depressed him at the same time. She'd lied to him. Eleanor had lied to him, and he didn't know what it meant or what he was going to do about it. But as he crept cautiously through the gate, he knew he was going to do something, something decisive and final, something dramatic, and there was no turning back now.

The sun bore down on him. Insects flitted through the air. He rubbed his eyes and stifled a sneeze. Then he was moving again, stealthy, wary, all his senses on alert. Fifty feet on he caught his first glimpse of the river, a bright liquid reflection trapped amongst the branches of the next irregular line of trees. He held his breath, studied his feet, stalked the open ground like a red Indian with a tomahawk clenched between his teeth. But there: what was that? Off to his left, through a stand of birch, wasn't that something moving? Or moving in place?

He dropped to a crouch, clung to the papery bark of the trees, inched forward. Step by step, closer and closer, drawn to that flash of movement that was now obscured, now revealed through the screen of leaves. And then all at once the object of that movement came into focus, and he saw that it was a man, a man with his back turned, a naked man, and that his right arm and shoulder were moving rhythmically over the center of him, as if, as if . . . Will wasn't prepared for what he saw next, could never have been, not in his fiercest imaginings, and it froze him where he stood.

He saw that there were two men there by the riverside and two women and that they were naked, all of them—completely, entirely, utterly naked, right down to their toes. The women were lolling on their backs, propped up on two logs at waist level, and one of the men stood between them, the stark white bunch of his buttocks facing the spot where Will stood concealed. The man's arms were extended on each side of him, his hands working between the women's legs. The other man—it was Badger—stood just behind them, masturbating himself. And the women? One of them, the one on the right, was Virginia Cranehill, her great tanned slippery dugs splayed out across her chest, her eyes closed and face transported in ecstasy. The other woman was Eleanor.

Eleanor. His Eleanor. His wife. His love. The moving hand was clamped to her, her nipples stood erect, her eyes were hammered shut and she was moaning—moaning. Like some animal. It was an image he couldn't contain. Something fell loose inside him, something primitive and ugly, and his hands scrabbled in the leaves for a weapon, the weapon of the Neanderthal, a club, a stick, the stark grainy leverage of murder. The stick was there, oak, walnut, beech, fit to the hand and tapered like a baseball bat, and in the next instant Will was on them.

Two pairs of startled eyes—Eleanor's, Virginia's—and then he was swinging at Badger from the side, his aim focused on that hateful swollen lump of bloated flesh between the man's legs, a snatch of rusty pubic hair, warts, pimples and crack!, a home run. And now the performance had music, piglike squeals, sorrow and woe and hurt, and the bat was slapping at the Teutonic buttocks suddenly, fencing with them, paddling, and the man turned his face abruptly to take the next rising blow across the bridge of the nose, the silvery disc of the monocle sailing out into the river in a sun-spangled arc. Virginia Cranehill screamed and he wanted to hit her, too, wanted to pound her flesh till it bled and shut the hole of her mouth, but he caught hold of himself.

Badger was on the ground, writhing, a flower of blood blooming between the knuckles pressed to his groin. The womb manipulator was on his haunches, holding his face. Virginia Cranehill, heavy in her suit of flesh, couldn't stop screaming. Will hadn't uttered a word. He stood there, chest heaving, the club dangling from his fingertips, and looked at Eleanor. She didn't scream, didn't whimper, didn't move. But he saw something in her eyes he'd never seen there before: fear. She was afraid of him. Afraid of the look on his face and the stick in his hand, afraid of the way the world had suddenly shifted beneath her. Her eyes darted to Badger, to the quack and to Virginia, and then back to him again. There was shame and guilt in the look she gave him, a plea, a promise, but most of all there was that new emotion, fear. Will dropped the stick in the dirt. "Get your clothes," he said, but he didn't wait for a response, his mind moving too quickly for that, and he had her by the wrist, her clothing—bloomers, dress, stockings, shoes, hat—bunched against his chest, and he was leading her, barefoot and naked, back up the path through the stand of birch, and away.

When they'd gone a hundred yards—and he didn't give a damn for her feet, let them bleed—he released her wrist, threw down her clothes and ordered her to get dressed. "I'm sorry, Will," she whispered, bending to her dress, the hair fallen round her face, her body lean and golden, tanned in every crevice, ripe as fruit. "I'm so ashamed."

He didn't want to hear it, didn't want to know. The rage and the hurt—he'd never known anything like it. He trembled with it, gritted his teeth, let it surge through him like some new kind of blood, like fuel—and he wouldn't let it settle in his stomach, not there, not anymore. Virginia Cranehill screamed in the distance. The sun tore through the trees. He held that rage in the back of his throat, that hurt, and he brought it up again and chewed it like a cud.

Eleanor hurried with her garments. She wouldn't look him in the eye, busy suddenly, so busy. Despite himself, despite his shock and disgust and the fierce seething wave of jealousy that ate at him like acid—he would never touch her again, never—he found himself growing hard as he watched her, harder than any mail-order belt or buxom nurse could ever make him. Her legs, he focused on her legs as she stood first on one foot to slip into her bloomers and then the other, and her breasts, swaying with the pull of the earth until the fabric of the dress enclosed them, and that excited him, too—she wore nothing beneath it, nothing but bloomers. "I-I don't know what came over me, Will," she began, and still she wouldn't look him in the eye, smoothing a wrinkle at her waist, tugging at her collar, her voice muted, buried. "It was *Freikorper Kultur*, it was therapy, it was—it was wrong, deeply wrong—" Her voice choked on itself. Her eyes were wet.

He hushed her. Took her hand, but gently this time, gently. "We won't talk of it," he said, and he couldn't breathe. The trees leaned over them, complicated, shadowy, limbs, digits, leaves. "We'll never talk of it, never again, never," he said, and he led her up the path and out of the woods.

At the same time, on the far side of Battle Creek, Charlie Ossining sat hunched in his misery on the doorstep of Chief William Farrington's gray-and-white clapboard house. The sun beat down on him, too, but he hardly noticed. His hands were manacled in front of him, his neck bowed like a postulant's, and he stared fixedly at the ground. The great black thick-soled shoes of the deputies who stood over him, one to each side, were the only objects in his line of vision, aside from the ants that crept obliviously across the step, and he sank deeper into himself as the minutes ticked by. All he could think of, all his body and brain could focus on despite the circumstances and against all odds, was escape. If only the deputies—open-faced men, reluctant, almost as embarrassed by the situation as he—would leave him for a second, just to get a cup of coffee or a slice of Mrs. Farrington's rhubarb pie . . . He stared at the shoes, stared at the ants, and saw himself running, leaping hedges and ducking down alleys, the wind in his hair, Battle Creek, Per-Fo, Kellogg, Mrs. Hookstratten and all the rest of it falling away to nothing behind him. It was all he could do to keep from springing up right then and there, but he restrained himself—he'd get only one chance, if that, and he couldn't afford to squander it.

Chief Farrington was inside, on the telephone, trying to arrange transportation to the county jail at Marshall, a place with which Charlie had become all too familiar through his dealings with George—two cells, no windows, heavy iron doors that swung to with a sound of finality and doom. He could hear the man's voice, patient, country-inflected, as he spoke into the mechanism, asking for Walter or Isaiah or Clinton, trying to scare up a vehicle on a day when the whole town was at the parade. Neither of the deputies said a word. The sun beat down. Off in the distance, snatches of music glorified the air.

When he finally looked up, out of boredom and misery and because he was still alive to the possibilities despite the face of utter defeat he put on for his captors, he found himself staring into the eyes of a boy in the yard next door. He couldn't have been more than six or seven, this boy, and he was wearing a clean starched white shirt, corduroy knee pants and a jacket of the same material. The way he was staring at Charlie, the way the whole focus of his world seemed to narrow until it enclosed only the front stoop of the police chief's house, you would have thought Charlie was Jesse James or William Bonney himself. The boy didn't look away when Charlie lifted his eyes, and that saddened him, hurt him in a way even Kellogg hadn't been able to. What was he then but a freak, a thrill, one more curiosity for a boy on his way to the parade? Charlie had to turn away, remembering himself at that age and how he and his friends would gather on Sunday after church to watch them let the Saturday-night drunks out of the lockup, and the thrill it would give him to be so close to these desperate men, these blinking criminals with their two days' growth of beard and slouchy clothes, men bewildered by the clarity of the day. Sure. And now he was one of them.

An hour passed. Two. The chief wasn't talking on the phone anymore—the house was quiet, in fact, and Charlie suspected he'd gone up to take a nap—and Mrs. Farrington, fat in the ankles and with a pouchy flushed suspicious face, had appeared twice to offer the deputies "a nice cool glass of water" or "a nice cool glass of lemonade," which both accepted, both times. She offered Charlie nothing. He sat there on the doorstep as if he'd sprouted from a seed while the sun moved overhead and the deputies sporadically conversed above him in soft whispering non sequiturs. Finally, at about four—Charlie was only guessing; he'd been relieved of his watch, billfold and rings by the constable—an open wagon, drawn by a pair of rawboned, skittish-looking horses, pulled up to the curb in front of the house.

Almost to the instant, the screen door swung open and Chief Farrington emerged from the house, dipped for Charlie's arm as casually as if he were scooping up a bucket on his way to the well and lifted him off the doorstep. They moved across the lawn in a little group, Charlie and the chief in front, the two deputies lumbering behind.

The man at the reins wore a stovepipe hat and an antiquated jacket polished with age at the seams. He was a farmer, obviously, dressed up for a day on the town, and he gazed out grimly on them from beneath the brim of his hat. "Isaac," the chief said, nodding a greeting, and the man returned it in a single clipped syllable, part of a ritual, nodding, too, "Bill."

The chief led Charlie to the back of the wagon, which was strewn with hay and clumps of dirt and torn sacking, and the larger of the deputies, the one with a face like the hind end of something you'd see in a pasture, helped him up. Farrington got up on the platform beside the driver, the two deputies scrambled into the back with Charlie and settled themselves in the straw with barely suppressed groans of pleasure, and they were off. As they pulled away from the house, Charlie caught a glimpse of the boy in the yard next door, motionless and patient, still staring.

The trees moved overhead. Shadows pursued them, a breeze came up, the sun dodged in and out of the branches. A few yards down, a dog lay prostrate on the lawn of a great looming meticulously kept house and lifted its head to give them a sleepy look before letting it drop back down again. The streets were quiet. Dead quiet. And that was a mercy, because Charlie knew these streets, knew the stolid sedate ranks of freshly painted houses and the ordered lives that went on within them. He'd wanted a piece of that prosperity, wanted the Daimler and the billiard table and the woman like Eleanor Lightbody that went with it—and was that so bad? Was that such a crime?

The wagon plunged precipitately and rocked back up again, lax on its springs, and Charlie took the sharp stab of it at the base of his spine and he shifted position, awkward with his shackled hands. The deputies were oblivious. They lay sprawled in the straw, their eyes slits, jaws working round twin stalks of grass, as snug as if they were home in their own beds. And what did they care? They weren't the ones going to prison, they weren't the ones abandoned by the world. He felt his stomach contract at the thought of it. For one terrible moment he held the whole thing in his mind, the lawyers in their fancy suits, the outraged witnesses against him, the term paid out in years and months of a young man's life, the prison grays, the stale incinerated world of the ex-convict. And who would help? Who would care? Not Mrs. Hookstratten, not his Auntie, that much was clear. He thought of the look on her face as she betrayed him, washed her hands of him, led him off to the chopping block as if there were nothing between them, as if all those years and all they'd shared amounted to nothing more than a bad memory. He should never have lied to her, he saw that now. Right from the beginning, right from the moment she got off the train, he should have told her the truth and pinned the blame on Bender, where it belonged.

Bender. The son of a bitch. So they'd caught up with him finally. At least there was that. But how could Charlie have listened to him?

How could he have been so stupid? And why hadn't he run when he'd had the chance and Will Lightbody's money to stake him? Because he was thinking of Mrs. Hookstratten, that was why, and look where it had gotten him.

Charlie stole a glance at the slumped spines and nodding heads of Farrington and the funereal driver, both of them already gone in a daze, and he thought of leaping, right then, right at that moment, leaping over the side and running cuffed through the streets like a runaway slave till they caught him or he dropped dead or got away clean, but the impossibility of it strangled the impulse in the instant it came to him, and he sat, merely sat, and rocked with the wagon. Lurching, heaving, it ground on with a faint percussive thump of spring and axle, endlessly repetitive, wearing him down as surely as if he were strapped to the wheel beneath him.

They turned onto Lake Avenue, and there was traffic now, farmers in traps and buggies coming in from the countryside for the parade and fireworks and all the other simple pleasures Charlie would be denied for who knew how many years to come. He was going to prison. He was a criminal. An outcast. The farmers and their wives drew even with the wagon and carefully looked away, as if a glance might contaminate them. Eleanor Lightbody had looked at him as if he were an insect, and she'd known, she'd known what was coming, and Kellogg, that blowhard, he'd really rubbed Charlie's nose in it. There was no call for that. The old goatbeard couldn't bear to see him quietly arrested—no, he had to make a spectacle of it, a lesson. God, how he'd like to even the score, just once, how he'd like to batter that self-satisfied goateed moonface until every last glimmer of superiority was bruised out of it, until the big shot went down on his knees and squirmed and pleaded and begged. . . .

Charlie never got to complete the fantasy. Because at that moment, the motorcar that was attempting to pass on their left—a midnight-blue Cadillac, so blue it was black, with its high open seat and gleaming headlamps—backfired. It was no fault of the driver, a Mr. Rudolph Jenkins, of Albion, who, with the veiled, hatted and satin-enveloped form of Mrs. Jenkins, was heading into town for the Sanitarium concert and fireworks display—it was just one of those things, too rich a fuel mixture, a spark too far advanced or retarded. Sudden, blood-quickening, loud as a gunshot in a closet, the flare of that erupting blast caused the deputies to snap their eyes open, the chief to duck his head in a reflexive huddle and the farmer, Isaac of the worn jacket and tall hat, to drop the reins between his legs. Which in turn caused the already spooked horses to attempt a sudden U-turn, lifting the back end of the wagon two feet clear of the ground in a crazy spinning tilt and ultimately slamming it into the right rear fender of Mr. Rudolph Jenkins's pristine Cadillac motorcar.

Ten seconds later, it was over. The Cadillac was impaled on a dec-orative stone wall twenty yards from the street, the Jenkinses and their baggage were strewn across the lawn behind it, and the farm wagon lay overturned in the roadway, its wheels spinning gratuitously in the warm filtered light of the late afternoon, its occupants trapped beneath its splintered planks. All its occupants except Charlie, that is. With his hands encumbered, he'd been unable to find a grip when the wagon pitched violently into the car, and he'd been thrown up off the floor-boards and into the dazzle of sunlight like a volleyball on the rebound.

There'd been an accident—he could see that from where he sat, unharmed, on the fine rich deep carpet of a well-tended lawn, assessing the scene. It took him a minute. He watched the wheels spin, heard the groans of the Jenkinses, saw the white pulp of an arm, the shirt torn from it, moving fitfully beneath the wagon. A minute, that was all. And then he was up and strolling off casually down the street, his hands folded up high under his jacket so that the chain of the handcuffs, draped across his chest, might have been nothing more than a glittering watch fob.

But what now?

He turned down a side street, quickening his pace, his eyes sucking at the fronts of the houses along the way, willing the doors to stay shut and the windows untenanted. He ducked into a driveway, cut through a yard, climbed a fence and dropped down into a vacant lot prickling with weed and wildflower. Crouched low in the vegetation, his back pressed to the naked slats of the fence, he took a minute to catch his breath and consider the situation.

The fire bell was ringing in the distance and he knew it would be a

matter of minutes before Farrington and his deputies climbed out of the
wreckage, brushed off their clothes, counted their teeth, toes, fingers,
limbs and ears, and recollected that something was missing. The fire
company would turn the wagon over, and Charlie wouldn't be there.
Then all hell would break loose. They'd start knocking on doors, dep-
utizing hayseeds and amateur marksmen, calling out the bloodhounds.
He had an hour, maybe less. He needed money, a change of clothes,
a place to hide. He couldn't go back to his room—Mrs. Hookstratten
would have alerted them to that—and he didn't dare go anywhere near
the rail yard. The smart thing to do—and from now on he was going
to do nothing that wasn't smart, he vowed it—would be to lie low
someplace in town for a day or two, in a cellar, a barn, a carriage house,
and find some way to spring the cuffs and free his hands. It was the
handcuffs that made the criminal, the handcuffs those farmers and their
dried-up wives wouldn't look at, and if he couldn't get rid of them, he
might just as well give it up and turn himself in.

The fire bell was closer now, shrill and urgent, and he could hear
voices raised over the tumult—he had to move. They'd start with these
streets, this neighborhood, this lot. Distance, that's what he needed,
and quick. He stood, hurried off across the lot and turned up the sidewalk, fighting to keep himself from breaking into a trot. Just then, a
blur of movement froze him in place, and two boys emerged from nowhere to dash past him in the direction of the fire alarm. It was a bad
moment—he thought he'd been taken—and he had to hold himself
there, hugging his shoulders, until he fought the panic down. When
he felt his legs moving beneath him again, he risked a quick reconnoiter
of the wide brilliant tree-hung street and found himself locking eyes
with an old woman on the porch opposite him. She was leaning on a
broom, her pinned-up hair like a helmet, and she gave him a long steady
look that ate through to his bones. He kept walking, studying his feet
now, his fists wedged up into his armpits to conceal the cuffs, but he
could feel her eyes on him all the way to the end of the block.

It was no good. The frenzy began to creep up on him—he wanted
to run, had to run, there was no reason or purpose to existence that
didn't involve legs and feet, the sure swift arrow of flight, escape, freedom, safety. He couldn't just stroll the public streets as if he were

invisible—they'd have him in ten minutes. What was he thinking? Had he gone mad? For all he knew, the old lady was on the telephone now. He looked suspicious, he knew it, sweat coursing down his face, bits of grass and lint clinging to his suit, coat sleeves dangling, his hat gone —and that was a giveaway right there, a dead giveaway. Who but an escaped criminal would walk the streets without a hat? He was practically cantering now, craning his neck left and right to look over his shoulder like a mad heifer in the midst of a stampede, doomed, all but doomed.

It was then, at the very brink of disintegration, that the architecture of his salvation appeared to him. Just as he was about to lose all control and fling himself howling down the street, he spotted something familiar—looming, tall, laminated in sunlight, a great stepped stairway cut out of the sky like a pyramid in profile. And what was it? He knew this place, didn't he? Stumbling, hurrying, no one in sight, he turned a corner and there it was: the ruin of the Malta-Vita plant.

A tumble of brick, walls without roofs, careening timbers, the great rusted three-story relics of the traveling ovens that had beckoned to him over the treetops: nothing had changed since that bitter November afternoon when he'd stood here and hammered the first nail into the coffin of his hopes. Or had it? As he crossed the deserted street, heart racing, holding himself back, inconspicuous, a decent citizen out for a holiday stroll, he saw that the place looked different somehow, softer, almost inviting. And then he understood: spring had come. Where the fire-blackened walls had stood stark against the barren ground, a testament to futility, now they were buffered by leaf, bud, stalk and creeper. A splash of wildflowers decorated the stripped doorway, saplings six feet high sprang up through the cracks in what had once been the packing-room floor. Six months ago the place had depressed him, shaken him to the core; now it was his sanctuary. There was no reason to get philosophical about it: he ducked behind the wall, and he was safe.

For a long while he lay there on his back in a clump of sumac, watching the swallows flit in and out of their nests in the ovens, his heartbeat winding down, the afternoon softening into evening. They wouldn't look for him here. They'd look on the roads, in the ditches, they'd prowl the Grand Trunk depot and the Michigan Central, poke through the refuse out back of the Red Onion and post a man outside the shabby building where he had his room. Here he was safe. Who'd even notice the place? Who even knew it was here? It was an eyesore, a monument to failure, the sort of place the Biggest Little City in the U.S.A. would just as soon forget.

He was safe for the moment, but where did that leave him? His hands were shackled, he was a thousand miles from New York, he had no wallet, no money, no watch, no food. And he was hungry, the first hot hard tug of necessity clutching at his insides even now. He'd had an egg and some toast at a tavern that morning, too excited about his prospects to hold much down, and he hadn't done anything more than rearrange the mattress stuffing they'd served up at the luncheon. *The luncheon.* The thought of it started up his breathing again, made his scalp twitch uncontrollably and sent something fluttering up his throat—but how the world had changed since the morning, how everything golden and shining had turned to shit. And was it only this morning? It seemed like ten years ago.

The sun held him in its grip, cupped him and held him, and despite himself, he dozed off. When he woke, it was as if no time had passed at all—the sun seemed to hang steady on the wall above him, and he guessed it must have been about five-thirty or six. Birds were pouring syrup into the air, crickets conspired, there was no sound of deputies or hounds or anything else, and nothing had changed. He was still shackled, still hungry, still at large. If he moved, it would be under cover of darkness, and it would be for one purpose only: to steal into a garage somewhere and make off with a hammer and chisel. He saw himself coming back here—leaving to scrounge food, maybe, from a smokehouse, an open kitchen, the trash, even—but always coming back here to sit within these blackened walls and wait on and on until they forgot he'd ever existed. . . .

But what was that?

He shrank into the ground. Held his breath.

A voice, a human voice, rasping and whispery, talking to itself—or, no, singing:

With the birds and the trees,
And sweet-scented breezes,

Good old summertime,
When your day's work is over,
Then you are in clover,
And life is one beautiful rhyme!

Cracked, drunken, obscene, the voice rose up over the lyrics as if it were raping them, eviscerating them, turning them inside out, and then there was a pause and it repeated the same verse again, once, twice, a third time. Charlie lay there, wrapped in a cocoon of fear, afraid to breathe, and it wasn't until the fourth repetition that he began to appreciate how his luck had changed. This was no ordinary concert he was enjoying, no usual drunk—*George*, it was *George*. Of course it was. With no one to pay his rent, Mrs. Eyvindsdottir had put him back out on the street, and he'd come home to his hovel under the flight oven. Sure he had. Where else would he go?

The knowledge invigorated Charlie, gave him new life—George would help him. If there was one person in the whole godforsaken dollar-crazed right-living town who would be able to straighten him out, it was George. Charlie rose up tentatively from his hiding place and tiptoed through the rubble in the direction of the sound. He found George slouched atop an outcropping of ruined machinery, a bottle between his legs, his face raised to the sun. "And life is one beautiful rhyme!" he howled, yelping at the words like a bitch in heat, and then he dissolved in laughter.

"George," Charlie whispered. "George Kellogg."

George barely reacted. At first Charlie thought he hadn't heard him, but then the slope-shouldered figure in the ragged coat swung slowly round on his perch—it was an old retort, rusted like an anchor—and let his black eyes and sullen mouth arrange themselves into an expression of mild amusement. "Charlie Ossining," he said, and it was almost as if he'd been expecting him.

Charlie took a step forward and raised his hands, the chain stretched tight between them. The sun held steady, just over the treetops. "I'm in trouble, George," he said.

"Who isn't?" George bawled, and then he laughed, a short whiskey-inflected bark of a laugh that made Charlie nervous all over again. He was pinning his hopes on a madman, a souse, a boozehound. George would no more help him than he'd help his own father.

"Your father did it to me," Charlie said, suddenly inspired. He hadn't moved his hands. He stood there in mute appeal, the chain catching the sun in separate hammered beads of light.

George's face changed suddenly. There was no trace of amusement in the eyes now and his mouth had fallen in on itself. He swung down from the big cylindrical retort, brandishing the bottle in one hand. "What are you saying? My father? Not that good-hearted man, not the Saint on the Hill himself?" Unsteady on his feet, he threw back his head to take a drink, and Charlie was impatient suddenly, angry—he wanted the cuffs off and he wanted them off now. "Here," George said, thrusting the bottle at him, "you need a drink."

What could he do—refuse? George was leering at him, teeth rotted to stubs, breath stinking like a dead thing, the miasma of his catastrophic odor enveloping him, the bottle waving in the air. Humor him, he told himself, humor him. Charlie fixed his hands on the bottle—it was pint-size, a label he didn't recognize—and drank. He felt the instantaneous heat of it in him, the charge of the alcohol, but there was something else there, too, something bitter and earthy, muddying the flavor. He took another drink above the gleam of George's eyes, the nod of the approving head, and he realized how much he'd needed it. "Jesus," he said.

George was grinning like a cadaver. "I've got a whole case of it tucked away under the oven over there—we're going to drink ourselves into oblivion tonight, Charlie, just you and me." He took the bottle back, pointed his chin to the sky and let his throat ripple. "I'm celebrating," he said, wiping his mouth with the back of a dirt-encrusted hand. "This is my last night in Battle Creek."

Charlie stood there beneath the fat mellow sinking sun, his hands chained together, his dreams obliterated, and conversed with a drunk. For lack of anything better to do, he reached for the bottle. "You know, I really do need to get out of these cuffs, George," he said, and took a hard swallow. And then, unaccountably, he began to laugh. It was all too ridiculous.

"Sure," George said, but he seemed distracted. "Aren't you going to ask me where I'm going?"

"Where you going?"

The yellow teeth, the stinking breath, the high sharp dog's bark of a laugh: "I don't know. But I'm damned if I spend another night in this pisshole." He lurched forward, caught himself. "One little visit to pay before I go," he muttered, and his look had gone cold again. "You say my father did that to you?" he slurred, tapping the cuffs and relieving Charlie of the bottle in one fluid gesture.

It took a while to explain, and they were well into the second bottle before George seemed to fully grasp his adoptive father's role in complicating Charlie's life, though Charlie had tried to fight down his own bowel-tightening terror and outrage and narrate as plainly as he was able. Charlie had been doing all the talking for some time, while George, silent save for the occasional epithet thrown in as a sort of punctuation, stared off into the distance as shadows seeped in to knock down the walls, and the last of the sunlight illuminated the forest growing up through the packing-room floor. They were lying side by side, stretched out in the weeds. A long suspended moment hung over them after Charlie had finished his recitation; he filled it by helping himself to another drink. Finally George drew himself up, coughed into his fist and observed, "He's a study, isn't he, the Saint on the Hill? A real study." Then he rose from the grass with a sigh and went off into the bushes to relieve himself.

Charlie listened to the birds and the crickets and the fierce rattling torrent of George's micturition, one more sound of nature, a nature he was going to know a lot more intimately now, at least for a while, and pressed the bottle to his chest. He'd begun to forget himself, drifting off for minutes at a time on the sheen of the alcohol, the handcuffs barely there, nothing at all, a minor inconvenience—didn't everyone wear them?—when George returned with a spike of rusted metal in his hand. It was a foot and a half long, blood-dark in its coat of rust—it might have been a lever once, or a connecting rod from some vital moving piece of machinery, a thresher, a sifter, one of the great standing ovens itself.

"Come over here," George commanded, and he led Charlie through the wreckage to the base of the nearer of the two big baking and sifting machines. And then, while Charlie strained against the chain that bound his hands, pulling it taut over the projecting edge of the bottommost tray, George lifted the rusted spike and beat the chain with an intense implacable rhythmic fury, beat and beat at it till the place rang with the echoing din and the chain recoiled, jumped, shrank in on itself and finally gave way. They had a drink to celebrate.

"You're a free man, Charlie," George said, tipping back the bottle, and the exercise seemed to have sobered him. "But listen, I've got something to do—for both of us. You wait here—and feel welcome to drink as much of this sheep dip as you want, didn't cost me a nickel, I just found it, you might say, on the back end of a car in the Grand Trunk yard. I'll be back late, after the fireworks, and they'll be looking for me by then, too—" He paused, and he seemed to relish the thought. "You can bet they'll be looking for me."

Charlie had no objections. He had nowhere to go and he was in no hurry to get there. He wouldn't have refused a bite to eat, but the elixir in the bottle had quieted his stomach even as it salved his wounds and stuffed cotton into his skull. He would drink, drink till he passed out. He settled himself down in the weeds. "What did you say this stuff was, anyway?" he asked, squinting at the label.

George stood over him now, ragged against the backlit sky. The hair stood out wildly from the dark globe of his head, his coattails hung in tatters. He looked grim, old, older than Charlie, older than anyone. "Read the label," he said, and he was already moving, already in action, off to do whatever it was he had to do to bid his proper adieus to Foodtown, U.S.A.—Charlie didn't ask, didn't want to know—but he came back a step and paused a moment on the edge of the darkness to add, "Biggest fraud going. They get a buck a bottle for that crap, can you believe it?" And the shadows swallowed him and he was gone.

Charlie propped the bottle on his chest and studied the label: *Lydia E. Pinkham's Vegetable Compound*, it read, *A Sure Cure for Prolapsis Uteri and all Female Weaknesses*. He was thunderstruck. Stunned and amazed (or at least as stunned and amazed as a three-quarters-inebriated ex-tycoon pursued by the law and wearing a freshly separated and matching pair of steel bracelets could expect to be). He'd been drinking patent medicine for the better part of the past hour and never even suspected it, but for the faint rooty taste of the stuff, a taste no worse or better than the intimation of charred oak you got from a good Kentucky bourbon. *Contains 15 Percent Alcohol,* he read, tipping back the bottle for another taste. *This Is Added Solely as a Solvent and Preservative.*

Yes. Well. Sure it is. He sipped again. Thirty proof and they floated the stuff on the market as a female remedy—and got a buck a bottle for it to boot. Now there was genius, he thought, as Venus showed herself in the east and the sky roiled to a deep quickening cobalt; there was genius on the order of the memory tablets. He took another long meditative pull at the bottle as night closed in around him, warm as a blanket, and somewhere between the moment his lips locked round the glass aperture and the hot certain stuff relit the hearth in his stomach, he experienced a moment of grace.

Per-To, he said to himself, and he said it aloud. *The Perfect Tonic.* Celery-impregnated, of course. He wondered if he could call it "pep-tonized," too, wondered briefly what "peptonized" even meant, and then dismissed it. Well, all right, maybe it wasn't peptonized—he'd come up with something else, something even better. It still Made Active Blood, didn't it? And why settle for thirty proof when it could be sixty—hell, eighty? *Per-To.* He liked the sound of it—it was catchy, unique. Almost irresistible.

Later, when the insects had taken possession of the night and all the familiar stars and constellations lay stretched out before him like jewels in a studded tapestry, the first distant rocket shot out into the nullity trailing a plume of gold. It went high, higher than he thought it could ever go, arcing over the sky like a lash of flame, and when it died, another followed in its path, and then another, and another.

Chapter 10

Decoration Day

ॐ

As the shadows lengthened across the South Lawn and the voices of his patients and staff, unified in song, drifted to him through the open window, Dr. Kellogg sat at his desk amidst the usual blizzard of papers, disposing of several small matters he didn't want to put off till after the holiday. He was no stick-in-the-mud—earlier, he'd led the Sanitarium Marching Band twice round the grounds, pumping a vigorous baton to the brassy thump of "El Capitan," and he'd inaugurated the picnic supper by tossing the first Protose steak on the outdoor grill while his immaculate chefs looked on and nearly two thousand patients, staffers and townspeople cheered—but time was money, and life, no matter how physiologic, was short. He was taking a brief hiatus from the festivities, that was all, accomplishing something, if only for an hour.

At nightfall, when the sky had gone fully dark, and not a moment before, he planned to meet Ella, Clara and the eight children still remaining at the Res for the fireworks display (child rearing had been a devotion of his earlier days; as he grew now into his middle years, he felt no qualms about reducing the number of youngsters in the house, along with the subdued yet omnipresent level of excitation, noise and dirt they inevitably brought with them). He was looking forward to it.

Fireworks. How he did love fireworks. Though Decoration Day was hardly his favorite holiday, never having been a military man himself (though you couldn't begin to count the generals, admirals and even secretaries of war he'd numbered among his intimates), the occasion provided him with a marvelous excuse to light up the sky over Battle Creek with a display second to none.

He worked on, his concentration unflagging. He prided himself on his ability to shut out the world no matter where he was, be it in a rattling second-class compartment in Gibraltar or a dhow in the Gulf of Oman, and focus on the matter at hand. Still, he couldn't resist tapping his foot in rhythmic sympathy with "Mother Was a Lady," which the two-thousand-voice chorus was even now bringing to a stirring close, and when they launched into "Daisy Bell," one of his especial favorites, he found himself irresistibly humming along.

As dusk settled in and he labored in the pool of light cast by his Handel desk lamp, he keenly felt the absence of Bloese and, for a moment, just a moment, regretted having given him the day off. But every man needed a break from the routine, particularly one so diligent and devoted as his secretary, and he comforted himself with the thought that, after all, he'd done the magnanimous thing. Thinking of Bloese, he lifted his head briefly from his papers and took a moment to listen to the ticks and murmurings of the great building that rose up above him, savoring its every least rustle and whisper. The Sanitarium was quiet, as quiet as it had ever been—nearly everyone, even the wheelchair-bound, was gathered on the lawn for the sing-along and the pyrotechnics that would soon take hold of their imaginations—and he settled into the feel of that quiet as he might have settled into a familiar chair or a pair of hearth-warmed slippers. Here was his institution, this grand edifice, this tangible representation of his will and his vision, and he had it all to himself for just this briefest sliver of time, while the voices of all those he'd brought together within its walls rose up just beyond the windows in health and jubilation.

It was then, while the Doctor sat there amongst his papers and allowed himself the small indulgence of pride of accomplishment, while his spirit gorged and a sense of the profoundest well-being seeped into his veins like a restorative, it was then that the smell began to invade his nostrils. A chemical smell, harsh with its load of petroleum distillates, the smell of fuel, coal oil, of old glass-chimneyed lamps and wicks burnt to the nub. And where could that be coming from? Was it some trick of memory, a nostalgic echo? He hadn't used a kerosene lamp since the days of the Western Health Reform Institute.

Curious, he rose from the desk, shoving back the celluloid eye-shade till it rested on the crease of his hairline, and crossed the room to the door. As he grasped the doorknob, he remarked how much stronger the odor was here, and as he pulled open the door and ventured out into the hallway, he nearly choked on it. But this was odd. The floor, the Italian marble floor he himself had chosen from a design from Favanucci, seemed to be wet, as if the janitors hadn't finished mopping up, or as if—but he stopped cold. It *was* wet. He bent a finger to the floor, brought it up to his nose: coal oil. Kerosene. He'd know it anywhere.

And then he looked up, puzzled, into the eyes and teeth of the greatest trial of his life, of the *cauchemar* come to life—George stepped out of the doorway of the next office down and leaned insouciantly against the wall. *George.* In his hand, a match. A single thin insubstantial stick of wood with a dab of phosphorus affixed to the fire-red tip of it. There was no manufactured smile this time, no mocking grin. There was only the bristling patchy beard of the boy-man with its grim slash of a mouth and the eyes black as the rim of the universe, so black they seemed to suck up all the available light and extinguish it. And that wasn't all: beyond him, at the far end of the hall, lay a five-gallon drum of coal oil, dropped casually on its side, bleeding its glistening contents over the surface of the floor. "Dr. Vegetable," George sneered. "Dr. Anus. Do you know why I'm here?"

All the peace he'd felt in his office, all the beauty of the evening and the sweet sentiment of its songs, all the exhilaration he'd felt over ensnaring that deviate Ossining character and liberating Amelia Hook-stratten from his spell, all of it dissolved in that instant. Damn that Farrington, he thought angrily, and he vowed to have him removed from his post—and why couldn't he and his twelve overfed deputies have dug George out from beneath whatever rock he'd been hiding under? He didn't move. Didn't breathe. Just kept his eyes focused on George's, on his son's.

"Do you?" George's voice echoed down the oil-slick corridor, that hateful familiar adolescent whine creeping into it for all the twenty useless years of his young manhood.

The Doctor said nothing. He tensed his muscles. Let him talk, let him rave—he was ready to spring, to fight for his life and the life of Battle Creek, ready to do anything, anything it would take to silence this insect, crush him, expunge him once and forever. Anything.

George threw himself back from the wall with a sudden violent thrust, and his eyes exploded with hate. "I'm here to give you a history lesson, Dr. Anus, that's what I'm here for—I'm here to make your life the cesspool you've made mine, here to cram all your zwieback and your enemas and all the rest of it down your throat once and for all." He lifted the match to his eyes and sighted down the length of it as if it were a rifle. "I'm going to burn this place to the ground," he hissed, and he was nearly choking on his rage, "—*again.*"

Again. The adverb dropped between them like a gauntlet, burst howling from the walls, electric, excoriating.

The Doctor came forward then, moving like a somnambulist, blind, goaded, the blood raging in his ears, and George flicked his thumbnail against the head of the match, the quick yellow spark springing up from his fist as if by prestidigitation. "That's right, *Father,*" he taunted, "*again,*" and as the Doctor rushed him he dropped the match to the floor and the flames fed on it, leaping up with an eager panting grace while George danced among them like some malignant hell-born thing with bituminous eyes and leathery wings.

"It was I!" he shouted, evading the Doctor's charge even as the flames rushed toward the barrel at the end of the hall, "me, I alone. Not Sister White, not your crabbed, ball-less, half-blind Elders, not a one of them, no." He was backing up the hall now, spitting it out, cavorting round the sudden churning troughs of fire. "Thirteen years old!" he cried in a hoarse rasping shriek that only seemed to fan the flames higher. "It was I, I, I!"

451

❖   ❖   ❖

Will Lightbody never said a word as he led his wife across the wide waving field and back out to the road. When they reached the highway, he looped his arm through hers, and they walked silently along the compacted dirt surface of the roadbed, neither hurrying nor dawdling, moving along as if they were out for an evening stroll on the cobbled streets of Peterskill. Will held himself erect, head back, chest thrust out, tie squared and vest buttoned up to the very last button, and he didn't need any posture coaches or shadowgrams to show him the way. Though his mind was in a ferment, his body was at ease, calm, filled with the sort of peace that follows on great exertion, secure in its own physicality. He strolled up that road like an athlete who's just vanquished the field and won the prize, and though vehicle after vehicle, from buggies to surreys to motorcars and even a farm wagon, stopped to offer them a lift, he steadfastly refused. It felt right to walk. It felt necessary.

Eleanor was on his arm, the day was golden, and though the scene he'd just witnessed, the primal scene, stark in its animality and horror, kept threatening to intrude on his consciousness, he fought it down. He would not relive that scene again, never, he refused to, and every time it crept back into his head he drove it out through sheer force of will. Happier times, he thought of happier times, five years ago, six, when the world was whole and the house on Parsonage Lane, with its smell of fresh paint and wallpaper paste, was their adventure. And so they walked, past farms and farmhouses, up and down hills, bisecting the fields on the sunlit ribbon of the Kalamazoo–Battle Creek road. And if Will hadn't known himself two hours ago, hadn't known where he was going or what he was doing, if he'd been uncertain and tentative, floating through life like a bit of fluff on the breeze, now he knew exactly who he was and where he was going and why.

For her part, Eleanor walked along beside him in silence, not daring to glance at him, her eyes locked straight ahead, never protesting. It was as if she'd been awakened from a dream, as if a spell had been broken. They hadn't discussed it, perhaps never would, but it was clear that she'd gone too far, over the edge, way beyond the bounds of reason and propriety; seeking health, she'd found disease and corruption. She knew it in her heart, he was sure of it. And he was sure, too, that things would be different from now on. Vastly different.

It was late in the afternoon by the time they reached the outskirts of Battle Creek, and it had been a long and hot journey, replete with dust, sweat and the ravages of pollinosis. Will could feel the moisture gathered round his waistband, and Eleanor, buttoned to the throat and with her hair falling loose and bonnet slightly askew, looked as if she could sit a moment in the shade. The first house they came to—the first city house, with lawns and flower beds and a pair of enormous old elms spread like parasols over the yard—had a well out on the side lawn, and someone had constructed a bench of white paling beside it. Will knocked at the door and asked for a drink, and the old woman who answered, stooped over a cane and looking confused and uncertain, misunderstood him at first. She gazed up into his face, then into Eleanor's, as if framing them. "They've all gone," she said, her voice too big for what there was of her. "They're down at the concert for the fireworks." When Will finally made himself clear to her, she shuffled off into the house and returned with a tin dipper, telling him to help himself and be welcome to it.

They sat there a long while on the bench beside the old woman's well, glad to be off the road and out of the sun. Will lowered the bucket, filled the dipper and handed it to Eleanor. She drank, arching her neck delicately, her lips pursed to receive the kiss of the cool tin dipper, and when she looked up at him, her eyes, which had been so cold lately he'd begun to wonder if they'd start to bead with condensation, were liquid and warm. She passed him the dipper and their hands touched. A breeze ruffled the trees. Everything seemed to fall away in the distance, and as he drank he came back to her eyes. "Do you think the gardener remembered to cut back my kitchen roses?" she said, and there was the faintest catch to her voice.

They went straight to the train station, and Will purchased a second ticket to go with the one he'd been carrying in his wallet for the past week and a half. It was understood that they'd stop a day in Chicago so that Eleanor could get some clothes, and he'd need a change himself—some underthings and shirts and socks at the very least. The next train was scheduled for eight, and since neither of them felt much like walking after the trial they'd been through, they found themselves seated on a bench outside the waiting room at the Michigan Central depot with some two hours to kill.

The place was all but deserted, the whole town absorbed in family celebrations or gathered round the San for the night's festivities. Eleanor freshened herself up in the ladies' room and then sat beside him, lost in her thoughts. Will found he didn't have much to say, either, and he was content just to sit there with her, but after a while he began to experience a sensation he hadn't known in so long, he didn't recognize it at first. It was a pressure in the region of his abdomen, a sort of internal swelling and constricting, as if he were carrying a disembodied mouth inside him, opening and closing on nothing. It took him a moment to identify the sensation.

He looked up into the sky, scanned the treetops, let his gaze rove from the big proud sign that was the first thing he'd laid eyes on in Battle Creek and out on down the tracks to the distant hazy point at which they grew together and disappeared in the east. And then, as if it were the most natural thing in the world, he turned to Eleanor and asked, "Are you hungry?"

George turned and fled up the hall, dashing past the overturned barrel of coal oil even as the flames reached it. Drunk as he was, as crazed, degenerate and congenitally mad, he'd planned it this way, that much was clear. He'd thought to make his escape as the barrel went up with a roar and a pounding thump of concussion that shook the building to its roots, but he hadn't counted on one thing—John Harvey Kellogg. Agile, quick, physiologically toned and clearheaded, he hadn't bothered himself with the fire, as the boy had obviously expected he would. No: what George didn't know or suspect was that the Doctor had built this structure to last an eternity, built it of stone and brick, with asbestos firewalls and beams of steel, built it to withstand tornadoes, floods, fires and all other disasters, natural and unnatural. The fire was an inconvenience, an outrage, but marble wouldn't burn and brick and stone were impervious. At worst the blaze would consume some of the furnishings in the lower offices and create a noxious stink that would have to be scrubbed out of the walls, pore by pore, but the fire wasn't the Doctor's first priority and it didn't begin to prostrate him in the way the dirty little firebug had calculated.

And so, instead of escaping scot-free as the wall of flame interposed itself between him and his adoptive father, George turned to watch the explosion, and the Doctor, who'd been right on his heels, hit him in the hips with a flying footballer's tackle. Down they both went in a roiling miasma of body odor, of filth and grease and the stink of unwashed underclothes and fungus-infested feet. They flailed at one another, the Doctor holding on grimly, more than a match, even at his age, for this obscenity, this ape, this sack of garbage. George lashed out with his fists, kicked away across the floor as if he were swimming in air, but his father came after him, as frenzied and omnipresent as ten men, moiling over him like a pack of hounds, tearing at his clothes and returning every blow with interest. *Now,* the Doctor thought, *now* we'll see what the physiologic life counts for and who wears down whom, the man of fifty-six or the boy of twenty—

But then the barrel went up and a brutal wind raked the hall and the Doctor somehow lost his grip. He was snatching at the boy, tearing at him, no healer, no doctor, no man of mercy, but one crazed beast of the jungle mauling another, when George, as slick with his grease as a pig at the fair, broke free. On his feet, scrambling, no sneers now, the face gone white in its mask of filth. Quick as a tumbler, the Doctor was up, too, and then they were off again on their desperate panting chase while the inferno roared out black and hot behind them.

George was running for his life. The Doctor was right behind him now, abbreviated legs pumping, eight hard inadmissible words pounding in his brain, *Again, I'm going to burn it down again!* "George!" he cried out in his rage, "George!" and it wasn't an injunction or even a curse, but a war cry, stark, terrible, stripped to the bone. At the end of the hall, George veered left down the stairs instead of taking his chances outside, and the Doctor's heart leapt—he knew he would run him down, just give him time enough and room. George hit the stairs at a bound and the quick panicky slap of his feet reverberated in the stairwell as he plunged toward the basement, the Doctor bouncing nimbly off the handrail and riding up off his bicycle-hardened knees as if they were carriage springs.

They took off down the long basement corridor lined with laboratories, an open field without obstruction, and the Doctor would have overtaken him here, run him into the ground, but George suddenly ducked to one side and threw himself across the tiles as if he were sliding under the catcher's tag in a game of baseball. It gave him a moment's purchase, as the Doctor, intent on the chase, hurtled on past him. George was up in an instant, reversing field and tearing back up the hallway. "Give it up, George!" the Doctor cried, bracing himself against the wall, swinging round and leaping forward again. "You don't have a chance!" he boomed, strangely exhilarated, already closing again on the narrow shoulders and the back of that flat greasy hateful fleeing head. He wasn't even winded.

But George surprised him. Instead of making for the stairway they'd just negotiated and having to choose between the outdoors and the flames, the boy burst through the door of the first lab on his right— "Fecal Analysis," the Doctor saw as he charged in after him. But then the Doctor caught himself. He stopped. Right there, right at the threshold of the darkened room. George might not have realized it, but he'd just run himself into a dead end—the room was long and narrow, divided and divided again by shelf after shelf of samples, and it had but one exit, and John Harvey Kellogg was blocking it. He didn't say a word. Just listened. Then he flicked on the light.

Nothing. If George thought he was going to play hide-and-seek, he was crazy. All the Doctor had to do was stand here till help came— someone would already have noticed the fire overhead, one of the skeleton staff or the revelers on the lawn. They'd deal with it—they were already dealing with it—and then they'd check the corridors, one by one. He folded his arms across his chest and settled in to wait. He'd almost begun to feel smug when all at once there was a noise behind him, loud as a rimshot, and a jar shattered on the wall over his head. The smell hit him then, rank, fecal, immemorial. It took him a moment to understand, and in that moment a second jar shattered against the wall, and then a third: George was destroying the samples. Desecrating Sanitarium records. Undermining the system at its very fount. He took a jar in the chest and it fell to the floor at his feet, discharging its load in a soft, almost shy, explosion. *George was throwing shit at him!*

That was it. That was the end. The Doctor lost all power of reason and threw himself into the room with a shout. It was a mistake. At that moment, George sprang into sight three rows down, and as the Doctor leapt for him he was suddenly confronted with the phenomenon of an entire shelf in motion, a moving wall of canned and encapsulated feces bearing down on him, and in the next instant he was buried beneath it. "Dr. Anus!" George shrieked in mockery. "Dr. Shit himself!" And the high ragged derisive laugh tore at the walls and trailed out into the corridor.

His jacket was white no more, his samples were destroyed, the lab was ravaged and a whole section of the building awash in flames, but Dr. Kellogg wasn't defeated, not he, not yet, not ever. He lay there half a moment taking stock of the situation, the odor gaseous and overpowering, the sad exposed secrets of all those autointoxicated bowels spread round him in every conceivable earth tone from raw sienna to ecru to tar black, and then he flung the shelf from him as if it were made of paper. He was back on his feet and out the door in an instant, but there was no one in sight. He stood there a long moment, wiping his glasses on the smear of his ruined coat, his hands black with filth and ordure, all his senses pitched keen. He seemed to be bleeding from a cut over his eye and he'd wrenched his shoulder somehow, but it was nothing. He had one object now, one object only, and that was all there was. He listened. He watched. Had George escaped upstairs? No, he wouldn't have had time, and there were voices crying out from above, the sound of footsteps, movement, hurry. He was here, damn him, he was here.

It was then that the Doctor became aware of a steady soft ratcheting sound, a sound he'd been hearing at low frequency for the past minute or so without being aware of it, a biological sound, the sound of air grating back and forth, in and out, across a rigid larynx. And what was it? He knew that sound, didn't he? He glanced round him warily. And then, from a doorway down the corridor, a shadow emerged. Sleek, lupine, low to the ground: Fauna, the pure white vegetarian wolf. Or parti-colored wolf, more gray than white since Murphy had no need to powder her except for performances—but where was Murphy? And how had she gotten loose? The question answered itself in the next instant as the shambling, loose-limbed, slope-headed form of Lillian the chimp slid out into the hallway beside the wolf: George. He was in there. In the animal lab. He'd freed them.

"Lillian!" the Doctor barked in his voice of command, "bad girl, back to your cage!" and he advanced on the animals, his arms spread wide to herd them. The chimp jerked up her head at the sound of his voice, but then she set her knuckles down on the floor and bared her teeth. *"Eeeee-eeeee!"* she shrieked in defiance, and the sound of it, raw and insolent, took the wolf's growling up a notch.

"Down, Fauna!" commanded the Doctor, and he swept up the hall, spectacles flashing, intent on one thing only—the open door and the agent of all his calamity and woe that lurked somewhere behind it. But Fauna didn't cower. The growl tightened in her throat until it was as if she were garroting herself, and she tensed her muscles to spring. "Down!" the Doctor roared and he threw his arms up over his head— no mere animal was going to intimidate him—and charged into them.

Still, and for all that, it came as a great disappointment to him when Fauna took hold of his right leg, just behind the knee, with a grip as savage and sudden as death—what had he ever done to hurt her?—and Lillian the chimp simultaneously fell on his throat with a pair of leathery long-fingered hands that could have crushed both of John L. Sullivan's fists as easily as they might have cracked open a nut. It was a bad moment. One of the very most disheartening moments of the good Doctor's life. What had he done to deserve this, he wondered, pitching to the floor beneath the combined weight of chimp and wolf, how could George hate him so immitagably and unconditionally, and these animals—didn't they appreciate him? He rolled instinctively, felt the incisors part and then dig in again, registered the cold wet feel of the

Italian tiles against his back as the shit-stinking jacket, shirt and un-dershirt were torn from him as if they were made of sacking, and for the first time in his physiologic life, he felt his faith flag.

Maybe, he thought, huddling under the onslaught of the pounding leathery fists and twisting his leg almost casually beneath the grip of the probing teeth, just maybe I've been wrong, maybe my entire life has been a sham. He saw the whole arena sweep before him then, the Elders and Sister White, the forty-two waifs, the countless faces of his countless patients and the open bleeding mouths of the wounds he'd made in them; he saw George, Charlie Ossining, the Lightbodys. Maybe I've been too single-minded, he thought, too sure of myself, too much my own guiding light and beacon, and that thought hurt him more than any fists or teeth or renegade son ever could. It hurt him so much he almost gave up. A voice rose up from within him and it said, *And so it goes: let them tear my flesh, let them strangle the breath from my lungs, let me die.*

But then, at the very nadir of that dark abandoned moment, that moment of despair and sickness unto death, he recalled a salient and telling point: he was no ordinary man. He was a man with a mission, a man with the strength of hundreds, thousands even—he was John Harvey Kellogg. The knowledge gave him new strength and he jerked his worried leg from the wolf's grip, and the wolf, in the heat of the moment, closed its jaws on the chimp's delicate, buffed-ebony toes. That was all it took. Lillian let out a screech of anathema and fell on the wolf as if she'd been set afire, one sinewy vinelike arm already jammed down its throat, the other locked across its eyes, and the two beasts rolled off down the corridor in a thrashing cataclysm of yips, shrieks, squeals and caterwaulings.

The Doctor shook himself and bounced promptly to his feet, the rags of his suit and undergarments stripped away to his waist and trailing behind him as if he were an enormous half-peeled banana, his right pant leg perforated and soaked with blood. He winced when he put his weight on the wolf-gnawed leg, and he found himself stiffly hobbling across the hallway to bend for the twin orbs of light that were his spectacles. Wiping them on one of the linen scraps that fringed his waist like a hula dancer's skirt and then forcing the bent wire frame back into shape over his ears, he straightened himself up and surveyed the field of battle, more determined than ever to track down the agent of this anarchy and make him pay the price of it.

Overhead: shouts, cries, the thump and pulse of vigorous movement. Down the hall: the two beasts, still going at it, surging and flapping against the walls like a pair of animated hearth rugs. Behind him: the excremental reek of the ravaged lab and a tile floor streaked with the unreadable message of its violated specimens. And directly ahead? The door to the animal laboratory stood open wide—and George must be in there still, smashing aquaria, freeing experimental rats, toads and lizards, lost in some obscene childhood reverie of annihilating his play-mates' toys. Well, let him, the Doctor muttered under his breath, and he approached the doorway on silent feet.

Noiseless, canny, stalking his quarry with the fierce and utter con-centration of the pygmy with his blowgun or the aborigine with his boomerang, Dr. Kellogg flattened himself to the wall and assayed a peek round the door frame. The lab stood unchanged. The lights were on, that was something, but otherwise all was as it should be. There was the faint odor of rodent urine—so faint that only the Doctor, with his hypersensitive nose, could detect it, and even in his extremity he made a mental note to have Murphy change the litter throughout—and the cages stood as usual on their shelves. He heard the muted scurry and shuffle of tiny feet and naked tails, and he was listening hard, listening for the untoward footfall, the squeal of hinges, the sound of glass shat-tering. And then all at once there was a hand in his face, George's hand, tearing at his spectacles, gouging at his eyes, his lips, his nose, and George spun out into the hall before him. "Well, Pater," he jeered, raising his voice to be heard over the unholy din of Fauna and Lillian, "and how do you like the physiologic life now? Stinks of shit, I'd say."

Though his spectacles were askew and his leg was stiffening, the Doctor made a lunge for him, but George evaded him, skipping off easily out of reach with a maddening laugh. "Catch me if you can," he taunted, and he fled the length of the hallway, past the ragged wolf and screeching chimpanzee, and disappeared into the Experimental Kitchens, as Lillian had done before him. The Doctor followed, slowed now by his leg—it didn't seem to want to bend at the knee—but all the more grim and dogged for it. This was a battle to the finish.

And here, finally, the balance swung in his favor.

When he came through the door and into the darkened room, dragging his leg, he found George crumpled on the floor beneath the nutbutter vat. He was clutching his ankle and whimpering, the same hateful intransigent boy he'd discovered in the root cellar, the boy who wouldn't hang his jacket on the peg, who tormented his siblings, set fires, refused to treat his adoptive parents with the respect—let alone gratitude— they deserved. The boy who couldn't be touched. The boy who lived only to refute and debase everything John Harvey Kellogg stood for. He was hurt. Whimpering. Clutching his ankle.

All in an instant, the Doctor saw that it was over. George had hurtled into the room, bent on destruction, but weak, essentially and in the deepest corrupt fiber of him, weak, weak, weak—and drunk, too, addled with drink—and he'd tripped over the three-foot lever that projected from the bottom of the vat, the lever that set the big mixing blades in motion and broke down the unyielding nuggets till they gave up their essence. From the way George was holding his ankle, from the angle at which the foot seemed to skew away from the tibia, the Doctor could see that it was broken, badly broken. George was breathing in quick shallow gasps and the pain clouded his eyes. He shrank into the shadows at the base of the vat.

Dr. Kellogg never hesitated—it had gone too far, and there was no coming back, not now. Sweeping across the floor in a single violent motion, he bent and snatched the boy to his feet, ignoring his shout of agony as he fell away from the broken ankle and staggered on his one good leg into the immovable wall of the vat. The Doctor slapped him, again and again, the pinched arrogant face shrunk to nothing, the flat head rolling loose on the shoulders, and he never thought back to the night in the hallway, never doubted himself for a second. Slamming the boy's spine into the sharp unforgiving lip of the tub, he sought to hurt him, only that, to give as good as he'd gotten, and he beat at him till his hands went numb and the rancid gutter stink of the boy gave way to the rich rising effluvia of macadamia butter.

A thousand pounds of it, half a ton, smooth and nutritious and replete, enough to restore three-quarters of the stomachs in Battle Creek and awaiting only the jars to contain it. A sea of pure golden oil floated atop it, richly glinting in the half-light cast through the doorway, trembling and dipping with the oceanic shock of the towering little Doctor's rage as he slammed into George again and again. And then a curious thing happened. In twisting away from the Doctor's blows, George, bent double at the waist and savage with the pain of his ankle and the imperative of staying off it, lost his footing and pitched forward into the vat. At first only his right arm plunged in, and he flailed back out of it, his hand, wrist and forearm glistening with oil, his shirt greased to the shoulder, but the Doctor was inspired now, and never vacillating, he forced the boy back down into the fragrant sloshing unguent froth, baptizing him, purifying him, and he held the boy's face there and fought it down with every ounce of outraged physiologic strength he could summon even as it lashed to the surface shrieking for air and fell back again into the oleaginous grip of the stuff.

The Doctor held George there until he stopped struggling. And in the end, his grasp became almost tender, and he imagined himself washing the boy in the big gleaming porcelain bathtub when he'd first come to them, digging deep with soap and washcloth, fighting down the dirt, laving and anointing the son George could never be. There was an infinite sadness at the core of it, infinite. But George was an experiment that hadn't worked, and there was no shame in that, not to a man of science. When an experiment went bad, you had to move on to the next one and the one after that, on and on into the shimmering universe of discovery and revelation that stretched out shining all the way to the very feet of God. George was weak. An aberration. He should never have been born, never have drawn breath, never have been allowed to add to the sum total of human misery and depravity that was dragging the race stubbornly down.

Dr. Kellogg drew himself up. Gently, with intimate touch and the most exquisite physiologic grace, he pressed the boy's limp and inanimate flesh to his own and lifted first one leg over the lip of the tub, and then the other. And then he let him go, let him drift away, face down, aglow with precious oil. It was a hard thing to do, as hard a thing as he'd ever done in his life. But even as he stood there, bleeding quietly into the tatters of his clothes, even as George bobbed gently away from him, he knew he would draw strength from it. For he was no weakling, he was no George. He was John Harvey Kellogg, and he would live forever.

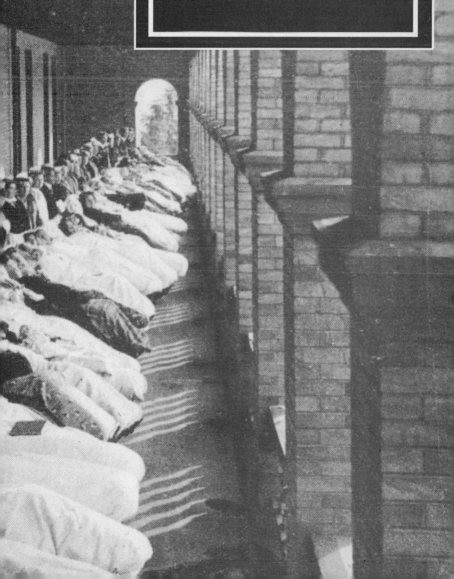

C W. Post, the man who brought Postum, Grape-Nuts and meretricious advertising to the world, was the first of the high apostles of health to succumb to the inevitable. He'd never really got over the stomach troubles that had brought him to Dr. Kellogg's doorstep in 1891, though positive thinking and the accumulation of a personal fortune that ranked him among the nation's wealthiest individuals helped keep them in check for a time. Tall, dynamic, the most photogenic and opportunistic of Battle Creek's breakfast-food barons, he fought his constitutional weakness with pamphlets and slogans (*Grape Nuts: There's a Reason; Postum: It Makes Red Blood*), and rejuvenated himself in 1904 by divorcing his suspender-sewing wife and marrying his typist, an ingénue thirty years his junior. When his appendix gave out in 1914, he was rushed by special train from his home in Santa Barbara to Rochester, Minnesota, where the Mayo brothers performed an emergency appendectomy while half the world held its breath. The operation was a success, but it was just the tip of the iceberg. Charlie Post was sick, sick at heart, sick at stomach. On May 9 of that year, in the bedroom of his home overlooking the bright snapping banner of the Pacific, he put a rifle to his solar plexus and ended it all. He was fifty-nine.

Battle Creek mourned his passing. Buildings were hung with black

467

T. Coraghessan Boyle

crepe, shops and factories were closed, a thousand Postum employees formed a guard of honor as the cortege rolled through streets packed shoulder to shoulder with mourners. It was a sad day for Battle Creek, though the Kellogg brothers—Dr. Kellogg, in particular—couldn't help feeling a private little frisson of triumph at the news. The health arena, so recently crowded, suddenly felt a whole lot roomier.

But if Dr. Kellogg shed no tears over the demise of his rival, Charlie Ossining did. The news reached him in Paris, where he was living in Saint-Germain-des-Prés with his Swiss-born wife, Marie-Thérèse, the ambassador's daughter who spoke five languages, composed music and poetry, and wrote for many of the leading intellectual journals of the day. Charlie had a house in Zurich, as well, and a two-hundred-fifty-acre country estate in northern Westchester, where he spent six months of every year, seeing to the affairs of the Per-To Company and living under his given name, Charles Peter McGahee. Both houses were roomy and extensive, as was the flat in Saint-Germain-des-Prés, and all three featured parlors devoted exclusively to billiards. In fact, Charlie was bent over the billiard table, engaged in a friendly small-stakes contest with the Baron Thierry de Villiers, when the telegram arrived from New York.

The news of C. W. Post's death hit him hard. The Baron later reported that Charlie, on opening the telegram, had set down his flute of Pommery & Greno, carefully leaned the cue against the bookcase and broke down in tears. Along with Lydia Pinkham and the anonymous purveyor of the memory tablets, Charlie Post had been his inspiration and guiding light, and, more than any other, the man in whose image he had tried to make himself. He was upset and out of sorts for days. His first impulse was to book passage for New York and take the train from there to Battle Creek for the funeral, but both his wife and the Baron talked him out of it—the cereal king's body would arrive from Santa Barbara in three days' time at most and would be long in the ground by the time Charlie arrived. Reluctantly, he agreed with them. But many years later, when he himself was an old man, Charlie made a pilgrimage to Battle Creek, the town which had inspired and rejected him, and stood before the big marble mausoleum in the Oak Hill Cemetery and paid his respects.

468

It was no idle homage, for Post had made Per-To possible, just as he'd made possible all the breakfast foods and cereal drinks that flooded the U.S. and Europe at the turn of the century. When Charlie had left Battle Creek, on the day after Decoration Day 1908, he had taken his hope and vision with him, not to mention the pair of steel bracelets the town constable had been good enough to donate, and the nine hundred dollars left over from Will Lightbody's investment in Per-Fo (or, rather, access to the account at the Central National Bank in which it was secreted). He was to found the Perfect Tonic Company, Inc., of Battle Creek, Michigan, with offices and production facilities in New York, Chicago, San Francisco and Boston, with that initial stake, and watch it grow into an empire. He considered himself lucky on several counts, but especially lucky to have escaped Battle Creek in the early hours of that June morning when all the town would have been looking for him and only the iron cot and musty cell awaited him.

He'd watched for George through the course of the long, rocket-festooned night, drunk on his dreams and Lydia E. Pinkham's potent brew, but George never showed up. An hour before sunrise he gave it up, and, tucking a pint of Vegetable Compound into his waistband for sustenance, he made his way along the darkened bed of the creek after which the town was named, traveling east and north until it was full light, when he settled down to sleep in the underbrush. Moving by night, sleeping by day, startling dogs on their chains and chickens in their coops, eating what he could scavenge and avoiding all human contact, he made a leisurely tour of the county's backwaters and finally left the state without incident. Eventually he made his way to Indianapolis, where he got work in a distillery and found a discreet black-smith, who, for a consideration, relieved him of his official jewelry. Closing his account at the Central National Bank by mail, he returned to New York in style, aboard the Twentieth Century Limited, eating oysters and fat rich dripping beefsteaks without a moment's regret.

Per-To was an instant success. It had an attractive and eye-appealing label of shiny embossed silver-and-gold paper, it was celery-impregnated, it made active blood, sturdy legs and sound lungs, and it was a specific for pleurisy, heart ailments, diphtheria, the flu, general weakness, men's troubles, women's troubles and rectal itch. Charlie floated its active ingredients—"Celeriac, Gentian, Black Cohosh, True & False Unicorn Life & Pleurisy Root"—in a forty-percent-alcohol solution ("Added Solely as a Solvent and Preservative"), and found that all he needed by way of a factory was a back room, a cast-iron kettle, some powdered roots and weeds, and a dependable source of white lightning. For the first three years, every nickel he made went into advertising.

Though eventually he became one of northern Westchester's leading citizens, widely recognized as a philanthropist and patron of the arts, he remained, at least in part, an expatriate, and he was never reconciled with Mrs. Hookstratten. When he was at home, he and Marie-Thérèse entertained lavishly, and many of the leading lights of the Peterskill circle enjoyed his hospitality, but Mrs. Hookstratten was conspicuously absent. He never invited the Lightbodys, either, though on Christmas Eve, 1911, four years to the day of making his investment in Per-Fo, Will received a check in the amount of five thousand dollars from a Charles Peter McGahee of the Per-To Company, thanking him for his generosity and hoping that his outlay had been sufficiently rewarded. Unfortunately, Charlie grew rather fat in his later years, glutted on the rich pâtés, chateaubriands and buttery sauces with which Marie-Thérèse plied him, and he died in 1945, sixty-three years old, of an overstuffed heart.

In all those years, Charlie had never heard news of Bender, except by rumor, though it was said that the man they'd detained in Detroit was a confederate—or, rather, a dupe—whom Bender had paid to assume his name and lord it about the finest hotel in town, presumably as a way of throwing the authorities off his track. With a man like Bender, the not inconsiderable sum he'd taken out of the Per-Fo scheme wouldn't have lasted long, and legend had it that he'd lost the better part of it in a Nevada silver mine. He surfaced years later in Montana, a man well into his eighties, his beard still parted and dyed, under the name Soapy Smith, and he earned his living, with a pair of shills, at the soap game. In a tavern or out front of the general store in any one of a thousand nameless rustic towns across the West, he would attract a crowd by conspicuously wrapping bars of soap in crisp new bills ranging in value from one dollar to a hundred, flashing a great many more of the latter than the former, and then he would wrap the bundles in plain paper and fill a basket with them. For a five-dollar fee, he would invite any of the onlookers to fish through the barrel and keep the bar of soap—and its precious wrapping—that they came up with. Somehow, though, the only contestants who ever managed to come up with the one-hundred-dollar bars were a pair of shifty-looking mustachioed men no one could remember having seen around town before. Bender did well with the soap scheme, as he always did and always had with his countless other schemes, a man blessed with flawless timing and a deep and resolute knowledge of his quarry. During the fall of his eighty-fifth year, so the story goes, he was shot three times in the face by a disgruntled soap dipper and was buried in his underclothes just outside Dawson, in the Yukon Territory.

As for the Lightbodys, Will and Eleanor, they returned to Peterskill to find everything in order on Parsonage Lane, though Dick the wire-haired terrier never quite got over their having deserted him and spent the rest of his life taking out his displeasure on the Persian carpets every time they left the house for more than an hour or two. The roses were in full bloom on the trellis outside the kitchen window, the sunny little room at the head of the stairs stood ready to receive its future occupant, and the familiar umbrageous town, with its sharp inclines and vernal walks, its uplifting views of the Hudson and Dunderberg Mountain to the west and Anthony's Nose to the north, seemed to cheer them both, and an air of normalcy and quiet fell over their lives. Admittedly, the question of their diet those first few weeks was a ticklish one, and Mrs. Dunphy, the cook, had to tread a fine line between the old physiologic order and the new one of moderation and laxness, but Eleanor ate an asparagus frittata, a poached shad or a veal chop without complaint, and Will found that the hard hot fist in his stomach had begun, ever so gradually, to unclench itself.

Dr. Brillinger had passed on in the interim, and the new man in town, a Dr. Morris Frieberg of the Johns Hopkins School of Medicine, examined Will casually, diagnosed a duodenal ulcer that was well along the way to healing itself, and prescribed absolutely nothing other than sensible eating and drinking and perhaps a stroll down the avenue after dinner. As the weeks and months drifted by, Will found that a glass of beer before dinner seemed to help with his digestion, and a brandy or two afterward just set him aglow. He took vegetables with his meat, ate his whole grains and his cereals, enjoyed the occasional pickled egg and strip of jerky. He slept well and contentedly at night, Eleanor breathing softly beside him in the big four-poster bed, Dick the wirehaired terrier at his feet, and when he felt like it, after eighteen holes of golf with one of his old school chums or a loping hike into the Blue Mountain Reservation, he took a nap in the afternoon. By the fall of that year, he'd returned to the factory on Water Street, but only to tender his resignation, pleading his health. In actuality, he'd never felt better, and he planned to devote himself to his own pursuits—reading the complete works of Dickens, building ships under glass, raising wirehaired terriers and preparing himself for fatherhood.

In February of the following year, Eleanor gave birth to their first child, a girl of seven pounds, two ounces, with eyes like twin specks of emerald glass, whom they named Elizabeth Cady and installed in the bassinet in the pink sunny room at the head of the stairs. She was followed two years later by Lucretia, and finally, after a hiatus of five years, by Julia Ward. The girls grew up to be leggy and lean, and they ate whatever they liked, within reason. Will was devoted to them.

Eleanor softened in motherhood, and the nervous condition that had so dogged her younger days seemed to become less and less a factor as the years went on. But though she was softened, and in a way chastened by her Battle Creek experience, Eleanor never lost her cutting wit or her reforming zeal. Where before she'd thrown all her energies into diet, as though control of the appetite were the source and foundation of all human endeavor, she now broadened her perspective, throwing herself into local and national politics, into charity work, education and the movement for women's suffrage, with the same fervor she'd once reserved for the Peterskill Ladies' Biologic Living Society or the Battle Creek Sanitarium Deep-Breathing Club. It was a shift of emphasis, that was all, and never a recantation. Whereas before it was vegetables that would save the world, now it was basic human rights, it was education, it was a giving and a selfless devotion to the cause. She became president of the Peterskill chapter of the National American Woman Suffrage

Association and in 1919 traveled throughout the country lobbying for passage of the Nineteenth Amendment. So involved was she, in fact, that it was often up to Will to look after their daughters, a responsibility he gladly and without prompting assumed. When she was home, and when they sat down to dinner, she accepted a slice of turkey or a choice cut of beef, and though she never did reconcile herself to meat, by the same token she didn't seem to miss Nuttose, Baked Cornlet or kumyss, and she never, or almost never, mentioned Dr. Kellogg.

By contrast, Will rarely traveled, rarely, in fact, went out, unless it was to take his constitutional, walk the girls to school or spend a quiet evening at Mapes' or Ben's Elbow (two drinks his limit—or, well, maybe three). When the girls were grown and the rumblings of the Second War making themselves heard, Eleanor pitched herself into the relief effort, and the house on Parsonage Lane gradually filled with refugees. There were Jews and Lithuanians, Czechs, Frenchmen and Poles, and they wrote, sculpted, played piano, gave speeches and argued politics, and they ate anything and everything that was put before them. It was a happy time for Will, the house full of talk and music, all three of his daughters (two now married) within walking distance, Eleanor shining like the polestar of that brilliant company, and as he slipped quietly into his sixty-seventh year, he felt at peace with himself, and if not exactly heroic, then a man who had risen to the occasion and taken charge of his life in that sunlit field by the Kalamazoo River so many years ago. He died in his sleep the night Hitler invaded Russia.

Eleanor outlived her husband by some twenty years, and as she got on into her seventies and the causes dropped away from her, she began, once again, and all those years later, to think of food. At seventy-eight, she was fitter, stronger, more mentally acute and physically active than women twenty years younger. She saw them in Woolworth's, feeding their great greasy globular faces with pork rinds and extra-buttered popcorn, watched them bend their heads to their chicken-fried-steak sandwiches and swell beneath their pedal pushers with appendages no human was meant to carry. She saw them, and she thought about it, and the more she thought about it, the more convinced she became that Dr. Kellogg had been right (maybe not Spitzvogel or Lionel Badger, dead of a stroke at forty-nine, and the thought of them and what had happened between them still made her blush and got her pulse racing all those many years later—not them, maybe, but Dr. Kellogg).

She felt like an apostate in the face of it, and she gave up what little meat she'd fallen into eating over the years, hardened her will, dug out her old pamphlets, her yeast powder and the crumbling pages of Dr. Kellogg's "Nuts May Save the Race." In 1958, at the age of seventy-nine, she got together with her youngest daughter, Julia, and opened Peterskill's first health-food store, stocking its shelves with fish-oil capsules, vitamin supplements, tahini, wonton wrappers and great open bins of sesame seeds, cracked-wheat flour, unhulled rice and dried soybeans. A juicer stood on the front counter, and local bodybuilders, Transcendentalists, Unitarians and chiropractors would stop by for a lecithin-yogurt shake or a glass of carrot juice. She died in 1967, at the age of eighty-eight, and no one knows why.

But Dr. Kellogg—Dr. Kellogg, that amazing high-wire act of a sprightly, proselytizing, tightfisted, food-altering, revolutionary great-grandfather, author and presiding genius of the whole alimentary business, what of him? He throve and he faltered, like anyone else, but he never let his guard down and he never missed a photo opportunity. We see him today, his portrait hung in that celebrated gallery alongside Sylvester Graham, Bronson Alcott, Thomas Edison and Old Parr, eternally smiling with a mouth full of physiologic teeth, his white cockatoo perched on his white shoulder. Or on his bicycle, at seventy, cutting figure eights in a pair of shorts for the camera, tossing Indian clubs and lifting barbells, doing a triple gainer from the high dive of the Miami–Battle Creek Sanitarium pool in Miami Springs, Florida, in 1933, aged eighty-one.

He fought his wars, and he had his triumphs. But on the evening of May 31, 1908, while rockets shot into the air and all the crowd of his inmates, his associates, his patients, devotees and familiars oohed and aahed and strained their eyes toward the heavens, he had some dirty work to do, some lies to tell, some dirt to sweep under the carpet. He appeared before an astonished Murphy, Linniman and some two dozen others who had sprung into the teeth of the fire and were even then driving it down to nothing, limping up the ground-floor hallway in his

474

rags and tatters. There was a sheen of blood and perspiration on his face, a glistening coat of macadamia oil pasted to the hard proud swollen knot of his bare belly, and he carried a reek of intestinal secrets with him that made two of the men, full-grown and eudaemonically sound, turn away and gag. "It was George," he cried, his voice trembling, face ashen, "he did it all. He attacked me, set the place afire, let the animals loose." He hesitated, overcome. They moved toward him, but he gestured them away. "I tried to save him," he choked, and then he said no more.

Those were the good years, the years of the San's heyday, the years when all the world came to him, John Harvey Kellogg, the one man, the unimpeachable, the authority, the king. The teens gave way to the twenties, the war years rose up and fell away like some sick red tide, women traded in their dresses and feathered hats for short skirts and cloches, ragtime segued into jazz, and the Battle Creek Sanitarium rode higher and higher on the current, unsinkable. John Harvey Kellogg's nimble fingers and razor-honed scalpel probed a thousand abdomens, ten thousand, and his enema machine irrigated the most celebrated bowels in the country, yea, the world. Johnny Weissmuller stopped by to have his plumbing inspected; Byrd, Amundsen, Grenfell and Halliburton paid their homage; J. C. Penney, Amelia Earhart, Battling Bob La Follette, Henry Ford. In 1928 the Doctor added a fifteen-story addition, sumptuous with marble, crystal, tapestries and murals, and sat back to watch its two hundred sixty-five new rooms fill with the physiologically wanting.

It never happened. The Crash came, the dyspeptic set took to dosing themselves with milk of magnesia, diet was whatever you could get. The San crashed under the burden of its debt, the glorious building that had witnessed the conversion of so many oceans of intestinal flora and the slow mastication of so many hundreds of tons of grits and granola, the Goodly Temple on a Hill, was sold at auction to the federal government and rechristened the Percy Jones General Hospital, and Dr. Kellogg retreated to Florida while his enemies—and they were legion—lifted up their parched old heads and sniffed something new in the air.

In the end, though he received and administered more enemas than any man in history, though he ate more vegetables, smoked less, drank less, slept less and exercised more than practically any man of his time, even Dr. Kellogg couldn't live forever. On December 14, 1943, like his nemesis, C. W. Post, before him, John Harvey Kellogg passed on into eternity.

He did die, yes. But could anyone ask for more?

In fourteen smart, funny, and richly crafted works, T. C. Boyle strips away the veneer of respectability draped across the American psyche, and exposes the comical truths beneath.

AFTER THE PLAGUE
These sixteen stories display an astonishing range, as Boyle zeroes in on everything from air rage to abortion doctors to the story of a 1920s Sicilian immigrant who constructs an amazing underground mansion in an effort to woo his sweetheart. By turns mythic and realistic, farcical and tragic, ironic and moving, these new stories find "one of the most inventive and verbally exuberant writers" (*The New York Times*) at the top of his form.   *ISBN 0-14-200141-4*

BUDDING PROSPECTS
All Felix and his friends have to do is harvest a crop of *Cannabis Sativa* and half a million tax-free dollars will be theirs. But as their beloved buds wither under assault from ravenous scavengers, human caprice, and a drug-busting state trooper named Jerphak, their dreams of easy money go up in smoke. "Consistently, effortlessly, intelligently funny." — *The New York Times*   *ISBN 0-14-029996-3*

DESCENT OF MAN
A primate-center researcher becomes romantically involved with a chimp. A Norse poet overcomes bard-block. These and other strange occurrences come together in Boyle's collection of satirical stories that brilliantly express just what the "evolution" of mankind has wrought. "Madness that hits you where you live." —*Houston Chronicle*
ISBN 0-14-029994-7

EAST IS EAST
Young Japanese seaman Hiro Tanaka jumps ship off the coast of Georgia and swims into a net of rabid rednecks, genteel ladies, descendants of slaves, and the denizens of an artists' colony. *The New York Times* called this sexy, hilarious tragicomedy a "pastoral version of *The Bonfire of the Vanities*."   *ISBN 0-14-013167-1*

GREASY LAKE AND OTHER STORIES
Mythic and realistic, these masterful stories are, according to *The New York Times*, "satirical fables of contemporary life, so funny and acutely observed that they might have been written by Evelyn Waugh as sketches for . . . *Saturday Night Live*."
ISBN 0-14-007781-2

IF THE RIVER WAS WHISKEY
Boyle, winner of the 1999 PEN/Malamud award for short fiction, tears through the walls of contemporary society to reveal a world at once comic and tragic, droll and horrific, in these sixteen magical and provocative stories. "Writing at its very, very best." —*USA Today*   *ISBN 0-14-011950-7*

RIVEN ROCK

With his seventh novel to date, T. C. Boyle pens a heartbreaking love story taken from between the lines of history. Millionaire Stanley McCormick, diagnosed as a schizophrenic and sexual maniac shortly after his marriage, is forbidden the sight of women, but his strong-willed, virginal wife Katherine Dexter is determined to cure him. "As romantic as it is informative, as colorful as it is convincing. Boyle combines his gift for historical re-creation with his dazzling powers as a storyteller."—*The Boston Globe*

ISBN 0-14-027166-X

THE ROAD TO WELLVILLE

Centering on John Harvey Kellogg and his turn-of-the-century Battle Creek Spa, this wickedly comic novel brims with a Dickensian cast of characters and is laced with wildly wonderful plot twists. "A marvel, enjoyable from the beginning to end." —Jane Smiley, *The New York Times Book Review*

ISBN 0-14-016718-8

T. C. BOYLE STORIES

"Boyle has the tale-teller's gift in abundance," writes the *Chicago Tribune*. And nowhere is that more evident than in this collection of sixty-eight short stories—all of the work from his four previous collections, as well as seven tales that have never before appeared in book form—that comprise a virtual feast of the short story. "Seven hundred flashy, inventive pages of stylistic and moral acrobatics."—*The New York Times Book Review*

ISBN 0-14-028091-X

THE TORTILLA CURTAIN

Winner of France's Prix Medicis Etranger for best foreign-language novel, *The Tortilla Curtain* illuminates the many potholes along the road to the elusive American Dream. Illegal immigrants Candido and America cling to life at the bottom of Topanga Canyon, dreaming of a privileged existence of the sort endured by L.A. liberals Delaney and Kyra. When a freak accident brings these two couples together, darkly comic events leave them wondering what the world is coming to.

ISBN 0-14-023828-X

WATER MUSIC

Funny, bawdy, and full of imaginative and stylistic fancy, *Water Music* follows the wild adventures of Ned Rise, thief and whoremaster, and Mungo Park, explorer, from London to Africa. "*Water Music* does for fiction what *Raiders of the Lost Ark* did for film ... Boyle is an adept plotter, a crazed humorist, and a fierce describer." —*The Boston Globe*

ISBN 0-14-006550-4

WITHOUT A HERO

With fierce, comic wit and uncanny accuracy, Boyle zooms in on an astonishingly wide range of American phenomena in this critically-applauded collection of stories. "Gloriously comic ... vintage Boyle ... [these] stories are more than funny, better than wicked. They make you cringe with their clarity." —*The Philadelphia Inquirer*

ISBN 0-14-017839-2

WORLD'S END

Walter Van Brunt is about to have a collision with history that will lead him to search for his long-lost father. This fascinating novel, for which Boyle won the prestigious PEN/Faulkner Award for American Fiction, showcases the author's "ability to work all sorts of magical variations of literature and history" (*The New York Times*).

ISBN 0-14-029993-9